A HISTORY OF THE ANCIENT SOUTHWEST

A HISTORY
OF THE ANCIENT SOUTHWEST

Stephen H. Lekson

SAR
PRESS

School for Advanced Research Press

Santa Fe

School for Advanced Research Press

Post Office Box 2188

Santa Fe, New Mexico 87504-2188

sarpress.sarweb.org

Co-director and Executive Editor: Catherine Cocks

Copy Editor: Margaret J. Goldstein

Designer and Production Manager: Cynthia Dyer

Proofreader: Kate Whelan

Indexer: Ina Gravitz

Printer: Cushing-Malloy, Inc.

Library of Congress Cataloging-in-Publication Data:

Lekson, Stephen H.

  A history of the ancient Southwest / Stephen H. Lekson. — 1st ed.

    p. cm.

  Includes bibliographical references and index.

  ISBN 978-1-934691-10-6 (pa : alk. paper)

  1. Indians of North America—Southwest, New—History. 2. Indians of North America—Southwest,

New—Antiquities. 3. Excavations (Archaeology)—Southwest, New. 4. Southwest, New—Antiquities.

I. Title.

  E78.S7L45 2009

  979'.01—dc22

2008039655

Front cover: top, red bowl, Fourmile Polychrome, UCM # 09634; center, owl, Ramos Polychrome from
Paquimé, UCM # 02061A; bottom, red jar, Salado Polychrome, UCM # 04765; photographs by Erin Baxter,
courtesy of the University of Colorado Museum of Natural History. Background image: Paquimé, photograph by
Stephen H. Lekson. Back cover: pot with animal handle, Wingate Black-on-red, UCM # 09641, photograph
by Erin Baxter.

Contents

Figures

Acknowledgments

This book is for southwestern archaeologists and for general readers with more than a casual interest in southwestern archaeology. The former is a small group; the latter, happily, quite large.

Southwestern archaeology is a tightly defined field, but it's difficult to put a precise number on its practitioners. I'd guess that the total number of southwestern archaeologists working in universities, museums, CRM firms, and governments is well over one thousand. That may seem like a lot of archaeologists, but the Southwest is a pretty big place. They (we) can be cantankerous at times, but I very much enjoy my colleagues. They are almost universally open, generous, and good company—not to mention trustworthy, loyal, helpful, friendly, courteous, kind, obedient, cheerful, thrifty, brave, clean, and reverent. To paraphrase Professor Higgins: by and large, we are a marvelous sect.

Those with more than a casual interest in southwestern archaeology constitute a much larger group. There are people out there with day jobs who know as much as any professor—and thousands more who know quite a bit, travel a lot, and generally enjoy thinking about ancient times. The high degree of archaeological literacy among southwestern aficionados should be the envy of other regions. To everyone out there who's intrigued by the ancient Southwest (whether or not you buy this book or agree with my interpretations): Thanks!

Striking a balance between a thousand professionals and thousands more keen, savvy "general readers," I've tried to write a text that is full of information but not hopelessly arcane and esoteric. (If you want academic minutia, read the notes!) Certain sections may irk particular archaeologists; other sections might bemuse general readers; the whole book may annoy Indians. It's pretty much a straight-ahead archaeology book, and not the kind of collaborative effort that gives us all hope for the future. I've benefited enormously from past collaborations and consultations with Native American officials and colleagues, but I wanted to sort out, archaeologically, what I think happened in the ancient Southwest. That was a book-length project. Now I look forward to bouncing these ideas around with Indians, archaeologists, and aficionados.

So it's an archaeology book. A lot of it focuses on archaeological personalities and peculiarities. I've tried to show how archaeologists think—where archaeological knowledge comes from. Not the details of pottery typology or tree-ring dating or stratigraphy, but the world of ideas that (for me) is the real domain of archaeology. Archaeology is only partly about discovering things; for me, archaeology is *thinking about things*. What we know about the past is exactly that: what *we* know, right now, today—not what my professors knew or what my students will know. That's not an admission of failure; it's a recognition of growth and learning. You can understand archaeology only by under-standing the archaeologists and the intellectual worlds in which they worked. That's not to say there is not a real past, which we can never really know. There is. But, as in every field of scholarship, the questions we ask and the things we focus on reflect our larger intellectual, political, and social worlds. Those worlds, of course, have changed over the century-plus that archaeologists have been poking and prodding around the Southwest.

I thought for a long time about writing this book. I actually wrote it during the spring and summer of 2004. The appalling first draft was almost a thousand pages long. The thing had more jarring twists and turns than a Disney eTicket ride. Peer reviewers' comments caused me to reshape and redirect the book: same story, different form. The new and improved second draft became the bane of a suffering group of graduate students, who unwittingly asked for it in a seminar at the University of Colorado in 2006. Further changes ensued. This, the third and final version, came together late in 2007 and early 2008, benefiting greatly from the editing of Nancy Dawson Mann and Zonnie Barnes (in Boulder) and Peg Goldstein (in Santa Fe). Thanks, Peg! Together, we chased most of the nitpicking academic arguments into notes, where they are now safely sequestered. Southwestern archaeology did not stand still through those various revisions, and I've tried to update both citations and arguments to reflect new data and insights through 2007. SAR Press (as always) has been a pleasure to work with. In addition to Peg Goldstein, I particularly thank Dr. Catherine Cocks, director of the Press. Cam's great! I hope this book repays her (and SAR Press) for taking a chance on an unconventional product.

I started off with standard archaeological illustrations: maps, plans, and profiles. Somewhere between the second and third drafts, I decided to replace them all with artists' reconstructions. Besides making a heavy-handed point about the nature of archaeological interpretation, I was struck by the quantity of archaeological art that's out there, much of it paid for by you and me. Some good, some bad, some ugly, but there's a lot of it. We've concentrated on the "good" category, and I thank the excellent artists who very generously allowed me to use their work, acknowledged in the figure captions. A few presses were more generous than others, and I should particularly mention Desert Archaeology, the Amerind Foundation, and the National Geographic Society for waiving or lowering fees.

The Mimbres images in this book come from the Rodeck Mimbres Archive at the University of Colorado Museum. Dr. Hugo G. Rodeck (biologist and director of the museum, 1939–1971) undertook an extensive study of Mimbres pottery, visiting collections and photographing thousands of vessels between 1952 and 1960. In preparation for a monograph (sadly, never published), Dr. Rodeck, his daughter Jean Rodeck, Joss Colony, and others redrew many images in ink. A few of these appear here.

I do not intend to trivialize Mimbres art or reduce it to mere decoration. Rather, I wanted images created by the people this book is about to balance the archaeological reconstructions and modern artists' interpretations. Mimbres images are specific to a time and a place and a people (chapter 5), but they stand, I hope, for the many different peoples and societies whose histories I'm trying to tell.

In the fall of 2003, I went on a fact-finding road trip through the Southwest, pestering people, asking questions, and being a general nuisance. The trip was supported by the American Council of Learned Societies and the University of Colorado. It was a great circle, south down the Rio Grande, west across the Butterfield route to Tucson, north to Phoenix and Flagstaff, through the Four Corners, over Wolf Creek Pass, and home. In alphabetical, not itinerary, order, these were the people I most annoyed (and enjoyed): Eric Blinman, Todd Bostwick, Gary M. Brown, Jeff Dean, Bill Doelle, Chris Downum, David Doyel, Mark Elson, Bill Gillespie, Dennis Gilpin, Kelley Hays-Gilpin, Jon Mabry, Peter McKenna, Barbara Mills, Peggy Nelson, Scott Ortman, Bob Powers, Jeff Reid, John Roney, Kate Spielmann, Wolky Toll, Mark Varien, John Ware, Stephanie Whittlesey, Dave Wilcox, Chip Wills, and my old friend Tom Windes. Everyone I bothered while gathering information for this book was admirably patient and pleasant. None of these nice people, of course, are responsible for my twisted renditions of their data and insights. Several institutions along the way were particularly welcoming: the Amerind Foundation, Arizona State Museum, Aztec Ruins National Monument, Chaco Culture National Historical Park, Crow Canyon Archaeological Center, Laboratory of Anthropology and Office of Archaeological Studies at the Museum of New Mexico, and Museum of Northern Arizona.

Throughout the long, lurching composition of this book, there were people I would go to for quick fixes of information—and for course corrections. Who dug this site? How do you spell that word? What's the current thinking? These wonderful go-to people were patient and generous—and they are totally blameless for what I've done with their information and insights. I list them by time period and specialty, so a few appear twice: *Paleo and Archaic*: Bruce Huckell, Brad Vierra; *Hohokam*: Todd Bostwick, Bill Doelle, David Doyel, Paul Fish, Henry Wallace, Stephanie Whittlesey; *Sinagua*: Chris Downum, Peter Pilles; *Mimbres and southern New Mexico*: Roger Anyon, Darrell Creel, Michelle Hegmon, Karl Laumbach, Steve LeBlanc, Peggy Nelson, David Phillips; *Mogollon*: Jeff Reid, Stephanie Whittlesey; *Anasazi*: Jason Chuipka, Dennis Gilpin, Winston Hurst, Richard Wilshusen; *Chaco*: Taft Blackhorse, Catherine Cameron, Andrew Duff, Rich Friedman, John Kantner, John Roney, John Stein, Tom Windes; *Salmon and Aztec*: Rex Adams, Gary Brown, Peter McKenna; *Mesa Verde*: Bill Lipe, Mark Varien, Rich Wilshusen; *Rio Grande*: Eric Blinman, Linda Cordell, Steve Post, David Snow, John Ware, C. Dean Wilson; *Kayenta/Hopi*: Chuck Adams, Jeff Dean, Jonathan Haas, Rich Lange; *Pueblo IV*: Kelley Hays-Gilpin; *northern Mexico*: Jane Kelley, Randy McGuire, Paul Minnis, Michael Whalen; *Hopewell*: Brad Lepper; *Mississippian*: Tom Emerson, Tim Pauketat; *Mesoamerica*: Chris Beekman, Art Joyce, and Payson Sheets. I could not, alas, consult several key scholars, now deceased, but my thinking on post-Chaco owes a lot to Cynthia Irwin-Williams, on West Mexico to J. Charles Kelley, and on Hohokam and (especially) Mogollon to Emil Haury.

As I note throughout the text, the recent publication of a number of "synthesis" volumes made this book possible. Other archaeologists did all the work, gathering and sifting data and producing summaries of various regions and time periods, which I then bent to my evil purposes. I especially thank Suzy and Paul Fish, editors of a forthcoming Hohokam volume (to be published through the Amerind Foundation and University of Arizona Press), for letting me ask their authors for advance copies of chapters; I thank the authors for generously sharing the chapters. And I'd like to thank John Ware for his outstanding leadership of the Amerind Foundation, which now fills a key role by hosting a series of remarkably useful southwestern seminars.

I'm certainly not the first to put the Southwest in a book. Among recent efforts, I enthusiastically recommend John Kantner's *Ancient Puebloan Southwest* (2004), Stephen Plog's *Ancient Peoples of the American Southwest* (1997), Jeff Reid and Stephanie Whittlesey's *Archaeology of Ancient Arizona* (1997), and, of course, Linda Cordell's *Archaeology of the Southwest* (1997). I'd like to think that my book might be the first to intentionally integrate the archaeology of the Southwest's three major regions—Anasazi, Mogollon, and Hohokam, taken together—with the parallel history of southwestern archaeology. How well that works I leave to readers and reviewers.

The title of this book is the same as a volume published in 1957 by Harold S. Gladwin. A diligent search for copyright revealed that Gladwin's title was available. I've used it because it describes concisely what I was trying to write and because I have a sneaking regard for old Harold. He is not today highly regarded, but a man who illustrates "nuclear fission in the Mimbres" with a progression of increasingly busy geometric pottery designs deserves our consideration.

Everywhere I go, these guys (and Earl Morris) were there first: David Wilcox and Carroll Riley. Long may they wave! For less specific but still fundamental inspiration, I thank Murray Gell-Mann, Alden Hayes, Mike Kabotie, Roger Kennedy, Ed Ladd, Peter Pino, Rina Swentzell, and Phillip Tuwaletstiwa. I've learned a lot from these people. I suspect that none will fully approve of the product, but what merit it might have comes, in part, from their observations and attitudes about what's important and what's not.

Friends and colleagues at the University of Colorado read various sections of this book, and created a very happy place for archaeology: Doug Bamforth, Larry Benson, Diane Conlin, Linda Cordell, Jim Dixon, Beth Dusinberre, Frank Eddy, Jim Hester, John Hoffecker, Bob Hohlfelder, Art Joyce, Payson Sheets, and Paola Villa. Thanks!

And I cannot fail to acknowledge with grateful thanks my wife and colleague, Catherine Cameron. It's great to have an expert in the house. She is in no way implicated in this book or its arguments. If she were the author, it would be a kinder, gentler, better book.

Finally, I nod to paired muses, whose art in other fields inspired or at least diverted me. In Anglophile moments, Plonk and Plum. For counterpoised Americana, Hoss and Hag. Of that million-dollar quartet, only the Hag still stands.

This book was inspired by actual events.

Figure 1.1. Paquimé, or Casas Grandes, in Chihuahua, Mexico—the Southwest's last and greatest city, 1300 to 1450. Painting by Alice Wesche, who illustrated Charles Di Peso's monumental report Casas Grandes. Wesche later wrote and illustrated a children's book about Paquimé: Runs Far, Son of the Chichimecs (1981). This image is on the cover. Courtesy Museum of New Mexico Press.

o n e
Fore! — *Orthodoxies*

Archaeologies: 1500 to 1850
Histories: "Time Immemorial" to 1500 BC

This book is about southwestern archaeology and the ancient Southwest—two very different things. *Archaeology* is how we learn about the distant past. The *ancient Southwest* is what actually happened way back then. Archaeology will never disclose or discover *everything* that happened in the ancient Southwest, but archaeology is our best scholarly way to know *anything* about that distant past.

After a century of southwestern archaeology, we know a lot about what happened in the ancient Southwest. We know so much—we have such a wealth of data and information—that much of what we think we know about the Southwest has been necessarily compressed into conventions, classifications, and orthodoxies. This is particularly true of abstract concepts such as Anasazi, Hohokam, and Mogollon. A wall is a wall, a pot is a pot, but Anasazi is... what exactly?

This book challenges several orthodoxies and reconfigures others in novel ways—"novel," perhaps, like *Gone with the Wind*. I try to stick to the facts, but some facts won't stick to me. These are mostly old facts—nut-hard verities of past generations. Orthodoxies, shiny from years of handling, slip through fingers and fall through screens like gizzard stones. We can work without them. We already know a few turkeys were involved in the story.

Each chapter in this book tells two parallel stories: the development, personalities, and institutions of southwestern archaeology ("archaeologies") and interpretations of what actually happened in the ancient past ("histories"). The century-long development of southwestern archaeology parallels, in odd but interesting ways, what happened in the much longer, three-millennium-long history of the ancient Southwest. Chapters 1 through 7 match sequences of archaeologies and histories, building frameworks and story lines for the last half of the last chapter—the point, the punch line, the nervous scraggly rabbit pulled out of a threadbare hat.

The first seven chapters are, in effect, extended notes for "A History of the Ancient Southwest," the last half of chapter 8. And each chapter has its own extended apparatus of notes—notes to notes. Impatient readers may cut to the chase: read the last half of chapter 8 first, and then browse through the earlier chapters. But it's all one big intertwined story. We can't understand the history of the ancient Southwest without also understanding the development of archaeological thinking, because what we know about the past comes through the filters and lenses of archaeology. Archaeology has a history of its own, focusing on different things in different ways at different stages of its development. So it's all history, or histories.

What's so interesting about *history*? Surely, that's what archaeology has been doing all along? Yes and no. The earliest southwestern archaeologists (chapters 1 and 2) considered themselves historians or prehistorians. Their goals—history—were those of European archaeology, a scholarly field that developed from written history and art history. Decades later, in the nineteenth century, American (anthropological) archaeology developed as a natural or social science with the work of Lewis Henry Morgan and Adolph Bandelier (chapter 2). History was not a major focus of anthropological archaeology because anthropologists weren't entirely certain that American Indians *had* history in the European sense. During the first half of the twentieth century, American archaeologists pursued "culture history" (chapters 3 and 4), but culture history was less history than *systematics*: geographically and chronologically structured diagrams of who was where when. No narratives tied together the rows and columns of culture history charts. Tree-ring and carbon 14 dating—and historical verisimilitude—arrived shortly before and after World War II, respectively (chapter 4). Archaeology then had precise dates with which to order events chronologically: what happened when. But before that chronological precision could be woven into a narrative, along came scientific "New Archaeology" (chapter 5). "New" in the 1960s, New Archaeology (in its most enthusiastic forms) eschewed history altogether, aiming instead for scientific laws or processes that transcended time and space (chapters 5 and 6). By the early 1980s, postmodern sensibilities—doubting science—had revived historical interests (chapter 7). Then several federal laws favoring Indians and historic preservation forced history down science's throat (chapters 7 and 8). Today almost all archaeology "does history" of one sort or another. But that's a recent development, only in the past ten years or so. We are still learning how to write history.

When we write southwestern history, what tales do we tell? Surprisingly dull stories, as it turns out. Apparently, nothing much ever happened in the ancient Southwest. Paul Martin and Fred Plog (whom we shall meet again in chapter 5) published a well-regarded textbook in 1973. One chapter lists "the great events" (273) in southwestern prehistory. There were precisely three: agriculture, towns ("an explanation based on technoenvironmental and technoeconomic determinism" [297]), and abandonment. People got corn, formed towns, and then left them for other towns. End of story.

The backstory, or master narrative, beginning with the first great Southwesternist, Adolph Bandelier, and continuing today, has been steady progress from rough rude beginnings to Pueblo life:

> The picture which can be dimly traced into this past is a very modest and unpretending one. No great cataclysms of nature, no waves of destruction on a large scale, either natural or human, appear to have interrupted the slow and tedious development of the people before the Spaniards came.[1]

We would not put it that way today of course. We know (and of course Martin and Plog knew) there were a few bumps on the road. The Great Drought of 1275 to 1300, for example, qualifies as a cataclysm. But a century after Bandelier and his "slow and tedious development," we still favor versions of the past that turn ancient people into modern Pueblos as quietly and efficiently as possible. Slow and tedious, perhaps, but along a fairly straight line leading to the Pueblos—serene, spiritual, communal, eternal. That's the version you see in museum exhibits, hear at Mesa Verde campfire talks, read in Santa Fe coffee table books. That's the orthodoxy.

I don't think it happened that way. I think the Southwest had rises and falls, kings and commoners, war and peace, triumphs and failures. Real history! Just like everyone else, the wide world over. And I think the story of the ancient Southwest was the story of the *whole* Southwest and beyond. The rise of kings at Chaco Canyon, for example, was a geopolitical reaction to the Colonial Period Hohokam expansion (chapters 4 and 5); the Hohokam Classic Period was the product of refugee Chacoan nobles chased off the Colorado Plateau by angry farmers (chapters 6 and 7); Casas Grandes was a failed attempt to create a Mesoamerican state (chapter 7); and modern Pueblos—so different from Chaco and Casas Grandes—developed not *from* their past but as a *deliberate rejection of* that past (chapter 8). Along the way there were cataclysms and destructions, and societies so big and bright we could rightly call them civilizations. That's a different history—not the sort of thing you'll read in coffee table books; it is a kind of history that archaeology has denied the ancient Southwest for reasons, honorable and not so honorable, that occupy many of the pages that follow. This book challenges the conventional view, our orthodoxies of the ancient Southwest.

How to Write a History of the Ancient Southwest

My goal is to write a narrative history of the ancient Southwest, specifically a political history. Why *political*? I will explain below. Why *narrative*? Simon Martin, in a recent essay, "On Pre-Columbian Narrative," explains:

> We cannot comprehend the meaning of time, or history, or personal experience outside the narrative form, making it a universal of mankind throughout the ages.... For all its centrality, and the weight of literature directed at the topic, defining exactly what is meant by "narrative" has seldom proved easy. At its broadest, we might include all discourses on human action, *especially as they concern change to an existing state of affairs*—usually describing both the reasons for that change and its consequences.[2]

An *eventful* history, a history in which *things happened*. We don't currently have that kind of history of the ancient Southwest. We have phase sequences, chronologies, and population graphs.[3]

Don't get me wrong: it took tons of work by many talented archaeologists to discover, analyze, and assemble those phase sequences, chronologies, and population graphs. Southwestern archaeology accumulated almost terrifying amounts of information and data. Making sense of it all is an enormous task. Fifty years ago, a committee of senior scholars—all wiser than I am—declared, "The time is not yet here when one man, or one committee, can write a new 'Southwestern Archaeology.'"[4] The following half century has not made the task any easier. The quantity of raw and processed data, of site reports and syntheses, has increased astronomically. It is inconceivable that a single person (or even a very large committee) could master that vast literature. What do I conclude from this? To write a history of the ancient Southwest, the aspiring author must be (1) completely bonkers or (2) highly selective. Or most likely both.

I leave it to others to judge my qualifications under criterion 1. I can more usefully address criterion 2, selectivity. Simon Martin again: "While we might consider any particular narrative self-contained, even the 'thickest' and most detailed description leaves a universe of crucial information unstated."[5] Let us be clear from the onset: I am not writing a comprehensive review of southwestern archaeology, presenting and weighing every model or idea. I pick and choose, and I do not exhaustively consider every alternative explanation. I attempt to reduce ten thousand years of glorious, messy, incompressible human history into a short, reasonably coherent narrative (the last half of chapter 8). Think of southwestern archaeology as a vast Iowa-size field of maize—variegated in corn's many varieties and colors—and think of the last half of chapter 8 as a shot of bourbon, neat. How do we get from corn to mash to still to barrel to bottle?[6]

Well, that depends. Is archaeology history or is it science? Science requires one set of procedures; history another. That question and its spin-offs occupied American archaeology for most of my career (which began during the distant, heady days of New Archaeology), and it's still unresolved. My contemporaries and I were trained in the 1970s and 1980s as scientists, and most members of my age group consider themselves scientists. But I've chosen to write history. (Sections to follow explore how that's done.) Since I've (temporarily) hung up my lab coat and (briefly) abandoned hypotheses for narrative, a short explanation is in order.

Archaeologists swim in theoretical schools. It's comforting—socially, intellectually, and professionally—to think, speak, and move together.[7] But which school? A recent review welcomes to this new millennium "a thousand archaeologies."[8] But I see only two: science and humanities. After four decades, C. P. Snow's "Two Cultures" (1959) have been rejected as a false dichotomy. But I reject those rejections. The differences are profound: sciences simplify understanding, reducing an unruly world to principles and *processes* (thus "processual archaeology," chapter 6); the humanities and arts multiply understandings, with as many valid insights as there are gifted practitioners—each a unique appreciation of unique events or phenomena. Schools formed along those two lines, following Lewis Binford (science) and Ian Hodder (humanities).[9]

Four decades ago, Binford (who dominated archaeology in the 1960s and 1970s and with whom I studied at the University of New Mexico) told us that we were poor scientists. Two decades later, Hodder (the leading British archaeologist, recently transplanted to Stanford University) told us that we were poor humanists. Both were right. They each found different deficiencies in American archaeology because they each had different ideas about what archaeology should be. Binford rejoiced in reduction and generalization and science; Hodder celebrated complications and particularity and humanistic understandings. Chalk and cheese.

Well known, but curiously underappreciated, is the fact that European and American archaeologies have very different histories and are in many ways different disciplines.[10] European archaeology may consort with anthropology, but it originated in written history and art history. European "prehistory is…a humanity and those who would call it a science are using the word *science* in a very special way."[11] We replied: "American archaeology is anthropology or it is nothing."[12] Anthropology, once the "science of man," remains very much at home with the social and natural sciences. "New" or scientific archaeology, at its most extreme, avoided history altogether: it sought laws and rules, not unique stories of particular places (Bruce Trigger rightly noted "the antihistorical bias of New Archaeology").[13] Despite recent humanistic turns in anthropology, American archaeology is still funded by the National Science Foundation and is featured regularly in *Science*.[14] British books and conferences address science *and* archaeology, or science *in* archaeology; American archaeology remains convinced that it *is* science.

"This disciplinary difference is far more than mere bureaucratic procedure: it mirrors the development of remarkably different methods and theories in Europe and the US."[15] Witness the appalled reaction of Europeans to the aggressive scientism of New Archaeology as expressed in *Explanation in Archaeology: An Explicitly Scientific Approach*, by Watson, LeBlanc, and Redman (1971). That book lit fires in Britain that have not yet burned out; our British cousins are still annoyed by scientific hypothetico-deductive Popperian falsification (which is curious because not many American archaeologists actually did archaeology *that way*). Conversely, American archaeologists are confused and bemused by the art school manifestos of avant-garde British archaeology, the introspective archaeology of Barbara Bender,[16] and the theater/archaeology of Michael Shanks.[17] (How many British archaeologists actually do archaeology *that way?*)

I've found myself swimming with one school and then the other, depending on where they were headed. Right now, I'm interested in history, for reasons that may or may not become clear in books yet to be written. But I'm not jumping in the deep end with the Brits. We differ on scale, and scale is important. Humanistic history loves small scales, even micro scales; it has been said that all history is essentially biography. The ancient Southwest must have had heroes and villains, elites and commoners, men and women of engaging interest. There would be plenty of biography if we could only know those long-gone characters and individuals. We can't—not without a time machine. So I'll essay history on a larger, geographic scale—which we *do* know, thanks to the hard work of pioneer, culture history, and New Archaeologists and their postmodern progeny. For more than a century, archaeologists have tramped back and forth across our quarter of the continent, finding sites and making notes. We know the geography of the ancient Southwest.[18]

Histories, Scales, and Connections

Modern history, however, favors smaller scales—a postmodern trend. Conventional biography (of course!) but also the micro scales of a medieval village in France, a woman's life on the American frontier—scholarly narratives constructed on the smallest possible scales dominate the literature. But there is also a countercurrent in contemporary history toward larger, even global scales. In the face of postmodern downsizing, globalization justifies Big History, which reemerged in recent years as "world history." Jerry Bentley, in a survey of "The New World History," defines the genre:

> The term world *history*…does not imply that historians must deal with the entire history of all the world's peoples, and certainly not all at the same time. It refers instead to historical scholarship that explicitly compares experiences across the boundaries of societies, or that examines interactions between peoples of different societies, or that analyzes large-scale historical patterns and processes that transcend individual societies.[19]

A flurry of recent studies focuses on the interconnectedness of the world's regions and continents: McNeill and McNeill's *The Human Web* (2003), David Christian's *Maps of Time* ("An Introduction to Big History," 2004), and Felipe Fernández-Armesto's *Pathfinders* (2006)—or, more to the point, his hemispheric *The Americas* (2003).[20]

Surely, *global* goals are unsuited for the Southwest—a small and insignificant bit of the great large world? Most readers, whether archaeologists or innocent civilians, probably share a view of the Southwest as neither mover nor shaker in world events. Rather, they see an

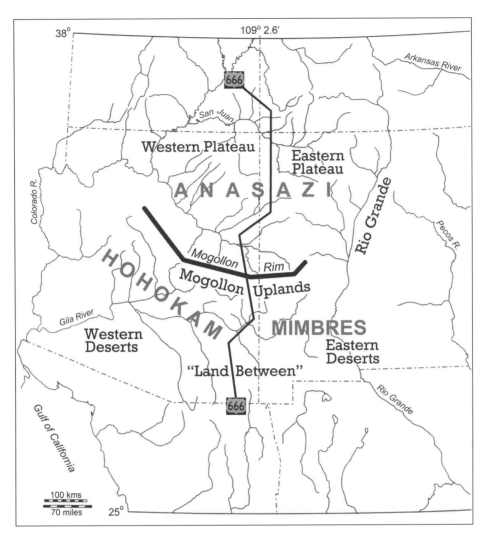

Figure 1.2. The Southwest. Courtesy of the author.

isolate, a backwater, an island of serenity amid the tumult and clatter of captains and kings. That idyllic detachment is one of the Southwest's particular (contemporary) charms. That's wrong. The ancient Southwest was not a prime mover in global events, but neither was it an island, entire unto itself (as we shall see in the chapters that follow). Do not fear: I am not trying to inflate the Southwest into a major player in world history.

I am inspired instead by the *scales* of world history, and particularly by the presupposition that *things were more likely than not interconnected*. If, as Big History tells us, the world and its continents were interconnected in historically important ways, it seems likely that smaller regions were too, in ways less dramatic but still consequential—within the Southwest, for example, across regions such as Anasazi, Hohokam, and Mogollon (figs. 1.2, 1.3), which we will explore in chapter 3. Southwestern archaeology views those three cultural regions as separate domains, separate professional specialties.[21] An Anasazi archaeologist is not required to know much about Hohokam, and vice versa. I'm troubled by that separation and specialization. It seems likely to me that the various regions of the Southwest were densely

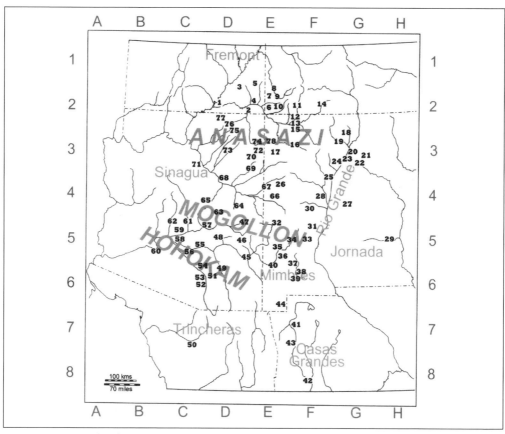

Figure 1.3. Sites and archaeological regions. Courtesy of the author.

29 SJ 423, 16 (F3)
Adamsville, 56 (C5)
Agua Fria, 62 (C5)
Alkali Ridge, 5 (E1)
Aragon, 32 (E5)
Archeotekopa, 26 (E4)
Awatovi, 73 (D3)
Azatlan, 61 (C5)
Aztec Ruins, 12 (F2)
Bad Dog Ridge, 70 (E3)
Bass, 7 (E2)
Betatakin, 77 (D2)
Black Mesa, 75 (D3)
Black Mountain, 39 (F6)
Bloom Mound, 29 (H5)
Blue Mesa, 11 (F2)
Bluff, 4 (E2)
Broken K Pueblo, 64 (D4)
Bronze Trail Group, 23 (G3)
Canyon de Chelly, 74 (E3)
Carter Ranch, 64 (D4)
Casa Grande, 56 (C5)
Cerrillos, 23 (G3)
Cerro Colorado, 66 (E4)
Cerro de Trincheras, 50 (C7)
Cerro Juanqueña, 41 (F7)
CH 151, 42 (F8)
Chaco Canyon, 16 (F3)
Chavez Pass, 65 (D4)
Chetro Ketl, 16 (F3)
Chimney Rock, 14 (F2)

Cliff Palace, 10 (E2)
Dolores, 8 (E2)
Escalante AZ, 55 (C5)
Escalante CO, 9 (E2)
Farview, 10 (E2)
Fort West-Lee Village,
 36 (E5)
Galaz, 37 (F6)
Galisteo, 22 (G3)
Gallinas Spring, 30 (F4)
Gatlin, 60 (B5)
Gila Bend, 60 (B5)
Gila Pueblo, 48 (D5)
Glen Canyon, 1 (D2)
Goat Hill, 45 (D5)
Grand Canal, 59 (C5)
Grass Mesa, 8 (E2)
Grasshopper, 63 (D4)
Great Sage Plain, 7 (E2)
Grewe, 56 (C5)
Gurley, 64 (D4)
Hawiku, 67 (E4)
Hay Hollow Valley, 64 (D4)
Homolovi, 68 (D4)
Hungo Pavi, 16 (F3)
Joyce Well, 44 (E6)
Keet Seel, 77 (D2)
Kin Cheops, 66 (E4)
Kin Li Chee, 72 (E3)
Kin Tiel, 69 (E3)
Kinishba, 47 (D5)

Kuapa, 24 (G3)
Kuaua, 25 (F4)
Kwilleylekia, 35 (E5)
La Ciudad, 59 (C5)
Las Capas, 53 (C6)
Las Colinas, 59 (C5)
Long House Valley, 76 (D2)
Los Muertos, 58 (C5)
Los Pozos, 53 (C6)
Lowry, 7 (E2)
Marana, 54 (C6)
McPhee, 8 (E2)
Mesa Grande, 58 (C5)
Mesa Verde, 10 (E2)
NAN, 38 (F6)
Owen's, 3 (D2)
Palo Verde, 62 (C5)
Paquimé, 43 (E7)
Pecos, 21 (G3)
Peñasco Blanco, 16 (F3)
Phoenix, 58 & 59 (C5)
Pine Lawn Valley, 32 (E5)
Point of Pines, 46 (D5)
Poncho House, 2 (E2)
Poshu'ouinge, 19 (G3)
Poston Butte, 55 (C5)
Pottery Mound, 28 (F4)
Pueblo Alto, 16 (F3)
Pueblo Bonito, 16 (F3)
Pueblo Grande, 59 (C5)
Pueblo Viejo, 45 (D5)

Redrock, 40 (E6)
Reeve, 49 (D6)
Ridges Basin, 11 (F2)
Roosevelt 9:6, 57 (D5)
Sacred Ridge, 11 (F2)
Safford, 45 (E5)
Salinas, 27 (G4)
Salmon, 13 (F2)
Sand Canyon, 7 (E2)
Shabikeschee, 16 (F3)
Silver Creek, 64 (D4)
Snaketown, 58 (C5)
Stove Canyon, 46 (D5)
SU, 32 (E5)
TJ, 34 (F5)
Tonto Basin, 57 (D5)
Tonto Cliff Dwellings, 57 (D5)
Twin Angels, 15 (F3)
Una Vida, 16 (F3)
University Indian Ruin,
 51 (D6)
Valencia Vieja, 52 (C6)
Victorio, 31 (F5)
White House, 74 (E3)
Winston, 33 (F5)
Woodrow, 35 (E5)
Wupatki, 71 (C3)
Yellow Jacket, 7 (E2)
Yucca House, 6 (E2)
Zuni, 67 (E4)

interconnected in ways we can see—and can't see. Anasazi, Hohokam, and Mogollon were not atomistic isolates, separate until proven otherwise. World history—Big History—offers a different perspective: human societies (even on Easter Island) existed only in the context of other societies. Local histories were always embedded in much larger narratives. This should be true of the Southwest too. We should *expect* interconnections between and among our carefully constructed culture areas.[22]

And I am pretty sure that the Southwest will never be understood except as a part of much larger North America. The Southwest was part of that larger world, not so much shaken as stirred by events beyond its borders. By the time the Southwest really got going—say, around AD 500—states and civilizations had been roaring along for two millennia in other parts of North America. Southwestern civilizations were late bloomers on a continent marked by active and intense large-scale, long-distance interaction. What picture would emerge if we began our thinking about the Southwest with the premise that it and its subregions were *more likely interconnected than otherwise?*[23]

Connecting the Dots

I write history by *connecting the dots*. The British call this method interpretive archaeology. "Filling in the gaps in the past…rendering it comprehensible," as one of the leading British archaeologists, Julian Thomas, says (nodding to Michael Shanks and Christopher Tilley) in his introduction to *Interpretive Archaeology*.[24] But here's the rub: what renders the past comprehensible *to me* may not work *for you*. Tilley tells us that "the 'truth' of an interpretation in archaeology, in effect, boils down to its acceptability to others"; "consequently, there is always resistance to novel interpretations."[25] Not only do I connect the dots differently, I see different dots! Different key sites, turning points, events. That's one reason we have seven chapters of windup—setting up the dots—before the pitch in chapter 8. To connect those dots, I follow three principles: (1) Everyone knew everything! (2) No coincidences! and (3) Distances can be dealt with. I err in many ways, I'm sure, but I err consistently in those three directions.

Everyone Knew Everything!

Of course, I do not mean that everyone in ancient North America had perfect social and environmental knowledge on a continental scale. Rather, I want to shift the burden of proof from the current default that ancient Indians (until proven otherwise with lead-pipe certainty) were ignorant hicks who knew little or nothing beyond their front yards or at best their valleys. We labor mightily—spending lavishly for laboratory tests of who made what where—to demonstrate that Indians on one side of the river knew about Indians on the other side of the river. Why start with such an unrealistic, even demeaning assumption? Why not instead assume that people were aware of what was going on over the hill and over the horizon? Assume interconnections!

I think, for example, that we can safely assume most Anasazi were well aware of Hohokam. People on the Dolores River during the ninth century knew that big things were happening on the Gila River, and more than a few had firsthand knowledge of those events. (As far as I know, no Hohokam sherds have ever been found on the Dolores River. So what?) Likewise Mexico: assume that southwestern peoples were aware of civilizations to the south and that the southwestern world was conditioned by that knowledge.

No Coincidences!

As scientific archaeologists, we were trained to assume that concurrent or sequential changes in different regions—for example, that in the tenth and eleventh centuries Hohokam fell while Chaco rose (chapter 5)—were causally unrelated unless proven otherwise. We do accept coincidence in regional and transregional *environmental* dynamics—El Niños, droughts, shifting westerlies correspond to cultural changes—but we eschew large-scale *historical* coincidences. If something goes up in one region and down in another, that's merely coincidence—in the sense of unrelated, random events. I think that's wrong, or at least wrongheaded. What happens if we take the opposite tack? [26]

Most coincidences (probably) were not coincidental. If something goes up or gets bigger in one area and goes down or gets smaller in another, or if similar things happen across several areas at the same time, or if series of events happen in parallel sequences, then I will assume that those things and events, more likely than not, were historically interconnected. Unless proven otherwise.

Distances Can Be Dealt With

Alice Kehoe inscribed the phrase "Distances can be dealt with" in a book she autographed. Long distances, as Kehoe rightly notes, did not intimidate Native North Americans. Why should distances intimidate *us*? Global or world histories of other continents show that human societies were almost never isolates. Polynesian societies offer us the incredible fact of their very existence: Polynesians *got there*, over vast and truly daunting distances. Distances *were* dealt with, in Polynesia and in North America, as we shall see in following chapters. Eric Wolf exhorted us in his classic *Europe and the People Without History*, "What difference it would make to our understanding if we looked at the world as a whole, a totality, a system, instead of as a sum of self-contained societies and cultures.… As we unraveled the chains of causes and effects at work in the lives of particular populations, we saw them extend beyond any one population to embrace the trajectories of others—all others."[27]

After some necessary stage setting in chapter 2, I'm fairly explicit about these three principles in chapter 3, so you can see how they work. Thereafter, they fade into the background—but they were posted over my desk throughout the writing of this book.

My Predilections

The rules and principles we just reviewed might be called methods or (in academese) methodology. Just as important are my innate prejudices: (1) I have outdated notions of politics, and (2) I'm down on parsimony. These are arcane archaeological concerns. Readers who are not interested in academic debates might do well to skip to page 14; we've had enough scholarly angst for one chapter already!

Playing Politics

I have unsubtle, undernuanced notions of "politics": I'm interested in hierarchies—a few people telling a lot of people what to do and enjoying it. The few enjoyed it, that is. But perhaps not forever. It's good to be king, until an angry mob rolls up a tumbrel. When small groups began making decisions for large groups and those decisions stuck, an interesting tipping point in human history and social evolution had been reached. Things happened that might not otherwise have happened, for good or ill (what *was* the lead lemming thinking?). Glorious Caesar or backroom cabal, somebody called the shots. (Of course, people don't always do what they are told; ask Louis XVI, Nicholas II, or any modern pope.) Most humans live with that kind of governance today, and it would be interesting to watch how it developed and operated in the past. Centralized, hierarchical governance is my narrow definition of "politics" in "political history."

In fairness to myself, my ideas of politics are not so much undertheorized as tightly focused (tunnel-visioned?). I'm sure there were plenty of communal nongovernments in the old Southwest, but they are relevant to my interests only in retrospect, as things that developed after the Southwest rid itself of conventional hierarchies and elites (chapter 7). I will suggest kinds of political hierarchy that may seem outré in the ancient Southwest—*kings*, for example.[28] In the 1980s, arguments about hierarchy and political complexity dominated southwestern archaeology (chapters 6 and 7). Today those topics are outdated, unfashionable. At the risk of being a bit retro, I think the potential insights of ancient southwestern political history are too important to dismiss like an old toy tossed aside by a kid with too many new toys. It seems sometimes that archaeology does not solve old problems; we simply tire of them or wear them out. Yesterday it was adaptation and complexity; today it is agency and ritual; tomorrow it will be something else.[29] It's too soon to abandon hierarchies; they have great interest for evolutionary sciences,[30] for political science,[31] and I think for the history of the ancient Southwest.

And it's a question of fairness, of equal coverage. Southwestern archaeology has long favored commoners over leaders. We've studied commoners for more than a century. Indeed, for the longest time we didn't even know there *were* leaders. Time for the leaders to take a bow.[32]

Hierarchy in the Southwest actually matters. For example, in the breach, the idealized perception (mistaken, I think) of communal, nonhierarchical societies in the ancient Southwest—through the work of Lewis Henry Morgan (chapters 2 and 8)—influenced Karl Marx and his followers. The cold war is over, so that interest is merely historical. But hierarchies in the ancient Southwest also offer insights into perennial, seemingly unanswerable questions: What's up with governments? Where do governments come from? I will suggest, in chapter 8, that southwestern hierarchies might even tell us something about states—secondary states. (For southwestern archaeologists, *states* are even worse than kings.) We can understand southwestern history only if we remember what was happening on the larger North American continent: two millennia of kings and empires to the south; great cities with kinglike "chiefs" to the east, in the Mississippi Valley. Even the California Coast, to the west, became politically "complex" during the era of Chaco and Hohokam. The Southwest was all but surrounded by "chiefs," kings, states, and "complexity." Politics in the Southwest had precedents, and if the Southwest had states, they weren't original. No southwestern king manqué had to *invent* kingship.

One of the more interesting aspects of political hierarchy is how some societies reject it, avoid it. Pierre Clastres called this situation "societies against the state."[33] Archaeological interpretations of southwestern societies were and are often cast that way: ancient North American societies were *not* states; they avoided the trap of government. And the ancient Southwest does provide, as we shall see, two remarkable instances of the rejection of state-level politics, "the defeat of hierarchy" as Barbara Mills termed it[34]—first, Hohokam, which should have been a state but wasn't (chapters 4 and 5), and second, Pueblo peoples, turning away from the hierarchical, statelike political arrangements of Chaco (chapters 7 and 8).

Hohokam is a puzzler (and one of the great pleasures of writing this book. I am mystified by Hohokam—and that's a good thing). Pueblo prehistory, in contrast, was not stateless or state free; early governments at Chaco Canyon and later centers set the historical circumstances for a Pueblo revolt, turning away from kings and toward the communal (chapters 7 and 8).

Hierarchy is a good theme for Big History because the forms and trappings of hierarchy move over distance—not just as empires or colonies but as ideas and practices.[35] Hierarchical governance is by definition an elite endeavor, and elites communicate on levels and over distances not often reached by commoners.[36] The Southwest developed kingdomlike polities at a time when Mesoamerica was rife with states and empires. The rise (and fall) of hierarchies in the Southwest was historically affected by or connected to that larger world. Fledgling governments often replicate or mimic older, bigger, better-known states (the sincerest form of flattery). As we shall see, southwestern leaders looked to the south, to Mesoamerica, to support their hierarchies, as did Pueblo and Hohokam looking for alternatives to kingship.

Once hierarchy starts, it spreads like rust or crabgrass or cancer. This is important, because hierarchies in the Southwest (if any) were neither original nor parthogenetic. Kings ruled in ancient Mexico for millennia before Chaco and Cahokia, and they begot other kings by inspiration and insemination; they begot other kings, and so forth. These things were known in the Southwest and the Mississippi Valley.

David Anderson mapped the spread of chiefdomlike governance pulsing out from the middle Mississippi across the southeastern United States (fig. 1.4; see chapter 5).[37] Starting with a "big bang" at Cahokia—the great Native city on the Mississippi and Chaco's exact contemporary—secondary and tertiary chiefdoms rippled outward, appearing first near Cahokia and then farther and farther away, much like the appearance of secondary and tertiary states on the margins of major civilizations. Anderson writes:

> Given the scarcity of evidence for chiefdom organizational spread through migration (something now suggested in only a few cases such as at Macon Plateau in central Georgia or the Zebree site in northeast Arkansas)…the spread of chiefly organization was more likely something of a reactive process. Following arguments of Carniero, if the first chiefdoms were predatory, chiefdoms may have emerged across the region as defensive reaction. Alternately or additionally, they developed to allow privileged lineages to participate more effectively in expanding trade and status-based, power-enhancing games through a process of competitive emulation.[38]

Ben Nelson proposed a similar "propagation" model for the spread of Mesoamerican traditions outward to the Southwest:

> Mesoamerican styles and practices spread northward along a time series of newly aggregated social groups whose formation demanded the introduction of symbols and practices associated with hegemonic order…. Small groups either assimilated to a growing politically coherent local center or moved away, eventually to face the same pressures again. Individuals joining local centers would naturally become subordinates, but they might establish their legitimacy by demonstrating special knowledge. Competence in Mesoamerican ritual and warring practices may have given some immigrants bases of power…. Neither the Hohokam nor any southwestern polity appears to have been Mesoamerican dominated, and yet Mesoamerican elements—including genes and languages—did appear there. Indeed, it may be the resistance to domination, both internal

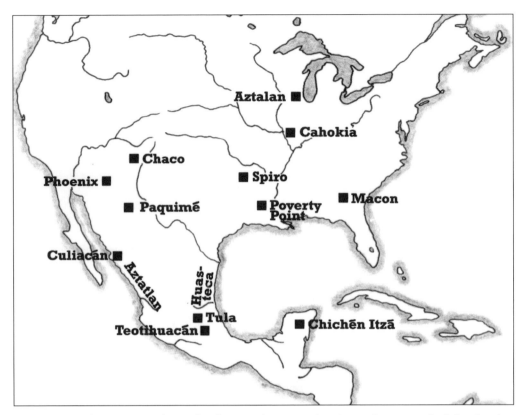

Figure 1.4. North America. On this small-scale map, Alta Vista and La Quemada are near the "z" in Aztatlan; and Teuchitlan is near the "n" in Aztatlan. Courtesy of the author.

and external, that fundamentally sets the Southwest apart from Mesoamerica, but that is another issue.[39]

Indeed, an issue central to this book, especially chapters 7 and 8. Throughout the following chapters, I try to frame southwestern events in the political context of Mesoamerica and the Mississippi Valley. Gordon Brotherston, who has looked more broadly at these matters than most archaeologists, laments the historical ignorance of a continental "native coherence ceaselessly splintered by Western politics and philosophy."[40] The Southwest mirrored larger Mesoamerican and Mississippian histories on smaller, local scales. Governance—its forms and protocols and sometimes perhaps its protagonists—moved across space, on both continental and regional scales. Some portion of southwestern political history might have been actual movement by displaced elites or would-be elites. And some portion might have been the adoption or emulation by local wannabes of ways of governance seen at other southwestern or Mesoamerican centers. Large-scale processes can indeed explain small-scale processes and at least make those small-scale processes something more than local history.[41]

Against Parsimony

My second peccadillo is a tendency to think that, all things being equal, the past was generally more interesting than not. This idea runs against a somewhat peculiar notion of "parsimony," a staple of American archaeology. Parsimony is a principle of simplicity, drawn like a gun to shoot down anything bigger than our customary breadbox, to mix metaphors. American archaeologists are encouraged to favor the simple over the complicated, the conservative over the daring. This approach (we think) makes us good scientists because we "stay close to the data." But consider: "the data" represent a small sample of a site that represents a small sample of a society's material remains that represent a tiny and indirect sample of its range of people, actions, and events—what actually happened in the ancient Southwest. No matter how much we dig, we work with impossibly small, unrepresentative samples of data. Any statement that stays "close to the data" almost certainly misrepresents the past.

I critiqued "parsimony" elsewhere as the sin of Occam: misapplication of the razor to the question of interest rather than to the logic of its answer.[42] Columnist Marilyn Vos Savant (once touted as "the highest IQ") writes a brain piece for the Sunday papers. She discounts parsimony thus:

> Many of us have heard that the simplest solution to a problem is the best one. This is a commonsense warning against unnecessarily complicated solutions, especially to practical problems. But some people think the statement also means: "The simplest answer to a question is the best one." This is just plain wrong. That's because problems and questions are different. Problems describe situations that need to be resolved.... By contrast, questions are requests for information, so the context of the question must be considered.... The best answer to a question will seldom be the simplest.[43]

I could not have said it better myself, because I am not as smart as Vos Savant. Marilyn and I don't like parsimony, but perhaps for different reasons. I think parsimony, as applied archaeologically, too often has the unintended consequence of underestimating Native accomplishments and—far more ominously—*keeping the Natives down*. Parsimony's real problems are not simply misapplied logic; the real problems are rather more sinister (chapter 8). We have been trained to think that Native societies north of Mexico *could not* have been large, complicated, or hierarchical, because our intellectual forefathers believed those societies to be simple and—here we go!—"savage" (chapter 8). Those were the assumptions of the forefathers of our field, who trained our teachers' teachers' teachers. But the societies of the ancient Southwest (and North America) were neither simple nor savage.

I anticipate objections to my interpretations in this book: too big, too complicated, too unparsimonious. Loud objections, strident objections—I've heard them already at conferences, in seminars, and over drinks. The things I suggest for the ancient Southwest seem unseemly for the kinds of societies we know—or think we know—north of the Rio Grande. "They couldn't have done that!" "That's beyond their capabilities!" "Remember the scales of these societies!" (These are real quotes.) To that I say bosh! Who are we to say what they could or couldn't do? Within very broad limits of environment and even more elastic limits of technology, anything was possible.

We should not limit Native history a priori. We should not say, "They couldn't have done that." Those limits, in both historical and archaeological thinking about Native Americans north of the Rio Grande, have unpleasant pedigrees—far more serious than mistaken theory. It was in our interests (I use the plural pronoun here to mean the United States of past times) to have simple, savage Natives—because essentially we wanted them gone. Our policies were less to assimilate than to eliminate, either by removal or destruction. (Efforts to remove or at least significantly diminish the Pueblos continued through the 1940s.) And it was morally easier to exterminate savages than it was to topple civilizations. So: No civilizations north of

Mexico. Mound builders were not Native; Aztec Ruins were, well, Aztec (chapter 8). It was convenient, morally, to portray the history of Native peoples north of the Rio Grande as simple and savage.[44]

Originally, unquestionably, these ideas were racist. Parsimony, used today as a scientific principle, runs the risk of perpetuating antique, racist notions about Native America. No archaeologist known to me is the least bit racist, but we are heirs to unwholesome traditions. Kings are demoted to chiefs, cities are leveled to chiefly centers, acts of will and courage are explained as adaptations to changing environments. We have edited their past to fit our present for almost five centuries.

The present isn't what it used to be. It's time to give ancient Native America back its complicated and impressive past, its *history*—insofar as that's ours to give. Too big? Too complex? I think not. My pumped-up versions of the ancient Southwest are still far shy of the mark, still too simple. The Southwest was a lively, dynamic, eventful place—a region with a history as rich and varied (and uneven) as any other in the New World. Parsimony, improperly applied, denies the political history that drove the ancient Southwest.[45]

Settings

The continents we call the Americas were transformed by European conquest: both calendars and place-names changed. After several failed experiments with decolonized terms and time systems (see chapter 8, note 50), I capitulate. I use Old World calendars and Old World geographic terms for Native times and spaces. Archaeology has so far been a Euro-American pursuit, and this book is written in a Euro-American language for an English-speaking readership. In this book we are looking at the "Southwest" from 1500 BC to AD 1500.

Defining the Southwest is actually a little tricky because the history of its Native peoples transcends modern political boundaries.[46] The history directly involves the northwesternmost parts of modern Mexico, the states of Chihuahua and Sonora. Indeed, the term *Southwest* is something of a misnomer. What we call the Southwest of the United States was in fact the northwestern frontier of ancient Mesoamerica and for quite a while the northern third of modern Mexico. One recent, popular correction is *noroeste/sudoeste*—Spanish, of course, so just as colonial as English terms. A precolonial term that has seen some use, *Chichimeca*—the Nahuatl name for the howling wastelands north of Mesoamerica—is a complex term too. It refers to a region, a people, or peoples and ultimately tells us as much about archaeologists' notions as about ancient geographies.[47] I'll stick with *Southwest*.

For the purposes of this book, the Southwest is framed by mountains and rivers: on the north and south by the Rockies and Sierra Madre, on the east by the Pecos River, and on the west by the Colorado River (see fig. 1.2). The northern Southwest is the southern half of the Colorado Plateau (hereafter the Plateau), a vast upland sitting about 1,500 m above sea level. Slicing right down its middle, cutting the Plateau into east and west halves, are the Chuska Mountains, which reach elevations of 2,500 m or more. The southern edge of the Plateau is the Mogollon Rim (hereafter the Rim), a long mountainous escarpment that runs right across Arizona and New Mexico, separating the Plateau to the north from the low deserts in New Mexico and Chihuahua and in Arizona and Sonora, to the south. Those deserts range from 600 to 1,200 m in elevation—much lower, hotter, and drier than the Colorado Plateau. A (low) upland, now in southeastern Arizona, separates the Chihuahuan Desert on the east from the Sonoran Desert on the west. The "Land Between," as Henry Wallace calls it, was an area of signal importance. The ancient social Southwest expanded far beyond the limits just sketched, but the land they enclose is the heart of its civilizations.[48]

The Mogollon Rim divides the region into northern and southern halves, and a modern feature, old Highway 666 from Douglas, Arizona, to Blanding, Utah, works as an axis dividing east and west.[49] The Rim, of course, is a natural feature, while Highway 666 is a modern road, conveniently routed for my purposes. The intersection of the Rim and 666 divides the Southwest into four quarters: the western Plateau, the eastern Plateau, the western (Sonoran) deserts and the eastern (Chihuahuan) deserts, representing—approximately, anachronistically, but usefully—natural, cultural, and historical regions. Highway 666, in the south, separates the Sonoran (western) Desert and the Chihuahuan (eastern) Desert very approximately. But to the north, the natural environments of the eastern and western Plateau are not notably different. The distinctions are historical: on the west side of 666 were Hohokam and Hopi—Uto-Aztecan speakers and societies that tended toward political equality and avoided hierarchy. On the east side of 666 were Paquimé, Mimbres, Chaco, Aztec, and the Rio Grande—speakers of the Pueblo "isolate" languages (Zuni, Keres, Kiowa-Tanoan) and societies that were, on balance, more hierarchically structured and authoritarian. From time to time, these easy generalizations spilled across, east to west and back again. But the north–south line along old 666—broad and zonal—marks a divide that meant something historically.

The Colorado Plateau's rolling plains—crossed by the north–south Chuska mountain chain, along the foot of which ran 666—were cut by erosion into deep canyons and tall mesas. Black volcanic plugs and peaks rim the Plateau (the Flagstaff volcano fields, the Mogollon Rim, and Mount Taylor; more on these below). The terrain of the southern deserts is "basin and range"—parallel, thin, jagged mountain ranges separated by enormously broad, flat, deep, sand-filled valleys, many of them indeed basins with no outlet for the rare rainfall. Huge playas (shallow salt lakes) fill each basin's center after exceptional storms and then evaporate with astonishing rapidity.

Separating the Plateau from the low deserts, the Mogollon Rim is mainly basalt and ash flow rocks—created by volcanic forces but not true volcanoes. At the Rim's west end, around Flagstaff, there are true volcanoes, at least one of which played a dramatic role in the history of the ancient Southwest. At the Rim's east end, in New Mexico, a series of huge, overlapped calderas—like gargantuan Olympic rings—formed from gigantic bubbles on the earth's crust. As these bubbles rose and then collapsed, forming calderas, their interlocking circles formed labyrinthine canyons. The Rim's higher elevation catches rainfall and snowfall—the headwaters of the Salt and Gila rivers, which flow west to the Colorado River. The Mogollon Rim and its uplands were a major east–west axis structuring the environment and history of the ancient Southwest—the only ecotone that really mattered.

Ten thousand years ago, the region was colder and wetter, with less desert and more grassland. Then the globe wobbled a bit, the glaciers melted, and the Southwest dried out. By two thousand years ago, it had reached its present condition, more or less. Through most of the story told here, the environment remained largely constant. There were minor oscillations of sun, rain, and water (and the living things that depended on them)—too small to affect the larger regional ecology but perilous for the very specialized economies of human societies. El Niños and El Niñas shaped the bigger picture. Local droughts shaped history.

The life the land supports is remarkably varied. The highest mountains are capped with arctic tundra; below that are broad bands of pine forest. Lower still, the vegetation varies with latitude. To the north, below the pine forest, are the piñon-juniper woodlands (P-J); scattered clumps of short piñon pines and junipers define the landscape of Santa Fe and Sedona and form a leitmotif of the Plateau and Anasazi. To the south, in place of piñon and juniper on the mountain slopes are thickets of scrub oaks and agaves ("century plants") that make up the encinal. Note those associations: P-J in Plateau highlands and encinal on the edges of the low deserts. Below encinal and P-J forests, both on the Plateau and in the deserts, are dry and drier grasslands (respectively). At least they once were grasslands; after decades of cattle and sheep ranching, little is left of the original grasses, which in good wet years grew thick and tall. Each of these biotic zones has its own wildlife and ecologies.[50] The Southwest is a desert—but a very complicated desert, with more fine-grained interweaving of environments than any comparable area north of Mexico.[51]

How did people live on this land before it had been colonized, reclaimed, irrigated, grazed, urbanized, industrialized? Some lived well on foods hunted and gathered from the wild; others farmed; most did both. Maize farming was the basis of southwestern civilizations. Even today, with the world's foods at every supermarket, Pueblo people maintain that "corn is life." Yet maize was profoundly out of place in the arid Southwest. It was originally a trop-ical plant, happiest in heat and heavy rainfall. Most of the Southwest gets less than 30 cm of yearly precipitation—summer rain plus winter snow. That's on the Plateau; the deserts get much less. (St. Louis gets 105 cm a year; Mexico City 75 cm; and Guatemala City 120 cm.)

Farming in the Southwest followed three general patterns: first, planting in naturally wet areas (even the desert has swamps); second, relying on rainfall ("dry farming"); and third, diverting waters from running streams to irrigate desert fields. All three can and did suc-ceed—after centuries of experimental hybridization.

Natural wet spots included rare areas around seeps or springs, but more importantly the moist floodplains of streams and *cienegas*—swampy patches along streams where natural con-strictions backed up water and saturated the soil. Cienegas were probably the first places where maize was grown, planted around the margins of the wettest soils. Dry farming was a much more problematic business. For most maize, 25 cm of precipitation a year is the rock-bottom, bare minimum. So on the Colorado Plateau, it was (just barely) possible to dry-farm (relying on rainfall)—most of the time. Chaco Canyon, perhaps the single most important ancient city on the Plateau, today gets only 22 cm of precipitation a year. The low deserts were bone dry: Phoenix, in the western (Sonoran) desert, today gets less than 20 cm of rain a year; El Paso, in the eastern (Chihuahuan) desert, gets only 22 cm. In Chaco, dry farming was merely precarious. In the low deserts, dry farming was simply impossible.

One solution was to take water from creeks and rivers and divert it to farm fields. Channeling water through ditches and canals requires a fair amount of labor, above and beyond the work of planting fields. If fields are directly alongside a stream, not much more than some sort of dam or intake is needed. But if fields are more distant, then canals must be dug—and carefully. They must be big enough to carry all the water needed to irrigate the fields they service, and they must slope enough (but not too much) to reach the farthest field. Intake dams and canals must be maintained, and rebuilt entirely if the river cuts deeper into its bed or if a flood destroys the system. The labor, planning, control, and maintenance of canals varied widely, but clearly canals required more effort and social coordination than dry farming. We tend to assume, understandably, that people first dry-farmed and later dug canals only when growing population or environmental circumstance made it absolutely nec-essary. But this might not be the case; the first great civilizations of the Southwest relied on canal irrigation (more on this below).

For nutrition, maize was not enough. Other crops were important, and some were critical. Beans and squash offered most of the missing nutrients, and that trio of crops—corn, beans, and squash—was planted and harvested all across the Southwest by 500, supplemented by other crops and many wild or partly domesticated plants.

Farming was seasonal, but hunting was constant. Meat was processed in many ways for storage, but it could never last as long as dried vegetables (corn stores for years). A major difference between the Old World and the New World was animals; the Old World had more species to tame and more time to tame them. Dogs and turkeys were the only domesticated animals in the Southwest. Turkeys were kept for feathers (not just fluff but down woven into winter cloaks); they became increasingly important for protein after 1150. Most meat came from game: deer, elk, pronghorn, mountain sheep, and (on the eastern edge of the Southwest) bison. More commonly, smaller animals such as rabbits, which lived in and around farm fields, found their way into the stew pot. Fish were sometimes eaten but most times not, and although the Southwest is today and probably was in ancient times on major migratory bird flyways, there is little evidence for harvesting wildfowl. Certainly by 1300, when game animals had been hunted out in the Four Corners, turkeys were being raised for food, a practice that moved to the Rio Grande and elsewhere in the fifteenth century.[52]

There were at least fifty different tribal groups—as Old World eyes saw them—in the Southwest when the Spanish arrived (fig. 1.5). We may question whether today's "tribes"—often the result of complicated colonial histories—were those of the ancient past. Colonial groupings often were administrative conveniences, foreign to Native ways. We speak today of "Pueblo Indians" as if they were a cohesive, self-identified group, but that's a five-century fiction. For the Spanish, *pueblo* simply meant permanent farming villages; there were many such pueblos throughout the empire. Today's Pueblo Indians speak dialects of four distinct languages. One (Kiowa-Tanoan) is related to a language spoken on the Plains; another (Hopi) is related to the language of the Aztecs; still others (Keres, Zuni) are isolates, unique on the continent and apparently representing local peoples who were displaced by Uto-Aztecan migrations (chapter 2).[53] There are today twenty-four federally recognized Pueblo groups, but many include a number of different, distinct villages. "Hopi," for example, encompasses twenty villages, administratively grouped for our government's convenience. While there is clearly a sense of "Hopi-ness," even near-neighbor villages can differ in many important ways (not the least in policies). Most other Pueblo groups have or had more than one village. And within each village there may be a dozen or more clans, each of which has its own history and traditions. The term *pueblo* means something but not something tribal.

The people we call Navajo and Apache both speak dialects of the same Athabaskan language (shared with other groups in Canada and Alaska). Science and history say that they came late into the Southwest, near the end of the story presented here. Navajos and Apaches tell different histories, which owe nothing to the Bering Strait and migrations from the north. Those who went to the Colorado Plateau became the people we call Navajo; those who went to the Mogollon Rim and the southern deserts became the people we call Apache. Those are our names; the people call themselves just that: people (*dine*). Neither the Navajo nor the Apache were coherent "tribes" historically. Each, in fact, consisted of scores of small local groups, fluid in membership and recognizing no higher affiliation. Sometimes groups cooperated, sometimes they fought. To us they were all Apaches or Navajos, and we forced them together in concentration camps and reservations, with sometimes disastrous results.

Like the Apache and Navajo, the Pima-speaking peoples of the Sonoran Desert were

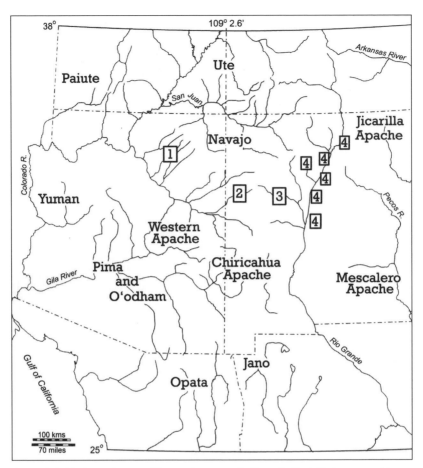

Figure 1.5. Modern tribes, pueblos, and nations. 1, Hopi; 2, Zuni; 3, Acoma and Laguna; 4, Rio Grande Pueblos. Courtesy of the author.

originally a score or more of separate local groups, with no overarching political leaders or governmental structures. Piman is part of the larger Uto-Aztecan language family that includes Nahuatl, the Aztec language. In the Southwest, Uto-Aztecan dominates west of 666, with Ute and Hopi branches to the north and Piman to the south. This is a fact of fundamental importance to the history of the ancient Southwest. Mark it well.[54]

From these many tribes, clans, and local groups, I have selected four southwestern peoples—the Pueblo, Navajo, Apache, and Pima—to illustrate the range of ways in which ancient southwestern people lived on the land. My presentations are idealized—almost caricatures of lifeways in the 1800s, after two or three centuries of Old World colonization, because nineteenth-century descriptions offer the best information we have on how Native peoples actually lived on this land.

The Pueblo, Navajo, Apache, and Pima all hunted game, gathered plants, and farmed, but the mix of strategies varied markedly from group to group. Some were mostly hunter-gatherers; others were farmers who hunted. Those differences were in part historical, the result of choices and decisions. But to a very great extent, those differences reflected differing local environments. Apaches represent successful hunter-gatherers of the Rim; Navajos, pastoralists of the Plateau; Pueblos, Plateau farmers; and Pimans, desert farmers.

The most successful hunter-gatherers were the Apache.[55] Apaches were mountain people who lived in the Mogollon uplands and on and below the Rim. That rugged area is high for maize—the growing season is short—but it was probably the very best environment in the Southwest for hunter-gatherers. The Mogollon uplands are wet, with the most rainfall in the entire region. Consequently, the variety of wild plants and the numbers of animals were remarkable. The encinal, along the Rim's flank, was a key zone for acorns (oak) and agave, the Apache staple. The Salt, Gila, and Mimbres rivers flowed out of Rim country and the mountains, and where they reached the desert, they created oases with permanent water and long growing seasons—great for farming. And the Apaches did indeed grow patches of maize in their mountain valleys. Not a lot, but maize was a useful backup to traditional wild foods in bad years—if the acorn harvest was small or if a new army fort impeded access to a favorite agave field. (In good years, maize might be brewed into *tiswin* beer.) Agave hearts and acorns from the encinal were the base of the Apache economy—they could be stored for winter and early spring, when other wild foods were scarce. So the Apache had a seasonal round in the mountains during the summer and fall and in the encinal in the winter and spring.

Pima speakers had a range of economies. One branch was the hunter-gatherers in the lower Sonoran Desert of southwestern Arizona, an impossible place for maize and indeed a rather difficult place for hunting and gathering. Piman hunter-gatherers were never very numerous—perhaps a few hundred at most—and they disappeared from the area almost immediately after the Spanish entered the territory (although they live on among modern farming Pimans). Historically, Pimans farmed desert wet spots or cienegas,[56] most successfully along rivers such as the Santa Cruz, Salt, and Gila, and they also farmed in isolated micro-environments deep in the desert itself. Cienegas were enhanced by minimal but effective modifications. For example, along the rivers, Piman farmers diverted flow into fields along the banks with small "scratch" ditches or by simply laying a log from the bank into the flow. The Salt and Gila river valleys contain broad floodplains and terraces of potentially excellent farmland; after the Spanish arrived, Pima people built large canal systems with substantial intake dams and became famous desert farmers, moving water well away from the rivers and cienegas out onto the broad desert terraces. Pima irrigation expanded historically: colonists (especially frontier garrisons) created a demand for more food than existing "low-tech" irrigation could grow, so Pimas revived Hohokam-scale canal irrigation to supply that increased demand. As we shall see, the Salt, Gila, and Santa Cruz rivers had long Native histories of canal irrigation, and we can assume that those histories were known to the Pima. However, even the largest post-contact Pima irrigation systems pale in comparison with the canals in place a millennium before the Spanish and Anglo-Americans arrived.

Over much of the Colorado Plateau, it was possible to dry-farm maize using rainfall alone—and that was a very good thing because the Colorado Plateau was an almost impossible place for hunter-gatherer economies. There were no large stands of dependable plants like the Apache's agave and oak encinals. The Plateau's most famous food plant was piñon nuts, but piñon pine stands produce large harvests only at long and largely unpredictable intervals. Nut crops vary from place to place; a great year for piñon in Santa Fe might be a lost year at Sedona. By spreading very few people very widely over the Colorado Plateau, a group might be sure of finding piñon somewhere every year. Still, piñon nuts could not provide even seasonal subsistence for large groups. To survive on the Plateau, people needed maize.

The Navajo, who (according to us) occupied the Plateau long after the ancient Pueblo people left, were excellent farmers. Navajos mixed low-tech irrigation and wet-spot cienega fields, along with a bag of other less important agricultural tricks. Because resources were thin and dispersed, Navajos lived in widely separated communities, with houses scattered up and down canyons, over ridges and hills. Each clan had its own historical ties to particular territories, but within those areas, Navajo life was mobile. Farming communities might last only a generation or so. Navajo homes were (and still are) abandoned after the death of a resident— a good way to keep people moving every ten or twenty years. Sheep, adopted early from the Spanish, also required movement to and from pastures and from parched grasslands to greener ones over the next hill.

With maize and sheep, the Navajo became long-term, migratory, pastoral farmers. Kit Carson knew this in 1863 when he led a small army deep into the Chuska Mountains—the heart of Navajo territory—burning cornfields and destroying stored food. Without those stored crops, there was no future. Hundreds of Navajos surrendered and were taken to a concentration camp on the Pecos River, at the eastern edge of the Southwest (a journey remembered today as the Long Walk). Many small, local Navajo groups were jammed together with groups from other tribes. The independent Navajo groups had to cooperate to survive, and a new tribal identity emerged from that terrible experience. When they were returned their old homelands in 1868, the Navajo became a nation. Their reservation and population has grown steadily ever since. Today the Navajo Nation is the largest Indian group in the United States.

Pueblos are the archetypical desert farmers, although most now farm in irrigated fields along rivers. Twenty federally recognized pueblos form a crescent along the southern margin of the Plateau, from Hopi on the far west, through Zuni and Acoma, and up the Rio Grande to the Keres and Tewa towns of northern New Mexico. Taos, the northernmost pueblo, marks the opposite end of the arc that starts at Hopi. Hopi country is arid and difficult; farmers use every trick in the book of desert agriculture (indeed, Hopis wrote that book)—*except* major canal irrigation, because Hopi lands today do not include major streams or rivers. All the other pueblos are located on creeks and rivers, and all irrigate with diversion dams and canal systems.

The Pueblos today are famously fixed in place. Pueblo towns like Oraibi and Acoma (which began around 1100 or even earlier) vie for the Chamber of Commerce honor of oldest town in North America. But in ancient times the Pueblos, too, were mobile. Whole villages moved, often great distances at remarkably short intervals. (The pace, place, and purpose of those movements are themes throughout this book.) When a village did stay in one place, Pueblo people traveled great distances, through expeditions and trade, to obtain the things they needed. Unless caught on the fly, however, Pueblos were indeed *pueblos*—the colonial category for settled Indians. Spain put an end to any movement (more or less). The king of Spain granted Pueblos deeds to their lands—4 leagues square, or about 100 square miles—within which they were expected to stay, live, pay taxes, and become Catholic. It was impossible: pueblos located on rivers could irrigate more acres, but other natural resources essential for body and spirit were beyond the king's grant.

When the United States acquired the Southwest, it promised to honor the royal grants. And it did, in the breach: Native titles meant that lawyers and speculators could legally buy Pueblo lands. By the late nineteenth century, the Pueblos owned only their towns and their immediate fields—and many fields were in legal doubt. The Pueblos lost much of the little granted to them by the king. Decades later, some attempt was made at compensation. Pueblos were asked, Where were your lands originally? The example of Zuni, one of the largest pueblos, is astonishing. Beyond their royal grants, the Zuni proved in a court of law that the lands upon which they had relied (the "area of Zuni sovereignty") extended from the Rio Grande on the east to the San Francisco Peaks (Flagstaff) on the west and from the Chuska Mountains on the north to the Mogollon Rim on the south—about 22,000 square miles.[57] (Today the Zuni Reservation totals 725 square miles—and it's one of the larger pueblos.) Remember that there are a score of pueblos today—two score if we count the various villages within each pueblo separately. When the Spanish arrived, there were even more. If each had a territory comparable to the Zuni's, there must have been considerable overlap in resource areas; good hunting, places where important plants grew, and other necessary resources must have been shared to some extent. Ancient Pueblos resolved overlapping territories through negotiation, but (as we shall see) they also settled disputes in more direct ways.

Many other people lived in the Southwest when the Old World arrived. The Apache, Navajo, Pima, and Pueblo fairly represent, I think, the range of economies that underwrote the southwestern civilizations, and they occupied the lands in which those civilizations rose, fell, and rose again.

Prehistories

This section presents a very brief introduction to southwestern archaeology. There are two reasons for this summary. First, for readers (bless you!) who are not deeply immersed in southwestern archaeology, to set the stage. Second, for readers (bless you too!) who are well up on southwestern archaeology, to present what I think *we* think—that is, my idea of the archaeological consensus. That's probably important for all readers to know, because I work both with and against this consensus (as I perceive it) in the chapters that follow.

All the Southwest was divided into three parts: Anasazi, Hohokam, and Mogollon. Other, less well-defined subregions sat out on the edges: Fremont, Patayan, and Jornada (figs. 1.3, 1.6).

A note on terminology: I use *Anasazi* as archaeological jargon, which it is—taken by archaeologists from a Navajo word but no longer Navajo.[58] There are Navajo and Pueblo terms for the people who built Chaco and Mesa Verde, but I do not use them—this book is based on archaeology, not on Navajo or Pueblo histories (those come into play, viewed through archaeological filters, as in chapters 7 and 8).

Roughly speaking, Anasazi equals the ancestral Pueblo peoples of the southern Colorado Plateau; Hohokam represents the several peoples of the Sonoran Desert of southern Arizona who were (at least in part) ancestral to the Piman peoples who live there today; and Mogollon names the people of the rugged uplands that separate Anasazi and Hohokam.

Mogollon is a bit of a catch-all, open-ended to the east and south. I have no definite ideas about what modern groups descended from the ruins of the Mogollon area (although others do).[59] Probably more than one modern Native community has Mogollon roots, while other Mogollon communities are probably not represented at all in modern, federally recognized tribes. They went south, into Mexico. I often substitute *Mimbres* for *Mogollon*. Mimbres was the precocious Mogollon subregion of southwestern New Mexico and the historical focus of the region.

It is useful, initially, to stereotype the three regions at about 600 to 1100. Anasazi was typified by stone masonry pueblos, pit houses, and kivas (see figs. 3.7, 4.12, 5.8); black-on-white decorated pottery and "corrugated" utility pottery (grayware) made by coiling; and rainfall dry farming. Hohokam, in contrast, was characterized by earth-and-timber, single-room

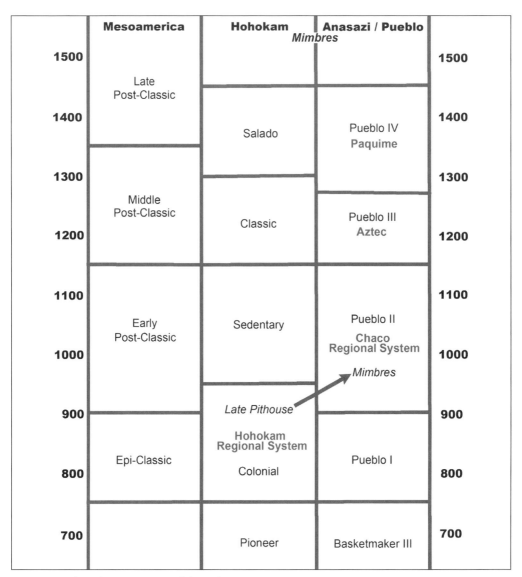

	Mesoamerica	Hohokam	Anasazi / Pueblo
1500			
1400	Late Post-Classic		
		Salado	Pueblo IV **Paquime**
1300	Middle Post-Classic		
		Classic	Pueblo III **Aztec**
1200			
1100	Early Post-Classic	Sedentary	Pueblo II **Chaco Regional System**
1000			*Mimbres*
900	Epi-Classic	*Late Pithouse* **Hohokam Regional System** Colonial	Pueblo I
800			
700		Pioneer	Basketmaker III

Mimbres

Figure 1.6. Chronologies. Courtesy of the author.

thatched houses (see fig. 4.6); ball courts (see fig. 4.7); red-on-buff decorated pottery made by paddle and anvil techniques (buffware); elaborate shell and carved/ground stone industries (see fig. 4.10); and farming with canal irrigation (see fig. 4.4). Mogollon, characterized by brownware pottery made by coiling, had both pit houses (before 1000; see fig. 3.1) and pueblos of stone or adobe (after 1000; see fig. 5.13) and farmed with rainfall (in the uplands) and canal irrigation in the Chihuahuan Desert.

Ritual and ceremony differed, particularly between Anasazi and Hohokam. Early Hohokam ritual focused (at least in part) on ceramic figurines and later on the ball game, played in modestly monumental ball courts. Hohokam cremated their dead in an elaborate burial ritual involving schist pallets (see fig. 4.8) and censers and buried the ashes in pits or jars in well-defined cemeteries. Anasazi ritual was expressed most clearly in kivas (see fig.

5.9). Anasazi dead were buried as inhumations in middens associated with each household. Mogollon dead were generally buried beneath floors of rooms, which were then refloored and replastered.

Hohokam villages between about 700 and 1000 consisted of a central plaza surrounded by single-room houses clustered, in threes or fours, into courtyard groups (see fig. 4.6). It is possible that the "houses" of a courtyard group were functionally differentiated: one structure might have been a house, another a storeroom, and so forth. Multiple courtyard groups formed a second-order grouping, or village segment, often associated with trash mounds and a cemetery for cremation burials. Larger villages often had one ball court (or sometimes two): oval surfaces defined by earthen embankments, presumably for a local version of a ball game pervasive across much of Mexico.

Anasazi villages were loose aggregates of independent households, or "unit pueblos." A unit pueblo consisted of a small masonry pueblo of five or six small rooms facing an informal plaza or work area; a subterranean pit structure, with its floor excavated deep below the plaza level and roofed with earth over a wooden framework; and, beyond the pit structure, a well-defined midden area for trash and burials (see figs. 5.8, 5.9). Much of the masonry pueblo was probably storage space; living took place under ramadas in the plaza, with sleeping and winter living in the pit structure. The pit structure was also a locus of ritual, and many archaeologists consider pit structures to have been kivas. Half a dozen to several score unit pueblos would have been loosely aggregated—the space between them ranging from nearly nothing to hundreds of meters—with a very large communal pit structure (Great Kiva) near the center of the community. Occasionally, a large clear area near the center of the village appears to have served as a community plaza.

Mogollon pit house villages generally lacked the courtyard groups of Hohokam villages or the formal storage facilities of Anasazi masonry pueblos but were often clustered into two larger aggregates, north and south of a clear plaza area. Frequently, to one side of the plaza, there was a large rectangular pit structure with a ramp entrance, probably a communal structure analogous to the Anasazi Great Kiva (see fig. 4.11).

Again, these descriptions are stereotypes—caricatures, really, of each region at about 600 to 1100. The history of agricultural villages in the Southwest starts about 1500 BC, so each area had two millennia of history before this archetypical span. And after 1100, the pace of change in each area accelerated dramatically. Hohokam ball courts fell out of use, replaced by rectangular platform mounds (see fig. 6.1). Anasazi unit pueblos aggregated into dense, apartment-style buildings, much like today's pueblos (see figs. 6.8, 6.9). Mogollon pit houses were replaced by masonry pueblos much like those of the Anasazi (see fig. 7.1). And those major shifts in material culture and architecture were just the beginning of five centuries of rapid change, from 1100 to 1600.

With the very notable exception of the Hohokam, tied to their canal irrigation systems, southwestern people moved in seasonal and multigenerational rounds and in large-group, long-distance migrations. Anasazi sites were usually single component (a single, short occupation) or, if multicomponent, discontinuous in occupation (for example, occupation at 600 to 700, a gap, and reoccupation at 1000 to 1150). Hohokam sites had deeper roots and were often continuously occupied for many centuries. But notably, many Hohokam sites were abandoned and relocated about 1150, about the time platform mounds replaced ball courts.

By 1300 the Anasazi heartland (around the modern Four Corners) was empty, "abandoned" in archaeological terms. Tens of thousands of people had migrated west, south, and east to where modern pueblos stand today. Many Mogollon districts had been abandoned a century earlier (by 1150), and the Mogollon uplands as a whole were largely depopulated by 1400. Hohokam towns beneath today's Phoenix ended around 1450, if not before. When the densely populated districts of 1150 to 1300 emptied, new population centers rose on the Rio Grande, at Acoma, Zuni, and Hopi, and in northern Chihuahua, in the Casas Grandes region (see fig. 1.3).

The history of penultimate "prehistory," from 1400 to Spanish colonization, about 1600, is surprisingly difficult to understand archaeologically. Pueblos reached immense sizes; some had several thousand rooms. The total regional population, however, declined sharply between 1400 and the arrival of the Spanish. Thereafter, European diseases and colonial policies decimated the remaining southwestern peoples. Some languages and "ethnic groups" effectively went extinct. From that nadir, southwestern peoples have recovered demographically, at least partially, and many modern Indian tribes and nations in the Southwest remain on the lands they occupied at European contact, maintaining enclaves of traditional cultures within the United States.

Archaeologies: 1500 to 1850 (Discovery and Exploration)

The discovery of Native Americans posed serious philosophical problems in Europe.[60] These were resolved in part by the *Sublimis Deus* of 1537, which declared that Native Americans did in fact have souls. But the size of the New World did not faze Old World explorers. Pre-Columbian Europe was well aware that the world was large and alarmingly diverse. Long-distance, nearly global interactions had a deep antiquity in the Old World.[61] The prehistoric Silk Road and many other long-beaten paths linked Europe, Asia, and Africa. Pre-Columbian Europeans were accustomed to distance. But they did not know what to do with Indians on that distant continent, a New World. Who were they? What were they? Where did they come from? What was their history?

In *Origins of the American Indians: European Concepts 1492–1729* (1967), Lee Eldridge Huddleston identified two European intellectual traditions in thinking about Indians and their history. The first, associated with Gregorio Garcia, was "characterized by a strong adherence to ethnological comparison [between Old and New Worlds], a tendency to accept trans-Atlantic migrations, and an acceptance of *possible* origins as *probable* origins." Garcians were not at all afraid of distance. The second tradition, associated with José de Acosta, was "marked by skepticism with regard to cultural comparisons, considerable restraint in constructing theories, and a great reliance on geographical and faunal considerations." Contemporary American archaeology follows the Acostans: local trumps global.[62]

Early explorers were no more daunted by distance than were Garcian intellectuals. Conquistadors marched large, expensive armies thousands of miles. Distance was something they did. Cortés burned his boats. Only his caballeros (and higher-ranking prelates) rode; the rest of his ruffians walked. That was true for all colonial armies. Yet Spanish forces ranged from Cuzco to Pecos in just a few decades. A few short centuries after Columbus, the new continents were crawling with Spanish, English, French, Dutch, and Portuguese intruders. These explorers *almost always had Native guides*. Native people had already been there and done that; distance was something *they* did too.[63]

Several armies sought Cibola, the fabled seven cities of gold; they looked to the north, toward the present-day Southwest. Histories of the Southwest typically begin with Cabeza de Vaca, the shipwrecked Spaniard whose epic wanderings took him through a corner of New Mexico or well south of New Mexico (depending on whom you believe) in 1536. De Vaca never saw the pueblos, but he heard rumors of great cities. Francisco Vasquez de Coronado, inspired by de Vaca's stories, mounted an expedition into the Southwest in 1540–1541.[64] Hoping to find the seven cities, an Old World myth transported to the New World, the expedition formed near Mexico City and marched to old Culiacán on the Sinaloa coast, the final outpost of Mesoamerican civilization (see fig. 1.4). From Culiacán, the soldiers marched north to Zuni. Zuni was a bust—all battles and troubles, no gold. Vasquez de Coronado and his men moved then from one pueblo to another, increasingly disappointed with the small farming towns empty of treasure. Each pueblo tolerated the Spaniards as long as it could and then directed the army to the next town; perhaps they would find what they sought up the river, over the mountains, across the plains?

At Pecos, the easternmost port of trade between Pueblos and the Plains (and all points east), the people furnished Coronado with a guide, whom the Spanish nicknamed the Turk. He was an Indian, but not a Pueblo Indian, who knew of the great city of Quivira far to the east.[65] The Turk led Vasquez de Coronado and a large contingent of his army across the southern Plains. The conventional interpretation is that the Turk deliberately led the Spanish on a wild goose chase, away from the Pueblos. Vasquez de Coronado lost patience with the Turk somewhere in Kansas and had him killed. The survivors of the expedition returned to Mexico, their exploration a failure. Almost sixty years would pass before a second official expedition, led by Don Juan de Oñate, colonized New Mexico.

For Europeans, the Southwest was a distant inland "island," needing discovery. Cabeza de Vaca found it by accident, and then only in passing. Vasquez de Coronado, inspired by de Vaca's traveler's tales (and other garbled reports), received official sponsorship and considerable financial support to chase a rumor. He found the Pueblos and was not satisfied, but New Mexico had finally been discovered. The clock of history could start.

That's the textbook story, written from the north. A seldom mentioned precursor gives us a slightly different view. In 1530—only a decade after Cortés took Tenochtitlán—Nuño de Guzmán, one of Cortés's more difficult lieutenants, assembled a large army at Culiacán to search for the seven cities. After looting Native coastal towns, Guzmán marched north following Native guides, including one whose "father traded into the back country, exchanging fine feathers for ornaments, by a forty days journey north, and one which involved passage of a wilderness."[66] This guide, Tejo, may have been from the Huastec area, but he reported his information to Spaniards in Mexico City and knew the western approaches over which his father traded. Tejo and other guides led Guzmán's army north out of Culiacán and into the Sierra Madres, where Native paths proved impassable for Spanish horses and wagons. After several failed attempts, political turmoil in Mexico City pulled Guzmán away from the expedition, and the first major attempt to find Cibola was abandoned.

We might draw two lessons from this historical footnote. First, Mesoamerican traders were familiar with the Southwest in 1530—sufficiently familiar to convince conquistadors to move armies. Second, history reads rather differently when we admit Native knowledge. Tejo knew what he was talking about and was not misleading Guzmán. His route north out of Culiacán would have led Guzmán to great cities; Paquimé, Chaco, and Aztec lie north of Culiacán. By the mid-sixteenth century, Chaco and Aztec were long gone (chapters 5 and 6), but Paquimé had closed its doors only eighty years before Tejo showed Guzmán the road to Cibola. If we are wrong in dating Paquimé's fall (our current guesses are about 1450, but 1500 is possible), it is possible that Tejo's father or his father's father actually visited the Southwest's greatest city (chapter 7) at its height, when it was a place of wealth, riches, and metals—copper, not gold.

Take a line from Tejo to the Turk. Let's assume that, like Tejo, the Turk was a knowledgeable and conscientious guide, just doing his job. Alice Kehoe, who thinks the Turk was Wichita, notes that he described in considerable detail "a Mississippian kingdom in the American South, on a wide river upon which the lord of the realm rode in a flotilla of canoes"[67]—the fading glories of Mississippian temple-towns. Stories of Cahokia, the greatest city in America north of Mexico (chapter 5), *must* have reached the Southwest. By 1540 Cahokia was gone, but smaller towns continued its traditions, including Spiro, Pecos's counterpart trading center in eastern Oklahoma. In April 1541—weeks out from Pecos—Coronado's soldiers camped in the Texas Panhandle, halfway to Spiro.[68] From there, the expedition went awry. History sees the Turk as a perfidious trickster or at best a martyr. Maybe he was simply doing his job: taking the Spanish to cities he had heard of—heard of as history, not as distant rumor.

Shortly after the Spanish toppled the Aztecs, archaeology (or something like archaeology) enters the picture. Archaeology's roots go deep into Classical and even pre-Classical antiquity. But the field as we know it was a child of the Enlightenment and the Age of Exploration. Archaeology was a colonial enterprise (a fact we consider in chapter 8), an Old World hobby transported to the New. It took odd turns in North America and particularly in the United States. William Adams named "Indianology" as the peculiarly North American form of Bruce Trigger's "imperial synthesis"—the historical, philosophical, and theological accommodation by Europe of a whole New World. How European and later American science and history viewed Indians—North American Natives—is a question and theme running throughout this book.

We have several good histories of southwestern archaeology—after the region was conquered by the United States. We have yet to see a useful account of Spanish and Mexican encounters with the Southwest's ruins. What did colonists think? What did the savants of Santa Fe, of Chihuahua, of Mexico City make of military reports of empty cities at Chaco, cliff dwellings in the canyon country? We have bits and pieces—mentions in travelers' journals, places on colonial maps, brief descriptions in official reports. But how did those fit into Spanish and Mexican historical visions of the region?

Some colonial savants saw the Southwest as Aztlan, ancient home of the Aztecs, who claimed their origin far to the north. Perhaps the ruins of Mesa Verde and Chaco Canyon (chapter 8)? Following Alexander von Humboldt, who codified local legends (in 1822 and 1829, based on explorations beginning about 1800), late Mexican and early American maps show specific "homes of the Aztec" at various places in the Southwest (first in the Four Corners, second at Casa Grande, and third and finally, the point of departure, at Paquimé). And both Pueblo and non-Pueblo groups spoke of Moctezuma as a native son.[69] Identification of the Southwest with Aztlan was strongly encouraged by Mexican authorities during the run-up to the Mexican War.[70] After that war disconnected Nuevo Mexico from its motherland, the story of Aztlan structured the earliest southwestern archaeology (chapter 2). It resonates today in modern intellectual and political life: Aztlan is a central theme of Chicano civil rights (chapter 8). And that matters.

Histories: "Time Immemorial" to 1500 BC (Paleo-Indian and Archaic)

This section, the first of the "histories" found in each chapter, covers the longest span—ten thousand years plus—but it is the shortest in length. My "History of the Ancient Southwest" really starts with agricultural villages, about 1500 BC (the Late Archaic). So this section is only prologue—Paleo-Indian (10,000 to 8500 BC), Early Archaic (8500 to 5500 BC), and Middle Archaic (5500 to 1500 BC)—and less a summary than a sermon on archaeological orthodoxies. Orthodoxies are not inherently or even mostly evil, but they provide an inexhaustible way to learn: they can always be challenged. It's almost always useful to question received wisdom. Sometimes challenges move us forward; more often orthodoxies prevail. (In the words of the poet: No need to be complaining / my objection's overruled.) I report a few queries about the epochs leading to 1500 BC that seem to be heading in useful directions. I do not report orthodoxies sustained; you can read about those in textbooks.

The first Native Americans (in the orthodox view) were Paleo-Indians. Paleo-Indian studies themselves are a study in orthodoxies,[71] four in number: (1) no Paleolithic in the New World; (2) no migration earlier than 10,000 BC; (3) no migrations save by a land bridge over the Bering Strait; and (4) no migrations other than a major first migration, followed much later by two more recent (Athabaskan and Inuit) migrations, all out of Asia. In the southwestern Archaic, a single orthodoxy is probably more important to this book than the four Paleo-Indian dicta: a seamless transition from Middle Archaic to Late Archaic to agriculture in the Southwest.

No Paleolithic in the New World

After late Renaissance and Enlightenment arguments about the people and peopling of the Americas were resolved, the actual antiquity of Native Americans was a matter of only mild interest. Prehistory was only a preamble to Aztecs and Incas. Real controversy erupted, however, after the discovery of Pleistocene humans in Europe—that is, after about 1860. Artifacts apparently comparable to those of Paleolithic Europe were found in North America, but the authorities denied them. Well into the early twentieth century, new discoveries were subject to the withering scrutiny of William Henry Holmes and Aleš Hrdlička at the Smithsonian Institution and consistently discounted. Claims for antiquity greater than about four thousand years ago were uniformly rejected—an orthodoxy!—until cowboy George McJunkin saw bison bones and fluted points eroding out of an arroyo bank near Folsom, New Mexico. The site, excavated in the late 1920s, had stone tools in clear association with Pleistocene fauna. Alfred Vincent Kidder (the most influential of southwestern archaeology's founding fathers) visited Folsom and gave his blessings, noted nationally. Orthodoxy fell, and the controversy was settled. Subsequent discoveries at Clovis, New Mexico, gave a name and a time for the first Americans; Clovis dated at about 11,500 years ago (9500 BC). There was a Paleolithic in the New World.

None Earlier Than 10,000 BC

The Clovis finds replaced the Holmes–Hrdlička doctrine with a new orthodoxy: the first settlement of the New World happened about 10,000 or 9500 BC, followed by two much later surges of people into the New World. Recently, Scotty MacNeish and colleagues have argued that a site in New Mexico, Pendejo Cave, evidences much greater antiquity for humans in the New World[72]—certainly pre-Clovis, with the West Mesa Phase deposits dated from just over 30,000 to 12,000 BP.[73] They claimed even older evidence for human occupation at Pendejo Cave, as early as 55,000 BP. Not everyone welcomed Pendejo Cave, and it remains controversial.

Perhaps southwestern archaeologists were wary, having been through a pre-Clovis false alarm a half century earlier at Sandia Cave.[74] But recent discoveries at other sites, such as Monte Verde in Chile,[75] Meadowcroft Shelter in Pennsylvania,[76] and Cactus Hill in Virginia,[77] demonstrate that people roamed North America long before Clovis. The "Clovis first" orthodoxy will go the same way as "no Paleolithic" doctrine.

Across the Bering Strait

The received view (of which many Indians are not fond)[78] demands migration across the Bering Strait land bridge, a "narrows" of immense width and length that linked Asia and America whenever sea levels sank—when water froze into glaciers. That happened several times in the past, during various ice ages, and humans and animals took advantage of the land bridge to move both ways, east and west. A land bridge makes sense, for terrestrial herd animals.

But the odd thing about people (and many animals) is that they solve problems multiple ways. It seems increasingly likely that if one came by land, two came by sea—certainly around the northern Pacific,[79] less certainly around the northern Atlantic.[80] Boats! They came in boats! The Bering land bridge orthodoxy joins *Titanic* as a legendary sea wreck. This is not to say that none came by land; of course they did. But others came by sea, faster and farther.

Men out of Asia

The accepted history calls for a single major migration in the distant past (Amerinds), followed by much more recent crossings via the land bridge by peoples who would become Apache and Navajo (Na-dene) and later still by Arctic peoples (Eskimo-Aleuts)—all out of Asia. There are, of course, other theories, mostly wacky: African Olmecs, the Chinese Formative, Polynesian Incas (or Inca Polynesians). But consider that many now think the New World was initially populated, at least in part, by boat people. If Paleo-Indians rowed over once, why not thereafter? It happened: Vikings colonized the New World around AD 1000,[81] and it looks increasingly likely that Polynesians landed, possibly in southern California and more certainly in South America, about the same time.[82] So we have bookends: Paleo-Indians around the North Pacific (and maybe North Atlantic?) sometime before 10,000 BC and Vikings and Polynesians around AD 1000. That's an eleven-millennium spread. Was there *nothing* in between? And nothing after, between Leif Eriksson and Columbus?[83]

It beggars belief that no one crossed the oceans between Paleo-Indians and Eriksson and between Eriksson and Columbus. I'll leave earlier Archaic seafaring to others. I'm more interested in the later end of that long, long span. From the thirteenth century on, both Europe and Asia were increasingly deep-ocean maritime powers—not just the court-sponsored explorers but also the irrepressible seagoing underclass: fishermen, traders, pirates. If a Chinese junk or a Genoa cog drifted onto American shores in the thirteenth century, that was not "peopling the Americas." The Americas were already fully and happily peopled. But if a tattered remnant of the Bristol fishing fleet (working the Grand Banks long before Columbus) washed ashore on Late Mississippian North America and a dozen bedraggled fishermen staggered ashore and coughed on two or three Natives, that may explain the Mississippi Valley's "Vacant Quarter." Transoceanic contacts may not have contributed greatly to the New World gene pool, but transoceanic disease vectors could have had a devastating effect on New World demography.

Why fill a page with near-fringe oceanic issues?[84] In part because the epidemiological possibilities are intriguing. But more to put southwestern squabbles into perspective: in light of Paleo-Indian oceanic and continental distances—the enormous distances covered in peopling the New World—why quibble over a few hundred miles between Chaco and Pueblo Grande or between Paquimé and Culiacán? Those small distances should not truncate our visions of the past. And finally to show that orthodoxies are just that: conventionally accepted beliefs. This book is, in large part, a critique of orthodoxies. Orthodoxies are comfortable, but they are not necessarily correct.

Middle and Late Archaic

The Early Archaic (8500 to 5500 BC) and Middle Archaic (5500 to 1500 BC) together cover more than seven millennia. There is much new, excellent research, and there are many new ideas.[85]

The orthodoxy for the southwestern Archaic is in situ evolution from rude hunter-gatherers to the earliest agricultural stages of Anasazi, Hohokam, and Mogollon. Even though maize itself came from Mexico, early maize seems sufficiently primitive that "domestication" in the Southwest would have more or less mirrored events in areas where crops were first invented and tamed. Various bits of the Southwest were somehow seen as so many separate Tehuacan Valleys, reinventing agriculture in sequences based on those of Mesopotamia or Mexico. This orthodoxy, promulgated by Emil Haury (1962) among many others (for example, Irwin-Williams 1973), is premised on the idea that early, primitive maize made little or no difference to Middle Archaic hunter-gatherers. Slowly and surely—but mostly slowly— maize adapted and hybridized to southwestern conditions, and from an Archaic continuum emerged the classic southwestern societies.[86]

Remarkable discoveries of the past ten years challenge the orthodoxy of slow, seamless transition from Middle Archaic to Late Archaic to agriculture. I review those data in some detail in chapter 2. But to conclude this discussion of past beliefs and present truths, I offer this observation: In a recent regional survey of *The Late Archaic across the Borderlands*,[87] few of the authors refer to the Middle or Early Archaic; the break between periods *was that marked*. As Bruce Huckell, reviewing the new discoveries, carefully notes, "Such sites suggested that the basic tenets of the Haury model"—the old orthodoxy—"were in need of revision."[88]

Figure 2.1. Maize, cloud terrace, and bird, Three Rivers petroglyph site near White Sands National Monument, New Mexico. Images at Three Rivers reflect Mimbres styles but appear to date after the Mimbres "collapse" of 1150. Digitally enhanced. Courtesy of the author.

t w o
Maze — Nationalisms

Archaeologies: 1850 to 1915
Histories: 1500 BC to AD 500

In this chapter, "archaeologies" and the earliest "histories" thread a maze of nationalisms. The history of the ancient Southwest, as we are accustomed to hearing it and telling it, reflects a 150-year-old foundational premise: the Southwest was *ours* and not Mexico's. The United States took Texas, New Mexico, Arizona, and California in the war of 1846–1848. If the Whigs had won in 1844, we might not have waged what U. S. Grant condemned as "the most unjust war ever waged by a stronger against a weaker nation," and the Southwest might still be Mexico's *noreste*. How would "southwestern" archaeology read, written from the south? Beatriz Braniff, the leading Mexican archaeologist of her generation to consider the question, shows us—the Southwest was, quite simply, the far frontier of Mesoamerica.[1] That's a very different perspective from ours: southwestern–Mesoamerican "contacts" and "interactions" are matters for research and debate.

The first US archaeological fieldwork, thirty years after the war ended, undertook to refute legends from Spanish and Mexican times suggesting that the Southwest was the original homeland of the Aztecs—mythical Aztlan. Pioneer archaeologists established that *our* Southwest was no part of *their* Mexican past—a conclusion based on data but predicated by nationalisms

Even today, inherited nationalisms color our perceptions of Mesoamerican "interactions." These are typically treated as extraordinary claims, requiring extraordinary proof: the smoking *pochetca*, the deoxyribonucleic acid, the crystal skull with jade eyes. Of course, we've found none of those things, but the Southwest has produced quantities of slightly less fabulous Mesoamerican and West Mexican objects. Even these—copper bells, macaws, mirrors—are often dismissed as inconsequential: "You could jam all that Mexican stuff into a single steamer trunk," or "They were curiosities, passed down the line from tribe to tribe." Is the cylinder jar half-empty or half-full?

Southwestern civilizations were maize based; maize was a Mesoamerican crop. The western half of the Southwest spoke Mesoamerican languages—Uto-Aztecan. Add in all those bangles, baubles, and feathers, and I'd say the beaker brims full. The Southwest was *fundamentally* Mesoamerican—right from the beginning—so we should be surprised if the Southwest was not closely engaged with Mesoamerica throughout its history. In chapter 1, I argued that interregional "interactions" *should be expected* throughout ancient North America. The absence of southwestern–Mesoamerican interactions then becomes the extraordinary claim.

Archaeologies: 1850 to 1915 (Pioneers)

Archaeology before World War I saw the world through lenses of nationalism, first refuting Aztlan (Mexico's prehistoric claim on the Southwest), then abetting—unwittingly—Manifest Destiny and Gilded Age imperialism by classifying southwestern Natives as uncivilized and therefore disposable. Southwestern archaeology, as we know it, began with explorers and self-trained pioneers from the East Coast. This is not to say that Spanish and Mexican savants were not interested in the region's ancient history. But early Spanish accounts have yet to influence our thinking about the Southwest. (That may change; see chapter 8.) The first excavators, surveyors, and field men worked as agents of conquest and colonialism: they were exploring newly won territories. Their language was (almost exclusively) English. They were not consciously complicit in imperialism; they were honest scholars doing their work. But they reflected a nationalism that had no room for Mexico or Mesoamerica in the ancient Southwest.[2]

Gallatin and the East Coast Historians

Albert Gallatin (1761–1849) died the year after the war ended; it was a war he deeply opposed. Swiss like the later Adolph Bandelier, Gallatin was a player on the national political scene (senator, cabinet secretary, ambassador). His idealism limited his success in the hurly-burly of federal politics. That idealism, however, made him one of the country's most respected statesmen. When Lewis and Clark named the three forks of the Missouri, they honored Thomas Jefferson, James Madison—and Albert Gallatin. We consider him here not for his public service but for one of his scholarly sidelines: Gallatin was one of the first US scholars—an ethnologist/historian—to reflect seriously upon the ancient Southwest.

Gallatin founded the American Ethnological Society in 1842. He was deeply interested in Indians—*interested* in the sense of both intellectual curiosity and social advocacy. His was a strong voice against the racism that denied Native civilization; in a massive volume on Indians in the United States, he concluded that the mounds of the East were entirely aboriginal and not the work of mythical "Mound Builders." He wrote a book-length introduction to another scholar's article in *Proceedings of the Ethnological Society*. One part of that introduction was a long essay titled "Ancient Semi-Civilizations of New Mexico, Rio Gila and Its Vicinity," based on Spanish accounts, military reports, and other sources.[3] It was his last major work.

Gallatin thought that the "semi-civilizations" of the Southwest "had attained a degree of civilization, inferior indeed to that of Mexico and Guatimala [*sic*], but very superior to that of any other tribe of North America. This singular phenomenon deserves particular attention."[4] Thus the Southwest was singled out, early in the history of American archaeology, as markedly more complicated than any other Native region in the United States, including the Mississippi Valley—an error it would take a century to correct. Gallatin noted that "the most popular theory is, that the country had been the abode of the Azteques [*sic*], whence they migrated to Mexico."[5] That "most popular theory" was based in part upon old and persistent Native southwestern stories and in part upon Mexican doctrines (promoted by Mexico City in the years leading to the war) fixing New Mexico as ancient Aztlan. But Gallatin questioned that "most popular theory." Maize, he argued, clearly came from Mexico into the Southwest, but the Aztecs were (according to their own legends) ignorant of maize when they arrived from the north into what would become their imperial capital in central Mexico. Gallatin suggested instead that "an ancient Tolteque colony...carried their civilization to the banks of the Rio Gila and the upper valley of the Rio Norte [Grande]."[6] There, the colony developed societies "intermediary between that of Mexico and the social state of any of the other aborigines" of North America.

Gallatin was much impressed with the egalitarian societies: "There was equality amongst them; they had neither king nor nobility; there were no serfs or degraded caste amongst them; they might have had a nominal chief, but government was in the hands of a Council of old men."[7] This is key—perhaps not the first but certainly the most important and influential early account of Pueblo nongovernments (undoubtedly influencing Lewis Henry Morgan; more on him below).

More important in Gallatin's time was his reconstruction of Southwest–Mexico history. Like him, many East Coast/New England historians of the second half of the nineteenth century connected the Southwest and Mexico. English-language accounts, from Josiah Gregg's *Commerce of the Prairies* (1844) through Lieutenant Simpson's descriptions of Chaco (1850) and William H. Jackson's pioneering pictures of cliff dwellings, "connected these ruins with the...Aztec culture."[8] Popular historian Hubert Howe Bancroft vigorously denied this, and his books were widely read,[9] but the idea of an Aztec or Toltec Southwest persisted in popular and scholarly imaginations through the end of the nineteenth century. It cut both ways: an Aztec Southwest could help or hinder national goals. We didn't really want the Southwest to be Aztlan, but if the Aztecs had indeed left the Southwest behind, then its magnificent ruins would not bolster land claims of the current Natives, who lived in pueblos much like the ancient ruins. Pueblo Indians could then be dismissed as johnnies-come-lately and mere copyists and could be dispossessed, as Indians in the Mound Builder East had been.

That canard would occupy archaeologists of the second generation, the second wave. Pioneer archaeologists came down firmly against any Mexican connection. What changed archaeological opinion, from Gallatin at mid-century to the pioneers at century's turn? In part, of course, it was the war. We had separated the Southwest from Mexico. Early US archaeologists, from government agencies and East Coast institutions, were sent to claim the Southwest's ancient history for the nation, to nationalize southwestern semi-civilizations.

Pioneer Southwestern Archaeologists

Through the nineteenth century and well into the twentieth, the Northeast and New England controlled archaeology (and American intellectual life in general). In the early decades of the twentieth century, leaders in New Mexico and Arizona revolted against the East Coast and attempted to establish a local archaeology. We'll look first at the real pioneer, Adolph Bandelier, and his mentor Lewis Henry Morgan, then at the larger second wave: Charles Lummis, Edgar Hewett, Byron Cummings, and others.

Adolph Bandelier (1840–1914) undertook the first major archaeological surveys of the Southwest.[10] He was commissioned by the Archaeological Institute of America (a thoroughly

New England institution) to investigate the ruins of New Mexico, Arizona, Chihuahua, and Sonora.[11] Bandelier walked or rode his mule thousands of miles—down river valleys, across deserts, over mountains—visiting and mapping ruins. Not every village in the valley welcomed him; the deserts were desolate and dangerous; and the mountains hid angry Apaches. Bandelier was undeterred. He went everywhere and saw everything (even things he was not supposed to see at pueblos). Strangely, his travels never reached the Four Corners. Bandelier *should have* discovered Mesa Verde, but he didn't.[12] And he never saw Chaco.

Bandelier was the particular protégé of Lewis Henry Morgan (1818–1881), whom we will meet again in chapter 8. Morgan deserves a digression; many consider him the Father of American Anthropology. Morgan's early scholarship and political influence convinced his contemporaries that anthropology was a science and that Indians were worthy of scientific study.[13] Morgan had a theory of social evolution in which societies evolved from rude savagery through slightly more refined barbarism and eventually up to civilization (those were his terms). Late in life, Morgan did a bit of fieldwork in the Southwest (and he was perhaps the first to recognize in print that Chaco extended far beyond its canyon; chapter 5). But Morgan's principal role for Bandelier and the Southwest is as a stern, censorious elder. Morgan was absolutely certain that the ancient New World had no states, empires, or complex political systems. Ancient America, declared Morgan, was communal. Morgan firmly believed that Indians had gone as far up the evolutionary ladder as they were ever going to go, stalled somewhere in "Middle Barbarism." Adolph Bandelier, who had read the Aztec literature, at first objected, but then he accepted his mentor's views, almost like a religious conversion. If the Aztecs were communal, so too, of course, were the ancient Pueblos—obviously much simpler than the Mexica Aztecs. As we shall see in chapter 8, Bandelier and his intellectual followers rejected ancient political hierarchies in the Southwest as they shunned sin.

If Morgan was the Father of American Anthropology, Bandelier was in many ways the Father of Southwestern Archaeology. We are all his followers, at least historically. Bandelier brought the ancient Southwest—filtered through Gilded Age nationalism and Morgan's ideas—into the United States. After the war, the boundary between the United States and Mexico jumped 700 kilometers south, from the Arkansas River in Colorado to very near its present position (the boundary was "fine-tuned" by the Gadsden Purchase of 1854). It was not empty country, unsettled territory. Spanish towns were older than Williamsburg, and Indian pueblos older still. And they had historical claims (and sometimes legal title) to the land that had to be addressed. Or did they? Were the Indians latecomers to a land originally home to greater civilizations now vanished? The Aztecs perhaps?

The ruins of Pecos Pueblo were a well-known landmark at the New Mexico end of the Santa Fe Trail. As Americans traveled that trail in the 1850s to occupy New Mexico, they pondered that ancient, mysterious place. Who built those ruins? Local Indians spoke of Moctezuma, the Aztec emperor defeated by Cortés. Indeed, Moctezuma—the Indians said— was born at Pecos Pueblo.[14]

Gallatin's conclusions on the "Tolteque" connection had been reported to the American Ethnological Society, a small, largely New England group of intellectuals, but every literate American had read, or knew of, William Prescott's *History of the Conquest of Mexico* (first published in 1843 and still in print today). Prescott hinted strongly that Aztlan, the mythic homeland of the Aztecs before their migration to central Mexico, lay somewhere in the

Southwest. Aztecs built those remarkable ruins! US administrators encouraged that claim, in a sinister way: if modern Pueblo peoples were merely imitators, not direct heirs, of the long-departed Aztecs, then Americans were justified in displacing Pueblos from the Southwest's best agricultural lands. The land grants of the Pueblos were in peril from the first arrival of US troops in 1846 to the defeat of the Bursum Bill in 1922. Aztlan (if not by that name) was a theme invoked by those who wished to send the Pueblos packing.

Bandelier was sent to New Mexico specifically to investigate and resolve this argument. The Archaeological Institute of America wanted to know whether the ancient ruins of the Southwest were in fact Aztlan. Bandelier concluded, definitively, that they were not and reported the facts in his *Final Report of Investigations Among the Indians of the Southwestern United States*, published just in time for the Columbus quatercentenary. Archaeologists happily followed Bandelier's lead, and the specter of Moctezuma faded from southwestern archaeology—but not from popular imagination (chapter 8).

Bandelier was a dedicated observer of Indians but perhaps not an admirer. In his voluminous reports, journals, and diaries, it's hard to find any indication that Bandelier thought the Gilded Age had anything to learn from the Southwest's Native peoples (that came later, from other scholars; chapter 3). Bandelier, his work done, wandered off to Peru, but he left intellectual progeny in the Southwest—most notably Edgar Hewett, a protean figure in New Mexico archaeology, and Charles Lummis, a journalist. In the early twentieth century, Southwesternists such as Hewett and Lummis—men of the West—rebelled against New England domination. They built a regional intellectual infrastructure: departments of anthropology, state museums, parks, and monuments in Utah, Arizona, New Mexico, Colorado, even California. Lummis, in his prolific writings, created a vision of the old Southwest that reverberates even today in the popular imagination. Lummis and Hewett set southwestern archaeology on a *southwestern* footing.

Lummis, Hewett, Dean Cummings, and others were the second wave, following (almost literally) in the footsteps of Bandelier. Indeed, early southwestern archaeologists did a lot of their thinking on their feet, or in the saddle like Bandelier. They were *field men*. Charles Lummis (1859–1928) first tramped across southwestern deserts and mesas in 1884, on a transcontinental hike from Ohio to Los Angeles.[15] It was quite a walk, and (by design) it made the papers. In the years that followed, he walked and rode over most of the Southwest, and he wrote widely read stories about the region and its ruins. Others had covered that ground—prospectors, mountain men, frontier riffraff—but Lummis wrote about it for mass media. (Bandelier's English was not up to the task; his most popular book about southwestern prehistory—the novel *Delight Makers*—required extensive editorial efforts by his friends.)

Lummis started at a Cincinnati newspaper and ended as a cultural patriarch in Los Angeles—from first to last a man of the West. He scorned the East Coast intelligentsia and wrote to rectify what he saw as their mistaken, "romantic" view of the Southwest, specifically Aztecs:

> Of course Montezuma—who was the war-chief of an ancient league of Mexican
> Indians, and emphatically not "Emperor of Mexico," despite Prescott and the Romantic
> School—never had anything more to do with our Southwest than Napoleon or Caesar
> did. The talk of Aztecs in New Mexico or Arizona is wholly absurd and without a
> shadow of foundation.... These myths die hard, and careless writers still keep them

current; but it is long since there was any possible excuse for them—since Lewis H. Morgan in "The North American Review" in 1866 pricked Prescott's iridescent bubble of Montezuma's "empire," and since Bandelier drove the last nail in the coffin of the Romantic School.[16]

(Note well Morgan's demotion of Aztecs to a tribe with a chief. We will meet Morgan and his Aztecs again in chapter 8.)

Edgar Lee Hewett (1865–1946)—follower of Morgan, friend of Lummis, and loyal student of Bandelier—was a key figure in the transformation of southwestern archaeology from East Coast exploration to a local endeavor, a regional specialty.[17] Hewett founded the School of American Research in Santa Fe in 1907 and assumed responsibility for the fledgling Museum of New Mexico that same year. In 1928 he founded the Department of Anthropology at the University of New Mexico. Hewett is best known for institution building and wheeling-dealing, but he began as a field man; Hewett walked or rode over most of the Southwest, including the Four Corners and Chaco, and he took a mule down the Sierra Madres to central Mexico just to see the country.

"Dean" Byron Cummings (1861–1956), Hewett's contemporary if not colleague, founded the Department of Anthropology (at first, Archaeology) at the University of Arizona and the Arizona State Museum in 1915.[18] Cummings's work in Arizona matched Hewett's New Mexican empire. A rivalry between Arizona and New Mexico institutions opened into a split. That split remains even today in southwestern work, and we shall cross the fault line often in chapters that follow. Cummings, like Bandelier, Lummis, and Hewett, was also a field man. His passion was exploring the canyon country of northeastern Arizona and southeastern Utah. He syllabified his wanderings for student credit in a "Summer Course Among the Cliff Dwellers."[19] The adventures of the summer course were perhaps not quite as challenging as Bandelier's pioneering treks or Hewett's mule ride through the Sierra Madres, but as one student recalled, "there were no maps."[20] Today interstates and hiking trails crisscross the region, but the *idea* of adventure still sells southwestern fieldwork.

Lummis, Hewett, and Cummings were all practical men, smart men, and above all westerners: men of their hands. None were recognized, then or now, as towering intellects. Thus southwestern archaeology began with brave pioneers but limited credibility. It was enough, in the early days, to declare independence from the Northeast and New England. The rest would come.

Hewett did not so much defeat the easterners as outlast them, and by the early twentieth century he had emerged as the leader of New Mexico archaeology, the biggest fish in a small pond. Hewett was comfortable in the public lecture halls of eastern museums and at the Cosmos Club in the nation's capital, but he was not welcomed in the salons of New York or the universities of New England. His external connections (and he had many) were to California, to Canada, to Europe—anywhere but Boston. Indeed, East Coast scholars dismissed him as a buffoon, a western bumpkin.

Easterners, Again

Who were these easterners? In the early days, federal agencies and museums in Washington sent John Wesley Powell, Jesse Walter Fewkes, Frank Russell, and others to explore the wild

Southwest. They collected artifacts and data, which then disappeared back to the District of Columbia.[21] A more substantial (and to Hewett more alarming) outsider presence came with a series of highly publicized expeditions, financed by New England or California philanthropists: the Hemenway Expedition in Arizona (1886–1889), the Hyde Exploring Expedition at Chaco (1896–1902), the Museum–Gates Expedition in the Mogollon country and at Hopi (California money, Smithsonian leadership; 1901–1905), and the Huntington Survey (1909–1919), among others.[22] The Hemenway Expedition into central Arizona was loosely affiliated with the Bureau of Ethnology, the employer of its main (and most colorful) character, Frank Hamilton Cushing (1857–1900)—a showman who briefly outshined Lummis.[23] The Hyde Expedition at Chaco Canyon and the Huntington Survey both enjoyed the aegis of the American Museum of Natural History. The intellectual world was small and interconnected but pointedly excluded Hewett.

All these surveys into Hewett's territory were enormously productive in the field, but most came to bad ends. Hemenway dissolved into "scattered and uncoordinated wreckage" (in the words of Charles Lummis, in a character assassination of Cushing).[24] The Hyde Expedition was driven out of Chaco in 1902 by a vengeful Hewett, who used his DC connections to evict the field party from federal lands. The Huntington Survey "fizzled out" (in the words of a contemporary observer), although its sponsor, the American Museum of Natural History in New York, denied this.[25] These expeditions, bright with promise, set an unfortunate precedent for major projects in the Southwest: much fieldwork, few publications.[26]

Hewett was furious. He saw the best sites of his generation destroyed and the best artifacts freighted to museums back east. By the turn of the century, "Smithsonian collectors had been shipping railroad carloads of archaeological and ethnographic objects from the Southwest to Washington D.C., for two decades."[27] More loot went to New York and Boston. Hewett called in the press, which responded with coverage of southwestern antiquities and the personalities of its leading archaeologists. In that era of illustrated weeklies, the papers dazzled Gilded Age America with the wonders of Troy and Schliemann, and (somewhat later) Tutankhamen and Carter. We wanted a past of our own, and the ruins of Mesa Verde and Chaco Canyon provided the material. We had our own vanished civilization!

Charles Lummis was the poet-propagandist of New Mexico and Hewett's close friend and colleague.[28] With Hewett's help, Lummis invented an *American* Southwest—not alone, of course.[29] Lummis, for all his objections to the "romantic" view, painted an exotic, idyllic picture of his adopted homeland: "a vast and incomparable treasure-house of artistic, pictorial, dramatic humanities which in any other land would have been for centuries famous in literature and on canvas."[30] And Lummis idealized and romanticized the pueblos—"Each Town a Republic[!]"—a chapter in his 1925 book, *Mesa, Cañon and Pueblo*. Lummis, like Hewett and unlike Bandelier, was a fan. An example, almost at random: "The people of Acoma naturally fit their romantic environment. They are picturesque, and have a dignity and thoughtfulness in keeping with their life."[31] Lummis wrote reams about the Pueblos (and about the Spanish Southwest). His prose was fervent and often romantic, but less romantic, in his view, than the old Aztec myth. Lummis's Southwest survives today in tourism, art, and letters—and at least a little in contemporary archaeology. We carry it forward, amplified by later writers and chambers of commerce. Anyone who has visited Santa Fe or Sedona knows the genre. James Byrkit, in *Land, Sky, and People: The Southwest Defined*, complained, "What Southwestern literature really needs is a good dose of Ambrose Bierce or Theodore Dreiser."[32] Amen.

Maize Maze, Part 1

Pioneer archaeologists were dubious or negative about Mexico in the Southwest, but the question was never completely closed. Artifacts of obvious Mexican origin, symbols and religious beliefs with close parallels in Mesoamerica, and maize itself—all these clearly connect the Southwest and Mesoamerica. Arguments revolve around particularities: what, when, and with what result? Bandelier answered the latter question, and many Southwesternists through the decades agreed: Mesoamerica had no *consequential* impact on the history of the ancient Southwest beyond maize. And maize diffused with an absence of drama. The plant arrived alone, unencumbered by cultural or political baggage.

Much depends on timing. Pioneer archaeologists generally assumed that southwestern prehistory was short—that is, compared to Europe, Mexico, Peru. Nineteenth- and early-twentieth-century archaeology did not enjoy the chronological precision for which the Southwest would later become justly famed; it had no tree-ring dates, no carbon 14, no archaeomagnetism. Careful relative dating (*this* was earlier than *that*, and so forth) and assumptions about progress produced standard archaeological litanies of "early-middle-late" and simple-to-complex, such as the Pecos Classification (see chapter 4). In those chronological schemes, each brief stage was followed in short order by another, slightly bigger and slightly better and—importantly—more like a Pueblo. Not yet discovered at the beginning of the twentieth century were Early Pithouse horizons, the very long Archaic Period, and the truly ancient Paleo-Indian.

The ruins of Chaco and Mesa Verde—so like the empty ancestral villages nearer Hopi, Zuni, and the Rio Grande Pueblo—did not suggest great antiquity. Indeed, at Mesa Verde, pots were found in place on the floor; baskets hung from pegs in the wall; sandals sat in the corner. It was as if the people had just left. How old could those places be, after all? So southwestern–Mexican interactions, if any, were conceived of as single-shot, dramatic events such as Aztec migrations headed south or Toltec invaders going north. (Discrete, staccato events shaped the histories later archaeologists such as Charles Di Peso and J. Charles Kelly —ardent Mesoamericanists.)[33]

A case in point: maize was Mexican, and since Mexican interactions were "events," brief and fleeting, the introduction of maize was often thought of as a single, germinal event: when *exactly* did maize appear in the Southwest? One senses, in early writings on southwestern maize, that the plant appeared with a mysterious stranger. After dropping off a few cobs and some mumbled words of horticultural advice, the visitor vanished, leaving to locals the real work of hybridization. There is something to this view of course. Mexican maize, a tropical plant, had to be hybridized into varieties better suited to the arid Southwest. But was that process exclusive and internal to the region?

Histories: 1500 BC to AD 500
(Late Archaic, Early Agricultural, Early Pithouse)

Recently, there has been much revisionist thinking about corn's arrival. Increasing evidence (and, importantly, shifts in our ground rules away from old nationalistic mores) reaffirms, of course, that maize came from Mexico. But it came with large numbers of people—in short, with migrations (fig. 2.2).

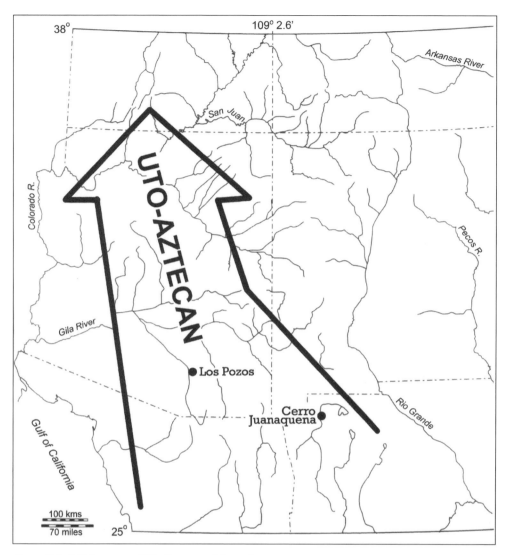

Figure 2.2. 2000 BC to AD 500. Courtesy of the author.

Maize Maze, Part 2

Maize, or corn,[34] is central to most Native societies in the Southwest: "Corn is our Mother."[35] Native histories and cosmologies offer many stories about its origins and roles.[36] Maize came from the gods, from underworlds, from the sun. Maize was sacred. But in this profane world, maize came from Mexico.

Maize was a truly remarkable artifact, perhaps the most genetically modified crop in human history: "No known wild ancestor, no obvious way to evolve a non-shattering variant, no way to propagate itself—little wonder that the Mexican National Museum claimed in a 1982 exhibition that maize 'was not domesticated, but *created*'—almost from scratch."[37] Most of that work was done in Mexico.

The exact date of corn's arrival is a southwestern grail. We seek the earliest maize like Indiana Jones sought the cup of Christ. And almost yearly, maize's ETA changes. (This book focuses on the Southwest long after maize became a staple, so the "correct" date for its first appearance is less important to me than it is to maize mavens.) Estimates currently range from 1400 to 2100 BC, with the smart money on the older end of that range, around 2000 BC.[38] Long before carbon 14 dating, Ted Kidder (whom we will meet in chapter 3) *guessed* that maize arrived in the Southwest sometime around 1500 to 2000 BC;[39] those early archaeologists were *good*. I go with 2000 BC for maize, give or take a century, and (as explained below) 1700 to 1500 BC for the first farming villages. These dates fall into a period once called Late Archaic and now called the Early Agricultural Period. Maize shows up on the western Plateau almost immediately after it appeared in the deserts, but it took almost a thousand years to reach the northern Rio Grande.[40]

The very earliest southwestern maize, at 2000 BC, may not have been cultivated for its puny cobs, a few centimeters long with tiny kernels, but rather for the sugar in its stalks (R. G. Matson calls this the "sweetness hypothesis"[41]). Maize was a sweet treat, a desert dessert. We could eat Archaic and have it too—as Ogden Nash once said. Larger maize, which actually could support farming economies and settled villages, arrived a few centuries later.

How did maize reach the region? Two major themes—diffusion versus migration—emerge from its large and contentious literature. Orthodoxy favors diffusion: an anonymous, ecological expansion of maize up from Mexico and into the desert valleys, invading the Southwest like kudzu or salt cedar. A variation on that theme came from Emil Haury (whom we will meet in chapter 3). Haury saw maize's initial introduction as a nonevent. Its immediate impacts were negligible; it took centuries, even millennia, for new, more productive strains to lure the Southwest's hunter-gatherers away from the liberty of the chase and into the hard life of the farmer.[42] Haury's views were influential in southern Arizona.[43] Stephanie Whittlesey and Richard Ciolek-Torrello, for example, argued that dependence on maize and the advent of sedentism were not sudden but very gradual: the process "began around 800 BC and was completed by AD 600."[44]

Let's look at the problem at a larger scale. The earliest maize in northern Mexico dates to about 3600 BC (another moving target) and in the Southwest to 2000 BC.[45] That's a long time. Apparently, early corn was not a hot brand, not a "must-have" product. And, as in the Southwest, maize in Mexico did not immediately translate into towns and cities and civilizations; those came much later. Farming towns popped up in Mesoamerica no earlier than 1700 BC, only a few centuries before farming villages in the southern Southwest![46] That's fast, compared with maize's initial slow march north. The very rapid march of village farming suggests better marketing, or a migration. I (and many others) think that's exactly what happened: migration.[47]

Maize, it must be understood, does not move on its own; it is famously dependent on people for propagation. People had to know how maize worked, how to grow it. Jane Hill suggests, on linguistic grounds, that maize arrived in the Southwest around 1500 BC as carry-on baggage with a migration of Uto-Aztecan-speaking peoples,[48] and that "water management techniques may have permitted the rapid spread of cultivation into the Southwest."[49] I accept that maize with its practitioners reached the southern deserts first and, a few centuries later, ascended the Plateau (more on this below). In this version, the first farmers on the Plateau spoke a language that later became Hopi (in contrast to other Pueblo tongues, Keresan,

Tanoan, and Zuni). Hill's linguistic hypothesis fits with Hopi migration stories in which several Hopi clans originated in central or southern Mexico.[50]

So—migration or diffusion? Haury's gradualism favors (but does not require) diffusion. There was, in this view, nothing dramatic or sudden about the onset of maize: the sweetness hypothesis? Hill and Matson represent the opposite: migration with the whole bag of tricks, including big maize, sophisticated canals, farming, and strong ideas about permanence.[51] It's possible to combine the two: corn candy diffused to Late Archaic hunter-gatherers as a causal treat, not a staple, sowing the seeds (so to speak) for a later migration of serious Uto-Aztecan farmers, dreaming of fields of maize.

New "races" of maize appeared in the Southwest several times after these beginnings, hybridized locally or imported from the south. It was not as if the first migrants arrived, built a gated community, and closed the door to additional immigrants. It may have been very difficult to draw a line, culturally, where the southern Southwest stopped and western coastal Mexico began. I suspect that Uto-Aztecan peoples kept up the old home ties with relatives to the south—a pattern not unknown in the region even today. Over the two millennia of what has been called the Early Agricultural Period, there were many opportunities to move people and ideas, and there was more than one direction in which people and ideas could move. These movements were probably less "events" than nearly constant traffic.[52]

Irrigation, almost as much as maize itself, launched much of what followed in the ancient Southwest. Basic techniques of water management could have been brought in by migrants and then greatly elaborated, or canal irrigation might have developed in the arid Southwest. John Mabry, writing about Las Capas (1200 to 400 BC), a large Tucson Basin Early Agricultural Period site, notes that "the Las Capas canals…were larger and more complex than the earliest known systems in Mexico."[53] This opens the intriguing possibility that maize came with Uto-Aztecan speakers, who then developed irrigation along the streams and cienegas of southern Arizona and possibly in the Land Between—and perhaps shipped that knowledge back south to the old country.

First Farming Villages

Maize made things happen, and those things happened first in the deserts. Throughout this book, the attentive reader will notice that the southern Southwest repeatedly scoops the northern Southwest. The deserts were almost always ahead of the Plateau. There was a time (chapter 3) when archaeologists considered the Four Corners the *fons et origo* of the ancient Southwest. As it turns out, many of the most interesting and important things appeared first in the western deserts (Hohokam) or eastern deserts (Mimbres) and showed up later on the Plateau (Anasazi).

Between 1700 and 1500 BC, small pit house villages appeared in the Tucson Basin and probably along most cienegas and creeks in the Land Between, in southeastern Arizona and southwestern New Mexico.[54] When archaeologists excavated those early villages, maize remains were ubiquitous. Thus begins the almost two-millennium-long Early Agricultural Period of southern Arizona. Sizable canal irrigation systems appear by 1200 to 1000 BC,[55] with—somewhat surprisingly—hints of the same in the Zuni area (discussed below).[56] Irrigation changed the deserts and, I think, set in motion a political history that can be traced over the Southwest up to the arrival of the Spanish.

Figure 2.3. The Santa Cruz Bend Site, an Early Agricultural Period settlement near Tucson. Artist's reconstruction by Ziba Ghassemi. Courtesy Center for Desert Archaeology.

What were the first farming towns like? Were the first agricultural sites of the Tucson Basin fully sedentary? Several Early Agricultural Period sites were impressively large, with scores of shallow pit structures (fig. 2.3). But size alone does not indicate permanence. George Custer, to his embarrassment, ran into a huge but temporary encampment of Indians. After eight thousand Cheyennes, Lakotas, and Arapahos dealt with the colonel, they dispersed to smaller camps and villages.

Did the Early Agricultural Period farmers continue, in some reduced way, the mobility of even earlier Archaic lifeways, or did they slip comfortably into stolid and respectable sedentism? Some say sedentary,[57] and some say semi-sedentary.[58] The arguments are summarized in an excellent review by Henry Wallace and Michael Lindeman.[59]

I vote for sedentary, based in part on a site nowhere near Tucson. The earliest solid evidence for sedentary villages in the Southwest was also the most spectacular: Cerro Juanaqueña in northern Chihuahua, which dates to about 1250 BC. Evidence there is literally rock solid. An entire hill (and it is not a small hill; fig. 2.4) was terraced with hundreds of stone walls and platforms, upon which sat structures no more substantial than those of the Tucson Basin. The massive investment in monumental terracing means, to me, more than a one-night stand. Cerro Juanaqueña was a sedentary agricultural village of perhaps two hundred people.[60] It was a real eye-opener. R. G. Matson remarked, "I know of no one who predicted such a community, indicating that the past is indeed independent of archaeologists and their wishes."[61]

Cerro Juanaqueña strongly suggests that some—perhaps most—Early Agricultural settlements were sedentary by 1250 BC. Early Agricultural Period sites of that age and later in

Figure 2.4. Cerro Juanaqueña, an Early Agricultural Period terraced hilltop village in northern Chihuahua, Mexico. Compare figure 7.9. Courtesy and copyright © Adriel Heisey.

the Tucson Basin—in many ways a more favorable setting—reached remarkable size, without stone terraces. Los Pozos, for example, had as many as *eight hundred* pit structures and substantial irrigation canals, which date between 350 BC and AD 150 (fig. 2.5).

Los Pozos, almost a millennium after sedentary Cerro Juanaqueña, typifies the debate over the nature of the Early Agricultural. David Gregory and Michael Diehl argue that Los Pozos, at any single time, consisted of only a handful of houses—used briefly, abandoned, and then built over by later residents, rather like much later Apache rancherias.[62] Their arguments are logical, but given permanence at Cerro Juanaqueña almost ten centuries earlier, why reduce these astonishingly large Tucson Basin agricultural villages to Apache camps? Moreover, Los Pozos's single, central "community house"—an oversized structure near the center of the site—suggests a larger plan, a larger community. Why would a handful of semi-sedentary farmers need a community structure? As Gregory and Diehl acknowledge, other calculations are possible, culminating in a Los Pozos village smaller yet comparable to Cerro Juanaqueña. And every time the city fathers of Tucson decree a new highway or strip mall, a new Los Pozos pops up. One gets a new and somewhat alarming view of life during the later Early Agricultural Period in the deserts: big, dense, impressive, dramatically nongradual.

How much of the Land Between—the gently elevated continental divide between Tucson and El Paso (see fig. 1.2)—sported sites like Los Pozos? The Tucson Basin was not unique in the region; it has its particularities, but sizable aceramic pit house villages are known from

Figure 2.5. Los Pozos, an Early Agricultural Period village in Tucson. Courtesy Desert Archaeology, Inc., and courtesy and copyright © Adriel Heisey.

other, similar drainages as far east as the upper Gila River.[63] They are hard to see, but they are there. The Tucson Basin today is one of the most actively investigated archaeological districts in the New World, while significant lengths of the Gila River valley and its tributaries remain essentially unknown. I suspect that the big Early Agricultural villages of the Tucson Basin are probably the tip of the iceberg.[64]

Continental Contexts

Terracing at Cerro Juanaqueña was primarily residential, but the terraced hill itself was monumental: a permanent and highly visible construction, sending its message over long distances. The labor involved was not inconsequential. As a monumental structure, Cerro

Juanaqueña was roughly contemporary with Poverty Point (1600 to 1300 BC) on the Mississippi and Olmec (1450 to 400 BC) on the Gulf Coast of Mexico, although decidedly more modest. For those with a predilection for diffusion, both Poverty Point and Olmec are key sites—centers from which all blessings flowed.

Poverty Point, with its huge central earthen pyramid and concentric rings of earthen berms covering 400 acres, was a seminal site in the Mississippi Valley. Yet there were monuments on the lower Mississippi earlier still.[65] North American prehistory may someday recognize a Mississippi Delta "mother culture." Olmec, the Mesoamerican matriarch, produced North America's first kings, pyramids, and all that: San Lorenzo, which hit its stride about 1400 to 1000 BC, two thousand years before Chaco Canyon.[66]

Surely, Poverty Point and Olmec have no bearing on Cerro Juanaqueña? Not directly, of course, but all three are symptoms of continental stirrings. Olmec was the first great Mesoamerican horizon, a sphere of art, ritual, trade, and other institutional "diffusion"—probably including institutions of governance. Archaeologists partial to the "mother" role for Olmec argue for Olmec colonies in Soconusco, 500 kilometers from San Lorenzo.[67] The web of long-distance interconnections that linked San Lorenzo and Soconusco may have reached southwestern deserts at many, many removes. How many removes and to what effect? We don't know, in part because we haven't asked those questions, at least not that way. Possibly too many removes and perhaps to no effect, but I suspect that Cerro Juanaqueña, Poverty Point, and Olmec could profitably be viewed as aspects of the same continental history. No coincidences!

Ethnic Divides on the Plateau

Uto-Aztecan migrations brought maize farming to the southern Southwest, and we can assume that the northern Southwest—the Plateau peoples—were well aware of that development, up to and including experiments with the new ways of feeding a family. Would-be Plateau farmers planted maize where it promised the greatest returns—along creeks and wet spots, as in the southern deserts.[68] But creeks and cienegas are few and far between on the Plateau, so even five centuries after the first farming villages in the Tucson Basin, maize was not particularly important over *most* of the Colorado Plateau.

Corn took root, so to speak, on the Plateau in a period called Basketmaker II, which dates roughly from 500 BC to AD 500.[69] Before Basketmaker II, the Plateau was sparsely occupied. As noted in chapter 1, there was not a lot for hunter-gatherer peoples to eat on the Plateau. R. G. Matson argues that the Plateau was in effect empty,[70] and he may be right: there are a few sites from the period 4000 to 2000 BC (the Middle Archaic), but not many.[71] This leads Matson (and me and others) to understand Basketmaker II as a migration, in whole or in part, from the southern deserts onto the western Plateau[72]—of which more anon.

Early maize showed up here and there on the Plateau as early as 2200 BC.[73] But the importance of that earliest maize among pre-Basketmakers is a matter of debate.[74] Kim Smiley, who has thought deeply on these matters, sees "significant reliance on food production...certainly before 3000 BP" (that is, 1000 BC).[75] Others delay any important role for maize to 500 or 600 BC (a date I favor),[76] 200 BC,[77] or even well into Basketmaker III (chapter 3). Since these estimates are for different areas within the large Plateau region, they could all be true. The appearance of maize at a few Plateau sites does not mean that everyone joined the (ancient) Future Farmers of America.

Basketmaker II—particularly in the west—was a true cultural break from the Plateau's preceding Archaic.[78] There weren't many people on the Plateau prior to Basketmaker II, but there were enough to leave the debris archaeologists call sites. Basketmaker II artifacts don't look like Archaic artifacts. Artifacts, language, and now DNA evidence indicate that Basketmaker II maize arrived *with people attached*.[79] It seems that sometime around 500 BC, waves of Uto-Aztecan migrants moved north out of the deserts and onto the *western* Plateau and became western Basketmaker II. (The directional adjective is important.)

It's not entirely clear what Native Plateau peoples, now shoved off to the east to become *eastern* Basketmaker II, thought about all of this. Whatever their possible reservations about the pushy Uto-Aztecans, eastern Basketmaker II picked up on corn almost immediately.[80] The situation was not without friction; there was violence.[81] In short order, the Plateau was effectively divided along Highway 666 (see fig. 1.2)—the Uto-Aztecan west aligned with once and future Hohokam, while in the east, the local, original inhabitants—fewer in number and overshadowed by the farming migration—*reacted to* these Uto-Aztecan intrusions and reconsidered their ways, means, and habits.[82]

I think there were long-term consequences: hierarchical, centralized governments developed in the eastern Plateau region, at Chaco and Aztec (chapters 5 and 6), but *not in the west*. Even today, eastern Pueblos are more authoritarian and centralized than the famously (if fictionally) egalitarian Zuni and Hopi—the Hopi being the westernmost and only Uto-Aztecan-speaking pueblo and presumably heirs of the immigrant Early Agricultural villages. Much if not most Pueblo history was sparked by migrations into the western Plateau in the first millennium BC—migrations fueled by the earlier successes of desert irrigation. The east–west division in Basketmaker II was a key event in the history of the ancient Southwest and structured Plateau prehistory for almost two millennia.

Brownware

Pottery is good to have around, especially if you are trying to store and cook corn, or stew it up with tastier ingredients. The first southwestern pottery was nothing flashy. At about AD 200, simple brown earthenware came into general use across most of the Southwest. At that time, the potters in central and western Mexico, Oaxaca, and the Maya regions were turning out some pretty interesting products, but the Southwest made do with simpler, functional wares.

Early brownwares were common from Sonora and Chihuahua into southern Arizona and New Mexico and throughout the Four Corners Plateau country. As with agriculture, brownwares in the south predated those in the north. Dates of AD 150 to 200 for the deserts[83] come in ahead of the best estimates for pottery on the Plateau: AD 200 to 500.[84] Brownware continued to be the pottery of choice in the mountainous transition zone thereafter (Mogollon is defined by its brownware; see chapter 3), but it was soon replaced by buffware in the desert and grayware on the Plateau. These colors had as much to do with local geologies as with cultural choices, but they soon became cultural traditions.

Brownware represents a default option, the easiest recipe; most common alluvial clays fired brown if no particular care was given to firing regimes (buffware and grayware require certain skills and particular clays). But there was almost certainly more to the brownware horizon than simple expediency.[85] The vessel forms, surface treatments, and contexts of brownware—settlement, subsistence, architecture, and mortuary patterns—were remarkably similar across the entire Southwest.[86] The initial spread of brownwares was something "cultural."

By AD 400 to 500, across the Southwest there was a substrate—spotty, discontinuous, but remarkably widespread—of agricultural pit house villages using brownwares. In the south, a few of those villages were very large, very permanent, and committed to canal irrigation. On the Plateau and in the Mogollon transition zone, settlements were much smaller—not really villages at all, but clusters of two or three households. Plateau "villages," even after agriculture, were short-term occupations lasting a decade or so, and they had no truck, it seems, with irrigation. (Five centuries had passed since the failed Zuni experiments with canals.) All parts of one big picture, but with definite differences in resolution—generally to the deserts' advantage.

Coda? Comma? Coma?

The "Southwest" was the northern frontier of the Mesoamerican south—a cul-de-sac but not a dead end. Olmec—the putative "mother culture" of Mesoamerica—had long since faded into myth and history when farming villages first appeared on the Plateau. Mesoamerican civilization was well into its long dynamic history of rises and falls, radiating flashes of brilliance that reached the Southwest like energy from distant stars. Southwestern peoples were making their own decisions, creating their own cultures, framing their own lives. On balance, however, the flow of people, ideas, innovations, and most of the things that shaped history moved, before AD 400, from south to north: from Mexico—probably western Mexico—into the southwestern deserts and then up over the Mogollon Rim onto the western Plateau. The package came together in the southern Southwest and especially in the Tucson region and the Land Between: large, permanent agricultural villages, powered by canal irrigation. Nothing on the Plateau at AD 400 matched or even approached those southern settlements, but soon Plateau peoples would try.

But it would be wrong to think of all historical dynamics moving from south to north, from Mesoamerica to North America. Better by far to consider North America entire, the North as eventful in its own way as the South. For example, perhaps the most extraordinary North American archaeology during the period covered by this chapter, after Poverty Point, was Hopewell (100 BC to AD 400).[87] Monumental Hopewell earthworks—perfect octagons, circles, and squares covering many hectares; cursuslike "roads" running scores of kilometers—owed nothing to Mesoamerica. Hopewell had maize, but it was not a corn-based culture.[88] Like Poverty Point before it and Mississippian after it, Hopewell might best be seen not so much as *independent of* but (ontologically) *equal to* its Mesoamerican contemporaries. Politically, Hopewell was nothing like Olmec or the great Mesoamerican city of Teotihuacán, (chapter 3) but it was (in its own idiom) equally astonishing. They all shared a continent, and ideas flowed both ways or pooled in their respective reservoirs.

The Southwest clearly owed much to Mesoamerica and to western Mexico specifically. But again, it's useful to see the two as an ensemble rather than core and periphery—a mixed ensemble with stronger and weaker players, to be sure. The Southwest was more than a passive receptor of Mesoamerica's foods, fads, and philosophies. The Southwest, as we shall see, was an *active* receptor. And that made all the difference.

Figure 3.1. Mogollon pit house reconstruction, New Mexico Farm and Ranch Heritage Museum, Las Cruces. Courtesy Toni Laumbach and New Mexico Farm and Ranch Heritage Museum.

three
Metes — *Space*

Archaeologies: 1910 to 1930
Histories: 400 to 750

Southwestern archaeology in the early twentieth century favored space over time—necessarily. Before tree-ring dating (chapter 4), archaeology could only guess about time, about exact dates. *Time* was tough, but early archaeologists covered vast amounts of *space* on foot, on horseback, or in clattering Model A's. They ranged the Southwest like latter-day conquistadors, looking for cities not of gold but of scientific import. The basic spatial structure that emerged—Anasazi, Hohokam, Mogollon—was defined by heroic field surveys covering entire states, even several states. Once the basic geography was worked out, archaeologists carved the Big Three into smaller working territories, trimmed and gerrymandered to fit modern political boundaries or the effective reach of competing museums and universities. Institutional competition was real and sometimes fierce. Turf wars could be ugly. Maps drawn (in blood?) during the 1930s set metes and bounds and shaped the spaces—geographic and intellectual—within which southwestern archaeology works today.

The archaeological patterns we call Anasazi, Hohokam, and Mogollon emerged, historically, between AD 400 and 700. And the archaeologists who first named those patterns emerged, professionally, from 1910 to 1930. The "archaeologies" of the era were directly linked to the "histories" of this chapter. Anasazi, Hohokam, and Mogollon were in fact variably real—it depended on which century we were talking about—but they were professionally useful, even necessary. The ancient Southwest had become too big and too busy to handle without compartmentalization and specialization.

But without an accurate method for telling time, it was hard to write history. History was the goal, but we couldn't do it —the record was too fragmentary. Southwestern archaeology was acutely conscious of its limitations, in contrast to ethnology's study of living Pueblos. Southwestern ethnology had a golden age in the first decades of the twentieth century, and its work became increasingly important in larger arenas of American intellectual life. Ethnology told archaeology that there was not much history to write: the ruins of Mesa Verde and Chaco Canyon were pueblos, just like Hopi, Zuni, Acoma, and the Rio Grande. And that's all we had to know.[1]

In the century since Bandelier's *Final Report*, we've filled in many blank spots on the map. We now know where almost all the big sites are.[2] That sentence demands clarification: I think we know the locations of almost all the larger, post-500 villages in the Southwest. Even with those caveats and conditions, Bandelier would be astonished—or at least highly gratified— at our geographic knowledge, our mastery of space. Much of that mastery developed in the decades between the two world wars.

Archaeologies: 1910 to 1930 (Culture History, without Dates)

It was easy to "see" the ancient Southwest: sites were highly visible, and many had standing walls! The towering walls of Casa Grande and the Pecos church were well-known travelers' landmarks, but less spectacular sites, reduced to rubble mounds, were evident everywhere. We stumbled over ruins. The region was an open book to the first cohort of twentieth-century professionals: A. V. "Ted" Kidder, Edgar Hewett, Dean Cummings, and others.[3] These men were humanists at heart. They spoke well of science, but they meant *systematic scholarship, informed by science*. They were historians (prehistorians really) who borrowed useful tricks and techniques from the sciences, such as stratigraphy, their first window into chronology. Stratigraphy was still in its infancy, and tree-ring dating was yet to come, so history was still beyond their reach. But it was possible to make maps and to learn the geography of prehistory, if not its chronology. And that's what they did.

Conquer, Then Divide

To be fair, the ruins did not suggest deep antiquity. Gustav Nordenskiold, in his account of Mesa Verde at 1891, noted, "To judge by the present condition of most of the ruins, no very long periods can have elapsed since their erection."[4] The cliff dwellings were not tells, nor were they deeply stratified sites spanning eons. Schliemann found many Troys, stacked like pancakes, but Cliff Palace (seemingly) stood alone, a single village in its singular alcove— something like this:

> Such silence and stillness and repose—immortal repose. That village sat looking down
> into the canyon with the calmness of eternity. The falling snowflakes, sprinkling the
> piñons, gave it a special kind of solemnity.… I knew at once that I had come upon the
> city of some extinct civilization, hidden away in this inaccessible mesa for centuries,
> preserved in the dry air and almost perpetual sunlight like a fly in amber, guarded by
> the cliffs and the river and the desert.[5]

Mesa Verde was (effectively) discovered in 1888 by Richard Wetherill and Charlie Mason, rounding up cattle on Mesa Verde in a snowstorm. Wetherill (1858–1910) later returned to the ruins and looted them seven ways to Sunday: pots, baskets, sandals, axes, knives, and more. He marketed this collection to the historical society in Denver as "Ancient Aztec Relics."[6] The historical society, recognizing the historical import of ancient Aztec relics in southwestern Colorado, paid him the astonishing sum of $3,000. Wetherill thereupon retired from the cattle industry and became an archaeologist—and eventually a very good one. He searched almost every cave in the canyon country of the Four Corners—or so it seems today.[7] We find his initials carved into alcoves accessible only by experienced technical climbers— with the added tag "What fools these mortals be" on one frighteningly elevated ledge.

Archaeological curiosity soon displaced the profit motive: Wetherill became genuinely interested in the Cliff Dwellers, where they came from, and where they went. In 1893, digging in the caves of southeastern Utah, he discovered that Cliff Dwellers had history. Deep beneath the cliff dwellings, below their masonry architecture and fine pottery, Wetherill found burials of earlier people with wonderful basketry but no pottery. His "Basket people" soon became Basketmakers—the term still used for the earliest Plateau farmers. And Wetherill had discovered *stratigraphy*: later cliff dwellings on top, earlier Basketmaker below. The principle was already well known in geology and in European and Mexican archaeology; it would soon be applied across the Southwest, most notably by Nels Nelson in 1914–1916 in the Galisteo Basin and by Ted Kidder in 1915–1929 at Pecos Pueblo.

In the 1910s and 1920s, the ancient Southwest was known mainly from its latest archaeology: Pecos in the Rio Grande, Hawiku at Zuni, and (later) Awatovi at Hopi. These sites were selected for excavation because they had mission churches that linked them to Spanish history. At Pecos, down deep under thick layers of trash and rubble, Kidder found black-on-white pottery and masonry walls that resembled those of Mesa Verde. A link had been forged between the empty ruins of the Four Corners and the modern Pueblos, across the hundreds of miles that separated Cliff Palace from Pecos Pueblo—something like history!

Alfred Vincent "Ted" Kidder (1885–1963) began his southwestern career in the Four Corners, working as Edgar Hewett's student-assistant. He understood the Basketmakers (he had done important work on the early period with Sam Guernsey).[8] Neither he nor anyone else at that time knew whether Basketmakers in fact became Pueblo people or whether Basketmakers were replaced by Pueblo people. Either way, the history of the Four Corners evidently started well before Cliff Palace, and the stratigraphy at Pecos Pueblo showed that Cliff Palace was much older than the pueblos of colonial times. There was history, but how much? How far back did the Southwest go?

Sherds offered a promising if somewhat shaky framework for chronology.[9] At Pecos, for example, pottery with black designs preceded more colorful later pottery. So sites with black-on-white sherds were (usually) earlier than sites with polychrome types. That didn't always work: a few ancient towns stubbornly continued to make black-on-white pottery while their neighbors flaunted polychrome wares. We might not be entirely certain where particular pottery types fell in time, but we knew where they fell on the ground, in space. Geographic distributions of types, styles, and forms were knowable and mappable.[10] So we mapped sherd and pottery distributions.

Maps showed us that the earliest-looking Basketmaker sites were found in the Four Corners—in the San Juan River area. It would be many years before really old Basketmaker-era sites were excavated beyond the Four Corners. And the sherds Kidder found deep below Pecos looked like the sherds he'd seen at Four Corners at Mesa Verde and Chaco Canyon. Those first, rudimentary understandings of the Southwest's history led, understandably, to the San Juan Hypothesis (an "age-area" argument): the Four Corners was the hearth from which came other southwestern cultures. The San Juan had the most spectacular ruins: Mesa Verde, Chaco, and the other sites that started all the early speculation about Aztecs and Aztlan. And, apparently, the San Juan area had the earliest Basketmaker sites. It stood to reason that the San Juan was the origin of the greater Southwest. But the various districts of the Southwest were coming into better focus, and archaeologists invested in those districts called for independence from the San Juan. More and more archaeologists questioned the San Juan Hypothesis: "My valley's different." Did all that emerging variety really originate in the San Juan? Or was there more to the Southwest than Anasazi?

The Tripartite Southwest

From hard-won firsthand knowledge, riding and walking over the territory, Edgar Hewett produced a remarkably accurate regional map of the ancient Southwest, first reported to Congress in 1904 and later recycled for a late-in-life dissertation.[11] He divided the Southwest—from Casas Grandes to Mesa Verde, from the Colorado to the Rio Grande—into five regions and thirty-nine districts, most of which stand up well today. We still use them, modifications of them, or independent inventions of them.

Hewett's work preceded by two decades a far better-known study by Ted Kidder, *An Introduction to the Study of Southwestern Archaeology* (1924). A. V. Kidder was the quintessential East Coast scholar, trained at Harvard. Throughout his long and productive career, he was associated with East Coast institutions. Kidder was sagacious, witty, and cultured—in contrast to Hewett and the other western men—and also, it seems, a nice guy.[12] Hewett claimed to have "pushed him off the pier"—Hewett's pedagogical style—by hiring Kidder and two other students, early in the 1900s, to survey the Four Corners country with minimal direction from the boss.

Kidder survived and even enjoyed that experience and went on to excavations at Pecos Pueblo and to write his *Introduction*. Like Hewett's dissertation, Kidder's *Introduction* was a strongly geographical work.[13] Kidder divided the Southwest into nine districts, of which number 1 was the San Juan, "considered first because it is in many ways the best known archaeologically of the major territorial divisions of the Southwest…[and] more important still is the fact that the San Juan appears to have been the breeding ground for many of the basic traits of Southwestern culture and center for dissemination."[14]

Not everyone accepted the San Juan Hypothesis. Harold S. Gladwin (1883–1983), Kidder's contemporary and sometime rival, funded and founded a research institution in Globe, Arizona: Gila Pueblo.[15] Self-trained, brash, opinionated, and defiantly nonacademic, Gladwin had deep financial resources and a passion for archaeology. He asked Kidder—the reigning authority—where best to invest his money and energy. Kidder recommended the Arizona deserts. No one was working there (other archaeologists favored the cooler climes and spectacular Anasazi ruins of the Plateau), but Kidder knew there was archaeology of some sort around Phoenix. A generation before, the showman Frank Cushing had dug there, with rumors of spectacular finds but few published reports.[16] That archaeology would come to be called Hohokam.

Gladwin took the Hohokam as his particular study. He built Gila Pueblo (over the ruins of the Gila Pueblo site) and staffed it with very good people (several of whom we will meet later). You can almost see Gladwin—businessman turned archaeologist—at the head of the boardroom table (he called it the Council Room), running Gila Pueblo in a crisp, efficient, nonacademic manner. The first order of business: Where is Hohokam exactly? Gladwin wanted to fix its limits. His method was simple, direct, effective: he sent field-workers out on field surveys, in all directions from the Hohokam center (ignoring political and academic turf), to find the boundaries, where sherds changed colors from Hohokam's red-on-buff pottery to something else. Gladwin's team went far, publishing thin volumes with stunning titles, for example, *An Archaeological Survey of Texas*, covering the Lone Star State in 164 pages.[17] The next year, Gila Pueblo published *An Archaeological Survey of Chihuahua*.[18] Gladwin's boys worked fast and far.

Where Gladwin's red-on-buff Hohokam pottery butted up against black-on-white Anasazi pottery, a boundary was drawn. That boundary survives today. To the north of that boundary, on the Colorado Plateau, the Anasazi; to the south, in the low deserts of Arizona, the Hohokam. The contrast between Hohokam and Anasazi seemed beyond argument: Hohokam had red-on-buff pottery (buffwares), cremation burials, and earth/thatch houses with earthen ball courts; Anasazi had black-on-white pottery on gray-firing clays (graywares), inhumations, and stone masonry houses with kivas. So Gladwin rejected the San Juan Hypothesis: *his valleys were different*. And for once, that claim—a notorious dodge in archaeology—was true. After some initial quibbling, the academics accepted Gladwin's new geography. Hohokam, after all, was confined to the blistering deserts of southern Arizona, where no one but Gladwin wanted to work. Hohokam was allowed to go its own way in peace; its freedom from orthodoxy had important repercussions, later. When Anasazi ruins were (and are) forced to become pueblos, the ancient Hohokam could evolve as they wished. As a result, Hohokam archaeology from mid-century on was by far the more interesting of the two (as we shall see in chapters 4 and 5).

The Hohokam–Anasazi boundary corresponds roughly to the Mogollon Rim (see fig. 1.2). That spatial division between Anasazi and Hohokam was, like the east–west Basketmaker split, a fundamental fact that shaped the history of the ancient Southwest—and many of the arguments in this book. But for Plateau archaeologists in the 1920s and 1930s, the Rim was more like a great wall. As long as Hohokam was contained in the desert, it would not trouble the archaeology and archaeologists of the Plateau. (We can wonder whether perhaps the amiable but canny Ted Kidder sent Gladwin to study Hohokam in part to keep the troublesome maverick away from the Four Corners and the Rio Grande.)

The western boundary of Hohokam was also fairly clear. Red-on-buff pottery stopped abruptly at the lower Sonoran and Mohave deserts. The early surveyors noted another ceramic tradition, Patayan, thin on that dry ground (chapter 5, note 186). To the south, sites with Hohokam pottery did not go very far into Sonora, bumping into the Trincheras culture (chapter 6), so that boundary seemed clear too. In any event, the southern boundary was well into Mexico and was no concern of Anasazi archaeologists.

The eastern boundary of Hohokam became something of a project. Working east, Gladwin and his gifted employee Emil Haury (1904–1992) defined a third major archaeological region in the mountains of southern New Mexico: the Mogollon.[19] The characteristics of Mogollon were not as glaringly distinctive as the differences between Anasazi and Hohokam, and Gladwin's insistence on defining yet another new culture struck many of his contemporaries as presumptuous. First Hohokam! And now this Mogollon farrago! Arguments raged for years over the reality of Mogollon. Twenty years later, Haury mentored Joe Ben Wheat's dissertation, a dense and detailed argument in favor of Mogollon. Haury arranged for Wheat's (1955) pro-Mogollon study to be published as both a memoir of the Society of American Archaeology and a memoir of the American Anthropological Association.[20] Every functioning archaeologist and anthropologist thus received the Mogollon gospel in the morning mail—market saturation—and the question was effectively put to rest, although a few lingering doubts remained (and remain).

What Harold Gladwin had done was to divide the Southwest into three parts: Anasazi, Hohokam, and Mogollon. Those three regions thereafter structured archaeological knowledge and the practice of archaeology.[21] Gladwin's contribution was truly foundational and owed almost nothing to universities, state museums, or the emerging professional structure of southwestern archaeology. The academy shapes and maintains our knowledge of southwestern archaeology, but that knowledge has been jolted from time to time by thunderbolt revelations from elsewhere: Gila Pueblo, climatology (chapter 4), and "salvage archaeology" (today's cultural resource management; chapter 6). Southwestern archaeology is not a closed shop.

Between the two world wars, the number of southwestern archaeologists increased slowly but steadily, and new practitioners began to specialize in one of Gladwin's three areas. Museums and laboratories similarly specialized in a region or even a subregion of the Southwest (chapter 4). One core function of all those institutions was continuing the survey of the ancient Southwest, infilling geographic detail. Each museum had its survey room, replete with maps and site files and sherd collections, bagged or boxed by site. Gladwin, for example, set up racks of "sherd-boards" at Gila Pueblo. These were squares of fiberboard about 2 feet on each side, each representing a site. "Diagnostic" sherds—rows of painted sherds and a smaller sampling of the plain, unpainted types—were glued to the boards. (Years later, Gladwin's collections were re-stored in bags and boxes. The discarded Gila Pueblo sherd-boards became obscure but treasured relics; there's one in my garage somewhere.)

Ethnography and Archaeology

Mesa Verde, the archaeologists had agreed, was not Aztlan of the Aztecs. The mysterious Cliff Dwellers were a matter of state and national pride: they were *our* ancient civilization. But if not Aztecs, then who? Cliff Palace might be empty and abandoned, but only a few days' walk away were Pueblo peoples who built towns that looked like Cliff Palace and who spoke of migrations from the north, perhaps from Mesa Verde. It was an easy step to connect "abandoned cities of the Anasazi" to the modern Pueblos. Indeed, Kidder had done it at Pecos, as others did at Awatovi and Hawiku.

The Southwest's Native peoples are one of the great blessings of southwestern archaeology. It's been my privilege to work alongside Pueblo, Navajo, and Pima archaeologists at Chaco Canyon, in the Mogollon uplands, and in the Tucson Basin. Dig all day, share meals, talk baseball, argue, and learn. A Navajo man told me exactly what happened at a site we were digging at Chaco, based on histories he had learned from his family and clan. Amazing! A blessing indeed, but not unmixed. Archaeologists, beglamoured by Pueblos and Navajos and Pimas, came to believe that the ethnographic present provided a full and sufficient account of the ancient past.[22] From southwestern archaeology's earliest days, media and museums routinely filled in details of ancient life by borrowing from the ethnography. (I recall a painting of Pueblo Bonito, commissioned for a famous national magazine, so faithful to photos of old Zuni that horses and sheep had to be airbrushed out.)

Hewett, Kidder, and Cummings routinely looked to Pueblo friends and "informants" (an ethnological term) for advice and insight. In a way, it was easy: archaeologists dug all summer and then asked Pueblo informants to explain what they had found. Neil Judd, who excavated Pueblo Bonito in the 1920s, relied heavily on Santiago Naranjo, governor of Santa Clara Pueblo,[23] among others, to interpret the site. Not surprisingly, Judd concluded that Pueblo Bonito was a farming village.

There are obvious dangers in that approach, and archaeology periodically purged itself of ethnographic prejudgment. The first "new archaeology" came in 1917 (a half century before Binford's New Archaeology; chapters 1 and 5), when Clark Wissler of the American Museum of Natural History challenged the orthodoxies of his time. Wissler and his colleagues rejected the ethnological approach of Bandelier, Hewett, and Judd. Wissler argued that "continuity in culture history was something to be demonstrated case-by-case, and not assumed out of hand."[24] But that first "new archaeology" failed. The allure of the Pueblos was simply too powerful; southwestern archaeology never weaned itself from the wholesale transportation of ethnographic detail to the distant past.

Conventional views of ancient history favor a steady progression from the inchoate past to the coherent solidity of the ethnographic present—from Basketmaker to Chaco to modern Acoma (for example)—so it made sense to seek (and not surprisingly to find) prototypes of Pueblo life at Mesa Verde. Strangely, ethnographies were trusted, but Native traditions were dismissed. Bandelier, Cushing, and Hewett paid attention to Native oral histories and "migration stories," but the brave new archaeologists of the 1920s and 1930s rejected Native oral histories as myths or folklore. The best basis—indeed the only sound basis—for understanding Natives past and present, they thought, was contemporary ethnology.

Ruth Benedict

Ruth Benedict, one of the most famous ethnologists of the golden age, noted, "Pueblo culture…has a long and homogeneous history behind it, and we have special need of this knowledge of it because the cultural life of these peoples is so at variance with that of the rest of [Native] North America. Unfortunately, *archaeology cannot go further and tell us how it came about*."[25] Ouch! Archaeology was merely a weak strategy to extend ethnology back into the past.

The most influential ethnographic work ever to come from the Southwest was Benedict's *Patterns of Culture*, published in 1934, in which she contrasted Zuni with two other cultures (one in New Guinea and one on the northwest coast of North America). Her theoretical interest was the link between culture and personality. The original culture–personality agenda faded in interest and importance, but Benedict's take on Zuni and southwestern Pueblo peoples continues to be enormously influential.[26]

Benedict's portrayal of Zuni established a vision of Pueblos enormously appealing for Americans between the two world wars. The 1920s and 1930s were not much fun. The almost unimaginable horrors of the Great War deflected political and intellectual life in Europe (and by extension in America) in somber and pessimistic ways. Before the war, they drank champagne, painted pictures, and went to ballets. After the war, they just drank. The twenties' brittle gaiety collapsed under the Great Depression, and the next decade saw the alarming rise of dictators: Mussolini in Italy, Franco in Spain, and Hitler in Germany. Against that bleak background, Benedict painted a picture of happy, peaceful Pueblo people, living communally in harmony with their environment—my words, not hers—and that picture powerfully attracted a reading public who might rightly conclude that the world in 1934 was no damn good. Others before Benedict had idealized Pueblos to fit their requirements—aboriginal democracies, embryonic city-states, the Shakers of the Southwest, and so on—but Ruth Benedict's book reached mass audiences and created a caricature that still sells by the quart in Santa Fe.[27]

For my focus—governance and hierarchy—Benedict's most important conclusions concerned Zuni's egalitarian ethos. To form her opinions of Zuni, Benedict relied on Ruth Bunzell; both studied Zuni in the early 1920s. Benedict quotes Bunzell in the following passage:

> Personal authority is perhaps the most vigorously disparaged trait in Zuni. "A man who
> thirsts for power or knowledge, who wishes to be as they scornfully phrase it 'a leader of

his people,' receives nothing but censure and will very likely be persecuted for sorcery,"
and he often has been. Native authority of manner is a liability in Zuni, and witchcraft
is the ready charge against a person who possesses it. He is hung by his thumbs until
he "confesses." It is all Zuni can do with a man of strong personality. The ideal man
at Zuni is a person of dignity and affability who has never tried to lead.... He avoids
office. He may have it thrust upon him, but he does not seek it.... A man must avoid
the appearance of leadership.[28]

Benedict's vision of Zuni and the other Pueblos as Apollonian (in Nietzschean terms)
achieved iconic status in American intellectual life: Pueblos are egalitarian and communal
and, in other sections of her portrayal, prayerful, peaceful, and contemplative. (What was that
bit about hanging would-be leaders by their thumbs, again?) Whether or not this vision
reflects realities at Zuni and other pueblos, it was uncritically applied by archaeologists of the
mid-twentieth century—painfully conscious of their inferiority vis-à-vis ethnology—to the
ancient past. I call this situation the Benedictine Fallacy—the assumption that Pueblo societies *always were* egalitarian, prayerful, peaceful, contemplative, and so forth.

"Archaeology cannot go further and tell us how it came about." It was hard for archaeologists
to counter Benedict's dismissive conclusion; we had only the vaguest control of time, essential to history. As we shall see in chapter 4, with the advent of tree-ring dating in 1929,
archaeologists rushed to provide the details of exactly how it came about: how Anasazi became
Pueblos through Benedict's "long and homogeneous history"—reminiscent of Bandelier's
"slow and tedious development."

Histories: 400 to 750
(Basketmaker III, Pioneer, Early Pithouse)

Archaeology from 1900 to 1930 lacked chronological tools to *tell the story*, so (as we have seen)
Benedict's archaeological contemporaries busied themselves defining geography, the spatial
structure of the ancient Southwest—space rather than time. The spatial emphasis of early
archaeology meshed well with historical events of 400 to 750, when the three major "traditions," or areas—Anasazi, Hohokam, and Mogollon—first came into focus (fig. 3.2; see fig.
1.3). Gladwin was not making this stuff up: there was a reality behind his maps.

Pots and People

Stephanie Whittlesey, armed with tree-ring dates, puts a date on it: "By AD 600, then, three
regional ceramic traditions were established. Each was anchored by a distinctive plainware":[29]
Lino Gray, Gila Plain, and Alma Brown, corresponding respectively to Anasazi, Hohokam,
and Mogollon. Those divisions, firm by 750, rose from a certain sameness. Recall that about
400, a horizon of small pit house sites, all sharing a common brownware, extended from
southern New Mexico and southern Arizona (and probably northern Sonora and Chihuahua)
north to the San Juan River drainage (chapter 2). Those early brownware sites were few and
far between, clustered along rivers and around cienegas. But over time, growing population,
the introduction (or breeding) of more useful, drought-tolerant corn, and happily wet weather
encouraged dry farming. Of course, the lucky few remained by the perpetually reliable creeks
and cienegas, and that's probably where differentiation began.

About 450, a slipped redware was added to Hohokam and Mogollon assemblages but not

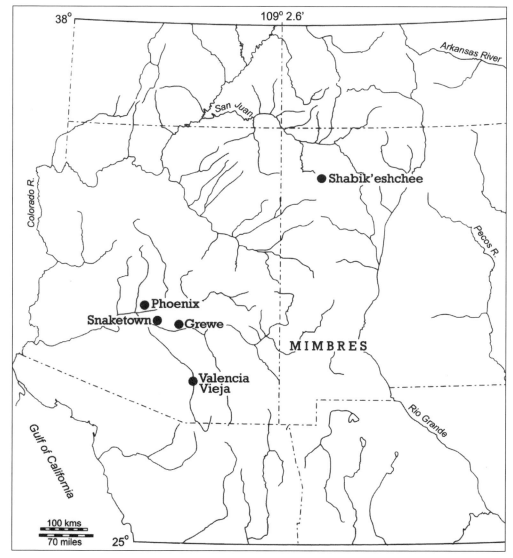

Figure 3.2. 400 to 750. Courtesy of the author.

to those of the Anasazi, who instead began to paint designs on their pottery. An Anasazi red-on-brown type (a color scheme conventionally associated with Mogollon!), dating about 550 to 600, apparently came first, in the southern San Juan Basin of northwestern New Mexico.[30] That was followed sometime before 600 by the first in a long line of black-on-white Anasazi types.[31] If those dates are right, Tohatchi red-on-brown predated Hohokam and Mogollon painted pottery by about a century.[32] That was the last time for the next several centuries that the Plateau led the deserts in anything.

By 600 (if not earlier), Plateau potters had quit digging clay in creek bottoms and had begun mining pottery clays from geological strata. They learned to grind those clays, temper them, and fire them a good gray color. Mogollon pottery stayed brown (or grayish brown), whether made from alluvial or local geological clays. The difference between gray and brown may simply reflect the differing geologies of the Plateau and the Mogollon region: sedimentary rocks on the Plateau, volcanic rocks in the Mogollon uplands. Clays from the latter apparently fire brown, and it is tempting to dismiss early "Mogollon culture"—defined by brownwares—as a quirk of geology. In the early stages of Mogollon, that may well have been the case.

Hohokam: The Buck Starts Here

Hohokam is an indefinite, fluid term with several meanings. It refers to an area more or less coterminous with the upper Sonoran Desert of southern Arizona. It also refers to an archaeological tradition marked by red-on-buff pottery (Gladwin's original meaning). More recently, *Hohokam* has come to mean a tight package of cultural practices that came together between 700 and 800 (chapter 4), with explosive results. I use the term all three ways, but I won't apologize overmuch; so do most of my colleagues.

Hohokam, in this section, refers to the region. As noted, the Hohokam region was almost always a step ahead of the rest of the Southwest. It was in the Hohokam area that, around 500, political complexity and hierarchical governance first emerged on the village level.[33] That would be in what is called the Early Pioneer Period (see fig. 1.6).

The scenario perhaps went like this: for almost one thousand years, farmers along the Santa Cruz and other small creeks of the Land Between had used small canals. The very earliest settlements may not have been permanent; small groups came and went (chapter 2).

By 150 that had changed. Recall the canals of Los Pozos in the Tucson Basin, marking (I think) a major commitment to place and permanence. Within a few centuries, at Pioneer Period Hohokam sites such as Valencia Vieja (fig. 3.3) and Snaketown, a small number of families had begun building conspicuously larger, distinctively roofed, square houses: "Big Houses" (fig. 3.4). These were once interpreted as communal structures, rather like kivas.[34] But following Henry Wallace and others,[35] I think they were in fact homes of politically important families. Wallace excavated Valencia Vieja, a large Early Hohokam site on a low terrace of the Santa Cruz River (see fig. 3.3): "The turning point in the development of Valencia Vieja and in the history of the region occurred sometime between AD 450 and 525…when populations aggregated. Valencia Vieja doubled in size, and it became a village."[36] At its center was a plaza area, and around the edges of the plaza were several very large, architecturally distinctive Big Houses. Location, location, location: Big Houses conspicuously faced the plaza, while smaller, normal houses were scattered farther away from the village center, behind the larger residences. Big Houses were the homes of important people: families that had better farmlands and more stuff (for example, turquoise)[37] than anyone else. Big Houses often included unusual features that appear to have been ritual or ceremonial. Big House families, I think, co-opted or created ritual that consolidated power—political, ritual, or both (see fig. 3.4). Wallace and his colleague Michael Lindeman conclude:

> For the AD 500 to 700 span—with oversized or otherwise special architecture fronting the plazas at Snaketown and Valencia Vieja, and the use of gable-roofed square structures as markers of social status—we think there is ample evidence of social differentiation. The developing mortuary ceremonies themselves signify the beginnings of institutionalized differences in status accorded to ritual and political leaders.[38]

What happened?[39] The canal technology (and perhaps peoples) of Tucson and the Land

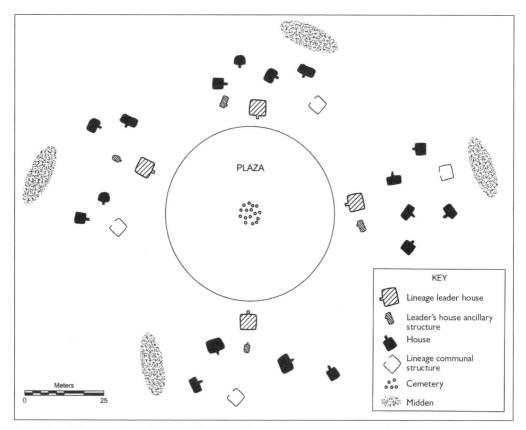

KEY

Lineage leader house

Leader's house ancillary structure

House

Lineage communal structure

Cemetery

Midden

PLAZA

Meters
0   25

Figure 3.3. Schematic plan of Valencia Vieja near Tucson, 500 to 650. "Lineage leader houses" equal Big Houses. Courtesy Center for Desert Archaeology.

Between spread into the Phoenix Basin about 400.[40] Then a new, more productive corn appeared in the late 400s.[41] Whether better corn meant more people or more people demanded better corn matters little. The result was the same: more and bigger canals. The social and political systems sufficient for canal irrigation on the smaller, more manageable streams of southeastern Arizona had to be ramped up—inflated, redoubled, amplified—for the Salt and Gila rivers, so much larger than Tucson's creek-sized Santa Cruz River. Building, maintaining, and administering Phoenix Basin canals required much more centralization and control than did irrigation in the Tucson Basin.[42] Big House political hierarchies already existed; the arrival of canal irrigation into the Phoenix area set the stage for dramatic increases in centralized political power.[43] Hohokam should have had kings. Curiously, they went another way (chapter 4).

There was more to Hohokam, of course, than budding elites ambitious to rule. Cotton arrived from Mexico about 500; the Early Hohokam grew it, although it did not become economically important until 700 (chapter 4). *Glycimeris* shell bracelets or armlets (a staple of Hohokam industry after 750; again, chapter 4) appeared first at Pioneer Period sites. Wallace (1995) identifies a pan-regional style (his Style I, with a terminal date about 800) in the earliest painted ceramics and rock art. It seems (with hindsight) that Hohokam was gearing up for something big. Prefiguring those later developments, I discuss two remarkable aspects of Pioneer Period Hohokam: figurines and mounds.

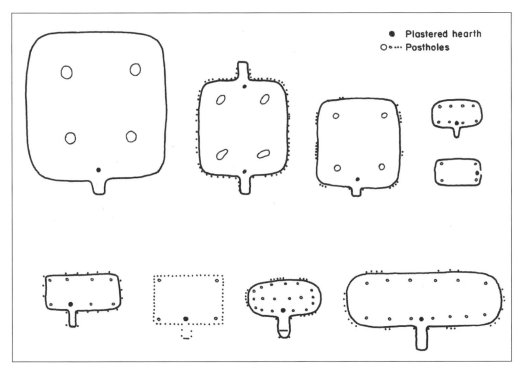

Figure 3.4. Hohokam Big Houses. Top row: three Pioneer Period Big Houses and two smaller, normal houses. Bottom row: two Colonial Period (left) and two Sedentary Period (right) normal houses. Courtesy David Doyel and the Amerind Foundation.

Clay figurines, used in ceremonies now beyond recall (rituals related to ancestors?), were common at Pioneer Period sites. David Doyel called the Pioneer Period "the age of the figurine"[44] (fig. 3.5). Of figurines at Snaketown, 90 percent date to the early Vahki and Snaketown phases, mostly from trash mounds.[45] At Grewe (a huge Hohokam site near Casa Grande), recent excavations recovered figurines mainly from house floors or household trash (but not trash mounds).[46] Although clay figurines were made throughout Hohokam's long run, they declined sharply in number after the Pioneer Period (chapter 4). Later figurines (Colonial and Sedentary periods; see fig. 4.3) were fewer in number, more elaborate in construction, and used in new contexts—as caches with cremation burials. Hohokam figurines were unquestionably, if distantly, of Mesoamerican inspiration; clay figurines appeared early and often in civilizations to the south.[47] The point here is, figurines were ubiquitous in the Pioneer Period and much less so through the following Colonial and Sedentary periods. At 700, something was about to change in Hohokam cosmology and the Hohokam world.

Earthen "mounds" (an unfortunately middling term for an important architectural form) were a time-honored element of Hohokam architecture, from modest trash mounds in the Early Pioneer Period through huge platform mounds of the Classic Period (chapters 6 and 7). Small but intentional piles of trash and unwanted fill—trash mounds—were part of Hohokam settlements from early on, but beginning in the Late Pioneer Period, some of those trash mounds were "capped" with a layer of caliche plaster.[48] That architectural treatment may signify that a mound's use-life was finished, or it may indicate a change in function, from a pile of trash to an architectural form ("dance platform" is one archaeological suggestion).[49]

Figure 3.5. Hohokam figurines from Snaketown, Arizona. Clay figurines were central to Pioneer Period beliefs and far less important in later Hohokam history. Courtesy Arizona State Museum, University of Arizona (photograph by Helga Teiwes).

We have little notion of the meaning of trash mounds and capped trash mounds in the Pioneer Period. Both forms—unlike figurines—continued through the following Colonial and Sedentary periods. It was only much later, in the Classic Period (chapters 6 and 7), that low capped mounds were replaced by tall, rectangular platform mounds. So the pace of change was not lockstep: figurines in the Early Pioneer Period, mounds through the Sedentary Period. Some things, such as figurines, fell by the wayside when Hohokam (in the sense of the package of practices) emerged around 700 to 800; other things, such as mounds, were incorporated into the new set of beliefs.

Mounds—solid forms built of earth and stone—were everywhere among North American farming societies, from Wisconsin to Panama. They served many purposes: sculptural (effigies), mortuary (burial mounds), discard (trash mounds), and architectural (platforms and pyramids that supported more conventional structures). Mounds and earthen architecture link Hohokam to that larger world—and separate it from Anasazi, which, as in so many other things, came much later to earthen architecture (chapter 5).

Transforming the Continent: Teotihuacán

When politically ambitious Hohokam families built the first Big Houses, they may have excused themselves: "Well, we're not really trying to be lords of Teotihuacán, you know." Or perhaps they claimed: "We *are* lords of Teotihuacán," no doubt to hoots of derision. But, more likely, they didn't have to say anything. Everybody *knew* there were lords in Teotihuacán, and everybody knew that if Big House families weren't quite those lords (*everybody knew everything!*), they were the best the Hohokam could hope for along those lines. The important thing was, Teotihuacán and rumors of Teotihuacán made it clear that lords were possible.

The central fact in the Southwest's larger world was thousands of kilometers away in central Mexico (*distances can be dealt with!*): the colossal urban center of Teotihuacán, the biggest city ever seen in North America until Aztec Tenochtitlán six centuries later. Teotihuacán began around AD 1, peaked between 400 and 500, and came to a dramatic, unpleasant end around 550–600.[50] The bigger they come, the harder they fall. Teotihuacán was unprecedented and unequalled, in George Kubler's terms a *prime object*: a unique, archetypical event that engenders and entails a long series of lesser replicas. "Prime objects resemble the prime numbers of mathematics because no conclusive rule is known to govern the appearance of either, although such a rule may someday be found.... Their character as primes is not explained by their antecedents, and their order in history is enigmatic."[51] Teotihuacán came out of nowhere (insofar as southwestern people could know) and set the North American agenda for many centuries.[52] Of course, the great city had an internal history, which began when "a powerful, probably charismatic, ruler decided to put Teotihuacán on the map with a bang" and caused the building of its principal monuments.[53] After a few centuries of "increasingly powerful rulers" came a period of reform: "permanent checks were placed on the exercise of arbitrary power" with the establishment of "collective leadership of a ruling bureaucracy," famously anonymous.[54] (That sequence of events had modest parallels, several centuries later, in Hohokam; chapter 4.)

Teotihuacán expanded earlier, Olmec proclivities for action at a distance. Teotihuacán colonies, scion princes, emissaries, or agents meddled in Maya politics, more than 1,000 kilometers from the great city.[55] That distance indicates the city's powerful reach and puts the Southwest into perspective: Teotihuacán was toppling kings and setting up puppet empires at 1,000 kilometers! *Distances can be dealt with!* (Chaco and Phoenix—southwestern centers and potential rivals in the ninth through twelfth centuries—were less than 500 kilometers apart; chapters 4 and 5.) In addition to enclaves and emissaries at distant capitals, Teotihuacán itself "collected" foreigners. Barrios—neighborhoods of people from particularly important, distant regions—formed among the city's one hundred thousand residents. The place was cosmopolitan and well connected to its world.

Teotihuacán directly affected societies as far north as Alta Vista and La Quemada, near Durango (and only 1,400 km from Phoenix [see fig. 1.4]).[56] Turquoise, almost certainly from the Southwest, was prominent in Teotihuacán art. It is possible of course that no southwestern Native ever saw Teotihuacán. But any organized farming group anywhere in North America would surely have *known about* the great city, heard the rumors. The great city must have reshaped the way Native North America thought about itself and redefined the possible courses of Native North American history. Ben Nelson (2000) offered a more specific model of how the *fall* of Teotihuacán might have affected the Southwest (chapters 1 and 4). How much more so *its rise?*

Conservatively, states had risen in Mesoamerica by 100 BC, more than five hundred years before the events in this chapter.[57] Less conservatively, states or statelike kingdoms began with Olmec, 1000 BC or earlier.[58] To understand the Southwest's continental context, it is important to realize that Mesoamerican states had been rising and falling for more than a millennium before Hohokam Big House families got the bug. If southwestern societies felt the need for central governments, they had Mesoamerican models and at least secondhand knowledge of how such things were done.

The Mesoamerican Classic was a many-splendored thing, and much of that splendor was only weakly relevant to Hohokam. Indeed, Teotihuacán may have been only a rumor—a very powerful rumor. In West Mexico, the Teuchitlán Tradition (see fig. 1.4) paralleled, but did not mimic, Teotihuacán. Teuchitlán cities, with their round, terraced, wedding-cake pyramids, flourished between 400 and 700.[59] They were much smaller and ultimately less consequential than Teotihuacán, but they would have been wonders to Hohokam farmers. With its deep, strong ties to West Mexico, Hohokam probably knew Teuchitlán, directly or by reliable secondhand accounts. If Hohokam leaders wanted role models, West Mexico was the obvious place to look.

La Quemada was closer to the Southwest than Teuchitlán. But it was east of the Sierra Madre, probably out of Hohokam's sphere, and perhaps of more import to Mogollon and Anasazi. And it came to prominence somewhat later than the events in this chapter; La Quemada began as early as 500 but really hit its stride from 650 to 750. It ended around 900, long after Teotihuacán's fall.[60] La Quemada, with an elaborate system of causeway roads and prominent colonnades, was a likely model of Mesoamerican urbanism for those southwestern groups whose interests lay east of 666: Mimbres and Chaco Anasazi. Around 900 to 1000, roads and colonnades appeared at Chaco (chapter 5). *No coincidences?*

No coincidences. Distances can be dealt with. Everybody knew everything. We should not doubt that southwestern societies knew, or knew of, Mesoamerican cities, lords, and civilizations. And we should not doubt that knowledge of Mesoamerica affected southwestern history. The simple fact that cities and kings *existed* altered the spectrum of options and possibilities. It was not necessary for Anasazi or Hohokam to "invent" villages and cities or to "evolve" complexity.[61] Mesoamerica had already done the heavy lifting. Southwestern societies could adopt, adapt, reject, or reinvent those social institutions. The point is this: everything that happened in the Southwest after 500 happened in contexts of urbanism, statehood, and hierarchy to the south. There may indeed have been scientific processes behind the emergence of political leadership at Valencia Vieja (that's another book, yet to be written), but *at the historical moment*, Big Houses were built, occupied, and understood in the context of Mesoamerican cities and states. Teotihuacán hovered over Valencia Vieja and Snaketown like Jerusalem over Europe of that same age—imperfectly known, constantly reinvented, a distant paragon.[62]

Mogollon: Mountain Men or Hillbilly Hohokam?

The Mogollon history included in this chapter encompasses the Early Pithouse Period and the first phases of the Late Pithouse Period (see fig. 1.6). I think that most of the Mogollon region before 750 was in many ways upland Hohokam. That may have been true right through the 800s and maybe into the 900s (chapter 4). Modern Mogollon archaeologists would recoil in horror from those assertions. Call me credulous, but early Mogollon pottery looks a lot like Hohokam pottery. Early Mogollon pit houses look like deep versions of Hohokam pit houses (compare figures 3.1 and 4.6; then look at figure 3.6). At higher (Mogollon) elevations, people dug deeper pits for their homes; at lower (Hohokam) elevations, people dug shallower pits. Deeper pit houses were better insulated and warmer in winter.[63] What would Hohokam look like, out on the diluted edges, if it lapped up into the mountains? Like early Mogollon, I think.

There's another way to look at this problem. Perhaps Gladwin and Haury were wrong and the Big Three were actually only two: Hohokam and Anasazi. The Late Pithouse Period in particular looks, to me, a lot more like Hohokam than Anasazi (chapter 4). Mogollon phases following the Late Pithouse Period looked a lot more Anasazi than Hohokam (chapter 5).[64] Archaeologists of the 1910s, '20s, and '30s detested that sort of cultural flip-flopping, and Mogollon's inconsistencies were "exhibit 1" in complaints against Gladwin's and Haury's third and final addition to the southwestern trilogy. Indeed, Haury acknowledged the problems, at least for later Mogollon. He very carefully proposed "Mogollon *prior to* AD 1000."[65] (We will follow Mogollon's contentious archaeological career in chapters 4 and 5.)

I think Mogollon prior to 1000 was very cozy with Hohokam. Of course, Mogollon wasn't a tail wagged by a Hohokam dog (probably one of those chubby little Colima dogs, bred to be tasty). Mogollon was a player. I focus here on the Mimbres Mogollon, in part because very interesting things happened there later (chapters 4 and 5).[66] Like Hohokam, *Mimbres* has multiple meanings. Mimbres is a river valley (the Río Mimbres, or "Willow Creek"), an area corresponding (more or less) to southwestern New Mexico, and the archaeological term for ancient peoples who lived there. It is also the name of an archaeological phase (the Mimbres Phase) of much later times, 950 to 1150 (chapter 6). Except in reference to the Mimbres Phase, by *Mimbres* I mean the region—southwestern New Mexico, its deserts and adjacent uplands.[67]

Early Mimbres and other Mogollon areas from perhaps as early as 200 (more likely 300 or 400) to about 550 had a notable predilection for high places: buttes, mesas, hilltops[68]—notably *unlike* Hohokam, who lived down by the river. Thereafter, river terraces were the favored Mimbres locales—notably *like* Hohokam—starting with the Late Pithouse Period and continuing through later Mimbres Phase villages (chapters 4 and 5).[69]

A number of interpretations have been offered for the earliest hilltop Mogollon sites:[70]

warm-weather seasonal farming camps; full-time farming villages avoiding cold-air drainage in canyon bottoms; resource-harvesting sites; ceremonial sites; defensive refuges;[71] or trophy homes on the hill.[72] Whatever they were, early Mimbres Mogollon pit house villages apparently were "short occupations by small groups of people, with frequent reoccupations over long time spans."[73]

Like Apaches who called the Mimbres area home a thousand years later, Early Pithouse Period villagers probably opportunistically farmed wetlands or cienegas, augmented with hastily built, temporary "scratch" canals. Early Pithouse peoples of course were not Apaches. They had very different histories and historical contexts. But the practicalities of "wet spot" agriculture structured similar settlement histories for the two very different societies.

Most Early Pithouse Period sites were small, a dozen or so structures. A very few had up to fifty-five structures, but sites that size were truly unusual (for example, the Thompson site).[74] In the following decades (the Late Pithouse Period), sites that big showed hints of hierarchy (something like Big Houses, as we shall see in chapter 4). Were Big Houses present in the 500s Mimbres Mogollon sites contemporary with Valencia Vieja and Snaketown? Probably not.

There were Early Mogollon populations—few and far between—throughout the mountains of central Arizona. Mimbres Mogollon may have been notably more engaged with the Pioneer Period Hohokam because the Mimbres country (unlike the wet Arizona highlands) was much like southern Arizona—desert, with desert rivers very much like Hohokam's middle Gila (the Rio Grande) and Santa Cruz (the upper Gila, the Mimbres). The beginnings of the Mogollon Late Pithouse Period, I think, were much like the beginnings of Tucson-scale irrigation in the Mimbres area. On balance, Mimbres Mogollon was in the Hohokam sphere, but a frontier remote from the hurly-burly of Tucson and Phoenix—and with its own local problems (defensive hilltop villages?). All that changed after 750. The Colonial Period Hohokam explosion (chapter 4) triggered the reorganization of the Mogollon throughout central Arizona and southwestern New Mexico.

Anasazi: Premature Politicization on the Plateau

The period from 400 to 750 is called Basketmaker III (see fig. 1.6). It started slow but really heated up after 550.[75] Indeed, when Basketmaker III began, large parts of the Plateau were essentially unoccupied or (perhaps) depopulated. For example, no one lived on Black Mesa from 400 to 800.[76] Basketmaker came late or not at all to many parts of northeastern Arizona and southeastern Utah.[77] Most uplands remained empty or nearly empty.

Basketmaker III people typically settled near or along streams and rivers (figs. 3.6, 3.7). Those settlements were small: most comprised one or two households (that is, one or two pit houses), often surrounded by a fence or stockade.[78] A really big Basketmaker site—a cause for archaeological jubilation—has a dozen structures.[79] Bad Dog Ridge near Ganado, Arizona, with as many as thirty structures, was truly exceptional (and may in fact be Pueblo I and thus belong in the next chapter).[80]

So that's Basketmaker III: small sites scattered unevenly across the Plateau, mostly along creeks. Against that unprepossessing background, two Basketmaker III sites at Chaco Canyon stand out as phenomenally large. Huge, gargantuan, colossal. These are Shabik'eschee and the prosaically named 29 SJ 423. Shabik'eschee, at the upper end of the canyon, had *at least* seventy structures,[81] and 29 SJ 423, at the lower end of the canyon, was probably even larger.[82]

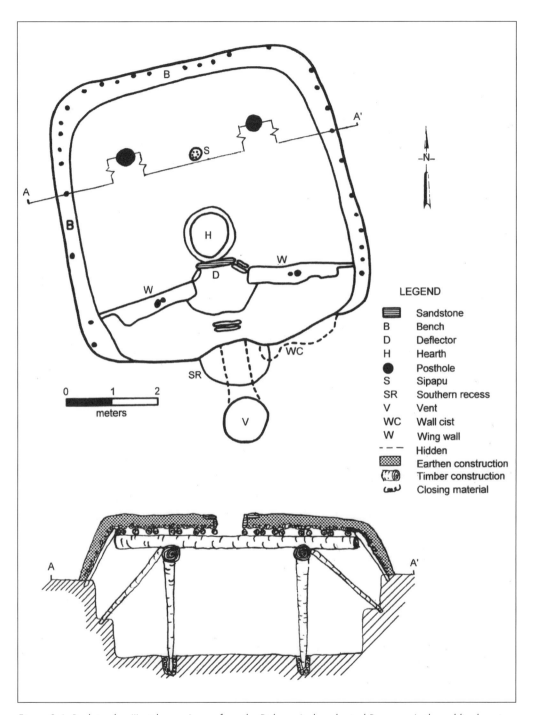

Figure 3.6. Basketmaker III pit house. Image from the Dolores Archaeological Program. In the public domain.

Shabik'eschee's three-score-and-ten pit houses, many with elaborate exterior storage pits, formed a village comparable in area to a medium-sized Hohokam town (fig. 3.8). No other Basketmaker III sites came close to that size. Shabik'eschee and 423 were Basketmaker III

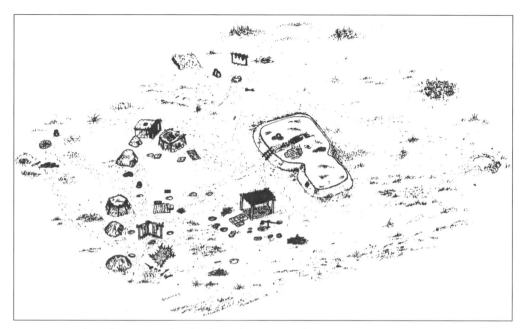

Figure 3.7. Basketmaker III Tres Bobos hamlet, Dolores River Valley, Colorado. Image from the Dolores Archaeological Program. In the public domain.

metropolises.[83] Some have argued that if the pit houses were all in use at once, these big sites represent many small sites, stacked up over many decades (much like Los Pozos; chapter 2).

Both sites had Great Kivas near the center of the settlement, in an ill-defined plaza area. A dozen or so Great Kivas are known throughout the Basketmaker III region. These probably served as the ritual and political focus of widely scattered communities of one- and two-household farmsteads. At Chaco, each of the two big Basketmaker villages merited its own Great Kiva. I think those Great Kivas tell us something about demographics. Chip Wills and Tom Windes argued that Shabik'eschee was actually a small permanent settlement periodically enlarged by other families attracted by piñon nuts—sort of a full-dress piñon camp.[84] Thus seventy (plus) pit houses. But 423, equally large, did not have Shabik'eschee's extensive piñon stands. *And why did they both need Great Kivas*? I think Shabik'eschee and 423 were truly villages. Not all pit houses were in use all the time of course but through most of the history of each site, they were really big—much, much bigger than any other Basketmaker III village.

At Shabik'eschee, the community pulled in tight around the Great Kiva and formed something like a town. A few houses nearest the plaza and Great Kiva are notably larger than the other houses (we don't know about 423; it's never been excavated). Archaeologists noticed this. "Pithouse F not only is the largest habitation, and not only is close to the communal pit structure [Great Kiva], but it also contained an inordinate quantity of rare artifacts, including turquoise"[85] and probably *Glycimeris* shell armlets.[86] Shabik'eschee was a Basketmaker III village trying to be a Tucson Basin town, and aspiring leaders at Shabik'eschee were trying to be Tucson Basin Big House elites.[87]

I say this because we know what happened earlier, in the Tucson Basin during the Early Agricultural Period: Big Houses (chapter 2). And because we know what happened next: Pueblo I Big Houses and proto-Great Houses (chapter 4). *Connect the dots!* For those who

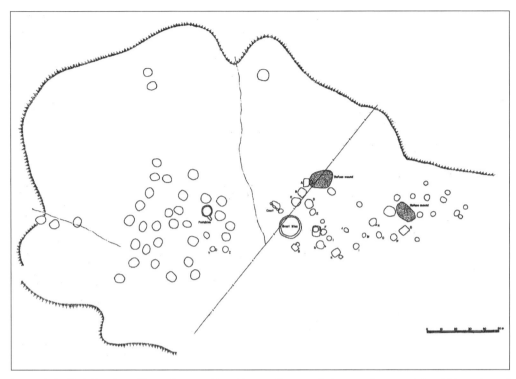

Figure 3.8. Shabik'eschee, Chaco Canyon, New Mexico. The straight line is a fence and the old boundary of Chaco Culture National Historical Park, now expanded to include the entire site. Courtesy Thomas Windes.

insist that data come only in bags, there is material evidence of Anasazi–Hohokam "connections": cotton on the Plateau before 900 almost certainly came from the south,[88] as did shell, and there were remarkable amounts of Hohokam shell in Basketmaker III, especially in the west.[89] *Glycimeris* shell armlets—such as those at Shabik'eschee—in later Colonial and Sedentary times became "badges" of Hohokam-ness (chapter 4). Pioneer Period shell bracelets or armlets, transposed to the Plateau, might well have been badges of Hohokam-inspired political leadership. Shabik'eschee's leaders need not appeal to kings of Teotihuacán or Teuchitlán. They could look closer to home and mimic the squires of Snaketown.

Did Shabik'eschee need a leader? Apparently not. If it was a town, it was not a very large town (only a few hundred people at most, small by Hohokam standards). It had no canals or other cumbersome infrastructure to control. The village didn't need a chief, but perhaps the chief needed a village. Someone of unusual charisma, ambition, luck, or ardor, inspired (at a distance) by tales of Hohokam and Mesoamerican leadership, brought together an unusual number of families. If that's the story, it didn't work for long.

Shabik'eschee and 29 SJ 423 did, however, establish a remarkable historical precedent. Both sites were phenomenal in their times. There was nothing else like them on the Plateau. People remembered whatever happened at Chaco Canyon during Basketmaker III. The Chaco towns (successful or not) established Chaco as an extraordinary place within the vast Anasazi region. As we shall see, developments in Pueblo I (chapter 4), Pueblo II (chapter 5), and Pueblo III (chapter 6) referenced Chaco as a point of signal significance, probably harking back to the first, failed experiments in hierarchy at Shabik'eschee.

Moving Forward

Kidder, Gladwin, Haury, and others of their era divided the Southwest into three regions: Anasazi, Hohokam, and Mogollon. Those three regions structure how later generations of archaeologists did and do their work. But boundaries changed; history played out over space, as well as time; borders moved, dissolved, reformed. (Gladwin in particular realized this, annoying his more conventional contemporaries.) As we shall see, Hohokam exploded outward from 700 to 950 (Gladwin's "Colonial Period") and then shrank back in on Phoenix. Anasazi Chaco boomed expansively from 950 to 1150, and then it too collapsed. Before 1930, archaeology could only guess about that. All we had was space, geographic distributions, and surveys. Archaeology was missing time, essential to any narrative.

Tree rings changed all that.

Figure 4.1. Pueblo I hamlet with palisade near Aztec, New Mexico. Artist's reconstruction by Cory Dangerfield. Courtesy Jerry Fetterman and Woods Canyon Archaeological Consultants.

f o u r
Pace — *Time*

Archaeologies: 1930 to 1960
Histories: 700 to 950

Before 1930, there was no way to link the history of the ancient Southwest to the modern calendar. After 1930, tree rings gave archaeology astonishing control of time and a new (and
somewhat unsettling) sense of change's pace in the ancient past. Colonial Period Hohokam
and Pueblo I Anasazi, once seen as plodding, necessary steps on the road to later cultural climaxes, began to look like cultural explosions—in large part because of their timing.

Actually, 1930 is approximate, a nice round number. The real year was eighteen months
long on either side of 1928—an *annus mirabilis* in southwestern archaeology. Three important institutions were founded: the Laboratory of Anthropology, Gila Pueblo, and the
Museum of Northern Arizona. Even more wonderful was the discovery, mid-summer in 1929,
of a specimen bridging the gap between the fledgling, "floating" tree-ring chronology and
our modern calendar, providing rock-solid dates for ancient sites and allowing the correlation
of past events with climatic changes—an immediate and still dominant theme in southwestern archaeology (chapter 6).

Southwestern sites—Anasazi and Mogollon but not Hohokam—produced quantities of
wooden posts, vigas, and latillas. (Hohokam remains for all practical purposes tree-ring free.)
In the early days, ancient beams and posts went into the campfire. After 1930 that wood
could be dated. Tree rings fixed the timing and rhythm of events with astonishing precision.

Competition among the new, regional institutions ensured that every area would be different, dancing to different drummers. Specialization made it harder and harder to comprehend the larger choreography. But there was indeed a pattern: a 2/4 rhythm of Hohokam and
Chaco. Hohokam jumped first (this chapter), while Chaco waited a century or two for its *gran
jeté*, its great leap forward (chapter 5). Was this a *pas de deux*—or punch, counterpunch?

Tree-ring dates require trees. Hohokam archaeology, in its bleak desert, had no tree rings,
so it fought, famously, over chronology, particularly during the middle third of the twentieth
century—the period of this chapter's "archaeologies." It was the fight of the century, or the
centuries: phases were cut off at the knees, bounced off the ropes, stretched out on the canvas. Gladwin's chronology accordioned from a "long count" of two-hundred-year phases

marching in stately progression, to a frenetic revision in which superfluous phases were jettisoned and the survivors were jammed into two short centuries.[1] Tree-ring-dated "trade" pottery, then carbon 14, and then archaeomagnetism rang in new rounds of chronological battles.

The winner came by split decision: Hohokam was both longer and shorter than anybody would have guessed. Hohokam, it turns out, was not just a region or culture area, steadily progressing to its Classic Period peak (see fig. 1.6). Hohokam as I and others now see it was a brief shining moment in the desert, set within that longer cultural history. Hohokam was an event—a century-plus-long event.

Tree rings fixed Chaco in time almost immediately and exposed a serious misapprehension: we had thought Chaco was roughly contemporary with Mesa Verde (Pueblo III, in the Pecos Classification described below). By the end of the 1930s, we knew that Chaco was actually much earlier (Pueblo II). That seemingly minor adjustment had remarkable implications, explored in chapter 6. In this chapter, we will watch the run-up to Chaco: Pueblo I, one of the most volatile, time-sensitive periods in Anasazi history.

Before 1929 there were no "absolute dates." Today we have tens of thousands. No one knows how many, but the total approaches fifty thousand. *Fifty thousand dates!* Of course, some periods and some places have more dates than others, but compared with southwestern archaeology before 1930, we now control time.[2]

Archaeologies: 1930 to 1960 (Culture History, with Dates)

In the run-up to World War II, the Southwest offered "stasis as aesthetic therapy"—the apt phrase of Curtis Hinsley.[3] Armies were marching, the world was changing. In contrast, the ancient, exotic Southwest was (we were told) unchanging and eternal, "a region that, while undeniably the locus of momentous past events, remained somehow *essentially* unchanged—a fly in amber."[4] But archaeologists and (of course) Indians knew better. There *was* a past, and with increasing chronological precision, it became clearer and clearer that the past was *different*. Indians kept their histories by memorization, by transmission across generations, and by commemorative acts in everyday life. Archaeology vacillated in its use and appreciation of Indian traditional histories. The earliest archaeologists, thinking the Southwest was relatively young, accepted Native tales as useful guides to events in the not-too-distant past. With the addition of time, that past became more distant. From the 1920s through the 1940s, archaeologists turned hard away from Native "myths" and toward the empirical record.[5] To craft "culture history," they schematized stratigraphy, potsherds, and especially tree-ring dates.

Tree Rings, Etc.

Working in the 1920s, the brilliant astronomer Andrew Ellicott Douglas discovered the principles of tree-ring chronology, allowing us to see, for example, that Chaco and Aztec were closely sequential but not (yet) providing actual dates. A temporal gap—literally an undiscovered piece of wood—separated his "floating," ancient tree-ring sequence from the tree rings of modern wood, tied to the modern calendar. A specimen bridging the gap between history and prehistory was finally found in 1929. The effects were immediate and profound. "Henceforth we will have tussocks of empirical certainty to guide our speculations across the fen of time,"[6] wrote Earl Morris (not in reference to tree-ring dating, but the sentiment fits). Tree-ring dating was cheap, and in many parts of the Plateau and Mogollon uplands, datable beams and posts were common finds. A burned pit house could fill boxes and boxes with beams, each a potential date to an exact year! Dendrochronology "blossomed into a full fledged focus of archaeological research between 1930 and 1942."[7]

Much of the Southwest, alas, is treeless desert. Calendrical, "absolute" dating in the deserts had to await the development of carbon 14 in 1946. Carbon 14 (or 14C) was experimental, costly, and imprecise, so it was not widely used until the massive Hohokam "salvage," or cultural resource management (CRM), projects of the 1970s and 1980s (discussed in chapter 6). Archaeomagnetic dating—based on the fact that magnetic north moves around true north—held out the promise of fairly inexpensive dates with perhaps five-year precision. Robert DuBois started his pioneering archaeomagnetic program in 1963, but later critical improvements mean that "for all practical purposes, archaeomagnetism is only 30 years old in North America."[8] Archaeomagnetic dates, while far less costly than 14C, require much greater investment of time in the field, and in practice they are seldom precise to a five-year span. The more we learned about the magnetic pole, the less precise became the dates; magnetic north wobbled around the pole like Santa on a bender, crossing its own path repeatedly.[9]

Tree-ring dating, largely unchanged since the 1930s and 1940s, remains the region's best option, the dating method of choice. Even in treeless deserts, tree-ring precision can be imported via "trade sherds," securely dated at their better forested points of production. It is fair to say that southwestern archaeology today is defined by dendrochronology: tree rings made the field what it is—for better, of course, but in a few subtle ways for worse.

Regional Sequences, Regional Centers

The privately funded museums and research institutions conceived in the Roaring Twenties staggered through the Great Depression. After regaining fiscal momentum, they carved up the Southwest into fiefdoms. Then they labored mightily to define phase sequences specific to their region and distinct from those of their rivals.

The Pecos Classification and Its Discontents

An Anasazi (or Pueblo) sequence was hammered out in 1927. The "Pecos Classification" was developed (after considerable wrangling) at a field conference at Ted Kidder's digs at Pecos Pueblo. Everyone who was anyone came to Kidder's camp for that meeting. Even Edgar Hewett appeared, briefly.

Kidder and company took up Ruth Benedict's challenge. Where did Pueblos come from? Could archaeology tell us how it came about? Everybody had ideas. T. T. Waterman, apparently a great conciliator, framed a compromise—the Pecos Classification, with Basketmaker I, II, and III followed by a succession of later Pueblo periods: I, II, III, IV, and V (see fig. 1.6).[10] The Pecos Classification was originally intended to define developmental stages or horizons and not spans of actual time. (It preceded tree-ring dating by a year or two.) The classification codified Bandelier's "slow and tedious development" in a series of steps or stages, incrementally adding elements necessary to modern Pueblo life: corn first, then pottery, then pueblos, then kivas, then kachinas, and so forth. That's not history; it's ontogeny.

With the arrival of dendrochronology, it became possible to assign dates, so people did. Pueblo II, for example, seemed to date from about 900 to 1150. But dates in one region did not always match those in another. That was taken, not illogically, as indicating something like history. The Four Corners was widely held to have been a center from which the Pecos Classification's developmental stages radiated (the San Juan Hypothesis, chapter 3). Places such as the Rio Grande, distant from the San Juan hearth, naturally lagged behind. So by that logic, Pueblo II (as a developmental stage) in the Four Corners might well predate Pueblo II in the provinces. Indeed, it seemed that Pueblo II lasted so late in the Rio Grande and Kayenta regions, at the edges of the Anasazi world, that it was almost embarrassing.

Not everyone was happy with the lockstep of Basketmaker II, Basketmaker III, and Pueblo I, II, III, IV, and V—particularly out in the provinces. No one wanted to hear that his or her region's sequence might be, well, *developmentally delayed*. Rival schemes were soon proposed, local phase sequences better suited to Walnut Canyon, the Tsegi area, or the Rio Grande. Five short years after the Pecos Classification, Gladwin (always the iconoclast) proposed an elaborate, dendritic "A Method for Designation of Cultures and Their Variations," which he felt better represented Hohokam and Mogollon chronologies.[11] Phase sequences sprouted like weeds in every valley—far too many to recount here or to reconcile.

A necessary apparatus of any report, then and forever after, was a full-page box chart (sometimes a foldout) with a half dozen or more vertical columns, each divided by horizontal bars like a slot machine spinning the sequences of rival chronologies, and a single column to one side (often in bold) labeled "chronology in this report." In that game, the house always wins.

Fiefdoms: The Lab, Gila Pueblo, and MNA

Regional chronologies reflected the emergence of regional research centers.[12] In 1907 Edgar Hewett established in Santa Fe the School of American Archaeology (later the School of American Research and now the School for Advanced Research). Two years later, he inherited the Museum of New Mexico. In the early days, neither institution was impressive. The state museum was underfunded and provincial, but Hewett soon transformed it from a colonial closet to a major cultural institution. The School of American Archaeology initially had the backing of the Archaeological Institute of America (AIA). AIA, an East Coast organization, had originally intended that the school be located in Mexico to study the high civilizations of Mesoamerica, but Hewett hijacked it to New Mexico to study Pueblo Indians. The classically oriented AIA soon lost interest in its Wild West branch.[13]

Hewett's East Coast enemies thought that he, his museum, and his school were not up to the task. Kidder was one of several archaeological luminaries who convinced millionaire John D. Rockefeller Jr. to fund yet another archaeological institution, the Laboratory of Anthropology in tiny Santa Fe—in direct competition with Hewett's museum and school. The Lab, as it came to be called, was chartered in 1928 as a museum/library/archive and as a base camp or field station for researchers from East Coast institutions conducting serious research in the Southwest.[14] It opened for business in 1931—two years after the stock market crashed. Not good timing.

Hewett was not fond of the Laboratory of Anthropology and no doubt rejoiced when the Great Depression gave Rockefeller pause—and better things to do with his money. Short on cash, the Lab limped on. After (and only after) Hewett died in 1946, the Museum of New Mexico swept up the Lab, saving it from bankruptcy. It might have become an outbuilding of the museum, which would have pleased El Toro (as Hewett was known to his students). But when the School of American Research split from the museum in 1959, the Laboratory of Anthropology found new life. It emerged as the research arm of the Museum of New Mexico, a position it enjoyed until very recently.

Neither was Hewett fond of the Pecos Classification. He never used it in his extensive writings; it was forever associated with East Coast men such as Ted Kidder and others who supported the Laboratory of Anthropology. The classification became the Lab's by default, to support or reject. The Lab—out from Hewett's and Kidder's shadows—did a bit of both, as we shall see.[15]

The same year the Laboratory of Anthropology opened in Santa Fe, Harold Gladwin established Gila Pueblo near Globe, Arizona, as his privately funded archaeological research center.[16] Gladwin was sometimes off target, but, as noted in chapter 3, among many other accomplishments, Gila Pueblo defined Hohokam and Mogollon. That's not bad.

After the war, Gladwin lost interest and Gila Pueblo ceased operations abruptly in 1950. Its collections and archives were transferred to the Arizona State Museum (ASM) at the University of Arizona in Tucson, which thereby became the undisputed world champion center for Hohokam research.[17] ASM had been established in 1893 but really came to prominence under Dean Cummings (who arrived at the University of Arizona in 1915) and then, most particularly, under Emil Haury. Haury—once a member of Gladwin's Gila Pueblo staff—became ASM's director in 1938. He transformed ASM from a small natural history collection into one of the leading anthropology museums in the Southwest. That took time; ASM moved into its own building only in 1936. Through the 1930s and most of the 1940s, ASM was overshadowed by Gila Pueblo and other, older museums.

The Museum of Northern Arizona (MNA) incorporated in Flagstaff, Arizona, in 1928—again, that wonderful year. It was several years before the present complex northwest of Flagstaff opened. Field research by MNA's founder, Harold Colton (1881–1970), was already well under way.[18] (Colton was present at the creation of the Pecos Classification in 1927.) Predictably, Flagstaff archaeology went its own way, with its own chronologies and local sequences, but Colton was more careful than most to synchronize his system with the Pecos stages.

Between 1930 and 1950, the Laboratory of Anthropology emerged as the leading research institution in New Mexico; Gila Pueblo dominated Hohokam studies until Harold Gladwin sent its collections to the Arizona State Museum; and the Museum of Northern Arizona became the preeminent institution for northeastern Arizona and Hopi.[19] Each institution wrote its own history of its chunk of the ancient Southwest.

The Plateau in Pieces: Regional Sequences

Three regional sequences developed from (or against) the Pecos Classification for the Anasazi or Pueblo world. Two were associated with the Laboratory of Anthropology, and one with the Museum of Northern Arizona.

Frank Roberts—a sometime instructor at the Laboratory of Anthropology before it was annexed by the Museum of New Mexico—proposed meaty names for the pallid Pecos Classification stages, with a rise-and-fall plot: [20]

- Basketmaker (Basketmaker II)
- Modified Basketmaker (Basketmaker III)
- Developmental Pueblo (Pueblo I and Pueblo II)
- Great Pueblo (Pueblo III)
- Regressive Pueblo (Pueblo IV)
- Historic Pueblo (Pueblo V)

The first acts of Roberts's story were set in the Four Corners—the San Juan Hypothesis. The denouement took place in the Rio Grande pueblos, at Zuni and Hopi. Roberts thought Pueblo history peaked in the Four Corners—Great Pueblo!—and then skidded into the Rio Grande and the western pueblos: the Regressive Pueblo Period.

"Great" and "Regressive" really offended archaeologists working in those later time periods, especially in the Rio Grande. The labels particularly annoyed scholars at the Laboratory of Anthropology, who felt Rio Grande archaeology was great, not regressive. Most northern Rio Grande archaeologists rejected the San Juan Hypothesis.[21] The vision of prehistory that emerged for the Rio Grande was one of steady progress—no regression—upward and onward toward the modern Pueblos and, in recent days, complete historical independence from the Four Corners. A separate-but-equal system was proposed by Fred Wendorf, working for the Laboratory of Anthropology.[22] His scheme owed little to the Pecos Classification. Wendorf proposed four long periods, the names of which told his tale:

- Developmental (1000–1200)
- Coalition (1200–1325)
- Classic (1325–1600)
- Historic (1600–)

Frank Roberts's "Great Pueblo" (Pueblo III of the San Juan area) was demoted to "Coalition," and "Regressive" pointedly became "Classic" (Pueblo IV). Stick that in your classification, Frank! Wendorf's chronology, with only minor modifications, remains the gold standard along the Rio Grande, in marked preference to the Pecos Classification.

The best story—in the sense of narrative—came from the Museum of Northern Arizona's (MNA) chronology for Sinagua, the archaeology of the Flagstaff area. The Sinagua sequence included a volcano—a real *event*—the kind of cataclysm that Adolf Bandelier had denied the ancient Southwest (back in chapter 2). A brief digression into MNA's provenance is necessary. MNA, unlike the Laboratory of Anthropology and Gila Pueblo, was a full-service natural history institution, embracing botany, geology, and all the natural sciences. Its director, Harold Colton, was trained in zoology.[23] He became an archaeologist after picnicking next to a ruin near Flagstaff during his honeymoon. Colton's terminology for pottery types and chronology reflected his natural science background, with "index wares," "keys," "branches," and "foci."[24] Importantly, he avoided value judgments like "Regressive" or "Classic." Colton preferred neutral, natural terms—"Turkey Hill focus of the Sinagua Branch," for example. That got a bit complicated; Sinagua had twenty foci in four branches.[25] I will not list them all here.

But the neutral, natural science terminology had a hook, a bit of business the rest of the Southwest could only envy. The Sinagua volcano (Sunset Crater) was the most dramatic natural event then known in southwestern prehistory. The Great Drought of the Anasazi (discussed in chapter 6) got lots of press and attention, but it couldn't compete with an eruption; dry weather pales before thundering, red-hot magma. Tree-ring dating allowed Colton and MNA to propose the very year it happened. As Colton told the story, Sunset Crater exploded shortly after 1063, covering the Sinagua area with a thin layer of "black sand"—the title of Colton's fine popular book.[26] It was a great story, almost biblical:

> The earth…quiver[ed] like a wounded animal and the world was full of horrible
> noises…the terrified inhabitants crawled forth and fled to the south…looking back,

they could see a great cloud hanging over their country; it was streaked with lightning and at night it glowed with a reddish glare.[27]

Scientific certainty carried over to Colton's denouement: The black sand acted as mulch, enriching the soil and sparking a land rush. Settlers arrived from every direction. The post-eruption land rush gathered new peoples into a great American melting pot. At Wupatki (the most famous Sinagua ruin), an Anasazi-style pueblo sat next to a Hohokam ball court. The pot bubbled and boiled, until the Great Drought of 1275–1300 brought Sinagua's story to The End. The specificity of when, where, how, and with what results—the terrible eruption, the beneficent black sand—added natural science credibility to the tale.

Similar, if less vivid, regional chronologies broke out in every quarter, and eighth, and sixteenth of the Southwest. It seemed that each area had its own, unique story to tell. The Rio Grande was different. Hopi was different. Flagstaff was different. Every valley was different. The Pueblo region—the Plateau, the Rio Grande—was riven to pieces, a vast pixilated mosaic.[28]

Hohokam Big Men: Gladwin and Haury

Harold Gladwin hired Emil Haury for his staff of outstanding archaeologists (joining such greats as Ted Sayles, Erik Reed, Irwin Hayden, and Julian Hayden). At Gila Pueblo, Gladwin was the boss. When Gila Pueblo dissolved and Haury moved to the University of Arizona, Haury became the boss, the unchallenged master of Hohokam studies, right through the rise of CRM archaeology in the late 1970s and 1980s (chapter 6). Snaketown, excavated by Gila Pueblo, was the key Hohokam site—the "type site." Gladwin (with Haury and the rest of the gang) excavated Snaketown in 1934–1935.[29] Haury, at ASM, re-excavated the site in 1964–1965.[30]

Gladwin and Haury, when they first defined Hohokam, posited a series of nine phases, encompassed within four periods.[31] Each phase was conveniently marked by a single characteristic pottery type. Lacking any independent means for dating, they estimated that each phase lasted about two hundred years. Those assumptions produced what has become known as the "long count" (a play on Maya calendrics), beginning at 300 BC and ending at AD 1400 (the disastrous last phase was cut short before its full ten-score years). Their chronology told the story. I'll pass on the many phase names. The four periods tell the tale (with my précis):

- Pioneer: Immigration into the Phoenix Basin
- Colonial: Crystallization of the Hohokam core and expansion into the peripheries
- Sedentary: Stasis and retraction
- Classic: Salado intrusions from the Plateau and the creation of a new society

No volcanoes but lots of action!

With the advent of tree-ring dating, well-dated Anasazi and Mogollon pottery types found at Snaketown shrank the original long count. In 1942 Gladwin revised Snaketown's history down to a mere five centuries, from 600 to 1100 (Snaketown lacked the final phases of Hohokam). The first six phases (each still with its very own pottery type) were shortened to about fifty years each. This revision became the Hohokam "short count." Gladwin couldn't let well enough alone. Six short years after he introduced the short count, he further compressed Hohokam at Snaketown down to only two phases spanning the brief period from 725 to 1100.[32] The first four phases were reassigned by Gladwin to the Mogollon and redated as contemporaneous with the two surviving Hohokam phases. The Pioneer Period became a local brownware Mogollon population, with whom, for a few short centuries, Hohokam co-resided at sites like Snaketown.[33] There was no longer a Hohokam developmental sequence, a steady progression from simple beginnings to complicated climaxes. In part because of the shortened fuse, Gladwin now thought that the Hohokam must have been migrants from Mexico. Hohokam was a historical event.[34]

Emil Haury stood by the original long count. He made his point in 1955 through his student Joe Ben Wheat (whose dissertation, *Mogollon Culture Prior to AD 1000*, we encountered in chapter 3). Wheat needed to correlate his Mogollon chronology with Anasazi and Hohokam. Not surprisingly, the Hohokam chronology Wheat used—a slight modification of the original long count—was Haury's.[35] Delivered to every American archaeologist via the leading professional journals, Haury's chronology became the standard version.

Archaeologists, of course, picked and prodded the long count. Among other things, Haury's Hohokam were annoyingly precocious. They did things before the Four Corners Anasazi and, for a San Juan archaeologist, that just didn't seem right. To make matters worse, while Hohokam got longer, Anasazi got shorter. More and more tree-ring dates on the Plateau made it clear that the Basketmaker–Anasazi–Pueblo sequence was much younger than originally estimated by Kidder and company. Kidder lamented: "[We] have a sneaking sense of disappointment as the pitiless progress of tree-ring dating hauls the Cliff-dwellers, and with them the Basketmakers, farther and farther away from the cherished B.C.s."[36] If Hohokam started in 300 BC, where did that leave Basketmaker III, now pushed forward to AD 500?

Debate over the Hohokam chronology convinced Haury to re-excavate Snaketown in 1964–1965. Based on the new data, he remained firm in his belief that the long count was basically sound. But somewhat surprisingly, he reached the same conclusion that Gladwin reached through his hypershort count: Hohokam had come up out of Mexico.[37] The key elements that made Hohokam *Hohokam* appeared together as a group, without precedents. Haury thought that meant they came up from the south. Turns out, he was probably right. On this, more later.

The chronological issues were bigger than Snaketown, bigger than Haury and Gladwin—who were indeed Big Men. The problem required the classic American fix: throw money at it. In the 1970s and 1980s, massive CRM projects funded thousands of expensive 14C and archaeomagnetic dates (chapter 6). In 1991 Jeffrey Dean synthesized all the new dates.[38] A chronological consensus began to form. Happily, both long and short counts could be (in part) accommodated: the Hohokam sequence defined in 1937 for Snaketown shrank upward, but newly discovered pre-Hohokam phases filled in the (briefly) vacant early centuries. Nature abhors a vacuum only slightly more than archaeologists abhor a gap in the sequence, and a new longer count fills gaps left by the new shorter count.[39]

Histories: 700 to 950 (Pueblo I, Colonial, Late Pithouse)

The period from 700 to 950 was perhaps the most dynamic in the history of the Southwest (fig. 4.2). The deserts exploded—that's the right word—during the Hohokam Colonial and Mogollon Late Pithouse periods. The Colonial Period expansion, driven by ideology as much as economy, was the main event of the eighth- and ninth-century Southwest. It engulfed the Late Pithouse Period Mogollon. On the Plateau, repeated attempts to forge political power, which failed in Basketmaker III, found degrees of success in large Pueblo I communities—

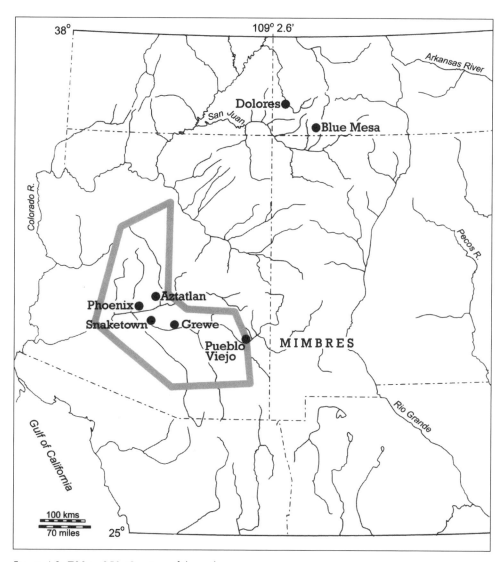

Figure 4.2. 700 to 950. Courtesy of the author.

perhaps in reaction to the astonishing developments in the desert. Town building, political aspirations, and spiraling violence entwined in a complex nexus of cause and effect—with dramatic results.

Continental Contexts: The Fall of Teotihuacán

Teotihuacán fell, with great violence, around 600. At 500 the city was the principal fact of central Mexico (and all points north). By 750 it was gone, removed to myth.[40] Ben Nelson offers a useful model for thinking, on a continental scale, about the implications of Teotihuacán's fall:[41]

> From 600 to 900 Alta Vista's ceremonial center was rebuilt [in northern Mexico], La Quemada flourished, and a later Guadiana Branch development began further north.

The latter eventually became connected with a similar expansion along the coastal corridor.... I suggest that the growth of these later polities was an artifact of political disintegration in the Mesoamerican core. Teotihuacán's demise may have involved a diaspora, as later myths suggest regarding the collapse of Tula. Warring factions may have spun off to establish the constellation of secondary states that did, in fact, arise out of the ashes of Teotihuacán's collapse, at which point the population estimates suggest that around 60,000 people may have dispersed.[42]

The span of this chapter, 700 to 950, equals the Mesoamerican Epi-Classic, a shadowy period that marked the shift from the colossus of Teotihuacán to many, smaller city-states.[43] Epi-Classic set the trajectories of Post-Classic dynamism (chapters 5, 6, and 7).[44] Southwestern–Mesoamerican interactions become clearer in the Epi-Classic and even more so after 900, in the Post-Classic.

Beatriz Braniff mapped "las grandes rutas sagradas y de comercio en Mesoamerica y en el Norte"[45] almost exclusively through West Mexico.[46] In West Mexico around 700, the Teuchitlán cities of Jalisco (see fig. 1.4) suffered a marked decline that ended in a "total and definite collapse" by 950.[47] Something like Nelson's political diasporas may well have linked failing Epi-Classic cities of West Mexico to the Southwest—domino-theory chains of events from Teuchitlán out to the coast and then north.[48]

Hohokam: The Colonial Explosion

Hohokam refers both to a huge region through many millennia (essentially the upper Sonoran Desert of southern Arizona from 2000 BC to AD 1450) and—more narrowly—to a specific cultural tradition, marked by ball courts, red-on-buff pottery, stone pallets, a complex cremation burial ritual, and more (fig. 4.3). Hohokam, in that narrowest sense, began in the Phoenix Basin about AD 700 and in less than a century expanded into most, but not all, of the larger Hohokam region. After a brief bright run, Hohokam hit its wall, shuddered to a stop, and collapsed back into the Phoenix Basin. New ideologies of the Classic Period replaced it in the eleventh century. By 1150 Hohokam was history.

It's confusing. Hohokam in the narrow sense was only a couple centuries in the long span of Hohokam history, and it did not even reach the entire Hohokam region. I use the term *Hohokam* for the larger region from the earliest Early Agricultural Period to the final Classic Period and hereafter the term *Hohokam Canon* for the eighth- and ninth-century complex of ball courts, particular styles of pottery, elaborate burial rituals—and forms of governance, which to me are the most interesting aspect of Hohokam.[49] Circumstances—big canals, burgeoning population, Big House families in the Colonial Period poised to take control—almost begged for political hierarchy. But despite a half century of extensive excavation, archaeologists cannot identify "chiefs" or leaders associated with the Hohokam Canon. Pioneer-style Big Houses continued into the Colonial Period, but none of those aspiring families made the leap from village head to the next level.

Modestly sized canal systems supported the towns of the earlier Pioneer Period in the Tucson Basin and the Land Between. Modest canals were appropriate to modest streams, such as the Santa Cruz, but even modest canals were big enough to require leadership (chapter 3). The Salt and Gila rivers were much larger than the Santa Cruz, and when canal infrastructure began to transform the Phoenix Basin (probably around the Pioneer/Colonial transition), those canals were necessarily *big* (fig. 4.4; see fig. 5.6).

Figure 4.3. Colonial Period Hohokam figurines (restored), found near Tucson. The shoulder pads and turbans on several figures resemble Mesoamerican clothing and ball game gear. Courtesy David Doyel.

The initial Phoenix Basin canals—up to 20 kilometers long but running low along the riverbed—could be "operated by a single community with a managerial authority embedded in kinship institutions,"[50] which I think fairly describes Big House elites working at the upper limits of their capabilities. By the end of the Colonial Period (900/950), Hohokam canals had reached levels of technological and organizational complexity unprecedented in the Southwest and indeed most of North America—well beyond the control of village-level authority.

The situation would have made Karl Wittfogel's mouth water. Those big canals could have (should have?) pushed political arrangements to the next level and beyond. But instead, the Hohokam Canon diffused governance and prevented the rise of political leadership. The canon provided ways to do impressive things on impressive scales without kings.

Hohokam political history reflects, at many removes and smaller scales, the Teotihuacán solution (chapter 3). Recall that the great city started with ambitious, even charismatic leadership (Big House families?) but reached its peak under a system of "collective leadership of a ruling bureaucracy"[51] (the Hohokam Canon?). Hohokam canal-based economies were of course rigidly linked to specific territories—it's hard to move a canal. Canals functioned, necessarily, with regular, periodic, modular tasks—a set of very different tasks, such as construction, maintenance, and water allocation. Those specializations were a perfect breeding ground for bureaucracies: the engineers, the ditch boss, the water judges. And of course the bells and whistles, smoke and mirrors that held it all together: priests.

It was the nature of the Hohokam heartland, the technology that tamed it, and, perhaps critically, the lack of outside threats (Chaco came later; chapter 5) that allowed the remarkable Hohokam Canon and the Colonial Period explosion. Colonial Period Hohokam had no peer polities, no warfare, and hence no pressing need for centralized political authority. As we shall see, they had problems, but they could run their show without showy elites.

Hohokam Heartland

The Salt and Gila rivers were many times larger than the Santa Cruz, and the irrigable lands of their valleys were far more extensive than the narrow floodplains and terrace systems of

Figure 4.4. Hohokam canal, Pueblo Grande Museum and Archaeological Park, Arizona, with Devin White. The shallow swale is the surface expression of a very deep, very wide canal. Only a few segments of the original Hohokam canals survive, but maps made before the growth of the Phoenix metroplex show their original extent (see fig. 5.6). Courtesy of the author.

southeastern Arizona streams. Canals along the Salt and Gila (fig. 4.4; see also fig. 5.6) became the most impressive "public works" projects undertaken in arid North America until the late-nineteenth-century reclamation boom.[52] Hohokam canals were bigger than any in ancient Mesoamerica.[53] The Phoenix Basin canals began in the Colonial and reached their most impressive extent in the Sedentary Period, so they are discussed at greater length in chapter 5.

Driven, I think, by the exponential increase in the scale of canals, the Hohokam Canon developed in the Phoenix Basin. That was the Hohokam heartland. The canon then radiated rapidly outward, upstream along the streams that feed the Salt and Gila rivers. Tree-ring-based estimates of stream flow for the Salt and Gila suggest that the Salt always had more water than the Gila[54]—often too much; destructive flooding at the end of the Pioneer Period (chapter 3) may in part have spurred the Colonial explosion as villagers headed upstream to find fresh farmlands.[55] Whatever the kicker, the Hohokam Canon was an ideological movement with Phoenix at its center, a "religious" expansion that transcended environments and economies.

The old social order of Pioneer Period Big Houses and figurine-based cosmologies (chapter 3) gave way to a coherent package of new burial rituals, ball courts, mound monuments, pallets, shell armlets, and sweeping cross-media stylistic change.[56] Emil Haury, before his second excavation at Snaketown, argued for gradual development of the Hohokam Canon from Pioneer Period beginnings through the Colonial and Sedentary periods. As noted above, after

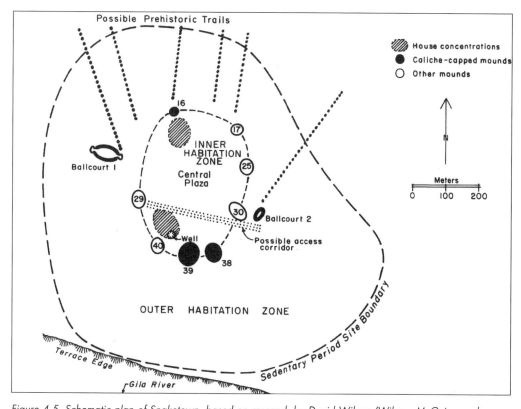

Figure 4.5. Schematic plan of Snaketown, based on research by David Wilcox (Wilcox, McGuire, and Sternberg 1981). Courtesy SAR Press.

rethinking Snaketown, Haury changed his mind: the canon came as a package from Mexico.[57] Its southern origins remain obscure, but many archaeologists now accept a strong West Mexican flavor to the canon.[58]

Haury felt "it was probably no accident that territorial expansion coincided with the climaxing of Hohokam culture" in the Colonial Period.[59] He held arts and aesthetics as the best indicators of cultural strength and coherence.[60] Through Hohokam's long history, he awarded artistic primacy to the Colonial Period, largely because of artifacts related to the canon. For Emil Haury, the Colonial Period was Hohokam's peak. I agree.

Hohokam Towns

Towns grew larger. Snaketown (fig. 4.5), the best-known Hohokam site, was big. But it was not the largest Hohokam site. That may have been Azatlan, on the lower Verde River (which reached its largest size in the later Sedentary Period).[61] Snaketown was near the top of the heap, and it is without question the most intensively studied Hohokam site, the "type site."[62]

How big was Snaketown? How big were the biggest Colonial Period towns? Snaketown's peak population is (of course) a matter of debate. Emil Haury estimated about two thousand people ("a figure which might be as much as 50 percent wide of the mark"),[63] peaking in the Sedentary Period (chapter 5). Others downsized the site,[64] suggesting populations ranging from only 200 to 350.[65] Excavations at Grewe, a site comparable to Snaketown, suggest that Haury was more right than wrong. Douglas Craig concludes that Grewe was home to about

Figure 4.6. Courtyard group, reconstructed at the Gila River Heritage Park on the Gila River Indian Community south of Phoenix, with John Stein. These structures face inward, into a small courtyard. Made of earth and timber, they are falling into disrepair (pit houses have a short use-life). A similar reconstruction, cast in concrete, can be seen at the Pueblo Grande Museum in Phoenix. Courtesy of the author.

one thousand people and suggests that populations of that size were probably resident at most large Hohokam settlements, including Snaketown, throughout their history.[66] Grewe (unlike Snaketown) peaked during the Early Colonial Period; there was a "30% decline during the late Colonial, stabilizing at about 500 to 600 people," and Craig attributes the decline to the settlement splitting, with "new settlements being established downstream from Grewe along the same canal."[67]

It is customary to speak of Hohokam settlements as villages.[68] That was surely so in the Pioneer Period. I refer to larger Colonial Period and later settlements, such as Grewe and Snaketown, as towns to make a point about increased size. Colonial Period settlements retained the older Pioneer Period village patterns, folded into much, much larger towns. Hohokam towns had a certain modularity, a repetition of structure, beginning with a courtyard group, a cluster of houses around a small common space (fig. 4.6).[69] Multiple courtyard groups clustered into barrio-like "village segments," each with its own cemetery and trash mounds,[70] and probably its own Big House leadership. Multiple segments made up a town, centered on a large plaza and—with the canon—a ball court or two (see fig. 5.5). Multiple towns and villages (typically half a dozen) along the same canal constituted a canal community.[71] Farmers on the same canal are necessarily of a community, although the members of a community needn't always get along. (We can be sure that Hohokam canal communities were just as contentious as modern southwestern irrigation districts: "Whiskey is for drinking, water is for fighting.") Coordination, adjudication, and even coercion would have been necessary to keep things rolling—or rather flowing—smoothly. The canon got it done.

The old Big House elites continued into the Colonial Period, but apparently they did not expand their scale beyond the village segment or the individual town. Certainly, there were Hohokam haves and have-nots; "differentially rich cemeteries and storage facilities at Snaketown and Grewe reveal that some individuals and groups were privileged over others with respect to high-value goods."[72] And it seems that the rich lived in Big Houses; many (most?) of the extraordinary objects found at Grewe (pyrite mirrors, remarkable shell and bone artifacts) were associated with Colonial Period Big Houses: [73]

> Some of the most spectacular artifacts were from the "Shrine Area."... The Shrine Area was not associated with any cemetery or isolated human remains. It was, however, immediately adjacent to the largest houses found at the Grewe site.... Their proximity to the caches of extraordinary shrine artifacts was surely no accident.[74]

Certain types of shell jewelry signaled leadership roles, at Grewe and elsewhere. *Pecten vogdesi* shell pendants, often with elaborate turquoise mosaic overlays, were "insignia of office" for priests, officers, and officials emerging outside of or parallel to traditional Big House power networks.[75] Big House families may have filled those new roles, but the important point is, they were *new roles*, requiring new regalia of the Hohokam Canon.

The architectural differences between Big Houses and normal houses diminished. Indeed, most archaeologists think the old Big House tradition ended sometime in the Colonial Period (see fig. 5.4).[76] I set great store by architecture; for archaeology, it's much easier to find a palace than to find a king.[77] *There were no palaces* in Colonial Period Hohokam (or Sedentary Period for that matter; Classic Period may be another matter; chapter 8). Nor were there easily identified kings or "chiefs"—no monumental tombs, no celebratory statues.[78]

We don't see paramount leaders, but there are hints that some towns were more important than others, hints of regional hierarchy. "Civic-territorial" organizations, in which particular settlements outpaced their neighbors and "show the beginnings of primacy," began to develop during the Colonial Period.[79] A few towns were notably larger than others and had more and bigger ball courts, monuments marking not the importance of individuals but the ascendance of the Hohokam Canon.[80]

Flattening the Hierarchy: Ball Courts

Ball courts were—in ways still opaque to science, art, and industry—central to the solution (fig. 4.7). Ball courts were large, earthen structures—essentially two symmetrical curved berms surrounding a level oval surface.[81] The largest courts were more than 55 meters long by 15 meters wide, with berms standing up to 5 meters tall. Most were much smaller. They were almost always embedded into a town. They were civic features.

Presumably, Hohokam ball courts were arenas for a local version of the Mesoamerican ball game[82]—not so much a game, perhaps, as a *social compact*.[83] The ball game was one thousand years old before courts first appeared in the Hohokam area. Many different ball games were played on formal, often monumental courts throughout Mesoamerica. Those games had many different purposes. On the one hand, ball courts were associated with the rise of governments,[84] as well as with the acquisition of wealth and power by elites.[85] On the other hand, ball courts functioned as community centers and places where political theater could resolve regional problems, "maintaining a balanced relationship" between competing factions.[86]

Many archaeologists think that Hohokam ball courts were of the latter variety, balancing communities and social classes within the larger region: "a social mechanism for region-scale integration."[87] Whatever was going on inside the arena, ball courts established the framework for a market system, circulating goods within the Hohokam core and perhaps beyond.[88] Ball courts united towns around communitywide events and synchronized regions through multiple-town events. (It's hard to not think of play-offs: fans don't have to get along, but they do have to get together.) Markets, organized around ball courts, probably began in the Colonial Period, if not earlier, reaching maximum extent in the later Sedentary and disappearing in the Classic.

Figure 4.7. Hohokam ball court. Artist's reconstruction by Peter Bianchi. A far cry from the monumental courts of the Maya, Hohokam ball courts were probably more elaborate than the plain dirt berms depicted here. There's no solid evidence, but we can safely assume that Hohokam people (fig. 4.3) invested more effort and energy in their principal civic monuments. Pennants and banners? Luxury boxes? Outfield landscaping? Courtesy National Geographic Image Collection.

Whatever happened in or around Hohokam ball courts, they were designed to provide views of events in the interior open space for large groups—in marked contrast to Big Houses. Big Houses housed their important residents and excluded the rest of the village. Hohokam ball courts, it seems, were public monuments to "communal ideologies"[89]—and not the political cockpits of the Aztecs and Mayas. I buy it, because we cannot find Hohokam rulers and leaders. If Hohokam ball courts created wealth and power, as in Mesoamerica, cui bono? Big Houses actually *decreased* in importance through the Colonial Period.

Ball courts are the best markers of the Hohokam "regional system"—a term introduced by David Wilcox in the late 1970s. When did that system arise? Ball courts are notoriously hard to date. (With a bit of digging, it's theoretically possible to date construction, but how do you date the last at-bat of the last inning of the last game? And very few ball courts have actually been excavated.) The two largest known ball courts (both excavated), at Snaketown and Grewe, were built in the Early Colonial Period.[90] There are (perhaps) a few earlier examples and many later Sedentary Period courts, but my reading of data suggests that most (and all of the largest) ball courts were built between 700 and 900.[91] I believe that ball courts, and the social experiment they represented, began during the Colonial Period and continued strongly into the earliest decades of the following Sedentary Period but thereafter most were decommissioned and fell out of use (chapter 5). (A few ball courts survived into the Early Classic Period; chapter 6.)[92]

David Abbott describes a Hohokam cultural geography that I think began in the Colonial Period: "Populations were linked across a vast swath of the Arizona desert via their participation in the ritual and exchange activities of the ballcourt network. Through this network, an abundance of commodities circulated. Many were probably produced by specialists, who supplemented their livelihood by satisfying demands across the region with their crafts."[93]

Figure 4.8. From left: Three Colonial Period pallets, three Sedentary Period pallets. Note the regular form and repeated, grooved border decoration of the Colonial Period pallets compared with the irregular shapes and variable border decorations lightly engraved on the Sedentary Period pieces. Pallets averaged about 15 x 8.3 cm (6 x 3.25 in) (White 2004). Courtesy of the author.

In Death as in Life: Burial Ritual

Along with ball courts, the Hohokam Canon featured new, highly formalized death rituals of cremation, often with urn burial.[94] These rituals involved—in poorly understood ways—stone pallets.[95] I focus on pallets over other aspects of the elaborate cremation ritual because they were a youthful fascination for me and because they offer fairly good evidence that the Hohokam Canon was indeed a cult or cultural movement emerging from the Phoenix Basin.[96] Carefully shaped schist pallets (fig. 4.8) were "one of the outstanding Hohokam hallmarks" according to Haury, and he should know.[97] Not every cremation was accompanied by a pallet—indeed, most were not—and pallets are sometimes found in nonburial contexts. But Haury noted that "cremation areas have always been the consistent producers" of pallets.[98]

Small, thin, rectangular slabs of the Pioneer Period are possible precursors, but "during the Colonial period, both the form and material changed"[99] dramatically.[100] Colonial Period pallets were very carefully crafted, highly stylized, almost standardized in shape and decoration. They were made almost exclusively of one material: micaceous schist or phyllite, probably from the Gila Buttes near Snaketown (there are a few exceptions made of sandstones, slates, and ceramics).[101] After looking at hundreds of pallets, I convinced myself that Colonial Period pallets were probably produced by specialist craftsmen in the Phoenix Basin and distributed outward to the provinces as finished products. Pallets and the elaborate burial ritual they represent typified the Colonial Period; all this continued (with major changes in style and production of pallets) through the Sedentary Period, perhaps outlasting ball courts (chapter 5). Then pallets disappeared with the sea changes of the Classic Period (chapters 6 and 7).

Wear It on Your Sleeve: Badges of Ethnicity

Hohokam shell production (figs. 4.9, 4.10) is almost legendary.[102] Shell was procured, in truly remarkable quantities, from the Gulf of California. The industry was highly structured. Much shell was processed at special sites deep in the arid deserts midway between the ocean and Phoenix, and most was distributed from the Phoenix heartland to the peripheries and beyond.[103]

There was a wide range of shapes, but *Glycimeris* shell bracelets were a signature Hohokam form (fig. 4.9). We call them bracelets, but they probably were armlets, worn around the upper arm. *Glycimeris* shell bracelets were more than fashion accents; they were,

Figure 4.9. Glycimeris *shell bracelets/armlets. Courtesy of the author.*

according to Jim Bayman, badges of "group membership and identity."[104] They meant, I think, that the wearer was a participating member of the Hohokam Canon. Most were plain, but many were elaborately carved, and their "major motifs...are unmistakably Mesoamerican in style."[105]

Shell bracelets/armlets are found in earlier Hohokam sites, but *Glycimeris* armlets were especially associated with the expansion of the Hohokam Canon during the Colonial Period. Consider, for example, the Tonto Basin, upriver from Phoenix. The Tonto Basin (see fig. 1.3) was only peripheral to Pioneer Period Hohokam.[106] During the Colonial Period, however, the number of Hohokam shell artifacts (of all types) increases enormously, and then drops just as dramatically during the following Sedentary Period. "*Glycimeris* shell bracelets accounted for more than half of the shell artifacts" at the height of the Colonial Period.[107] Shell bracelets were part of Hohokam's big bang.

The Colonial Explosion

The term *colonial* was meant by Gladwin and Haury to be both geographic and dramatic. The Colonial Period package appeared suddenly in the Phoenix Basin and thereafter spread throughout most of the Hohokam region. Gladwin and his gang thought that meant colonization, out from Phoenix and into the peripheries of southern Arizona.[108]

There are endless arguments over colonization versus diffusion versus interactive dialogue.[109] But I think there is agreement among Hohokam archaeologists that the cluster of behaviors, artifacts, and monuments that I call the Hohokam Canon formed first in the Phoenix Basin.[110] Then it radiated out—by colony, emulation, adoption, co-residence, or sheer bloody brilliance—into the river valleys of desert Arizona. I think versions of the canon went even farther, into Mogollon and even Anasazi regions.

Many of the motifs and elements of the Hohokam Canon were clearly Mesoamerican, or rather West Mexican, adopted and adapted to Hohokam requirements.[111] Hohokam, however, would not fit comfortably into West Mexico. For example, Hohokam's oval, earthen ball courts were not much like I-shaped, masonry Mesoamerican courts. The motifs seen on *Glycimeris* armlets were "unmistakably Mesoamerican," yet we have trouble finding exact duplicate images in contemporary Mesoamerica.[112] If we adopt Haury's sensible view that connections between the Southwest and Mexico were constant, varying only in degree,[113] the Hohokam Canon might be seen as a bundle of ideas, beliefs, and practices from West Mexico, brought by Mesoamericans who went north or acquired by Hohokam who visited the south.[114] The Hohokam Canon cherry-picked the rich possibilities of West Mexican civilizations and created a local fix for what the deserts needed in the eighth century. But the canon deliberately referenced older, stronger, distant traditions. A brilliant charismatic prophet can get things going with a few rousing sermons, but it also helps to have recognized authority on your side.

So the founders and propounders of the Hohokam Canon were selective shoppers, and connections with West Mexico varied over time. Hohokam sites of both Colonial and Sedentary periods had impressive quantities and qualities of West Mexican things, but the Colonial Period things were different from the later Sedentary Period things (chapter 5). For example, there are about one hundred pyrite mirrors from the Hohokam area, and almost all date to the Colonial Period.[115] There are very few copper bells from Colonial Period contexts and many more in the Sedentary Period (chapter 5). Both mirrors and bells probably originated in West Mexico.

How did it work exactly? I don't know. But somehow the Hohokam Canon managed the big towns, with their markets and astonishing canals—perhaps like Balinese water temples,[116] the Ilocano of the northern Philippines,[117] or other "plausible ethnographic analogies for the …Hohokam."[118] Presumably, Big House lineages retained a degree of power within the village, but the remarkable canon took care of all the major business, maybe through protobureaucracies and priesthoods.

The next step, toward something like a state, was—we are told—never taken.[119] As discussed in chapter 1, societies may indeed avoid the urge to statehood,[120] but few had as powerful provocation to political complication as Hohokam with its phenomenal canals. However the Hohokam Canon worked, it managed dense populations, big towns, and a remarkable economy without kings and palaces. The rich got richer,[121] but they did not get royal. What political institutions are represented by the artifacts and monuments of the Hohokam Canon? Priesthoods? Sodalities? Societies? NGOs? We don't yet know, and (for once) I am not willing to guess.

Mogollon: Mountains and Deserts

During the Late Pithouse Period (550 to 950), the Mimbres Mogollon region paralleled, in important ways, Hohokam developments. The western Mogollon region—the Arizona uplands, larger in size but smaller in population—was also variably engaged with Hohokam. At least one upland Mogollon site boasted a ball court (Stove Canyon, discussed below). But the well-watered uplands neither required nor encouraged canal irrigation, the fundamental infrastructure of both Hohokam and Mimbres Mogollon. For Arizona Mogollon, rainfall sufficed.

Down by the riverside, things got interesting. By 700, dozens of sizable pit house villages crowded the low terraces where creeks and rivers left the mountains and flowed into the sunny Chihuahuan Desert of southwestern New Mexico. Permanent water plus a long, long growing season! Many of those Mimbres villages expanded considerably around 825–850,[122] and a few grew quite large: the Fort West–Lee Village site in the Cliff Valley of the Gila River had as many as two hundred pit houses.[123] Of course, not all the pit houses at big sites were contemporary, but Fort West–Lee Village was as big as many Hohokam towns and probably for the same reasons—canal irrigation. The situation in the Mimbres and upper Gila valleys was essentially identical to Hohokam's and auspicious for those willing to invest in proper canals. Late Pithouse Period farmers in the Mimbres area did just that. Irrigation required new technology and knowledge and, very likely, new ways of organizing villages. Mogollon people could have invented all those things, but they didn't have to. Their pals to the west in southern Arizona had already worked things out.

Hohokam in Mogollon

Canal irrigation appeared in the Late Pithouse Period—that is, just as Colonial Period Hohokam was rumbling upstream from Phoenix. The Hohokam Canon and quite possibly Hohokam colonies popped up along the middle, then the upper Salt and Gila rivers. We know much less about the upper Gila than we might wish,[124] but here's a clue: one of the very largest Hohokam ball courts *anywhere* was in the Safford Valley (see fig. 1.3), at the eastern edge of Hohokam proper, the westernmost fringe of Mimbres. Ball courts did not (as far as we know) make it into Mimbres Mogollon, but remarkable commonalities—pottery, shell, cremation rituals, architecture, town plans, and of course canals—tied the Phoenix Basin to the Mimbres Valley.[125]

Widespread ceramic styles—divided by archaeology into dozens of different local types—crossed the Arizona deserts, the Land Between, the valleys of southwestern New Mexico, and even northernmost Chihuahua. First, a style of broad-lined, red-on-buff or red-on-brown pottery from 650 to 750; that was followed from 750 to 950 by a widely adopted style of fine-lined design.[126] Local types and traditions came into focus during the latter, fine-line period, and by 850 there were western (Hohokam) and eastern (the Land Between and Mimbres Mogollon) ceramic spheres.[127]

To anticipate subsequent developments, things fell apart after the Colonial Period. The old Hohokam world balkanized, with (for example) the Tucson Basin becoming an independent ceramic province (chapter 5). A similar model could be applied to much of the Land Between and to the upland and Mimbres Mogollon; they parted company with Hohokam and went their own ways. But the emerging regional desert traditions were still notable for their commonalities, particularly when contrasted with contemporary Plateau (of which, more below).

Mimbres sites were notably rich in shell artifacts. Much and probably most Late Pithouse Period shell came from the Hohokam. Figure 4.10 juxtaposes two plates from two different books. The first is from William Wasley's work at Gila Bend.[128] Wasley intentionally set it up to mirror the second image, a plate from a much earlier publication of shell artifacts from the NAN Ranch Ruin in the Mimbres Valley.[129] Obviously, it's a setup: picking pieces that look alike. Even so, the similarities are scary! Gila Bend was the far western edge of Hohokam, almost 500 kilometers from NAN Ranch at the center of Mimbres.

Some Mimbres burials had dozens of *Glycymeris* shell bracelets, worn on the upper arm. Many were clearly of Hohokam manufacture, with Hohokam carving on the hinge of the

PAINTED ROCKS RESERVOIR

Fig. 77. Shell objects from Citrus site selected and arranged to simulate those illustrated from Swarts Ruin (Cosgrove and Cosgrove 1932, Pl. 76.) Length, lower left, 7.8 cm.

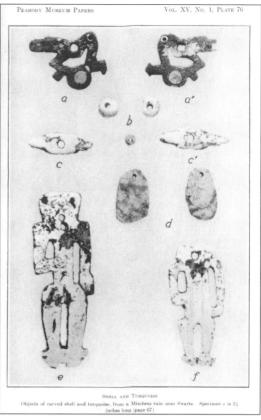

PEABODY MUSEUM PAPERS   VOL. XV, No. 1, PLATE 76

SHELL AND TURQUOISE
Objects of carved shell and turquoise, from a Mimbres ruin near Swarts. Specimen e is 3⅛ inches long (page 67)

Figure 4.10. Hohokam and Mimbres shell artifacts. William Wasley directed our attention to these plates, the left showing Hohokam shell from Gila Bend, Arizona, and the right showing Mimbres shell artifacts from the NAN Ranch Ruin in southwestern New Mexico. Left: from Wasley and Johnson, Salvage Archaeology in Painted Rocks Reservoir, Western Arizona (1965), courtesy University of Arizona Press. Right: from Cosgrove and Cosgrove, The Swarts Ruin (1932), courtesy Peabody Museum, Harvard University.

bivalve shell. Shell debris suggests that after the Late Pithouse Period, Mimbres Phase people made their own *Glycimeris* bracelets—out-Hohokaming the Hohokam. (We will return to Mimbres's shifting loyalties below and in chapter 5.)

Cremation was widespread, if not exactly common, among the Mimbres towns.[130] Inhumation had been the custom, usually below house floors or outside houses. Cremation, if unusual, was also unusually prominent, taking place in central plazas (not unlike cremations at Late Pioneer Period Tucson Basin sites). Mimbres sites also produce more than a few pallets—not the standardized Colonial Period schist pallets but local interpretations on local materials.[131] Were these converts to the Hohokam Canon—locals adopting or adapting Hohokam strategies for water management?

Mogollon architecture and town planning during the Late Pithouse Period also echoed Hohokam. Hohokam villages had clear central plazas, around which clustered courtyard groups. Mogollon pit house villages generally consisted of two groups of pit houses, north and south of a central plaza (a pattern that carried forward into a few of the large pueblos of the later Mimbres Phase; chapter 5).[132] The plazas of Hohokam and Mimbres Mogollon sites contrasted sharply with earlier Anasazi sites such as Shabik'eschee (chapter 3) and contemporary Pueblo I villages (discussed below).

Courtyard groups—clusters of three or four houses facing inward to a small courtyard—were a fundamental unit of Hohokam towns (more fully described in chapter 5). It's possible to recognize similar groups at Late Pithouse Period Mogollon sites.[133] Mimbres Mogollon courtyard groups were less well defined than Hohokam, but, as with plazas, the similarities between Mogollon and Hohokam pit house groups stand out clearly when compared with the standard Anasazi domestic building, the six-rooms-and-a-kiva "unit pueblo" (below). Even the details of the simple, short ramp entries of Hohokam pit houses (see fig. 4.6) and the longer ramp entries of Mogollon pit houses (see fig. 4.1) were far more similar to each other than either were to the elaborate entries of Anasazi pit structures (discussed below; see figs. 3.6 and 3.7). Similarities between Colonial Period Hohokam and Late Pithouse Period Mogollon are not glaring and obvious, like the contrived yet instructive figure 4.10, yet they are real and become clear when contrasted to Anasazi. In a two-point comparison of Hohokam and Mogollon, we notice the differences; in a three-way comparison including Anasazi, we see the similarities.

We know of no ball courts at any Mimbres sites.[134] Evidently, they didn't buy into that part of the program, or perhaps they played their game in sandlot settings. One ball court was found at an upland Arizona Mogollon pit house site, the Stove Canyon site at Point of Pines[135]—much closer to Phoenix than was the Mimbres Valley. Stove Canyon is even more interesting because the site had both a ball court and a Great Kiva, a distinctly Mogollon form to which we now turn.

Instead of a ball court, big Mogollon pit house villages usually had a large central structure (fig. 4.11), which I call a Great Kiva (more cautiously termed a "communal structure").[136] Mogollon Great Kivas were rectangular pit structures, 1.5 meters deep (or more) and up to 10 to 12 meters on each side, with three or four stout posts supporting a massive peaked or semiconical roof and with a long, narrow, sloping entry ramp. Typically, a village had only one such structure up and running at any one time,[137] off to the side of the central plaza.[138] Around 950 the Late Pithouse Period ended with a shift from pit structure to pueblo-style architecture (chapter 5). In the Mimbres area, that shift entailed the abandonment of most (but not all) Great Kivas.[139] In the Mogollon uplands, however, Great Kivas continued in use well into the thirteenth century.

Uneasiness over the term *Great Kiva*—many of my colleagues prefer the safer *communal structure*—stems from *kiva*'s Anasazi connotations. Anasazi Great Kivas were round; Mogollon, square. But that obvious distinction is not enough. Mimbres archaeologists seem to fear Anasazi and work hard to secure the Mimbres homeland against those ancient people of the north (discussed in chapter 5). Not me—open borders for all, I say. And I say Great Kiva.

I think both Anasazi and Mogollon Great Kivas served essentially the same purpose: they furnished a large open auditorium for village or community functions—social, ritual, and political. Square, round—different strokes for different folks, as the poet said. Importantly, Mimbres and Anasazi had them; Hohokam did not (the three-point comparison). The Late Pithouse Period was not a Hohokam clone. Interactions were consensual; Mimbres played the field.[140]

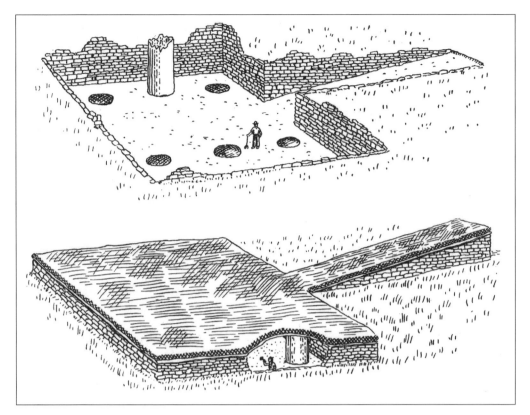

Figure 4.11. Top: *Mogollon Great Kiva in process of excavation. Artist's reconstruction by Gustaf Dalstrom.* Bottom: *restoration of Mogollon Great Kiva. The roofline of this conjectural reconstruction is problematic. The roof was probably pitched, not flat, and the upward slope of the entry ramp roof seems unlikely. This image was used in Paul S. Martin's* Digging into History *(1959), his summary of highland Mogollon and my introduction to southwestern archaeology. Courtesy Fieldiana, Field Museum.*

Technology Transfer: Canals

We know the Mimbres Mogollon used canal irrigation in the valleys of southwestern New Mexico from strong inference,[141] as well as stronger direct evidence—the actual remains of canal systems.[142] But our knowledge is far less perfect than it is for the Phoenix Basin, where canals have been mapped in great detail (see fig. 5.6). No one thought to map Mimbres canals before they were co-opted by later farmers; I suspect that many modern canals in the area follow ancient lines.

Large Mimbres villages, like Hohokam towns, were located at key locations on canals, usually above the best sites for diversion dams—places where local geology created narrows in the streambed.[143] These villages, like Hohokam towns, were occupied for centuries and reached impressive sizes—for the same reasons: natural hydrology and canal infrastructure fixed them in place.

Hohokam, of course, perfected canals centuries before Mimbres Mogollon. Mimbres people could have independently invented canals, but why would they? We know that Mimbres Mogollon was deeply engaged with Hohokam on many levels. Technology transfer was probably less an event—Hohokam to Mimbres—than a prevailing condition. Sustained, long-term connections brought Hohokam canals to Mimbres Mogollon. But it's also quite possible that Mimbres leaders invited Hohokam irrigation specialists—priests or engineers—to lay things out and advise on operations.

Mimbres Late Pithouse Period Considered

The Late Pithouse Period was in many ways the most dynamic era of Mimbres Mogollon history, much like the contemporary Colonial Period in Hohokam. Its earliest days continued the ways and means of the Early Pithouse Period, with the addition of red-slipped pottery. (Indeed, I poached the earliest Late Pithouse Period back into chapter 3.) Things really heated up about 700, when a red-on-brown pottery (much like Early Hohokam broad-lined styles) showed up. Riverside villages launched histories that spanned (in many cases) three centuries, ending only with the collapse of the Mimbres Phase (chapters 5 and 6).

The real detonation, however, came around 825–850 with the Three Circle Phase.[144] Pow! Really big sites—and lots of them. From that I infer that canals really kicked in about 825. Population jumped like the dot-com market, and the Hohokam "presence" became distinctly more present.

Things continued to boil and bubble right through 900[145]—and then, by 1000, a swift transition from pit houses to aboveground, pueblo-style masonry structures! The old pit house form—hallowed for at least five centuries—was replaced by five- to seven-room stone masonry "pueblos," often with an attached or associated kivalike pit structure.[146] *That's* not Hohokam. As we shall see, Mimbres architecture after 1000 was much more like Anasazi unit pueblos (below and chapter 5). Changes reflected a realignment of Mogollon away from the Hohokam world to the emerging Anasazi world of Chaco (chapter 5). Mimbres Mogollon's interests shifted with the prevailing political winds.

Late Pithouse Mogollon may not have been the cheerfully leaderless, egalitarian society long assumed by regional archaeologists.[147] Hierarchy may have raised its ugly head in the later Late Pithouse Period.[148] If there were leaders, they were neither great nor dreadful. A recent review concluded, "For the most part, any leaders would have had authority in some contexts and not in others."[149] Frustrated wannabe Big House leaders?

Anasazi: The Rise of Great Houses

The span from 700 to 950 equates roughly with the Pueblo I Period on the Plateau (see fig. 1.6). Our knowledge of Pueblo I increased exponentially in the mid-1980s, largely as a result of the Dolores Archaeological Program (a huge CRM project; see chapter 6) in southwestern Colorado.[150] They dammed the Dolores River, and forty sites were excavated in advance of the reservoir and the agricultural developments that would use that water. The Dolores research was followed by revelations from the Animas–La Plata CRM project,[151] as well as important Pueblo I studies by Richard Wilshusen (an alum of Dolores) and his colleagues—all of which revolutionized our knowledge of Pueblo I.

Meeting Pueblo I

The Dolores project completely changed our view of Anasazi history. Before Dolores, Pueblo I was simply a stage in the Pecos Classification between Basketmaker III and Pueblo II. (In the early days of the Pecos Classification, some archaeologists questioned whether Pueblo I

Figure 4.12. Pueblo I unit pueblo—one of the famous museum dioramas at Mesa Verde National Park, even better than the real thing. Courtesy Mesa Verde Museum Association.

was even real.) Pueblo I was known best from Mesa Verde, where small sites of the period (fig. 4.12) seemed like a predictable step in the steady progression of Pueblo prehistory[152]—culminating, of course, in Cliff Palace (chapter 6).

But there were anomalies, unsettling exceptions. In 1931 J. O. Brew excavated an alarmingly large Pueblo I site at Alkali Ridge in southeastern Utah.[153] A really big Pueblo I site! Earl Morris excavated a few fair-sized Pueblo I sites in Colorado and northern New Mexico, but none as big as Alkali Ridge.[154] Happily, Alkali Ridge was way over in Utah, and we could dismiss it as a bit of an aberration. The Dolores project showed that Alkali Ridge was not an aberration (fig. 4.14); many Pueblo I sites were big—but not the best-known Pueblo I sites, on Mesa Verde. Pueblo I sites were much larger than Basketmaker III farmsteads. Those earlier settlements, in the northern San Juan, generally consisted of a pit house or two, sometimes enclosed in a circular "stockade" (see fig. 4.1). By 860 there were at least twenty major Pueblo I villages or towns, with an average size of 123 aboveground rooms and fifteen or more pit structures.[155]

Brew and Morris worked in the early days of tree-ring dating. Advances in chronology and huge CRM budgets (chapter 5) changed things. Precision dating of the Dolores sites not only put better dates on Pueblo I as a period but also showed us that the Pueblo I period was remarkably dynamic: they moved around a lot.[156] Villages bounced around the San Juan River drainage like balls in a particularly lively pinball machine. In some areas, Pueblo I was never even there! Two examples: sites in La Plata Valley of northern New Mexico often consist of Basketmaker III and Pueblo II components; Pueblo I was absent.[157] And the same is the case at Yellow Jacket, the largest site in the northern San Juan—lots of Basketmaker III, Pueblo II, Pueblo III—and no Pueblo I.[158] But in other areas—Dolores, for example—Pueblo I sites were many and sizable. Pueblo I was sometimes the other side of the coin: a massive Pueblo I occupation in a valley was essentially all there was—no earlier Basketmaker III or later

Pueblo II. That was roughly true for both Dolores and Animas–La Plata. Of course, there were "persistent places," where short hops around a specially favored locale kept the whole sequence on a very short leash.[159] But in general, Pueblo I was surprisingly peripatetic. These people got on the good foot—they needed room to move.

All this suggested that big Pueblo I villages were short-lived. In the early days of tree-ring dating, archaeologists were delighted to date a site to a century or half century. Advances in dating (and CRM budgets that could afford those advances) made it clear that big Pueblo I villages were indeed only brief stops. Richard Wilshusen aptly described big Pueblo I sites as "trailer parks" lasting a generation or less.[160] Apparently, after Pueblo I people set up a new village, they proceeded to cut down all the nearby firewood, hunt out all the nearby game, and farm out the nearby fields. After exhausting local resources, they then jumped to the next valley and did it all again. After a few moves (three or four generations), the original home valley had time to recharge and regenerate. As long as there were not too many people, that sort of thing worked.

Pueblo I sites apparently were fewer and farther between in the southern and western Anasazi areas.[161] We know a bit about Pueblo I in the western Anasazi area (northeastern Arizona),[162] and it appears to have been less—in every dimension—than in the San Juan. Like Pueblo I sites on Mesa Verde, western Anasazi sites were small, consisting of five or six rooms and a pit structure (a unit pueblo, discussed below). They were not the sizable towns of Dolores and Alkali Ridge.[163] The uplands of northeastern Arizona had been more or less empty during Basketmaker III; sites of that period were mostly down along rivers (chapter 3). After 800, small Pueblo I populations moved into upland areas (Black Mesa, Cedar Mesa, Red Rock Plateau, Glen Canyon, and much of upland northeastern Arizona and southeastern Utah).[164] And Pueblo I populations bounced around among those areas thereafter, much like the busier San Juan but on smaller scales. (Indeed, western Anasazi Pueblo I sites were generally smaller than the earlier Basketmaker III sites!)

There is much we still do not know about Pueblo I (especially in the southern Anasazi area), but it's my impression (based on conversations with Pueblo I aficionados) that Pueblo I was really bigger, stronger, and more interesting in the northern San Juan area (and Chaco, as we shall soon see). From Alkali Ridge on the west to the Animas River on the east, the northern San Juan was the center of Pueblo I history. Indeed, Blue Mesa, high above the Animas River south of Durango, Colorado, was probably the very largest of all Pueblo I sites.[165] Blue Mesa is only part of a much larger complex that came to light during the work of the Animas–La Plata project (ALP, a major CRM effort just south of Durango). The ALP worked on Pueblo I sites in Ridges Basin, immediately to the west of Blue Mesa.[166] To me, Blue Mesa and Ridges Basin were one site—just as later Chaco Canyon was all one site (chapter 5). In contrast to the tight, linear room blocks of Alkali Ridge, Blue Mesa–Ridges Basin sites—more than 150 pit structures—were loosely strung east–west over almost 10 kilometers, with two major concentrations, on Blue Mesa itself and around Sacred Ridge (a key site in the center of Ridges Basin), about 5 kilometers apart. (That's comparable to "downtown Chaco," chapter 5).[167]

Sacred Ridge, a low isolated knob near the center of Ridges Basin, was at the heart of this remarkable site. Sacred Ridge was, for Pueblo I, unusually permanent. It began well before Blue Mesa and persisted through Blue Mesa's span and indeed until the entire ALP area was abandoned.[168] Its architecture was remarkable, quite extraordinary in the Pueblo I world. It included a group of oversized pit houses (discussed below) and *truly* unique structures—a cir-

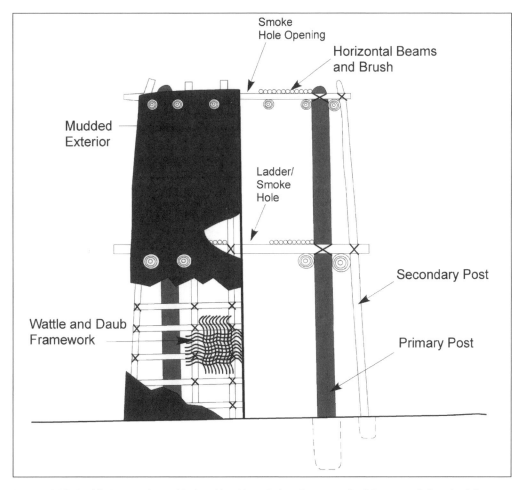

Smoke Hole Opening

Horizontal Beams and Brush

Mudded Exterior

Ladder/ Smoke Hole

Secondary Post

Primary Post

Wattle and Daub Framework

Figture 4.13. Pueblo I tower, Sacred Ridge, Blue Mesa–Ridges Basin, south of Durango, Colorado. Schematic reconstruction by Jason Chuipka. Courtesy Jason Chuipka and SWCA and courtesy Kiva, Arizona Archaeological and Historical Society.

cular domed structure, an enclosed plaza, and a multistoried tower (fig. 4.13).[169] Nobody's ever seen anything like that at Pueblo I sites! Blue Mesa–Ridges Basin was by far the largest Pueblo I site anywhere, and Sacred Ridge—at the heart of the site—had the strangest, most impressive architecture known from Pueblo I. Not quite a city but a very big town!

Blue Mesa–Ridges Basin dated from 750 to 810, with limited occupation into the 830s.[170] The whole complex popped up without any significant precedent population. (An interesting but much earlier Basketmaker II occupation had come and gone by 500.) Essentially, no one was home (or even in the area) for a century before Blue Mesa–Ridges Basin. Blue Mesa–Ridges Basin must have *come from somewhere else* or from several different somewhere elses. There is much evidence that Ridges Basin and Blue Mesa represented several groups from several very distinct areas, east and west.[171] And there was nothing after. There was no significant Pueblo II or Pueblo III occupation of the Durango area following Blue Mesa–Ridges Basin.

Oddly, Blue Mesa–Ridges Basin, the largest, most interesting Pueblo I site, was due north of Shabik'eschee and 29 SJ 423, the largest, most interesting Basketmaker III sites.[172] Surely a coincidence!

PI Peregrinations

Following the movements of Pueblo I villages has become a favorite spectator sport in south-western archaeology. The game is very complicated, and the players change with every new research project. It appears that people moved into the northern San Juan in waves. Once they got there, they didn't stand still. Villages moved, splintered, reformed, and moved again. It's like figuring out football without knowing the rules—very confusing.

We are pretty sure that Pueblo I started with migrations into the area, because there weren't nearly enough Basketmaker III people in the northern San Juan to produce the high populations we see in early Pueblo I. They came from the south, or rather from several souths, as we shall see. "By AD 860, at least one third to one half of the known population in the Anasazi world was in the Northern San Juan"[173]—a relatively small corner of the Anasazi region.

Pueblo I in the San Juan split into three subregions, each with slightly different house forms and village layouts, and, most notably, three very different ceramic traditions. From west to east: redwares in southeastern Utah; "classic" San Juan Basketmaker III black-on-white pottery in southwestern Colorado (Mesa Verde, Dolores, Durango); and, at the east end, a remarkable enclave of glaze-painted pottery (north-central New Mexico and around Chimney Rock in Colorado; see fig. 5.12). The glaze paint (pigments that turn glassy when fired) is notable because in eastern Pueblo I it was precociously early. And a short-lived experiment. That peculiarly southwestern technique vanished after Pueblo I and returned to favor (a reinvention?) centuries later in Pueblo IV (chapter 6).

These three areas may represent different groups, coming into the San Juan from several souths. The Utah redware group presumably followed Uto-Aztecan Basketmaker II and III; they came from Arizona. Mesa Verde Pueblo I were most likely descendants of the people who built Shabik'eschee and 423, from northwestern New Mexico. And the glaze-paint group... we don't know. They may have come from the south or from left field. In politics, we follow the money; in southwestern archaeology, we follow the pottery. For early glaze-paint pottery, that trail starts and ends in Pueblo I.[174]

These territorial divisions were not hard and fast and may to a degree reflect the history of archaeology as much as ancient verities. House and village forms from one area popped up in neighboring districts, and of course pottery got around. People were sloshing back and forth across the northern San Juan, from one subregion to the next, in small groups and village-sized assemblies. At least that's how it looks: the demographic center of gravity bounced around, and that probably tracked population movements. Unraveling the cultural geography has been largely the work of Richard Wilshusen and his colleagues.[175] Through a combination of many new tree-ring dates, refinements in ceramic chronology, and a great deal of fieldwork, Wilshusen and company developed a trial version of Pueblo I regional dynamics. The details will undoubtedly change, but the general picture seems clear. The first Pueblo I center—Blue Mesa–Ridges Basin and a surrounding cluster of villages around Durango—was the biggest. Thereafter, centers of population formed and failed more or less as follows:

> 750 to 810: Durango
> 770 to 830: southeastern Utah
> 810 to 860: Mesa Verde, Mancos

840 to 880: Montezuma Valley/Great Sage Plains/Dolores

880 to 900: upper San Juan and southeastern Utah

880–900 to 1020: northern San Juan effectively empty; Pueblo I in Chaco

Of course, this itinerary changes with each new CRM project, but the general picture will hold of Pueblo I skipping back and forth across the northern San Juan. After a few centuries of frenetic musical chairs, everyone left the San Juan. The party was over. Redwares headed south, Mesa Verde Pueblo I went to Chaco, and the glaze-paint group beamed back up to the mother ship—or something like that. We will follow Pueblo I to Chaco in chapter 5.

Kivas?

Kivas: the round or square ceremonial buildings we see today at modern pueblos. Every pueblo has kivas (although only a few pueblos call them that). Kivas have become a southwestern icon, central to Santa Fe style. The word *kiva* names retail products, home amenities, businesses, dogs, and horses. There are probably counterculture kids out there named Kiva.

When did kivas first appear in prehistory? Pueblo II? Pueblo I? Earlier? It's a chestnut and a standard exam question: "When is a kiva?"—the title of a classic study.[176] Even with an accommodatingly broad definition—"a kiva is a chamber specially constructed for ceremonial purposes"[177]—the original Pecos conferees were uncertain: perhaps kivas were on board by Pueblo II, but probably they were earlier, Pueblo I. The Pecos Classification listed the parts needed to make a Pueblo—corn, pottery, kivas, and so on—and added them into the mix in proper sequence. At the end of that sequence, all the parts were in place. Bingo! Modern Pueblos. That's more than a tad teleological—every day in every way, more like Hopi. You can almost see the Anasazi of 850 counting the days until someone would invent kivas.

Proto-kivas are archaeology's gift to those anxious Pueblo I people, waiting to do their duty. "Oversized pit structures" at Dolores (and elsewhere) have been identified as proto-kivas—that is, early kivas.[178] Oversized pit structures looked like regular pit houses but much bigger. Many had (in addition to normal domestic furniture) more esoteric, presumably ritual features. If we want to find the earliest kivas, oversized pit houses fit the bill—proto-kivas.

Here's an alternative take: oversized pit structures were the Anasazi equivalent of Hohokam Big Houses. Pioneer and Colonial period Big Houses were notably larger versions of normal houses and often included esoteric, ritual features alongside normal domestic furniture. But unlike putative proto-kivas, Big Houses housed elite families, lineages, or village heads (chapter 3). Ritual was of course one path to power—probably one of several strategies alongside more pragmatic options, such as grabbing the good farmlands, glad-handing, and winning friends and influencing people. Big House braggadocio at Shabik'eschee in Basketmaker III came to nothing. But I think would-be Big House families resurfaced in Pueblo I at sites like McPhee Village (below). I think oversized pit houses at Pueblo I sites were Big Houses, not proto-kivas.[179]

If we seek precursors to modern kivas, we will do better to consider Great Kivas, present at some but not all Basketmaker III and Pueblo I villages. I do not suggest a straight line from Basketmaker III Great Kivas to the kivas at modern pueblos—too much changed between Pueblo III and Pueblo IV for that kind of genealogical precision (chapter 7). But Great Kivas make much more sense as the forerunners of modern kivas than do pit houses, normal or oversized. Pit houses (small and large) were *houses*, and the house form continued in Pueblo II and III, even when dressed up in masonry (chapters 5 and 6). All those small round "kivas" at Cliff

Palace and Pueblo Bonito…weren't. They weren't kivas. They were the last, most formal versions of the centuries-old Anasazi house: a pit house.[180] When tracing political power in the early Pueblo world, we'll see that this distinction actually matters.

Towns?

The pit house did not stand alone. An Anasazi home in Pueblo I times consisted of a pit house (conventionally called a kiva) in front of a half dozen contiguous aboveground masonry rooms (conventionally called a pueblo). The pit house was home; the pueblo was mainly storage space: closets, pantries, whatever. That combination—six rooms and kiva—describes a *unit pueblo*, another conventional term but this time a useful one (see figs. 4.12, 5.8, and 5.9). Six is nominal. The number of rooms varied from two to ten, but most unit pueblos had six rooms or less. That was a house from 700 to 1300—Pueblo I, Pueblo II, and right through Pueblo III (chapter 6).

Big Pueblo I towns may have been short-lived, but they were dense, tightly packed settlements—lines and lines of unit pueblos (fig. 4.14).[181] That unprecedented aggregation reflected, at least in part, increasing levels of violence.[182] Every society is capable of ugly behavior, and Anasazi was no exception. Low-level beastliness was background noise throughout Basketmaker III. Population growth and disruptive migrations during Pueblo I escalated the pushing and shoving into raiding and feuding. Hatfields and McCoys, MacDonalds and Campbells, Maple Leafs and Senators—something like that. By 800 the Plateau was lurching toward war—not organized armies but fairly widespread and constant killing. People circled the wagons and clustered in large villages—those big, short-lived Pueblo I towns.

How to hold a big town together? Richard Wilshusen and Scott Ortman have shown that there were at least two notions of how a Pueblo I town should work, typified by Grass Mesa and McPhee Village on the Dolores River (fig. 4.14).[183]

Grass Mesa was a large village with at least twenty-five pit houses arranged in one very long row and two shorter rows—in effect, lines of unit pueblo row houses, side by side, all facing south.[184] Of course, there are familiar issues of contemporaneity (were they all occupied at once?), but Grass Mesa was by any estimate a big site. Importantly, no one unit pueblo or cluster of unit pueblos was larger than any other. There were differences, of course, but nothing conspicuous. And there was no indication of segmentation into separate "megahouses" or neighborhoods. The place was a Levittown of identical little pink boxes—or, following Wilshusen's trailer park analogy, an Airstream camp. At the west end of the site sat a Great Kiva—a large, shallow, round structure much like the Great Kiva at Shabik'eschee (chapter 3). Apparently, the Great Kiva came first and the town (very rapidly) thereafter.[185]

McPhee Village had a very different plan and history (fig. 4.14). About sixty-five pit houses were scattered over a much larger area—three or four times the size of Grass Mesa—many in stand-alone unit pueblos and most in arcs of two or three unit pueblos.[186] (Again, not all were contemporary.) In the larger groups, lines of five to eight conjoined unit pueblos curved shallowly in on themselves. McPhee was much more segmented than Grass Mesa.

Importantly, there was no Great Kiva at McPhee Village. In its place, at the west end of the town, was a large, massively built, U-shaped arch of five unit pueblos, pulled tight around a small plaza. In the middle of the plaza was a single, very large, "oversized pit structure." Like most oversized pit structures, this one had interesting and esoteric floor features. A proto-kiva? Or a Big House—the home of a politically important family? I'm guessing the latter.

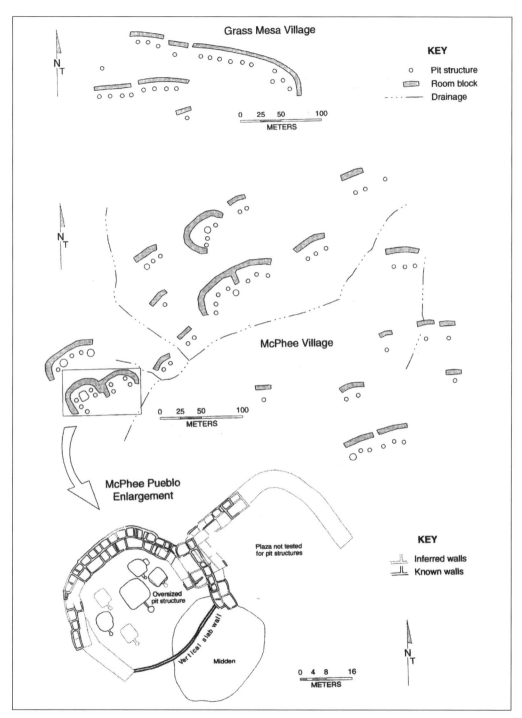

Figure 4.14. Grass Mesa and McPhee Village, 840 to 880, Dolores River Valley, southwestern Colorado, with "proto-Great House" detail. Courtesy Richard Wilshusen and Scott Ortman and courtesy Kiva, Arizona Archaeological and Historical Society.

The big U-shaped room block and its oversized pit structure at McPhee Village (see fig. 4.14) was, I think, one of the very first "Great Houses"—another jargon term but an important one.[187] Great Houses, a century later, were the sine qua non of Chaco and its region, so the term will be discussed with Chaco in chapter 5. But that's jumping ahead. The McPhee proto-Great House was a wonder or perhaps a burden to McPhee villagers, who had no idea what might or might not happen ten decades later at Chaco Canyon.

If I'm right about kivas and oversized pit houses, the proto-Great House incorporated a Big House—the oversized pit house in the middle of the plaza. I realize this terminology—unit pueblos, proto-Great Houses, Big Houses, and so forth—is getting silly, but there's a point to all this. I think that the arc of unit pueblos that formed Pueblo I proto-Great Houses (there were others) represented families or households directly allied with, answering to, working for, and serving under the Big Family in the Big House (that is, the people who lived in the oversized pit house in the middle of the plaza). It is important to note that the Big House at McPhee Village was *not* part of a unit pueblo (see fig. 4.14). That is, it did not have the standard, associated six-room "pueblo" (storage rooms). The Big House stood alone, without storage. The people in the oversized pit house ate other people's food.[188]

Grass Mesa had a Great Kiva, and McPhee Village had a Great House. That difference was so striking that Richard Wilshusen suggested that the villages represented different ethnic groups: McPhee was Chacoan, and Grass Mesa was Mesa Verdean.[189] There is something in that suggestion: Great Houses like McPhee's moved from Dolores into Chaco and were only later reintroduced to the Mesa Verde region and northern San Juan as Chacoan "outliers" (chapter 5).

The two village plans may have been two ethnic groups or may represent two experiments in governance—or both. Grass Mesa, with its row houses and Great Kiva, looks like community. McPhee, with its segments and Great House, looks like an organizational chart. For Anasazi, the Great Kiva was the default option: Great Kivas were standard from Basketmaker III on (chapter 3). Most big villages or communities had a Great Kiva. Dispersed scatters of Pueblo I unit pueblos often had a Great Kiva tucked away somewhere, like a prairie church in Iowa farmlands.

What were Great Kivas? In Basketmaker III and Pueblo I, I think they were town halls in which the community or its representatives (elders? heads of households? initiated men? initiated women?) could meet in solemn assembly and transact the community's business, sacred and profane. Part-time church, part-time grange hall. In Pueblo II and III times, things got more complicated.

The re- or dis-placement of the Great Kiva by a Great House at McPhee Village suggests to me that Big House families were shortcutting the process, junking the solemn assembly of elders, and so forth. Would-be rulers proposed to make decisions for their friends and family in the Great House and (in their dreams perhaps) for the larger community. Great Kiva meetings were no longer necessary, so Great Kivas were not necessary. Indeed, whatever happened in Great Kivas was probably inimical to centralized leadership.

McPhee villagers must have bought into this argument—there was no Great Kiva there. Pueblo I Great Houses marked the first faint successes of Anasazi political hierarchies—people accepted the *idea* of rulers.[190] People had tried, and failed, to establish themselves in ruler roles at Shabik'eschee. In Pueblo I, it finally worked. The families who lived in McPhee's oversized pit houses thirsted for power, wished to be leaders of their people, to paraphrase

Benedict. A thousand years later at Zuni, those ambitions would hang them by their thumbs. But their great-grandchildren became kings and queens at Chaco.

Politics!

Pueblo I in the northern San Juan was a period of unprecedented aggregation, rapid (almost random) movement, jarring dislocations, and violent turmoil that strained the old ways—the more or less egalitarian social systems represented by Basketmaker III and Pueblo I Great Kivas. Not quite chaos, but close enough. People (as always) wanted stability, and stability in those conditions demanded leadership. By strength or snake oil, whoever delivered peace and quiet attracted followers. The office sought the man, or vice versa. In the end, it didn't matter. Individuals and families stepped up, claiming that they could fix the problem.

The historical precedents for early Anasazi political leadership—at McPhee and elsewhere—lay in the Hohokam experience. Recall Shabik'eschee and the first hints of Hohokam-like Big Houses on the Plateau. Those failed, but if at first you don't succeed, try, try again. Oversized pit structures in Pueblo I were Basketmaker Big Houses, version 2.

It worked in Pueblo I, but not wonderfully well. Anasazi leaders couldn't quite pull it off: towns splintered and reformed. The great difference between Hohokam and Anasazi leadership was Hohokam canals versus Anasazi rainfall farming. Hohokam farmers were stuck in their villages. They couldn't move. They needed canals. So they had to put up with political shenanigans—up to a point, when they threw the bums out and converted to the Hohokam Canon. Anasazi people, however, were not tied to infrastructure. Rain watered their crops, and rain was everywhere (sometimes, and sometimes nowhere). If would-be leaders tried to bring together too many people, promulgate too many rules, or extract too much stuff, the people could follow the clouds and move. Everybody involved—leaders and led—recognized this reality. But inspired by Hohokam elites, Anasazi leaders kept trying. In retrospect, we can see they made mistakes: Pueblo I was not yet ripe for political hierarchy. Caught up in the moment, Anasazi Big House families were not thinking anthropologically about canal infrastructure versus variable rainfall. They thought about life and how they'd like to live it. The idea of political power is awfully hard to stop once it starts, and it started thousands of years before McPhee Village, far to the south. Aspirant elites plotted their moves as kings to be crowned, not as pawns of precipitation. But in the end, it's indeed a desert. Great House communities rose and fell in rapid succession, at least in part responding to rainfall, finally moving out of the San Juan and to the south.

Pueblo I in the northern San Juan ended around 880 with an abandonment of the Four Corners that presaged the more famous "Mystery of the Anasazi" abandonment in 1300 (chapter 6). By 900 Pueblo I villages had vanished even from the margins of the San Juan "heartland." Next stop: Chaco.

Figure 5.1. Chetro Ketl. Artist's reconstruction by Robert M. Coffin. From Edgar Hewett's The Chaco Canyon and Its Monuments (1936b). Hewett hinted that Chetro Ketl (his site) was in fact prettier than Pueblo Bonito (Neil Judd's site). Courtesy School for Advanced Research.

f i v e
Grain — *Scale*

Archaeologies: 1960 to 1975
Histories: 900 to 1150

This chapter is about *scales*, in past history and in present archaeology, and about *grain*, the resolution with which we see things. In the distant past, from 900 to 1150, things got big: Chaco flared out like a supernova, affecting most of the Plateau. In the near present, from 1960 to 1975, things got small: New Archaeology demolished old ways of thinking—smashed the tablets, broke the icons—and replaced those discredited ideas with more scientific methods, smaller in scale and finer in grain. Adaptation replaced sweeping culture history; small "natural laboratories" replaced large culture areas. Alas, the scales of New Archaeology misfit the events of prehistory recounted in this chapter—"regional systems" that were just coming into archaeological focus in the mid-1970s. In the Hohokam area, ball courts defined a region covering most of southern Arizona. On the Anasazi Plateau, Chacoan Great Houses did the same over all four of the Four Corners.

Postwar prosperity, a flood of new students (baby boomers), and truckloads of federal research dollars drove universities ahead of museums as the lead institutions of southwestern archaeology. The nature and style of research changed. The old museums and research institutions operated with staffs. A research organization (such as Gila Pueblo) might have a ceramic specialist, an ethnologist, and a few field archaeologists; a museum (such as MNA) might add a botanist and a geologist. They were expected to collaborate, to work as a team—to excavate and analyze Snaketown, for example. For university professors, the professional structure was distinctly different. Tenure was awarded to individuals, not to groups. The single-authored monograph was the required standard. And it was publish or perish! So whatever you hoped to publish better not take too long to write—no time for extended research programs. Gladwin had a stable of field-workers to figure out Hohokam, in all its vastness. New professors in the 1960s and 1970s focused on short segments of single rivers. The scales of early CRM operations were often comparable, focused on a small reservoir, a highway right-of-way, or a power plant. (CRM got big in the 1970s and 1980s; chapter 6.) Those projects *seemed* big at the time, but compared with the events of prehistory, they really weren't. Together, boomer demographics, New Archaeology, and early salvage archaeology set the scales for southwestern work—scales much smaller than Gila Pueblo's or the Laboratory of Anthropology's.

The small scales of New Archaeology simply could not handle regional phenomena between 900 and 1150 such as Chaco and Hohokam. The fieldwork that defined those very large arrays came later, in the 1970s and 1980s, after New Archaeology stalled and staled (chapter 7). And that work did not come from universities. The geography of Chaco "outliers" was delimited by two teams of nonacademics, the first working for a regional power company,[1] the second working for the National Park Service (NPS).[2] In contrast, the distribution of Hohokam ball courts was worked out by a single scholar, David Wilcox,[3] who went on to a museum career and many other large-scale studies—a remarkable exception to my generalizations about single scholars and small scales!

Scale is our field of view—macro, close-up, portrait, landscape. *Grain* is how we see things—the resolution of the image, pixels and DPI in this digital age. We can get very fine-grained resolution on small-scale objects—scanning electron microscopes measure nanometers—but (unless we have access to spook satellites) really big pictures are necessarily coarse grained. And that is how archaeology works: great detail at the scale of artifact, feature, or even site, while larger scales and big pictures require more impressionistic or at best pointillist renderings (a dilemma of Big History).[4]

The first southwestern synthesizers worked with coarse data (chapter 3). Regional data files—manila *files*, kept in cabinets at the Laboratory of Anthropology or the Arizona State Museum—proved too much data for graph paper, adding machines, and slide rules (or even IBM punch cards, for those of a certain age). Big pictures were literally that—maps, mental or cartographic abstractions. Many of the early large-scale maps were remarkably useful. We still use Kidder's, Hewett's, and even Gladwin's maps of the ancient Southwest (chapter 3). As we shall see (chapter 6), computational power eventually caught up with massed data. GIS and digital cartography put us on the cusp of large-scale regional studies with fine-grained data.

But we aren't quite there yet. This book was written with the methods and tools of an older age: abstractions and impressions based on data of course, but—like Kidder's and Hewett's efforts—the product of mental maps and personal perceptions. So here's what I think happened: between 900 and 1150, Hohokam began its long slide down while Chaco pumped itself up. Mimbres, once closely allied to Hohokam, shifted its fickle attentions to the busy, bustling north.

In Mesoamerican terms, this period is Early Post-Classic, with the rise and fall of Tula. Textbooks and review articles generally ignore or dismiss this coincidence as, well, coincidence. I think those histories, southwestern and Mesoamerican, were surely linked. But how? Past proposals—and there have been several (below)—failed to persuade. My suggestions may fall short too. But wrong answers do not negate or invalidate the question.

Archaeologies: 1950 to 1975 (New Archaeology)

Postwar prosperity, cold war research, and the baby boom turned quiet campuses into research mills and degree factories. The life of the mind survived in archaeology (more or less), but new directions reflected new realities and opportunities.

Hohokam Culture History, Continued

At mid-century, the report on Gila Pueblo's 1934–1935 excavations at Snaketown still stood as the Old Testament of Hohokam.[5] It was the foundational text. Other digs—Roosevelt 9:6 in the Tonto Basin (excavated by Haury)[6] and Kelly's work at the Hodges site in the Tucson Basin in 1938[7]—confirmed what Gladwin knew from Gila Pueblo's wide-ranging surveys: Hohokam was bigger than the Phoenix Basin. It covered much of the upper Sonoran Desert. But little additional work was done there in the noonday sun; summer field schools—the modi operandi of academic archaeology—aren't much fun in the blistering desert. Professors preferred the cooler Mogollon uplands and its stone pueblos—which also needed research of course—or the high Plateau and its Anasazi ruins.

Moreover, Anasazi was still the big deal. It was famous. It belonged to the NPS and therefore to the American people, a proud part of our national heritage. Hohokam, however, was something of an orphan. Of the scores of NPS archaeology parks in the Southwest, the vast majority featured Anasazi ruins. The Sonoran Desert has only a few NPS archaeology units: the Casa Grande Ruins and the Tonto Cliff Dwellings. The former is one of very few Hohokam sites with standing walls; the latter of course is a cliff dwelling and not Hohokam.[8] Between the NPS and *National Geographic*, many Americans knew of Mesa Verde and Cliff Palace, but only a few had ever heard of Snaketown. (*National Geographic* did a Snaketown story in 1967; see fig. 4.7.) Anasazi research accelerated with many field schools, public works excavations (in the 1920s and 1930s), and NPS projects. Scores of big Anasazi sites were excavated. Hohokam plodded along with a few public works projects (such as University Indian Ruin and Pueblo Grande) and, after Gila Pueblo's demise, no institutional spark plug, no staff fully devoted to the deserts.

In their enthusiasm for stone pueblos and black-on-white pottery, state universities drew and quartered Anasazi: Utah did Glen Canyon,[9] Colorado did Mesa Verde,[10] New Mexico did Chaco.[11] The fourth of the Four Corners (in northeastern Arizona) was on the Navajo Reservation. Its archaeology—Poncho House, Canyon de Chelly, Keet Seel, and many other major ruins—was hit and run by a dozen different institutions. Chaco's region, as we later learned, was fragmented by state lines and archaeological politics (revisited below). The Hohokam regional system presented itself entirely within the boundaries of southern Arizona, ripe for inspection.

From the wreck of Gila Pueblo, the Arizona State Museum inherited Hohokam and (indirectly) Emil Haury. Haury was the undisputed heavyweight champion of Hohokam, but he was a man alone (with a few grad students). Pueblos and pine trees drew the main force of the University of Arizona away from the deserts and up into the Mogollon highlands. Thus began a series of three epic Mogollon field schools—big crews digging hundreds of rooms— first at the huge ruin of Kinishba (1931 to 1937, about the same time Gladwin and Haury were excavating Snaketown), continuing with long-term projects at Point of Pines (led by Haury, 1946 to 1960)[12] and ending at Grasshopper (1963 to 1992).[13] The University of Arizona tradition of Mogollon pueblos continued, on scales better suited to end-of-the-century archaeology, with the Silver Creek Project (1993 to 2004).[14] The foci of all those field schools were big Mogollon pueblos. So real Anasazi archaeologists were not overly alarmed by incursions onto the edge of the Plateau. Indeed, the Mogollon area was big enough to host big field schools and long-term research from Chicago's Field Museum, directed by Paul S. Martin (more on him below). "Outsiders" working in the Mogollon uplands did not provoke the irritated reaction that, for example, any university other than New Mexico's might at Chaco Canyon.

Hohokam archaeology was, in effect, neglected; a slow desert tortoise to Anasazi's jackrabbit and Mogollon's badger—comfortable in its hole but capable of alarmingly fast short sprints. Looking back on those years, Emil Haury noted, "The archaeological story was unfolding slowly."[15] Absent major new excavations, Snaketown's chronology was revisited and revised again and again (chapter 4), leading to Haury's second campaign (a fine Old World archaeology term!) at the site in the mid-1960s.

Snaketown defined Hohokam, and it cast a long shadow. Our views of Hohokam were mostly extrapolations from this one key site, so it's worth visiting its archaeology. In both the 1934–1935 and 1964–1965 excavations, Sedentary Period (950–1150) houses were by far the most numerous. The total one hundred Sedentary Period houses equaled all houses from earlier periods combined.[16] Quite sensibly, the Sedentary Period (reviewed in this chapter) seemed, to Haury and others, the demographic peak and the maximum geographic extent of Hohokam.[17] It is important to understand that Hohokam phases and periods were assumed to be homogeneous blocks of time: one type of pottery, one style of house, one set of ritual practices, and a steady history from beginning to end. The Sedentary Period, in that view, saw no internal changes, twists, or trajectories—Sacaton red-on-buff fore and aft, and steady on to the somewhat mysterious Classic Period (chapters 6 and 7). Snaketown did not have extensive Classic Period remains.

Haury thought that Hohokam expanded throughout the Sedentary Period, but he did not believe that bigger was necessarily better. He saw Hohokam material culture and population size as independent variables, with material culture "peaking from A.D. 700–900; followed by a population rise but with an associated decline in aesthetic values" in the Sedentary Period.[18] I agree, and so do many others.[19]

Haury's magnificent report on the second excavation at Snaketown appeared in 1976, with important new data from the "type site." But Snaketown no longer stood alone. Data from other sites were about to arrive by the truckload. Salvage archaeology—early CRM—began on small scales in the early 1960s, with projects such as Painted Rocks Reservoir at Gila Bend in 1958–1961.[20] After 1975 the size and number of CRM projects increased exponentially (chapter 6), eclipsing Snaketown and all earlier excavations. CRM's importance for Hohokam studies was enormously greater than its contributions to Anasazi and Mogollon. CRM archaeology helped us understand Pueblo I on the Plateau, for example (chapter 4), but most Anasazi research was university or NPS driven. And CRM contributed almost nothing to Mogollon. Today Hohokam archaeology *is* CRM (chapter 6).

New Kid on the Block

New Archaeology arrived in the mid-1960s as a self-proclaimed revolution, with high words and higher hopes. The established ways of doing archaeology had to go—now! And very often, the established archaeologists had to go too. Dissatisfactions with conventional culture history had surfaced long before, most notably in Walter W. Taylor's widely discussed *A Study of Archaeology* (1948), which marks the beginning of this chapter's "archaeologies." Taylor's dissertation was published as an *American Anthropologist* memoir. Like Joe Ben Wheat's Mogollon manifesto (1955), it could not be ignored (chapter 3).[21] Taylor complained that culture historians wrote bad history. It was neither rich nor textured nor "conjunctive" (his solution to archaeology's ills). He wanted archaeology to be anthropologized history. But he was insufficiently revolutionary: thrones did not topple, heads did not roll.

Lewis Binford read Taylor's *Study* repeatedly.[22] Binford (whom we met in chapter 1) also wanted archaeology to be anthropology. But more than that, he wanted anthropology to be a science—and *not* part of the humanities, *not* Taylor's history. A new archaeology! Binford's seminal "Archaeology as Anthropology" and "A Consideration of Archaeological Research Design" outlined a theory of practice for New Archaeology in the 1960s. Science! Binford's classes at Michigan and Chicago inspired the first wave of new archaeologists, and a pipeline from Chicago's Field Museum brought lab-coated junior scientists into the Southwest. (They didn't really wear lab coats, but they probably wanted to.) They spoke the language of science, taking as their texts philosophers of science seldom seen in archaeology bibliographies.[23]

Most of the eager young scientists worked at the Field Museum's Vernon Field Project, run by curator Paul Martin in the Mogollon uplands of eastern Arizona.[24] Martin was open to ideas. In 1950, perhaps in response to Taylor's critique, Martin added a chapter, "The Social Organization of the Mogollon Indians," to an otherwise unremarkable site report. That chapter anticipated later work (on Martin's projects) by James Hill at Broken K Pueblo and William Longacre at Carter Ranch—two 1970 southwestern manifestos of New Archaeology as (scientific) anthropology. Two other paragons of Binford-style research came out of Martin's Vernon Field Project. Ezra Zubrow's *Prehistoric Carrying Capacity* (1974) was stridently scientific, replete with flow charts, systems diagrams, and ecological microanalysis of the Vernon Valley. But Fred Plog's *The Study of Prehistoric Change* (1974) was in the end more influential.

Plog and Di Peso, for Example

Plog's book was one of two profoundly contrasting works that appeared in 1974, representing the old and the new. Charles Di Peso's *Casas Grandes* (out with the old) and Plog's *The Study of Prehistoric Change* (in with the new) marked the changing of the guard. Di Peso's *Casas Grandes* was an old-style site report—data, analysis, conclusions, and more data—from his ambitious project at the ruins of Paquimé (chapter 7). It was the biggest site report in the century-long history of southwestern archaeology (pre-CRM)—more than thirty-five hundred pages in eight oversized volumes, tipping the scales at just over 30 pounds, 14 ounces (14 kilograms). The first three summary volumes were richly illustrated and ornamented in faux-codex style.[25] The last five volumes were detailed definitions, descriptions, and discussions of architecture and artifacts (all in 9-point type), accompanied by thousands of tables, charts, maps, profiles, figures, and photos.[26] Too big for conventional publishers, *Casas Grandes* was published by (and almost bankrupted) Di Peso's Amerind Foundation, a private archaeological research organization at Dragoon, Arizona.

Much more than a site report, *Casas Grandes* was the last and perhaps greatest of the Southwest's culture histories. Di Peso tried to write ancient enthography (not unlike Longacre and Hill), exploring society, economy, and ideology at Paquimé. Most importantly, he tried to write history (going well beyond Taylor's requirements). Di Peso told the history of Paquimé's rise and fall as a Mesoamerican outpost. The publication's scope was continental, embracing the whole "Gran Chichimeca"—the greater Southwest and a good bit of northern Mexico. Di Peso's approach was his own, engagingly idiosyncratic, but his thinking was firmly grounded in culture history, pre-Binford. (Di Peso cited Binford just once: Binford and Quimby's 1963 study of "Indian Sites and Chipped Stone Materials in the Northern Lake Michigan Area.")

Plog's *Study* (reworking his 1969 University of Chicago dissertation) was published by Academic Press (the edgy archaeology press of that era). It was a small volume, half the size of *Casas Grandes*, with only two hundred pages of text. Hardcover, it weighed just over 1 pound (less than half a kilogram). Plog did not write a site report; he offered a case study in New Archaeology centered on the excavation of four pit houses at the Gurley site (again, one of Paul Martin's projects). Plog's book was not so much about data as about *new ways to think about data*, citing six Binford works, starting with "Archaeology as Anthropology."[27] The first half of Plog's book set up the problem much as Binford had decreed, with chapters on goals, methods, the local environment, dynamic-equilibrium models of change, test implications, and research strategies, defining the questions and the "natural laboratory" in which to answer them. The next four chapters—only one-quarter of the book—analyzed data. The rest of the book was summary, conclusions, and end matter.

Plog's *Study* became a basic text for New Archaeology, at least in the Southwest. Plog wasn't trying to write history. His goal, for the book and for archaeology, was a general and generalizing question: "Why do cultures change as they do?... Explaining change should be our primary undertaking."[28] The explanations of change should not be specific to time, place, or history; they should be processes valid across cultures—"cross-cultural," a key concept of New Archaeology. This was New Archaeology in a nutshell: a study of process (whence came processual archaeology, New Archaeology's immediate progeny; chapter 6).

In 1974 Plog's archaeology won and Di Peso's lost. But today Plog's *Study* is seldom cited, while Di Peso's *Casas Grandes* fuels scores of papers, theses, and monographs. Di Peso banked data for new alchemies: a mother lode to be refined and rendered useful by eager young scientists and (later) nonscientists. *Casas Grandes* was the tome that launched a thousand critiques. Dissertations, theses, conference presentations, and term papers interpreted and reinterpreted Di Peso's data. To be fair, Di Peso's longevity comes in large part from his site. One Paquimé trumps four pit houses.

Scalar Issues

New Archaeology accomplished its science in "natural laboratories"—an idée fixe and a sure shibboleth of the times. Natural laboratories were areas big enough (but not too big) to test hypotheses, typically about ecological adaptations. (Ancient societies were understood to be, first and foremost, adaptations to local environments.)[29] The large-scale staples of 1950s culture history—vague influences, migrations, and diffusions—were anathema, dismissed as "non-explanations."[30] Generally, a natural laboratory was about the size of a small creek's watershed or drainage. Plog's natural laboratory, for example, was the Hay Hollow Valley, about 65 square kilometers of desert grassland in east-central Arizona—about a two hours' walk on each side if transformed into a square.

Labs need not be that small. With the same level of effort required to completely survey 65 square kilometers, a much larger lab could be investigated, statistically, by scattering (often randomly) sixty-five individual 1-square-kilometer sample units over much bigger areas. New Archaeology eagerly embraced sampling, with its appearance of statistical precision. But hide-bound "old archaeologists" delighted to demonstrate, for the benefit of brash

"New" colleagues, how hypothetical random sampling in the Basin of Mexico consistently missed Teotihuacán. The brash youngsters replied: Any archaeologist in the Basin of Mexico who did not know about Teotihuacán should have his or her license revoked. It was grudgingly agreed that sampling fairly represented the common or ubiquitous but was no tool for discovering the rare or unique.

Multiple natural laboratories sometimes collaborated in larger projects, such as the Southwest Anthropological Research Group (SARG), with a dozen projects scattered over the Plateau and a bit beyond.[31] SARG projects give us an idea of New Archaeology research scales. At the high end was the Grand Canyon, which was pretty big, but the investigators covered only a tiny sample of its vastness. Next after the canyon came two survey areas in central Arizona, measuring 4,500 square kilometers and 2,300 square kilometers; these were sampled at 5 percent or less. The rest ranged from 500 square kilometers to 80 square kilometers, with sampling from 7 to 20 percent. Only one research area was surveyed completely; it was just over 40 square kilometers. At the high end, 100 to 200 square kilometers of actual data; at the low end, 40 to 50 square kilometers. Those scales were typical of the time; my MA thesis reported a project of about 55 square kilometers, a little smaller than Plog's natural laboratory.[32]

Those aspects of New Archaeology that most clearly separated its operations from those of old archaeology—small scales, natural laboratories, sampling, and the rejection of large-scale "non-explanations"—hobbled the new regime when it confronted two major ancient entities: Hohokam and Chaco. At 80,000 square kilometers (Hohokam) and 150,000 square kilometers (Chaco), these regions were many times larger than even the largest natural laboratory. Hundreds of ball courts marked the Hohokam region; hundreds of Great Houses marked Chaco's. Each region had an evident and obvious center—the teeming Phoenix Basin and the smaller Chaco Canyon.

It was impossible to tackle Chaco or Hohokam questions with 50-square-kilometer natural laboratories. Not too many people tried. Ball courts were ball courts (whatever those might have been), but within the confines of a natural laboratory, Chaco Great Houses became, simply, large Pueblo II sites.[33] Indeed, the recognition of these "regional systems" came only after the first enthusiasms of New Archaeology faded in the late 1970s and 1980s. Tensions between the two scales—natural laboratory and regional system—in many ways paralleled the tug-of-war between science and history in southwestern archaeology after 1975 (recounted here and in chapter 6): science worked small; history, it seemed, ran big.

Histories: 900 to 1150 (Chaco, Sedentary, Mimbres)

Pueblo II was the apex of Anasazi (fig. 5.2). The trademark Anasazi sites—cliff dwellings at Mesa Verde—came in the next age (chapter 6). Surely, that was the zenith? No—I think the centuries from 900 to 1150 were arguably the biggest, busiest, and best in the long history of the Plateau. In the deserts, Hohokam reached and quickly passed its peak. In the Mogollon region, Mimbres had a bright, brief, precocious run, commemorated by its remarkable art.

The Early Post-Classic

The Mesoamerican era from the fall of Teotihuacán to the rise of the Aztec capital Tenochtitlán is called the Post-Classic, conventionally divided into three subperiods: Early

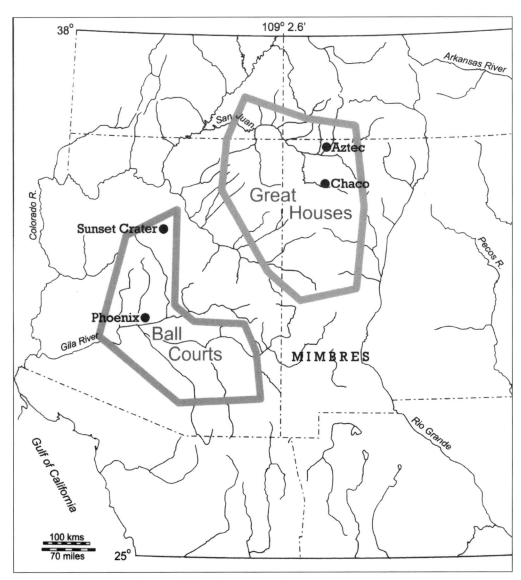

Figure 5.2. 900 to 1150. Courtesy of the author.

Post-Classic (950–1150), Middle Post-Classic (1150–1350), and Late Post-Classic (1350–1500).[34] Those chronological divisions did not play out simultaneously over all of Mesoamerica; West Mexico, particularly relevant to the Southwest, marched to a slightly different drummer.[35]

"Post-Classic" is as much an archaeological value judgment as a time period. *Post* gives the game away: a general perception of a fall from Teotihuacán's Attic grace to Roman commercialism—showy, militant Toltec and, worse yet, come-lately parvenu Aztecs. As with most generalizations, there's something in it. The Post-Classic was indeed an age of hustle. Michael Smith and Frances Berdan list its salient characteristics: population growth, proliferation of small polities, greater diversity of trade goods, commercialization of the economy, and new iconography[36]—to which we should add rampant militarism.[37] This list more certainly describes the better known *Late* Post-Classic, and we will revisit the Post-Classic zeitgeist in more detail in chapter 7. But those characteristics, in varying or embryonic degrees, can also be assumed for the Early Post-Classic.

The scale of many Post-Classic polities was actually rather small. In the Late Post-Classic (for which we have the best information), the total population of a ministate might be as few as ten thousand to twelve thousand.[38] Southwestern regional systems were larger than that. Chaco Canyon, with only twenty-five hundred people, would have made the cut for a small Post-Classic city.[39] Cahokia would have placed well among the larger cities.

The titan of the Early Post-Classic—in myth and scholarship if not in fact—was Tula in central Mexico, with an urban population of at least thirty thousand.[40] Tula had a "twin city" that was remarkably similar in architecture: Chichén Itzá, 1,125 kilometers away in the Yucatán.[41] The nature of their relationship is far from clear, but the two were importantly connected.[42] Tula and Chichén Itzá demonstrate the geographic scale of Early Post-Classic history —more than 1,000 kilometers! Post-Classic long-distance shenanigans reached even farther than those of the preceding Classic Period (themselves impressive—recall the long arm of Teotihuacán; chapter 3). The Post-Classic world was markedly and remarkably expansive.

Other major Early Post-Classic centers included El Tajin and huge Cholula.[43] The rise of El Tajin in the Huastec area of northeastern Mesoamerica probably had implications for the Mississippi Valley (of which, more below). Cholula, in central Mexico, had monumental architecture rivaling Teotihuacán's. But, unlike that Classic polity, Cholula flourished, apparently, in the Late Classic and all through the turmoil of the Post-Classic. Perhaps Cholula was less militaristic than its neighbors and rivals. Instead, "through a combination of trade and religion, Cholula was able to…reinvent itself [in the Post-Classic] as a new entity based on cultural diversity, supernatural authority, and international trade," signaled by the "international" Mixteca-Pueblo style of pottery and art.[44] International trade and "international styles"—iconographically charged art that transcended political boundaries—were hallmarks of the Cholula and the Post-Classic generally.[45] (Something similar happened later in the Southwest with Pueblo IV "art" and in the Southeast's Ceremonial Complex; chapter 7.) Cholula's trade-based international relations probably had more impact on the Southwest than Tula's more conventional empire building, but Tula and the legendary Toltecs get all the attention.

Tula and the Southwest

Tula—acting through piratical filibusterers,[46] merchant diplomats,[47] or a generalized deus ex machina—has been invoked, repeatedly, to explain events in the Southwest.[48] La Quemada and Alta Vista in Zacatecas, Mexico (chapter 3), and Paquimé in Chihuahua (chapter 7) have all been nominated as northerly outposts of Tula. But the timing is off. The first two preceded Tula by several centuries,[49] and Paquimé followed its fall by a century or more. Toltecs themselves, sans middlemen, have been implicated for Chaco,[50] and that timing works. There may indeed be historical connections—but probably not the direct string pulling of past models.[51] Tula represents one peak, perhaps *the* peak, of the Early Post-Classic, and the Early Post-Classic shaped the larger world in which Chaco and Hohokam went about their business. What happened in Tula did not stay in Tula. But if Toltec notions reached the Southwest, they probably came indirectly. [52]

Early Post-Classic cities and states in northern and especially western Mesoamerica were probably more directly important to the Southwest than was Tula. In the Early Post-Classic, "much of west Mexico was drawn into Mesoamerican economic and religious orbits."[53] The first rumblings of what would become the powerful Tarascan Empire—which later fought the Aztecs to a standstill (chapter 7)—came in the Early Post-Classic, perhaps linked to the final demise of the West Mexican Teuchitlán polities around 1000,[54] or initiated by an influx of elites from abandoned Classic Period centers in the north,[55] perhaps La Quemada in Zacatecas.

The Pacific Coast and Aztatlan (South)

West beyond the soon-to-be Tarascan heartland, a chain of temple-towns developed in coastal valleys of Nayarit and Jalisco. Mesoamerica, in its West Mexican form, rippled north well into Sinaloa. The Aztatlan "horizon" brought the Post-Classic to the Pacific coast from 800 to 1100 (or maybe a bit later; Spence says AD 900–1250).[56] Aztatlan was not a unified political system. Rather, it was a series of city centers along 800 kilometers of coast (a horizon of shared ideas rather than a polity or even a phase). The Aztatlan cities were linked by long-distance exchange of prestige goods and "international" art styles—later the Mixteca-Puebla style from Cholula—that signaled new ideologies and social forms. The network of Aztatlan temple-towns extended north beyond Culiacán (see fig. 1.4) and inland as far as Durango, 200 kilometers and a major mountain range distant from the coastal centers.[57]

Foot-sore traders, climbing over the Sierra Madre and crossing the Chihuahuan Desert, no doubt played a role in Anasazi history of this period, but trade moved far more easily along the Pacific coast—both by foot and by boat—from the Bay of Banderas to Guasave, only 750 kilometers from the Tucson Basin.[58] Metallurgy surely came up along the Pacific coast by sea, leapfrogging from Ecuador to the intermediate zone and then to West Mexico, reaching the latter no earlier than 800.[59] Distinctive styles of clothing did the same. Patricia Anawalt argues that similarities in the cut of clothes and the cloth from which they were made link Ecuador, West Mexico, and the American Southwest. There is no reason to dismiss out of hand coastal trade to the head of the Gulf of California.[60]

It was probably no accident that a great deal of Mesoamerican wealth was found at Gila Bend, Hohokam's southwesternmost bastion on the Gila River—closest to the coast, farthest downstream, and nearest the Colorado River's mouth. Hohokam owed much to West Mexico; indeed, Hohokam *was* West Mexican in many important ways (chapter 3). Colonial Period Hohokam mostly likely controlled or at least channeled early Anasazi connections to the south (chapter 4), until the rise of Chaco (below).[61]

Less important land-based *rutas* went over the Sierra Madre Occidental through J. Charles Kelley's "Topia Gate" or straight north out of Aztatlan cities such as Culiacán (chapter 7). Those routes had considerable antiquity if not heavy traffic; they seem to become more important after 900.[62] In any case, studies of copper, shell, and textiles do in fact suggest two routes, one coastal and the other over-mountain.[63] Both routes started in coastal West Mexico, but one connected coastally to the Hohokam area while the other swung east around the Hohokam sphere and ended, ultimately, on the eastern Plateau and Chaco Canyon (a path we will trod again below).

Cahokia and Aztalan (North)

Cahokia, the great city in the Mississippi Valley, was the exact contemporary of Chaco, Sedentary Period Hohokam, and Mimbres—all Early Post-Classic. Cahokia (across the

Mississippi from St. Louis) rose rapidly about 900 and fell more gradually after 1150/1200. The city's site is marked today by scores of earthen "mounds"—pyramids, tombs, monuments. The biggest, Monk's Mound, was one of the very largest pyramids in North America, *including* Mexico. Cahokia's population was ten thousand to fifteen thousand, as big as most Mesoamerican cities and four or five times bigger than the largest southwestern towns.[64] Its lords were powerful people, buried with impressive quantities of high-value goods and alarming numbers of human sacrifices.[65] The Cahokia site itself was the largest of a cluster of large mound centers on either side of the Mississippi River in the rich American Bottom,[66] which together formed an urban center much larger than almost all cities in Mexico of that time— or in Europe for that matter. The population of the American Bottom metroplex probably doubled that of the Cahokia site alone, perhaps to thirty thousand or more.

Cahokia, like Chaco, was extraordinary but not unprecedented. "Emergent Mississippian"[67] in the lower Mississippi Valley was immediately antecedent. But Cahokia had even deeper roots, more ancient histories and practices to build upon and transform. It was heir to millennia-old traditions of monumental building (older than Olmec perhaps; chapter 2); symbolically charged exotic goods moved over long distances—metallurgy more ancient than Mexico's,[68] obsidians and chert from the far west, and shells from the Gulf Coast (and later the Pacific).[69] Hopewell's symbol systems—centuries before Cahokia—were of continental scope (chapter 2). And Cahokia could, if it wished, borrow from or share with Mesoamerica via the Mississippi and the Gulf of Mexico—a coastal trade surely as open as West Mexico's.[70]

The distances involved in southwestern "regional systems" pale by comparison with those accepted—or at least taken seriously—by Mississippianists. The Aztalan site in Wisconsin was a Cahokia "outlier," comparable in many ways to Chaco "outliers" (below). Note there are multiple Aztlans and Aztalans and Aztatlans; watch your t's and z's! Set amid woodland populations of southern Wisconsin, Aztalan appeared as out of place as Chimney Rock, a monumental Chacoan outlier towering above the rustics of the upper San Juan River (of which, more below). Some suggest that Aztalan was a Cahokia colony, some argue that it was an "emulation" (a local copy), but only a very few would argue that there was no connection to Cahokia whatsoever.[71] Here's what's impressive to me: Aztalan is 495 kilometers north of Cahokia. That's the distance from Phoenix to Chaco and twice the distance from Chaco to its most distant outlier! There were other important ties between Cahokia and Spiro Mounds on the western frontier—555 kilometers away,[72] the distance from Flagstaff to Santa Fe or from Casas Grandes to Zuni.[73] A third example of Cahokian interaction at a distance—a large colony at the Macon Plateau site (Ocmulgee) in Georgia, 900 kilometers from Cahokia—is even more impressive, if more hotly contested. (Cahokia to Macon is comparable to Tula to Chichén Itzá.) Many archaeologists believe that Macon Plateau was a Cahokia outpost that "failed." Others (of course) deny that, asserting local autonomy from all things Cahokian.[74]

Think of those Mississippian distances: 459, 555, and 900 kilometers! Distances of 200 kilometers trouble southwestern archaeologists dealing (for example) with Chaco and its region. Mississippian archaeologists debate comparable questions framed at 500 or more kilometers. Those, it seems, were the scales of ancient Mississippian histories. Then again, Mississippianists balk at talk of Mexico, while Mexico–Southwest connections are healthy subgenres of southwestern archaeology—legitimate subjects for debate. But in the Southeast, linking Mississippian and Mexico can end an archaeologist's career.[75]

Did Cahokia know its southwestern contemporaries, and did the Southwest know the Mississippi? It would be remarkable if they did not. Recall the tale of the Turk in chapter 1.

We've found no Cahokia artifacts at Chaco and no Chaco black-on-white at Cahokia, but what of that? *Everybody knew everything.*

Hohokam: Rise and Fall

Sometime during the Early Sedentary Period, Hohokam reached its peak and began to ebb. Perhaps it got too big and stretched beyond the tensile strengths of the Hohokam Canon holding it together.

Sedentary Perceptions

"Sedentary," in Gladwin's original scheme (chapter 4), was the culmination and consolidation of "Colonial"—the preceding growth phase of 700 to 900 (chapter 4). From 900 to 1150 (the story went), the Sedentary Period Hohokam were settling in and setting up shop in their newly colonized territories, consolidating gains, and investing in infrastructure.[76] Excavations at Snaketown—our sole source until CRM in the 1970s—suggested that Sedentary was the demographic peak. Gladwin's Gila Pueblo surveys—the best maps of the past well into the 1960s—had Sedentary Period sherds marking Hohokam's greatest geographic extent. Putting those two pieces of information together, it seemed likely that Sedentary was the climax of pre-Classic Hohokam.

New data and new understandings suggest that the Sedentary Period (which consists of a single phase, called Sacaton in Phoenix and Rincon in Tucson) had an internal trajectory, a history. At some point in the Sedentary Period, the momentum and energies brought forward from the Colonial Period dissipated and Hohokam took a downturn. The skid probably began around 1050; after 1075, things fell apart.[77]

The Sedentary Period remains the public face of Hohokam, the aspect of their history that we most often and most easily see. Large Hohokam sites were impressively long-lived, with pit houses stacking up for centuries (insofar as pit houses stack). The later Classic Period was marked by shifts in settlement, away from earlier town centers (chapter 6). So at many sites (importantly at Snaketown), the Sedentary was the last major occupation and therefore the most visible to archaeology.

During the decades when Snaketown was the sole source for big Hohokam towns, its demography was projected over the whole region. CRM changed that picture. At the equally large Grewe site (excavated ahead of a highway interchange), population peaked in the Colonial and fell sharply during the Sedentary (chapter 4)—unlike Snaketown. Apparently, Hohokam towns did not march in demographic lockstep. During the Sedentary downturn, many of the largest Hohokam sites "were depopulated between A.D. 1050 and A.D. 1075 (e.g., Snaketown, Gila Butte, Grewe, Poston Butte, the Buttes, and Orme reservoir areas), while growth occurred at other villages (e.g., Adamsville, Gila Bend, Grand Canal, Palo Verde and Azatlan)."[78]

Regionally, population may have peaked early in the Sedentary Period, but given the alternating rises and falls of population at various towns, it seems a toss-up whether Colonial or Sedentary was actually largest. In any event, by the Middle and Late Sedentary, political disorganization, territorial contraction, and demographic downturns had started the slippery slide into the following Classic Period (chapters 6 and 7).

Despite Haury's aesthetic preferences for the Colonial Period and despite our foreknowledge of Classic troubles to come, the Sedentary Period was very impressive—more remark-

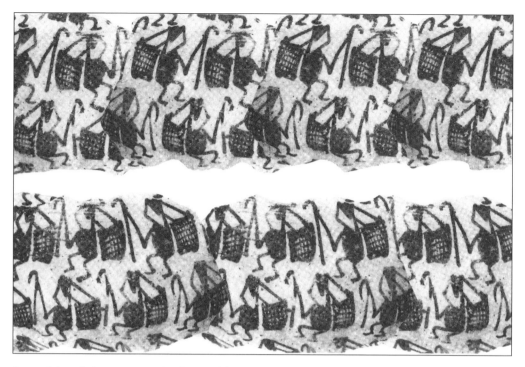

Figure 5.3. Hohokam porters, a familiar motif from Hohokam red-on-buff pottery. Digitally enhanced. Courtesy of the author.

able on most counts than the more hyped Chaco. Market economies blossomed under the aegis of the ball court system (see fig. 5.3). Some towns probably specialized in the production of pottery,[79] particular crops,[80] or other products that moved through the markets. The Sedentary Period economy—like that of the Late Colonial Period—involved regular movements of bulk goods.[81] Disparities in agricultural production between Gila and Salt probably encouraged craft specialization along the Gila; much of the pottery used in more prosperous Salt River towns was made in hard-luck Gila River communities.[82]

In a recent review, David Abbott described Hohokam regional economies in terms seldom if ever used before for Anasazi or Mogollon: "Populations across large tracts were interdependent for the supply and demand of a large variety of goods and services, including utilitarian pottery, comestibles, and other basic necessities. A sophisticated division of labor and probably calendrically timed, centralized marketplaces [around ball courts] assured an unimpeded flow of commodities across a wide territory."[83]

Big Houses all but disappeared; more accurately, the differences between Big Houses and normal houses decreased (see fig. 5.4; see also fig. 3.4). Sedentary villages continued the patterned modularity of the Colonial Period: courtyard groups, village segments, central plazas, ball courts, low capped mounds, and so forth (see fig. 5.5; see also fig. 4.6). And they were tied to the same canals, with significant additions.

Canal System 2, for example, was a group of about a dozen canals that tapped the Salt River (fig. 5.6).[84] Geology created an underground "dam," or ledge, in the river bottom, just below the narrows of Tempe Butte. The "dam" forced water seeping through the riverbed to the surface and, more importantly, ensured that the river could not cut down below canal

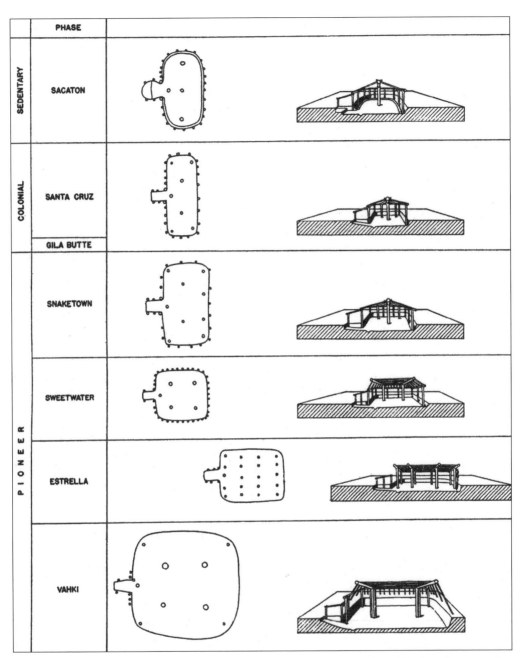

PHASE		

SEDENTARY — SACATON

COLONIAL — SANTA CRUZ / GILA BUTTE

PIONEER — SNAKETOWN / SWEETWATER / ESTRELLA / VAHKI

Figure 5.4. "Postulated reconstructions of dwelling units found at Snaketown." The Vahki Phase house is in fact a Big House and not the progenitor of the later forms. From Gladwin and others' seminal Excavations at Snaketown (1938). Courtesy University of Arizona Press.

intakes. Canals were too important to trust to the vagaries of hydrological cycles. At Canal System 2's maximum extent, nine canals ran up to 25 kilometers over the low terraces above the river, from Tempe, across downtown Phoenix, almost to Glendale. The combined length of all the canals reached more than 100 kilometers. The canals were substantial: cross sections of the largest were up to 20 meters wide and 6 meters deep.[85] They brought water to more

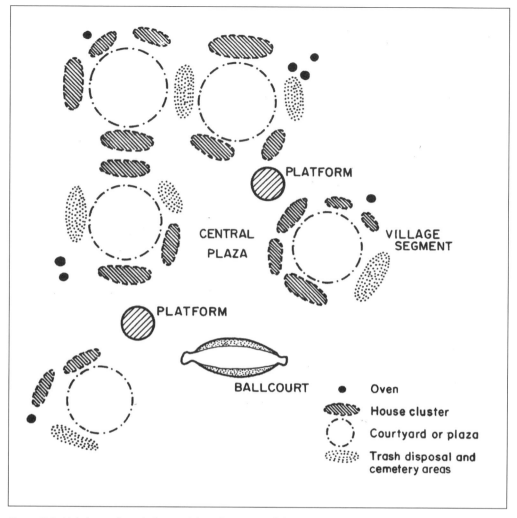

PLATFORM

CENTRAL PLAZA

VILLAGE SEGMENT

PLATFORM

BALLCOURT

● Oven

House cluster

Courtyard or plaza

Trash disposal and cemetery areas

Figure 5.5. Hokokam village (schematic) based on research by Jerry Howard. Courtesy David Doyel and the Amerind Foundation.

than 15,000 acres (60 square kilometers) of excellent farmland. That was just one (albeit one of the largest) of a half-dozen canal systems on the Salt River. And there were contemporaneous large systems on the nearby Gila River.[86]

Big canal systems and all the infrastructure required to make them work were major construction projects. Operating them—allocating water, adjudicating disputes, and all the other fun that comes with irrigation—required formal, institutional decision making. The biggest canals passed through many towns and villages, creating canal communities. All these facts seem like an invitation to centralized hierarchy. But, as we saw in chapter 4, that didn't happen.

Canals expanded throughout the Sedentary Period, fanning outward and bringing water to higher terraces, farther from the river. Was there enough water in the river for all the new lands? Tree rings at the upper reaches of the rivers' watersheds—high in the Mogollon uplands—say yes.[87] "Water flow in the Salt River was mostly reliable and predictable

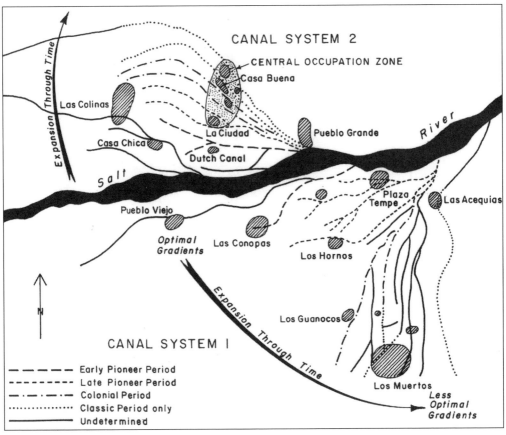

Figure 5.6. Hohokam canals on the Salt River near Phoenix, Arizona. Early maps by Omar Turney and Frank Midvale and later research by Jerry Howard and many others record the remarkable extent of ancient canal systems now destroyed by agricultural and urban development in the Phoenix Basin. Courtesy David Doyel and the Amerind Foundation.

throughout the Sacaton phase" (Sedentary Period).[88] One Hohokam archaeologist referred to these decades of felicitous stream flow as "the salubrious Sedentary." Yet, this was when Hohokam—as expressed by the canon—fell apart.

Hohokam Scales

Ball courts are the sine qua non of Hohokam. In chapter 4, I argued that most were built during the heady days of the Colonial Period. New courts were built during the Sedentary Period, of course, but by the Middle to Late Sedentary, courts (both old and new) were apparently being abandoned. Still, ball courts marked the Sedentary Period maximum, and a discussion of their geography belongs in this chapter, briefly here and at more length below.

There were 238 ball courts at 194 sites[89]—numbers curiously close to the two hundred or so outlier Great Houses of the Chaco region (discussed below). There are, of course, quibbles about a few of the features designated as ball courts—were they or were they not?—but there is no reason to doubt the approximate number and the general pattern. Two of the farthest out, biggest, no-doubt-about-'em ball courts were near Wupatki to the north and at Pueblo Viejo near Safford to the east. These were 240 and 250 kilometers distant from

Phoenix (see fig. 5.2; see also fig. 5.12). A few small ball courts have been reported at slightly greater distances in southeasternmost Arizona.

That was the home territories. Hohokam had more distant interests. The shell industry—huge during the Colonial Period—expanded even more during the Sedentary Period.[90] The sources remained the same: the Gulf of California, about 280 kilometers from Phoenix.[91] Tons of shell were procured at those distant shores. (For comparison, Chaco was only 180 kilometers from the Cerrillos turquoise mines; of which, more below.) Several species were procured at much greater distances.

And of course, Hohokam reached back deep into western Mexico. Copper bells (for example) were numerous, although they were curiously concentrated into only a few caches.[92]

Sedentary Governance

As in the Colonial Period, governance during the Sedentary Period is surprisingly hard to see. Despite dense populations,[93] increasingly large and elaborate canal systems,[94] impressive quantities of prestige goods,[95] and a developing market economy,[96] *we can't find Hohokam rulers.* Elite or economically favored families carried over, but Sedentary Period sites have not produced princely houses or burials.[97]

There are two main competing views of Hohokam governance within its regional system. The first emphasizes ritual obligations among local elites;[98] the second stresses economic networks built around markets and ball courts.[99] The two views are not mutually exclusive of course. Village-level Big House families were probably more important in the earlier Colonial Period and less so in the Sedentary. Elite lineages did not disappear; they may have directed or even sponsored the construction of ball courts, co-opted by the canon. At Grewe, for example, the houses of rich families were notably near a new ball court.[100] Yet ball courts denoted a diffusion of governance—the Hohokam Canon—that held in check would-be leaders and leading families (chapter 4). The canon repressed or avoided political hierarchy. But sometime during the Sedentary, the canon failed.

Beginning of the End

Around 1050 Hohokam wobbled off course.[101] Ball courts were decommissioned or abandoned. At Grewe, for example, "during the second half of the eleventh century…the large ballcourt had fallen out of use."[102] In a recent review, David Abbott and his coauthors conclude, "The ballcourt network was in rapid decline, if not totally collapsed, by the end of middle Sacaton times, around A.D. 1070."[103] The regional system unraveled: Tonto Basin connections to the Phoenix core "significantly decreased" in the Middle Sedentary.[104] The same thing happened in the Tucson Basin,[105] the New River drainage,[106] the lower Verde,[107] and even Gila Bend.[108] As the old Hohokam world Balkanized, more distant districts spun off in new directions. Mimbres, for example, shifted diplomatic interests from Hohokam to Chaco (below).

Pallets illustrate the decline. Pallets of the preceding Colonial Period were remarkably standardized (see fig. 4.8) and uniformly well made.[109] Sedentary Period pallets, in contrast, varied greatly in size, workmanship, form, and decoration: "During the Sedentary Period, while the materials remained the same, the manufacturing precision declined, life-form additions were almost completely lost, and decorations were mostly simple running patterns lightly incised or occasionally painted on the borders."[110] The Colonial standard of neat, long

Figure 5.7. Hungo Pavi, Chaco Canyon. Modified from the original image by Richard Kern, an artist who accompanied Lieutenant James H. Simpson's pioneering investigations at Chaco Canyon in 1849. Kern's was one of the first images of Chaco to reach the scientific world. This version comes from William Thayer's Marvels of the New West (1890), a popular book that introduced much of the East to the West. Image in the public domain.

rectangles with slightly concave sides gave way to imprecise, rounded rectangularity. Colonial Period pallets almost invariably had deeply incised parallel grooves running around their margins. Sedentary Period pallets had broad, flat margins that were lightly incised with a chaotic variety of geometric designs, some familiar from pottery and rock art, others unique to particular pallets.[111] The designs seem almost idiosyncratic and suggest the work of many different individuals—in contrast to the patterned regularity of Colonial incised grooves. Sedentary pallets appear to have been hastily made blank slates on which the end user scribed his or her own ideas and symbols.

It takes a saguaro a long time to realize it's dead—as many southern Arizona homeowners have discovered after paying good money for a transplanted cactus, roots cropped fatally close. It looks good for a year or so, but then the facts of its fate catch up. Likewise, timing cultural declines is difficult. Absent cataclysm, we can expect stylistic lags and anachronisms. Ball courts almost certainly continued to function locally in many areas long after the larger Hohokam regional system ceased to function. But long before 1150, the Hohokam Canon was over.

Anasazi: Chaco

Chaco was a phenomenon, a prodigy, a rare bird. Or maybe it was an abnormality, a grotesque, a sport of nature. One distinguished archaeologist, exasperated, called Chaco the simultaneous deus ex machina and bête noire of southwestern archaeology. And there's something in that. After a century of investigation, archaeological interpretations of Chaco vary so widely, it's sometimes hard to believe that we are all looking at the same small canyon in the deserts of northwestern New Mexico.[112]

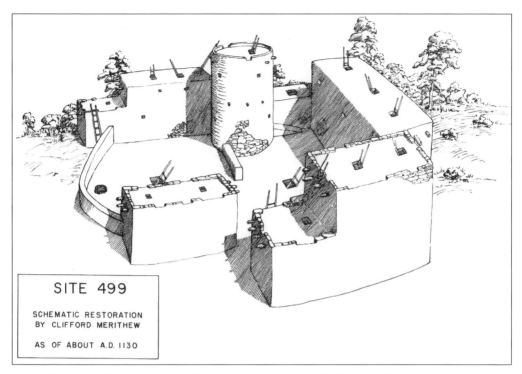

SITE 499

SCHEMATIC RESTORATION
BY CLIFFORD MERITHEW

AS OF ABOUT A.D. 1130

Figure 5.8. Unit pueblos near Farview House, Mesa Verde National Park, Colorado. Artist's reconstruction by Clifford Merithew. Site 499 was excavated by the University of Colorado in 1953. It consists of two contiguous unit pueblos, each with five or six rooms and a kiva (indicated by two square man-holes in the plaza) and an attached tower. All of this was built over an earlier unit pueblo (see fig. 5.9). Courtesy University of Colorado.

Chaco Hype

Archaeological interest in Chaco centers on a dozen remarkably large sandstone masonry buildings called Great Houses (see fig. 5.1; fig. 5.7). Chaco Great Houses began about 850–900, reached some sort of critical mass around 1000, and then exploded (or metastasized) in a century-long building boom from 1020 to 1125.

The idea behind Great Houses began, I think, in oversized pit structures at sites like Shabik'eschee as early as Basketmaker III. Basketmaker Big Houses presumably housed elite families—knockoffs of Hohokam Big Houses (chapter 3). The specific form of Chaco Great Houses, however, originated in the northern San Juan region, in the 700s and 800s, as U-shaped room blocks surrounding elaborate, oversized pit houses (chapter 4). These "proto-Great Houses" were short-lived—typically built, used, and abandoned in no more than a few decades, a generation or two. Proto-Great Houses bounced around the northern San Juan, finally moving up the Chaco River, where, for reasons that elude us, they took. Chaco Great Houses were permanent, lasting centuries. The visible ruins of extraordinarily large Basketmaker III villages at Chaco—Shabik'eschee and its sister site, 29 SJ 423 (chapter 3)—probably played a role: *those* villages, at *that* place, were remembered.

Great Houses at Chaco in the mid to late ninth century were monumentally scaled-up versions of unit pueblos.[113] Recall that a unit pueblo was six rooms and a kiva—the cookie-cutter house of the Anasazi (chapter 4; figs. 5.8, 5.9). Great Houses looked like really big unit

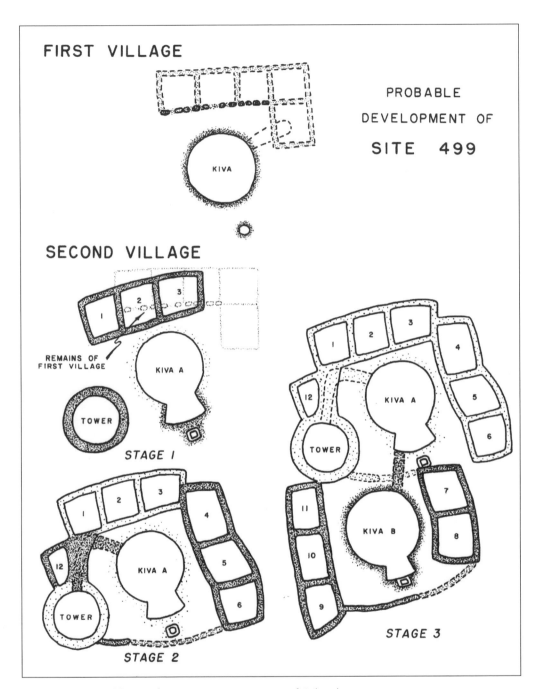

Figure 5.9. Unit pueblos (see fig. 5.8). Courtesy University of Colorado.

pueblos. Most of a unit pueblo—the home of the common people—could fit into a single room at Pueblo Bonito—the home of uncommon people. Great Houses were geometrically more formal, massively constructed, and quite costly in labor—extravagantly so, compared with unit pueblos. But the basic form of early Great Houses was clearly domestic: Great *Houses*. They began as trophy homes; they became palaces.

Figure 5.10. Downtown Chaco. Artist's reconstruction by Richard Friedman. The image was created using an elevation surface based on photogrammetry from 2001 aerial photography, 1-foot contour data published in 1934, and a digital orthophoto produced in 2004. Surface modifications were based on excavation reports and survey-grade GPS data. Courtesy Richard Friedman and John R. Stein and the Navajo Nation Chaco Protection Sites Program.

Ciudad Chaco

Chaco was a city—different in conception and detail from Post-Classic Mesoamerican cities but modestly urban nevertheless (fig. 5.10).[114] The reader may recoil from terms such as *urban* and *city* applied to a southwestern site, and indeed Chaco did not look like New York or Chicago or like the progression of crowded, busy, metropolitan sites—from Ur to the Big Apple—leading through the millennia to stormy, husky, brawling modern urbanism. Not all cities were like that; not all roads lead to or through Rome. There are many other, non-Western ways to build cities.[115]

What then is a city? Bruce Trigger offered a useful cross-cultural definition: "The key defining feature of an urban center is that it performs specialized functions in relation to a broader hinterland."[116] Chaco did that.

Why *not* a city? North America in the eleventh century was a continent of cities, big and small, from Cahokia to Cholula. Chaco was no Cahokia and certainly no Cholula, but it was by far the largest "site" on the Plateau from 900 to 1150. Between 2,100 and 2,700 people lived there.[117] Corn farming in and around the canyon could support only a tenth that many at best.[118] Twenty-four hundred people qualifies as a small Post-Classic city; twenty-four hundred people being supplied with corn from a hinterland qualifies as a capital.

For its time and place, Chaco offered an extraordinary concentration of impressive architecture.[119] A half dozen of the largest Great Houses concentrated in an urban "epicenter" 2 kilometers in diameter—a central district dubbed Downtown Chaco by some nameless wag. A remarkable number of Great Kivas were built in and around the Great Houses, perhaps relocated into the canyon from outlying communities.[120] Notable architecture extended up to 8 kilometers beyond that central zone. Chaco's major buildings were carefully placed and sited according to an overarching design that could be called urban planning, ritual landscape, or geomancy, depending on your interests.[121] The architectural repertoire encompassed massive earthen platforms ("mounds"), roadways, and waterworks—not the least of Chaco's wonders. Imagine the impact of Chaco's ponds and gardens on a traveler who had just crossed the surrounding desert. Water and waterworks were important architectural elements, planned into the larger cityscape.[122] Hundreds of regular unit pueblos crowded the south side of the canyon, at a respectful distance from the Great Houses.

We think of cities as densely packed, but those are *our* cities. Chaco (like modern Sunbelt cities) had an advantage many cities lack: lots of space. Chaco was spacious—impressively so. Broad open areas separated major buildings, increasing visual drama. Intervisibility gave Chaco an openness that counters our preconceptions about urban densities.[123] Visibility over great distance was (literally) a worldview inspired by the Plateau's vast vistas. Distance itself defined Chaco and its region, and distance was a key element of their urban aesthetic. Chaco city planning followed different rules than that of Ur or Chicago, because Chaco was not primarily an economic hub; transport and efficiency were secondary to political theater. Chaco was a city of palaces.

Palaces

A century of archaeology has led many of us, independently, to conclude that Great Houses were not pueblos—that is, they were not the communal dwellings, apartment buildings, or row house towns we characterize today as pueblos.[124] If not Ruth Benedict's pueblos, then what? Many archaeologists seem comfortable with Great Houses as elite residences.[125] I go one step further: Great Houses in Chaco Canyon were *palaces*, the homes of elite rulers.[126] The term means more than southwestern social climbing: *palaces* connects Chaco and Post-Classic Mesoamerica.[127]

Pueblo Bonito was not Versailles or the Alhambra. As with *city*, we should understand *palace* in New World terms.[128] There was a proliferation of palaces during the Post-Classic;[129] Chaco was part of that world. Mesoamerican "palaces are the residences of individuals of wealth or high social rank, along with their families and retinues, and they include facilities appropriate to the ritual, political, recreational, and economic functions of elite households and individuals as foci of social power."[130] So too were Great Houses.

Great Houses were almost certainly elite residences, the homes of persons or families of high rank and their followers. We have seen their burials—two rulers and their retinues interred in crypts in the oldest part of Pueblo Bonito.[131] We have seen their homes in the monumental domestic sectors of Great Houses.[132] And we are fairly confident that large portions of almost every Great House were *not* elite residences—indeed not residences of any kind— but instead warehouses, ritual facilities, "offices," and perhaps even temporary quarters for visiting elites, whose primary residences—marked by round rooms or kivas—were elsewhere, perhaps at outliers. Those spaces were "facilities appropriate to the ritual, political, recreational, and economic functions of elite households and individuals as foci of social power."[133] Those nonresidential spaces were ritual, political, recreational, and economic foci of social power.

A triangle of palaces—Pueblo Bonito, Chetro Ketl, and Pueblo Alto—formed Chaco's core. Pueblo Bonito was the oldest. Chetro Ketl may have been the largest, but Pueblo Alto, according to some Native accounts (chapter 7), was the actual seat of power, the place where the paramount rulers lived. A half-dozen other palaces, smaller and farther from the center, lined the canyon. Think of a northern Italian Renaissance town with competing princely houses. Chaco was something like that.

Great Houses were nothing if not monumental statements of purpose. I think the architecture of the three central buildings (Bonito, Chetro Ketl, and Alto) proclaimed adherence to different political factions, with competing views of Chaco and its future. I would not pretend to understand the intrigues and rivalries, but we can infer different politics from different cosmologies, different schemas for how the world was (or should be) ordered. Chaco had at least two conceptual frameworks for social and political life: solstitial and cardinal.[134] Solstitial buildings faced southeast, with their long rear walls aligned more or less to the solstice, as had most other Anasazi building for centuries. Cardinal orientation followed rigid north–south, east–west layouts (perhaps prefiguring Paquimé? chapter 7). Solstitial was traditional; cardinal was new—in buildings. The cardinal directions may have a respectable antiquity, pre-Chaco, in landscapes. I've noted that in Basketmaker III and Pueblo I, the biggest, most interesting sites were more or less on a meridian—Chaco's. That interesting fact will resurface in hints and innuendos and in various notes.

Orientation may seem a small thing, to us a matter of degrees. But Chaco was all about building and the act or process of construction. The planners of Pueblo Bonito argued, in architecture, about orientations. Through excavation, we can see the unused foundations, the building raised, razed, and rebuilt.[135] Orientation was a big deal.

The cosmological contrasts were stark and structured. Pueblo Bonito began, in the 900s, as solstitial. In the 1020s building boom, Chetro Ketl followed a traditional solstitial orientation, while Pueblo Alto was conspicuously cardinal—a bold departure from centuries of Anasazi practices! And here is a key event: Around 1100 Pueblo Bonito adopted Alto's new ways. Bonito—the oldest, most important building in the canyon—shifted from the old ways to the new, cardinal cosmologies. The remarkably true north–south wall that transects Pueblo Bonito's plaza signaled its new allegiance. In the cosmological (and political) competition between upstart Pueblo Alto and the older order at Chetro Ketl, Pueblo Alto apparently had won. When a new capital was built at Aztec Ruins (chapter 6), the site selected was due north of Chaco—clearly a cardinal decision—but the city plan itself was solstitial. Compromise? Or a competition played out through landscape and architecture?[136] We will return to those questions in chapter 6.

Theological tussles could not have been rare in the ancient Southwest. Consider the rise and fall of the Hohokam Canon (chapter 4). And Pueblo IV must have been one long cosmological argument (chapter 7). Chaco's philosophical discord is unusual in the history of the ancient Southwest for its clarity, the stark monumentality of the evidence, and the fact that it played out at the very highest levels of society, with political consequences for centuries thereafter (chapter 6).

Chaco's Origins

Cities? Palaces? Lords? Competing princely houses? Where did all *that* come from?

To understand Chaco at its height, we must look back to its origins. Chaco's beginnings, around 900, marked the end of Pueblo I (chapter 4) and the beginning of Pueblo II (chapter 5). In its later Pueblo II days, Chaco's central functions were political and ritual; initially, at the very end of Pueblo I, they were probably economic. Chaco was an inland island, a slightly favorable patch of land at the center of a very difficult desert, the San Juan Basin—a vast shallow bowl, 200 kilometers in diameter. The circle of mountains and rivers around its rim was better watered than the lower desert interior. Consequently, the rim was far more heavily settled than the center.

Traditions of movement had led Great House communities into Chaco by the late ninth/early tenth century but perhaps could not lead them out again; there was no longer an empty "next valley over" into which they could move. By 1000 the more livable edges of the basin were full. Political tensions that in an earlier age would have prompted a move were overcome, and Chaco's three Great Houses—Peñasco Blanco, Una Vida, and the largest and most important Pueblo Bonito—defied tradition by growing in place from 900 to 1125. Shorter-lived Great Houses of the preceding age marched or died, yet these three stood solidly in place for two centuries. Something had changed.

Anasazi political power had found an economic base. Proto-Great Houses in the northern San Juan housed aspirant leaders whom no one really wanted; Chaco's Great Houses were institutions for the common good. Early Chaco operated as a kind of corn bank, where surpluses from villages on one edge of the San Juan Basin were available to even out shortages in villages on the opposite edge. Farming varied unpredictably around the edges of the San Juan Basin, both yearly and regionally. Communities banked surplus corn and other products at Chaco, the basin's center place. When in need, they counted on Chaco to supply the want.

That reconstruction was first proposed by James Judge in New Archaeology language: "the development of a complex cultural ecosystem in the Chaco [San Juan] Basin."[137] That was New Archaeology's best attempt to grapple with Chaco-sized problems. Judge's model was ecological. It was evolutionary (for *development*, read *evolution*). It eschewed history both by commission and omission: indeed, it was a pointed response to Charles Di Peso's history of Chaco as a Mesoamerican outpost,[138] and it omitted historical triggers in favor of timeless processes. It was framed on much larger scales than the typical natural laboratory; the San Juan Basin was about 200 kilometers in diameter.

Judge's "complex cultural ecosystem" was counted among the triumphs of New Archaeology in the Southwest. But a short decade later, Judge disavowed his ecological model in favor of ritual explanations: Chaco was a pilgrimage center[139]—the sort of thing that might drive Binford to apoplexy. (The resurgence of ritual unfolds in chapter 7.) There were several reasons for the renunciation and reformation of Judge's arguments. His original model was criticized—unfairly, I think—because ceramics and lithics did not appear to support it. The model was about corn, not pots and rocks.[140] And the distances involved, some said—incorrectly, as we shall shortly see—exceeded the practical limits of foot-borne bulk goods. But most importantly, the ecological basis of Judge's model was strained past credibility by the later discovery of Great Houses far beyond the limits of the San Juan Basin—out past Mesa Verde, well into southeastern Utah, and deep into northeastern Arizona, almost reaching Hopi. Whatever the "complex cultural ecosystem's" merits, they could not possibly apply to that greatly expanded regional system. Chaco's reach exceeded New Archaeology's grasp, and Judge recanted.

He needn't have and probably shouldn't have. It's a matter of history. I think Judge's model applied to Chaco's *beginnings*. Early economic and political success fueled Chaco's expansion, through colonies or emulations, out to the farthest fringes of the Anasazi world (with the notable exceptions of the Kayenta and Rio Grande areas). But the rules of engagement changed. Corn was not redistributed to and from the farthest fringes. Instead, lighter, more precious prestige goods traveled between Chaco's lords and local elites.

I believe that Judge's model still holds as a historical prelude to that greater, grander Chacoan world. Back in their terminal Pueblo I/earliest Pueblo II beginnings, elite families at early Pueblo Bonito, Una Vida, and Peñasco Blanco administered Judge's system and grew fat (metaphorically) on the margins. After sputtering failures at Shabik'eschee oversized pit houses and San Juan proto-Great Houses, Anasazi rulers at last had a *reason* to rule. I think Chaco's rise was in large part a function of its central place and its central place was a part of its function.

Chaco Canyon was also a historically important place, the site of the largest settlements of the sixth and seventh centuries (Shabik'eschee and 29 SJ 423; chapter 3). Those remarkable early towns were surely remembered and commemorated through the mnemonics of place. Chaco Canyon's early history may have given Chaco leaders a regional authority—and edge—that their ambitious predecessors lacked at Dolores and other early San Juan Great Houses.

That nod to history, added to their economic roles, made them effective leaders. Their spheres of competence and control expanded. They became peacemakers and keepers of order. Steven LeBlanc chronicled the escalating levels of feuding and raiding in the eighth and ninth centuries. With the rise of Chaco, that violence suddenly ended. A remarkable era of peace— which someone illiterate in Latin dubbed the Pax Chaco—blessed the countryside from 900 to 1250.[141] Indeed, the times required statesmen. Peacemaking may have been as important as commodities trading in the rise of Chaco's lords.

I think a third factor played an important—perhaps critical—role in Chaco's rise. That was Hohokam's Colonial expansion (chapter 4; see fig. 4.2). The emergence of political leadership among the eastern Anasazi in Basketmaker III (chapter 3) and Pueblo I (chapter 4) was at least in part a response of Zuni, Keres, and Tanoan speakers to the alarming actions of Uto-Aztecan societies in the western Southwest and, most importantly, to Hohokam. Chaco was a geopolitical riposte to the astonishing Colonial Period expansion. At 900 Hohokam was going strong. The following Sedentary Period was a decline only when viewed in retrospect, through history's eyes. Hohokam people and ideas of both the Colonial and the Sedentary periods were vigorous, expansive, and truly foreign *to the eastern Plateau*. Ball courts? Figurines? Cremations? *Everybody knew everything*: Plateau people were well aware of Hohokam and must have been impressed and even alarmed.

I do not suggest that a council of Chacoan leaders met to discuss the Hohokam crisis and to formulate appropriate responses—although that scenario is not impossible. More likely (or perhaps more palatable), Hohokam's career created both models and excuses for the rise of Chaco-era leadership. Big House leadership in the Hohokam area was constrained by the canon, but elite families on the Plateau flourished after 1020 perhaps because Anasazi communities—uncertain how to respond to the remarkable events to the south—felt a need for leadership. Economy, war, geopolitics: the office sought the man—or men, or women, or families—who could make sense of it all. Aspirant leaders were readily available in proto-Great House clans. Chaco became the political, economic, and ritual center of an immense region—comparable in scale to the older Hohokam ball court network but evidently far more centralized.

Curiously, Chaco—the largest, most interesting Pueblo II site—was due south of Blue Mesa–Ridges Basin—the largest, most interesting Pueblo I site—which itself was, oddly, due

Figure 5.11. Chimney Rock, "the ultimate outlier." Computer reconstruction by John Kantner on a photograph by Frank Eddy. A Chaco Great House perched high on a ridge west of Pagosa Springs, Colorado. Its location was undoubtedly fixed by the twin spires, between which the moon rises every eighteen-plus years. But it was also dictated by the Great House's connection via line of sight back to Chaco Canyon. Chimney Rock could see Huerfano Peak, atop which were fire-signaling features; Huerfano Peak could see Pueblo Alto at Chaco Canyon. Courtesy John Kantner and University of Arizona Press.

north of Shabik'eschee and 29 SJ 423—the largest, most interesting Basketmaker III sites. Surely a coincidence.

Outliers or Outliars?

Two hundred small Great Houses—"outliers"—scattered over most of the Plateau defined Chaco's regional system (see fig. 5.2).[142] The term *outlier* suggests a center—which Chaco

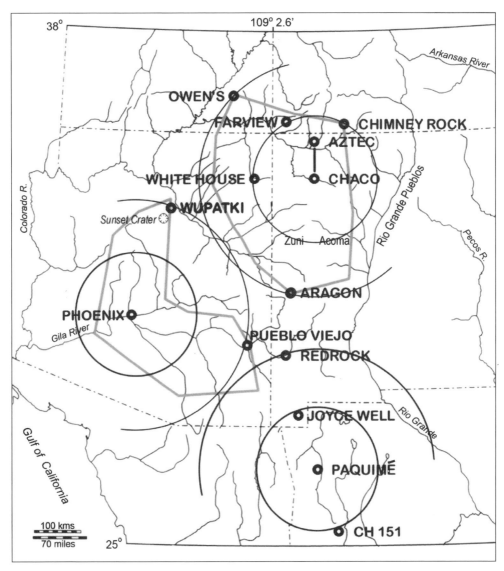

Figure 5.12. Chaco, Hohokam, and Casas Grandes regions with selected sites. The outer arcs represent 240- to 250-kilometer "outer limits," the inner arcs are 140- to 150-kilometer "inner circles," and the gray polygons delimit the distribution of Chaco Great Houses and Hohokam ball courts. Hohokam and Chaco were roughly contemporary (about 900–1150), Casas Grandes much later (1250–1450). See note 144. Courtesy of the author.

Canyon surely was—and *regional system* implies interconnection—which less surely was the case. But beyond those two stipulations, Chaco's "regional system" should be understood as a pleasantly vague and indefinite appellation, with loads of potential meanings. Some Great Houses, such as Chimney Rock (fig. 5.11), were probably Chacoan colonies or impositions, while other outliers were local families mimicking (emulating) Chacoan styles. Still, both were part of the larger regional system.

The Chaco regional system—whatever it was—completely overshot the research scales of 1960s and 1970s southwestern archaeology. Each individual outlier, with its attendant community nestled in a convenient valley, could serve as a New Archaeology natural laboratory—and a few did. The scale of the Chaco region was indeed prodigious and evoked understandable skepticism: "Can sites halfway across Arizona, hundreds of miles from Chaco Canyon, be considered 'Chacoan' in any meaningful sense?"[143]

How far is too far? What are realistic scales for Chaco—and for the ancient Southwest?[144] As with "cities," we should shed modern preconceptions. Our world is at once very small and very large. We think nothing of flying 4,000 miles to Paris, but we balk at walking 4 miles to a restaurant. Archaeologists often frame ancient space in terms *we* find comfortable, reasonable—a day's walk, for example, 10 to 22 kilometers. But the sites themselves suggest that those scales are too small for understanding Chaco (and Hohokam, and later Paquimé, as we shall see in chapter 7). For Chaco, there was an inner core of undeniable outliers out to about 140–150 kilometers (fig. 5.12)—"undeniable" in that if a contrarian denies them, I ignore the contrarian. Out at 150 kilometers sat Chimney Rock ("the ultimate outlier"),[145] Farview (a classic Chacoan Great House at Mesa Verde), and White House (ditto at Canyon de Chelly)—three archetypical outlier Great Houses. The most distant outlier candidates—such as Owen's Site at the head of Grand Gulch and Aragon in the Mogollon highlands—were another 100 kilometers out—that is, about 240–250 kilometers from Chaco (see fig. 5.12). These uttermost outliers are, in all important respects, identical to outlier Great Houses within the 150-kilometer inner core. They had local ceramics, of course, and local stone masonry. Mostly because of distance, these outermost outliers are subject to doubt and skepticism, but they were the same kind of buildings.

Tumpline Economies

What mean these radii when the sandals hit the road? Chacoan commerce was foot driven, delivered by tumpline backpacks on porters.[146] No carts, no horses, no boats, no rivers. How far and how much could people move on their feet and their backs?[147]

Travel distances have obvious implications for economic interactions. Let's go for the throat, or rather the gut, and look at basic, subsistence economy: the transport of bulk foodstuffs such as maize. Kent Lightfoot suggested a 50-kilometer limit for "prehistoric food redistribution" at Chaco;[148] beyond that limit, transport was uneconomical (the porter ate the portage). Lightfoot's 50-kilometer limit became a rule of thumb—and another nail in the coffin of "complex cultural ecosystems." That radius around Chaco gets you only the stinking deserts of the interior San Juan Basin, so Lightfoot's limit was cited as proof that Chaco's regional system was not economic, at least not in subsistence economy.[149] The 50-kilometer rule is far too short, however. Robert Drennan, looking at bulk food transport in Mesoamerica, set a much longer limit for regular commerce—an absolute (and extreme) maximum distance of 275 kilometers. "Ordinarily, we should expect transport of such staples to be restricted to substantially shorter distances."[150] More recently, Nancy Malville (who studies porters worldwide) concluded that "foot transport of food stuffs and durable goods would have been feasible in the pre-Hispanic American Southwest on a regular basis over distances of at least 100 to 150 km and on an occasional basis over much longer distances."[151] The inner limit for regular bulk goods transportation was on the order of 140 to 150 kilometers (Malville's 150-kilometer limit), while occasional movement of bulk goods might have reached 240 to 250 kilometers (Drennan's 275-kilometer limit). Certainly, precious prestige goods—macaw feather artifacts, copper bells, and so forth—could easily reach out and touch someone at 250 kilometers. The inner circle (150 kilometers) might mark the bulk goods economy;[152] the outer limits (250 kilometers), the political economy (see fig. 5.12).

The huge and hugely important turquoise mines at Cerrillos were about 175 kilometers from Chaco (see fig. 1.3)—a bit beyond the 150-kilometer radius but well within the 250-kilometer limit. Turquoise was central to Chaco's political economy. The canyon was one big lapidary workshop. Turquoise went out to the provinces and went south to Mexico, but much of it stayed at Pueblo Bonito and the other princely houses. Chaco's rulers decked themselves out in more blue stones than a Santa Fe matron on the make. It irks Rio Grande archaeologists to have Cerrillos under Chaco's "control"—but I suspect it was.[153]

Distances like 150 and 250 kilometers don't faze Hohokam archaeologists. The ball court system compares favorably with the most expansive reading of Chaco's regional system (see fig. 5.12). As discussed above, bulk transport was routine throughout the central Hohokam region, although no one suggests regular bulk economies on 250-kilometer scales! (We are only beginning to appreciate the scale and complexity of Hohokam commerce; it was probably big.) To anticipate a third, later system, Casas Grandes' interior region (chapter 7) also fits nicely within a 150-kilometer radius; 250 kilometers reaches Redrock, the source of ricolite, the most important commercial import (after shell) to the Casas Grandes capital of Paquimé (see fig. 5.12). (The vast quantities of shell found at the great fourteenth-century city came from shores even more distant; chapter 7.)

They did it in the deserts. It seems very likely that they did it on the Plateau too. They routinely moved masses of materials, including food, within the inner circle of 150 kilometers and sporadically to and from the outer limits of Chaco's region at 250 kilometers from the canyon.

Mogollon: Mimbres Moiré

Mimbres, well beyond the 250-kilometer territorial limit, was an extraordinary development in Mogollon southwestern New Mexico, but it was neither a major regional system nor (apparently) a fledgling hierarchical government.[154] Mimbres is worth thinking about because (1) Mimbres vividly shows the one-two historical punch of Hohokam and Chaco, and (2) Mimbres may well have been the place where Pueblo people first lived like Pueblos—in permanent, aggregated, dense, apartmentlike villages held together without hierarchical government. Ruth Benedict's ideal Pueblo world was neither entirely false nor entirely unprecedented. Mimbres rituals and ideologies, which made all of this possible, prefigured the ceremonialism of modern Pueblos. We usually look to the Four Corners and the Colorado Plateau for Pueblo origins, but it seems that some of the key things that characterize modern Pueblo life started in the south.

Mimbres, like many southwestern archaeological terms, refers to both a place and a time within that place. The Mimbres area was essentially southwestern New Mexico, with a bit of southeastern Arizona and northernmost Chihuahua thrown in. The Mimbres Phase, from 950 to 1150, is the best-known archaeology of the Mimbres area. Mimbres was a precise contemporary of Chaco, Sedentary Hohokam—and Cahokia. Those coincidences were probably not coincidental.

Mimbres Archaeology

After several large excavations in the 1920s and 1930s,[155] looting outpaced science. Mimbres sites were gutted for their pots—some of the worst looting on record—and archaeology wrote off the region as a sad loss. Mimbres was left to the cruel mercies of pot hunters until the late 1960s.[156] New projects, most driven by the ideas of New Archaeology, then began.[157] Small scales, small budgets: Mimbres projects in the 1960s and 1970s were field schools—intrinsically poor—or otherwise chronically underfunded. Mimbres escaped big CRM. That was good for the region, since no big CRM meant no huge destructive undertakings. But that was bad for archaeology, since big CRM budgets potentially advanced prehistory.

More than money, small scales reflected New Archaeology. Steven LeBlanc, one of the leading Mimbres archaeologists of the 1970s generation, was a standard bearer of "an explicitly scientific approach."[158] The Mimbres Valley was a fine natural laboratory for local ecological adaptations and evolutionary sequences (for example, Paul Minnis's 1985 study of Mimbres Valley's "social adaptations to food stress"—a study that still holds up well).

But Mimbres history was bigger than that. New Archaeology projects created useful, separate local histories for the Mimbres and the upper Gila river valleys. Archaeologists naturally considered how sequences in various valleys compared. It came as something of a surprise to learn that the histories of different valleys were intertwined. Apparently, populations from one valley colonized and recolonized other valleys, shifting about much as in Anasazi Pueblo I (chapter 4).[159] The Mimbres region was regional, not an accumulation of local sequences and local adaptations. The sum was greater than the parts. We are still a long way from disentangling that history with anything like Pueblo I precision.[160]

And Mimbres itself was part of a much larger world. In chapter 4, I argued that the Late Pithouse Period in the Mimbres area was deeply engaged with Colonial Hohokam. In the Mimbres Phase, those interests turned like a weathervane to the north, toward Chaco.

Mimbres = Hohokam + Anasazi

Mimbres was an Anasazi lifestyle built on a Hohokam infrastructure.[161] That's a slogan—my slogan, which I've mumbled at meetings, annoying many Mimbres archaeologists. It means that the economic base of Mimbres pueblos was canal irrigation, almost certainly borrowed from the Hohokam (chapter 4)—a "Hohokam infrastructure." The Mimbres Phase continued and expanded the canals, but its architecture shifted to masonry pueblos with small "kivas" and its pottery, to black-on-white and corrugated types—all of which paralleled, reflected, or perhaps even inspired Anasazi developments—the "Pueblo lifestyle"[162] Note that these were *sequential* episodes: Hohokam flared out during the Colonial Period (750 to 950, the Late Pithouse Period; chapter 4), and Chaco exploded outward in Pueblo II (900 to 1150, the Mimbres Phase)—the one-two punch.

Many archaeologists agree that Hohokam was an important influence during Late Pithouse and even Early Mimbres times (chapter 4). But don't go talking that Anasazi trash for the Mimbres Phase! There is nearly universal resistance to any Anasazi role whatsoever in later Mimbres prehistory. It's easier for a camel to pass through the eye of a needle than for Mimbres to consort with Anasazi—even hypothetically. Anti-Anasazi feelings are deeply entrenched, dating back to the convulsions of New Archaeology. The old guard—Haury, Kidder, and others—saw the changes so evident in the Mimbres Phase as "Anasazi swamping" or "Anasazisation" around 1000.[163] New Archaeology had a programmatic distaste for migrations, diffusion, and "swamping." So Mimbres projects of the New Archaeology era denied absolutely any Anasazisation.[164] But I think Mimbres from 950 to 1150 was far more engaged with Anasazi than it had ever been with Hohokam. More than that, I think

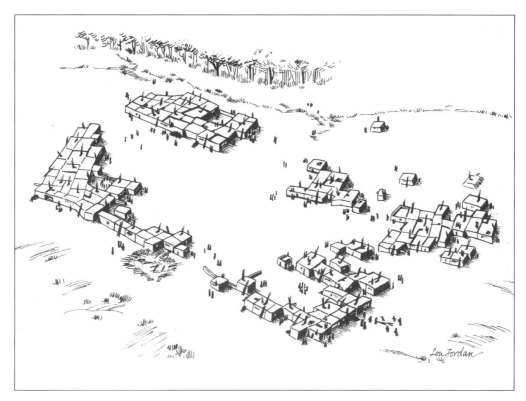

Figure 5.13. The Galaz Ruin, a large Mimbres site in southwestern New Mexico. Artist's reconstruction by Lou Jordan. Galaz was one of the largest eleventh- or early-twelfth-century towns in the Mimbres River Valley; two towns in the upper Gila River Valley (Woodrow and Redrock) were twice this size. Courtesy Roger Anyon and Steven LeBlanc.

Mimbres—well beyond the 250-kilometer limit—was still within Chaco's larger sphere of influence, *and vice versa*. It was a two-way street.[165]

Mimbres was an Anasazi lifestyle built on a Hohokam infrastructure. Mimbres's debt to Hohokam was merely fundamental: canals. While elements of the Hohokam Canon slipped into Mimbres life in the Late Pithouse Period (chapter 4), the most important contribution of Hohokam in the end was irrigation technology. Mimbres's affiliations with Anasazi were importantly superficial: they looked alike. Appearances were important—clothes, as it were, made the man. When Mimbres suddenly started looking Anasazi, there was probably a reason.

The Galaz Ruin, one of the largest and best-known Mimbres towns, did not look exactly like Pueblo Bonito (fig. 5.13); neither did most Anasazi buildings. Comparing the celebrated masonry of Chacoan Great Houses with Mimbres walls—artfully stacked river cobbles at best, with plenty of mud mortar—would not suggest close kinship. But that's apples and oranges: Mimbres towns were not Great Houses. Simpler Anasazi forms serve us better. Unit pueblos (*not* Great Houses) were the characteristic Anasazi house form from 950 to 1150—and before and after. Their masonry was markedly less perfect than Chaco's. In both Anasazi and Mimbres, people built with what they had and what they knew, but they were building the same kinds of buildings. The unit pueblo was a common Mimbres house form, especially around 950/1000—the time of the critical shift between Mimbres pit houses and pueblos.[166]

At the turn of the first millennium, six rooms and a kiva constituted the common family home from Mesa Verde to the upper Gila. Structures much like unit pueblos formed the nuclei around which grew larger, later pueblos of the Mimbres Valley, such as the Galaz and Swarts ruins. Those big Mimbres towns began as loose clusters of small room blocks—rather like a small community of Anasazi unit pueblos.[167]

The "pit house to pueblo transition" in the Mimbres area meant more than a cameo by unit pueblos. Something actually happened, and it was *big*: population jumped dramatically from the Late Pithouse Period to the Mimbres Phase. That's why unit pueblos disappeared almost immediately, subsumed by big pueblos. The jump was so dramatic that several archaeologists suggest significant in-migration.[168] People poured into the Mimbres Valley and probably into the Gila as well.

Where did these new people come from? Around 1000, it turns out, substantial Anasazi populations migrated into the Mogollon Rim country of Arizona,[169] and into the Mogollon highlands of west-central New Mexico.[170] Population spiked throughout the Mogollon uplands. Existing Mogollon people may have been bumped south into the Mimbres—but we still come up short, I think, for the Mimbres boom. Why not Plateau people moving a bit farther south, into the Mimbres area? If we reunite Mimbres with the larger Southwest, we can solve its demographic problems. For centuries, Plateau populations sloshed back and forth like water in a wash basin, and in the eleventh century, people spilled into and over the Mogollon uplands—and, I think, beyond into the Mimbres area.[171]

Chaco was clearly implicated, perhaps at the center of these events. Chaco may not have been that nice a place. Whatever Chaco was, it drove people outward—north into the Four Corners (empty in the tenth century and repopulated in the eleventh), south into the Mogollon uplands (above), and beyond, a vast penumbra of Anasazi-like sites in far-distant areas previously innocent of stone pueblos, painted pottery, and corn. Something like Anasazi popped up in Wyoming, southern Nevada, and even the northern Rio Grande—a penumbra around Chaco's regional system. This was the "Pueblo II Expansion," a staple of pre-1960s archaeology. Discarded by New Archaeology, it turns out the Pueblo II Expansion was real—or at least describes a real pattern in prehistory, Chaco's sphere of influence. By expansion or by contagion, concentric zones around Chaco—reaching out 600 kilometers or more—suddenly looked a lot more Anasazi than they had before or after. Mimbres, in the context of the Pueblo II Expansion, was the southern counterpart of Anasazi wannabes in northern Utah and Colorado (aka Fremont).[172]

But Mimbres was not a backwater like Las Vegas or Wyoming in the twelfth century. (Today, of course, viva Las Vegas and the equal rights state!) Nor was it a silent partner, a tail wagged first by Hohokam and then by Chaco. During the Mimbres Phase, at least five or six thousand people (perhaps twice that) built two dozen big pueblos and irrigated thousands of hectares of corn. Their world was wide, reaching far beyond their particular valleys. Mimbres was cosmopolitan. Its painters depicted exotic animals from distant rain forests and seas: ocean fish,[173] armadillos, and possibly monkeys.[174] Macaws appear on many Mimbres pots, establishing a motif that would culminate in the parrot pots of Paquimé (chapter 7).[175] Indeed, researchers note that "Mesoamerican-like motifs" increased notably during the Mimbres Phase (that is, after about 1000).[176]

Mimbres was a player. During the Late Pithouse Period, Mimbres was on the receiving end of Hohokam ideas. During the Mimbres Phase, it cranked out ideas that had profound effects on the Plateau. Some—perhaps most—of the Mesoamerican objects that so famously marked the lords of Chaco Canyon may have come through the Mimbres—not directly from Mexico or via Hohokam (a topic to which we will return below). But it was Mimbres's contributions to later Pueblo life that marked its most lasting achievements.

Proto-Pueblos

Mimbres villages were the first real *pueblos* in the Southwest, if by that term we mean large, permanent, high-density, "apartment house" settlements (see fig. 5.13). Before 1200, Anasazi villages were almost always small and short-lived, with the important exception of Chaco Canyon. Mimbres villages, in contrast, were large and permanent, like Hohokam towns. The very largest Mimbres sites, on the upper Gila River, reached four hundred rooms and spanned two centuries.[177] Like Hohokam, big Mimbres towns did their work without leaders; they developed other mechanisms for holding towns together. Chaco-style governance, if it ever reached Mimbres, did not leave robust evidence of its workings.[178] Mimbres devised other ways of doing business, which may well have been a source (the source?) for fourteenth- and fifteenth-century Pueblo arrangements that avoided hierarchy (chapter 7).

In the vacuum left by Hohokam's collapse, one obvious alternative would have been Chaco-style hierarchy. Everyone knew everything, and Mimbres was well aware of the 800-pound gorilla to the north. A few Mimbres structures may represent emulations, or local copies, of Great Houses. But the emulations are barely recognizable as Great Houses, and elites (foreign or domestic) were so muted as to emerge only now from Mimbres archaeology.[179]

Throughout the Late Pithouse Period, selected elements of the Hohokam Canon kept Mimbres politics in check. With retrenchments of the Sedentary Period Hohokam, Mimbres people looked to their own devices. They created frontier liturgies, like Catholics isolated in colonial New Mexico. Mimbres went another way—kachinas—not precisely as in modern Pueblos but the development of forms and practices that eventually became kachina ritual and ceremonies. Kachina societies are one of several institutions that act as a social glue in modern Pueblos, and Mimbres art is the earliest place in which archaeologists and art historians recognize kachinas.[180] That was not Mimbres's only ritual or social contribution to Pueblo life, but the images evident in Mimbres art mark an important event in the history of the ancient Southwest—insofar as archaeologists can tell it.

Mimbres managed canals, which in turn supported large, long-lived towns with kachinas, not kings. And then they too failed (chapter 6). Real hierarchy—with pomp and grandeur—rose in the region decades after the Mimbres collapse at Paquimé (chapter 7). But the lessons learned by Mimbres townspeople carried over into the modern Pueblos, refined in the cosmological evolutions of Pueblo IV (chapter 7).

Hohokam, Mimbres, Chaco, Cahokia, and Mexico

What was the bigger picture? How was all this playing on the continental stage? Recall that Early Hohokam was, in significant ways, West Mexican. Other early societies were variously but more distantly engaged with the south. After 900, that changed: relations between the Southwest and Mesoamerica became notably more formal and "patterned."[181] That clarity may reflect, in part, long-distance proclivities of Post-Classic Mesoamerica, but it also represents new strategies of engagement with the south by southwestern leadership. Southwestern leaders wanted what Mesoamerica offered: a way to demonstrate and validate their importance to the people they hoped to lead.

Hohokam

In Hohokam, around 900 the nature of the engagement changed. Pyrite mirrors—most abundant in the Colonial Period (chapter 4)—gave way to copper bells. More than 110 copper bells—almost certainly from western Mexico—were found in Sedentary Period contexts, compared with only a handful from Colonial contexts.[182] That's an impressive number, compared with other areas: less than thirty from contemporary Chaco, about twenty from Mimbres, and (I'm told) none from Tula.

Macaws were relatively numerous at key pueblo sites—at Chaco and Mimbres and later at Point of Pines and Wupatki (chapter 6)—and were spectacularly numerous at Paquimé (chapter 7). The colorful, talking birds were all but absent at Colonial and Sedentary Hohokam sites. We've found about five.[183] Differences in preservation might account for the disparity, but macaws and parrots were also conspicuously absent from Hohokam imagery, in which birds of many other species were common. Haury noted, "The Hohokam seldom painted the parrot."[184] Mimbres painted lots of macaws. So did Mesa Verde, later and far to the north—at a time when macaws were hard to come by (chapter 6). And Paquimé potters positively doted on the birds (chapter 7). Either Sedentary Period Hohokam was not into noisy, nasty, natty birds or (more likely) was unable to connect with macaw suppliers. Mimbres may have cornered that market.

Hohokam connections went west, then south. A cluster of Hohokam towns was established during the Colonial Period at Gila Bend,[185] at the southwesternmost edge of Hohokam and a "hard boundary" between Hohokam and Patayan peoples of the lower Colorado River.[186] Gila Bend prospered through the Sedentary, as the Hohokam town closest to the coast. Coastal trade routes were a straight shot from Gila Bend through the western Papagueria, a region ribboned with ancient trails.[187] It developed as a "gateway community…coordinating the flow of goods through inter-regional routes of commerce."[188] But Gila Bend did not last long into the following Classic Period: shifting trade networks of the Classic bypassed Gila Bend (chapters 6 and 7).

Mimbres

Mimbres kachina ceremonialism had roots deep in Mesoamerica: "Ultimately, certain of the ideological concepts embodied by the kachina cult may be traceable to Mexico. Tlaloc-like rain gods, conceptually related to rainmaking kachinas, as well as the masks themselves" are among the things linking kachinas to the south.[189]

During the Late Pithouse Period, Mesoamerican objects that reached Mimbres probably came via the Hohokam. As that partnership dissolved, the Mimbres turned away from the west and to the north. And to the south, I believe. Mimbres developed their own routes to West Mexico, bypassing or outflanking the Hohokam—over the mountains and through the woods to Aztatlan. The Sierra Madre Occidental is a barrier more in our perceptions than in Native interactions.[190] During the time covered in this chapter, Mimbres and Chaco had the same kinds of Mesoamerican objects, and these objects differed from those found at Hohokam sites.[191] Witness macaws: Mimbres and Chaco had them, Hohokam did not.[192] And Mimbres may have developed its own supply for Mexico's demands. Prehistoric turquoise mines dotted the Mimbres region (Santa Rita, Tyrone, White Signal), with one of the very largest in the Southwest, rivaling Cerrillos in size, at Old Hachita.[193] Mimbres towns produced turquoise beads and mosaics, both for their own use and presumably for their new trading partners.[194] Mimbres had what Mesoamerica wanted.

Chaco

What was the relationship between Chaco and Mesoamerica? That question has sparked hundreds of debates, many heated. Almost every consideration of this question moves from south to north, sometimes very specifically from Tula to Chaco.[195] Mesoamerica was the cause, and Chaco the effect.

That's a reasonable perspective, of course. Mesoamerica was enormously more developed than Chaco; it's easy to identify junior and senior partners. And southwestern turquoise, which Chaco had in impressive quantities, was of great interest to the civilizations of ancient Mexico.[196] Turquoise alone may have been sufficient cause for Mesoamerican meddling in the Southwest.

But perhaps motivation also moved from north to south. Chacoan and other southwestern leaders served their own interests, obtaining Mesoamerican objects and alliances to further their political agendas at home. Would-be kings needed all the gewgaws, gadgets, and symbolic alliances they could get. Mary Helms has eloquently essayed the problems of pop-up polities out beyond the edges of real civilizations. She says:

> Potential or hopeful local leaders may seek support from outside personages believed to be unusually powerful or may themselves seek to experience direct contact with the outside in order to derive exceptional powers by "walking in the wilderness" or by visiting distant lands and foreign sacred centers...leaders...have also taken great pride in the acquisition of sea shells, copper bells, and a wide range of curious relics and other material goods from places beyond their realms. Similarly, both great kings and lesser tribal leaders, who are often believed to be the most ardent keepers of conservative ancestral traditions, may in fact be the first to receive representatives of new foreign faiths and customs, to accept new charms and protective amulets, to adopt foreign modes of personal deportment, official dress and regalia, and to accept foreign advisors, or even new political ideologies and models of rule.[197]

Helms's model works well for Chaco.[198] Mesoamerican objects reached Chaco, or Chaco reached out for Mesoamerican objects, so the men who would be kings could impress their followers, cement local alliances, and legitimize their rule.[199]

Many Mexicos

Hohokam, Chaco, and Mimbres engaged Mesoamerica in intriguingly different ways. Emil Haury argued that Hohokam *was* essentially Mesoamerican, or rather West Mexican.[200] Major elements of the Hohokam Canon came from the south, whoever brought them to or used them in Arizona. Interconnections between southern Arizona and West Mexico were the rule, not the exception. Mesoamerican objects filled roles in social and political life that were well understood and expected. Hohokam domestic and monumental architecture referenced Mexico: courtyard groups re-created, in local idioms, the patio-focused domestic architecture of northern and western Mexico, and ball courts were ball courts. (Hohokam mounds may or may not represent local versions of Mesoamerican monuments; we will revisit that issue in chapter 6.) And of course there is a lot of West Mexican *stuff* from Hohokam sites: tons of shell always, mirrors early, bells later—but macaws almost never.

Chaco and Mimbres had some of the same stuff, but far less of the architecture. Chaco boasted platform mounds at Pueblo Bonito and a colonnade copy at Chetro Ketl. Mimbres, in the Late Pithouse Period, had something like Hohokam patio groups, which ultimately referenced Mesoamerican domestic architecture. But nothing about unit pueblos—Anasazi or Mimbres—looked the least bit Mexican.[201] Unit pueblos were notably *unlike* sunken patio groups in concept and detail.

In contrast to Hohokam, Chaco and Mimbres had fewer mirrors, more bells, and many macaws. Mimbres had been a part (however distant) of Hohokam's remarkable Colonial Period, but after 900, Mimbres went its own way, engaging the Chacoan north and—more importantly—forging new trade routes south to Aztatlan.

Great House leaders at Chaco wanted to be the equals of Hohokam elites, but they did not want to *look like* them. They wanted to be kings, like rulers in Mesoamerica. Perhaps that explains the different emphases on macaws, and feathers for regalia. Feathered objects were new symbols of power, referencing the great civilizations of the far south (and, pointedly, not the alarming Hohokam, who had no parrots or macaws). Just as Chacoans made mistakes with their colonnade (see fig. 5.1), they may not have used bells and macaws in precisely the same way as west or central Mexican elites, but Chaco elites used them in ways that worked for Anasazi society.[202] At Chaco, macaws signified power; they were confined to and controlled by Great Houses. In the Mimbres area, macaws were recruited into emerging beliefs that worked *against* political power: they appeared broadcast on everyday pots and rock art. Elites did not control Mimbres macaws, because there were no elites.

Chaco and Cahokia

In the eleventh century, there were two clear centers of political hierarchy north of Mexico: Chaco and Cahokia. Cahokia makes Chaco look puny. In every possible dimension, the Mississippian city outshone the Anasazi capital. And they had very different engagements with Mesoamerica.[203]

Cahokia, with its pyramid "mounds" and huge plazas, mirrored Mesoamerican ideas of the city—or perhaps vice versa. Whatever the deeper history, Cahokia, El Tajin, and Chichén Itzá were members of a circum-Gulf school of urban planning. As far as we know, there were no Mesoamerican objects at Cahokia—no bells, no mirrors, no macaws. Cahokia did not need them. The lords of Cahokia were not wannabe kings. They *were* kings, and they didn't need to prove anything. Unlike Chaco, Cahokia was heir to ancient traditions of monumental building. And unlike Chaco, Cahokia's symbols of power did not need to be borrowed or imported. The lords of Cahokia could employ objects and materials empowered by millennia of symbolism, understood over half a continent—metal, shell, exotic stones—and ancient images, motifs, and icons that could be bent to political purposes.

Cahokia was an equal to Mesoamerican societies. It was not first among equals by a long shot, but in fact Cahokia was larger than most Mesoamerican cities. Its lords did not require Mesoamerican baubles. The men who would be kings at Chaco, however, were making up kingship on the run. Chaco elites had to create and then sell their own brand of power. Their people were aware of kingship but not used to kings. They faced the same challenges as a medieval king—perhaps mythic, perhaps pythonic—when he rode past a peasant woman grubbing in her field:

KING: How-de-do, good lady. I am Arthur, King of the Britons.

PEASANT: Didn't know we had a king. I thought we were an autonomous collective.

Would Anasazi people have known a lord when they saw one? What should a king look like? The best references, the most compelling models, came from Mexico. The lords of the Great House were trying to be Mesoamerican kings, and they wanted to dress the part. They needed all the bells and feathers, smoke and mirrors they could get.

Figure 6.1. Pyramid Point, a Tonto Basin platform mound 90 kilometers east of Phoenix, Arizona. Artist's reconstruction by Ziba Ghassemi. Pyarmid Point was one of a half-dozen platform mounds and scores of other sites excavated by the Bureau of Reclamation's Lake Roosevelt project, a huge CRM endeavor in the late 1980s and early 1990s. Courtesy Center for Desert Archaeology.

s i x
Clime — *Ecology*
Archaeologies: 1975 to 1990
Histories: 1150 to 1300

Southwestern archaeology between 1975 and 1990 became big business: cultural resource management (CRM) transformed the field. In the last quarter of the twentieth century, CRM—archaeology for hire—far surpassed academic and museum archaeology as the primary producer of data and as the major employer of new BAs, MAs, and PhDs. Most of CRM's new recruits were trained as second-generation New Archaeologists. The government bureaucracies that oversaw CRM (staffed by shiny new MAs and PhDs) fixed aging New Archaeology as the new American standard: processual archaeology.

The immense scale of the large CRM projects embarrassed even the most ambitious academic research. The National Science Foundation-funded projects could not compete with a big coal mine or major reservoir. University field schools—once elite training—devolved into summer activities for undergrads, who could as easily (and perhaps more profitably) have spent their holidays at tennis camp.

CRM was only one thread in a larger skein of environmental laws. Natural history profited even more from environmental concerns than did archaeology. Not surprisingly, paleo-environmental studies advanced stride for stride with CRM. The lingering influences of ecologically based New Archaeology, coupled with finer- and finer-grained environmental data, ensured that adaptation decisively replaced culture history as the requisite framework for archaeological storytelling.

Tree rings über alles! Dendroclimatology—the science of "retro-dicting" rainfall from tree rings—came of age in the 1970s. It was wonderfully well suited to the events of 1125 to 1300, an era closed by the Great Drought of 1276 to 1299. (Hereafter, I use a nominal 1275 to 1300 for the Great Drought.) The Great Drought was a chestnut brought forward from the earliest days of tree-ring dating (chapter 4). Tree-ring science moved quickly beyond epochal great droughts and by the 1980s offered yearly and even monthly records of precipitation and stream flow back to the very beginnings of Hohokam and Anasazi. With increasing precision, archaeologists linked every Anasazi hiccup to minor rainier or drier periods, while fifty- and one-hundred-year floods—again, known through tree-ring studies—fixed key moments for Hohokam canal irrigation and history.

The events of 1150 to 1300 absolutely require big thinking—abandonments and retrenchments, migrations, rises and falls painted on broad canvases. In Mesoamerica, this period was the Middle Post-Classic—the end of Tula and consequent regional reorganization, marked by audacious long-distance trade and flamboyant political adventures. Southwestern history was no less dramatic. On the eastern Plateau, a new town at Aztec Ruins attempted to re-create Chaco's rule, moved north into the Mesa Verde region. On the western Plateau, volcanic fireworks inspired a rival political center at Wupatki. In the end, neither Aztec nor Wupatki worked. By 1300 tens of thousands of people had left the Plateau, both east and west. Hohokam entered its misnamed Classic Period, an accelerated decline from the Early Sedentary Period high-water mark (chapter 4). And far to the south in Chihuahua, the first stirrings of the Southwest's last great city: Paquimé.

Archaeologies: 1975 to 1990 (Americanist and CRM)

New Archaeology—at least in its most extreme logico-deductive-evolutionary-systems-paradigm form—sputtered out after about a decade, two academic generations. We no longer talked like that. But ferment did not cease. The revolution had become permanent and institutional. The best thing an aspiring new professional could do was name and claim a new theoretical approach in a quest for better science. Young Turks spun off New Archaeology and made careers from newer and newest archaeologies: behavioral, Darwinian, processual, and many others. From that thicket of competing ideas emerged a modified form of the older culture history, braced by the systematic thinking of New Archaeology and transformed particularly by New Archaeology's cross-cultural and ecological predilections (but shorn of its aggressive hyperscience).

The winner was not a new intellectual movement but a safe middle ground: *processual* archaeology.[1] We focused on ahistorical, cross-cultural *processes* set in the context of conventional culture history. We just couldn't part with culture history. The Southwest had too many good narrative elements—dramatic settings, colorful characters, and (above all) a plotline pegged by thousands of tree-ring dates! We could not avoid telling stories. Processes might be the adoption of agriculture, aggregation into villages, the emergence of complexity. If economy was X, population density was Y, and prior settlement patterns were Z, then pit houses would turn into kivas, or people would aggregate into villages, or complexity would emerge. Processes could and should be studied as repeatable, if ex post facto, experiments in the natural laboratory—processes were science. But natural laboratories had their own cultural and historical contexts. Process and history—the best of both worlds.

Two important legacies of New Archaeology, greatly amplified by processual archaeology, were (1) small-scale human ecology informed by (2) cross-cultural analyses. Ecology was in the air in the 1970s and 1980s—Earth Day and all that. More importantly, southwestern archaeology, with its demon child dendroclimatology, was primed for ecological analyses. Cross-cultural studies had a long, if uneven history in cultural anthropology, institutionalized in the Human Relations Area File (HRAF, founded in 1937). HRAF is a giant, indexed collection of ethnological facts, categorized and coded for comparative study. A fictitious example: in cross-cultural studies, most societies with round houses are matrilineal; therefore, round houses in ancient sites suggest matrilineality. That was cross-cultural theory building.[2]

The master narratives of cross-cultural prehistory came not from HRAF but from the political evolutionary schemes of Marshall Sahlins and Elman Service.[3] Their work first appeared in the 1960s but penetrated archaeology a decade later.[4] Sahlins and Service had done the cross-cultural work, and they gave us an atomic chart of political development, a regular progression of increasing political complexity from simple bands to larger tribes to more complex chiefdoms and finally to states—the way we live today. Archaeologists could plug their data into that chart and diagnose political development! Another fictitious example: ethnographic chiefdoms have a three-level hierarchy of settlement (one town, many villages, myriad farmsteads); therefore, a river valley with one big site, three medium sites, and twenty small sites was a chiefdom. Sahlins and Service gave us a cross-cultural language with which to compare one valley with the next and made communication possible between Mesopotamianists and Mississippianists. (The former had states; the latter had chiefdoms.) "Band-tribe-chiefdom-state"—a sequence called neo-evolutionism—became the litany of political prehistory and became archaeology's orthodoxy through the 1980s. It was "neo" because it marked a return to the evolutionary principles of Lewis Henry Morgan (chapter 2), which had fallen out of favor in anthropology. Unlike the work of Morgan, however, neo-evolutionary theory allowed states in the New World—but not north of Mexico![5]

CRM

Thanks to historic preservation and environmental laws passed in the late 1960s and early 1970s, CRM boomed in the 1980s. Not just more jobs, but bigger projects. Huge projects hired hundreds of archaeologists, surveyed or dug thousands of sites, recovered millions of artifacts—and cranked out millions of pages of technical reports. This work was the beginning of "gray literature," unpublished reports (many excellent) prepared not for general dissemination but as contract deliverables for the clients and agencies that paid the tab. There's no way to estimate accurately, so I'll guess: the number of gray literature pages since 1980 probably represents fifty times the total *publications* from nine or ten decades of southwestern archaeology before CRM. And I think that's a good guess. Since 1980 the vast majority of southwestern archaeology has been performed by large engineering companies with CRM divisions, medium-sized CRM corporations, or small mom-and-pop consulting firms.[6] University and museum research now represents only a small fraction of recent work.[7]

CRM completely transformed Hohokam archaeology. It was hard to get professors and students interested in Hohokam—way too hot for summer field schools. But neither rain nor sleet nor 120 degrees in the shade could stay CRM from its contractual obligations and fieldwork. Sunbelt cities built roads and pumped water through canals. Freeways and the Central Arizona Project (a huge canal, running uphill from the Colorado River to Phoenix and Tucson) produced tons of CRM data and thousands of new dates. There was so much new data that the lead federal agency, the Bureau of Reclamation, held a conference in 1988 to take stock of Hohokam,[8] as well as another in 1995 to synthesize Salado.[9] *Salado* was the problematic term for Late Classic Period Hohokam archaeology in an upland reservoir of the Salt River, where CRM teams excavated almost as many platform mound sites in a few short years as Hohokam archaeologists had managed to do in the preceding century. (We will meet Salado again, below and in chapter 7.)

CRM work generally was (and is) excellent archaeology. But CRM itself is essentially an environmental check-off: before construction of a highway or reservoir can proceed, the agency in charge must account for endangered species, soil and slope, wetlands, ownership and rights-of-way, construction codes, and—thankfully no longer an afterthought—archaeology. Government agencies that had never before heard of archaeology added archaeologists to their staffs, a few in positions of authority.[10] And—here's where it gets interesting—in the Southwest, the people who filled those agency jobs and who developed policies for CRM had been weaned on Binford and *Archaeology: An Explicitly Scientific Approach*.[11] They were trained in New Archaeology. Long after academic archaeology (fickle in its faith) moved away from hypothetico-deduction and "test expectations," CRM research designs remained rife with scientific phraseology. Federal regulations are hard to write and harder to change. Policies developed in the late 1970s have been much amended, but the intellectual roots are still recognizable. The systematic ethos of New Archaeology suited CRM as a business: explicit hypotheses and test expectations lent themselves to rational budgeting and realistic work plans. That hasn't changed. Construction companies won't pay for postmodern noodling (chapter 7).

Agency officials and CRM professionals negotiated a brand of research that revitalized southwestern archaeology with an infusion of big money, tagged with accountability. And that was new. Academic field schools might never be published, with no penalties for the professor, but tank a contract and you landed in court. CRM meant that some small part of the Southwest was being bulldozed, dammed, leveled, or otherwise molested, and of course that wasn't great for the landscape. But, in my opinion, CRM has been wonderful for southwestern archaeology. Many of the key links and most of the data behind this book come from CRM.

One thing that didn't change, immediately, was the relatively small scale of archaeological thinking. Even the largest CRM projects were always strictly limited in area: a highway right-of-way, a reservoir take line, a well pad, a strip mine. Some projects, such as Black Mesa, Dolores, and the Central Arizona Project, *seemed* large, covering large areas and costing millions of dollars. But to understand the history of the ancient Southwest, they were still too small—as was, of course, most academic research. Normal life expectancies and average NSF budgets don't lend themselves to truly regional research.

We are choking on our own data. How can one person *actually use* all those excellent CRM projects and NSF projects and field schools (and their warehouses of artifacts and data) to build a big picture? I have no idea; after three decades of Big CRM, it probably can't be done by one person. Big pictures still come from armchair synthesis, necessarily selective and idiosyncratic (like this book), or from collaborations of many scholars and projects (a few of which I highlight in this and the following chapter).

The sheer mass of CRM data drives us to specialize in smaller and smaller areas. Indeed, the administrative and regulatory structures of CRM often fragmented knowledge along jurisdictional lines. Much CRM work was on federal lands, which constitute a remarkably high proportion of the Southwest. Arizona, for example, is 70 percent federal, including Indian lands. Thus seven-tenths of Arizona is administered by half a dozen federal and state agencies, each with its own policies and staff archaeologists, and by a number of politically astute tribes—each of course with its own agenda.

Agencies and tribes are jealous of their jurisdictions. For example, New Mexico has four national forests, each surprisingly independent under a distant regional administration. And each forest is subdivided into a number of districts, each with its own headquarters and—potentially—its own archaeologists. CRM decision making is, shall we say, broadly distributed. Other vast tracts are administered by the Bureau of Land Management, with a similar substructure of districts, smaller resource areas, and so forth. CRM planning in the 1980s was often done on the scale of a district, a forest, a resource area. And archaeological thinking was often constrained, contractually, to those same small scales.[12]

Misfits between agency administrative units and actual prehistory were obvious. A remedy rose at the state level: by law, each state had a Historic Preservation Officer to coordinate CRM within that state. State historic preservation programs commissioned overviews and studies that overarched boundaries between various federal agencies and boundaries between federal and nonfederal lands—within each separate state. New Mexico was a leader in that effort, producing a remarkable archaeological synthesis and "state plan" in 1981.[13] Other Four Corners states followed suit, with statewide, thematic, or subregional documents, many excellent.[14]

Still, the ancient Southwest would not be confined to state lines. The Chaco world, delimited in surveys during the 1980s,[15] spread outward from the canyon and soon crossed state boundaries, to the consternation of archaeologists in Arizona, Colorado, and Utah. It was not unusual to hear indignant objections to Chaco in Utah, or in northeastern Arizona, or at Mesa Verde. Territorial resistance was eventually beaten down by cold, hard data: Chaco really was *that big*. Today an official Chaco "Interagency Management Group" crosses state lines and agency jurisdictions. Hohokam ball courts were almost entirely contained within southern Arizona.[16] They stretched far across those wide open spaces and through no fault of their own ended up on a crazy quilt of land jurisdictions and ownerships. Paquimé—as presented by Di Peso (1974)—crashed the international boundary. And, to anticipate chapter 7, NAGPRA—the Native American Graves Protection and Repatriation Act of 1990—ignores political divisions (save tribal and national ones) altogether. The law recognizes a fact long known to Native Americans: state lines, agency boundaries, reservation borders, academic research domains, and other administrative subdivisions had no relevance in the past. NAGPRA profoundly changed archaeological thinking, in ways we shall see in the next chapter.

Anasazi Cyber-Ecology

Two iconic documents demonstrate the dominance of ecology (and the tension between large and small scales) during the late 1970s and 1980s. These are Linda Cordell and Fred Plog's "Escaping the Confines of Normative Thought" (1979) and George Gumerman's edited volume *The Anasazi in a Changing Environment* (1988).

"Escaping the Confines" was written partly in reaction to the authors' involvement with government-sponsored CRM regional syntheses.[17] Cordell and Plog urged us to snap the chains of the Pecos Classification and to appreciate the diverse and profoundly *local* chronologies and archaeologies that made up the Southwest: "It is only through an understanding of the nature of this diversity that we will ever come to comprehend the prehistory of the area. A prehistory based on generalizations that are also inherently oversimplifications tests the boundary between science and fiction." Our grain should be small, and our story the sum of many parts—kind of like a sandpainting. The key themes should be those strategies employed by societies "for coping with the changing environments in which they find themselves," both social and natural. Since the environment provided the independent variables for social histories, ecology (as reflected in subsistence economies) should be the primary concern of southwestern archaeology: "Prehistory is best understood through a focus on the efforts of local groups to sustain themselves."[18] "Escaping the Confines" was an important essay, required reading for archaeologists of that era. It set the tone for processual archaeology in the Southwest.

Dendroclimatology underwrote the second iconic work, *Anasazi in a Changing Environment*, a carefully structured collection of demographic, environmental, and ecological reconstructions for the Plateau. The volume realized the dream of SARG (chapter 5), the consortium of archaeologists who, in the early 1970s, pooled their natural laboratories to answer this question: Why were sites located where they were?[19] *The Anasazi in a Changing Environment* presented "a model of Anasazi behavioral adaptation"[20] that linked environmental (mainly climatic) change to demographic shifts through ecological models, and thence to behaviors such as colonization, mobility, abandonment, migration, subsistence mix, intensification, storage, "alliances," and so forth.[21] *The Anasazi in a Changing Environment* was a strong effort, a shining example of the potential of research consortia, realized.

I refer—fondly, admiringly—to southwestern archaeology's pervasive reliance on dendroclimatology as the "fungus model": sprinkle the right amount of moisture on the right kind of soil and up pops a pueblo. Dry it out and the pueblo vanishes. Fungus models were based on multiple indices (pollen, hydrology, and geomorphology, in addition to dendroclimatology), but tree rings ruled. The precision of dendrochronology far exceeded that of any other environmental measure. Indeed, the incredible resolution of tree-ring data was far finer than the best chronologies and phase sequences we could devise for archaeology itself. That posed problems, as we shall see.

Everybody wanted dendroclimate—even in the desert. Oddly enough, vagaries of rainfall were less important in the desert Hohokam and Mimbres Mogollon areas because in the desert, there was *never* enough rainfall. Irrigation drove those ancient societies; rainfall and snowfall, in mountain headwaters far upstream, drove irrigation. Too much rain in the mountains might prove worse than too little rain in the valleys: flooding rivers destroyed canals. Dendroclimatology could do canals too! Rings from trees in the river's upland watershed produced precise schedules of flooding and indices of their magnitude.[22] Magnitude mattered: damage from small floods could be repaired, but a real stem-winder destroyed whole canal systems (for example, mid-fourteenth-century Hohokam; chapter 7). Thanks to tree rings (and a lot of hard analysis), we know the exact years when floods of biblical proportions scoured the Salt and Gila rivers. We now arrange Hohokam prehistory around those disasters, just as droughts frame Anasazi prehistory. If the changing environment of the Anasazi leads us to fungus models, we could call Hohokam's floods a "flushing model"—flushing out canal systems and sending Hohokam right down the toilet. Again, I use *flushing* with the deepest respect and admiration.

Dendroclimatology (droughts) and dendrohydrology (floods) are amazing tools and the envy of archaeologists everywhere. The Southwest is a desert—a bedrock, undeniable fact. Rainfall and stream flows are critical. As the title of a classic southwestern book said, the sky determines. Fungus models and flushing models explain a great deal of what happened in prehistory—*but not all*. Unexplained residuals and exceptions are often matters of singular interest.

Dendroclimatic data lend themselves to quantification: we have exact dates for climatic events. If we can approximate population numbers by half century (better yet, by decade), the rest, as they say, is history. Or, more accurately, the rest is correlation. The urge to quantify is particularly strong on the Plateau, where easy visibility lends itself to counting sites and rooms and converting those counts into numbers of people. Two current computationally high-powered projects—the Artificial Anasazi Project and the Villages Project—are modeling the lives and hard times of the ancient Plateau peoples. (I discuss them in this chapter because their roots lie in the 1980s.) The Artificial Anasazi Project is the heir apparent of SARG and *The Anasazi in a Changing Environment*: agent-based modeling of the Long House Valley of Arizona from 200 to 1300, undertaken by several SARG alumni and the Santa Fe Institute.[23] The Villages Project, a collaboration of Washington State University and the Crow Canyon Archaeological Center, focuses on the northern San Juan or Mesa Verde region.[24] A recent joint summary in *Scientific American* reviewed the successes and failures of high-resolution environmental modeling.[25] Both projects mirrored actual settlement patterns from 800 to 1250 with admirable accuracy. Problems rose, however, with the abandonments of the regions, in both cases after 1250. There were unexplained exceptions, misfits between the models and reality.

Those misfits were not minor. Neither model predicted complete abandonment. Yet it happened. That's perplexing. In the *Scientific American* summary of the Long House Valley model, Kohler, Gumerman, and Reynolds write, "We can only conclude that sociopolitical, ideological or environmental factors *not* included in our model must have contributed to the total depopulation of the valley." Similar conundrums beset the Villages Project: "None of our simulations terminated with a population decline as dramatic as what actually happened in the Mesa Verde region in the late 1200s."[26] These cyber-Anasazi projects (and earlier, trend-setting models by Carla Van West, 1994) indicate that, even during the Great Drought, the region could have supported substantial populations—up to half the peak population of the mid-1200s. Moreover, from archaeological data, it appears that abandonment began long before the Great Drought; people were leaving in large numbers in the early to mid-1200s, when the climate was relatively clement. Pueblos were not fungi.

Flushing fares no better. Canal-busting floods unquestionably were key historical events. As we shall see, epochal floods clearly punctuated Hohokam, just as the Great Drought ended Anasazi. But, as discussed in chapter 5, Sedentary Hohokam began to fall apart as early as 1050, during an era (950–1150) of "optimal conditions for irrigation agriculture in the Salt River valley" (but not so good along the smaller Gila River).[27] Climate completed changes that were already well under way.

Why then *did* the Anasazi leave the Four Corners? Thousands of little cyber-agents make up their minds based on environmental and behavior rules; ancient people thought otherwise. A problem with agent-based cyber-Anasazi is that history accumulates from the bottom up. One thing missing (by design) from bottom-up agent-based models is top-down dynamics: regional economies and pesky governments. Working stiffs have agency, but so do kings.[28]

Bigger, Better Scales

It was clear by 1980 that many archaeological problems—Great Houses, ball courts, Paquimé, and others—required larger scales than those to which we were accustomed. Steadman Upham's *Polities and Power* (1982) was a landmark book of early processual archaeology, on the right scale: Pueblo IV, taken entire, Hopi to the Rio Grande. Upham analyzed every major late Pueblo site.[29] You could do that with Pueblo IV: there weren't too many big Pueblo IV sites. We really could think big with data!

Chaco "outlier hunts" produced a comparable "big site" atlas for Pueblo II, with about two hundred outliers (chapter 5). Pueblo III was next. A conference at Crow Canyon Archaeological Center in 1990 produced a synthetic volume and database of big sites (more than fifty rooms) of that period[30]—and revealed some surprising large-scale patterns (below). The Pueblo III effort inspired a return to Pueblo IV, and a parallel volume recently appeared, with equally provocative results (chapter 7).[31]

Big thinking was not confined to the Pueblo region. As noted above, the Bureau of Reclamation sponsored a 1988 conference to pull together the flood of new Hohokam CRM data.[32] Carefully structured edited volumes looked at even larger scales. *Chaco and Hohokam* (Crown and Judge 1991) compared those two regions; *Dynamics of Southwest Prehistory* (Cordell and Gumerman 1989) took on the whole Southwest, region by region; and, more recently (slightly out of this chapter's time frame), *Great Towns and Regional Polities* (Neitzel 1999) compared the entire Southwest and the entire Southeast. At the largest scale, a flurry of books and articles reevaluated the Southwest's continental connections to Mesoamerica, spurred by Charles Di Peso's *Casas Grandes* (1974).[33]

The logical next step was to systematize the data over time across the whole Southwest, in a real atlas of southwestern prehistory. SARG provided a successful model for research consortia, and variations were played on that theme. But it's surprisingly hard to compare multiple projects, the work of multiple researchers. Currently, an alliance of the Center for Desert Archaeology, the Museum of Northern Arizona, and Geo-Map, Inc., is working on a project called Coalescent Communities, building GIS data of all sites with more than thirteen(!) rooms from 1200 to 1700 from all regions of the Southwest: Anasazi, Mogollon, and Hohokam.[34] Those data are massaged and manipulated in various ways to produce detailed, time-series population estimates and maps. The Coalescent Communities database includes more than three thousand sites.[35]

Histories: 1150 to 1300
(Pueblo III, Early Classic, Animas–Black Mountain)

The year 1150 (give or take a decade) was a rough one for North America. Tula fell; Cahokia and Chaco crashed; and Hohokam fell apart, gluing itself back together in the problematic Classic Period (fig. 6.2).

Middle Post-Classic and Post-Middle Mississippian

By 1150 Tula was gone. Tula's collapse may have been a minor local disturbance or a shattering continental cataclysm, depending on whom you ask.[36] Other major Early Post-Classic centers also declined around 1150, most notably Tula's "twin," Chichén Itzá, and El Tajín in the Huastec area.[37] Each had been the premier city of its region. Perhaps their simultaneous implosions were just another curious archaeological coincidence, but I doubt it. Cholula remained constant,[38] and it may have been of some consequence to the Southwest: the great city was the central Mexican terminus of the Aztatlan trade network, which presumably reached north into the Southwest.[39]

Southwestern connections with Mexico intensified or (perhaps) democratized after 1150/1200. There was no lack of Mesoamerican objects and ideas before 1150, concentrated at key sites. After 1150 the floodgates opened.[40] Everybody had a parrot or a copper bell, or so it seems. Surely, things changed within the Southwest (below), but it also seems likely that

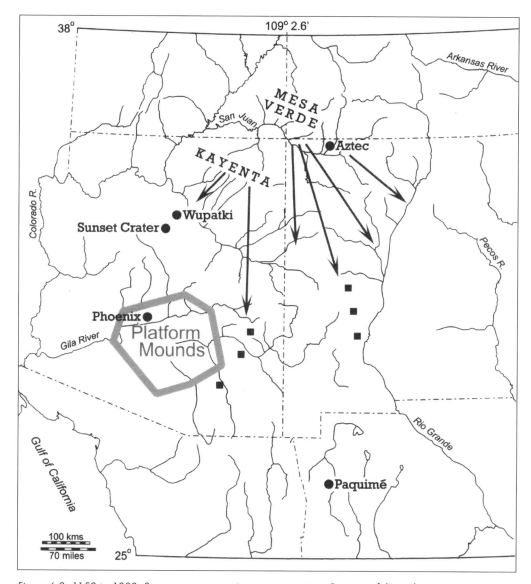

Figure 6.2. 1150 to 1300. Squares represent migrant communities. Courtesy of the author.

the long-distance proclivities of the Early Post-Classic were jacked up another notch in the Middle Post-Classic. There were probably more Mesoamerican things to be had, from more distributors.

Tula and the Early Post-Classic were obscured by later Native mythologies—was Tula the fabulous city of Tollan or just another tin-pot polity? Mesoamerica comes into clearer focus after Tula's fall, with the Middle Post-Classic.[41] A view of the world that found its most dramatic (or at least best-known) expression in the Aztec Empire developed. Michael Smith and Frances Berdan, in a recent summary,[42] characterized the later Post-Classic as an era marked by

1. *Population growth* over much of Mesoamerica
2. *Proliferation of small polities*
3. *Increased quantity and diversity of long-distance exchange*, including "the conversion of former prestige goods into commercial luxury goods"
4. *Commercialization of the economy*, "based in marketplaces"
5. *New forms of writing and iconography* that replaced phonetic writing systems, tied to particular languages, with more universal symbol systems, for example, the Mixteca-Puebla style
6. *New patterns of stylistic interaction*: "the Postclassic international symbol set" largely congruent with Mixteca-Puebla

To their list I would add (7) *Heightened militarism*. The militaristic Post-Classic was once contrasted to the peaceful, philosophical Classic, but the once-halcyon Classic has now been recast as bellicose.[43] This new and presumably more accurate reading of the Classic should not blind us to the wars of the Post-Classic, an age of battles and strife.

I list these characteristics here because *that was the Southwest's world*. When we ponder Mesa Verde or Pueblo Grande, the Post-Classic should be our frame of reference, because it was *their* frame of reference. We may think of Hopi and O'odham and modern descendants, but people at Mesa Verde and Pueblo Grande knew nothing about those future societies. Ancient people didn't think about Hopi and O'odham; they thought about the Post-Classic—that was their reality.

Across the continent, Cahokia began a precipitous decline between 1150 and 1200.[44] That was the beginning of the end of what archaeologists call the Middle Mississippian—the primacy of the American Bottom metroplex. Small numbers continued to occupy (or at least to use) the city, but by 1300 Cahokia was empty and derelict. Cahokia was gone and, remarkably, all but forgotten by Native peoples.[45]

Moundville, 650 kilometers to the southeast in Alabama, took Cahokia's place atop the (size) hierarchy of Mississippian cities and towns.[46] Moundville was by far the largest Mississippian site of its age (the span covered in this chapter), but still it was less than a quarter the size of Cahokia. Moundville was Cahokia diminished. There is little evidence of a Moundville region comparable to Cahokia's. Moundville's region was tucked tight around the Black Warrior River.

Moundville, and the many smaller chiefdoms that followed (chapter 7), surpassed Cahokia only in art—in the eye of this beholder. An astonishing generation of ideologically charged art in many media, termed the Southeast Ceremonial Complex (SCC), began at Cahokia but truly flowered in the centuries that followed.[47] I am not alone in my admiration for SCC, one of the most important artistic traditions of ancient Native America.[48] The remarkable dynamism of SCC art recalls the equally remarkable murals of Pueblo IV (chapter 7)—both were nearly complete breaks from the stiff, sketchy, geometric imagery of preceding traditions.

Comparisons to Chaco and Aztec Ruins (below) are irresistible and provocative.[49] Cahokia = Chaco; Moundville = Aztec; and the Southeast Ceremonial Complex = Pueblo IV art (of which, more in chapter 7)—except, of course, that the Mississippian sites eclipsed the junior partners in the Southwest. Still, the geopolitical shifts were parallel: social energy moved from Chaco and Aztec southeast into the Rio Grande and from Cahokia similarly southeast to Moundville and the later Southeaastern chiefdoms. And there were parallel after-

Figure 6.3. Aztec West model, Aztec Ruins National Monument, New Mexico. Courtesy National Park Service.

maths: when they imploded, Chaco/Aztec and Cahokia both left smoking craters. The "abandonment of the Four Corners" and the "Vacant Quarter" on the Mississippi and Ohio are historical chestnuts. The vast depopulated middle Mississippi, which so perplexed French and Spanish explorers, was the counterpart to the Mystery of the Anasazi: where did *they* go? History? Process? Both?

Mississippian after Cahokia presented many (but not all) of the characteristics of the Late Post-Classic: the proliferation of smaller and smaller polities, increased long-distance exchange, and new iconography and stylistic interactions—the SCC. And heightened militarism. Post-Middle Mississippian warfare reached levels previously unknown in the Southeast.[50] There was no writing, of course, and no commercial economy (at least, so far recognized). Demography remains problematic. Population boomed in the Mesoamerican Post-Classic. Southeastern population fell dramatically in the Protohistoric, much as in the Southwest (chapter 7).

Anasazi: Chaco to Aztec

After 1125 the Anasazi center of gravity and gravitas shifted north, from Chaco Canyon to Aztec Ruins (hereafter Aztec) (fig. 6.3). That move was commemorated with a remarkable earthen monument, the Great North Road, connecting the two sequential capitals.[51] Chaco was never a very powerful capital—compared with, say, Tenochtitlán, Moscow, or Sacramento. Aztec was even weaker. But both Chaco and Aztec *were capitals*.

North!

Chaco ended about 1125 and rose again 60 kilometers due north at Aztec, where major construction began about 1110. That was the final outcome, but there might have been a false start or two. Aztec was preceded by almost two decades by Salmon Ruins on the banks of the San Juan River. Salmon Ruins may have been the first choice for a second capital, and Aztec an alternative site after Salmon Ruins proved a bad choice.

To mark the spot, a four-room unit, now encased in Salmon Ruins' east wing, was built as early as 1068.[52] About 1090 major construction began on the actual Great House, a building the size and shape of Hungo Pavi back at Chaco Canyon.[53] The timing is important: Chaco's shift to the north began four decades *before* an 1130–1180 drought, often blamed for Chaco's demise. And after the initial four-room unit, there was nothing tentative about the move. Salmon Ruins was as large as the largest individual construction events at Chaco Canyon. This was not a casual experiment, knocking together a hut or plunking down a Tuff Shed.

Salmon Ruins was a big investment, but it didn't work out. The San Juan River—a real river, not a southwestern river-by-courtesy—must have seemed inviting after centuries of coping with the trickle of Chaco Wash. But the San Juan River floods, unpredictably, on magnitudes far beyond the abilities of Chaco engineers (or even Hohokam perhaps) to tame. After a few years—perhaps less than a decade—the error was obvious. Plan B: the Great North Road line was extended north from Salmon to a stream of more appropriate size, the Animas River. That was the place; construction started on Aztec Ruins about 1110.

Strangely, Aztec Ruins—the largest, most interesting Pueblo III site—was due north of Chaco—the largest, most interesting Pueblo II site—which itself was, curiously, due south of Blue Mesa–Ridges Basin—the largest, most interesting Pueblo I site—which itself was, oddly, due north of Shabik'eschee and 29 SJ 423—the largest, most interesting Basketmaker III sites.[54] Surely, a coincidence.

The New Chaco?

Aztec Ruins began about 1100 with a small block of four to eight rooms, much like the initial core of Salmon Ruins. Very shortly thereafter, construction began in earnest. In less than twenty years—probably no more than a decade—the large West Ruin was effectively finished. That was a big job. The West Ruin at Aztec was comparable to the very largest Chaco Canyon Great Houses, which took centuries to complete.

If Aztec was built in a decade, that's saying something: the people in charge at Aztec organized labor on unprecedented scales. Aztec was not the last gasp of a disintegrating society, Chaco on the skids. Aztec West was *huge*—the biggest single thing ever built in the Chacoan tradition. Aztec out-Chacoed Chaco. The guys who started Pueblo Bonito, back in 850, would have been deeply impressed, or perhaps appalled.

After that, you'd think they'd rest on their laurels, or better still, on their derrieres. But massive new construction began almost immediately (as early as the 1120s), on the equally large East Ruin (fig. 6.4).[55] Construction on the East Ruin continued through the late thirteenth century, more like the incremental construction of Chaco-era Great Houses. We know less about the construction dates of the other Aztec Great Houses (there are several more).[56] Three tri-wall structures defined the Aztec Ruins cityscape, with tri-walls pinning the key points in the layout (fig. 6.4; see also fig. 6.7).[57] At Aztec Ruins National Monument, the big

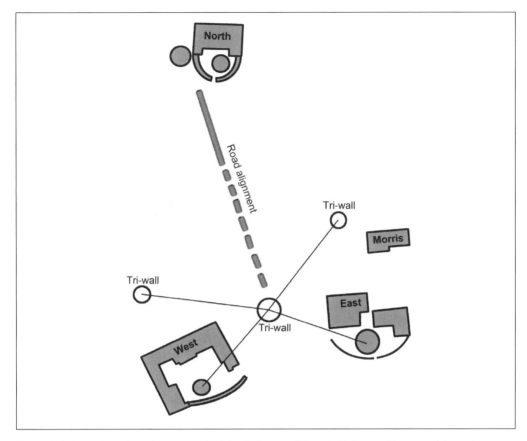

Figure 6.4. Aztec Ruins based on a map by John R. Stein and Peter J. McKenna. Courtesy of the author.

West Ruin is the focus, and the tri-walls a sideshow. But that may invert the importance of these buildings. Tri-wall (and bi-wall) structures were the defining points of Aztec's city plan. The central tri-wall, the pivot of Aztec's geometries, was the largest ever built (Mound F). Bi- and tri-wall structures were Aztec's particular contribution to Anasazi architecture and a key to understanding Aztec's political region (of which, more below).

Chaco Canyon had a deep history, perhaps going back to Basketmaker III (chapter 3). Aztec was a new town, planned from the beginning as a monumental city. Aztec was a new take on the old idea. Aztec's site, of course, was profoundly cardinal: at the north end of the North Road. But its urban plan was unquestionably solstitial.

Weather, Religion, and Politics

I greatly admire the science and precision of dendroclimatology—despite my fungus and flushing jokes. But in this book I honor it mainly in the breach—what changes, what actions, what events does climate *not* explain? Voltaire once pondered the differences among New World civilizations. Climate, he concluded, was important but not compelling: "The climate has some power, the government a hundred times more, and religion joined to government still more."[58] *D' accord.*

Chaco got drier around 1080, but the drought had surprisingly little effect on building

Figure 6.5. *Sacred Eruption by Michael Kabotie (Hopi). Permanent installation at Sunset Crater National Monument, Flagstaff. Copyright © 2004 by Michael Kabotie; courtesy Michael Kabotie.*

projects in the canyon and around the region. After a short dip, construction surged, including (most importantly) Salmon Ruins. The weather got good (that is, wet) about 1100, and things were decidedly damp for the next three decades. But after an initial burst of very large scale building in the early 1100s, construction at Chaco Canyon declined sharply and ceased entirely by 1125—that is, *just before* the nasty drought of 1130–1180. The weather was still good when the really big decisions were made—to move north. And when they got there, they made a decision and took a step curiously untaken by most Anasazi: they dug canals.[59] Perhaps canals had failed on the San Juan River at Salmon Ruins. The San Juan was too big and unruly. The Animas River was smaller and far more manageable—about the size of the Mimbres River. And it might well have been Mimbres canals that Aztec's rulers copied. They did not want their capital held hostage by inconstant rainfall, so they turned the river to their will. Climate had power, but religion joined to government had still more.

The biggest—or at least the most spectacular—challenge faced by Chaco and Aztec was not drought but a bedrock change in the land itself. A volcano erupted near the San Francisco Peaks. This was noticed; things happened.

Under the Volcano

Sunset Crater (figs. 6.2, 6.5) erupted sometime between 1050 and 1100.[60] It wasn't a big volcano—not as deep as Vesuvius or as wide as Krakatoa—but 'twas enough, 'twill serve. It was the first eruption in the Southwest in more than a thousand years. Its plume of ash, smoke, and continual lightning—the mother of all thunderstorms—was seen in Phoenix and may have been visible from high points at Chaco Canyon. Everybody knew everything—but

Figure 6.6. Macaws of Wupatki by Jim Thomas. Wupatki had remarkable quantities of exotic objects and tropical birds. Courtesy Jim Thomas (http://JHThomas.imagekind.com).

in this case, even the most reclusive anchorite was glued to the tube. Sunset Crater was a fiery marvel.[61]

The eruption attracted attention and gathered in a remarkable array of esoteric architecture. The buildings rose, sometime after 1125, a safe distance from the smoking mountain's base at Wupatki (fig. 6.6). (The eruption may have ended, but who could predict the mountain's next move?) Wupatki had a ball court, a Great Kiva, and something mighty like a Great House. Ball courts were not new to the area; courts were in use around the flanks of the San Francisco Peaks as early as the Colonial Period (part of the Colonial explosion, chapter 4). What was exceptional was a new court—a very large masonry ball court—built at a time when courts were going out of use in the Hohokam heartland (chapter 5). (There were only one or two other masonry ball courts, and one was at another edge of the Hohokam world, at Gila Bend.)[62] The new elements in Wupatki's mix were Chacoan: the Great Kiva and Great House. Even at Chaco's most expansive, the regional system went no farther west than Hopi. Wupatki—70 kilometers beyond Hopi—was more than 300 kilometers from both Chaco Canyon and Aztec Ruins.

The volcano blew right about the time Chaco ended. Wupatki was contemporary with Aztec Ruins. Construction at the Great House began about 1145—as soon as it was safe to build?—with a four-room block, much like the initial constructions at Salmon and Aztec. The initial room block was built with "carefully selected sandstone slabs, chinked with sandstone pieces, in what many have referred to as a Chaco style."[63] Major construction continued through the 1190s, with additional building until 1215.[64] I think Wupatki rose as a rival to the twelfth-century centers of the northern San Juan—and especially to Aztec Ruins.[65]

If Aztec out-Chacoed Chaco in monumental construction, Wupatki seriously out-blinged Aztec. Wupatki was loaded with wonderful and exotic things: more than forty macaws, nine bells, and remarkable regalia ("jewelry").[66] Aztec had little. Wupatki's West Mexican goods probably came through Hohokam—recall its ball court, one of the last in use anywhere. In Mesoamerica, trade often followed the flag. Something like that may have characterized commerce among the Late Sedentary and Early Classic Hohokam. Perhaps Wupatki had to "buy in" before they could buy, period. A big, stone ball court: build it and they will come.

Voting with Their Feet

Wupatki moved *toward* the Hohokam, at least obliquely. Ties between western Anasazi and Hohokam were deep: Uto-Aztecan languages and—in the distant past—western Basket-maker origins in the south (chapter 2).

Aztec moved *away* from Hohokam—I think, deliberately. The shift from Chaco to Aztec marked a political retreat deeper into unreconstructed eastern Anasazi territory, up into the Mesa Verde and northern San Juan areas. In a sense, Aztec was a return: five centuries earlier, the Rio Animas had been the setting of the largest of all Pueblo I sites, Blue Mesa–Ridges Basin. Like Blue Mesa–Ridges Basin, Aztec was pretty much at the northeastern edge of the Anasazi world—about as far away from Phoenix as one could decently go (see fig. 6.2). Aztec took itself out of the game.

Whatever Chaco was, Mesoamerican objects and tropical birds figured prominently in its pomp and circumstance. With the demise of Mimbres and beginnings of Casas Grandes (below), no royal road connected the San Juan and the south. Aztec could no longer deliver what Chaco promised. Where were the prestige goods that underwrote the Chacoan regional system, feathers sent out to the fringes? Gone but not forgotten: instead of macaws, Aztec's Anasazi contented themselves with hundreds of images of the birds on pottery, rock art, and kiva murals. Trade ceramics and exotics dropped almost to zero.[67] Only three macaws were found at Aztec,[68] and a few copper objects. If exotics were the political tokens marking and linking Chaco's region, Aztec could offer only IOUs.

What was Aztec's region? Indeed, was there an "Aztec region"?[69] I think there was (albeit smaller than Chaco's); others do not.[70] It might be possible to map Aztec's region with Mesa Verde black-on-white, the predominant pottery at Aztec Ruins, but ceramics had little to do with Chaco's region, either in operation or in archaeological definition. I look instead to the novel architectural features clearly associated with Aztec: bi- and tri-walled structures (fig. 6.7).

Bi- and tri-walled structures were built at many (but far from all) communities within the northern San Juan and along both flanks of the Chuskas,[71] but most were found in south-western Colorado, around Mesa Verde National Park and west to the Utah state line. That distribution, I think, maps Aztec's region, less than a fifth the size of Chaco's. Mesa Verde and the Great Sage Plains—setting of the very largest Mesa Verde sites, such as Yellow Jacket—stood perhaps in the same relation to Aztec as earlier the Chuska Valley had to Chaco: a western breadbasket and population center. It worked for Chaco: Chuska pottery, high-end lithics, construction timbers, and corn flowed into the canyon. But it is not entirely clear that the rulers of Aztec Ruins convinced Great Sage Plainers to play that role.

We don't really know what bi- and tri-walls were.[72] Some say ritual; others think they were the homes of politically or economically important families; still others suggest that tri-walls were solid-fill structures, wedding-cake-like ziggurats.[73] Current consensus seems to be that bi- and tri-walls were ritual, political, and domestic—the homes of very important people ("key people or segments of the village," according to Donna Glowacki).[74] Great Houses were still elite houses, but the uppermost crust moved to tri-walls to differentiate themselves from mere nobles. The upper strata of post-Chaco society were getting top-heavy.

Many Chaco-era Great Houses (for example, Lowry and Bluff) continued to be used and

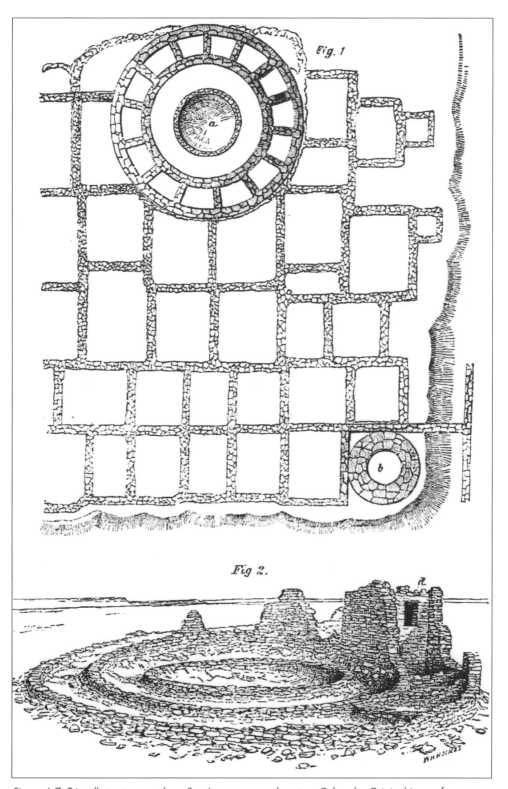

Figure 6.7. Tri-wall structure, northern San Juan area, southwestern Colorado. Original image from W. H. Holmes, Report of the Ancient Ruins of Southwestern Colorado (1878). In the public domain.

even expanded through the post-Chaco twelfth and early thirteenth centuries. Several new ones were built.[75] During Chaco's times, distance separated the Great House and unit pueblos. In the thirteen century, unit pueblos lapped the very foundations of Great Houses: many "latter-day great houses [were] embedded in a residential roomblock."[76] Commoners crowded around the palace. Proximity bred familiarity and ultimately perhaps contempt; a palace embedded in room blocks is far less formidable than a palace alone on a hill—the Chaco tradition. Aztec failed to maintain Chaco's solemnity and grandeur. Perhaps the move from distant Chaco to Aztec, closer to the people, had been a mistake.

Aztec started strong but faded fast. The bustle and excitement of building a new city maintained, convincingly, the aura of Chaco—monumental construction was that canyon's constant. By accident or hard work, the Pax Chaco was prolonged through the twelfth century. Aztec-era settlements initially continued the open, dispersed homesteads of Chaco's times—people had nothing to fear. But a fifty-year drought from 1130 to 1180 showed that at least two generations of Aztec leaders failed in their jobs. Dissent and unrest stirred the countryside. I infer this because late in the twelfth century, there were unmistakable signs of repression. A landscape of peace was marred by instances of almost unspeakable violence. I believe these violent acts—few in number, concentrated in fury—came out of Aztec: an iron fist but an admission of failure. Things were going badly.[77]

Archaeology reveals about two-score mass executions of families or small settlements, with great brutality and even desecratory cannibalism.[78] These violent events may well have emanated, at first, from Chaco in its final days,[79] but most date to Aztec's time.[80] I believe that these executions were official sanctions, attempting to enforce a failing political system.[81] In any case, violence spread and social order disintegrated: village attacked village.[82] The scattered farmsteads and hamlets of Chaco's golden days were abandoned. Farmers "circled the wagons" and aggregated into big, defensive towns on the Great Sage Plains. Others built havens high in sheltered alcoves, the cliff dwellings of Mesa Verde.

Many of the towns formed by panicked villagers quickly reached impressive sizes. In the Great Sage Plain, Yellow Jacket was the largest, with twelve hundred rooms, twenty towers, and two hundred kivas (fig. 6.8).[83] Its size alone was sufficient defense. Smaller (but still large) towns, such as Sand Canyon Pueblo,[84] surrounded themselves with walls and towers (fig. 6.9). The Late Pueblo III Period in the Four Corners area saw increasing aggregation into larger and larger towns,[85] and increasing warfare.[86] Trouble bred trouble. By the late thirteenth/early fourteenth century, war and violence had spread south as far as Zuni, with much the same results (chapter 7).

The deterioration of Aztec's region is written in its ruins. Architecture tells the tale. In the late thirteenth century, the largest post-Chaco Great Houses changed radically from palaces to pueblos.[87] Apartments first built as elite residences were taken over by commoner families, like scenes from postrevolutionary Russia. These events have been called reoccupations.[88] Changing adaptations? Or political convulsions? Or, as Cynthia Irwin-Williams often said about Salmon Ruins but never committed to paper, squatters in the ruins? Whatever spin we chose, by 1270 Aztec West's Chaco-sized rooms had been subdivided into tiny unit pueblo rooms, and family "kivas" had been jammed into adjacent Chaco chambers. Other Great House rooms were turned into dumps or burial crypts, neither of which, in Anasazi life, carried negative connotations. That pattern was repeated at Great Houses throughout the Four Corners.

This would not have happened at Pueblo Alto in 1070. I agree with Irwin-Williams: this

Figure 6.8. Yellow Jacket, southwestern Colorado. Artist's reconstruction by Jean Kindig, based on her research and that of Joe Ben Wheat and J. McKim Malville. Arthur Rohn and Crow Canyon Archaeological Center have made other maps of this largest of all Mesa Verde towns. Courtesy Jean Matthews Kindig.

Figure 6.9. Sand Canyon, southwestern Colorado. Artist's reconstruction by Glen Feltch. Subsequent excavations altered a few details—most notably the discovery of a Great Kiva in the southwestern corner of the village (lower left). Courtesy Crow Canyon Archaeological Center.

was a reoccupation of princely houses by local populations. Peasants taking over palaces? As we shall see (chapter 7), revolution was not unknown in the ancient Southwest.[89]

The final act was the "abandonment of the Four Corners" (see fig. 6.2).[90] Modern Pueblo people insist that the region was not and is not "abandoned"; the ancient villages, now in ruins, mark their ancestral lands in spirit if not proprietary fact. But the fact remains that between 1200 and 1300, tens of thousands of people left, never to return. The conventional story holds that the Four Corners region was abandoned between 1275 and 1300—the period of the Great Drought. But it turns out that people were leaving in large numbers in the middle 1200s and perhaps even earlier.[91] By 1250—twenty-five years before the Great Drought—the rush was on.[92]

Weather was important of course. A major volcanic eruption at 1259, somewhere outside the Southwest, dropped temperatures and dimmed Anasazi hopes,[93] and a general breakdown of annual predictability of precipitation, beginning about 1250, made farming increasingly chancy.[94] Resource unpredictability bred war, and Aztec could no longer keep the peace.[95] People fled not only from a changing environment but also from a landscape of fear. The Great Drought—when it came in 1275—was the last straw for a sad remnant, much reduced by exodus, war, and (perhaps) negative demographics.[96]

But here's the kicker: our most advanced environmental modeling—the cyber-Anasazi (above)—shows us that *they didn't all have to leave*. Even the worst periods of the Great Drought could have supported substantial numbers of people, and—overlooked in most computer models—they could have shifted gears and dug canals. The Hohokam had been doing just that for a thousand years, and the Mimbres for several centuries. The leaders of Chaco and

Aztec were surely aware of both. The San Juan River was too big, but its tributaries were calm, reliable Mimbres-sized streams—apparently suitable for southwestern canal irrigation. Chaco and Aztec could organize the necessary labor—that was no problem. In fact, there were ancient canals at Aztec Ruins.[97] But for the larger region, that decision was never made—or if made, the decision was not carried out. No one else dug canals. (I'm not sure whether agents in agent-based models are given that option; if not, they should be.) Instead, people left, migrating hundreds of kilometers to new lands.

When the last villagers left the Mesa Verde area, sometime after 1280, the homelands were truly empty. If anyone stayed behind, we can't see them archaeologically. The totality and finality of the evacuations suggest to me political rather than environmental processes. Complete depopulation is unusual in history. When it happens, it often follows immense natural calamities, disasters of biblical proportions, not just a drought—"great" but no worse than several the Anasazi had previously weathered. The disaster that ended Chaco and Aztec was at least in part, and I think largely, man-made: failure of the political system.

Why did Aztec fail? There must have been many reasons, but among them, consider the differences in how Chaco and Aztec came to be. Chaco grew from a fortunate (perhaps fabled) setting and a deep history reaching back to Basketmaker III, as well as (initially at least) from the needs of people within what would become its inner region (chapter 5). Aztec was de novo. And Chaco had advantages of space and distance. It was out there, a place everyone knew about but perhaps only key people visited. In contrast, Aztec—created by the heirs of Chaco—was imposed, a new capital created by a class of elites entitled to rule. They were not central to their reduced region, but they were far more accessible to the people they hoped to rule. Easy access to the capital may have diminished its mystique and power. Aztec's ideas of social order did not match well with the larger forces of the times, and out of that misfit came repressive violence of a nature seldom seen in the Southwest.

The differences were reflected in the divergent histories of the post-Chaco north and the post-Chaco south. The north was racked to pieces; the south held together. Mesa Verde (roughly Aztec's region) had a southern counterpart or close cousin in the Tularosa horizon, a densely occupied region characterized by Tularosa black-on-white pottery, stretching at least 300 kilometers from the Rio Grande to the Tonto Basin (see fig. 1.3).[98] The Tularosa horizon filled the southern third of the old Chaco region, much as Mesa Verde filled the northern San Juan. In between was something of a doughnut hole. For decades after the move to Aztec Ruins, Great Houses and Chaco-style communities continued to function in the southern third of the old Chaco region—far beyond Aztec's reach. New Great Houses were built amid dispersed farmsteads as late as 1225.[99] Local leaders maintained some semblance of the old order, without the central support of a capital, Chaco or Aztec. The political executions and pocket pogroms that ended Aztec's era in the northern Anasazi never reached the south.[100] Real, Hobbsian warfare eventually did, a few decades later (below and chapter 7).[101]

Migration Situations

As the Four Corners emptied, waves of migrants sought new homes. The size of the migrating groups varied, no doubt, from families to clans to whole villages. Most settled in a broad arc or crescent around the southernmost Plateau, where Pueblos are today—from Hopi on the west through Zuni and Acoma to the northern Rio Grande on the east (see figs. 6.2 and 1.5).[102] It's very important to remember that at 1200, that entire arc was already well settled.[103] Four Corners clans joined villages that most knew only through rumor or hearsay. Trading partners, fictive kinship, common clans, or shared religious societies probably eased in-migration, but the arrival of strangers strained the existing social order, and adjustments were necessary.

Long before the final migrations, ties between the Four Corners and the Rio Grande were particularly close. Sarah Schlanger, who knows both areas well, recently suggested: "We might argue…that the Mesa Verde region extended as far east as the northern Rio Grande and…rather than a migration to the Rio Grande, we might consider a consolidation along the Rio Grande—the far eastern end of the northern tier—as a better model of the events of the late AD 1200s."[104] Population jumped dramatically on the Rio Grande and in other Pueblo areas. The notable rise in Rio Grande population began in the late twelfth and early thirteen centuries—about the time people started leaving the Four Corners—and took off like a rocket in the later thirteenth century. Demography seems crystal clear, but the archaeological evidence—architecture and pottery—is puzzling. We want to see Mesa Verde people (with Mesa Verde pottery, Mesa Verde kivas, Mesa Verde arrowheads, and so forth) suddenly appear in the Rio Grande, but (with a few exceptions) they are hard to spot. Two things were probably happening: migration of very small groups and—far more importantly—a conscious rejection of Chaco and Aztec and all they entailed. They no longer wanted to *look like* Mesa Verde people.[105]

Small groups—families, extended families—joined existing villages and quickly adopted the material culture of their new homes. People accustomed to eating meals from Mesa Verde black-on-white pots quickly accepted Tularosa black-on-white or Santa Fe black-on-white. Artifacts formerly essential to life in the northen San Juan—ceramic mugs, a distinctive form made almost exclusively in the Mesa Verde area—were never made again. Mugs were not simply for drinking; if they were merely useful forms, everyone would have made them, but only Mesa Verde did. Mugs *meant something* that people did not want to remember or continue in their new lives. "Keyhole kivas," once requisite architecture at every Mesa Verde home, were likewise made no more. They had no place in the new society. So population rose dramatically without obvious archaeological evidence of immigration; the "smoking gun" is not a pottery style or house form but the precipitous rise in numbers of people.[106]

In other places, larger units retained, at least for a while, the practices and styles of their past. We see these as "site unit intrusions"—to use dated jargon. In brief, a unit intrusion is a site that sticks out like a sore thumb. These are most obvious when large, migrating groups moved beyond the heavily populated Pueblo crescent and out into lands beyond, farther south. Sizable villages appeared, profoundly out of place in the Chihuahuan and Sonoran deserts— Mesa Verde towns in the Magdalena region of southern New Mexico;[107] Kayenta communities in southern Arizona.[108] Why did these few big groups hang together? Perhaps groups that big were not welcomed at existing pueblos; they could not be integrated as easily (or as safely) as single families. Importantly, Kayenta villages kept many of the features used in the old homelands (they are classic site unit intrusions); the big post–Mesa Verde towns did not. There are no San Juan kivas or mugs at even the largest Magdalena site. Even big communities chose to discard Mesa Verde elements formerly key to their lives and histories.[109]

The migrations took decades, but even with that slow pacing, things did not go smoothly. About 1275, signs of war appeared in the south.[110] In response, post-Chaco Great House communities (which continued the openness of Chaco times) were quickly replaced by huge towns, planned with Chaco precision as giant circles and squares (fig. 6.10),[111] but without Mesa Verde's "latter-day Great Houses": no thirteenth-century Great Houses were embedded in big Tularosa towns. They were finding other ways to control communities.

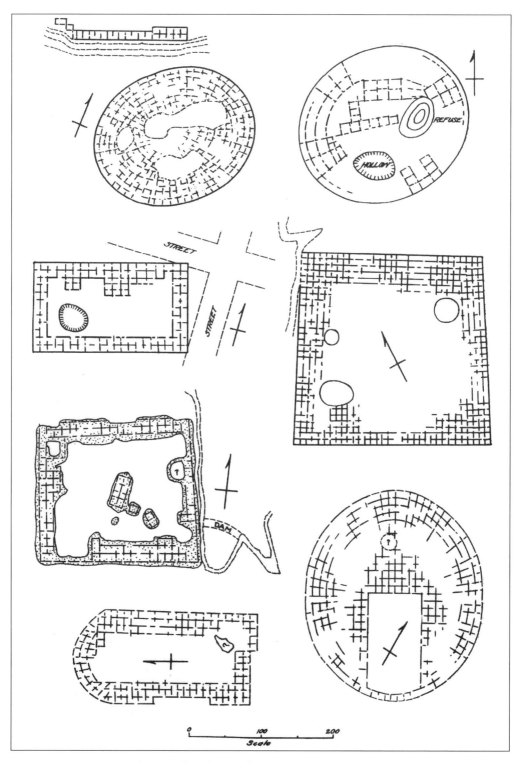

Figure 6.10. Zuni ruins; early maps of a selection of sites. From Leslie Spier, An Outline for the Chronology of Zuñi Ruins *(1917). The geometric formality is perhaps slightly exaggerated in this schematic rendering. Courtesy American Museum of Natural History.*

Compare Yellow Jacket (see fig. 6.8), the largest Mesa Verde town, with twelve hundred rooms, to its southern contemporaries, the largest Tularosa sites, which ranged up to fourteen hundred rooms (see fig. 6.10). At Yellow Jacket, line after line of contiguous unit pueblos formed straggling "streets." To the north stood a Great House and Great Kiva, reminders of Chaco; to the east, a bi-walled "Great Tower" complex, the signature structure of Aztec. An ill-defined plaza lay near the center of town, offset to the west. A halo of detached unit pueblos surrounded Yellow Jacket—the suburbs. Yellow Jacket, taken entire, looks haphazard compared with the tidy Tularosa circles and squares. The circles and squares were densely in-filled with rooms and apartments. It is my impression that the outer walls of big Tularosa sites were laid out as an act of corporate will and that the subsequent in-fill was a bit of a jumble, the work of many smaller groups. Most Tularosa sites were smaller, and many were less geometrically precise, but Tularosa town planning clearly adapted Chacoan conventions for Pueblo III—the democratization of Great House architecture? The principles of Chacoan architecture persisted, at least for a while, in big Tularosa towns, but the principals of Chacoan leadership vanished. There were no more palaces, no more kings. Gone south? We may meet those last Chaco elite families again, far to the south in Classic Period Hohokam (chapter 7).

In the eleventh and twelfth centuries, the Mogollon uplands were the broad no-man's-land separating Chaco and Hohokam, with low population densities, high mobility, and a casual commitment to agriculture. We can only imagine how Chaco and Hohokam leaders—living in (small) palaces in (small) cities with (modest) luxury and (limited) power—regarded Mogollon highlanders. As Plantagenets regarded Scots?

In Pueblo III, that no-man's-land filled with villages—no doubt an effect of the great migrations.[112] At the headwaters of Hohokam's rivers, big Tularosa towns represented the closest juxtaposition of eastern Anasazi and Hohokam in their long histories. Anasazi sagged south, over the Mogollon Rim and into the deserts. Pueblo Viejo in Safford Valley of the upper Gila River had been the eastern frontier of Hohokam (chapter 5). After 1150, Pueblo Viejo and Safford sites had Tularosa-style pottery, in quantity.[113] Northern peoples using Tularosa-like pottery shared the Tonto Basin with Early Classic Hohokam groups.[114] Farther east, big Tularosa towns sprung up on the margins of the old Mimbres area. Tularosa towns carried traditions of Chaco, untrammeled by Aztec's failures—they had not been part of that mess. The south continued local Great House rule for decades after the original capital moved far to the north, effectively out of the Tularosa world. Eventually, with the onset of war, even the southern post-Chaco Great Houses vanished. Those Great House families—where did *they* go?

Hohokam Early Classic: Meltdowns and Floods

Platform mounds (see fig. 6.1) replaced ball courts, marking the onset of the Hohokam Classic Period. *Classic*: "having high quality that is unquestioned; of the highest quality or rank." That was the idea: the Classic Period was the acme, the apex, the top. Harold Gladwin called Classic Period Hohokam "the Golden Age of southern Arizona."[115] Gladwin's view prevailed for four decades, but several Hohokam archaeologists raised doubts. (David Doyel was an early skeptic,[116] a Cassandra of the Classic.) As it turns out, Gladwin was probably wrong. The current view of the Classic is—in a word—bleak. David Abbott's recent book (2003) bears the grim title *Centuries of Decline during the Hohokam Classic Period*. "The transition to the Classic Period was marked by the collapse of the ballcourt network and significant population dislocations [from uplands back into river valleys].... Exchange networks were cut, and the volume of trade goods declined."[117] Gladwin's golden age turned to dross.

The Déclassé Classic

Small-scale conflicts between and among canal communities were endemic after 700, perhaps indicating social strains that eventually overwhelmed the Hohokam Canon. With the Classic Period, violence escalated to real warfare engaging "entire canal systems."[118] Defensive trincheras sites—terraced hillsides built for defense—proliferated in the Early Classic, as did hilltop "forts."[119] Warfare escalated throughout the Classic, culminating in the spectacular sackings of later Salado pueblos (chapter 7).

The unpleasantness was exacerbated by big floods, periodically destroying headgates and intakes. We have detailed history of stream flow in both the Salt and Gila rivers, building on the tree-ring work of Don Graybill.[120] From 1150 to 1300, "destructive floods were sporadic, averaging about one per generation."[121] Early Classic Period Hohokam society could survive sporadic floods. They had no choice. When it stopped raining, the Anasazi could move over the hills to the next valley; Hohokam did not have that option. When floods scoured canals, the Hohokam dug more canals. That worked—more or less—through the 1100s and 1200s, but monster floods in the mid-1300s would put an end to things (chapter 7).

There were social and demographic disruptions as well. Gladwin saw the golden age Classic Period as the vibrant combination of hidebound Hohokam and vigorous new peoples rolling down from the north like a bracing cold front—the Salado. The Salado invasion was a staple of both Gladwin and Haury. Salado's calling card was a flashy, un-Hohokam pottery called Gila Polychrome (which properly belongs in chapter 7). With the gaudy new pottery came Pueblo-like adobe compounds and platform mounds. That was Gladwin's (and Haury's) model of the Classic: Hohokam + Salado = Classic.[122]

Fieldwork in the 1960s and 1970s showed that, in the Hohokam heartland, adobe compounds and platform mounds long predated Gila Polychrome, which arrived in most places after 1300. I postpone Salado, sensu Gila Polychrome, for chapter 7, in its proper chronological place. But what became of Salado, sensu Gladwin—peoples from the north, with or without polychromes? New Archaeology and processual archaeology discounted and rejected invasions, migrations, and diffusions. Gladwin's Salado invasion was ruled off the court and consigned to the dustbin of culture history. But the new millennium revived both historicity and migration. Salado's back, but with historical tweaks and corrections.

Let's look first at Early Classic Hohokam and then at its times, both rich with incident. The Early Classic, from 1100 to 1250, is much less well known than the Late Classic (1250 to 1450, chapter 7) because at many sites Late Classic structures were plunked down right on top of the key Early Classic features: platform mounds.[123] Only a few Early Classic platform mounds survive without extensive, later, superimposed construction—most famously at the Marana site, north of Tucson.[124]

Marana is a great example of one salient feature of many Classic settlements: they were *new towns*, established at some distance from earlier Sedentary Period sites. Many of the largest Sedentary sites were more or less abandoned and (presumably) reestablished elsewhere.[125] Relocation was of course constrained by canals. Towns could only slide up or down the canal system. The large Sedentary population at the Grewe site, for example, shifted down-canal a few kilometers to found Casa Grande[126] (not to be confused with Casas Grandes, Chihuahua, below and chapter 7).

In that regard, Marana was *not* a typical Early Classic town. Suzanne and Paul Fish, who excavated Marana, note that the site "was not situated among long-established [Sedentary Period] populations in the most favorable riverine or upland locales, but in a recently settled and agriculturally secondary area."[127] Perhaps that choice of location was not wise: Marana did

Figure 6.11. Platform mound with elite residence, Marana Site; commoner compounds in distance. Artist's reconstruction by Pamela Key, based on the research of Suzanne and Paul Fish and others. Courtesy Pamela Key.

not survive into the Late Classic. But the absence of Late Classic overlays makes it our best example of an Early Classic site.

Marana is a big site—1.5 kilometers long (east–west); one-half kilometer wide (north–south). It was the center of an even larger community on the gently sloping west flanks of the Tortolina Mountains. At Marana itself, twenty-five adobe compounds, evenly spaced along a rough east–west axis, represent the residential form that replaced courtyard groups of earlier Hohokam periods. The one excavated example consists of a quadrilateral compound of more than 5,000 square meters, defined by a low adobe wall. Inside the wall, about twenty adobe-walled rooms were built as individual units or in small structures of three to five rooms. Rooms either were very near to or actually backed against the compound wall. The center of the compound was an open plaza. Outside the compound walls were several low middens or trash mounds, domestic debris from the compound.

Marana compounds were rather larger than other Early Classic examples, most of which average about 1,600 square meters,[128] but they were comparable in room counts to many Classic compounds.[129] That is, most Early Classic compounds were about one-third the size of the Marana example but had about the same number of rooms jammed into a smaller area. Perhaps Marana (like Chaco?), in its unusual location, had more available space than did Phoenix Basin sites, jammed tight between canals and fields.

Archaeologists argue that small Early Classic compounds represent the characteristic Hohokam courtyard groups transformed by adobe walls.[130] That suggests, they say, continuities between Late Sedentary and Early Classic domestic architecture. Those continuities were real, but we should not lose sight of the differences: pit houses had been replaced by above-ground, adobe-walled homes. That's a big difference. And the formerly open courtyard group was now surrounded by a closed, compound wall; I think something important had changed.

A rectangular platform mound (fig. 6.11) stood at the center of the Marana site. The mound was small by Phoenix Basin standards (as we shall see) but still impressive. A rectangular compound wall surrounded the mound. Atop the platform was a compound within a compound: "A massive adobe wall, 60 centimeters wide, probably surrounded the entire top of the platform mound. It enclosed the mound-top rooms in a compound-like arrangement."[131] Suzanne and Paul Fish and their colleagues interpret the platform and its compound as an elite residence with attendant ceremonial and community functions.[132]

Marana, built de novo after the decline of the Hohokam Canon, of course did not have a ball court. Nor did most "new towns," such as Escalante (near Casa Grande),[133] or the Classic Period communities of the Tonto Basin.[134] But many towns in the crowded Phoenix Basin had both platform mounds and ball courts, in stylized architectural opposition.[135] The placement of mounds vis-à-vis earlier ball courts was carefully considered and sent a powerful message. If platforms represent a new order, the new order that raised a platform could easily have leveled a ball court. That kind of architectural obliteration was either unnecessary or impolitic. People may have given up on the canon but still revered its monuments. Or perhaps the message was a disused ball court, weedy and eroded, no more a field of dreams. The ideological contest between the old Hohokam Canon and the Early Classic played out architecturally in the town's public spaces. The new ways clearly won (chapter 7), but—significantly—there is no known instance of a platform mound built directly over a ball court.[136] That kind of heavy-handed superposition happened when platforms were built over earlier capped Hohokam mounds.

Platform Mounds, Begun

Platform mounds became the most conspicuous and (presumably) important monumental form of the Classic Period.[137] Conventionally, archaeologists derive platform mounds from earlier Hohokam "capped" mounds—low, rounded oval mounds built with trash and sterile fill (and thus clearly architecture), sometimes surfaced with coats of caliche-rich mud plaster. Low capped mounds, with their gently rounded surfaces, were stages, a sort of theater-in-the-round for a surrounding audience. The space atop low mounds was open to all (in something of a contrast to ball courts—sunken enclosed spaces, open only to those who crowded the berms).[138]

Capped mounds are properly features of chapters 4 and 5. I describe them here because they are critical to the history of platform mounds. For clarity, hereafter I call the earlier rounded mounds simply "mounds" and the later Classic Period rectangular structures "platform mounds" or "platforms." They were two different things.

Classic platforms—in contrast to Hohokam mounds—were large, tall, rectangular, sheer-sided, flat-topped constructions. They were built by first erecting a rectangular enclosing wall (adobe or stone) and then in-filling to create a level platform. Platforms, in contrast to mounds, towered 1.5 to 2 meters or more above the surrounding town. Because the platform's broad surface was flat, it provided public viewing only around the edges (that is, along a narrow proscenium, a few meters deep from the mound edge)—and then only from the direction faced by that face of retaining wall. Actions and events in the center of the platform were not visible to those below. What happened on the platform stayed on the platform.

Mounds and platforms seem to me to be very different monuments built in very different ways. Yet the archaeological urge to find continuities in the sequence is strong—very strong in this case because with the rejection of Salado invasions, continuity became necessary: unbroken threads between Sedentary and Classic. If platforms did not signify outsiders, then they must be a development of local folks. How to get from A to B, from low, rounded mounds to imposing rectangular platforms? The most often cited models for continuity and local origins of platforms are David Gregory's, expanded by David Doyel.[139] According to Gregory, Mound 8 at Las Colinas (a large Phoenix town) represented "a bridge between the earlier mound forms...and the later [platform] morphology that appears so consistently at the Classic period sites."[140] Mound 8 was a Sedentary mound covered by a Classic platform; Gregory suggests that this sequence will be found at some (but not all) Classic mounds, especially in the Phoenix core.[141] Extrapolating from "scattered exposures" in deep excavations at Pueblo Grande, Chris Downum and Todd Bostwick propose that the very largest Classic platform mound probably covered a "circular Sedentary mound or mounds."[142] Thus, many platforms were built directly over mounds, covering and obscuring the earlier mound features —unlike the deliberate placement of platforms at some distance from earlier ball courts, which preserved the abandoned monuments. Mounds made a very different architectural statement.

The generally accepted scenario goes like this: early low mounds developed into small Late Sedentary platforms supporting simple "temples," which developed into Early Classic platforms supporting elite residences, culminating in Late Classic Great Houses such as Casa Grande (a tease: we will meet Hohokam Great Houses in chapter 7).[143] That sequence is widely accepted, and indeed it has come to be expected.[144] And certainly that's the sequence of what happened, particularly at Phoenix Basin sites where new Classic towns were built atop older Sedentary Period villages. But what message was sent when the people of Pueblo Grande saw the imposing new platform rising over their familiar old mounds? Classic Period town planners preserved decommissioned ball courts—that's continuity of a kind, if only in the breach. They built platforms, in contrast, over Sedentary mounds, as the Spanish built churches atop pyramids—that, perhaps, is discontinuity.[145]

It's generally agreed that platforms began (or "evolved") in and around the Phoenix Basin and then spread outward to Tucson, Tonto, and other peripheries—much like ball courts in an earlier age.[146] Platforms spread like wildfire; they must have filled a need. What need? That same question rephrased: What were platforms? It's hard to say, because the original architecture of Early Classic platforms was almost always replaced or obscured by substantial Late Classic structures. Phoenix Basin archaeologists see Early Classic mounds as temples or as public ceremonial spaces, continuing the presumed function of earlier Hohokam mounds.[147] But the Marana mound—one of the few Early Classic platforms unencumbered by later construction—was clearly an elite residence[148]—a small sample of one, to be sure, but the best we've got.[149] I think our hopes for continuity color our perceptions of Early Classic platforms.

Might most early platforms, like Marana, be elite residences? If so, that's a major discontinuity. Whatever the earlier low rounded mounds might have been, they were almost certainly *not* elite residences.

Let's turn continuity on its head. As we shall see, there is general (but not unanimous) support for elite residences on platform mounds in the *later* Classic Period (chapter 7). The conventional interpretation of continuity moves earlier Sedentary mound functions onto the elevated surfaces of Early Classic platforms and then replaces them with Late Classic elite residences. Or were early Classic platforms (like Marana) really elite residences and markedly discontinuous with earlier mounds? Pay your money, take your choice. William Doelle, David Gregory, and Henry Wallace in a review of all platform mounds questioned the conventional view, albeit cautiously:

> The proposition that concepts embedded in the Classic period forms owed something, perhaps a great deal, to earlier forms is not to be denied.... However, Classic period mounds also differed from their architectural predecessors in *both* form and function. The most important functional difference was that later forms served as residential spaces. But the overall change in form was substantial as well and cannot be explained solely by change in the functional use of space atop the mounds.[150]

Treading carefully but opening the door for...discontinuity.[151]

Whatever view ultimately prevails, platform mounds clearly marked the replacement or displacement of the Hohokam Canon. The canon was unraveling throughout the late twelfth and early thirteenth centuries. With the arrival of platform mounds, it withered to nothing. As noted above, no ball courts were built after 1150, and existing courts fell out of use. Cremation burial diminished sharply (but continued nevertheless in some places at least until 1250). Pallets ceased to be made, and presumably the old cremation burial ritual of which pallets had been part ended. And a sea change occurred in styles of pottery and rock art.[152]

Platforms marked a major break with the past. Classic period platforms, I think, were a political response to social crisis, mixing a fresh round of West Mexican ideas (via the Gatlin site?) with the stern realities of Anasazi political life (Chaco via Tularosa?). That tale must wait for chapter 7.

Trincheras: New Views from the Mountaintop

People in the Hohokam region were looking for new models—the end of the canon and the rise of platforms show us that. One new model that came and then went was trincheras. (The history of the ancient Southwest included many false starts, dead ends, and failed attempts; history did not move in the steady progression of Morgan's stages or neo-evolutionary ladders.) *Trincheras* is a term applied to a wide range of terraced or walled hills.[153] The first monumental construction in the Southwest—the terraced hill of Cerro Juanaquena (chapter 2), dating to 1250 BC—was technically a trincheras site. Walled hilltops, presumably defensive, were also conspicuous in Early Pithouse settlements in the southern Southwest (chapter 3). But between 500 and 1100—the happy days of Hohokam—there was apparently little construction or use of trincheras.

A renewed burst of trincheras building began in the twelfth century in the deserts around Tucson and particularly in Sonora (with a few late examples in southwestern New Mexico and northwestern Chihuahua). Most (but not all) of the Tucson hill towns were features of the

Early Classic Tanque Verde Phase.[154] In northern Sonora, the region most associated with trincheras (chapter 7), terraced hill sites were marked by a purple-on-red pottery peculiar to that area. Apparently, the need for terraced hills crossed divisions that balkanized the old Hohokam world in the Late Sedentary and Early Classic—terraced hills appeared all over southern Arizona and Sonora, even into New Mexico and Chihuahua, but far less in the Phoenix Basin.

Some see these impressive sites as short-term defensive refuges.[155] Others view them as long-term villages.[156] Still others emphasize the ideological or ritual importance of monumental hilltops.[157] I think defense played a major role but trincheras may also have represented a new way of understanding a world absent the Hohokam Canon. The move from low terraces to hilltops certainly changed worldviews, figuratively and literally. Recall that many Classic Period towns shifted deliberately away from older Sedentary and Colonial sites. Perhaps trincheras' use of previously empty hill slopes was something like that.

Where might those new ideas come from? Southwestern trincheras sites followed much older traditions of hilltop settlement in northern Mesoamerica,[158] as well as much closer, not-quite-so-old sites in northern Sonora.[159] Trincheras construction probably began a century earlier in Sonora before reaching Tucson.[160] Trincheras ideology—if that's what it was—did not survive the Classic Period in the Tucson area and failed, shortly after 1400, over most of Sonora (chapter 7).

The collapse of the Hohokam Canon by 1150, followed a century later by the final fall of the Chaco/Aztec world, left immense ideological voids throughout the Southwest. The ideas that ordered existence for centuries no longer worked. Platform mounds and trincheras sites represent new sets of ideas, variably successful in replacing Hohokam. Pueblo people experimented with a remarkable array of new beliefs, finding ways to replace rather than re-create Chaco. The interplay of those competing ideologies shaped the remarkable fifteenth and early sixteenth centuries (chapter 7). One of the strongest forces in that animated era—Casas Grandes—surfaced first in the mid-thirteenth century.

What's Local and What's Distant in the Origin of Casas Grandes?

Casas Grandes in northwestern Chihuahua was one of the key sites—and the last great city—of the ancient Southwest. Its story rightly belongs in chapter 7, but its origins lie in the period and events covered here.[161] *Casas Grandes* names both a region and a site, the central city also known as Paquimé. I prefer to call the site *Paquimé* and the region *Casas Grandes*. But following the usage of other archaeologists (some of whom are quoted below), I'll use *Casas Grandes* and *Paquimé* interchangeably for the site.

The great city rose around 1250. Rose from what? And from where? The central question of Paquimé's origins: local or distant?—a phrase taken from "The Local and the Distant in the Origin of Casas Grandes," an important article by Michael Whalen and Paul Minnis.[162] As we shall see, the origin of Casas Grandes is critically important to our understanding of the ancient Southwest. Consequently, the following section contains the kind of detailed quibbling that I've mostly banished to footnotes. If you don't care for academic disputes, skip to page 179.

The origins of Casas Grandes have long been the subject of heated argument. The site's original excavator, Charles Di Peso, thought Paquimé was the result of deliberate actions by Mesoamerican agents, a colony of southern civilizations.[163] I argued that Casas Grandes leadership came not from the south but from the north, from Chaco.[164] Whalen and Minnis (the leading experts on the site) think the answer lies within the Casas Grandes region: Casas Grandes was local.

Whalen and Minnis certainly acknowledge "the importance of distant contacts in the rise of Casas Grandes…within the context of local initiatives and aspirations."[165] But local was primary, and distant a distant second. Nodding to Chaco and Mexico, Whalen and Minnis conclude that Paquimé was essentially local, a product of local ecological and social processes.[166] Their model of Casas Grandes origins appeals to processes that might be (should be!) repeated in other contexts and cultures. That's a processual account (and thus belongs in this chapter).

I place a higher value on the distant. I've convinced myself that to understand Paquimé's origins, we have to look far beyond the Casas Grandes region. There are too many coincidences in timing between events at Casas Grandes and elsewhere, too many objects and ideas that clearly referenced distant sources, both Chaco and Mesoamerica.

A caveat: despite the excellent efforts of Whalen, Minnis, and many others, the archaeology of Chihuahua is still in its early days, decades behind Hohokam and Anasazi. Historian Victor Lieberman, in a fascinating parallel to Paquimé, reconnected Southeast Asia (an area "of limited local data," much like Casas Grandes) to its larger continental context. As an aside, he noted:

> Scholars usually have sought to explain the rise of Pagan, the collapse of Angor, the First Toungoo conquests, and so forth in purely local terms, institutional or political. But the fact that these changes coincided with more general regional transitions obliges us to treat skeptically explanations that are entirely *sui generis*.[167]

Whalen and Minnis have labored mightily to build a local, sui generis sequence for the Casas Grandes Valley.[168] But much of what we've learned recently about the Southwest suggests that *there is no such thing as a local sequence*. Thus, like Lieberman, I treat skeptically explanations that are sui generis—especially for a southwestern city with three *real* Mesoamerican ball courts, five hundred macaws, and more fancy copper artifacts than most sites in central Mexico—not to mention some surprisingly Chaco-like or Chaco-esque architectural tricks.[169] We will consider the role of the distant in chapter 7. In this chapter, I focus on the role of the local, because my "local" is larger than Whalen and Minnis's, and its role hinges on events prior to 1300 (the terminus of this chapter's "histories").

No one—not Di Peso, I, or anyone else—thinks that Casas Grandes' population moved en masse from far distant places (Chaco or Mesoamerica). Rather, distant roles were rarer and more rarified: leadership. Both Di Peso and I would count Paquimé's elites in scores, perhaps hundreds, but certainly not thousands. So where did the thousands of people who actually built and supported Paquimé and the other Casas Grandes towns come from? It's the reverse of the mystery of the Anasazi: "Where did they go?" The mystery of Casas Grandes is "Where did they come from?" I think they came not from the local Casas Grandes Valley but from places a bit more distant.

Down with Mimbres…

After two decades of looking—and looking hard—Whalen and Minnis have not found substantial twelfth-century populations in the area immediately prior to Paquimé (a bald statement, discussed further below). There are sites preceding Paquimé. People lived there of course, but not enough people to create and populate a city.

So where did they come from? The best place to look, I think, is north, to Mimbres. With our new understanding of the geographic scale of southwestern regions (such as Chaco and Hohokam), Mimbres should be considered "local" for Casas Grandes. Recall that Mimbres ended about 1130, the same time Chaco ended. Some Mimbres archaeologists recognize that fact as a matter of interest;[170] others dismiss it as a fluke;[171] still others argue that Mimbres did not in fact end.[172] (Of course, Chaco didn't end either; it moved to Aztec.) But *something* happened. At 1100 there were five to ten thousand people living in Mimbres towns throughout southwestern New Mexico. By 1150 there weren't.

Here's a summary of recent thinking: Margaret Nelson[173] concludes that some took to the hills—the uplands around the Mimbres Valley. Darrell Creel[174] suggests that a few more hung on in the old Mimbres towns—the aptly named Terminal Classic. Harry Shafer thinks that "geographically separate groups [within the Mimbres region] went their own ways when the breakdown of the Classic Mimbres tradition occurred and many of the large towns in the Mimbres Valley were abandoned…with the collapse of the networks responsible for managing the river's water."[175] Shafer thinks that Mimbres of the upper Gila merged north into the Tularosa horizon. Others went up into the hills of the eastern Black Range (as Nelson argued), while the bulk of the Mimbres Valley population went south: they "shifted their ranges southward…eventually becoming part of the Casas Grandes sphere."[176] I agree with all three—but *especially* with Shafer.[177]

The post-Mimbres era was fluid. We might call it liminal, if we chose to use such words. It's hard to get a handle on those times because people and villages bounced around like popcorn. Ben Nelson introduced the idea of "short-term sedentism" for post-Mimbres times, with pueblos flitting from valley to valley,[178] and then projected that idea back in time and over greater space with an influential article on "fallow valleys": the episodic, sequential occupations and abandonments of valleys all over southwestern New Mexico (traced in astonishing detail).[179] "Fallow valleys" meant that in one century a valley stood empty; in the next it was filled with villages; and in the next it was empty again—the people relocated to another valley, over the hills and far away. (Parallels with Pueblo I come to mind.) Nelson and Roger Anyon's mapping of that intricate demographic dance was neatly confined within southwestern New Mexico. But their "fallow valley" model makes even more sense *if it is extended across the border into Chihuahua.* (For some reason, archaeologists are hesitant to do that—oh, those state lines and national boundaries!)

I think the Casas Grandes Valley was more or less empty—fallow—in the century before Paquimé. And I think that the run-up to Paquimé involved the in-migration of substantial numbers of people (of which, more below). Mimbres falls, Casas Grandes rises. Surely, those two events were not unrelated.

But there is a problem with timing. Mimbres ended around 1130. Paquimé began around 1250. How to account for the missing century? Mimbres people were still around; they moved and altered appearances. Most of them simply changed clothes and slipped out of town, heading downstream and south into the deserts.[180] They made a remarkably complete break with their past and covered their trail (making it hard for archaeologists to track them). Mimbres people, until 1130, elaborately painted black-on-white bowls, built stone masonry pueblos, and buried their dead beneath the floors of special rooms (predominately but not exclusively—Mimbres treated their dead with both inhumation and cremation, depending, I

Figure 6.12. Firecracker Pueblo, a small El Paso Phase site near El Paso, Texas. Artist's reconstruction by George Nelson. Courtesy George Nelson and the Institute of Texan Cultures, USTA, #6-9-219.

suppose, on the deceased's enthusiasm for the Hohokam Canon; see chapter 4). After 1150 the people formerly known as Mimbres ceased painting pottery, built with adobe, and generally cremated their dead. There were continuities, of course,[181] but the changes were sufficiently dramatic to convince some archaeologists that the Mimbres area was actually briefly abandoned and then quickly reoccupied by new people.[182] I think they were the same people, struggling through the same sort of identity crises that shook Hohokam at 1150 and Anasazi at 1300 (chapter 7). Hohokam solved their problems by becoming "Classic"; Anasazi turned into Pueblos; but Mimbres just quit being Mimbres and marked time (archaeologically at least), waiting for the Next Big Thing: Paquimé.

The other post-Mimbres interpretations are probably right, in part: some went north and some headed for the hills, but most just turned their back on the old ways and moved into the desert. Deserts to the east—the Jornada Mogollon area, joining or becoming the Early El Paso Phase (fig. 6.12). And deserts to the south—down the Mimbres River, becoming the Black Mountain Phase, a key but curiously understudied event.[183]

The Black Mountain ruin sits about 15 kilometers northwest of Deming, New Mexico.[184] This enigmatic and now almost mythical site is conspicuous by its near absence from most discussions of Mimbres archaeology.[185] A curious omission: Black Mountain was one of the largest sites of any time period in the Mimbres Valley and certainly the largest post-Mimbres town.

Black Mountain was at the lower (that is, desert) end of the Mimbres Valley. The Mimbres River, confronting that desert, gives up and sinks into alluvial oblivion miles above the site. At Black Mountain, the "Mimbres River" is a small sandy wash with a thin thread of water forced to the surface by underlying rock. Apparently, that small flow was enough. Survey data from 1974, when the site was still more or less intact, recorded three hundred rooms in a dozen large adobe room blocks, with ceramics suggesting post-Mimbres, pre-Salado, pre-Paquimé times—that is, about 1150 and 1300.[186] There were other, smaller Black Mountain Phase sites, farther out in the desert, but the Black Mountain site alone could solve the puzzle: Where did Mimbres go between 1130 and 1250? Several hundred ex-Mimbres parked themselves, for a while, near Deming. Black Mountain and smaller sister sites in the Jornada and Animas districts marked a century-long wandering in the wilderness that ultimately took once-Mimbres peoples finally to the Rio Casas Grandes.[187] Not as straggling refugee families but as organized town-sized groups, tanned, rested, and ready for business.[188]

So here's what we have: at 1100, thousands of people in scores of big Mimbres towns and only a few bedraggled farmers scratching out a living on the Rio Casas Grandes; at 1200, an empty Mimbres Valley, murky but substantial Black Mountain Phase settlements in the deserts, and no perceptible change in Chihuahua; at 1250, a bustling, packed Rio Casas Grandes Valley in and around Paquimé—leaving only a few bedraggled farmers rattling around the old Mimbres region's now permanently fallow valleys. Looks like migration to me.

...Up with Paquimé!

We've considered things from the Mimbres north. Let's look to the north, from Chihuahua in the south. On one fact we all agree: there were *a lot* of people in Chihuahua by 1300.[189] The question is, were there a lot of people there at 1200? As far as Charles Di Peso could tell, the Casas Grandes Valley was thinly peopled before 1200 or even at 1250.[190] Di Peso called this time the Viejo Period. He excavated several small Viejo sites and cast about, widely, looking for others.[191] Whalen and Minnis's recent work in the Casas Grandes region has, at least for me, largely confirmed Di Peso's conclusions. They have found only thin evidence of twelfth-century populations in the area, but thin evidence is *some* evidence and from that evidence Whalen and Minnis argue for a sizable pre-Paquimé population.

They see the cup as half full; I (and Di Peso) see it as all but empty, with only a few lingering hints of Viejo. We've learned that it's okay for a valley to be empty, from time to time, in the ancient Southwest. That's not a scary thing, not a gap we must rush to fill. Should it surprise us that the Casas Grandes Valley might have been all but empty at 1200? No. From time to time, almost all parts of the Southwest (except for Phoenix and Tucson) were depopulated and repopulated: fallow valleys. So I think there was (essentially) nobody home at 1200 but by 1300 northern Chihuahua was one of the most densely settled areas in the Southwest.[192] Casas Grandes, between 1200 and 1250, sucked in people like lunch in the park attracts pigeons. They flocked to Chihuahua from the Mimbres north and from valleys farther south.[193]

It happens: consider Cahokia, Chaco's and Mimbres's contemporary in the Mississippi Valley. Its urbanization drew in immense numbers of previously dispersed people. Cahokia emptied its hinterlands.[194] Whoever occupied the American Bottom before Cahokia, they were responsible for only a small fraction of the city's population. That kind of explosive urbanization began with Teotihuacán and ended with Mexico City.

Paquimé too was a strange attractor, both locally and distantly. Population influxes were both cause and effect of Paquimé's rise—much like Cahokia's. Perhaps in dramatic migrations or perhaps more gradually; perhaps into an empty valley or perhaps overwhelming existing communities. Whatever—clearly, something *happened*. Events, not adaptations! If any place in the Southwest had *history*, it was Paquimé. I think that history starts with massive in-migration from the Mimbres area, building a base population that created Casas Grandes: the commoners. We'll deal with rulers and the really distant in chapter 7.

That kind of history had no place in processual archaeology—the archaeology of the 1970s and 1980s. I think it fair to say that Whalen and Minnis's account of Paquimé is largely processual—simply a description, not a judgment (or more accurately, "processual plus," to anticipate theoretical developments in chapter 7). To explain the rise of Paquimé, they borrow a staunchly processual account of Chaco's emergence from Lynne Sebastian's *Chaco Anasazi* and apply it *as a process* to Paquimé "to support the idea of local developments as primary factors in the rise of Casas Grandes."[195] They find that the Chaco model works well at Paquimé. The two processes (Chaco's and Paquimé's) were parallel but unrelated, historically separate but processually equal, "a simple local development model that is a Chihuahua adaptation of one used for Chaco Canyon."[196]

That's classic cross-cultural, processual archaeology! And a good illustration of how archaeological thinking shapes our views of the past. If we assume that cross-cultural processes shaped human affairs, what happened at Chaco might well apply to Paquimé—or to sites in Mesopotamia or Africa. However, sliding Chaco onto Paquimé ignores Galton's Problem, the bane of cross-cultural studies. A nineteenth-century gadfly and anthropomotrist (don't ask), Sir Francis Galton questioned cross-cultural enthusiasts: if two cases are alike, how can we be sure that similarity represents real cross-cultural patterns or processes and not simply a historical connection? Cross-cultural generalizations are not so convincing if all round house/matrilineal societies (if you remember my hypothetical example) were in fact daughter colonies from an original matrilineal mother culture. That's Galton's Problem, and it applies to Paquimé.

If Chaco and Casas Grandes were similar (as Whalen and Minnis suggest), *perhaps there was a reason*. Were they, perhaps, historically connected? That possibility—historical connection—avoids the disturbing déjà vu of two parallel narratives, chronologically sequent, in nearly adjacent regions. Whalen and Minnis say that Paquimé walked, talked, and acted like Chaco—but that could happen anywhere. I say Paquimé looked like Chaco because Paquimé *was* Chaco, revised and transferred to a new region—not a process but a very specific historical progression. Whalen and Minnis of course value history, but filtered through local processes.

The kings of Chaco moved south—perhaps the disenfranchised cardinal faction that lost its bid to plot Aztec's course—and found post-Mimbres towns looking for leaders (chapter 7). The details we may never know, but I feel cautiously confident that *something like that happened*. Certainly, we should feel entirely confident that *something happened*—that Paquimé had a history above and beyond local adaptive processes. Through historical events and coincidences we are only beginning to understand—and processes we may yet discover—migrating Mimbres farmers and displaced Chaco elites came together in northwest Chihuahua and joined with local Chihuahuans and strong personalities from farther south. The result, I think, was Paquimé—the Southwest's greatest and last city, and the star of chapter 7.

Figure 7.1. Kinishba, a reconstructed Mogollon pueblo near Fort Apache, Arizona, excavated by Byron Cummings of the University of Arizona in the 1930s. Cummings restored and rebuilt a large portion of the pueblo, most of which has now fallen back into ruin. This photo shows the site as Cummings left it, probably around 1940. Courtesy Arizona Historical Society, Tucson.

s e v e n
Tale — *History*

Archaeologies: 1990 to 2005
Histories: 1250 to 1600

In 1492 the Old World declared war on the New. The New World lost.

The "declaration" was piecemeal and prolonged: royal charters, papal edicts, and executive orders issued over several centuries. But it was war—with no quotation marks—and truly a world war. War reached the Southwest (and history, as conventionally written, began) with Coronado's army in 1540, a half century after Columbus landed on Guanahani. The conquistadors failed to find golden cities and returned to Mexico disappointed. Smaller expeditions—slave raids excused as explorations—came and went. In 1598—two generations after Coronado—Don Juan de Oñate finally colonized the region. 1600 is close enough—the end of history for the ancient Southwest.

We know these things because conquistadors and colonizers had clerks and clerics who wrote reports. Those documents, with hints of what came before, make the last centuries of prehistory more historical and less anthropological.[1]

The "histories" in this chapter (1250 to 1600) cross the somewhat arbitrary boundary between anthropology and history. There are parallels in archaeology: "archaeologies" in this chapter (the final years of the twentieth century) move away from science and toward history or, more accurately, historically tinged humanism—a British import. This is "post-processual" archaeology, rejecting American processual scientism with its theories and generalizations. Post-processual archaeology glories in humanistic particularities: each story is unique and every account valid. Remember the Two Cultures (chapter 1)? They're back.

Southwesternists did not go over to British ways wholesale. Indeed, the Southwest little noted, nor long remembered, what the first, most enthusiastic British post-processualists said in the late 1970s. British thinking didn't really impact the Southwest until the mid-1990s. (Things move slowly in the Old West.) While the British were spinning hermeneutic circles and pondering Heidegger, southwestern debates of the 1970s and 1980s centered on *pre-post*-processual political hierarchy—couched in scientific, neo-evolutionary terms (chapter 6).

Hierarchies in the fourteenth-century Southwest—yes or no? Compared with slippery British metaphysics, southwestern arguments were simple and blunt. (John Wayne meets David Niven?) Our "debates" turned fierce, furious, and seemingly endless. (More like John Wayne meets Victor McLaglen, in *The Quiet Man*.) A summary of the contest—not quite blow-by-blow or round-by-round—comes in the following sections.

It was in part to escape these bloody processual battles that young Southwesternists turned, at last, to the consolations of British philosophy. Arguments over fourteenth-century political complexity found resolution, or rather quietus, around 1990, when post-processual notions transmogrified (sensu Calvin) tired, old neo-evolutionary hierarchies into exciting, new, historically unique arrangements, reflecting a newly appreciated difference or "otherness" of the past. Hoary "chiefs" gave way to intriguing "ritualities." (We will meet more of these ancient novelties below.) Most of these new arrangements were communal, ritual, and generally nonhierarchical—Benedict's Pueblos still exert a strong teleological tug. In any case, arguments about hierarchy were rendered moot, unproductive, and—the ultimate sin!—stale and boring. Who wants yesterday's papers? Interests shifted and the old order passed. British notions changed southwestern archaeology—not so much with its convoluted rhetoric and arcane vocabularies, thank God. (Trust me, early British post-processualism was far denser and far more lexically impenetrable than the preceding paragraph—a lapse into jargon for which I apologize). The major impact came from interesting ideas behind the abstruse words. In short, *history*. Southwestern archaeology rediscovered history.

But the most revolutionary transformation came not through Anglophile theorizing but in a federal law: the Native American Graves Protection and Repatriation Act of 1990 (NAGPRA). The law effectively shifted control of the past from archaeologists to Native peoples. New Archaeology and processual archaeology ignored Native Americans. NAGPRA made us take Indians seriously. NAGPRA was a product of a lot of hard work by Indian lawyers and legislators. It was also a symptom of the same postmodern milieu that led British archaeology to post-processualism: questioning science and emphasizing instead history and human rights. So NAGPRA agreed well with post-processual approaches, and vice versa, and archaeologists of that persuasion had little trouble accepting NAGPRA's aims—which were not altogether friendly to archaeology, old or new.

Archaeologies: 1990 to 2005 (NAGPRA and Post-Processual)

We are still too close to the 1990s to pretend to useful histories of its archaeological trends. I offer here (as in all other chapters) my personal observations on how intellectual convulsions in the larger world of ideas rippled to the secluded backwaters of southwestern archaeology.[2]

Archaeology beyond Process

History—the realization that one thing leads to another—was the great divide between American processual and British post-processual approaches. It comes full circle to the Two Cultures, science and humanities (chapter 1). British archaeology always was history; American archaeology tried to be science. In a nutshell:

- Processual archaeology = natural/social sciences = generalizing/evolutionary accounts

• Post-processual archaeology = humanities = particularizing history

It might seem odd that archaeology would "rediscover" history, but for several academic generations, we were trained to think of ourselves as scientists. And it might seem odd that being trained as scientists somehow barred history: evolution itself is profoundly historical. But the emphasis on *processes*, which were ostensibly timeless and universal, reduced history to background noise. For Americans, history was chance events cluttering up the picture, something to filter out (Galton's Problem; chapter 6). For Brits, history was the goal. Hodder's humanism superseded Binford's science (chapter 1).

Despite healthy infusions of British post-processualism, southwestern archaeology is still solidly in the processual camp. I still have a lab coat; I wear it on Halloween to scare the kiddies.[3] We've made changes: "processual plus" (Michelle Hegmon's happy phrase) adds tricks and chops from the British school to our familiar practices.[4] Much of our funding comes from NSF or from CRM regulated by aging New Archaeologists. We remain more comfortable with natural and social sciences than with the more avant-garde humanistic approaches, efforts like Barbara Bender's multivocal *Stonehenge* or Michael Shanks's arty *Traumwerk* Web page—intriguing, even illuminating, but not what we call archaeology. Americans held out for process and—with reservations—science. (Our few recent flirtations with real history—in the 1980s, a handful of brave souls cited the French Annalistes—proved fleeting.) But we finally got our noses rubbed in it; NAGPRA legislated that archaeology would henceforth be history.[5]

History and Particularity

NAGPRA directed archaeologists to determine the "cultural affiliations" of their sites—that is, to determine which tribe or pueblo *now* is affiliated with a fifteen-century-old pit house village *then*. The law forbade osteological and genetic research to answer that question, which left us with the old standbys: pottery and architecture. Overnight, the most science-happy processual archaeologists were worrying about culture areas, index wares, migrations, historical linguistics, diffusion, and a host of concerns banished from thought since the 1930s.[6]

NAGPRA caught us by surprise. Archaeologists of my generation (and younger) had never really thought much about migration and diffusion. Those topics were off-limits during New Archaeology and processual archaeology. Now we had to, but (as noted in chapter 6) the tools and concepts we brought to the task were relics of the 1930s and 1940s. Pottery once again became people; masonry styles meant something beyond compression strength; kiva features marked ethnic identities.[7] Migration went from nowhere, in the days of New Archaeology, to a major theme of CRM reports and dissertations.

The one-two punch of British post-processualism and NAGPRA turned us away from processes and back toward history. History was back, with a postmodern spin: particularity. Postmodern history (and post-processual archaeology) detested metanarratives—Big History—and gloried in local complications. Each story was unique, particular, and, more often than not, markedly local (history's version of "my valley's different"). NAGPRA, in its own way, also promoted particularity. The key archaeological task, under NAGPRA, was to determine "cultural affiliation": which modern tribe is affiliated with (that is, descended from) the archaeological remains in question. The standard archaeological approach would have been to study the issue systematically and reach general conclusions: all archaeology that looks like X equals modern tribes Y and Z. But after a few attempts at large-scale generalization failed spectacularly, the federal agency in charge of NAGPRA directed that each instance should proceed case by case, tribe by tribe, and even artifact by artifact. It's hard to imagine a method more particularizing than that.

If history was to be local and particular, every site could have a unique and particular history. Absent general processes, two nearly identical platform mounds can support two very different historical interpretations, and both can be right. (Indeed, for the more extreme British post-processualists, *one* platform mound could have two or three or four very different historical interpretations, and all would be right!) Or two seemingly similar Mogollon pueblos might have been subtly, historically, and qualitatively *different* (thus avoiding the Chavez Pass–Grasshopper debate, below). And of course, every Chaco outlier could be *different*—and beautiful in its own particular way.

To me, our major accomplishment of the 1970s and 1980s was the recognition of Chaco, Hohokam, and Casas Grandes as regional systems—or at least, regional issues. Those regional systems transformed our vision of the ancient Southwest and how to think about it. Historical particularity introduced in the 1990s could refragment those hard-won worlds, deconstructing them into myriad tiny local histories—curiously, on about the same spatial scale as the old natural laboratories. Every outlier, potentially, had its own history, and Chaco became a vague annoyance, miles away and largely irrelevant. Slip-sliding away, back to the 1960s.[8]

Hierarchies on Trial

The periods covered in this chapter—Pueblo IV, Classic Period Hohokam, and Medio Period Casas Grandes—framed southwestern archaeology's three major battles over the nature of ancient political systems: the Grasshopper–Chavez Pass debate, Hohokam platform mounds, and Paquimé's provenance. More than battles, these were wars—academically speaking—with many skirmishes and a few bloodbaths, intellectual Verduns. There were casualties—careers wrecked, research programs derailed. The stakes were merely academic; the scars were sometimes real.

Two campaigns tore up central and southern Arizona; the third, Chihuahua. None of the battles were fought on Pueblo turf, but Pueblo egalitarianism hung in the balance—and hovered over every conflict. Did ancient southwestern societies evolve steadily toward the happy ideal of Benedict's Zuni, or were there ancient episodes of un-Pueblo-like hierarchy and government? It seemed important, to many archaeologists, to defend interpretations congruent with Benedict: a more or less steady progress from the inchoate past to the egalitarian, ethnographic present. For others, it was important to attack that position.

The battles over these fourteenth- and fifteenth-century political systems were fought by processualists in the late 1970s and mid-1980s. In retrospect, it sounds like an obscure medieval ecclesiastical debate: Did they or did they not have chiefs? Or elites, or some other euphemism for *rulers*? Seems silly, but it was serious stuff. The arguments wound down. After a stunned armistice, the 1990s saw an intellectual reaction that effectively realigned the Southwest with British post-processual programs—*particularly* regarding political history. Younger archaeologists—watching their elders duke it out—decamped to neutral ground and sought new ways of thinking. Softer British approaches rejected neo-evolutionary political schemes (the old rules of engagement) and instead "foregrounded" the halcyon, almost mystical roles of ritual, ceremony, and nonhierarchical alternatives. And that's how many archaeologists and much of the public now view the ancient Southwest. You can't talk about the ancient Southwest without using the words *ritual* and *ceremony*.

The Grasshopper–Chavez Pass debates went public around 1982.[9] They reached a sort of climax just before 1990.[10] At issue were two comparably large fourteenth- and fifteenth-century masonry pueblos in the Mogollon uplands (see fig. 7.1, a similar site, not involved in the debate).[11] Grasshopper was the long-term field school of the University of Arizona, under the direction of J. Jefferson Reid (and, earlier, William Longacre). Chavez Pass was a shorter, smaller project of Arizona State University, under the direction of Fred Plog, Sted Upham, and others. Upham and Plog—in search of universal processes—maintained that Chavez Pass had managerial elites (that is, political complexity). And because those processes were universal, they suggested that something similar would be found at Grasshopper, if only the University of Arizona looked harder. Reid and his colleagues (Michael Graves, Stephanie Whittlesey, and others) felt they had a good handle on Grasshopper and its particular history and stoutly denied managerial elites.[12] The Chavez Pass contingent thought *they* saw elites at Grasshopper. The Grasshopper group questioned elites at Chavez Pass. It got unpleasant.

The "debate" dominated discussions of ancient southwestern political history through the 1980s.[13] Spin-offs involved political "complexity" in other times and places, but the heart of the issue was Pueblo IV, the era of this chapter.[14] In *Polities and Power: An Economic and Political History of the Western Pueblos* (1982), Steadman Upham argued that there were elites and political power throughout the Pueblo IV world. Not just elites, but multivillage clusters that represented political units or polities. What Plog's *The Study of Prehistoric Change* was to the 1970s, *Polities and Power* was to the 1980s: a provocative must-read.

Upham's ideas were rooted in his view of western Pueblo ethnology, and his views of western Pueblo ethnology were disturbingly unlike Ruth Benedict's (chapter 3). He (and others) argued for a revision of our understanding of modern western Pueblo political arrangements. Upham said that historic Hopi and Zuni political organizations were in fact hierarchical. But Benedict's peaceful, communal, egalitarian Pueblos had deep purchase with the public and within the academy—we really *wanted* to believe it. So Upham's arguments were not popular. As it turns out, Upham was right: Hopi and Zuni were (and are) politically complicated and not egalitarian utopias; the eastern Pueblos, even more structured and authoritarian.[15]

The question I asked at the time (timidly, from the back of the classroom) was why Upham had to make this argument at all. Chavez Pass and Grasshopper dated to the fourteenth and early fifteenth centuries. What did twentieth-century Hopi and Zuni have to do with it? Why would the social and political structures of modern Pueblos apply to Grasshopper and Chavez Pass—much less Chaco, Aztec, or Paquimé? I never got an answer to those questions (I never actually asked Upham), but I can guess: it would have been extremely difficult for Upham or anyone to present a past that was politically more elaborate and complex than the Pueblo present. That would imply some sort of past peak, a climax followed by a modern regression. Remember Pueblo IV as "Regressive Pueblo" (chapter 4)? That idea was no more popular in the 1980s than it had been in the 1930s. For Upham's argument to persuade, things had to keep moving upward, so Benedict's Pueblos had to be adjusted upward. If Pueblo IV was more complex than Hopi, then Hopi had to be revised, made more complex.[16]

It's still hard to talk about rises and falls, ups and downs in the history of the ancient Southwest. Post-processual (and postcolonial) sensibilities make it awkward to suggest that

Pueblo society was significantly more politically complex in the twelfth century than it was in the fourteenth or fifteenth. It just seems *rude* to propose that Pueblos, in the past, might have been "more" or "bigger" or "higher" or otherwise *greater*—even if those adjectives are used in a numerical or theoretical sense and not as value judgments.[17] We may have abandoned band-tribe-chiefdom-state, but a form of Victorian progressivism remains.

Platform Mounds, Continued

The second battle was set in Hohokam. Did platform mounds support palaces, high above the peons? Or were they stages for communal ceremony, watched prayerfully by the people in open and lawful assembly? That question forms a large part of the "Histories" section, below. It also divided Hohokam "archaeologies" during the 1970s, '80s, and '90s, paralleling the Chavez Pass–Grasshopper debate.

Anasazi had to be tailored or "pre-adapted" or somehow destined to become Pueblos, but (until NAGPRA) historical continuity did not constrain the Hohokam. It was not at all clear, in the 1970s and 1980s, who the Hohokam were, who they became. It's still not clear, but NAGPRA won't take no for an answer. The Pima and O'odham of southern Arizona seemed most likely descendants.[18] But (in an ironic variation of the Pueblo IV predicament) the argument was made that ethnological Pima were *not* Hohokam because the Pima *were much less complex* than the Hohokam.[19] Many archaeologists reject that kind of rise-and-fall argument for Hohokam–Pima. As with the Anasazi–Pueblo, "devolution" was presumed unlikely or even impossible.[20] So instead of reinventing the Pima as a complex society (on a level with Classic Period Hohokam), we simply cut them out of the picture.

Classic Period Hohokam (the era considered in this chapter) featured many things missing from later Pima and Pueblo repertoires—for example, platform mounds. Nobody today builds platform mounds, Pueblo or Pima. So it was possible to think creatively about Hohokam platform mounds—for example, to propose "managerial elites" living on top. Huge CRM projects in the Tonto Basin targeted platform mound sites, which the lead researchers initially more or less *assumed* were the elite residences. But the unpleasantness of the (slightly earlier) Grasshopper–Chavez Pass debate soured the Southwest on managerial elites; they were damaged goods. By the mid-1990s, platform mounds had become monuments to community ritual. Post-processual fascinations with ritual and ceremony substituted those benign activities for unwelcome managerial elites, and everyone was happy.[21]

Platform mounds were flattened, socially. But as we shall see, those mounds may rise again. So too Salado (chapter 6): with NAGPRA and the rise of migration studies, archaeologists are once again open to the idea that events *and people* from the Plateau and the Mogollon Rim might have had historical consequences for the Hohokam:

> Based on recent CRM work in the Tonto Basin and academic research in other regions, many scholars have embraced a more sophisticated version of Haury's concept of Salado.... The basic scenario has a variety of ancestral puebloan groups migrating into central and southern Arizona during the late 1200s, in response to deteriorating environmental and social conditions on the Colorado Plateau. These migrants co-resided with...Hohokam.... The exchange patterns of exotic and decorated ceramics suggests the emergence of intensive trade networks and information flow that traversed, if not completely dissolved, previous cultural boundaries.[22]

The import of these new developments will become clear below. My point here is that what post-processual approaches could not do (did not want to do), NAGPRA accomplished—breaching the Iron Curtain separating Plateau and Deserts.[23]

Paquimé Pretrial Motions

The third disagreement about political hierarchy was Chihuahuan. It was less a battle than a changing of the guard: the avant-garde dismissed the old guard, in this case Di Peso. Charles Di Peso (1920–1982),[24] the excavator of Paquimé, was a free man. He headed an independent research institute—the Amerind Foundation, in Dragoon, Arizona—and was accountable only to his board and his conscience. Working in northern Chihuahua, he had no public perceptions of Natives to color or constrain his imagination; Chihuahua was not (then) part of the popular Southwest. Native peoples were hidden up in the rugged Sierra Madre and were no longer a serious presence in the Casas Grandes Valley. And Chihuahua had no Ruth Benedict. Indeed, the most widely read English-language survey in the 1970s was Robert and Florence Lister's *Chihuahua: Storehouse of Storms*—not a peaceful, happy image.

Before Di Peso, we knew essentially nothing about Casas Grandes. After his work, we had Di Peso's Paquimé: *Casas Grandes: A Fallen Trading Center of the Gran Chichimeca* (a monumental work discussed in chapter 5). Di Peso invented Paquimé—in the best sense of the verb *invent*. Mesoamerican lords ruled Di Peso's city. ("Managerial elites" does not begin to describe his vision.) The pomp and circumstance of Casas Grandes governance was lifted, literally, out of Mesoamerican codices. The incidental illustrations of his report mimicked codex styles. This was new for the Southwest and alarming.

We all agreed that Paquimé was something else. Through the 1980s and early 1990s, people seemed more or less okay with Paquimé as a Mesoamerican trading outpost. It was, after all, actually in Mexico. And there was nothing in the Southwest like it, with its Mesoamerican ball courts, effigy mounds, pyramids, and astonishing wealth (described below). So there were no actual battles over Paquimé's politics, because there weren't two sides. Di Peso stood alone as the one guy who actually knew Casas Grandes archaeology. We might object to the details (in particular his dating),[25] but no one could seriously challenge his larger vision because until the early 1990s, Di Peso had the data, momentum, and credibility.

Di Peso's Paquimé survived until processual archaeology caught up with it and joined forces with post-processual leveling to diminish and deflate—in a word, to *normalize*—Di Peso's dramatic vision. Decades after Di Peso left Casas Grandes (he died in 1982), new projects took the field. The most important, led by Michael Whalen and Paul Minnis, was staunchly and proudly processual (see chapter 6). Local adaptations replaced Di Peso's continental history: no Mesoamerican lords. Casas Grandes was not so much a hot war—a heated debate between two camps—as a cold war, a shift in ideologies.[26]

Jury Selection: Alternative Leaderships

Debates about hierarchy were so '80s! New thinking from across the Atlantic redirected archaeological energies. But the result, curiously, sustained the Benedictine vision of the Southwest: no kings! In the 1980s, ancient southwestern political leaders were poking their diademed heads through Benedict's (and Lewis Henry Morgan's) glass ceiling. On the table were trial histories that challenged an endlessly egalitarian Southwest: Chaco as a "complex" political system (chapter 5), Hohokam elites atop platform mounds, Paquimé as a sort of little Tula—and Chavez Pass of course, with its managerial elites. At the end of the century, post-processualism smacked them down again like whack-a-moles at the county fair.

The Chavez Pass–Grasshopper debate left us skeptical of complexity claims and turned many away from processual approaches—if a process explains my site, it jolly well should explain your site too. Things were calmer if every valley was different. Evolutionary stages and schemes (based on cross-cultural data) were ruled off the court: no more bands-tribes-chiefdoms-states.[27] Arguments about political complexity were condemned as unproductive and unsophisticated; alternative approaches were required. The British had plenty of alternatives, and we came up with a few of our own: pasts that were fundamentally *different* from anything we might see in ethnographic tribes, truly unique local histories. Post-processual interpretations of ancient societies often (but not exclusively) emphasized ritual, communalism, and egalitarianism[28]—echoing, in eerie ways, Morgan's and Engel's "primitive communism" (chapter 8). Stonehenge, for decades a chiefly exercise, became a place of communal worship—or something even more diffuse.[29] Other Neolithic monuments, formerly manifestations of political power, became "loci of high devotional expression" (a term applied to Chaco Canyon in an oft-cited application of British sensibilities to southwestern situations).[30]

Much of the British post-processual smorgasbord was not to southwestern tastes —a bit too out there—but the idea of a past detached from the band-tribe-chiefdom-state neo-evolutionary ladder (chapter 6) appealed very strongly indeed.[31] Post-processual approaches offered intriguing alternatives. We all agreed that some sort of leadership was needed to build Chaco and engineer Hohokam canals. But what was the nature of that leadership? That was an excellent question, most usefully asked by Barbara Mills and contributors to her volume *Alternative Leadership Strategies in the Prehispanic Southwest*.[32] Alternative to what? Well, to band-tribe-chiefdom-state, among other things. Alternative leadership strategies favor ritual and ceremony over conventional power politics.[33] Of course, there are all kinds of rituals and ceremonies out there: courtly rituals of Manchu emperors, the ceremonies of Hitler's Nuremberg rallies, whatever went on atop Aztec pyramids. "Ritual" does not necessarily equal "nice." But the ritual alternatives proposed for the ancient Southwest are invariably more corporate, communal, spiritual, and, frankly, Pueblo-like. (Modern Pueblos of course are famously ritual.) Or, following the British, southwestern alternatives might be true novelties, things ethnographers and neo-evolutionists never considered. Perhaps the Southwest was unique, its societies unlike anything in the neo-evolutionary locker: ritualities, communidades, antistructures, hierocracies. That would be interesting indeed! (And that might very well be true for the Hohokam Canon; I think Chaco and Paquimé were more like garden-variety states; chapter 8.)[34]

Chaco Great Houses, in the alternative view, became ceremonial structures (certainly *not* palaces). Hohokam platform mounds allowed the masses to view the shamans (*not* elite residences). Paquimé proved more resistant to revision. But even there—in the Southwest's greatest city—political hierarchies were trimmed and tailored to southwestern tastes.[35] It was made safe for theocracy with shaman-priests—albeit shaman-priests of Mesoamerican extraction—arranging the city's affairs.[36] Ancient southwestern societies, it seems, did great things with a remarkable variety of alternatives to actual government. Anything but kings!

Political edifices were leveled, southwestern social climbing denied. Not everyone jumped on the dissolution bandwagon. David Phillips and Lynne Sebastian, on the downsizing of Chaco: "We agree with many ideas within these approaches, but we fear that the current reaction to 'neo-evolutionary' models could easily drift into what we have termed 'neo-egalitarianism.' For at least some scholars, that is in fact the goal.... We view such statements as whistling one's way past the unromantic truth of social inequality, and thus past important insights about life in the past."[37] Kings?

Pueblos and other southwestern societies did indeed develop remarkable ritually based social and political systems that discouraged centralized political hierarchy. It's tempting to project those systems back into prehistory, but time does not work that way. Rather than paint the past in the colors of the present, I think the question we should ask is, When did those ritual alternatives arise? And why? In this chapter and chapter 8, I will argue that Puebloan egalitarianism—based in ritual and ceremony—rose after 1300 *in reaction against* more familiar forms of political power: men who would be kings at Chaco, Aztec, and Paquimé.[38] Ancient complexity caused modern simplicity.

Angry Indians

NAGPRA told southwestern archaeology to do something we had not done in a long time: listen to Indians. Archaeologists (as anthropologists) have always respected Native societies, but archaeology's interest in Native traditions *as history* varied over the years.

Early archaeologists, such as Bandelier, Cushing, Fewkes, and Hewett (and many of his students), paid close attention to Pueblo friends and informants and tried to find archaeological traces of Native origin stories. Then the first "new archaeology," just before World War I, explicitly rejected Native traditions as unreliable myths and legends (chapter 3). That attitude carried forward into the 1960s, with notable exceptions in the land claims cases of the 1940s and 1950s, in which archaeologists worked both for and against tribes, confirming or denying Indian traditions.[39] The New Archaeology of the 1960s and 1970s reaffirmed the first new archaeology's dismissal of Indian "myths" and engaged Indians rarely, and then mainly through published ethnography.[40]

The 1960s and 1970s were times of social ferment, including Indian civil rights and "Red Power."[41] Indians told us what they were thinking. Anthropology, it turned out, was not well regarded by its Native research "subjects," and archaeology was loathed and abhorred (to put it bluntly). Vine Deloria Jr. (my late colleague at the University of Colorado) led a blistering Native critique of the field,[42] beginning with an indictment of anthropology, veiled in parody in *Custer Died for Your Sins*, and later specifically targeting archaeology in *Red Earth, White Lies*. In the latter book, Deloria targets the peopling of the Americas and Pleistocene "overkill." He wraps up archaeology in a general condemnation of the Western sciences that study those events: "In our society we have been trained to believe that scientists search for, examine, and articulate truths about the natural world and about ourselves. They don't. But they do search for, take captive, and protect the social and economic status of scientists." Archaeology and anthropology were part of the colonial program, Deloria concluded, and "much of Western science must go."[43]

Deloria was controversial, even among Indians. It's my impression that few share his disdain for science in general, but most Indians I know are dubious about anthropology and openly disapproving of archaeology (fig. 7.2). That disapproval found legal expression in NAGPRA, which (along with other laws) directed archaeologists and the agencies that regulated archaeology to notify and consult with Indian tribes and nations.[44] Consultations were taken very seriously, and tribes and nations soon acquired substantial power over archaeological research on federal lands and CRM projects. (Procedures and policies vary from agency to agency, but the balance of power now tips heavily toward Indians.)

Figure 7.2 *Pot Hunters #2*, 2002. Oil and collage on panel, 48 x 72 in., by Mateo Romero (Cochiti). Credit: Phil Karsis, original photo; credit for photo-transfer image: Jennifer Esperanza. Courtesy Mateo Romero.

As we shall see, the upshot of all this was positive. But the rhetoric surrounding NAG-PRA was, to say the least, uncomfortable for archaeologists. ("Grave robbers" was one of the milder pejoratives.) That anger took many of us by surprise. If we thought about it at all, we thought we were recovering history that might interest or even help descendant peoples. That was not the case. Consequently, the 1980s and 1990s were marked by careful circumspection in the focus and language of archaeology, vis-à-vis Native America.[45] The tenor of the times discouraged narratives that strayed from steady progress or steady states. The Native past may have had high points and low points, good and bad, but Indians didn't need to hear it from archaeologists.[46] In 1999, bombshell books such as Christy and Jacqueline Turner's *Man Corn* (about cannibalism) and Steven LeBlanc's *Prehistoric Warfare in the American Southwest* seemed, to many Natives, like another round of Indian bashing.

Native Histories

At a meeting of tribal representatives, the governor of one of the Pueblos told me to leave Chaco alone: "Let it remain a mystery. There are things we are not supposed to know." A quandary. My job at that time was to investigate Chaco—not with new excavations but by rethinking a century of previous excavations and research. I asked the larger group what we (non-Indians) should know about Chaco. After a moment's pause, a representative from another Pueblo suggested, "How they farmed. How they made pottery. The yearly cycle. Daily life." Heads nodded in agreement. But, I objected, there was a lot more to Chaco than daily life: politics, history, stories. Silence. I had my marching orders.

I didn't follow those orders. I declined, with real uneasiness, the good-faith request by tribal representatives, wiser than I. I couldn't do what they asked—my job as an archaeologist is to learn about the ancient past. I try to do that job with respect for Native peoples, but I'm aware that simply *doing* that job, *doing* archaeology is inherently disrespectful. The most respectful thing I could do would be to get a different job.

I might, but first I must finish what I've started. How to proceed? How to write a history of the ancient Southwest, engaging Indian knowledge, when many Indians are not particularly interested in engaging archaeology? I proceeded by looking, selectively, at written texts, transcribing what ethnologists and folklorists call myths and legends, and listening to Indian people who chose to discuss that history with me, however obliquely. Because I am writing Big History, I've sought accounts that describe big events. Of course, no one from whom I've learned—from the anonymous "informants" of early ethnologists to modern leaders and poets—is responsible for the interpretations or spin I put on his or her words. (Which is part of the problem: I take traditions and *interpret* them, which of course is offensive.)

For the most part, I've tried to learn larger lessons, not details. For example, it's extremely important for archaeologists to understand that Indian traditional histories and origin stories are narratives of change and transformation. The past recounted in those stories was *very* different.[47] In "Histories," below, I summarize traditional stories about four key themes that seem useful for understanding the ancient Southwest—stories of Mesoamerican origins, of Chaco, of Hohokam platform mounds, and (perhaps) of the founding of Paquimé.[48] (In chapter 8, I present tales of a fifth tradition, but not an Indian one: Aztlan.)

Histories: 1250 to 1500 (Pueblo IV, Late Classic, Paquimé) ⚡

The Coalescent Communities project (chapter 6) concludes that population peaked across the whole Southwest between 1300 and 1350 and then plummeted sharply, decreasing by 1500 to the levels of the eighth and ninth centuries.[49] After the Spanish arrived, Old World diseases took their predictable, terrible toll, and regional population fell even further, sinking to the earliest preagricultural levels. The difficult years from 1300 to 1500 must have transformed southwestern societies as fatefully as colonization.

It cannot be stressed too strongly that the year 1300 was a watershed, a demographic zenith for the region, followed by catastrophic population decline, nearly complete reorganization of peoples and polities—and *then* centuries of colonization. The southwestern societies we know, imperfectly, from ethnography were studied in the nineteenth and twentieth

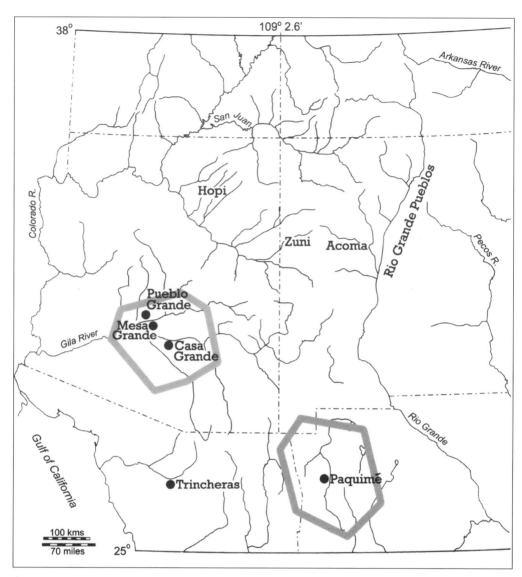

Figure 7.3. 1250 to 1500. Courtesy of the author.

centuries—six hundred years or more after that critical divide, 1300. That year of course is a convenient tag for several decades on either side of the nice round number. Around 1300 (plus or minus a few decades), one cycle of stories ended and another began. The first step toward the future: migrations. Great migrations from 1250 to 1450 shifted tens of thousands of people across the region, shaping a new Southwest (fig. 7.3).

Migrations frame much of Pueblo traditional history; the movement of clans and larger groups over long distances seems crucial to Pueblo heritage.[50] The early archaeologists tried to trace specific migrations from site to site; NAPGRA is essentially asking us to do the same. I'm not sure archaeology can do that. But our understanding of the past can benefit from the larger lessons of migration stories.

For example, the scale of the longest migrations: several Hopi clans came from or went to Palatkwapi, the Red City of the south.[51] Where was Palatkwapi? I have heard Hopi elders declare it was Teotihuacán,[52] while other Hopi scholars insist it was Paquimé—"the last stop on the road to Hopi."[53] Some of the Hopi clans may well have begun in the Classic Period at Mesoamerica's first great city (perhaps, I was told, as oppressed lower classes, building pyramids) and then tarried a while at the Southwest's last great city before finally moving on to Hopi. Other clans may have moved south to Paquimé, perhaps as post-Mimbres migrants. Palatkwapi ended badly, with fire and flood and earthquake and violence. Perhaps those stories recount the final dissolution of Paquimé—the last major southwestern political event before the arrival of Europeans. (The rise of Paquimé has been hotly debated; chapter 6. Much less attention has been focused on its fall; below.)

The Red City appears in Hopi tales as an admonitory episode, recalling past errors and reminding Hopi people of proper behavior in the present. But the Red City was surely also a historical event or series of events, with conflicting details. Moving beyond details, the larger lesson may be this: histories of migrations out of central or even southern Mexico broadly parallel early movements of Uto-Aztecan peoples into the Southwest and onto the western Plateau (chapter 2). Were southwestern migrations continental in scope? Probably.

Late Post-Classic Mesoamerica and Late Mississippian

The Mexica, who would become the Aztecs, arrived in the Valley of Mexico sometime around 1300. They were only one of many Chichimec tribes moving through, and from the north. The Mexica established their capital, Tenochtitlán, in 1345. A century later, they were masters of central Mexico.

According to their official histories (as interpreted by modern scholars), for about one hundred years, the Mexica wandered from their original homeland, Aztlan, far to the north, before reaching the Valley of Mexico. The Aztec king Moctezuma I was curious about Aztlan. Around 1440 he sent an expedition to find it, with mixed results. Aztlan was a myth (and political propaganda), but perhaps also a place. As we shall see in chapter 8, a sizable portion of the American electorate believes that Aztlan encompassed the US Southwest.[54] They may be right.

Aztecs get all the attention, but a rival empire immediately to their west, the Tarascan state, was every bit their equal.[55] The Tarascans (aka Purépecha) fought the Aztecs to a standstill along their mutual border. With the Southwest's close connections to west and Pacific coastal Mexico, the Tarascans may have been of more consequence than the Aztecs to Classic Period Hohokam, Paquimé, and Pueblo IV.[56] A gaggle of smaller secondary states and would-be states extended west from the Tarascan Empire to the post-Aztatlan polities along the Pacific coast.[57] These smaller states may have been as close as most southwestern pilgrims ever got to Tzintzuntzan, the Tarascan capital, or to the Aztec's Tenochtitlán. But it's worth looking at the Tarascans to see what sort of stories and ideas might have reached the far Southwest.

Tarascan royalty, like the Aztec kings, claimed Chichimec ancestry (or so the Spanish wrote, using that Nahuatl word). Either they came from the north, or they aspired to the warrior-hunter ideal of a mythic north.[58] Unlike Aztec emperors, who loosely presided over a large bureaucracy of priests and lords, Tarascan *cazonci* were powerful autocrats "who shared power with no one."[59] (If southwestern leaders shopped around for ideas about kingship, West Mexican models were far toward the authoritarian end of the scale.) Their capital,

Tzintzuntzan, reached a population of about thirty thousand. Their second-tier cities averaged four thousand people (Chaco or Paquimé size).[60]

Unfortunately, we know very little about the "trans-Tarascan" states and the post-Aztatlan coastal cities of the Late Post-Classic. Long-distance trading, which marked the Aztatlan horizon (chapter 5), certainly continued into the Late Post-Classic. The northern focus was Culiacán, a local capital and trading center and the northwesternmost Mesoamerican city (see fig. 1.4).[61] Culiacán would become the jumping-off point for conquistadors headed toward Cibola and the Southwest—about 800 kilometers from the Classic Period Hohokam and 650 kilometers from Paquimé. The city flourished in the very late Post-Classic[62]—that is, from about 1400 to the arrival of the Spanish (who relocated the capital several kilometers upstream to its present location).

And to the east? In the Mississippi Valley, Cahokia was gone. The once great city was now empty. Moundville, its successor in sequence if not in extraction, peaked in the late fifteenth century. Over most of the Southeast, small, short-lived "chiefdoms" appeared and then vanished (much like Post-Classic polities in Mesoamerica but on slightly smaller scales). David Anderson calls this pattern cycling.[63] A chiefdom would rise along one river and flourish for a few generations. Then it would fall, to be replaced in a nearby valley by another temple-town. That was the political landscape that met the Spanish when they arrived: scores of small chiefdoms throughout the Southeast. In the middle Mississippi, where Cahokia had once ruled, was a vast "vacant quarter." Mississippian continued its Post-Classic ways but on diminished scales. As noted in chapter 6, population in the Southeast decreased long before the arrival of Europeans—much like the Southwest.

The Natchez Indians seen by European explorers were a late—perhaps the last—lower Mississippi Valley polity. They were a pale reflection of Cahokia's glories. Still, Natchez political arrangements were impressive, with kings, nobles, and commoners. Their king, "the Great Sun," was carried aloft on a regal palanquin while commoner "stinkards" cringed below.[64] The exaggerated class distinctions of Natchez government seem slightly ridiculous, given their reduced circumstances. Their capital, the Grand Village (aka the Fatherland site),[65] could be easily mistaken for a fourth-tier village of Cahokia's time. Natchez rulers inherited the pomp but not the potency of Mississippian society. (How much greater must have been Cahokia?!) Strong governments in the Mississippi Valley, throughout the long Mississippian era, show that southwestern hierarchies were far from exceptional. In that continental context, princes at Chaco and kings at Paquimé were no big deal.

Anasazi/Pueblo

The year 1300 divides Pueblo III and Pueblo IV and divides "Anasazi" as an archaeological entity from "Pueblo" as historical and modern societies.[66] In previous chapters, I've used *Anasazi* as an archaeological tag (probably to the annoyance of some readers; see chapter 1, note 58). Make no mistake: Chaco and Aztec were Puebloan—and also part of histories and worlds far beyond the modern Pueblos. The term *Anasazi* seems less useful, less necessary for the final centuries of "prehistory." Compared with the many long centuries before 1300, the last three hundred years of Plateau and Rio Grande archaeology might seem fairly straightforward: becoming Pueblos. It was *not* a straight run to the modern Pueblos—there were twists, turns, and dead ends. Much of Pueblo IV remains surprisingly murky. Linda Cordell recently wrote, citing with agreement Kidder's 1924 précis of Pueblo IV, "We have not yet

Figure 7.4. Pueblo III versus Pueblo IV. Pueblo III Mesa Verde black-on-white (right) and Pueblo IV Fourmile Polychrome (left). Courtesy University of Colorado Museum of Natural History (right, UCM 9369; left, UCM 9634).

written the culture history that would 'trace the complex series of events—the migrations, the wars, the developments and clashes of societies and cults'" in those final centuries.[67]

Signs and Symbols: Pottery, Kiva Murals, Rock Art

Pueblo IV was an era of religious and ceremonial experiment, a flowering of new ideas and cults. *Cult* is a loaded word and probably an unfortunate one. It suggests religious pathologies ending with spiked Kool-Aid or sarin gas. What Kidder meant in the quote above, I think, was religious movements that rose suddenly and spread rapidly: the Virgin of Guadalupe in Mexico, Shugendo in Japan, or even early Islam and Christianity. For their practitioners, these were positive (if not easy) beliefs. Cults, in Kidder's sense, had the potential to become world religions. In competition with other belief systems, they also had the possibility of failure.

Something like that happened in Pueblo IV, a period of intense religious creation—an "adaptive radiation" after the "extinction" of Chaco/Aztec ideologies (if I may be allowed a natural science metaphor). New ideologies rushed to fill the vacuum, and not all of them survived. Kidder would call them cults.

The principal evidence for archaeologists, looking from the outside in, was art (fig. 7.4).[68] The evidence for art in Pueblo IV is dramatic. Without really knowing what it means, we can still trace the evolution of Anasazi artistic traditions through centuries of relatively simple, repetitive geometric designs on black-on-white (or, more rarely, black-on-red) pottery, culminating in the pottery of Pueblo III.[69] During Pueblo IV, those long-held traditions of fussy black-on-white were replaced by multicolored polychrome and glaze-painted pottery with bold, dynamic, asymmetrical images.[70] There was not a single, unitary Pueblo IV style; rather, there were a dozen vibrant styles, united only by the visual repudiation of what came before. Pueblo II and III art was as different from Pueblo IV as Geometric was from Attic Black Figure or—perhaps more relevant for older readers—as 1950s button-down was from 1960s flower power.[71] The shift came fast—a few decades at most. Elements of Pueblo IV art can be traced to earlier times, but the fully realized expression marked a clear break from the past.

The new styles crossed media: pottery, kiva murals, rock art, textiles.[72] This explosion of ideologically charged art had contemporary parallels in the flamboyant "international" styles of the later Post-Classic and in the Southeast Ceremonial Complex of the Mississippi Valley and the Southeast.

Post-Classic international styles—Mixteca-Puebla the most famous of several—were busy, dynamic, and polychromatic in a "codex" style. Mixteca-Puebla pots "were widely exchanged and highly prized, and…contained high information content."[73] Pottery in these styles might well be elite markers; that interpretation is widely but not unanimously held.[74] But recent reinterpretations suggest that the remarkable international designs represented new, competing religious beliefs (cults?)—elite, or perhaps not.[75]

The Southeast Ceremonial Complex (SCC) was likewise "a symbolic system of communication,"[76] carried by extraordinary objects, traded or otherwise traveled over extraordinary distances.[77] Like Pueblo IV art, SCC was expressed on many media—copper, stone, and other forms, but not pottery—at sites from Oklahoma to Georgia. The SCC originated at Cahokia.[78] After Cahokia's fall, its most elaborate forms developed in a range of regional styles, some of which continued up to the sixteenth century.[79] I believe Pueblo IV art repudiated the old, hierarchical order. In contrast, SCC is generally thought to "validate the power of a stratified elite social order,"[80] perhaps like Post-Classic international-style pottery—unless international styles indeed signal new "cults" and not old regimes.

Pueblo IV polychrome ceramics were also once interpreted as "elite" artifacts.[81] But, more likely, they reflect fourteenth- and fifteenth-century attempts to rebuild Pueblo society—post-Chaco—*without* a stratified elite social order. Salado redwares,[82] Sityaki polychromes,[83] and other Pueblo IV polychromes represented "cults" or emerging belief systems—most famously kachinas[84] and probably many other ritual-based beliefs. Diverse ceremonial systems competed or melded throughout Pueblo IV.[85] Some of these ceremonial systems came from the remarkable syncretism of Wupatki, where Anasazi met and mingled with Hohokam (chapter 6). Others had deeper roots in Pueblo–Anasazi history: they were with the people from the time of emergence, and they expanded in importance after Chaco and Aztec ended. But many of the new ideas came from, or were deeply influenced by, Mesoamerica.[86] For Pueblo societies seeking new ways to understand their world, west and central Mexico were again obvious places to look.

Why did people need new ways? Why, in Pueblo IV, a sudden search for ideological novelty (with intriguing parallels to post-processual archaeology!)? I argue below that with the central authority of Chaco and Aztec gone, Pueblo people needed new ways to live, to order their universe—without kings.[87]

Towns and Clusters

In Pueblo III (chapter 6), people made homes almost everywhere on the Plateau, in thousands of small farmsteads and bigger villages. By 1450 almost everyone was gathered into about one hundred large towns, clustered at Hopi, Zuni, Acoma, and Laguna and in the Rio Grande Valley from Socorro in the south to Taos in the north. That was a very big change.[88]

Some of the earliest Pueblo IV towns were enormous, with thousands of rooms. These included Late Pueblo III–Early Pueblo IV towns in the Chama Valley, the Mogollon uplands of Arizona, and the upper Little Colorado and—most spectacularly—the huge Tularosa towns near Zuni, with their Chaco-esque formality and perhaps remnants of Chacoan order (see fig.

6.10; chapter 6). Post-Chaco, post-Aztec social institutions could not hold them together. The strains were too great. The big, early Pueblo IV towns fragmented into smaller (two-hundred-room), less formal villages with Pueblo IV polychromes and glaze-painted pottery.[89] Town plans remained broadly similar: rooms massed around plazas with only a few (real) kivas. Some Pueblo IV kivas continued old Great Kiva forms and (presumably) functions, while others reflected new ideologies and religious associations.

Families lived in apartment-like suites of rooms, side by side in "row houses." The old unit pueblo—six rooms and a pit house/"kiva"—had been the basic Anasazi house form from 700 to 1300. After 1300 the form disappeared, as a freestanding structure or as an element of larger aggregations (chapter 6). This, too, was a big change. A large Pueblo III village in the Mesa Verde region had hundreds of small "kivas," one for each five or six rooms (see fig. 6.8). I believe these so-called kivas were actually pit houses; others consider them ceremonial chambers (see chapter 4, note 180). After 1300 most Pueblo IV towns had only two or three large kivas. Something happened around 1300, which shows quite clearly in house forms: people gave up on millennia-long traditions of pit house living, or they jettisoned family-level ceremonial architecture, or both. House form is an essential reflection of society, more surely denotative than portable, mutable pottery.[90] The ideological ferment that shows positively in art was also reflected in negative evidence: the absence of small Pueblo III "kivas." Ceremonial chambers or pit houses, Pueblo III "kivas" were freighted with symbolism and meaning, and their disappearance is strong evidence...of *something*.

The huge, earliest Pueblo IV towns fragmented after no more than a generation (not unlike the final Anasazi Pueblo III settlements of the Four Corners). Unrest and rising levels of violence (below) made bigger seem better. People wanted the safety of large towns but no longer had the social and political institutions to hold them together. "The explosive growth in settlement size after AD 1400, where the typical village size jumped to over 500 rooms, required social mechanisms in all surviving clusters that effectively subjugated the needs of the few (cross-culturally, kinship groups) to the will of the many."[91] How to do that without Chaco-like kings? Where to look?

Two centuries before, Mimbres successfully sustained large (up to five-hundred-room), permanent, densely aggregated towns. Some of the lessons learned by Mimbres were transformed in Pueblo IV and adapted to the new political realities.[92] It took time to revive and redevelop old (and new) ideas into successful cosmologies—to reinvent a world for new realities. For the first century of Pueblo IV, social frictions were "solved" by division (fissioning) into separate smaller towns or by movement: if it didn't work in one place, try it again somewhere else. The preceding sentence glosses hundreds of migration stories told at every pueblo—repeated movements from old towns to new towns, seeking a shifting center place, *where things finally worked*. A few pueblos sank roots—both Acoma and Oraibi claim twelfth-century beginnings—but most thirteenth- and fourteenth-century pueblos were footprints of migration, short-lived stops on paths to the middle place.

The year 1300 marked the end of migrations out of the Four Corners, but migrations continued thereafter throughout Pueblo IV. Clans and other groups bounced around in already settled districts (Zuni, for instance) and into areas empty or only sparsely settled.[93] Towns were built, abandoned, and rebuilt, with populations moving to new towns or splitting into "daughter" villages. That pattern is well attested at Hopi in the west, a clear case because of its splendid isolation,[94] but short-term, short-distance movements from village site to village site were typical of the entire region.[95]

Figure 7.5. Poshu'ouinge, a large village in the Chama River Valley, New Mexico. Artist's reconstruction by Mary Beath. Copyright © Mary Beath; courtesy Mary Beath.

There was more movement than simply "settling in" within local Pueblo territories. Between 1400 and 1450, a second large-scale "abandonment," rivaling the Four Corners of the thirteenth century, emptied the southern Pueblo region—the big pueblos of the Mogollon uplands and along the toe of the Plateau. Thousands of people, moving as villages, clans, and families, joined towns to the north.[96] A dozen towns at Zuni and Hopi got bigger and bigger through the late fifteenth century, absorbing population from the Mogollon uplands (total population actually *decreased* after 1450; see below). That second "great migration" out of the southern Pueblo area is less famous than the Mesa Verde migrations, but it was probably just as important in Pueblo history.

Pueblo IV was the Rio Grande's golden era, a time of enormous towns that are properly called Classic.[97] Rio Grande Classic Period towns developed new institutions to cope with increasing size, more political than western pueblos but far less centralized than Chaco models.[98]

Poshu'ouinge (fig. 7.5), on the Rio Chama, was not the largest Classic Period town (that might be Sapawe, just north of the Chama, or Kuapa, near Cochiti Pueblo), but it was big, with eighteen hundred rooms in linear blocks around three football-field-sized plazas. Pueblo Bonito would have fit inside the largest plaza.[99] There were scores of comparably large Rio Grande towns, from Taos in the north to Socorro in the south and from the Galisteo Basin in the east to Acoma in the west.[100]

The Rio Grande Classic was a vibrant and fascinating period, but it was not untroubled.

"Classic," as in Hohokam, does not mean Edenic. Population rose sharply and then fell catastrophically. All across the Pueblo world, from Hopi to the Rio Grande, population increased from 1250 to 1300/1325—doubtless from relocations from the Four Corners. Then population fell in the west (despite the influx of Mogollon upland groups). Numbers continued to increase in the east, along the Rio Grande—particularly in the northern Rio Grande.[101] Thus the western Pueblo world diminished while the eastern Pueblo world and the Rio Grande increased dramatically—for a time. Population along the Rio Grande peaked around 1400 and then dropped like a rock through the fifteenth and sixteenth centuries—as it did over the entire Southwest.[102] That was the Late Pueblo IV world in which modern Pueblo life crystallized—at 1300, dramatic growth; after 1450, catastrophic decline. Things only got worse with European intrusions: more than fifty large Rio Grande pueblos were abandoned in early historic times, leaving only twenty towns today.[103]

Demographic collapse was reflected in changing political landscapes. During Pueblo II and III, Anasazi towns and villages were thick on the land: "Virtually the whole North American Southwest was a single contiguous settlement system at that time [1200–1250] during which it was possible to walk a path from one community to another throughout almost the whole area without having to go more than one day between neighboring sites."[104] During the fourteenth and fifteenth centuries, Pueblo settlements contracted into a score of isolated groups, each group consisting of a half-dozen large villages or towns. These town groups almost certainly represented intervillage political alliances,[105] confederacies,[106] or, more prosaically, "clusters."[107]

The fundamental reason for clustering of big towns was defense—safety in numbers and distance from potential enemies in other clusters. The warfare that marked the end of Pueblo III (chapter 6) increased markedly in Pueblo IV.[108] New ideologies might integrate a large town, but they could not pacify the region. Warfare between and among towns and clusters became endemic and continued long after the arrival of the Spanish.[109]

Pueblo Transformations

Pueblo IV was a sea change, a break from what came before. What came before, of course, were Chaco and Aztec, central governments that held together the Anasazi world with varying success. By 1500 no vestige remained of that earlier, Anasazi political world: there was no central government. Indeed, there was little we would recognize as government at all.[110] Anasazi became Pueblo, developing the remarkable lifeways and worldviews captured, or stereotyped, by Ruth Benedict.[111]

In chapter 3, I caricatured Benedict's stereotype: *happy, peaceful Pueblo people, living communally in harmony with their environment.* That vision of the Pueblo past has been amplified and reinforced at ten thousand campfire talks at national parks, in hundreds of coffee table books, and through scores of museum exhibits. It forms the intellectual bedrock that underlies a great deal of serious scholarship. And it's true—I'm sure Pueblo people are all those things, when possible. They worked hard to become so, today and in the past.

Benedict (back in chapter 3) told us that archaeology could never tell us how Pueblo life came about. I think we can. During Pueblo IV, people made hard decisions to re-form their societies after a history of unhappiness, war, hierarchies, and environmental catastrophes. They created societies that avoided hierarchy while coping with violence, change, and the periodic unhappiness that is the human condition.

In pueblos today, there is a clear separation of church and state, with elective, democratic, secular governance taking the lead in secular affairs. In practice, the temporal is subordinate to parallel, older ritual offices. Ritual and ceremonial knowledge is a potent form of power. Modern Pueblo religious life is wonderfully varied, elaborate, and (to an outside observer) eclectic.[112] Kachina ceremonialism is only the most visible of the multilayered network of ritual that threads through village life, binding communities into workable wholes that prevent the fissioning of Pueblo IV. Individuals and small groups make decisions, which we could call ritual, that ramify throughout the economy and governance of the community.[113]

So, too, secular leadership. Governors and councilmen have power. It's impossible for a pueblo to operate without people making decisions that affect the entire village. But individual political power (leadership, rulership, kingship) is effectively discouraged by a complex net of "leveling" mechanisms—ritual and social checks and balances "level" and prevent personal, political advancement. Benedict had it right (chapter 3): "A man must avoid the appearance of leadership."

Neither spiritual nor temporal power materially benefits those holding ritual roles or political offices, nor can it. It has been famously said that the most powerful man at Zuni lives in the meanest house. That was decidedly *not* the case at Chaco: the most powerful men lived in the biggest palace. That contrast in house form (if you will) encapsulates Pueblo political history.

Pueblo IV people had been there, done that—and never wanted to do it again. I think that reaction against Chaco was deliberate but not calculated. A plethora of reformation ideologies flowered in Pueblo IV. Not all of them survived into modern times. There was a Darwinian weeding of competing "cults," rituals, and ceremonial systems. Ones that worked were kept; others were set aside. It took centuries of tinkering, from 1300 to 1600, to get the balance right. Christianity, when it came, was just another entry in that crowded field—a new ideology for coping with the colonial state.

Pueblo IV was a remarkable ideological and cosmological experiment. It was first and foremost a rejection of Chaco and Aztec and thereafter the creation of new worlds and worldviews that sustain Pueblos today.

Native Histories: Chaco and After

My impressions of Chaco (and "Anasazi" in general) began to change fifteen years ago, when I was working on an exhibit at the Museum of New Mexico with a remarkable group of Native consultants and collaborators. Prior to that, I was more or less in the Benedict bandwagon: happy, peaceful, and so forth. While working on the exhibit, the subject of Chaco kept coming up. People from several Rio Grande pueblos said the same thing in different ways: we know all about Chaco, but we don't talk about it because bad things happened out there. The tone of the comments—there were no details—made me wonder.[114]

Chaco and all the Four Corners sites were clearly sacred places for Native peoples, but I had uncritically equated sacred with good—and good with happy, peaceful, egalitarian, and all that. I was not alone, I think, in a naive, sixties-influenced view of sacred, ritual, and ceremony. Many southwestern sacred places, I've since learned, were places where people overcame obstacles, made mistakes, learned lessons—sometimes the hard way. The places might be sacred, but they were not necessarily happy.

Traditional histories told by Pueblo and Navajo peoples recount much that was difficult, challenging, *eventful*—and these are the accounts that most interest me now. It's not that I am obsessed with disasters, failures, misery (a charge I have heard leveled by Native scholars against archaeology). To trace the lineaments of history, we need to nail the hinge points, the times of change. Those times are often turbulent and troubled. When things were working, we can write archaeologies of daily life. But history requires the times when things were *not* working, when things shifted to something new.

It is my impression that, from modern Pueblo perspectives, what happened at Chaco and in the Four Corners was *not right* for Pueblo people—that's one reason for the "abandonment." Pueblo people left to start anew. Bad things happened at Chaco in particular. People learned from those errors and thenceforth conducted their lives differently. These events are wrapped up in the stories of White House, an amalgam of Chaco and Aztec Ruins, to which we will shortly turn.

Many Pueblo stories speak of Chaco as an important place in migrations, a meeting spot for many peoples, and surely it was that.[115] But in many accounts of Chaco and the Four Corners—sometimes veiled, sometimes clear—there are also themes of political power and contest. Several respected Pueblo people have chosen to address these matters "on the record," in public arenas.[116] Although the names are available, I omit them here (and in the notes for this section).

> A Laguna man:
>
> In our history we talk of things that occurred a long time ago, of people who had enormous amounts of power: spiritual power and power over people. I think that those kinds of people lived here in Chaco.... Here at Chaco there were very powerful people who had a lot of spiritual power, and these people probably used their power in ways that caused things to change and that may have been one of the reasons why the migrations were set to start again, was because these people were causing changes that were never meant to occur.... There are some things in our migration histories that we don't understand, but I think that some of those things were never meant to be understood. They served a purpose when they were needed and now that purpose is, or that need is no longer there. It's no longer necessary to repeat that portion of the story.[117]
>
> A Hopi man:
>
> Perhaps, over time, the original premises on which they began to develop these places could have been corrupted. And some people who come here feel that there was an aspect of this place that was, perhaps, darker.[118]
>
> An Acoma man:
>
> I think that they were so "in tune" with the natural forces that they were able to control these forces. And sometimes it's been said that this [control] could be abused by people; and that perhaps there were decisions made in the past not to continue this accumulation of knowledge, of control of the natural forces.[119]
>
> A Santa Clara woman:
>
> [Chaco was] full of energy, a different energy than before or after.... A hierarchical structure: it was not the idea of Pueblo society that we know today, where everybody is equal...a different ideology.[120]

And again:

My response to the canyon was that some sensibility other than my Pueblo ancestors had worked on the Chaco great houses. There were the familiar elements such as the *nansipu* (the symbolic opening into the underworld), kivas, plazas, and earth materials, but they were overlain by a strictness and precision of design and execution that was unfamiliar.... It was clear that the purpose of these great villages was not to restate their oneness with the earth but to show the power and specialness of humans...a desire to control human and natural resources.... These were men who embraced a social-political-religious hierarchy and envisioned control and power over place, resources and people.[121]

Two key traditional stories—one Pueblo, one Navajo, and both well known—represent these events. Chaco and Aztec are remembered, I think, in Navajo tales of the man that ethnologists and folklorists call the Great Gambler and in Keresan stories of White House, versions of which are shared by many Pueblos.[122] These are my retellings, primarily from published accounts, augmented by conversations with Navajo and Pueblo colleagues.

The Great Gambler (in Navajo stories) was neither Navajo nor Pueblo. He was a persuasive stranger. By staging and winning betting games, he subjugated all peoples—Pueblo and Navajo—to a condition close to slavery. He made the enslaved people build him a house (usually identified as Pueblo Alto) and then more houses for his associates (the other Chaco Great Houses). After years of oppression, the people rose up and overthrew the Great Gambler. There are several versions of his end, but in one account they shoot him straight south into Mexico. As noted in chapter 5, a Navajo man from a clan near Chaco commented that the person we call the Great Gambler could more accurately be called king.[123]

White House (in Pueblo stories) was an extraordinary town where all the people lived before they split into the modern pueblos. It was a good place: the rain fell, food was plentiful, and the people were at peace. Wonderful things (shell, turquoise, macaw feathers) were available at White House. Most importantly, at White House, spirits that would become kachinas lived side by side with people. Frictions between people and kachinas led to violence, a battle between the two. The kachinas then left the people, after teaching them ceremonies and dances necessary to continue the vital converse between spirits and people. The cause of that dramatic separation was improper behavior by some people—gambling and (importantly) the accumulation of wealth and power, which fostered disrespect toward the kachinas. After the battle, White House was afflicted by many troubles. The people were instructed to move on, to the south. On the way to their new homes, they held "ceremonies of forgetting" to ensure that the mistakes made at White House would never be repeated. I think White House refers to Chaco and Aztec and combines their histories. My reading, several Pueblo people have told me, isn't right in all particulars, but it isn't wrong.[124]

Native stories tell of an eventful past, a past with history. Of course, I have drawn upon histories and story fragments congruent with my narrative—or, more accurately, that inspired my narrative. My use of Native history is selective, as is my use of archaeology. But the important point here is that Native histories consistently show that *the past was different*, and well-known episodes like the Great Gambler and White House suggest that a key dimension of that difference was political. People in the past acquired power far beyond that known or allowed in today's southwestern societies. *Things like this happened* and were remembered.

Figure 7.6. Pueblo Grande, Phoenix. Artist's reconstruction by Michael Hampshire. This mural combines a Hopi-like ceremonial (left edge, center) with Hohokam pomp and circumstance (the lordly figure holding forth lower left center, with conch-tooting attendants). The split personality of platform mounds: ceremonial and/or elite residential? Chris Downum constructed a magnificent model of this platform mound, which can be seen at the Pueblo Grande Museum. Courtesy Pueblo Grande Museum.

Hohokam: Terminal "Classic"

Late Classic Hohokam was a period of archaeological contradictions. In the Phoenix Basin, population increased and political power reached its peak, marked by the largest monuments ever constructed by the Hohokam and by astonishingly crafted, elaborate artifacts—things early archaeologists understandably called classic. But all this happened as the fabric of Hohokam unraveled, disastrously. Demographic collapse, warfare, floods, famines—ending in the dissolution of Hohokam society.

Pobre Pueblo Grande

Pueblo Grande is Phoenix's archaeological showcase—the best place in town to see a platform mound, ball courts, and Hohokam canals (fig. 7.6).[125] The Pueblo Grande mound was the largest of all platforms: a rectangular structure, 47 by 90 meters, with a flat surface elevated 4 meters above the surrounding Salt River valley bottom. It was larger than all but the very largest mounds at Cahokia. The mound was surrounded by a walled, rectangular compound.

Big as it was, the huge platform is the tip of the iceberg. A new highway just east of the Pueblo Grande park cuts through the eastern half of the much larger site, which extends far beyond the current park boundaries. That narrow highway corridor produced seven hefty volumes of CRM data.[126]

The Pueblo Grande project changed our view of the Hohokam Classic. Far from "classic," the era was (it seems) one of collapse, retrenchment, and isolation. Pottery and other artifacts tell a tale of a disrupted region and balkanization. War, which marred the Early Classic, redoubled in the Late Classic.[127] Violence flared first between the Phoenix Basin and its old peripheries and later between competing towns within the core. Health deteriorated, particularly among children.[128]

Overall population grew at Pueblo Grande, but only through a massive influx of people from Hohokam towns in the peripheries. Waves of migrants, fleeing war, had different histories and customs—undoubtedly straining social relations, rather like the situation in contemporary western Pueblo IV towns.[129] Resources of the Phoenix Basin had been depleted by almost ten centuries of Hohokam civilization: farmed out, hunted out, fished out.[130] Diet lacked the nutrients found only in wild resources. Corn, beans, and squash would keep people alive, but without other foods, those basic crops would not keep people healthy. Still, the only answer was to expand canals farther and farther into the deserts, away from the river itself.[131] Without the addition of substantial numbers of displaced people, Pueblo Grande probably would have dwindled into nothing, but those additional people quickly overshot the resources of the Phoenix Basin. In that context, Pueblo Grande's huge platform seems grimly ironic—a monument amid misery.

Platform Mounds, Concluded

There are today essentially two schools of thought on platform mounds, summarized by Mark Elson and Dave Abbott: (1) "Mounds were ceremonial and used by relatively undifferentiated groups for ritual, feasting, and other socially integrative activities," and (2) there was "residence on top of mounds by managerial elites."[132] Those are very different views, but a compromise was possible (chapter 6). Platform mounds may have *begun* in the Early Classic Period as ceremonial structures. After 1250 platforms shifted to elite residences.[133] That became the accepted view (chapter 6): early, ritual; late, elite.

Alas, the compromise seems to be tilting back toward ritual for *both* Early and Late Classic.[134] The arguments used *against* the elite residence interpretation are almost the same as those that elsewhere (Chaco?) might suggest palaces—elevated (with all that that entails), exclusive, surrounded by high compound walls.[135] Like early Chaco Great Houses, they look like commoner house forms scaled up: monumental houses. Remarkably massive construction, overly large rooms, disproportionate storage, attached spaces for ritual and perhaps for administrative/ritual assistants—the second assistant minister in charge of shamanism, perhaps. As at Chaco, an absence of work-a-day, quotidian features. Those arguing for ritual functions use all these features as evidence for ceremony; I read this list and think Great House. I think the structures atop Late Classic platforms were elite residences.[136]

So I accept the compromise: platforms were initially public spaces, later co-opted for elite residences. That diplomatic solution allows both schools of thought to be right. In the service of harmony, let us accept that it was thus. (I still have doubts. I don't see evidence that Early Classic mounds, like that at Marana, were strikingly different from later Classic mounds, but I'm working other people's turf.)

Perhaps, the most famous "platform mound"—Casa Grande, 75 kilometers south of Pueblo Grande on the Gila River (figs. 7.7, 7.8)—was not a platform mound.[137] Casa Grande, built around 1300, was an impressive four-story tower rising more than 10 meters from a base

Figure 7.7. Casa Grande, south of Phoenix. A palace overshadowed by a monumental tin roof. A hailstorm at Casa Grande today is a truly astonishing experience.

only one-twentieth the size of Pueblo Grande. It was built of adobe, poured or packed into meter-wide walls.[138] The first story of Casa Grande was intentionally filled, creating something like a platform; many Hohokam archaeologists believe that Casa Grande was in fact a hyperbolized Late Classic Period platform mound.[139]

What was Casa Grande? Casa Grande has been explained as an observatory used by stargazing shamans.[140] Native histories name it as the home of an oppressive ruler (below). I think that Casa Grande (see figs. 7.7 and 7.8) was just what its name says: a Great House, towering over the surrounding town. Casa Grande, Pueblo Grande, and all the Late Classic platform mounds were, perhaps, the apotheosis of the Chacoan Great House.

Meet the New Boss

In the decades after 1250, Chacoan ruling families were looking for work. Aztec was falling apart. The Great House elites of Zuni were conspicuously excluded from huge, geometric, late-thirteenth-century towns. About the same time, elite residences appeared atop Hohokam platform mounds. Coincidence? Not in this book—no coincidences! We may be looking at supply and demand. Hohokam needed leaders, and the Plateau had a surplus.

Things around Phoenix began to deteriorate in 1075, if not earlier, and went from bad to worse right through the Classic Period. The old ways failed. Ball courts were abandoned, and platforms were built over mounds. Whatever transpired atop Early Classic platform mounds—shaman shows?—was not up to the challenge. Civic life spiraled downward.

Figure 7.8. Casa Grande, Arizona. Bird's-eye view of Compound A from the south. A combination perhaps of early aerial photography and advanced museum model-making. Original image from Jesse Walter Fewkes, Casa Grande, Arizona (1913). In the public domain.

Nothing could halt the "centuries of decline."[141] Just as the Late Pioneer Period villages welcomed the remarkable Hohokam Canon, the people of Pueblo Grande looked for answers, for leaders—ritual or political—who offered solutions. But where were leaders to be found? The Hohokam Canon had held political power in check for four or five centuries. Hohokam Big House families, if they still existed, had long since forgotten or forsaken their Archaic ambitions. Whatever vestiges of leadership they retained would have long since been reduced into roles appropriate to the canon

Hohokam lacked the political tools and traditions to fix, or attempt to fix, the Phoenix Basin. They had no roles or models for hierarchical leadership. For half a millennium, they had purposefully avoided Mesoamerican-style political power. The Chaco Anasazi, in contrast, courted and copied southern leadership styles. Chaco's rulers were knockoffs of Post-Classic kings. They might or might not have had the knowledge to fix Hohokam's problems, but they certainly had the credentials.

Their families had real or fictive histories of many generations of rule. From the capital cities to two-hundred-plus outliers, they numbered many hundreds or even thousands and (taken together) formed something like a ruling class. Leading families in the Bluff Great House, for example, had more in common with the kings of Chaco than with commoners of southeastern Utah. Elite connections were essential to their status in Bluff, as they were for every outlier Great House family. Like ruling families in Mesoamerica and in the Mississippi Valley, they probably felt entitled—indeed obligated—to practice their craft. Kings were kings, whether or not they had countries or followers. Recall Ben Nelson's account of elite diasporas from fallen Teotihuacán: rulers looking for people to rule (chapter 4). That was the Plateau after 1250.

Would it be strange for Hohokam to accept or invite rulers from the Plateau? Stranger-kings—princes without portfolios—were a familiar theme in Mesoamerica. Kings were often foreigners or pretended to be. Otherness enhanced their kingship.[142] Something like that—diluted, reduced, a comic opera to Teotihuacán's Greek tragedy—brought Chacoan and post-Chacoan elites into the deserts of the south.

In the context of the conventional Southwest that we've come to know and love—Benedict's Southwest, the Southwest of Hopi and Taos and Santa Fe—that suggestion seems outrageous. *But that was not the world of Pueblo IV and Classic Period Hohokam!* Their world was Post-Classic and Mississippian, and in those contexts the suggestion is not incredible. Don't think about Zuni at 1890. Think about elite diasporas leaving Teotihuacán (chapter 4); the Post-Classic world, predatory and active (chapter 7); "chiefdoms" rippling through the Southeast from a middle Mississippi epicenter (chapter 1); Cahokia as a great city, its leaders far greater than chiefs (chapter 5). Remember that Hohokam *was* Mesoamerican and Chaco *wanted to be*. Both were part of that larger world. In those contexts, Chaco elites setting up on Hohokam platform mounds seem less outré. It might even be what's known in the trade as a "plausible scenario."[143]

Thinking about that larger world might change our views of what was possible or likely in the ancient Southwest. Recall the Natchez, a pale reflection of Cahokia's glory: kings, nobles, groveling commoners. All the mounds at the Natchez Grand Village, scooped up and carried west in dump trucks, would not fill a tenth of Pueblo Grande's platform—upon which, we say, shamans danced.

Both were societies in decline. The Natchez village was undersized and shabby. Pueblo Grande was still a very impressive place, meriting the title "classic." It surpassed the Natchez in every dimension: population, infrastructure, economic organization, even artifacts (subjectively). The Natchez had one essential advantage: history. The Great Sun was heir to the lords of Cahokia; they were part of the Natchez past. The Hohokam did not have that history. By choice, they had no kings. Chacoan traditions, carried by post-Chaco elite families, could bring hierarchy into the desert.

New, hierarchical political structures—more like Chaco than Snaketown!—were now in place, atop the ailing but still impressive Classic Period Hohokam. For a short, swift time—a century, maybe two—Classic Period Hohokam was on the bubble, ready to move to the next level. David Abbott speculates (his verb) that "the Hohokam will be shown to have been on the verge of forging a multi-community, centrally controlled hydraulic network. Such accomplishments are usually associated with politically advanced, state-level societies."[144] But it didn't work. "Unfortunately, the uptick in sociopolitical complexity was short lived and ineffective."[145] Their new leaders did not have the answers. Phoenix Basin Hohokam continued to suffer war, famine, pestilence, death, and floods—and in the end, something like class revolution (below).

Floods

"The long-term pattern that had defined optimal conditions…in the Salt River Valley since about AD 900 changed radically in the mid-1300s."[146] Changed and not for the better.

Along the Salt, there were destructive floods three years in a row—1357, 1358, and 1359—followed by two years of deep drought, 1360–1361.[147] The Salt River systems may or may not have been repaired after 1360. They could not survive the final stem-winders: enormous floods in 1381, 1382, and 1384. The 1382 flood was twice as big as any in the preceding 480 years, and two years later came another! That calamity was followed by a ten-year drought,

1386 to 1395.[148] Population in the Phoenix Basin, already in serious decline, plummeted. "Even during a time when leaders exercised new ritual and managerial authority, their efforts to master environmental and economic adversity were undone by circumstances and events that were too unwieldy to control."[149] By the end of the fourteenth century, most of the great Hohokam cities and towns were understandably empty.[150] A few people rattled around (the Polveron Phase), particularly along the Gila, which had relatively better stream flow from 1150 to 1420. But the thin good times on the Gila ended with huge floods in 1420 and again in 1428.[151]

Why did the Classic Period end? Floods, of course! The flushing model indicates demise at 1360 or 1385 for Salt River sites, perhaps extended to the 1430s for the Gila River. It might have all ended in the 1380s; the Gila Valley was the weak sister, economically dependent for trade, perhaps even for food, on the stronger Salt. The Salt River Classic, when it was fully and finally flushed, may have sucked down Gila River valley towns too. Or perhaps Gila Valley peoples rose up and overthrew Salt River rulers. Perhaps there was more to Hohokam's end than floods and flushing.

Native Histories: The End of Hohokam

The Hohokam region, historically and today, was the home of Piman-speaking O'odham tribes. (*Hohokam* is an anglicized version of a Piman phrase meaning "things that are all used up.") There are scholarly debates about whether or not the O'odham are the lineal descendants of the Hohokam (discussed above). The O'odham might well be heirs of the Hohokam—and yet a different people.[152]

Some of the traditional O'odham histories have been published in *The Short, Swift Time of Gods on Earth: The Hohokam Chronicles*.[153] The stories tell of a war waged by the O'odham against oppressive ruler-priests, who lived on platform mounds and in Great Houses. The rulers were Hohokam—ethnically different from O'odham. Perhaps they were gods.[154] Perhaps they wanted to be. The ruler-priests were arrogant and arbitrary and offended O'odham's culture hero, Elder Brother. Elder Brother rallied the O'odham, who rose up and destroyed their oppressors. There are various versions of the revolt story, with battles ranging from Gila Bend to the lower Salt River. Lynn Teague reconstructed the O'odham revolt: it started at Casa Grande (the Hohokam Bastille?) and ended at Pueblo Grande, and heads rolled from platform mounds along the way.[155] At about the same time, there was a terrible flood: "This flood was said to have followed a period of drought and wind, when the people became hungry. In a similar tale, but one that is not specifically identified with the fall of the platform mound system, Morning Green, the chief of Casa Grande, lost control of the rain and wind gods so there was a period of drought followed by flood."[156] The revolt was connected to floods and droughts—they were the ultimate cause—but the O'odham uprising adds political history to Hohokam's end. (After the revolt, the O'odham did not remain in the Hohokam core, the Phoenix Basin. They returned to the south, where they became today's Pima or Akimel O'odham.)

I interpret these stories as a class revolt. The oppressed O'odham rose up against Hohokam leaders, who lived in Great Houses on platform mounds. Alternatively, the stories could recall a regional contest between politically simpler people to the south (Tucson?) and an oppressive regime in the Phoenix Basin. I suspect that the traditions include both events, conflated. I am persuaded that class revolt toppled Classic Period leaders, who were caught

Figure 7.9. Cerro de Trincheras, northern Sonora, Mexico. Compare figure 2.4. Courtesy of and copyright © Adriel Heisey.

up in events and forces beyond their control and beyond remedy: demographic collapse, environmental degradation, and ultimately floods.

Notably, the stories make clear that Classic Period rulers were "foreign" to the O'odham. I think they were literally foreigners, from the north. The hierarchy represented by platform palaces was indeed foreign to centuries of Hohokam traditions of governance. The Classic Period towns thought they wanted leaders, until they got them.

Cerro de Trincheras

Terraced hills had deep antiquity in the southern deserts: recall Cerro Juanaqueña about 1200 BC (chapter 2). During Early Classic Hohokam (chapter 6), after a long hiatus, terracing reappeared on hills across much of southeastern Arizona and in the eponymous Trincheras "culture" of northern Sonora—home of the biggest and the best. At this time, a few terraced hillsides appeared in southern New Mexico and northwestern Chihuahua.[157]

The largest, most monumental terraced hill was one of the last: Cerro de Trincheras in Sonora (fig. 7.9).[158] Cerro de Trincheras dates to 1300–1450. More than nine hundred substantial stone terraces step up the north face of a 150-meter hill, the tallest prominence on that stretch of the Rio Magdalena. The terraces were residential, with a population between one and two thousand.[159] Cerro de Trincheras was contemporary with Paquimé and may have rivaled the Chihuahua capital as a producer of shell jewelry.

Figure 7.10. Colonnade, Paquimé, northern Chihuahua, Mexico. Artist's reconstruction by Alice Wesche, based on the research of Charles Di Peso and others. Colonnades were numerous and conspicuous at Paquimé. Elsewhere in the Southwest, we know of precisely one, at Chetro Ketl in Chaco Canyon (see fig. 5.1). Courtesy Amerind Foundation.

There was a Trincheras region or area, also comparable in size to Casas Grandes (see fig. 7.3).[160] Cerro de Trincheras was a big, central site but apparently not the capital. These things are only now being worked out. Like Casas Grandes (chapter 6 and below), northern Sonora saw some isolated, early work; a handful of dedicated archaeologists maintaining interest; and a recent boom in research.[161]

The terraces at Cerro de Trincheras are massive affairs, standing up to 2 meters tall. Enormous amounts of fill were required to create level surfaces upon which homes were built. The houses built on those massive terraces were surprisingly ephemeral; they left scant archaeological remains. Enormous quantities of artifacts (mostly plainware pottery; Cerro de Trincheras made little decorated pottery) show that a large population lived at Cerro de Trincheras. There are apparently only two public or ceremonial structures. One is a rectangular (14 by 54 meters) open stone enclosure (La Cancha) that hints of a ball court, except that someone plunked down a circular stone hut at mid-court. La Cancha was on the lower slopes of the hill, in a natural amphitheater: "Any activity here would have been visible over most of the densely occupied north face."[162] The second ceremonial structure is El Caracol, a dry-stone spiral enclosure on the hill's crest. Transported several hundred kilometers north, into the broken country of central Arizona, El Caracol might be called a fort. But surrounded by two thousand people living on terraces, who needs a fort?

Cerro de Trincheras was a big town and the biggest town in its region. But there remains something inescapably defensive about Cerro de Trincheras and *trincheras* sites in general.[163] Perhaps terraced hills were some form of Star Wars defense, expensive and impractical. A monumentally impressive, highly visible hill might suffice to discourage rough stuff.

If they were thinking defense, whom were they worried about? Where did Cerro de Trincheras stand geopolitically? The site produced remarkably little painted pottery. Among the few sherds, only about twenty were Late Classic Hohokam's signature Gila Polychrome, while five hundred were Ramos Polychrome—the calling card of Casas Grandes.[164] Randy McGuire and Maria Elisa Villalpando (the site's principal researchers) discount Cerro de Trincheras's links to Paquimé (admittedly minimal) and state with some vigor that "it is not an extension of the Hohokam civilization to the north, nor is it an outpost of Mesoamerican civilization."[165] Cerro de Trincheras, apparently, stood alone. And there we shall leave it. Sonora reenters history later, along its namesake river (below).

Casas Grandes

Chaco rose in reaction to Hohokam (chapter 5), but I suspect Chaco never worried Hohokam overmuch. Far to the north, in their cold stone palaces, Anasazi leaders were too busy keeping the peace to meddle in the affairs of their larger, older, much more impressive southern neighbor. That may have changed in the Classic Period (above), but Chacoan influences during the Late Classic Period, if real, were merely political.

In the Late Classic Period, Hohokam faced for the first time a serious *economic* rival: Casas Grandes in Chihuahua. Paquimé (the Casas Grandes capital) was the grandest city ever in the ancient Southwest (see figs. 1.1, 7.10, 7.11). No other site was as cosmopolitan, as ostentatiously connected to the larger Post-Classic world. If southwestern elites were trying to become Mesoamerican lords, then the rulers of Paquimé came closest to that ideal.

Paquimé

There had been a few earlier visitors, but Adolph Bandelier put Paquimé on the archaeological map. A huge adobe city, a long day's journey into Chihuahua, Paquimé was clearly important. Bandelier urged excavations "at the earliest possible date."[166] But border troubles through the 1920s discouraged research. Neither US nor Mexican archaeologists seemed interested in Chihuahua. The first major fieldwork was undertaken in 1958–1961—thirty years after Judd's work at Pueblo Bonito, twenty years after Gladwin excavated Snaketown—when Charles Di Peso of the Amerind Foundation excavated one-third of the site.

Di Peso's monumental report (see chapter 6) confirmed Paquimé as a key site in southwestern prehistory.[167] But fifteen years passed and Di Peso died before another major project—a survey of the Casas Grandes region, directed by Michael Whalen and Paul Minnis (now the region's senior scholars)—was undertaken.[168] The 1990s witnessed a welcome burst of new field projects by the Instituto Nacional de Antropología e Historia and institutions in New Mexico and Canada—and a cascade of papers on Paquimé.[169] If only it had been possible, back in the 1980s, to invest in Paquimé futures! Happily, there's no end in sight. It's still a bull market for Casas Grandes archaeology.

Di Peso's Paquimé was an outpost of Post-Classic Mesoamerica, established by state-sponsored explorer-merchants, similar to later Aztec pochteca. His interpretation made sense: Paquimé boasted a remarkable array of Mesoamerican architectural forms and artifacts. As far

Figure 7.11. Mound of the Cross, Paquimé, northern Chihuahua, Mexico. Artist's reconstruction by Alice Wesche, based on research by Charles Di Peso and others. The Mound of the Cross was the principal cardinal monument at the north end of the city. Courtesy Amerind Foundation.

as Di Peso could tell, the preceding Viejo Period population was far too small and underdeveloped to account for the great city (chapter 6). So Di Peso spun a tale of pochteca corvéeing the local Viejo Period populations, constructing Paquimé, and leading it into the Medio Period—Paquimé's golden age. That sort of historical "explanation" did not sit well in the 1970s and 1980s. A spate of conference papers and theses quickly corrected Di Peso, bringing Paquimé back into the southwestern fold.[170] Many (but not all) researchers now reject Mesoamerican origins for Paquimé, favoring a local evolutionary development. I once doubted Di Peso, but now I doubt local development.[171] Di Peso was fishing the right waters but may not have thrown his net out far enough (chapter 6).

Paquimé was not the largest southwestern site of its era—1250 to 1450.[172] Classic Period Hohokam towns spread over larger areas, prefiguring the urban sprawl of modern Phoenix.[173] The largest Rio Grande pueblos were in fact the very largest *pueblos*—larger by far than Paquimé. But Paquimé was not a pueblo, not a Rio Grande farming village. It was a city—the most urban, urbane, and arguably important southwestern city of its time.

A massive, four-story adobe "high-rise" (Di Peso's term; see fig. 1.1) formed the core of the city, a giant U around a central plaza—pueblolike in form (think Taos) if not in function. The massed buildings incorporated many small enclosed plazas.[174] To the west: five masonry-faced mounds (pyramids, in Di Peso's terms) and effigy mounds (a serpent, a bird, and a cross; see fig. 7.11); two or three ball courts in the I-shaped form typical of Mesoamerica (and not Hohokam); two large reservoir/settling ponds for water channeled to Paquimé from distant springs; courtyards with pens for raising turkeys and macaws; huge ovens for roasting agave (a succulent local succulent); and other esoteric structures unique in the Southwest.

Consider, for example, the effigy mounds. The effigy mound of a plumed or horned serpent, 110 meters long and running north–south, marked the city's western edge. Another north–south serpent mound (in my opinion) may have stood high above the city at the mountaintop signal station of Cerro Moctezuma.[175] Who builds effigy mounds? Nobody in the Southwest. Hopewell did that sort of thing half a continent and eight centuries away. There were no southwestern precedents for Paquimé's monuments or for its Mesoamerican I-shaped ball courts. Ball courts and colonnades (a Post-Classic signature) reinforced Di Peso's conclusion that Paquimé was a Mesoamerican outpost.

Yet the multistoried, terraced compounds of Paquimé more closely recalled Pueblo architecture than the domestic architecture of northern Mexico and Mesoamerica. North and West Mexican homes were more Hohokam-like, with three or four freestanding, single-room structures facing into a small central patio, often with a central shrine. That's not Paquimé. In my opinion, Paquimé's massing, multiple stories, and suitelike apartments place it in the Pueblo architectural tradition.[176] There was even a Mogollon-style Great Kiva,[177] but no Pueblo IV plaza-kivas. The Mogollon Great Kiva says much about Paquimé's base population—probably Mimbres (chapter 6). (Even if the whole city was transplanted Anasazi, we would not expect to see the small kivas of Pueblo III; they vanished everywhere in Pueblo IV.)

Casas Grandes conspicuously employed historical and exotic architecture—for example, the T-shaped doors of Chaco and Aztec.[178] A map of T-shaped doors would track the movement from Chaco to Aztec. They appeared first at Chaco Great Houses (but not commoner dwellings) and after 1150 at Aztec and throughout its region. A map of the Southwest after 1300 would show T-shaped doors all but gone from the Plateau and Pueblo region, only to reappear throughout Paquimé and its region during the Medio Period. Colonnades were famously prominent at Paquimé; the form was almost definitive of Post-Classic Mesoamerican architecture and elsewhere in the Southwest was found only at Chaco. Its pottery was remarkably varied in form and decoration. The core techniques of the ceramic industry lay largely (but not entirely) within southwestern ceramic traditions.[179] Ramos Polychrome, the calling card of Casas Grandes, recalls in many details the much earlier Mimbres, which ceased production 150 years before. Barbara Moulard perceptively notes the deliberate "archaism and emulation" of Casas Grandes pottery, recycling Mimbres motifs.[180]

In other crafts, Paquimé may have been unique in the Southwest. "Crafts" hardly covers it. Paquimé was a factory, or series of factory workshops, with industrial-scale breeding of macaws and turkeys (and probably the creation of feathered objects, seldom preserved), agave processing in huge ovens, shell carving on Hohokam scales, and almost sculptural production of serpentine stools and remarkably formed metates—clunky compared with Panama's best but extraordinary for the Southwest.[181] Paquimé made lots of high-end stuff.

Equally remarkable were its imports. Two examples: tons of shell from the Gulf of California (and farther, as far away as Mazatlán) and large quantities of serpentine from Redrock, New Mexico. Those were brought in as raw materials for processing and manufacture. Many equally remarkable things were imported as finished objects. Huge amounts of pottery came into Paquimé from the Jornada, Salado, and other southwestern areas. As David Wilcox points out, Paquimé produced far more El Paso Phase pottery than any excavated El Paso Phase site.[182] More distant sources supplied prestige goods, most notably, copper artifacts and macaws, in quantities unknown elsewhere in the Southwest. Turquoise was the Southwest's gemstone (or so we like to think). Only 2 kilograms of the blue stone were found—very curious, given that extensive prehistoric mines at Old Hachita, New Mexico, were only 180 kilometers north of Paquimé.[183] Perhaps Hachita turquoise was processed and shipped south—an export? Somebody had to pay for all those birds and bells.

Di Peso considered Paquimé's craft shops and remarkable imports as prima facie evidence of a mercantile economy. Paquimé, he thought, was a trade center, set up by Mesoamerican merchants who knew how these things should work. Whalen and Minnis downplay commerce and suggest, instead, elite hoarding.[184] I see a bit of both—or rather a whole lot of both.

There were, unquestionably, elites.[185] Whalen and Minnis—dubious of Di Peso's unsouthwestern Paquimé—conceded elites with "authority and control...at an intermediate level of development."[186] ("Intermediate" means more than hunter-gatherer, less than state; chapter 8.) Gregory Johnson, a famous deflator of southwestern political pretensions, once remarked, "Casas [Grandes] looks elite—even to me."[187] Paquimé had rulers. Rulers of what exactly?

The Casas Grandes Region

Paquimé was by far the largest site in the Casas Grandes region and northwestern Chihuahua, four or five times larger than any other Medio Phase site.[188] Like Chaco before it, Paquimé was clearly the center of a region. How big? Di Peso's Paquimé was the political and commercial hub of a very large region indeed, reaching far into southern New Mexico and southeastern Arizona. Other archaeologists extend Casas Grandes' reach even farther.[189] But deep-seated processual proprieties are shrinking Paquimé faster than a punctured balloon.

Di Peso put Paquimé "sovereignty" in excess of 200,000 square kilometers.[190] Whalen and Minnis suggest that the entire Casas Grandes region was 70,000 to 100,000 square kilometers—pretty big but "about the same size as Chaco and Hohokam regional systems."[191] That, however, was the culture area and not the polity. The outermost limits of Paquimé's "political economy" were the "near peripheries," within 70 kilometers of Paquimé (a theoretical circle enclosing about 15,000 square kilometers). And Paquimé's actual political control was limited to its innermost core, a 15-kilometer "radius of daily interaction" of less than 1,000 square kilometers. That's tiny.[192]

Whalen, Minnis, and I agree (generally speaking) on the evidence; it's the interpretation that varies. I think Paquimé threw its considerable weight around far beyond the "near peripheries." Rather than build outward from Paquimé, let's work from the outside in (paralleling the arguments I made for Chaco in chapter 5; see figure 5.12). Several adobe pueblos in extreme southwestern New Mexico have architectural features markedly characteristic of Paquimé, among them, countrified versions of I-shaped ball courts and quite acceptable copies of a unique, raised adobe firebox form seen throughout the central city.[193] Most archaeologists see more than casual relations between the southwestern New Mexico sites and Paquimé.[194] The largest of these sites is Joyce Well, "on the frontier of the Casas Grandes world."[195] Joyce Well and the other New Mexico sites are approximately 140 kilometers north of Paquimé. Working from the outside in, I think that Joyce Well sets a conditional northern limit for Paquimé's region.[196]

To the south, Jane Kelley and her colleagues defined a southern boundary at site CH 151, about 155 kilometers from Paquime.[197] Those distances—140 and 155 kilometers—are comparable to those given in chapter 5 for Chaco's "inner core" (see fig. 5.12). I think Paquimé's inner core, similarly, was not 15 kilometers, but ten times that radius.

Of course, Chaco and Hohokam reached farther than 150 kilometers (chapter 6), and so did Paquimé. For example, I noted above that one of the major material imports to Paquimé was serpentine, a hard, green-banded stone that was crafted into extraordinary four-legged stools (presumably to support important behinds). The source of the serpentine was at Redrock, New Mexico, about 270 kilometers to the north of Paquimé.[198] A large Salado site near the serpentine source—the only site at Redrock contemporary with Paquimé—was probably the supplier (Paquimé pottery was recovered from the site, in burials).[199] Redrock was about the same distance from Paquimé as the outermost Chacoan outliers were from Chaco Canyon and the outermost ball courts were from Phoenix (chapter 5).

I think Redrock marked some sort of outer limit, Joyce Well and the southern Medio sites marked a Chaco-sized inner core, and Minnis and Whalen's 15-kilometer "radius of daily interaction" represented something like the "halo" of settlements around Downtown Chaco. In chapter 5 I interpreted Chaco's "halo" as the city's suburbs, the 140/150-kilometer radius as the limits of bulk economic exchange, and the outermost outliers at 240/250 kilometers as the farthest reaches of Chaco's political economy.

Paquimé was Chaco on steroids, or Chaco gone to finishing school. The southern city was everything Chaco had tried but failed to be. And I think its region was at least as large as that earlier, simpler city.[200]

Whalen and Minnis see Paquimé as a local development, distantly affected by distant dynamics—a conventional, processual sense of scale (chapter 6).[201] I see Paquimé as the conclusion of a political history begun far to the north at Chaco Canyon (if not before). Whatever their origins, Paquimé's rulers purposefully sought to integrate Casas Grandes into the much larger Post-Classic world—as demonstrated spectacularly at Paquimé. Contemporary scholarship favors local development and reclaims Paquimé from Di Peso's pochtecas and from the Post-Classic—but it runs the risk of removing Paquimé from that critical larger context.

I once described our unseemly hurry to downsize Paquimé as the "devaluation of Di Peso," and indeed his stock is now low. But, in retrospect, I feel that Di Peso was working on the right scales and even in the right way. Paquimé and the Southwest, however, were not passive recipients of Mesoamerican-driven changes. For many centuries, southwestern leaders were active partners in the engagement. It all came together at Paquimé more than any other place: Mesoamerican I-shaped ball courts and Anasazi T-shaped doors.[202]

A decade ago, I suggested that Chaco or Aztec elites had something to do with Paquimé.[203] My interpretation was based on chronology, architecture, and the nature of hierarchy. Paquimé followed close on the heels of Chaco's demise and actually overlapped the end of Aztec. Chaco's fall and Aztec's rise were associated with a bold new architectural vision: cardinality (chapter 6). Architecturally, Paquimé was stridently, emphatically cardinal; Di Peso (with no prompting from me) called it a cardinal city.[204] A suite of monumental architectural features, known from only Chaco and Aztec, were also used at Paquimé.[205] Even the details of "high-status" burials of Casas Grandes leaders closely paralleled those of Pueblo Bonito.

Paquimé's engagement with Mesoamerica and West Mexico extended and perfected

Chaco's. Why? Leaders of emerging polities at the margins of great states often seek legitimacy by associating themselves with those great states—typically using (or misusing) their symbols and architecture.[206] This was a common strategy throughout the Americas—and at Chaco and Paquimé.

Astonishingly, Paquimé—the largest and most interesting Pueblo IV site—was due south of Aztec Ruins—the largest and most interesting Pueblo III site—which was, strangely, due north of Chaco—the largest and most interesting Pueblo II site—which was, curiously, due south of Blue Mesa–Ridges Basin—the largest and most interesting Pueblo I site—which itself was, oddly, due north of Shabik'eschee and 29 SJ 423—the largest and most interesting Basketmaker III sites. Surely a coincidence?[207]

Native Histories: Paquimé and Beyond

Many Hopis think that Paquimé was their Red City, Palatkwapi. We met Palatkwapi above, as an illustration of the vast distances implied by traditional histories. The stories are also suggestive for understanding Paquimé's end. The Red City was overthrown by earthquake and flood (according to Courlander),[208] or by strife among the clans, ending in siege, destruction, and escape (according to Waters)[209]—or by other means, not known to these two often discredited chroniclers of Hopi history.[210] But it seems that the Red City died hard, with calamity and violence.

The role of violence at Paquimé is a matter of considerable debate. Di Peso said that Paquimé was sacked and burned—probably around 1450 and certainly by 1500.[211] The Casas Grandes region was no stranger to the later Southwest's war of all against all, but there is little direct evidence of violence, except Paquimé's unburied dead, trophy skulls and trophy bones,[212] and the proliferation of defensive cliff dwellings in the Casas Grandes hinterlands.[213] Paquimé's end and the depopulation of the southern Southwest constitute a legitimate mystery. How did it end?

Other Native accounts might address its origins. When Oñate's conquistadors marched to New Mexico through Chihuahua in 1598, they recorded stories of Native peoples—tribes unknown today and languages perhaps gone. One of those stories told of two large groups of people—warriors, women, children—marching boldly out of the north from the Pueblo region, led by two brothers. On their journey to the south, they encountered an immense "mass of solid ore...so smooth and polished and free from rust as though it were the finest Capella silver." A terrible hag carried this huge rock, which she "hurled...through the air with the speed of a lightning bolt." After that she vanished. "No sooner had this missile struck the ground than the whole earth trembled." One brother took this portent as a sign to found a city (or, in another version, to turn around and head back north!), which the Spaniards later saw on their march north as "the ruins of a great capital." The second brother led his group southward into central Mexico, and they were lost from memory.[214] We may meet them again in chapter 8.

Paquimé is famous among astronomers for its 1,500-kilogram meteorite, discovered by looters in a "temple" at the ruin, in the 1860s. The extraterrestrial omen is now in the Smithsonian.[215] Does the Spanish retelling of obscure Native tales describe some aspect of the founding of Paquimé and of the migrations of the Chichimec tribes out of the north? Many Chichimec tribes marched through the north before the Mexica—the most famous of that ilk (chapter 8)—arrived in central Mexico to found the Aztec Empire. Some Chichimec groups may have originated in the Southwest. We will revisit this question—pregnant with political ramifications—briefly below and more fully in chapter 8.

Statelets of the Rio Sonora: A Parable and Postscript

The Rio Sonora—south of the Trincheras district—was a western slope counterpart to the well-watered Rio Casas Grandes. Its valley may prove critical to understanding the later history of the ancient Southwest. Or not—southwestern archaeology seems oddly ambivalent about Rio Sonora archaeology. There has been good work in the Rio Sonora[216]—but far less, alas, than even the sadly under-researched Trincheras and Casas Grandes regions. Compared with Anasazi, the Rio Sonora is still terra incognita.

In the late 1970s, Carroll Riley suggested that the Rio Sonora was the setting for "statelets." The term was Riley's, based on sixteenth-century historic accounts:[217]

> The Sonoran statelets in my reconstruction were aggressive multitown units, each with a primate center and outlying villages and hamlets. The largest towns had at least several hundred terraced houses, some perhaps multistory, of adobe or jacal construction.... There were temples, ball courts, other public buildings, and an elaborate irrigation agriculture with double cropping.[218]

Here's a conundrum for archaeological consideration, couched as personal history. In my early work in the Mimbres region, I compared Mimbres and the Rio Sonora and found the latter wanting, unimpressive. Even the biggest Sonoran sites were simple scatters of individual houses, evidenced by bare rectangles of upright cobbles, foundation stones (*cimientos*). There wasn't much else. Mimbres sites might not be much to look at, but in comparison with rubble mounds and Great Kivas and that sort of thing, they were monumental. Years later, looking south from Chaco Canyon, I was even less impressed with the Rio Sonora's archaeology.

Mimbres (we then thought) were simple, egalitarian farmers, and nobody at that time (except Dave Wilcox) called Chaco a statelet, much less a state. Surely, Sonoran "statelets" had to be Riley's mistake.[219] Yet there were those sixteenth-century accounts. In the sixteenth century, the Spanish (and, later, Carroll Riley) were much impressed by Sonora.

When I dismissed Sonoran statelets, I still considered each region—Chaco, Hohokam, Mimbres—as a separate evolutionary sequence, bigger than most natural laboratories but still essentially self-contained. But what if (as we assume in this book) everybody knew everything, and there were no coincidences? Statelets in the Rio Sonora in the sixteenth century might then be part of a larger story, the last in a long series of centers. The Four Corners crashed in the thirteenth century. In the Pueblo and Hohokam areas, population fell catastrophically after 1350. The "classic" periods of the Rio Grande and Hohokam were not so much cultural peaks, I fear, as last gasps. Demographically, both were downslope declines—calamitous times in Arizona and New Mexico.

Demographic centers of gravity bounced around the Southwest. As the north fell, the south rose, first in Chihuahua (chapter 6) and later, perhaps, in Sonora.[220] Casas Grandes peaked from 1300 to 1450 and then collapsed and emptied—a true southwestern mystery. By the seventeenth century, if we accept Riley's and Spanish accounts, Sonora was perhaps the most densely settled area in the greater Southwest—yet its archaeology is singularly uninspiring.

Nowhere in Sonora do we see sites to rival or recall Chaco, Aztec, Phoenix, or Paquimé—yet there are those Spanish reports. Was Sonora the last refuge of political complexity, remnant ideologies inspired by political systems that started at Chaco and ended at Paquimé and Late Classic Phoenix? Remember, again, the parable of the Natchez, the last of the Mississippi kingdoms. Not much to look at—but their king, the Great Sun, was heir to centuries of pomp and glory. And despite his paltry kingdom, he was no man to trifle with. Sonora, perhaps, was the last site for southwestern hierarchy, the Avalon for her defeated kings.

Pueblos Suspended

Are the migrations over? Yes. Many Pueblo towns have remained in place, give or take a few kilometers, for the past five centuries. But that formidable permanence reflects, at least in part, foreign interventions. Spanish colonial policies "reduced" Indians to settled life. Indians were easier to count, control, and convert if they stayed put. Pueblos, after centuries of short-hop movements, were granted four square leagues and instructed to stay there. They did, but enforced permanence required profound changes in social and ideological systems.

Permanence was not the Pueblo norm. Recall that in Pueblo I, Pueblo II, Pueblo III, and most of Pueblo IV, most towns and villages lasted only a generation or two or three, continuing traditions millennia old. One early ethnologist described Pueblos as "agricultural nomads." That was true until Oñate and colonization.[221]

As we've seen in the preceding chapters, the history of the ancient Southwest was as eventful and dramatic as any human history. I've focused on events specific to political history and accessible to archaeological inquiry: geopolitics of the greater Southwest; the failure and rejection of Post-Classic political systems; the devolution from kingdoms to egalitarian, communal societies. A lot happened in the ancient Southwest.

But perhaps more important to understanding Pueblos, as they exist today, is not ancient history but the colonial experience. Beyond obvious impacts—new economies and religions, economic oppression, disease, assimilation—*the end of migration* must have been enormously important. After millennia of movement, a sudden fixity.

Pueblo people have told me that if it weren't for Spanish and US colonialism, they'd be somewhere in Mexico now. Their peoples would have continued to migrate to the south. (For many Pueblos, movement south is correct and movement north is not. That directionality is widespread but not universal.) Other Pueblos would have stayed put, because they had found their middle places.

If the Old World had not invaded the New, Pueblo peoples would have continued south into Mexico and Mesoamerica. I would not be surprised if some clans and towns did exactly that, long before Coronado. Many Pueblos have memories of clans gone south, never to return. Aztlan in America is a modern political and philosophical construction, but there may be something in it. And to that we now turn.

e i g h t
Post — *Ends and Beginnings*

Archaeologies: Pre-Columbian to Postcolonial
Histories: Then and Now

Each of the preceding chapters has broad themes—orthodoxies, nationalisms, space, time, scale, ecology, and history—that play across both "archaeologies" and "histories." Chapter 8 recapitulates and proposes, looking Janus-headed backward and forward in time. So—*post* as an end or a postscript and *post* as a beginning—to your posts!

Looking forward: for a large segment of the US population, the ancient Southwest has turned or returned to its mythic past, its past before anthropology got hold of it—Aztlan, homeland of the Aztecs. For many Mexican Americans, we've come full circle. Aztlan has repercussions for diversity, civil rights, and immigration. Archaeology seems curiously disconnected from or dismissive of that enormously important vision of the ancient Southwest.

Looking backward: American anthropology, in its infancy, incorporated troubling colonial beliefs about American Indians. Lewis Henry Morgan, the "Father of American Anthropology," thought that Indians were savages or, at best, barbarians and that that's all they ever could be. Those anthropological prejudices—for such they are—were internalized and carried forward by American archaeology for many decades, like dormant pathogens or recessive genes. Today they are endemic and unquestioned. They limit a priori what was possible for past peoples. *Of course* there were no states north of Mexico! (It's silly even to consider that possibility.) Biases inherited from American anthropology and now axiomatic in American archaeology constrain the histories we hope to write.

"Archaeologies" of earlier chapters, tracing the century-plus development of southwestern archaeology, were more than an imperfect parallel to prehistory. The story of southwestern archaeology—from its earliest days to today—is *essential* to understanding ancient history. There are other ways to know the past, but if you want archaeology, you have to understand the thinking behind the research and interpretations.

The first part of this chapter, "Archaeologies," reframes southwestern archaeology in terms not southwestern but Aztec—an unconventional postscript to the more conventional "archaeologies" of preceding chapters. First, we look back to Aztecs as seen by Europe in the age of expansion, and then we look forward to the Aztec heritage in American society today. Enlightenment Europe's understandings of Aztecs underwrite current visions of the ancient Southwest—and then as a modern, politicized history: Aztec interests in American society, today and tomorrow, require archaeological rethinking of southwestern prehistory and how we tell it.

The second half of the chapter, "Histories," first considers briefly how we might write narrative histories of ancient times (to your posts!). Then the bulk of the chapter attempts to do just that: A History of the Ancient Southwest.

Archaeologies: Pre-Columbian to Postcolonial

In 1492 Columbus discovered America but not Mesoamerica. Hugh Thomas credits *The Real Discovery of America: Mexico, November 8, 1519*, to Hernán Cortés, who first met Moctezuma's Aztecs twenty-seven years after Columbus landed on the Caribbean island of Guanahani. Europe had something truly new to deal with—not just new worlds (whose Natives may or may not have had souls) but new *civilizations*. Aztecs were the principal problem in early thinking about the suddenly larger world. Philosophical reactions to Aztecs carried over into early American anthropology and archaeology and extend even into today's study of the political architecture of the ancient Southwest.

Aztecs, Again

In chapter 1, we noted how the discovery of the New World shook Old World cosmology. Columbus was upsetting, but his Taínos could not have prepared Europeans for what was to come. Cortés stumbled into a new civilization that rivaled those of Europe. The Aztecs were fundamentally disturbing.[1] At first, Europeans dismissed as bluster conquistadors' tales of teeming cities, vast empires, and vaster riches. But the influx of wealth that fueled Spain's sixteenth-century power drive proved those tales true. Aztecs were taken seriously.

How to think about Aztecs? *How to Write the History of the New World?*—the title of Cañizares-Esguerra's intriguing historiography of seventeenth- and eighteenth-century accounts of the Aztecs. Early explorers' reports were revised and re-revised to suit Old World agendas. By the eighteenth century, generations after the initial encounter, two competing schools had formed, southern and northern. Spanish (and Spanish American) authors developed a "patriotic epistemology"[2] that glorified the ancient Aztecs and made them equals or more than equals to Europeans. Northern European (and US) authors were inclined to see New World Natives as decidedly inferior to European civilizations. They discredited Spanish accounts of the Aztecs as propaganda or hyperbole. The two schools argued Aztec history, even in the Aztec homelands. "On the eve of the wars of independence [circa 1800] the pages of Mexican periodicals carried both articles dismissing the glorious reconstructions of the Aztecs' past as unreliable and replies questioning skeptics" and venerating the fallen Native empire.[3] The Aztecs became the focus of Mexican political symbolism, particularly after the revolution of 1910—the first great nationalist rising that included mestizos and Natives.[4] Today Aztec heritage is firmly embedded in Mexican national identity and *indigenismo* (chapter 1) and in Chicano/Latino ideologies of Aztlan, the Aztec homelands in the southwestern United States (below).[5] Aztecs and Aztlan have been, and remain, politically potent.

Morgan, Revisited

The divergent Mexican views of Aztecs played out in early American anthropology. Five early scholars—Prescott, Bancroft, Morgan, Bandelier, and Hewett—personify American attitudes toward Aztecs through the nineteenth and early twentieth centuries.[6] Of these, Morgan (as we shall see) was by far the most influential—for good or ill. Morgan set the agenda for American archaeology. He worked in reaction to earlier works, so a brief history of earlier American attitudes toward Aztecs is in order.

William H. Prescott's (1796–1859) enormously successful *History of the Conquest of Mexico* was published a few short years before the Mexican War. His book was a huge best seller in a time before best-seller lists. Prescott wrote of powerful Aztec kings, glittering courts, and vast empires and compared the Aztecs, favorably, to ancient Rome, Egypt, and "Hindostan."[7] He was not an uncritical admirer, and his views were colored by the nineteenth-century racism that was a largely accepted part of American intellectual life. Prescott's glorious portrayals of the Aztecs' past were reinforced, after the war, by eyewitness accounts of returning army officers and government officials. They had seen the Halls of Montezuma and stormed them. Santa Anna's Mexico (in their view) might be fit only for conquest and filibuster, but its ancient monuments were indeed impressive, even humbling.

Hubert Howe Bancroft (1832–1918) carried Prescott's view forward in the initial volumes of his monumental West American Historical Series—another widely read and hugely influential source of ideas about Native Americans. His volume on the Aztecs (published in 1875) reached much the same conclusions as Prescott: the Aztecs were a great empire and a brilliant civilization, and Moctezuma was their king.

Of course, there had been counterarguments (prior and post) to that enthusiastic view of the Aztecs—for example, from Albert Gallatin (chapter 2). But the pivotal critique came from Lewis Henry Morgan (1818–1881). Wary of attacking the enormously popular Prescott, Morgan used Bancroft's book as a surrogate to demolish "the romantic view" of Aztecs. Morgan announced his intentions in a letter to another key anthropologist, Frederick Putnam of Harvard: "Our first dead weight to be got rid of is the Aztec monarchy and the Aztec romance."[8] In a blistering 1876 review of Bancroft's book (a review later republished as "Montezuma's Dinner," a seminal essay for American anthropology), Morgan demoted the Aztec emperor to a petty chief and reduced Moctezuma's palace to a simple pueblo, the communal dwelling of a communal society. Morgan argued—insisted—that *all* Native American societies were, at heart, communal. Morgan reached his conclusions by considering data (in very odd ways, to be sure) filtered through racism. Morgan was a mild, paternalistic, Victorian racist—a man of his times, even enlightened for his era, but a racist.[9] Morgan thought that Indians didn't have states and empires because Indians *couldn't have* states and empires. They weren't capable of such things.

Morgan was also colonial. He was, by any standard, a friend to Indians, and he worked toward their betterment (as he understood it). But he was living in colonial times. The United States was still colonizing its continent, and the continent was fighting back. The year Morgan died, 1881, the Apache leader Nana led his warriors on a spectacular, bloody raid through New Mexico. Morgan imbibed colonialism with the morning paper, over breakfast.

He may have deplored America's treatment of its Natives, but he would not question that his country was rightly replacing First Nations.

Morgan stated categorically that no Native society anywhere on the North American continent—including the Aztecs—ever rose to the political status of a "state." He didn't use that term (he said "civilization"); I'm translating Morgan into today's anthropological parlance. And while I'm taking liberties, I'll call this Morgan's Maxim: *No states in the forty-eight!* Another anachronism on my part: in Morgan's time, there were only thirty-eight states.

Morgan's views prevailed in the United States.[10] But seminal Mexican historians and archaeologists such as Manuel Gamio, Alfonso Caso, and Ignacio Bernal brusquely dismissed or simply ignored him.[11] Morgan was not the Father of Mexican Anthropology.

North of the border, Morgan's ideas carried well into the twentieth century—even his ideas about Aztecs. Benjamin Keen, in his magisterial survey *The Aztec Image in Western Thought*, notes Morgan's intellectual influence on Adolph F. Bandelier, an early and influential convert (see chapter 2), and then traces the thread through the late nineteenth and early twentieth centuries in the works of Marshall Saville, Herbert Spinden, Eric Thompson,[12] and (as we saw) Frederick Putnam.[13] Morgan's line ran right through the 1920s and 1930s. "As late as 1940 anthropologists of the eminence of George C. Valliant and Robert Lowie [two of the greatest anthropologists of their times] accepted the validity of the key elements in the Morgan-Bandelier doctrine."[14] These were not minor or marginal figures in American anthropology. They were key players, the professors who taught the professors who taught the professor who taught me. Morgan's Maxim—now an unspoken truism—was brought forward through generations of teaching. No states in the forty-eight.

You can see it in archaeological thinking even today. We have been trained to value parsimony—simple is always preferable to complex. As I noted in chapter 1, we've transposed that rule of thumb for logic onto the people we study: understandings that make *them* simpler are always preferable to understandings that make *them* more complex. I've heard this idea in hundreds of conversations, read it in scores of papers and articles: "An egalitarian Chaco is more parsimonious than a Chaco with kings," or variations on that theme. It may be true that Chaco, or Paquimé, or Cahokia was not hierarchical in the ways I've argued here. But that's a matter for open debate, not to be foreclosed by parsimony. That's not just a misapplication of the principle; it's Morgan's Maxim—now an unquestioned, bedrock principle. Indeed, no states in the forty-eight!

Morgan's views were racist and colonial. Modern anthropologists are neither racist nor colonial—quite the reverse. And carried unquestioned into the twenty-first century, Morgan's Maxim is neither racist nor colonial; it is merely embarrassing and counterproductive.

Morgan was particularly influential in the Southwest. Two of his earliest adherents were also men of enormous influence in southwestern archaeology: Adolph Bandelier and Edgar L. Hewett (chapter 2). Bandelier literally defined the field in his *Investigations among the Indians of the Southwestern United States*.[15] Morgan was Bandelier's mentor. Morgan told Bandelier what to read and how to think about it. And Morgan used his considerable influence to secure funds for Bandelier's fieldwork. Not surprisingly, Bandelier became a doctrinaire Morganite. Hewett was of the next generation. In his student days, Hewett read (and approved of) Morgan's writings. Bandelier took Hewett under his wing when the younger man's fancy turned to archaeology. Hewett welcomed Bandelier's exegesis and instruction, "Hewett deferring to Bandelier even as Bandelier had been influenced by Morgan."[16]

Edgar Hewett was the kingpin of New Mexico archaeology through the first third of the twentieth century (chapter 3)—or maybe the kingfish. A successful empire builder and educator but a second-tier scholar, he trained cohorts of the Southwest's future archaeologists. And throughout his many decades at museums and universities, he remained firmly loyal to Bandelier's and Morgan's views of North American Native civilization. For Hewett, Aztec society and all New World societies were communal and democratic, nothing like states. For the Southwest, this situation was of particular consequence because Hewett controlled Chaco, the most statelike of pueblo polities: he published many widely read, popular books and articles about Chaco while reports of other expeditions languished, unpublished.[17] Hewett, more than anyone, shaped ideas about Chaco Canyon through the mid-twentieth century, and Hewett's Chaco was communal and democratic—and certainly not a state.

Morgan's Aztecs infiltrated the Southwest: if the Aztecs were communal, democratic, and stateless, then the southwestern peoples who found themselves in Hewett's gaze *must* have been even simpler—communal, democratic, and egalitarian—and that's how Hewett portrayed them.[18] Morgan, Bandelier, Hewett, and later Ruth Benedict (*not* a Morganite)[19] set firm limits on the modern and ancient Southwest—the kinds of societies that archaeologists should expect to find.

No States in the Forty-eight?

Mexican archaeology barely acknowledges Morgan, but his ideas hold tenaciously north of the Rio Grande. Morgan's Maxim has become axiomatic. Modern archaeologists apologize for any discussion of Cahokia or Chaco that strays, however tentatively, toward the forbidden territory. Students learn this in North American Archaeology 101: there were no states north of Mexico.[20]

The State We're In

Norman Yoffee, Suzanne Fish, and George Milner formed a high-powered panel ruling on the political achievements of the ancient Pueblo, Hohokam, and Mississippian peoples. They dismissed any political pretensions for the Pueblos, modern and ancient, "whom we can't even pretend formed states." They skirted unsettling, statelike aspects of Hohokam by offering arguments for why Hohokam was not or could not become a state—thereby triggering a semiserious rule of thumb referred to (affectionately) as Yoffee's Rule: "If you can argue whether a society is a state or isn't, then it isn't."[21] Even Cahokia, with its enormous pyramids and spectacular high-status burials, did not qualify:

> Nothing remotely like these finds [Cahokia] exist in the SW, so it was hard for SE archaeologists—to a man, downsizers—to convince their [southwestern] colleagues that…Cahokia was not fundamentally different than its Mississippian counterparts elsewhere.… No one doubts that SE societies conformed to many (but not all) of the attributes commonly thought of as defining a chiefdom.[22]

We *know*, a priori, that nothing like a state ever happened north of Mexico, so it's pointless to think about it. Maybe so. But those ancients at Chaco, Phoenix, and Paquimé (and Cahokia)—perhaps *they* thought about it. They knew what states were; that knowledge was part of their world. Post-Classic states and civilizations were roaring along on the same small continent as Chaco, Phoenix, and Paquimé (and Cahokia)—and *everyone knew everything!*

How could they not? Kingship began with Olmec, two millennia before Chaco or

Cahokia.[23] Kingdoms rose and fell throughout Mesoamerica, on larger or smaller scales, thereafter.[24] It beggars belief that the elites of Chaco and the lords of Cahokia—whose business it was *to know*—would *not know* of Mesoamerican kingship.

Small scales are a legacy of New and processual archaeology; many older archaeologists (including me) were trained that way. So we evaluate Cahokia's and Chaco's political evolutions as if they were clinically isolated in natural laboratories, each in its own petri dish. Papers and dissertations discuss "the evolution of complexity *at* Chaco" or "*at* Cahokia," as if all the necessary events and ingredients were found within the San Juan Basin or the American Bottom. Whatever the political histories of those cities (and others in North America), they surely encompassed regions and ideas from far beyond their particular places. To ignore Mesoamerica, the lords of Cahokia or Chaco would have to have been deliberately isolationist (and clearly they were not) or flat-out stupid (and we can assume that they were not). Chaco and Cahokia were not petri dishes on a lab shelf. They were corners of a huge terrarium.

In his brief, brilliant "hemispheric history" of the Americas, Felipe Fernández-Armesto says of Chaco, Paquimé, and Cahokia, "In North America, cultures which made contact with the great civilizations of the south fell under their spell and imitated their models."[25] It's not surprising that Chaco or Cahokia fluttered around the notions of Mesoamerican statehood; it's only surprising that it took them so long to get around to it.

I will not claim that any southwestern polities were great and mighty empires. Most importantly, I do not claim that any political formation north of the Mexican border was a *primary* state—that states "evolved" parthogenetically in situ at Chaco or Cahokia in the neo-evolutionary progression from band to tribe to chiefdom to state. Other, older, greater states in Mesoamerica had already gone through all the preliminaries. They'd done the heavy lifting. The Southwest did not have to invent any of this stuff. Chaco and Paquimé and Cahokia were *secondary* states, inspired by the historical, economic, ideological contexts of North America. Not just semantics, that's a huge difference for anthropological archaeologists. Primary states are evolutionary miracles; secondary states are historical by-products.[26]

States of Being

The ancients didn't read our textbooks. They were making it up, borrowing, or cobbling together whatever worked or didn't work. The rules we write for states come from successes, not failures. What do we call states that didn't know they were supposed to have all those things?[27]

All of this would be doubly true for secondary states: small, starter-kit kingdoms out on the edges of civilization. If an era's iconic symbols for leadership were those of an emperor living in a grand capital city, an ambitious hill chief might well adopt the habits and customs and accoutrements of that exalted but distant lord. The hill chief might not understand that he (or she) needed attached specialists, or a standing army, or any of the other goods and services we've declared necessary for a true, successful state. Sometimes it worked, sometimes it didn't. But seldom would it not look like a primary state: the few, the proud, the Yoffee-approved.

We've heard Yoffee's Rule. Well, here's Lekson's Corollary: "If you can argue whether a society is a state or isn't, then it's *really interesting*." And if it's in North American, it's probably a secondary state.[28]

Primary states? Secondary states? Wait a minute: *what's a state?* The anthropological literature has almost as many definitions for *state* as it has for *culture*. Yoffee sets the bar high; I'm aiming low. How about this: a state will have a central government, a capital city and a surrounding region, perhaps a regional economy, a hint of sanctioned force, and a degree of permanence. Those all seem stately qualities, whether primary or secondary. But they also seem chiefly. Those who traffic in such things might say I'm describing neo-evolutionary "chiefdoms." Well, yes: many chiefdoms in North America were probably secondary states. But I'd prefer to stay away from those old categories and reexamine the whole issue of political development.[29]

My understanding (not a definition) is, rather, a loose description of the kinds of polities found throughout North America during the Post-Classic. I insist on "states" because North American polities *must* be so designated to occupy the same intellectual space as their peer polities across the border in Mexico.[30] In the Post-Classic period, they were all distant cousins; all were secondary states, variations on themes first worked out by Olmec and Teotihuacán. So we *can* argue whether or not later southwestern, like Post-Classic, societies were states, and that is *really interesting.*

Southwestern secondary states were mix and match. Chaco, for example, had a central government, however diffuse or non-Western. It had a capital city—the focus and center of a large region, gossamer perhaps but archaeologically evident nonetheless. The same could be said for Paquimé but perhaps not for the Phoenix Basin. It's likely that Chaco had a regional economy; Hohokam and Paquimé certainly did. And perhaps Chaco and its successor, Aztec Ruins, had the use of force; witness the brutal but apparently socially sanctioned events of the twelfth and thirteenth centuries. Force was less clearly a prerogative of Phoenix and Paquimé. All three—Chaco, Hohokam, and Paquimé—had degrees of permanence. Their spans measured centuries, a half-dozen generations or more.

Chaco (and Phoenix and Paquimé) does not fit, exactly, classic neo-evolutionary "chiefdoms." We must look, I suppose, to the Southeast for those. Nor would it qualify as a neo-evolutionary *primary* state—it doesn't have the history, or rather the *absence* of history (no long slog up the evolutionary ladder). But I submit, Chaco, Phoenix, and Paquimé can be understood as failed copies (literally impersonations) of states to the south. Not Tula, precisely, but a distant murky reflection of an idealized Tollan filtered through northern and western Mexico.

Chaco and other southwestern polities were one thousand kilometers and two thousand years removed from the beginnings of Mesoamerican kingship. Government was so old a fixture in North America that Chaco would not even have known its origins. To think that Chaco's political developments occurred in ignorance of southern kingship is to force an atomism and isolation on ancient southwestern peoples that is not simply wrongheaded and unrealistic but also transparently colonial—a relic of Morgan's nineteenth-century prejudices, brought forward (unwittingly) in contemporary anthropological archaeology.[31]

Once and Future Aztlan

The Aztecs called the wild north—including today's Southwest—*Chichimecatlalli* or *Chichimeca.* (Pedro Carrasco notes that *Chichimec* referred to all Early Post-Classic displaced wanderers—there were many—but *Chichimeca* meant specifically the north.)[32] Chichimeca was the "house of darts," a place of misery and suffering and *rocas secas*, a barbaric land, whose people survived by hunting and by eating dogs.[33] Yet, the Mexica Aztec proudly claimed

Chichimec heritage. It was important, apparently, to start out rough and end up king. But Aztec histories—often state propaganda—were disingenuous about their humble origins at a place called Aztlan or Aztatlan.[34] Aztlan was a place of mists, reeds, and herons—a wet haven in a dry land.[35]

Aztlan, like the Aztec histories, was legendary. It may have been a fabrication or more likely an embellishment. Considerable scholarly energies have been spent on Aztlan's reality and possible location, beginning with Moctezuma I, the Aztec ruler who sent an expedition to find the fabled homeland. The expedition returned with mixed results—part myth, part geography.

Aztlan remains elusive—"Aztlan of the Aztecs, whose legend knows scarce a ruin."[36] Archaeology places Aztlan, if real, in northwestern Mexico, "in the present day states of Guanajuato, Jalisco and Michoacán,"[37] or perhaps alongside the ocean, in "the lagoon named Mexcaltitlan on the Pacific Coast of Nayarit"[38]—both well south of the Estados Unidos de America. But much modern scholarship relegates Aztlan to myth. Carroll Riley, in his recent account of the ancient Southwest, *Becoming Aztlan*, concludes that Aztlan "really represented a sort of land of faery, *somewhere* in the distant north and west but with no geographical parameters."[39]

But Aztlan is not so easily disposed of. It lives. It has important constituencies outside archaeology: Mexican Americans. "Aztlan!" was the rallying cry of the 1970s Chicano civil rights movement. The "Plan Espiritual de Aztlan," declared in Denver in 1969, proposed that the Southwest was indeed "the northern land of Aztlan from whence came our forefathers." That is, the ruins of Mesa Verde and Chaco Canyon were, in fact, the "first home of the Aztecs"—as they were labeled on early-nineteenth-century maps.[40] La Raza—the Mexican mingling of Native (Aztec) and Spanish peoples—was therefore indigenous to the Southwest. Going north meant going home. (And you shouldn't need a Green Card!)

In the 1980s and 1990s, Aztlan shifted to a literary and philosophical metaphor—a powerful symbol but not a territorial claim.[41] Recently, however, territorial Aztlan has reemerged with a new wave of "Mexica nationalism." A few Chicano (or "Xicana/o") splinter groups (La Voz de Aztlan, for example) advocate a separate nation of Aztlan, encompassing the US Southwest and northern Mexico—claims repudiated by most Chicano or Latino writers and organizations. Separatists are a small minority, but the idea of a southwestern Aztlan has reemerged, reconsidered, in arts, letters, and political thinking.[42]

Aztlan is popular and pervasive—far better known to many Americans than the latest archaeological theories about Chaco or Mesa Verde published in scholarly journals or presented at professional conferences. Aztlan appears in striking mural art in neighborhoods, parks, barrios, and communities from Chicago to LA. Many communities are justly proud of well-trained, wonderfully costumed, multigenerational Aztec *grupos danzantes*. Aztecs are part of Mexican American—and therefore American—life.

Interest in the Aztec heritage of course does not necessarily imply a southwestern location of Aztlan, but the larger identification of Mexican American communities with ancient Mexico is a cultural phenomenon worthy of note by archaeologists. The Mexican American community—self-identified on census forms—is sizable: twenty-two million and growing, according to the most recent census.[43]

Perhaps archaeology should not too hastily dismiss a southwestern Aztlan.[44] There is nothing inherently implausible about an active southwestern role in the extraordinarily dynamic history of Late Post-Classic Mesoamerica—if not as Mexica Aztecs, then as part of other migrations out of the north.[45] Clans and villages and whole peoples migrated left, right, sideways, and *south*. We are only beginning to understand the scale and the convoluted history of demographic movements in and out of the ancient Southwest. Many Pueblos tell of clans that went south and never returned. The first dominoes in long braided chains that ended at Tenochtitlán?

Southwestern archaeology has been shaped by nationalisms (chapters 2 and 3). The Mexican War gave us a continent. We then colonized our country, internally, with the Indian Wars. American anthropology was born in that colonial era as the study of our "vanishing" Natives. Of course, they didn't vanish, and anthropology shed many preconceptions and attitudes inherited from colonial times. Vestiges remain. To fully "decolonize" southwestern archaeology, two steps seem necessary and obvious: tear down the wall built in 1848 between the Southwest and Mexico and remove the glass ceiling hung over Native America by Lewis Henry Morgan forty years later. The border nationalized the Southwest and kept its Indians ours, not theirs. And Morgan's Maxim kept our Indians down: no civilizations, no states. Both barriers are relics of nineteenth-century racist and colonial thinking, and both should go.[46]

Histories: Then and Now

In chapter 1, I suggested a way to write a Big History of the ancient Southwest: *connect the dots*. Toward that goal, I offered three rules: (1) *Everyone knew everything*: assume interconnection; ancient isolation is an extraordinary claim, requiring extraordinary proof. (2) *No coincidences*: interregional coincidences were (mostly) not coincidental. (3) *Distances can be dealt with*: distance did not intimidate the ancients; distance should not intimidate us. Not so much rules as what ye call guidelines—to paraphrase Captain Barbosa.[47]

A History of the Ancient Southwest

The whole book has been leading up to this: a history of the ancient Southwest.[48] The sections that follow are based directly on the "histories" in chapters 2 to 7. (Chapter 1's primeval speculations are relegated to time immemorial.) Each chapter provides the data, sources, citations, and arguments for its corresponding section here. For example, chapter 4's "Histories: 700 to 950" (and notes) underwrites "Phoenix Ascending, AD 750 to 900" (below). This history of the ancient Southwest is told without intrusive scholarly apparatus. You'll find all that stuff in the preceding pages and the notes.[49]

I've tried to eliminate as much archaeology jargon as possible. Of course, it's not possible to expunge all technical terms, but I hope they are few. *Plateau* means Anasazi and Rio Grande; *western desert* means Hohokam (the area); and *eastern desert* means Mimbres and Casas Grandes. Some things need naming: *Chaco* (the regional system) and *Hohokam* (the cult—or whatever it was). Otherwise, most names are geographic.[50]

Of Maize and Men, 1500 BC to AD 400

Maize, a useful but ancillary plant, percolated up from the south, from western Mesoamerica, well before 2000 BC (see fig. 2.2). Early corn spread throughout the Southwest, both in the deserts and on the Plateau. But the tiny cobs of the first corn did not transform the region. Five centuries passed before farming villages took root in the low deserts, around 1500 BC. Perhaps people and maize made slow, mutual adjustments. More likely, new strains arrived together with new people who really knew how to farm. It took special knowledge to grow maize and even more specialized knowledge to hybridize it, to adapt it to new soils and climates. That bag of tricks probably included rudimentary irrigation, necessary as maize moved from wetter to drier climes. From the beginning, desert farmers planted first in the few naturally wet bottomlands and especially around treasured cienegas in the western deserts and the Land Between. As those favored settings filled with fields, farmers diverted water from creeks and streams, running it through small ditches to new fields above the creeks. They had to: maize needed more water than desert rains could provide; it did very well with simple irrigation. The basic principles of irrigation may have come with maize, but the Southwest would develop water technologies far beyond anything attempted in Mesoamerica.

All that knowledge was embedded and distributed in social structures, ceremonial practices, political relationships, and languages: a Uto-Aztecan mother stock that later became Piman, Hopi, and other western languages. There were indeed new ideas about maize and about many other things. From Poverty Point in the lower Mississippi Valley to Olmec in Veracruz, North America was waking up. The first Mesoamerican civilizations formed along the Gulf Coast and across the isthmus on the Pacific. Faint currents eddied north into the Southwest's deserts.

It was a package. Maize *farming* came to the deserts with maize farmers, in sufficiently large numbers to form an agricultural vector—in short, a migration. The new southwesterners did not forget their roots. A chain of Uto-Aztecan-speaking groups linked the western deserts and West Mexico. Shared histories ensured that desert communities looked south throughout the following centuries, just as related West Mexican communities looked north. The roads were open.

Desert villages, by 1000 BC, consisted of a score of small pit structures—family homes—around a plaza. Near the center of some villages stood a single large building, a place for community affairs. The large building was the place where family and clan representatives could meet in closed session to settle the village's business, spiritual or temporal. Decisions were made in the community house, by councils. Age and wisdom undoubtedly carried weight, but no one family was more important than any other.

Around the villages were thin hunter-gatherer groups that populated every region of North America. Thin in numbers and probably in physique, with a lean and hungry look. Cornfields and *milpas* were rich new resources, ripe for the picking. Apparently, there were frictions between farmers and their hunter-gatherer neighbors. Defensive sites such as Cerro Juanaqueña—an impressively terraced and walled mountain—attest to a certain edginess and attitude. Cerro Juanaqueña (1250 BC) was a large town and probably did not fear hunter-gatherers. Its massive terrace walls said: "We are here, and we are not going away." It was not Poverty Point, nor was it an Olmec city, but Cerro Juanaqueña was a big, permanent village and the Southwest's first monumental construction.

Boom times in the deserts! The Native peoples of the Plateau—people speaking languages that would become Zuni, Keres, and Tanoan—noticed. Some surely saw, with their own eyes, the thriving villages around Tucson and the terraced mountain of Cerro Juanaqueña. Small canals were dug around Zuni as early as 1000 BC, only a couple centuries after Cerro Juanaqueña. But the maize in hand—successful in the deserts when irrigated—did not prosper in the higher, cooler climate of the Plateau. Centuries would pass before they hybridized or imported maize that could be grown with the scanty rainfall of the Plateau—only marginally moister than the deserts.

When maize-based villages finally arrived on the Plateau, they came up from the western deserts, in another wave of Uto-Aztecan migrations around 500 BC. The western desert people moved north onto the western Plateau, displacing Plateau natives to the east.

The maize-based way of life in small farmsteads spread among the local people of the eastern Plateau. But some Plateau peoples may have resisted the intrusion of new crops and new people, as did Native peoples of the desert around Cerro Juanaqueña. There are hints of violence between the eastern and western halves of the Plateau. The divide between the Uto-Aztecan west and the Zuni–Keres–Tanoan east structured Plateau history. It cast long shadows. Many centuries later, hierarchical governments would rise in the east, among the "locals," but not among the peoples of the west, who harked back to different, desert ways.

Plateau families clustered into villages near the best farmlands, creating social and economic problems unprecedented in their preagricultural social histories. The customs and habits of hunter-gatherers could not solve the problems of villages. They lacked the deeper traditions of the desert farmers, brought from the south: long histories of village life and governance by council. Where to find solutions? Leaders—marked by age or knowledge or skills—sought out other leaders, pooling ideas to address novel challenges. And they surely looked to the south, to the successful villages of the deserts.

Brownware pottery spread throughout communities of both deserts and the Plateau between AD 200 and 400. Its initial appearance, in the deserts, may have signaled the arrival of more new people from the south—there were constant comings and goings between the deserts and West Mexico. Everyone in the Southwest, regardless of language or history, quickly embraced pottery. A brownware "foundation" formed across the eastern and western Plateau and the deserts, a craft shared among villages with different histories and backgrounds. After mastering the basics, potters built on that foundation, inventing techniques and creating styles increasingly characteristic of each area.

Maize fueled southwestern civilizations, but in fact the Southwest was a terrible place to grow corn. Corn's failures were as important as its successes. The environmental mismatch between corn and the Southwest played out in unequal production, agrarian tensions, droughts, famines, and—above all—the many measures, social and political, taken to support maize-based societies in blistering deserts. It's not that maize worked in the Southwest; it's that *they made it work*—most of the time.

This Desert Life, AD 400 to 750

At AD 400, more than a millennium after farming villages first appeared in the deserts, perhaps a hundred small settlements flanked small desert streams, irrigating crops with short, small, simple ditches (see fig. 3.2). Three short centuries later, the western deserts were crossed by dozens of massive canals—25 meters wide and up to 30 kilometers long—rerouting enormous quantities of water from the major rivers, the Salt and the Gila. Those canals soon became one of the largest irrigation systems in North America (and indeed in the New World). And the small farming villages grew with them and became very large towns. The remarkable upshift in scale demanded new political structures. Or new political structures allowed larger village sizes—or a bit of both. In any event, new political practices replaced the older, inclusive village councils.

New ways of living in the Southwest reflected, distantly, a new idea in North America: urbanism at Teotihuacán, far to the south. It was not the first Mesoamerican city, but

Teotihuacán was by far the greatest. Teotihuacán dominated Mesoamerica during the first half of the Classic Period (200 to 950), sending emissaries and enclaves to the heart of the Maya region and to the northernmost boundaries of Mesoamerica at Alta Vista, 1,200 kilometers from the southwestern deserts. Rumors and repercussions of Teotihuacán reached the deserts and Plateau, faint but clear.

Teotihuacán redefined the possible. No one ever again had to "invent" villages, towns, or cities. Every wandering hunter-gatherer, far into the tundra waste, was at least dimly aware that people could live in densely packed, permanent cities. Peoples of the Southwest knew of Teotihuacán—the capital of a great state with hundreds of thousands of citizens. They may not have known its real name (nor do we), but they surely understood its idea. When history and environment pushed southwestern communities toward larger, more complex social arrangements, Teotihuacán's prodigious urbanism provided an obvious, if mythical, model for how to proceed.

There were of course many other, smaller cities. Those of Teuchitlán in western Mesoamerica rose in or around the ancient Uto-Aztecan homelands, with clearer connections to the farmers of the southwestern deserts. Teuchitlán cities reflected Teotihuacán at several removes—smaller, with distinctive plans and organizations. They were likely conduits for urbanism (or the idea of urbanism) into the Southwest. Desert townspeople translated and transformed the forms and protocols of distant Mesoamerican cities yet again, into local languages and patterns. City cosmologies shrank to serve villages and towns. Desert leaders did not try to re-create the great southern cities (which they may have never seen), but concepts of political leadership surely reflected—in pale emulation—Mesoamerican originals.

If you wanted to set yourself up as king, you might have considered how real kings in real cities did it. The people you were trying to rule would judge your performance against that ideal—a distant, filtered knowledge of Teotihuacán, the Teuchitlán cities, and their successors. And strategies of leadership necessarily respected local realities: customs, economies, landscapes, and histories that generated new forms. The results, in the deserts and later on the Plateau, looked very little like Teotihuacán or Teuchitlán—how could they? But southwestern political leaders owed some part of their success to the existence, the *fact*, of those southern cities and their ideas of kingship.

But why would the desert need leaders? What happened was this: the farming villages along the creeks and small rivers of the western desert succeeded and grew. The small, simple ditches got deeper and longer, extending out to upper terraces to meet the need for new farmlands. Irrigation—even on those modest levels—demanded centralized decision making, a few making decisions for the many. That is political authority—small and almost invisible at first, but increasing in step with each increase in infrastructure and with the personal successes of particular leaders. Power breeds power, and (unless society steps in) the rich get richer. Around 500, a few desert families got power. They liked it or accepted it as an obligation, or both, and they took steps to keep it, for themselves and their descendants.

At villages like Valencia Vieja, at about 500, emerging leaders built Big Houses. A few prominent families with more lands, more wealth, and more power built notably larger residences, combining conspicuously larger domestic space with interior ritual features. From its very beginnings, political power in the Southwest was symbolized and signified by architecture. Big Houses were built in prime places, immediately adjacent to the central plaza. Less fortunate families built smaller houses behind the inner circle of Big Houses, farther away from the plaza. The council houses of earlier times disappeared, their governance functions having shifted to the Big House families.

Big House political power was modest, appropriate to small early ditches—insignificant by Mesoamerican measures. When irrigation tapped much larger rivers—the Gila and the Salt—the scale of decision making expanded exponentially. Canals got big and Big Houses got bigger. Big House families could have—should have?—promoted themselves to the next level. At Snaketown, Grewe, and a score of other early towns in the Phoenix Basin, leaders began to really matter. Their spheres of interest and control expanded beyond farming and its rituals to encompass other sorts of mischief.

At Snaketown and Grewe, leaders drew attention to themselves—predictable behavior for aspiring leaders—through travel back to the source, to western Mexico and Mesoamerica, returning with impressive stories and fabulous objects. Reciprocally, people to the far south began to hear of fertile farmlands, impressively irrigated, in the western deserts. No one in West Mexico had canals like that.

People on the Plateau noticed too. Agricultural villages of any size were few and far between and relatively impermanent—still in a sort of transitory sedentism. Settlements were more permanent around permanent water—valley bottoms, upland pockets of wetlands, and so forth. Those lands were limited. Plateau farmers discovered that, unlike in the deserts, it was possible to farm away from streams or permanent water, relying on precipitation: rainfall farming.

Rainfall farming reshaped life on the Plateau, for both the Uto-Aztecans of the west and the local populations of the east. The two groups were increasingly difficult to tell apart, but the old divisions remained in language and history. The eastern peoples continued many of the old ways, most importantly, an inclusive system of governance. As in the earliest desert villages, decisions were made in a large community or council house: the Great Kiva. Great Kivas were round chambers, often roofed but sometimes not and big enough for representatives of families or clans to meet, perform ceremonies, and make decisions.

Unlike desert farming, tied to canal systems, rainfall farming required no investment in infrastructure and therefore no commitment to any particular place. Plateau peoples already knew—but farming sharply reinforced—that rainfall varied from year to year and place to place. Families and small villages moved often, on cycles of a generation or less—a fluidity that did not encourage permanent political leadership.

Yet, in the end, leaders put themselves forward. Inspired by first- or secondhand knowledge of desert Big House elites, individuals or families decided to try it on the Plateau. Form probably mattered more than function. Just as desert leaders looked to Mesoamerican cities, Plateau leadership borrowed ideas from the desert—a different world economically but the closest model for how hierarchy might work. In the deserts, political leaders lived in Big Houses prestigiously near the plaza. And at a few Plateau villages around 500—such as Shabik'eschee in Chaco Canyon—the first feeble attempts at political leadership appeared as exceptionally large pit houses, built prestigiously near the village center and the Great Kiva.

Big House elites at Shabik'eschee and other Plateau villages weren't needed to control elaborate canal systems. Indeed, they may not have been *needed* for any economic or agricultural reasons. Political forces—the tensions between the eastern and western Plateau—created a context for political leadership. Alarming things were happening in the Phoenix Basin, where elites were behaving more and more like elites. Western Plateau villages had historical and linguistic ties to the deserts. They literally understood each other. But the east did not. Eastern Plateau villages needed tighter organization. Rather, aspirant leaders *thought* they did, and they built Big Houses. They were wrong: political leadership did not "take" on the Plateau. Unlike canal communities of the deserts, Plateau families—if annoyed by would-be leaders—could simply leave, move to a better (or at least different) place. Rainfall was equally spotty everywhere. If a leader became obnoxious, the led could leave.

The people of the deserts, tied to canals, did not have that option. Single families couldn't build canals. Desert people stayed where their parents and grandparents had lived. Towns got bigger and bigger. Canals on the Salt and Gila rivers created a breadbasket, the richest farming economy in the Southwest. It had maize hybridized for irrigation; long, hot growing seasons; abundant water in the rivers; canal technologies capable of capturing and using that water; and a Big House political system to organize it and make it all work. Desert farmers needed leadership, but maybe not the kind they got.

The deserts at 700 were a civilization waiting to happen. The region was primed to produce the food surpluses needed to fuel great things: kings, empires, whatever. But Big House rulers did not become kings. Desert civilization took a different path.

Phoenix Ascending, AD 750 to 900

Hohokam began perhaps with another wave of people and most certainly with a new wave of ideas from Mesoamerica, drawn by and to the thriving canal farmlands of Phoenix—which attracted attention to the south. Hohokam, as it came together around 700, was more than a "people" or an ethnic group (see fig. 4.2). It was an ideology that united many groups—newcomers, long-settled migrants, and converted locals. A crystallization of ideas, symbols, and practices—heavily but selectively Mesoamerican—transmuted into a Big Idea that crossed lines between church and state. Hohokam was like Hopewell, whose monumental mound building in the Ohio Valley had ended a couple centuries earlier. It was a supragovernmental or antigovernmental or instead-of-governmental cosmological arrangement that encompassed large areas and many people, and it got big things done without kings.

In the western deserts, Hohokam presented a new way of life revolving around ball courts, elaborate (but democratic) burial rituals, bold new styles of art, and, most importantly, decision-making structures that diffused political power. As at Teotihuacán (but on a far smaller scale), individual political leaders in Big Houses were replaced by a government of bureaus and committees—in the guise of priesthoods and councils. Perhaps these were innovations; perhaps they were existing institutions elevated to new levels. For a few short, brilliant centuries, Hohokam ideologies allowed an enormous, elaborate irrigation economy without centralized political power—and propelled an astonishing cultural explosion out from Phoenix and across the deserts.

Some elements of what became Hohokam already existed in the deserts, part of the continuous interchange from the deserts to western coastal Mexico and back again. Some parts of Hohokam were endemic, local developments. But the key elements were new, brought in from the south. The transformation into Hohokam almost certainly involved *people*: new arrivals, established figures, or prophets out of the deserts. A small charismatic group—perhaps an individual—got it going. It took off in directions that no one could foresee. Hohokam ideologies replaced and overshadowed conventional Big House leadership (which remained for a few more centuries at the village level).

People *became* Hohokam. Perhaps the most conspicuous and widespread markers of Hohokam were armlets of *Glycimeris* shell. Bivalve shells from the Gulf of California were carefully shaped into armlets and sometimes carved with symbols—birds carrying snakes, desert toads, and the like. Shell bracelets or armlets became a badge or marker of Hohokam; they had once been rarities, but after 700 they were ubiquitous. Someone in every sizable settlement had armlets prominently displayed on an upper arm.

Inward-facing groups of several shallow pit houses, clustered around a courtyard, formed the typical home—in both the southwestern deserts and in northern Mesoamerica. A score or more homes were grouped into small neighborhoods circling the plaza, which remained the center of the town or villages. Ball courts displaced Big Houses as the iconic architecture, the central monument. Not *re*placed: Big Houses and their elite families continued, but their leadership functions were transferred, very concretely, to another arena. The whole village watched and witnessed the action in a ball court, a "game" that (as in Mesoamerica) played out political issues, territorial dilemmas, difficult decisions. The social apparatus behind ball courts—the people who arranged the "game" and its appurtenances—was a new class, group, or bureaucracy or perhaps old leading families, transformed. Each village of sufficient size had a ball court; very large villages had two.

Around the plaza were earthen mounds, usually round or oval. Mounds were architecture—something new or greatly transformed versions of older trash piles. A site was selected, fill was brought in and sculpted to shape, and a smooth plaster surface applied. The first mounds were elevated slightly—a meter at most—above the surrounding ground, well below the peaked roofs of surrounding houses. They supported ceremonies and small presentations (all the action had to fit on a small stage) performed for large groups. The village could see the action atop the mound's elevation, like a stage above groundlings. Mounds were inclusive; events that would be restricted in the old community house or private in Big Houses were now public. At the same time, the raised performance space separated actors from audience. In that way too, mounds differed from plazas. Plazas were a level playing field; everybody could be involved. Mounds combined architectural inclusion and exclusion. That contradiction sowed the seeds of future political developments.

In sum, Hohokam was a new way of doing business, getting things done without elite individuals or families. Not a return to village councils—Hohokam society had become far too large and complex for that—but rather a decentralized, inclusive stew of ritual, power, and decision making. Individuals had power of course, but they did not flaunt it with Big Houses, palaces, and tombs. Whatever Hohokam was, it controlled individual political ambitions and curtailed social stratification and hierarchy.

To the south, it was a time of kings and rulers. Mesoamerica was going the opposite direction from Hohokam. The fall of Teotihuacán (about 550) sent tsunamis of political power outward, rulers looking for places to rule. In the following decades, displaced, dispersing elites transformed cities and towns throughout Mesoamerica. The aftershocks of Teotihuacán's fall—real, not just metaphorical—reached the Pacific Coast with the temple-towns of the Aztatlan horizon and reached the very northernmost frontiers of Mesoamerica at La Quemada.

Petty chiefs and Big House leaders, far beyond those frontiers, were tempted to emulate southern kings. As Mesoamerican polities popped up nearer and nearer to home, they provided models and perhaps a threat, real or imagined. Hohokam quashed those Big House impulses. It rejected seventh- and eighth-century Mesoamerican political models while using a wide range of Mesoamerican forms and symbols.

For almost three centuries, Hohokam worked. More than worked, it prospered and expanded out from Phoenix in one of the more remarkable events in the history of the ancient Southwest—like early Islam without armies. The rapid spread of ball courts, Hohokam pottery, and burial ritual followed creeks and rivers upstream, up to the very edges of the Plateau and out beyond the Land Between. Surprisingly, it did not go very far downstream, stopping short at Gila Bend, a short distance west of Phoenix. If Hohokam had reached the Colorado Delta, what might have been?

But on a continent of kings and empires, it was hard to contain hierarchy. A geographic pecking order emerged. The very largest towns, such as Snaketown, Grewe, and Aztatlan, had the very largest ball courts. That correlation might be simply scalar: larger audiences required larger facilities. By 900 there were hints of hierarchy not within but between towns, with the largest occupying positions of control at the heads of canal systems—positions of power.

One of the largest ball courts was built highest up the Gila River, at Pueblo Viejo (the Buena Vista site, 250 kilometers east of Phoenix). Beyond Pueblo Viejo, Hohokam elements reached deep into the Mimbres region, where mountain streams flowed out of the Mogollon highlands into the sunny Chihuahuan Desert. Mimbres settlements were less permanent than the villages of the Tucson or Phoenix areas. Pit house groups moved from one valley to the next, allowing depleted soils, hunted-out game, and gallery forests to replenish and regrow. It was a successful way of life—so successful that rising numbers filled the valleys. The best farming lands—cienegas, wet bottomlands—soon were overtaxed.

Like the societies of Phoenix and Tucson, Mimbres farmers dug ditches from streams and rivers to open new fields. Mimbres rivers were much smaller than the Salt and middle Gila. The farmers learned the tricks of irrigation from Hohokam, but Mimbres canals were modest and easy compared with the huge Phoenix systems. Mimbres accepted, selectively, a range of Hohokam beliefs: cremation burial rituals (for some), ideologically charged designs on pottery, and—conspicuously—Hohokam *Glycimeris* armlets. Not every Mimbres person wore them, but some were buried with dozens.

As in the western deserts, canals fixed Mimbres villages in place. Pit houses, which had a fairly short use-life, stacked up (insofar as pit structures can stack). Newer houses cut into older abandoned structures. Some villages grew to hundreds of houses—untroubled, it seems, by hierarchy. Their canals were too small to need it, and their borrowed Hohokam ideologies discouraged conspicuous leadership. Mimbres did not accept the whole Hohokam package; ball courts, essential for Hohokam life and governance, were absent. Apparently, they were not needed. Great Kivas kept pit house communities together, serving some of the purposes that ball courts played, far to the west, for Hohokam.

Hohokam reached north, as well as east. Western Plateau peoples shared languages with the Phoenix Basin. They had deep historical connections—so deep (by this time) to perhaps be almost mythical. The two areas reconnected, sharply, when Hohokam ball courts were built in the north, among the western Plateau's piñons, junipers, and pine trees. Mimbres had taken canals but only a selection of Hohokam ideologies. On the western Plateau, Hohokam ideology came without Hohokam irrigation! Over the long haul, western Plateau peoples resisted hierarchy more successfully than those of the eastern Plateau and Chaco. Around 800, Big Houses reappeared on the Plateau—not among the Uto-Aztecan kin in the west but among the Native peoples of the eastern Plateau.

With corn adapted to the Plateau and increasingly sophisticated knowledge of land and weather, population grew and villages got larger. People grew up in, and over generations became accustomed to, the strictures and structures of village life. They had to: there were fewer open valleys, no place to go to start over. More rules, more conventions, more possibilities for hierarchical leadership. And intervillage squabbles escalated after 700, occasionally reaching levels approaching warfare by 850. Increasing violence also called for leaders, military or diplomatic.

Over the short term, shifting rainfall favored some areas over others. In the ninth century, rains fell on the great Sage Plains, northwest of Mesa Verde. Population concentrated there. Towns expanded. There, people built the first Big Houses on the Plateau since the false start at Shabik'eschee, three centuries before.

Of course, basic house forms had changed, somewhat, since the pit houses of Shabik'eschee. Plateau peoples now used more stone masonry in the architectural repertoire. Behind the pit structure (which was still the primary living space), they added a low, small masonry building of a half-dozen rooms used mainly for storage: pantries, equipment lockers, and so forth. With food and equipment housed safely above, the pit structure itself could be made smaller and easier to heat. That combination—six rooms and a pit structure—became the standard for Plateau housing (and a clear contrast to the courtyard homes of the western deserts). The new, ninth- and tenth-century Big Houses used that form: six rooms and a pit house built *really* big. Big Houses became Great Houses.

Great Houses—Big Houses by another name—were essentially residences, built on the same ground plan and of the same material, but much larger and more substantial and built with greater craft and care. The heart of the house, in both Great Houses and normal residences, remained the pit structure. Great House pit structures were larger, deeper, and better built than normal pit houses. Significantly, they included more formal, unusual ritual facilities. Just like the early Big Houses of the Tucson and Phoenix basins, Plateau Great Houses combined secular and ritual architecture in conspicuous, even modestly monumental elite residences. That was the key: both Big Houses and Great Houses were *houses*, not public facilities like ball courts or Great Kivas.

Great Kivas—the people's council chambers—continued to be built, especially in villages (happily?) lacking leaders. One village might have a Great Kiva but no Great House. Another might have a notable Great House but no Great Kiva. Often both were present but at some distance apart. Great Kivas were the buildings of the people, while Great Houses were buildings of the leaders.

Great Houses popped up over much of the eastern Plateau. The western Plateau stayed out of it, for now. In western villages, homes were often jammed together in long rows. Each home was essentially identical to the next. These villages often had Great Kivas. Eastern villages were, superficially, more dispersed, with clusters of freestanding homes or scattered short segments of three or four conjoined homes. Large settlements had scores of these separate housing segments and one or more Great Houses—and no Great Kiva. The people were architecturally fragmented, without a common hall or communal center. Looming over them, the Great House offered the coherence and regulation needed, perhaps, for village life.

Plateau peoples still moved as they had for centuries, but in larger groups than in earlier times. Rising violence urged safety in numbers. Ruling lineages emerged as a few important families maintained their status from old village to new village, from one generation to the next. They began to think it was their right, or duty, to rule.

Chaco Nova, AD 900 to 1150

Supernovae—stars visible in daylight—lit the skies in 1006 and 1054 (see fig. 5.2). There had been no stellar explosions for many centuries. Those of the early/mid-eleventh century must have been wonders and portents. That of 1006 signaled Chaco's ascendancy. At Chaco Canyon, from about 1020 to 1125, the Plateau saw its first and greatest city. And the star of 1054 foretold Hohokam's decline. By 1075, at the latest, Hohokam had begun to unravel.

The decades from 900 to 1150 were momentous in North America. Three centuries of uncertainty and reorganization that followed Teotihuacán's fall (around 550) ended with the rise of Tula and the beginning of Mesoamerica's Post-Classic Period (950 to 1500). Tula was much smaller than its Classic Period predecessor and less consequential. It was first among several equals and many lesser yet independent states. Long-distance, "international" interactions —commercial, military, or ideological—latticed over a politically fragmented Post-Classic Mesoamerica. Early Post-Classic (900 to 1150) interactions-at-distance were impressive: Tula in central Mexico and Chichén Itzá more than 1,000 kilometers away in the northern Yucatán replicated in remarkable detail each other's major monuments.

In eastern North America, Cahokia rose in a remarkable "big bang," urbanizing the middle Mississippi Valley and setting the course for subsequent political history, much as Teotihuacán had set the agenda for Mesoamerican urbanism five centuries before. Cahokia was the size and shape of a major Mesoamerican city. The lords of Cahokia would have been taken very seriously at El Tajin or Tula. The same could not be said for the would-be rulers of Chaco Canyon.

On the Plateau, Great Houses, with elite families now accustomed to their status, moved south of the northern San Juan and into Chaco Canyon. Perhaps Great House leaders saw themselves as the heirs of Shabik'eschee. Perhaps Chaco was simply the last empty valley. At any rate, the people who promoted Great Houses at Dolores—their descendants or their spiritual heirs—built three Great Houses in Chaco Canyon by 900. Unlike earlier, short-lived Great Houses, these sank roots. After a century-long germination, Chaco burst forth to dominate the Plateau from 1020 to 1125.

Pueblo Bonito, for example, was built over the course of three centuries (850 to 1150). The building lasted longer, perhaps, than it should have. Masonry that worked well for the older, one-generation Great Houses failed after three or four. Rather than move and rebuild—as had been done in the past—people maintained and expanded Pueblo Bonito and the other Chaco Great Houses. Chaco *as a place* had come to mean something. Eventually, ten Great Houses were built at Chaco. The people who lived in those imposing Great Houses transferred power from one generation to the next; Chaco's massive architecture expressed that transcendence of time. Great Houses became monuments. The labor invested in a Great House equaled that required to build a medium-sized Mississippian pyramid. The act of building was an important social and political event that brought together people and resources from every part of Chaco's expanding region. Planning and coordination reached levels rivaling the Phoenix Basin canals. There was an important difference between desert canals and Plateau Great Houses: canals delineated an economy; Great Houses manifested an ideology of power.

Great House families lived privileged lives. They probably did not farm or hunt. They did not make pottery or chip arrowheads or grind corn. Others supplied their food and everyday crafts. They traveled far to the south (certainly to Mimbres and probably to Mexico) and brought back colorful macaws, metals, and other wonders. When they died, they were buried with pomp and ritual in the oldest parts of the building. Thus, they stayed with the Great House and became part of its history. Chaco Great Houses were the houses of generations of elites—kings of the Plateau. Or so they saw themselves, modeling their actions on Mesoamerican rulers.

The massive buildings began as great *houses* but later encompassed much more than elite residences and tombs. Construction after 1020 added wings of warehouses, ritual spaces, public monuments, and barracks perhaps, or at least group housing. Great Houses became centers of government, ritual, and, to some degree, economy. They became palaces, unmistakably differentiated from normal five-rooms-and-a-kiva dwellings. Chaco was a palace culture—not Minoan Crete but nevertheless a monumental city defined by huge elite houses.

With the rise of would-be kings at Chaco, the people found themselves redefined as commoners. Many declined that dubious distinction, but most found the arrangement necessary if not congenial. Villages with scores of separate individual homes dotted the landscape. Set on a low hill or prominence above the village stood a Great House, and off among the commoners' homes, a Great Kiva—the traditional community center. In many cases, Chaco elites were sometimes able to co-opt Great Kivas. The largest Great Kiva of its age was built *within* the walled plaza of Pueblo Bonito—the first and greatest Great House—about 1050. Great Kivas of outlying communities were moved and rebuilt—"collected"—within the limits of Chaco's canyon. But the two forms coexisted, perhaps uneasily, throughout Chaco's reign.

Chaco created a degree of political integration over the Plateau, offering economic and political security. What threats worried Plateau villages? The threats posed by other villages. Escalating intervillage violence ended with Chaco's rise. And the Hohokam. Eastern Plateau peoples were well aware of the remarkable Hohokam expansion of 750 to 900. Eastern Plateau peoples knew their histories. Zuni, Keres, and Tanoan speakers remembered the much earlier Uto-Aztecan expansion onto the Plateau. Their western Plateau neighbors were a constant reminder. Great House leadership recalled, distantly, the earlier desert Big House elites, and on some level, Chaco itself was a geopolitical response or reaction to Hohokam.

Chaco's rise was also a gift of geography and climate. Chaco Canyon itself was a dry and cheerless place, but it was central to a ring of villages, 80 to 150 kilometers from the capital, around the better-watered margins of what would become its interior region—the San Juan Basin (and a bit beyond). Chaco, from its beginnings, served as a central resource center for the basin, evening out the short-term problems of its surrounding villages. Bulk goods—building timbers, pottery, corn—moved freely within that 150-kilometer radius. Many things came to Chaco and stayed there, in the service of the kings. Maize moved into and through the canyon, from places that had plenty to places that had none. Consequently, violence and raiding almost ceased. Its successes, from 900 to 1000, allowed Chaco's leaders to expand their horizons. Its influence soon reached far beyond its original domain. Outliers—colony or copy Great Houses—popped up, up to 250 kilometers away. Local leaders almost everywhere on the Plateau joined with or deferred to Chaco. And it worked. The weather cooperated; rain fell. From 900 to 1200, Chaco kept the peace, promoted the general welfare, enhanced its own glory, and *got things done*.

Chaco could not compete with Hohokam and did not try. Leaders (or their representatives) surely exchanged visits. But beyond courtesy calls, the region's biggest powers maintained a decent distance over the Mogollon Rim. Chaco's kings would not welcome Hohokam's diffusion of power. And Hohokam had no use for Chaco's palaces and would-be kings. (Decades later, they would reconsider.) Chaco and Hohokam acknowledged but did not engage each other.

Very few objects from Phoenix reached Chaco, and very few objects from Chaco reached

Phoenix. As measured by pottery, the western deserts had far more commerce with the western Plateau (the two areas had deep connections). Yet Chaco's rulers needed Mesoamerican objects and symbols to legitimize their tenuous rule. They may have first obtained these in Phoenix, but Chaco quickly negotiated separate routes of interchange well east of the Hohokam sphere, through Mimbres.

It would probably be wrong to think of Chaco's rulers as aggrandizing, avaricious, ambitious feudal lords. Leadership may have been a duty, probably intertwined with ritual and religion. As with many rulers, the leaders of Chaco may rightly be called priestly elites. They no doubt had the dignity of Pueblo elders, but they also enjoyed worldly privileges and luxuries denied commoners—fruits of power shunned by Pueblo leaders today. And Chaco's rulers perpetuated political leadership through following generations. The best model might be Mesoamerican lords, who ruled both by right and by duty. Ideally, the Mesoamerican lord came from a particular class or clan, trained to the task. In many cases, the king was a stranger—actually or fictively from a distant place. Chaco's leaders distanced themselves from commoners through architecture and personal embellishment, using (or misusing) elements of Mesoamerican elite symbolism. Chaco was the idea of a Post-Classic polity translated into Plateau idioms of architecture, space, and cosmology.

In the deserts, Hohokam shifted from explosive expansion to consolidation. Canal systems grew. To a large degree, each canal system was independent. There was water enough for all. Key social dynamics played out among settlements along single canals. The flows of the Salt and the Gila were, in most years, sufficient to supply all canals, up- and downstream. On lesser rivers, an advantageous upstream location might have propelled one canal and one town to preeminence over its downstream peers. But that did not happen. A dozen independent "irrigation communities" emerged within the Phoenix Basin, and the Hohokam ideology ensured that power was diffused within those communities. Surely, there were shifting alliances and mutual obligations, but these were not structured by dramatic differences in agricultural productivity, geographic location, or control of a scarce resource. Hohokam political life—and social life—was relentlessly modular.

It was different at Chaco. Chaco was enormously larger than other Plateau settlements of its time—orders of magnitude larger. Chaco, uniquely, kept the peace and took the credit for decades of abundant rainfall. There was a price to be paid for Pax Chaco and prosperity: support of Chaco's elite families. But that price was not too high. At 900 there were only a few (perhaps three) elite families; by 1100 there were a few score. Chaco Canyon itself was decidedly top-heavy—a city of palaces—but the tip of the social pyramid was in fact rather small: perhaps a thousand or fifteen hundred elites. And the pyramid had a broad base— one hundred thousand or more commoners across the wide Plateau. By 1100 Chaco's reach expanded west into Uto-Aztecan areas. Within that vast region, smaller outlier Great Houses represented the local, second-tier elites who visited Chaco, perhaps regularly. Outlier Great Houses symbolized that connection. Beyond Chaco's sphere, local leaders copied Chaco ways, building emulation copies of Great Houses—the form without the political entanglements, much as Chaco mimicked Mesoamerica without actual, burdensome obligations.

Chaco propelled, directly or indirectly, movements of people out, away from the center, in almost every direction: to the north, back into the Four Corners area (largely abandoned from 900 to 1000); and to the south, into the Mogollon highlands. The outermost penumbra—far beyond Chaco's control—reached as far north as corn would grow, west to the Colorado River, east to the Rio Grande, and south into the Mimbres valleys.

As Chaco waxed, Hohokam waned. Energy shifted swiftly from the deserts to the Plateau. The high-water mark in the deserts came between 900 and 1050; on the Plateau, between 1020 and 1200. In the decades after 1050, Hohokam's remarkable expansion reversed and shrank back in on the Phoenix Basin. The hallmarks of Hohokam civilization—ball courts, shell insignia, elaborate cremation burials, low mounds, and (most importantly) regulation without kings or governors—continued into the early 1100s, but the energy was gone. Most ball courts fell out of use. The desert fragmented into local polities. Phoenix and Tucson went separate and unequal ways.

Even in decline, Hohokam remained far more impressive as an economic landscape than Chaco—or anything else, then or thereafter, on the Plateau or the Rio Grande. The canal systems, already enormous, continued to expand, bringing more water to more desert to feed growing populations and to replace lands spoiled by salinization or depletion. Larger populations in the Phoenix Basin came less from local population growth than from the relocation of villages. Thousands of people moved in from the edges of the old Hohokam world, back to the heartland. The demographic implosion accelerated through AD 1300. With all those new people, the farmlands of Phoenix—once inexhaustible—were reaching their limits.

Mimbres registered the shift from the desert to the Plateau, like a weather vane swinging to the winds. Mimbres pit house villages once looked west to Hohokam; after 1000 they looked north to Chaco. Pit houses gave way to small stone-masonry homes of a half-dozen rooms, not unlike the Plateau house form. Emulation Great Houses, 400 kilometers from Chaco, were built at a few villages, with much larger rooms, more formal layouts, and more massive masonry than was customary in Mimbres pueblos.

Chaco's political power never directly reached Mimbres, and would-be Great House elites never took hold. Through a remarkable combination of old Hohokam ideologies, new Plateau forms, an influx of Mesoamerican ideas, and their own local genius, Mimbres people developed new ways of living that allowed for large towns, complicated (if not huge) irrigation systems, and interactions as equals with the Chaco world—but that avoided Chaco's hierarchies and political complications. In many ways, Mimbres invented the Pueblo way of life. Mimbres institutions live on, much changed, in modern Pueblos.

Going around Hohokam, Mimbres villages established direct trade relations, over the Sierra Madre, with western Mexico and the Aztatlan cities of the Pacific Coast. Mimbres, unlike Hohokam, had a straight shot down the east flanks of the mountains to the Post-Classic states of central Mexico. More than a few Mesoamerican ideas central to Mimbres thinking—and later passed on to Pueblos—referenced central rather than western Mexican ideologies.

Chaco elites came to rely on Mimbres for Mesoamerican objects, symbols, and contacts. There were many elites—a thousand or so in Chaco Canyon and twice that in outlier Great Houses—and a large demand. Mimbres people became middlemen and supplied the Plateau rulers. Long-distance trade shifted, permanently, from the Pacific side of the Sierra Madre to the inland side. Inland routes pioneered by Mimbres reached their fullest expression with the rise, two centuries later, of Paquimé in the southern Mimbres region.

Chaco prospered. Then, 300 kilometers west of Chaco Canyon in the western Plateau, a wonderful awful thing happened. A volcano erupted. By a remarkable coincidence (it happens), the thing blew up at the northernmost frontiers of the Hohokam world. Sunset Crater was a small volcano, a pimple on the earth, but it was spectacular. No volcano had erupted in the region for thousands of years. Travelers' tales of smoking mountains in central Mexico could not have prepared anyone for Sunset Crater. The plume of fire and smoke was visible from highpoints on the eastern Plateau—probably from Chaco—and from the Phoenix Basin.

Chaco could not compete with Hohokam, and it certainly could not compete with a volcano. Take your pick: jumped-up kings at Pueblo Bonito or an exploding mountain showering fire, lightening, bombs, and sooty rain? For decades, vivid memories of the eruption made the area around it a more important place—*as a place*—than any other on the Plateau. More important than Chaco.

A flood of new people repopulated the volcano-devastated area (and discovered that ash made excellent mulch). The volcano was a strange attractor. An extraordinary aggregation of structures and monuments converged around the smoking mountain's flank, at a place with a good view from a safe distance: Wupatki. The place was known to Chaco: a small Great House there actually preceded the volcano by perhaps a decade. A larger, later Great House— or something very like a Great House—rose after the eruption, after 1125. By then, Chaco was gone and Aztec Ruins was ascendant on the Plateau.

The post-Chaco Great House was only one of several remarkable monuments. Just below Wupatki, a Great Kiva sat a long stone's throw from a large masonry Hohokam ball court, among the last ball courts ever built. A strange brew of ideologies—Hohokam, Chaco, and the magic mountain—intermingled at Wupatki. Wupatki had elaborate turquoise artifacts, macaws, and Mesoamerican objects that rivaled Chaco at its height. Chaco and Hohokam met, at last, under the volcano. But by 1135, when Wupatki was built, Hohokam was greatly diminished and Chaco was coming to its end.

Internal rifts at Chaco came to a head well before Wupatki. The physical orientations of major Great Houses showed two competing cosmologies. The old, original worldview (of 850 and perhaps even earlier) was represented by a southeastern, solstitial alignment. A newer, north–south cardinal cosmology was introduced at several Great Houses built after 1020. Cardinal directions had a long history in ritual and ceremony; now one Chaco faction appropriated cardinality for political purposes. A matter of a few degrees but a fundamental difference in world views between Great House groups at Pueblo Alto and Chetro Ketl. In the end, Pueblo Alto's cardinal cosmology came to dominate Pueblo Bonito (the oldest and most important palace) and the cityscape, but Chetro Ketl and several other Great House palaces retained the older, solstitial outlook. The crisis came around 1070—about the time of Sunset Crater?—when discussions began about a new capital. It was agreed that it should be built to the north, toward the edge of the Pueblo world—away from Hohokam? Away from Wupatki?

The location of the new Chaco was fixed by cardinal direction: due north, up the Great North Road, to the San Juan River. So far, the new cardinality prevailed. But when planned and built (1068 to 1088), Salmon Ruins' layout was distinctly solstitial. After a few seasons of floods and near floods, the large and dangerous San Juan River was seen to be a poor choice for the new capital. Another cardinal move, a few kilometers farther to the north, found the right place. About 1110 construction began at the place we know today as Aztec Ruins.

Again, as at Salmon Ruins, the cityscape of Aztec was profoundly solstitial, a near-perfect parallel of Chetro Ketl. The cardinal party prevailed in the location of the new capital (no small thing). But when all was said and done, the solstitial bloc determined the new capital's form and cosmic vision. The leading families of Pueblo Alto and Pueblo Bonito—both cardinal—lost the fight for Chaco's future. The cardinal factions turned away from the north and from Aztec and reversed directions. They went south. That split may have happened at Chaco at 1125 or at Aztec a century later.

The End of Order, AD 1150 to 1300

The philosophical schism—solstitial versus cardinal—had very practical political consequences (see fig. 6.2). Aztec was, literally, only half the capital that Chaco had been. And its region was greatly reduced to the northern San Juan and flanks of the Chuska Mountains. That region included Mesa Verde and, more importantly, the densely settled Great Sage Plains of southwestern Colorado.

Things that worked at Chaco failed at Aztec. Chaco responded to needs—first for food, then for peace—and presented the Plateau's answer to Hohokam's unasked question. Aztec, in contrast, simply perpetuated a dynasty. The new capital was unable to keep the peace or to bring the rain as Chaco had done. A major drought hit from 1135 to 1180—while Wupatki flourished. A second burst of monumental construction at Aztec marked a brief rebound. But about 1250 rainfall became erratic and unpredictable. At 1275 an even worse drought began; it would last for a quarter century. Villages battled other villages over farmland, food, debts, slights, whatever. Violence spun out of control. Farmsteads—previously scattered freely among their fields—clustered into large, walled towns or huddled together in alcoves high on the cliffs of Mesa Verde.

To enforce its failing rule, Aztec unleashed lethal force. At farmsteads, squads of warriors fell upon families failing in their duties, old and young. They were executed to intimidate other villages that might be thinking of slipping Aztec's yoke. Men, women, and children were brutally and publicly killed and left to rot, unburied, in the ruins of their homes. These horrible scenes replayed a score or more times, but even terror could not hold Aztec's failing polity together.

It was a classic case of unintended consequences and opposite effects. Aztec's use of force drove away already wavering groups. Beginning as early as 1220 (decades before the Great Drought of 1275), villages began leaving Aztec's stressed region. Grandparents and great-grandparents had previously moved their villages over substantial distances, but always within the confines of the Plateau. Now people moved much farther away, setting off cascades that rippled out beyond the Plateau into the deserts.

Collapse is a difficult word: pejorative, clichéd, now (in deference to Pueblos) avoided. But it accurately describes Aztec's end. The city and its region were abandoned, an exodus of tens of thousands of people, complete and permanent, seldom if ever paralleled in history. They and their descendants returned only as pilgrims praying over the bones of ancestors, but never to reestablish villages and farms.

Most who left the Four Corners region went to the modern pueblos: Hopi, Zuni, Acoma, Laguna, and the many towns of the Rio Grande area, spiking population in an arc from Hopi to Taos. Those were the southern edges of the old Chaco region or, in the case of the Rio Grande, slightly beyond. (Chaco had interests in the Rio Grande Valley—turquoise—that Aztec let lapse.) Some went farther; whole villages relocated far to the south in the deserts, at places later known as Tucson, Arizona, and Cañada Alamosa, New Mexico. In the western deserts, Mogollon pueblos and Hohokam towns grudgingly accepted newcomers. The welcome was not warm; migrants often settled atop buttes and mesas. A generation later, they were joined by more people from the north, following paths into the upper Gila and Salt drainages. These newcomers integrated into fading Hohokam societies—this time on their own terms.

The old order passed. The elites of Aztec Ruins and its outliers filed out of their palaces and went south. If they were like Mesoamerican kings, they probably still believed in their right, and duty, to rule. Chacoan ideas of hierarchy surely survived Chaco's and Aztec's fall. Chaco elites in the deepest south (beyond Acoma and Zuni) maintained their status decades after Chaco removed to distant Aztec. Perhaps, to commoners, Chaco was always (and only) a remote, near-mythical place—Rome to an ancient Pict, Jerusalem to a medieval serf. In any event, southern elites kept up appearances, brooding in their Great Houses on hills above their towns. A second wave of immigrants—who knew what was really happening up north and wanted no more Great Houses—drove those relic elites out and south. We shall meet them again.

Authority vanished, refugees arrived, and violence ensued. Two centuries of Pax Chaco ended after 1175. More than a resumption of pre-Chaco raiding and feuding, violence escalated quickly to village-on-village warfare. Towns reorganized into safer arrangements. As in the northern San Juan, scattered southern farmsteads clustered into larger and larger villages. But unlike those in the north, southern villages were not hodgepodge affairs. They were carefully planned, with the organizing principles of Chaco applied to thousand-room pueblos. Central decision making shows in these huge new towns, which began with tall, defensive perimeter walls, laid out as precise squares and circles. Homes in-filled the town in a bit of a jumble; within those walls, no single house was "great." From the Rio Grande on the east to the mountains of central Arizona on the west, aggregated towns employed elements of Chacoan planning but rejected the ruling elites—rejected and perhaps ejected.

We do not know the fates of the northernmost elites—the lords of Aztec and their San Juan Great House allies. Not all who died in the violence of the thirteenth century were commoners. What of the southern Great House leaders, elites around Zuni and Acoma? Their lives were disrupted first by the end of Chaco, then by the fall of distant Aztec, and finally by a popular movement—literally a migration—away from hierarchy and toward a new social order. Some elites surely converted; many moved. North—a region and direction of ill omen—was no longer possible. There was no one left to rule. To the south, Hohokam beckoned from the deserts—a civilization without kings.

The root causes of warfare on the Plateau did not obtain in the deserts, but refugees from the violence brought the means and perhaps the disposition. Young people brought up in Aztec's reign of terror were perhaps inured to and inclined toward violence. Disorder around Phoenix was less pervasive than to the north, but the reestablishment of defensive trincheras sites in the twelfth and thirteenth centuries showed cracks in the tottering Hohokam edifice. For many generations, Hohokam ideologies supported diffuse governance, collaboration, cooperation. Desert dwellers lacked leaders who could react quickly and decisively. They lacked the social tools to deal with violence spilling out of the Plateau—or with the displaced Plateau elites looking for someone to rule.

Architecture tells the tale. For many centuries, desert homes were clustered into small groups or neighborhoods. These clusters were intentionally open, visible, and patterned. Their pervasive modularity reflected the nonhierarchical nature of Hohokam society. About 1150 the modular house clusters were replaced by adobe walled "compounds": walled or fenced enclosures containing pueblolike rooms and houses built of puddled adobe. In marked contrast to the open house clusters, compounds were closed, rigid, exclusive spaces. That architectural development (inspired at least in part by Plateau building traditions) marked the breakdown of the old Hohokam way of life.

Ball courts—the sine qua non of Hohokam—were replaced, around 1150, by platform mounds. The courts were not leveled or razed; they were simply forsaken, left open and unused. The contrast between the sunken surfaces of ball courts and the raised surfaces of platforms was a clear indication of new ways of doing business.

Nor could platforms be confused, architecturally, with the earlier Hohokam mounds. In contrast to the low, rounded mounds—which had served as stages for public viewing of ceremonies and rituals—the new platform mounds were large, tall, sheer-sided, and sharply rectangular structures. Some platforms—square, massive, controlling—were built directly over earlier low mounds, making a statement. The tall platforms lifted the buildings and activities they supported far above the people. An audience below could see figures only at the platform's edge—criers, priests, those who reported, ordered, and communicated. Events at the center of the platform were screened from public view. Priests and leaders did their work above and beyond ordinary people's reach. Platforms were the architectural antithesis of both earlier low mounds and ball courts. They paralleled the shift from open courtyard groups to closed compounds. Something had changed in Hohokam thinking. Indeed, "Hohokam," as a suite of beliefs and practices, ended.

Hohokam fell apart as Plateau populations spilled into the deserts, into the upper Gila River, and into the Tonto Basin of the upper Salt River. In the Tonto Basin (and perhaps elsewhere), large rectangular masonry structures—a few with columns—were built in existing towns. They had no precedent in the deserts. They resembled, perhaps, emulation Chaco Great Houses—very distant variations on the Great House theme. But the desert peoples did not want Great Houses. Tonto Basin quasi–Great Houses were quickly converted into rectangular platform mounds—filled with rocks and capped with a flat adobe surface. The old Hohokam world, for at least a few decades, fended off Plateau adventurers and hierarchies.

While Hohokam shifted shape, Mimbres went through parallel changes to the east. Chaco's fall reverberated in the eastern deserts. It was no coincidence that around 1130, when Chaco's move to Aztec was complete, the people of the Mimbres region rejected, completely, the ideological and political forms that had held their societies together for almost a century. The change was sudden and complete—as if someone had thrown a switch. Once bustling Mimbres towns emptied. Mimbres pottery—for a century the focus of intense artistic energies, with scenes of myth and history—became antidesigns: black, burnished interiors, dimly reflecting the viewer's eyes and nothing more. The people formerly known as Mimbres even changed how they built their new homes—from stone masonry to puddled adobe, usually at new towns some distance removed from the old pueblos. Many Mimbres people moved up into the hills and declined; others moved north and joined the big towns around Zuni and Acoma. But most moved south, out of their old valleys and into the desert.

New adobe towns with black burnished pottery were built where there were no streams —just dry desert channels. With no streams, there were no canals. It is not entirely clear how people supported themselves—at small cienegas, perhaps, a throwback to the very earliest farming villages. Short-lived Post-Mimbres settlements skipped from valley to valley in a fast-tempo dance. When the music stopped, around 1250, many came to rest in the valley of the Rio Casas Grandes. They would become the commoners of the Southwest's last and greatest city, Paquimé.

It should not surprise us that the greatest city ever built in the Southwest was the southernmost. After 1150 *everything* sagged south, so to speak, with migrations out of the northern Plateau bumping people of the southern Plateau farther south into the Mogollon uplands. The people of the Mogollon uplands spilled south into the deserts, and the Mimbres moved south out of their mountain-edge valleys and into Chihuahua. A row of dominoes toppling toward Mexico.

Not only a push from the north but also a draw to the south: the Middle Post-Classic of

Mesoamerica. Tula fell about 1150. The implications of that fall are a matter of debate: truly momentous or merely legendary? In any event, with Tula's end, the Post-Classic pattern came into focus in vibrant clarity: expansive politics, long-distance dynamics, power plays and upheavals, and a swirling world of migrations, invasions, expulsions, and fragmentation. That was the world of Paquimé.

Blood Meridian, AD 1250 to 1450

Violence did not end with the migrations out of the northern San Juan (see fig. 7.3). The influx of migrants fleeing the troubled north strained the existing communities at Hopi, Zuni, Acoma, and the Rio Grande. Violence flared. Wars broke out, with villages sacking other villages. Larger towns were safer but inherently unstable. Settlements of several hundred people—many of them new immigrants—tended to split apart. How to hold together big towns? No one wanted the kind of leaders who had created cities like Chaco and Aztec—thousands had left the Four Corners to escape those failed kingdoms. New ideologies rose and old ideologies were revived and transformed to unite and consolidate large villages without the evils of elites or kings. The new ideologies replaced political power with ritual authority. After several centuries of experiments and false starts, the foundations of modern Puebloan society emerged from the crucible of post-Chaco chaos: egalitarian, ritually based, antihierarchical.

It was not a seamless transition. Through the 1300s and 1400s, rival ideologies competed. New "cults" appeared, some looking to Mesoamerica and some homegrown. Important ideas came from Mimbres and from the remarkable amalgam of Wupatki. Elders and priests evaluated ceremonies and rituals and accepted those that seemed most likely to help their people. New images of kachinas and other supernaturals bloomed on pottery and rock art like flowers after rain.

Old symbols of power were rehabilitated and deliberately transformed. Mesoamerican objects—macaw feathers, copper bells—had signified personal political power at Chaco, Aztec, and Wupatki. They now became the accoutrements of ritual—from princely regalia to priestly vestments. The macaw, whose feathers had once distinguished Pueblo nobles, became a close affiliate of kachinas.

Chaco faded to a bad memory. Elders composed histories to remind their children's children's children to shun hierarchies and spurn elites. For many Pueblos, Chaco and Aztec became White House, remembered as a great city led by rulers who had too much power. White House came to a bad end, with violence, famine, and migration. For Navajo people who lived later in those same lands, Chaco was remembered as a place where a kinglike ruler—neither Navajo nor Pueblo—enslaved all the peoples of the region and forced them to build palatial homes for him and his family. In this history, the people rose up and overthrew the tyrannical rule.

New ceremonies were central to the new way of life, and devout attention to ritual ultimately reshaped Pueblo society—away from the Post-Classic hustle and toward a quieter communalism. Life now revolved around ritual and ceremony. New town plans and new pottery reflected new ways of living. Black-on-white pottery gave way to a polychrome revolution: unprecedented pigments, symmetries, and icons that mirrored changes in worldview and cosmology. It worked well at the local level.

But the larger picture remained grim. Regional population fell sharply after 1300 and continued to fall. Paradoxically, people jammed into bigger and bigger towns. Compared with earlier times, towns were few and far between. Several towns might group into a defensive alliance or cluster. Clustering put safe distances between battered populations—de facto demilitarized zones. Those empty, neutral buffers decreased but did not end war. The frequency of violent incidents declined, but not their severity. Wars still raged between villages, between clusters.

Troubles on the Plateau accelerated the transformation of Hohokam, but on the opposite tack—away from bureaucracies and toward hierarchy. These were bad times in the western deserts. Large areas within the old Hohokam sphere were abandoned. Many people retreated back into the Phoenix Basin, taxing the diminishing productivity of those long-farmed lands. At places like Pueblo Grande (one of the largest Phoenix Basin towns), health suffered. Babies died; many of those who survived to adulthood died young. The old Hohokam way of life was long gone, the intricate web of beliefs abandoned. New forms of governance were needed to stem the downward spiral.

Out on the margins of the old Hohokam world, there were out-of-work rulers: Great House families pushed off the Plateau. In the upper Gila and the Tonto Basin, local people had earlier rejected Great Houses, filling their rooms with rocks and rubble and converting them to platform mounds. Would-be rulers—either from the north or inspired by the north—riposted by building new houses atop those same platforms. Great Houses rose from platform mounds along the desert–Plateau borderlands, and soon after in the Phoenix heartland and the Tucson Basin. Kings had come to the deserts.

Just like platform mounds built over earlier low mounds, Great Houses atop platform mounds were a blunt architectural statement, a stratigraphy of power. Pima people who live today amid the ball courts and mounds of the Phoenix and Tucson basins recall in their histories the elites who lived atop platforms. They were foreigners, even supernatural—certainly not Piman. They came into the heartlands and imposed their rule, tyrannical and oppressive. But the new regime could not reverse the social and economic decline. The people suffered under these rulers for a time and then rose in revolt. They went from platform mound to platform mound, killing the kings. Pima stories ring true. Something like a class revolt toppled the new governments.

The drought of 1135 to 1180 marked the end of Chaco. The Great Drought of 1275 to 1300 closed the book on Aztec. The Phoenix Basin's bitter end was punctuated by huge floods on the Salt River in 1357–1359 and again in 1381–1384. These destroyed the Phoenix canal systems. Equally disastrous floods hit the Gila River in 1420. After centuries of decline, the heartlands were unlivable.

While Pueblo peoples took themselves out of the Post-Classic world, desert societies more closely engaged the south. Two weeks' walk (500 kilometers) to the east, Paquimé rose as western deserts fell. That was probably not a coincidence; distance was no obstacle to political (or even economic) interaction in the Post-Classic world. Prior to Paquimé, the valley of the Rio Casas Grandes had been a quiet backwater. Many centuries before, at 1250 BC, Cerro Juanaqueña, at the northern end of the valley, had been the first monumental structure in the ancient Southwest. Long after, the Casas Grandes Valley became the southern margin of the old Mimbres region and the frontier beyond, with a thin scattering of pit house villages (which probably knew of Mimbres and may not have approved). Even after canals on the Mimbres and upper Gila rivers created large Mimbres towns, peaking in population in the early 1100s, to the south the Rio Casas Grandes Valley remained sparsely inhabited.

A century later, by 1250, the Mimbres and Gila were empty and the Rio Casas Grandes teemed with people—Mimbres peoples, shifted south through a string of short-lived desert towns, built far from the rivers. They knew the Casas Grandes Valley was perfect for irrigation, but in their desert hegira they had lost the skills. The institutions that regulated construction and maintenance of canals were long gone. Equally important, the remarkable ideologies that had united Mimbres villages for major public works, such as canals, had been left behind, dramatically rejected a century before. If large populations were to live on the Rio Casas Grandes, major irrigation would have to be grafted into the valley—lock, stock, and barrel—and quickly.

New towns on the Rio Casas Grandes surely sought help from the west, perhaps even experts fleeing the troubled Phoenix Basin. But Hohokam canal irrigation was an intricate balance of enormous public works administered by deliberately diffuse governance. It was a complicated, obscure system, fine-tuned to the Phoenix Basin. It might be possible to transfer technology, but not that administrative culture (which was already on the skids in its homelands). Neither Hohokam nor Mimbres had traditions and institutions of strong central leadership. In the Southwest, Chaco alone had those skills. Chacoan elites were accustomed to organizing labor to get things built. They had dug canals at Aztec Ruins, their final Plateau capital. And the direct heirs of Chaco and Aztec Ruins—or at least its cardinal factions—were conveniently available.

Pueblo histories tell us that, after the fall of White House, the people were instructed to go south. Most stopped at Acoma, Zuni, and other pueblos. But others continued straight south beyond the modern pueblos, in search of macaws (we are told), and through the empty Mimbres Valley, once the source for Chaco of macaws and other regalia. Migrating precisely south from Chaco (or from Aztec) to Mimbres might take decades, a span of time consistent with other Pueblo migration stories. By the time cardinal Chacoans reached the Mimbres Valley, that once-busy region was empty. The energy had already shifted south.

Native peoples in southern Chihuahua told Spanish conquistadors of two large groups coming into the region from the north, led by two brothers. The brothers found an old hag perched on a huge iron boulder. On this omen, one brother stopped to found a city. The second brother and his people continued south. An exceptionally large iron meteorite was found at Paquimé. Was that the omen? Paquimé became a famous breeder of macaws, on astonishing commercial scales (the goal of groups leaving White House).

The people who became the modern Pueblos voted with their feet against hierarchy— by moving away from Aztec and by *not* moving on to Paquimé. But many northerners joined their leaders' move to the south; the late thirteenth/early fourteenth centuries saw extraordinary population increase in Chihuahua. And with the post-Mimbres thousands who had settled in the Rio Casas Grandes and other valleys, the region became one of the most densely settled areas in the entire Southwest.

It was a new and brilliant city. Many architectural and organizational details—for example, the verticality of multistoried Great Houses—purposefully recalled Chaco, Aztec, and the now fabled cities of the north. Paquimé was constructed of poured adobe, a desert technology adopted by Mimbres people in their desert wanderings after they had ceased being Mimbres. Adobe was a poor fabric for Paquimé's towering five-story walls. Form trumped function— or perhaps symbolism trumped compressive strength. The city was a congeries of separate, multistoried compounds, each the scale of a small or medium-sized Great House. The houses were palatial—expansive and expensive and filled with treasures. Around the urban core were platform mounds and masonry pyramids; at least three I-shaped masonry ball courts (direct copies of Mesoamerican models, not the peculiarly Hohokam earthen ovals); and, most remarkably, monumental effigy mounds, unique in the Southwest. At least two of these, a four-armed cross and a north–south snake, commemorated cardinality.

Paquimé was more closely tied to Mesoamerica—both west and central—than were any other southwestern polities. The city represented southwestern elites' last and strongest appeal to the Post-Classic. Architectural forms—colonnades, ball courts, and (modest) pyramids—and astonishing quantities of ideologically charged Mesoamerican objects far surpassed Chaco, Mimbres, and Hohokam. Although all three southwestern traditions played parts in Paquimé, the city's leaders redefined (or refined) themselves as Mesoamerican kings. Southern objects and architectural details were no longer simply stage props or window dressing, reinterpreted in local contexts for local politics. Paquimé's leaders were trying to *be* Mesoamerican.

The basis of power shifted, from Chaco to Paquimé, from political to commercial—mirroring economic developments of the Late Post-Classic. Chaco and Aztec justified their rule by ideology, adjudication, and geopolitics. (Chaco had little but turquoise to offer. Aztec had even less. Neither was particularly successful in trade.) Paquimé was a capital, but it was also a commercial center. The lords of Paquimé amassed huge quantities of shell, precious minerals and stones, copper bells and objects, and macaws. Some of these treasures were used to demonstrate their power and to cement local alliances. But most were traded to the north, where the new Pueblo ceremonial systems redefined old Chacoan power symbols into ritual equipment. The new Pueblo ideologies were deliberately inclusive, so demand for one-time luxuries was broadly based. There were big markets for macaws on the Rio Grande, in pueblos along the Mogollon Rim, and at Hopi.

The rulers of Paquimé were delighted to oblige. Pueblo people, in their histories, recall that the White House group that went far south later returned as traders with macaws and shells. The Pueblos had turquoise, much in demand in Post-Classic Mesoamerica, and other things of value perhaps (cotton cloth?). Paquimé's commercial region encompassed the Pueblos, West Mexico (via the old Mimbres routes over the Sierra Madre), and—in a route prefiguring the later Camino Real—central Mexico.

The new city formed the eastern end of a desert axis, with fading Phoenix at the west. Paquimé and Phoenix were "peer polities"—one on the way up, the other on the way down. Casas Grandes population increased dramatically. Even as migrants retreated into the Phoenix Basin, its total population fell.

Paquimé undercut the western deserts' commerce. The Plateau's demographic center of gravity shifted east to the Rio Grande, well out of Hohokam's established trading circuits but a straight shot north for Paquimé. Phoenix's sphere was reduced to Hopi—its linguistic cousin—and a dozen large but short-lived towns in the Mogollon uplands that soon were abandoned, one after the other. Clans from those Mogollon towns shifted to the Hopi mesas and Zuni (as always, a middle place), but overall, population declined sharply in the west, both in the western deserts and on the western Plateau.

Hopi was famously poor in material terms. It was a difficult, challenging place to live. Zuni was better for farming. But the Rio Grande was rich, with fine farmlands, access to the Plains and bison, and, importantly, turquoise. Acoma, Laguna, and the Rio Grande pueblos saw marked growth in the thirteenth and fourteenth centuries, while the Hopi and the western Plateau diminished. So Paquimé had an up market and Phoenix did not.

Indeed, Paquimé may have meddled in Phoenix Basin politics, building outlier embassies in and around the Phoenix Basin. The largest candidate outlier was Casa Grande, the home of the greatest, principal Hohokam lord (according to Piman accounts), one of the first to be killed when the people rose up against their rulers. Hierarchies, imposed late over a failing, nonhierarchical system, could not fix Hohokam's problems. By 1450 little was left of Hohokam's earlier glories, save stories and histories.

Patterns of Culture, AD 1450 to 1600

Paquimé fell, taken and sacked by unknown parties, between 1450 and 1500 (see figs. 1.5, 7.2). Hopi clan histories recount origins deep in Mexico at a place called the Red City, which some identify as Paquimé. The Red City's end—war and ruin (plus flood and earthquake in some versions)—fits Paquimé. Paquimé's fall was the last and greatest historical incident in the political history of the Southwest and may have occurred within a few decades of the Spanish arrival in 1540. The historical haze around that epochal event reflects history itself: when Paquimé fell, some may have gone to the pueblos, but many survivors (and they must have been legion) did not return to the north. Their histories led south, following factions gone south two or three centuries earlier. The people who came out of the Southwest may not have been the Mexica Aztecs, who founded the great empire of central Mexico. Rather, southwestern peoples were subcurrents in a vast swirl of migrations, mostly north to south, which created a complex patchwork of northern and western Mesoamerican societies later conquered by Spain.

It is hard to find kings and cities in traditional Pueblo and Pima histories because they have been, in essence, deliberately repressed. They show up as foils and "bad examples" in accounts of White House and Pima revolts. Pueblo historians know the nature of Chaco and Aztec but recount those stories only when needed, as admonitions of how *not* to behave. The heirs of Chaco's kings, if they could be found in Mexico, might remember things differently.

Or perhaps not: Chaco and Aztec and Paquimé and Pueblo Grande did not end well. The century and a half between 1450 and the arrival of Spanish colonists in 1598 was almost certainly as dramatic and violent as the preceding centuries—and it was not happy.

Population continued to plummet over the entire Southwest. The number of towns decreased. Whole districts were depopulated, continuing the alarming pattern that began in the Four Corners at 1300. For example, scores of towns—big towns!—in the western deserts, in the Mogollon uplands, and along the southern Rio Grande were abandoned before Spanish conquistadors entered the region.

The pueblos from Hopi to Taos absorbed new peoples, not always of the same language or history. The unsettled social conditions created by constant but erratic in-migration must have tempted pueblos (and Pueblo individuals) to reassert a degree of political authority, to bring order out of something like chaos. There are hints of that kind of authority in the Rio Grande. But the bitter lessons of Chaco and Aztec were still fresh. The Pueblos avoided political hierarchy and suppressed potential leaders through a complex mesh of ritual and social practices. In one researcher's words, they "defeated hierarchy."

The Pueblos that survived those turbulent times thrived, to a degree. Rio Grande pueblos stabilized and expanded. The fifteenth century saw renewed connections with Mexico, almost certainly tied to the fall of Paquimé, which had controlled inland trade routes. Turquoise was still much in demand in Late Post-Classic Mesoamerica. (The turquoise trade may have been at least partly coastal, with a large proportion of southwestern turquoise entering central Mexico through Pacific ports.) The eastern Pueblos also forged economic connections across the Plains. Chaco and Cahokia surely knew of each other in the twelfth century; so too Pecos and Spiro, two great trading centers at the outer margins of their respective regions.

The people who would become Navajos and Apaches arrived from the north, after the fall of Chaco and probably after the end of Aztec—but not long after. Athabaskan speakers may well have been on the Plateau during Aztec's reign. Certainly, Navajo clans have detailed knowledge of the times and places of the ancient Plateau cities.

Piman peoples recovered slowly from the final, tumultuous centuries of Hohokam and their rebellion against the platform mound rulers. Desert populations, like that of the Plateau, were only a small fraction of their earlier heights. It would take the deserts many years to rebound from centuries of intense canal irrigation, overhunting and overgathering, and the depletion of firewood and other resources. Before they could, Europe arrived.

Coronado's army entered the deserts in 1540, looking for cities of gold. The memory of a rich, urban Southwest lived on in the stories of Mesoamerican traders. Those traders (or their children's children) guided Coronado and other conquistadors into what should have been the new Mexico. The stories were true: there were cities. But the Spaniards came too late—a century too late for Paquimé and the Phoenix Basin, three centuries too late for Chaco and Aztec. The pueblos they found were nothing like cities: no gold, no wealth, no commerce, no kings. The Spanish could not know that those seeming deficiencies and poverties reflected the Pueblos' conscious decisions to turn away from cities and kings. Discouraged, the conquistadors returned to Old Mexico.

Sixty years later, Don Juan de Oñate returned with colonists seeking not cities but farmlands and metals. They stayed. Not without incident of course: Native revolts, political revolutions, Yankee invasions, and all the alarms and excursions of modern history.

The Spanish brought Aztec tales into the Southwest with their Mexican auxiliaries. But versions of those stories were already being told: tales of Moctezuma and Aztec palaces. In later years, the Aztecs' first home was said to be in the Four Corners, their second home at Casa Grande, their third and final southwestern home at Paquimé. Over the decades, ancient Aztlan infused southwestern lands—not by that Nahuatl name but as the original homeland of the Aztecs and their emperors.

El mundo nuevo y bravo, AD 1600 to 2005

The history of the ancient Southwest ends at 1600. After 1600 the Southwest was no longer Native, no longer aboriginal, no longer "ancient." Native people remained of course, and their stories continued in the face of crushing colonization. They had become threads and themes in a larger global history.

In 1598 the Southwest became part of a world system directed first by Madrid, then by Ciudad de Mexico, and finally by Washington. Of course, the Southwest had always been linked to larger worlds, most notably Post-Classic Mesoamerica. But European colonization was brutally different. Southwestern societies and institutions, at 1600, were the products of long, complex, and "nonlinear" histories. Thereafter, their histories were trimmed, compressed, repressed, nearly obliterated. Native groups coped with even worse demographic collapse and with displacement, economic domination, religious repression, and political subjugation by European colonizers. Perhaps most importantly, *they were no longer allowed to move*. Pueblos with long histories of movement and migration were confined to the four square leagues of royal charters. Traditional governance went underground. Shadow cabinets directed village life through public officials, with constitutions and titles approved by the colonial authorities. The real power remained with the older system, working behind the scene. The remarkable Pueblo Revolt of 1680 was one of the final major southwestern confederacies. The revolt of 1680 was not the first "pan-Pueblo" political organization; it was the last. It came two centuries after the collapse of the last major southwestern political system. And the revolt failed, ultimately, because Pueblos themselves had made it impossible to maintain regional polities.

Pueblo or Pima or Athabaskan peoples today are both like and unlike Chaco and Hohokam, or Mesa Verde and Tularosa. The histories and traditions are there, but today's Native societies are profoundly different. Indeed, modern tribes and Pueblos are not very much like southwestern societies at 1600. How could they be? They live in or in spite of the twenty-first century, in a world totally changed from that of the fifteenth. Yet, Native societies survive, and many even thrive in the face of astonishing adversities. Traditions, histories, and truths endured through changes in regime, ancient and modern.

The Southwest today is dramatically different from the Southwest before 1600, and the Southwest of 1600 was a very different place than it was at 1100, and at 1100 very different than it was at 500. We should honor those differences and honor the ancient societies that rose and fell. The descendants of those societies are still here, but their ancient kingdoms are gone.

Conclusions?

This book is half history, half archaeology. The best conclusion for history is "the end"—and we hope they lived happily ever after. For archaeology, it's more complicated.

There's no "the end" for archaeology. Archaeology, like most science and scholarship, is open-ended. The whole point is to learn new things, correct past errors, and offer fresh hypotheses—which others will then correct. We whittle away at competing ideas and maybe get closer to the truth. That's as it should be. If long-suffering readers slog through this book's notes, they will know that there are a half-dozen competing interpretations for each of the many events—minor and major—that I've cherry-picked and strung together in narrative. Picking a different interpretation would send the history off on a different course. And we are always learning. If I rewrite this book ten years from now, it should be a substantially different book.

But this is the book I wrote now, in my thirty-fifth year as a southwestern archaeologist. It's not "right," but I'm reasonably confident that it's closer to the truth than much of the competition: coffee table books, museum exhibits, PBS shows, and perhaps even conventional textbooks. Because I think that my assumptions, going in, were more realistic. Everybody knew everything. No coincidences. Distances can be dealt with. These assumptions lead us to an ancient Southwest that I think fits better in its time and place than many other versions currently on offer.

The next archaeological steps are obvious: professors and professionals will bemoan the fact that this pernicious claptrap is now in the literature, cluttering the course of careful scholarship. And eager graduate students will sharpen their knives and their wits and carve away.

After three decades in the Southwest, I've come to understand that archaeology is less like butterfly collecting and more like ice hockey. (There's some truth in Indiana Jones, especially his really bad days.)

Since I'm the one to be eviscerated, I'd like to beg several small favors: Slice away, but think big! Don't sell them short! Because this matters!

Think Big

The Southwest was part of North America. We will never understand Yellow Jacket, Grewe, or Old Town without considering Mesoamerica and the Mississippi Valley. Ancient southwesterners engaged their continent or rejected it. Either way, their history was framed in a Big Picture. Consider two dimensions of bigness: space and time.

Space first. Over its century-long history, southwestern archaeology painted itself into tighter and tighter corners, until a small valley (during the hyperscience 1970s) became a self-contained "natural laboratory," culture in a petri dish. State lines and ranger districts further fragmented the region. Recognizing larger entities—for example, Chaco and Hohokam "regional systems"—was not easy, because they crossed research areas and jurisdictions. There's still surprising resistance to thinking on those scales—or, more unsettling, resistance to thinking that *ancient people thought on those scales*. We've been trained to think that *they didn't*, that anything beyond their immediate horizon was a mystery and a marvel. That's a presupposition about ancient southwesterners that won't bear up under close analysis (more on this below).

We need to look well beyond our site, our valley, our district, even our "culture area." Hohokam, Anasazi, and Mogollon will probably make sense only together, as a historical ensemble, a ménage à trois. The histories of Hohokam, Chaco, and Paquimé formed an equilateral triangle, 500 kilometers on a side. And larger still: the Southwest was an active player in the North American Post-Classic. So what context is appropriate for understanding the history of the ancient Southwest or any site or small part of the Southwest? Continental!

And time, Big Time. Our vade mecum for understanding the past is the present: ethnography. Modern Hopi infiltrates interpretations of even the earliest agricultural periods. For societies after 1300 in the north and after 1450 in the south, ethnography has something useful to say. But those dates marked cataclysmic changes; life after was hugely different from life before. Bandelier thought the history of the ancient Southwest was slow, tedious, and gradual. He was wrong. Native peoples have traditional *histories* of those earlier times—histories about *change*. In their traditions, their present differs dramatically from their past. That is, there was a *tradition of change*, of learning new ways, of moving to new places. Yet we look to ethnographies of Pueblos and Navajos and Piman peoples for our interpretations and conventions. An offended cultural anthropologist once asked me, "What other societies could possibly be more appropriate for archaeological interpretation?" I would say *Post-Classic societies* elsewhere in North America. Tula and Cahokia are legitimate "triangulation points" for understanding Chaco and Hohokam, and they are almost certainly more useful than ethnographies of Native groups written a thousand years after the fact. Thinking back at the past, at Epi-Classic and Post-Classic, Emergent Mississippian and Middle Mississippian, will actually move southwestern archaeology forward. Forcing Chaco into a Pueblo mold will not.

Our work is freighted with a century of ethnographically saturated interpretation, and that received wisdom needs an infusion of less teleological insights. Before you carve me up, check out the Post-Classic; look at Mississippian. *That's* what was happening when Chaco and

Phoenix and Paquimé were alive. Those great cities knew nothing about the twentieth century; they knew a lot about the eleventh. In space and time, think big!

Don't Sell Them Short

North America encompassed a vast range of societies, many of which shaped or framed the ancient Southwest at various removes. Kings, states, and empires of course had more impact than hunters and gatherers. Is it presumptuous to link Pimas and Pueblos to Mesoamerican kings and Mississippian lords? I don't think so. There is ample evidence that the ancient Southwest played or wanted to play on the Mesoamerican and Mississippian level.

And what level was that, exactly? What is the proper frame of reference for southwestern societies? It is a rock-solid anthropological truth that Native societies north of Mexico were "intermediate" or "middle range"—an archaeological euphemism for groups more than hunter-gatherers but less than states. All American Indian farmers were intermediate and no more; we learn this with our archaeological ABCs. Writing this book, I've come to realize that "intermediate" is a useless category—useless but with negative consequences. For southwestern archaeology, "intermediate" means that we are absolved from thinking about Chaco and Paquimé as states because we already know they were "intermediate." We limit, a priori, what they could or could not have done. That's not fair to Chaco and Paquimé.

Were there kings at Chaco? Of course! After their own fashion. There had been kings in Mesoamerica for two millennia before Pueblo Bonito. How could aspiring southwestern elites *not* know about these kings—and shape their actions in light of that knowledge? Kingship was a part of Chaco's historical context. Was Paquimé a state? Again, of course! Not a primary state, evolved in place, but a secondary (or pick-your-power) state. And a state that did not, in the end, succeed. Most don't.

We want our Southwest simple. Why? Well, in large part because our archaeological forefathers told us so, as their forefathers told them. We should carefully consider their (and our) enthusiasm for a simple Southwest. There is more than a hint of colonial prejudice in the wisdom we received from Bandelier, Hewett, and even Kidder—and from the ethnographers. Reexamine the foundational narratives and weed out the colonialism. Don't sell them short!

This Matters

Modern visions of the ancient Southwest have repercussions—faint, perhaps, but real—in political theory and popular thought. Anthropology presented an image of peaceful, egalitarian, communal Pueblos; that image of utopian communalism inspired Marx and Engels and their followers.[51]

That Pueblo image later found popular expression in Ruth Benedict's Zuni, with influences far beyond nineteenth-century political philosophies. Benedict's Zuni (and their sister Pueblos) were unique in the Americas and deliberately so:

> It is not possible to understand Pueblo attitudes toward life without some knowledge of the culture from which they have detached themselves: that of the rest of North America. It is by the force of the contrast that we can calculate the strength of their opposite drive and resistances which have kept out of the Pueblos the most characteristic traits of the American aborigines.[52]

As it turns out, among those traits were hierarchical governments—in Post-Classic times. That's what Pueblos detached themselves from. Benedict didn't know the history behind the "opposite drive and resistances." Now I think we do. Pueblos did not exist time-lessly in a happy condition of "primitive communism" (Morgan, Marx, and Engels's term). They struggled and staggered and tacked, historically, from villages to kings to chaos to equality. Pueblos developed after 1300 as a reaction to state-level governments, conscious rejections of earlier hierarchies. They deliberately replaced the kings of Chaco with the priests of Zuni. Ruth got it right, more or less, for Pueblo IV. Karl and Friedrich got it wrong. That mattered: there were consequences.

The cold war is over. Marxism, at least in this country, lives on only in universities. It's become academic. The ancient Southwest still matters, however, in current events of some consequence: our relations with Mexico and Latin America. The past, both ancient and colonial, frames our thinking on immigration, NAFTA, and the "melting pot" turned "salad bowl." So it's important to get it right. Was Native North America a fragmented continent, culturally divided into a simple temperate north (ripe for European exploitation) and a complex tropical south? Or was the continent a historical whole? The latter, I think: Native histories of what later became the United States and Mexico were intertwined. Our thinking about Mexico and Latin America should build upon that historical foundation: *Aztlan* or something like it.

Not perhaps the Aztlan of Mexica myth or of Chicano civil rights—although that Aztlan has enormous importance. I'm thinking of the Aztlan that led open-minded (that is, naive) colonists to name an earthen pyramid in Wisconsin and a Pueblo ruin in New Mexico after the Aztecs. Mistakenly, perhaps, but a useful mistake—a recognition that Native North America was an interconnected whole, a vast association of overlapping and interconnected civilizations. They shared *histories*.

Colonialism and intercolonial squabbles (the Mexican War, for example) fragmented the continent and reduced its Native societies to administratively and philosophically convenient sizes: small and smaller. We should not reinforce or reify colonial tactics by projecting them back into the past. In our efforts to understand that past, we owe it to the ancient people to shed colonial biases, if we can. We'll never scrape them all off, but two are easy to identify and rectify: Lewis Henry Morgan's glass ceiling, a racist limit for what American Indians could or could not do, and the international border, a legacy of colonial wars that seals off our Indians from their Post-Classic. Morgan said Indians could not create states. Bandelier said Indians were ignorant of Post-Classic politics. These were the founding fathers of southwestern archaeology, and both were terribly wrong. Shatter the ceiling and erase the border. This matters!

Notes

Chapter 1

1. Bandelier 1892:592.

2. Martin 2006:61, emphasis added.

3. Adolph Bandelier wrote a *Histoire* for Pope Leo XIII, but that was mostly documentary history—explorers, proselytizers, martyrs—with a final, disconnected chapter on prehistory (Bandelier 1887). Edgar Hewett, Bandelier's loyal student, wrote the Handbooks of Archaeological History series (e.g., Hewett 1936a; Bandelier and Hewett 1937). Hewett's prehistories were pretty much modern Pueblo lifeways projected uncritically back into the past. *A History of the Ancient Southwest* by Harold S. Gladwin (1957) was the first (and last) attempt to write a real narrative history. (No doubt there's a reason it's been tried only once, and I'll probably figure out that reason before I'm done writing.) Gladwin sponsored his own research institution, Gila Pueblo (chapter 4), and wrote many of its reports (the Medallion series). He published *A History of the Ancient Southwest* through a commercial house, for a larger audience. A few chapter titles: "The Enemy at the Gates: AD 1000 to 1100," "The Quick or the Dead: AD 1100 to 1200," and "The Gathering of the Clans: AD 1200 to 1300." Those titles not only tell the story but also tell us that Gladwin was *telling a story*. Gladwin himself, of course, is problematic: he was a nonacademic maverick; he enjoyed writing and slipped easily into humor and word play; and he had interests in forbidden subjects, such as transoceanic contacts, which alienated his few friends in the field (Gladwin 1947, 1979). I court derision by co-opting his title, but I admire the man for his vision and his amused disregard of academic proprieties. I caution young archaeologists, however, to shun Gladwin as they would shun their elder's jargon. Gladwin died discredited. And so, most likely, shall I.

Charles Di Peso was another, more successful prehistorian. Di Peso spent his career at the Amerind Foundation, like Gila Pueblo, a privately funded research institute. Di Peso's *Casas Grandes* (1974)—his magnum opus—was an enormously detailed site report on his excavations at Paquimé, but it was much more. It was a history of the Gran Chichimeca, Di Peso's label for the greater Southwest. Di Peso's Chichimeca was the northwest of Mesoamerica, and he linked almost everything interesting that happened in the ancient Southwest to Mexico. Another scholar of astonishing vision and verve, but again, probably not a man for aspiring young scholars to follow; the academy did not welcome his Mexican enthusiasms.

Neither Gladwin's nor Di Peso's history is well regarded today—although their substantive archaeological contributions are rightly held as seminal. No one cites *History of the Ancient Southwest*, and Gladwin has been reduced to a footnote (the founder of Gila Pueblo and Emil Haury's first sponsor). Di Peso is honored as a scholar (Reyman [ed.] 1995; Woosley and Ravesloot 1993), but his massive *Casas Grandes* report has been dissected in dozens of articles and dissertations, almost all of which conclude that he was wrong. Di Peso's focus on Mesoamerica and the Southwest was sustained by a few scholars, most notably Carroll Riley, who has written several volumes comparable in vision to *Casas Grandes* (Riley 1987, 2005), and J. Charles Kelley (see Riley and Hedrick 1978). But the tides run against his brand of history (e.g., Cobb, Maymon, and McGuire 1999; Whalen and Minnis 2003).

Other Southwesternists have succeeded with nonnarrative syntheses of the region. Linda Cordell's textbooks (1984, 1997) are exemplary, standard references, but they are neither historical nor narrative—nor were they intended to be. Cordell's books are honored, as are other textbooks and overviews (e.g., Kantner 2004; Plog 1997; Reid and Whittlesey 1997), but the professional rewards of synthesis can be problematic. Ted Kidder, who wrote the first (Kidder 1924), recalled that "everybody said it was a swell job, except in the region that they knew about" (quoted in Givens 1992:148). A few more brave contemporaries who have inspired me with their wide-ranging historical studies include David Doyel (Doyel and Lekson 1992), Steven LeBlanc (1986b, 1989a, 1989b, 1999), and David Wilcox (e.g., 1986, 1999a), as well as Linda Cordell and George Gumerman (1989), who bravely attempted to forge a truly regional chronology—a series of stages that accommodated *both* Anasazi and Hohokam.

4. Jennings 1956:120.

5. Martin 2006:61.

6. Selectivity—and heavy reliance on secondary sources! Readers may wonder, Where are the numbers, charts, tables, regression analyses, and data crunching? My data came precrunched. References to the work of others, I hope, are extensive and, insofar as possible, complete; if I failed to cite an author whose ideas or interpretations I use, that was honest error, or the neurological decay of age. Where it is necessary to present and analyze data qua data, I've done so in notes.

7. For an amusing or depressing—but suitably crusty and codgerly—analysis of archaeological flocking, see Bentley's (2006) statistical analysis of the words *agency* and *nuanced* and their rises and falls in current literature. Archaeology, as so often happens, was a bit behind the curve. Elsewhere in the academy, *agency* took off in 1991–1992; American archaeology, I think, caught the wave about 1996–1997. The Southwest, as also so often happens, was even further back in the pack; fifteen years after *agency* first broke big, it was only beginning to make a substantial mark on southwestern literature. It lurks today in dissertations, theses, and conference papers. Presumably, those will turn into print over the next several years. But by then the larger intellectual world will probably be on to something new. (Of course, Bentley's analysis offended some, who refuted his facts and figures, suggesting that jargon is not a problem [Chrisomalis 2007]—but it truly is for me.)

8. Hodder and Hutson 2003:206.

9. Both Binford and Hodder were (and are) larger than life, and I invoke them here not so much as names but as *numen genii*, as that term was used in antiquity and today in acuity. For me (and I think for many of my colleagues), Binford and Hodder typify very different ways of thinking. The past half century was marked by much intellectual Sturm und Drang in American archaeology, mostly between their two "schools," as I call them here. This book is no place to analyze in detail those turbulent times. I organize my thoughts throughout around simple histories or schemas, and, rightly or wrongly, that's how I remember archaeology's key debate in the second half of the twentieth century. I think my simplified memories truer than not. Americanist archaeology in the twenty-first century redefines itself (at southwestern archaeology's flagship university) as "human evolution and social change," while Lord Renfrew (no flaming radical) juxtaposes archaeology and modern art in *Figuring It Out: The Parallel Visions of Artists and Archaeologists* (Renfrew 2003; see also Renfrew 2007). Two archaeologies, "Two Cultures"—sensu Snow (1959) *and* Shott (2005).

10. Of course, European archaeology is more comfortable with history and historians. When Hodder noted (in 1987) that archaeology had figured out how to deal with "large scales and long term" history, he must have been thinking about the Old World. European archaeologists routinely argue about migrations, diffusions, and histories over areas that make the Southwest look tiny. For example, they argue about Linearbandkeramik (LBK), a type of early Neolithic pottery found from the Black Sea to the English Channel, a distance of almost 2,000 kilometers. That's approximately the distance from the Four Corners to Mexico City. When I discuss southwestern problems with archaeologists working in Europe, Africa, or Asia, they are universally bemused by the small scale of our arguments. *They* may have figured out how to deal with large scales and long-term history, but I think *we* still have some work to do.

Hodder sees two historical scales: one small and personal, the other larger and impersonal; "both are needed," but "different types of theory are relevant to the different scales" (Hodder 1999:130, 147). Having successfully grappled with larger scales (e.g, Hodder 1987, 1990), Hodder seems to be turning his considerable energies to the micro, household, and even individual scales: "The movement of the mass…is built up from the micro-details of life—where and when and how one sits by a hearth, how one plasters a wall, how one cooks, and what one does with the leopard bone" (Hodder 2006:258). History is the sum of its many tiny parts, a stream of micro events: "Everyone…agrees that 'large scale processes cannot be invoked to explain small scale processes'" (Hodder and Hutson 2003:144, citing Knapp 1992; for variations on this theme, see Morris 2000).

After a brief flirtation with European, macro-scale *annales* (e.g., Bintliff 1991; Knapp 1992), American archaeology came down hard in favor of particulars, microhistories, "individual time." I see in many recent southwestern studies a rising skepticism toward large-scale processes or narratives, part of the larger tide of postmodernism, late to hit the Great American Desert. I'm more interested in large-scale history, for reasons that will become clear throughout this book. Unfortunately, the professional structure of American archaeology encourages us to think small (chapters 2 and 3), while the "cultural affiliation" clauses of the Native American Graves Protection and Repatriation Act of 1990 (NAGPRA) direct us to write highly particularistic, very local histories (chapters 5 and 6). All of this makes it rather awkward to think publicly about large-scale history in ancient North America.

11. Daniel (1962:156), responding no doubt to the first stirrings of Binford's New Archaeology. Hodder wrote, "Ultimately the main reason why the New Archaeology never really took hold in Europe to the extent that it did in America may be that in Europe archaeology is intellectually and administratively (in universities) closely linked to history, not anthropology" (Hodder 1991:10).

12. Willey and Phillips 1958:2. In British universities, there are about thirty-five academic departments or units teaching archaeology. Of these, 70 percent are stand-alone archaeology faculties; 25 percent are combined archaeology and history; only two are parts of anthropology departments or faculties. Cambridge is one of these exceptions. The Disney Chair of Archaeology at Cambridge was originally endowed for classics; later it shifted to prehistory (Clark 1989:27–29).

Glyn Daniel gets almost three-quarters through his 1981 *A Short History of Archaeology* before anthropology is even mentioned. It appears as a separate field and a source of "ethnographic parallels." At American universities, of course, one can find archaeology courses in art history, history, religious studies, classics, and elsewhere, but "prehistoric" archaeology is firmly at home in anthropology. There are only two or three stand-alone archaeology departments, most notably at Stanford.

"Archaeology is anthropology or it is nothing!" was a rallying cry of American archaeology in the 1960s and 1970s. The phrase is still heard today. George Kubler offered a useful study of its provenance, which is well worth quoting here (bereft of his citations and footnotes):

> Phillip Phillips was first to say this in 1955, and the aphorism is often used with approval by archaeologists (e.g., L. Binford), although it is sometimes wrongly credited to Gordon Willey (e.g., K. Flannery), because Willey and Phillips later collaborated, re-using the dictum in joint authorship and altering "New World" to "American."… Phillips originally credited the English legal historian, F. W. Maitland, with the format of his own aphorism, as a "famous dictum." Maitland's remarks first appeared in 1899 in an essay on "The Body Politic." The eminent Cambridge historian had said this about progress in the writing of history: "Of course I am including under the name of history what some people call archaeology; for to my mind an archaeology that is not history is somewhat less than nothing…" and he went on to imply that archaeology is no more important to history than the Rule of Three is to mathematics. (Kubler 1975:764–65)

13. Trigger 2006:409.

14. And by the National Endowment for the Humanities, in one of life's little ironies. Indeed, archaeology is (I think) the only discipline specifically named in the missions of both the National Science Foundation and the National Endowment for the Humanities, and I know archaeologists who have received money from the National Endowment for the Arts too. The National Endowment for the Humanities' archaeology leans more to classical and historical brands.

15. Morgenroth 2001:157. Attempts at reconciliation (e.g., Hodder 1999:ch. 2; Van Pool and Van Pool 1999) fail to persuade (me); the goals of the two archaeologies are fundamentally different and divergent. "Processual-plus," as Michelle Hegmon (2003) named it, adds agency, gender, symbolism, and materiality (staples of British archaeology) to familiar Americanist agendas. With a shift of emphasis, Timothy Pauketat's (2001) "processual-historical" archaeology attempts a similar Vulcan mind-meld across two archaeologies separated by a common language. I think both processual-plus and processual-historical are trying to be science. They make American archaeology much more lively and interesting, and I fit somewhere in that stew, but I'm not sure exactly where.

16. Bender 1998 and most recently the wonderfully jargon-free Bender, Hamilton, and Tilly 2007.

17. Pearson and Shanks 2001.

18. In North America, comparisons of large archaeological regions are an established genre in Mesoamerica (e.g., Clark and Knoll 2005, in a remarkable continental-scale study; Blanton et al. 1993, in a classic interregional comparison). Very few Mesoamericanists actively engage the Mississippi Valley (but see Clark and Knoll 2005), and the Southwest's role in cross-regional comparisons is usually as a spoiler or an

admonition. For example, Norman Yoffee (2005) uses the Southwest as a cautionary tale in his comparative study of Archaic states (or myths thereof). There are exceptions, usually Mesoamericanists who trained in the Southwest. The Southwest played a more active role in intriguing conference sessions comparing Hohokam with Mississippian, and Anasazi with the Neolithic Near East, and several laudable publications treated the Southwest as a comparative equal to other parts of the world, for example, with Mesoamerica (Feinman, Nicholas, and Upham 1996) or with the US Southeast (Kowalewski 1996). Jill Neitzel's *Great Towns and Regional Polities: In the Prehistoric American Southwest and Southeast* (1999) is an outstanding, sustained analysis, with disappointing results. The Southwest Anthropological Research Group (SARG) compared smaller areas within the Anasazi region (chapter 6), and Patty Crown and Jim Judge's *Chaco and Hohokam* (1991) was an exemplary comparative study on larger scales but still firmly within the Southwest.

Big History is not the same as regional synthesis. The Southwest surely does not lack the latter—far from it! Outstanding works synthesizing large areas or particular time periods made this book possible and are cited throughout. I call your attention to recent syntheses that convinced me the time might be right for a narrative history, supported by the hard work of other people. For the southwestern Archaic: Vierra 2005. In the Anasazi area: Reed 2000 (Basketmaker III), Wilshusen 1999b; Wilshusen and Ortman 1999 (Pueblo I), Lekson, ed. 2006 (Pueblo II), Adler 1996 (Pueblo III), and Adams and Duff 2004; Dean 2000; Spielman 1998 (Pueblo IV and Protohistoric). For Mesa Verde specifically: Lipe, Varien, and Wilshusen 1999. In all Hohokam periods: Doyel 1987; Doyel, Fish, and Fish 2000; Gumerman 1991; and especially Fish and Fish 2007. For Mogollon: Hegmon et al. 1999; Mills, Herr, and Van Keuren 1999; Shafer 2003. For the "Land Between" Hohokam and Casas Grandes (that is, southeastern Arizona and southwestern New Mexico): Wallace and Lindeman forthcoming. For the Rio Grande: Vierra 2007. Without these regional and temporal syntheses (and others cited throughout the book), I could not and would not have attempted this project.

19. Bentley 2002:393.

20. Some other seminal or useful works: Bentley's *Old World Encounters: Cross-cultural Contacts and Exchanges in Pre-Modern Times* (1993) and Philip Curtin's *Cross-cultural Trade in World History* (1984). An excellent recent summary—playing off a history title (Carr's classic "What Is History?") as iconic as "When Is a Kiva?"—is Pamela Crossley's *What Is Global History?* (2008). Patrick Manning provides another guide to developments and resources: *Navigating World History* (2003)—critical of Bentley!

Big History has become something of a marketing slogan, and a somewhat different animal. Titles like Fred Spier's *The Structure of Big History* (1996), Cynthia Brown's *Big History* (2007), or David Christian's *Maps of Time* (2004) attempt to varying degrees to tell a coherent narrative of extreme time depth, Big Bang to today. I find these books interesting but a bit too much like Toynbee or Durant, extrapolated to cosmological and geological time. I use the term *Big History* here and in lectures because it sounds good, but I'm really thinking more along the lines of Bentley's world history.

"Comparative civilizations" is an established genre with its own professional societies, meetings, and journals (*Comparative Civilizations Review*, the journal of the International Society for the Comparative Study of Civilizations). Defining *civilization* is (of course) a stumbling block, but once out of the gate, comparative civilizations covers just about anything, anywhere, anytime—not just the lifestyles of the rich and famous.

21. Michael Berry (1982) attempted to correlate events and trends in the Anasazi region to those in the Hohokam area. He was raked over the coals for his efforts. Cordell and Gumerman (1989) attempted a southwestern chronology that encompassed both Anasazi and Hohokam. Unfortunately, it is not widely used.

22. Of course, I am not alone in wishing for larger scales. I have plenty of good company grousing around the bar at meetings and conferences. Jeffrey Quilter, in the introduction to *A Pre-Columbian World*, catches the tone of those conversations when he notes

> the natural tendency of experts in particular areas to resist having their specificities lumped into larger categories that dilute the special features so carefully delineated in their research. And, scholars make their careers mostly in cleaving off or isolating part of a larger corpus of data or discourse into their own areas of expertise. The generalist is always in danger of being criticized by the specialist because of exceptions to the rule. The reluctance to see the forest instead of concentrating on trees is also part of the rhythmic cycles of scholarship that swing between periods of generalization and others of particularist studies. Another important factor is archaeological conservatism. Although the New Archaeology was optimistic in its outlook, archaeologists are generally a pessimistic lot, reminding themselves of how much they don't know and restricting their interpretations to not venture too far from the bits and pieces of the past that serve as the source of their knowledge. A cautionary stance in approaching prehistory is appropriate in the same way that any conservative position has the advantage of avoiding mistakes by refusing to make a commitment. But if nothing is ventured, nothing is gained. (Quilter and Miller 2006:10)

There is a difference between regional synthesis and what the historians call Big History or global history, and that difference is *interconnection*. John Vincent surveyed regional versus global histories and concluded, "There are world histories, and good ones…but they are more the sum of various professional regional histories, than a cultural new departure…. World history, then, is the thing that is most obviously missing as the century ends" (Vincent 2006:147). The *assumption of interconnection* (versus the assumption of isolation) constitutes, I think, a *cultural departure* for archaeology: Big Archaeology to match Big History.

The East leads the way. *Native American Interactions*, edited by Michael Nassaney and Ken Sassaman (1995), examines interactions over the eastern United States, an area about three times the size of the greater Southwest. Nassaney and Sassaman's analysis of the history of archaeological thinking on these matters (1995:xxi–xxiv) presaged the arguments presented in this book, although we reached our parallel conclusions independently. We all see the same developments in American archaeology, which is comforting. Nassaney and Sassaman find cause for hope in the intellectual developments of the 1980s and early 1990s, yet they caution: "Despite these positive influences, however, there seems to be resistance on the part of many—if not most—North American archaeologists to discuss interaction at pan-regional scales" (Nassaney and Sassaman 1995:xxiv). Amen.

A remarkable exception—a book almost unique in American archaeology—was James A. Ford's *A Comparison of Formative Cultures in the Americas* (1969), the acme of culture history–era diffusion. In maps and tables, Ford traced the ebb and flow of dozens of traits across the continents. Diffusion, alas, was shunned by New Archaeology in the late 1960s, and Ford died in 1968, before the book was published, so he could not defend, much less promote, his approach. Recent reevaluations (Clark and Knoll 2005) show that Ford was wrong in detail but perhaps not in vision and scope: "History matters, and it can reach across great distances, either across Olmec Mesoamerica or around the Gulf [of Mexico]" (Clark and White 2005:300).

In the Old World, Colin Renfrew and the McDonald Institute for Archaeological Research are headed toward Big History (e.g., Bellwood and Renfrew 2002; Boyle, Renfrew, and Levine 2002). And others: Steven Mithen covers the globe in the early Holocene in his remarkable book *After the Ice: A Global Human History, 20,000–5,000 BC* (2003). *Atlantic Connections and Adaptations* (Housley and Coles 2004) is an archaeological approach to the North Atlantic but reaches into the New World only with the Vikings. Barry Cunliffe's *Facing the Ocean* (2001) is a superb archaeological treatment of a huge region—the Atlantic Coast of Europe—and a model for the genre. *African Connections* by Peter Mitchell (2005) is an admirable attempt to put sub-Saharan Africa on the map. LaBianca and Scham's *Connectivity in Antiquity: Globalization as a Long-term Historical Process* (2006) is a demonstration of independent invention, or convergent evolution; the editors do not mention Wallerstein, although one contributor tips the hat, briefly. (Their inspiration for ancient connectivity was Manuel Castells's *The Information Age: Economy, Society and Culture* [1996, 1997, 1998]—a work I have not fully explored.) I am particularly impressed with Philip Kohl's view of archaeology expressed in *The Making of Bronze Age Eurasia*:

> Such macrohistorical processes are impossible to detect archaeologically if one focuses on developments in a single region or over a relatively restricted chronological horizon of a hundred years or so. The basic task of the archaeologist as culture historian is not to compile and order new data and ceaselessly refine local chronological sequences, though those are both essential and necessary activities; the culture historian also must take advantage of the only real strength of the archaeological record: its coarse-grained, spatial and temporal macroperspective on the basic activities carried out by different groups, and then attempt to discern how these various activities relate to one another or are interconnected. As E. Wolf (1982) argued persuasively for the modern historical era, cultures continuously imbricate and get caught up in shared historical processes that extend far beyond the areas they occupy. (Kohl 2007:258)

The assumption of interconnection is not new or exclusive to a handful of modern mavericks. Many archaeologists study interconnections under the aegis of the "world systems" theories of social historian Immanuel Wallerstein (1974, 1980, 1989). Wallerstein's interest was, in effect, globalization since the Age of Exploration and colonization. Over the past two decades, two schools of archaeological world systems have emerged—one driving Wallerstein's modern world systems back deeper into Old World prehistory (e.g., Abu-Lughod 1989; Frank and Gills 1993) and the other abstracting the *idea* of world systems and applying the concept across a wide range of preindustrial, premodern societies in the Old and New worlds (e.g., Chase-Dunn and Anderson 2005; Chase-Dunn and Hall 1995, 1998). Both varieties face the charge of overstretching concepts from Wallerstein's historically specific study of modern Europe (see, for example, Wallerstein's own 1995 skeptical review).

Still, I think world systems partisans are right about *how* to think about things. The world—within and sometimes among its several continents—was densely interconnected long before the rise of the first states and even more so thereafter (e.g., Chase-Dunn and Hall 1995, 1998; Hornburg and Crumley 2007; Peregrine 1992; Peregrine and Feinman 1996; Sanderson 1995; Schortman and Urban 1992; among many others). Truly alarming for most of us (including your author), world systems archaeologists often jump right into *real* theory—the kind of thing historians sometimes do (e.g., Chase-Dunn and Anderson 2005; Friedman and Chase-Dunn 2005). That's scary. Most of us are still trying to figure out *how* to think about archaeological stuff, and we are still streets away from *what* to think about it—that is, real theory.

K. R. Dark's (1998) *Waves of Time* should be cited here too, and Bertrand Roehner and Tony Syme's *Pattern and Repertoire in History* (2002). Dark is an archaeologist. My political science colleagues wonder why archaeologists do not pay more attention to his global-scale, very long-term archaeological study of political cycles in prehistory and early states. I wonder too. Like Roland Fletcher's astonishing *The Limits of Settlement Size* (1995), is Dark's book far behind or too far ahead of its time? Roehner and Syme (2002) propose a VLC (Very Large Chronicle) project. I love the name, since I've worked near and occasionally in the VLA, west of Magdalena, New Mexico. VLC is a proposal for grand-scale, quantified, sociological history, which does not (yet) encompass prehistory.

It was only when I had finished the first draft of this book that I became aware of Kristian Kristiansen and Thomas Larsson's *The Rise of Bronze Age Society: Travel, Transmissions and Transformation* (2005). This bold book tackles matters of scale in a way I find entirely admirable:

> The processual and postprocessual archaeologies of the last generation have one thing in common: an autonomous perspective. The local or regional unit is their favourite frame of theoretical and interpretive reference.... If processual and postprocessual archaeology may be said to have provided archaeology with the theoretical and methodological tools for understanding prehistoric social organisation and cosmology at local and regional levels, they have failed in extending this beyond local and regional borders. (Kristiansen and Larsson 2005:5–6)

How well Kristiansen and Larsson succeed in writing a large-scale history of Bronze Age Europe I leave to specialists in that area to judge. But I second their call for continental, comparative, interconnected, "intercontextual" (their word) histories. And, as a last-minute postscript to this endnote, I note with pleasure that *The Rise of Bronze Age Society* won the "best book" award at the 2007 Society for American Archaeology meetings. Things are looking up!

23. The tension between isolated evolution and cross-cultural connections is a chestnut in anthropology called Galton's Problem. How much of local history was in fact local and internal, and how much was the result of "diffusion" or "influences" from other areas? I answer Galton in the affirmative (he favored diffusion) and err on the side of connections.

My assumption of historical interconnection does not discount *process* and the stuff of science. Historical interconnections, I think, place processes in more realistic contexts than heretofore allowed. What constitutes "more realistic contexts" is a central question of the chapters that follow, and the answers are generally couched in terms of geographic scale. I will also argue that perhaps we have been studying the wrong processes. In chapters 6, 7, and 8, I will suggest that some processes may be more important than others.

24. J. Thomas 2000:4.

25. Tilley 1993:6. James Schoenwetter, reviewing *America before the European Invasions* by Alice Kehoe (2002; a book I view with sympathy and approval), notes that Kehoe does two things differently than most conventional summaries of New World archaeology. First, Kehoe views complexity as historical, not evolutionary. Thus, "the decline of Hopewell is no more or less an unusual historical phenomenon than the development of Mesoamerican civilization." Second, "Kehoe unapologetically tells the story she considers most likely. There is often little discourse on the range of evidence…and even less concern with counterargument of alternative historical scenarios" (Schoenwetter 2005:791). He concludes, "I wonder if syntheses that come across as personal perceptions rather than as attempts to express professional consensus are not the sort of anthropological archaeology that is to be expected as more archaeologists adopt a "processual-plus" view of how archaeology should be understood" (Schoenwetter 2005:791). To Schoenwetter, this is a matter for regret. For me, it's the first faint glimmer of method.

How do we distinguish Kehoe's work, or this book, from historical fiction? Fiction is not eschewed in post-structural anthropology. Indeed, ethnographic novels and ethnologies that are part fiction win awards. A familiar post-structural deflection: "We are constrained by the data." But so were Robert Graves, Mary Renault, and Patrick O'Brian. What's the difference? This is a methodological question that interests me deeply but that I cannot currently answer.

26. For example, papers in Crown and Judge (1991) comparing Hohokam and Chaco, including one by me, reached the predictable conclusion that the two were curiously parallel but historically unrelated. Stay tuned.

27. Wolf 1982:385. And one could cite Giddens's admonition to "redevelop a concern with large-scale, long-term processes of social transformation" (1987:41), *hommage á* Braudel.

There, it's done. I've dropped a few Names. I recall a grad student's paper at a recent SAA meeting that led off with a machine-gun burst of social theory savants. After rattling off the Names, she paused—perhaps in irony, but I fear not—and said, "There, I think I got them all in." For the record, the reader may wish to know whether I have read de Certeau, Bourdieu, and Giddens. I have. And E. O. Wilson and K. R. Dark and Stuart Kauffman—and Sewell and Hobsbawm and Gaddis and Lowenthal, among others. I read a lot of theory, some of it archaeology, some of it history, geography, anthropology, ecology, and art history. Reviews of early drafts of this book (and my other publications) suggest that I failed the field by ignoring social theory, or the French and Brits of the moment. Since this aspect of my scholarship seems to be on trial, I must state that I bought early Shanks and Tilley and Bradley (whose writing I admire) directly from British and Scottish publishers, paying substantial postage (but curiously no duties). I'm pretty sure I owned the first copy of *Phenomenology of Landscape* west of the Pecos and east of the San Francisco Bay. And, yes, *I read it* (carefully; Lekson 1996a). I note these matters because two reviewers of early versions of this book accused me of being "anti-intellectual" because I'm not beglamoured by the currently fashionable theorists, and Giddens specifically. The social theory gang may be smart people, but their work is not necessary to mine.

And, frankly, the obscurantism of post-structural rhetoric is no longer amusing. I've met French scholars who freely acknowledge that most of their colleagues can't understand Foucault and Bourdieu (*particularly* Bourdieu), yet many post-structural archaeologists consciously mimic their convoluted discourse. Why? To paraphrase the poet, I don't want that much obfuscation in my life. A memorable obituary of the postmodern novel noted that it seems there are only a limited number of ways to avoid telling a story. And there is a story to tell. The truth is out there; theory should help us find it and tell it, not obscure it.

Or find parts of it. I have odd notions about theory and its uses. I read many, subscribe to none. Most theories seem fairly useful for specific questions or for particular places and times. All theory is local! (A slogan I heard first from Murray Gell-Mann; it may have older origins.) Yet in the marketplace of ideas, competing theories are often treated as absolute or exclusionary. Agency *replaces* evolution: theoretical change is paradigmatic change, à la Kuhn. Rather than march lockstep with doctrines de jour over the wreckage of yesterday's ideas, might it be possible to find some good—or rather some utility—in multiplicities of thought? Many years ago, I wrote an essay on metatheory (a term that means something else today). My argument was Gell-Mann's: few if any theories are universal; all theory is local. Ecological theories are more helpful in thinking about early hominids than is economic theory; economic theories work better for modern economies than does optimal foraging; and the key problem for archaeology is finding theory or theories that might work in between. When in the course of human events ecological theories cease being useful and economic theories begin to explain more satisfactorily, this tipping point may tell us that ancient societies crossed an interesting divide. Metatheory meant (to me) that we could use the succession or local successes of competing theories to learn about history. The fact that evolutionary ecology works well for hunter-gatherers but less well for urban societies does not reflect badly on evolutionary ecologists; rather, it tells us that human beings marched in step with evolutionary ecology more in some settings than in others. That's something gained, and perhaps something very important. Theory itself becomes method: metatheory. Alas, no journal wanted that essay, so I did not pursue metatheory as a program. But I still like metatheory, and that's pretty much how I think: ecology for early societies, economics for later societies, and, the key problem for archaeology, finding theory or theories that work in between. A key point for me was the conservation of good thinking: metatheory offers a way to salvage old ideas driven out by new regimes. Maybe there is a way to use *both* art and science without mashing them into pasty consilience. But that's another book.

So I declare no theoretical allegiances. No bandwagons, no esoteric vocabularies (I hope! I hope!). I use what works best for my purpose, a stew of ideas culled from history, geography, anthropology, ecology, and art history. For this book, William McNeill, John Gaddis, Karl Sauer, Amos Rapoport, John Vincent, and George Kubler were more useful than were social theorists (Gaddis honored in the breach). Indeed, my pole star is Kubler, the great art historian of an earlier age, for his vision more than his methods. In his classic *The Shape of Time*, Kubler wrote, "Unless he is an annalist or a chronicler the historian communicates a pattern which was invisible to his subjects when they lived it, and unknown to his contemporaries before he detected it" (1962:13). I read Kubler long before I read anthropology, and his challenge has always seemed a worthy goal.

In archaeology, I have found Colin Renfrew and Bruce Trigger inspirational. And Norman Yoffee, for urbanity and style (again, honored in the breach). Among the younger Turks, I am much in sympathy with Tim Pauketat's "historical processualism" (2001), save his insistence on Agency over Larger Forces. The two can coexist. And with Richard Bradley, for his writing and of course his ideas.

Of course, I'm influenced by scores of other scholars, whose names I've forgotten but whose ideas I've internalized (that is, lifted, nicked, copped, ripped off). In the text, I discuss a few recent books that deflected or redirected my arguments. If I had written this book ten years ago, or ten years from now, I certainly hope that my theoretical leanings would have been, or would be, different. Theory may or may not be local, but certainly it is transitory. How will we regard social theory in thirty years? Probably the same way we view New Archaeology today.

My apologies for this note, but I'm tired of critics who seem to feel that if I don't think what they think, I don't think. Can we agree to disagree? If not, you go your way and I'll go mine. At least with this note, I (like the harried graduate student) have named the Names. If this note gets Giddens and Bourdieu into the index, perhaps their partisans will cut me some slack.

28. Jan Vansina, in *How Societies Are Born: Governance in West Central Africa before 1600*, asks and answers this question: "Why focus on governance? Because, as a well known Arab leader might put it: 'The history of governance is the mother of all history! Common governance creates and maintains societies, which, in turn, form the matrix in which much else flows" (Vansina 2004:2). Political narrative is an established genre in history, "one that needs no justification" (Pedersen 2002:36; see also Gardiner 1988). It seems that if we *can*, we *should* write archaeological political histories. It's just the right thing to do. Mayanists (for example) write political history, and it's riveting stuff (Rice 2004; Schele and Friedel 1990). I think we can do that for the Southwest too.

We used to call this complexity (Lekson 2005), but that word is damaged goods. No longer fashionable. The Big Question of the 1970s: Was Chaco or Chavez Pass or Paquimé or Cerros de Trincheras politically "complex"? And the answer from this brave new millennium: Who cares? I do. A few questions from the 1970s retain their interest and, alas, remain unanswered. I discard the old term *complexity* in favor of *hierarchy* or *hierarchical* governance, but not my old interests.

Complexity is out of favor in the Southwest. But that's shooting the messenger. Expunging *complexity* does not eliminate the thing it was trying to describe. There's still something at Chaco and Aztec that was more organized, more hierarchical, more political (in our terms) than Zuni. In Mesoamerica, those would be *elites* (Chase and Chase [eds.] 1992), a term with at least two meanings: a class of rich, powerful, and privileged and "those who run society's institutions" (Chase and Chase 1992:4). I'm thinking of the latter: leaders, becoming rulers, becoming kings (Haas 2001; Oakley 2006).

The terminology is always difficult (e.g., Diehl 2000; McIntosh 1999; Redmond 1998; Yoffee 2005). In these nuanced times, binary categories like hierarchical/egalitarian seem quaint or counterproductive. Yet there's something important in recognizing those poles, and we have to call them *something*:

> The term *nonhierarchical* is not an ideal one, because it is based on the lack of certain attributes rather than their presence. It signifies societies in which decision making is largely consensus based and permanent positions of status and leadership based on ascription are lacking. *Egalitarian* is another possible term. In reality, however, purely egalitarian societies do not exist. (Spielmann 1991:1)

My argument will be that not all southwestern societies were nonhierarchical, and I suppose, among those double negatives, this means that they *were* hierarchical. This sort of early hierarchy is what was meant by *chiefdom* back in the neo-evolutionary days. Interest in chiefdoms—a concept that has been stretched far beyond its early definitions—is still strong (Earle 1991, 1997; Feinman 2005), but the term itself has fallen far out of favor in the Southwest. In later chapters, for reasons to be explained in chapter 8, I use *king*, a term that will undoubtedly alarm many southwestern archaeologists. My kings might be someone else's chiefs, if that helps, but they might be something else too (chapter 8).

29. Because I have been severely scolded for ignoring Agency, I will take this opportunity to comment. (I capitalize *Agency* here so that I can use the word lowercased in its general meanings later in this book.) Agency was a huge deal in the 1990s in American archaeology, although enthusiasm seems to be waning. Basically, Agency means that human beings made decisions and took actions independently of (or in spite of) their political superiors and—more importantly—the large and ponderous processes that New Archaeology studied: cultural evolution, adaptations, climate change, and so forth. Anthony Giddens, the British guru of Agency, put it this way: "An individual is the perpetrator, in the sense that the individual could, at any given phase in a sequence of conduct, have acted differently" (Giddens 1987:9).

A few years ago, when Agency was in full cry, two of its most perceptive advocates lamented, "Agency has become the buzzword in contemporary archaeological theory...there is little consensus about what 'agency' actually means" (Dobres and Robb 2000:3). Archaeological Agency, as Dobres and Robb suggested, has become many things to many people—objects now have Agency! Agency in every form is handmaiden to Practice, another enthusiasm that seems to have peaked. (Practice was removed from my text to this note in the several years it took to publish this book.) Michelle Hegmon (2003) bundles Agency and Practice, correctly I think, in her recent review of theory in *North American Archaeology*. Hegmon concludes, with a touch of irony, "Agency is everywhere":

> The term *agency* was brought to the fore recently by Giddens, who defines it as individuals' capacity for doing things, regardless of their intent.... Practice and agency have to do with similarly conceptualized processes, but the terms emphasize different components of the processes. *Agency* is more "behind the scenes," in that it has to do with capability and is sometimes (I think wrongly) associated with motivation. In contrast, *practice* refers directly to what people do. (Hegmon 2003:219–20)

In another paper, Hegmon and Kulow caution that "if agency is omnipresent, then it becomes a catchall with little theoretical or explanatory power" (Hegmon and Kulow 2005:329). They go on to refine the concept and apply it, but their caution is quite correct.

In any event, in the nineties Agency was all the rage. Graduate students got their knuckles rapped if they failed to use the word two or three times in the first page of whatever they were writing. Agency was a good thing, I think, because it restored a sense of history to American archaeology (Dobres and Robb eds. 2000; Gardner 2004; Pauketat 2001, 2007; among others). But I do not love it. Agency pushes us toward smaller historical scales, which I want to avoid. Individuals aren't history's only motor; there *are* larger forces. In that sense, Agency is nothing new.

Agency could be understood as the tension—old as Gilgamesh, old as history itself—between "Great Men" and "Larger Forces," writ small. Or writ large, or writ jointly, or writ corporately, or writ whichever way you like your Agents cooked. Great Men can of course be Great Women, or Little Women, or an anonymous corporate group, or a town council, or the oppressed masses, singly and severally. Larger Forces are all those vast impersonal things—environment, economy, ideology, social trends, processes, structures—that smack of metanarrative, generalization, and simplification (that is, the kinds of things processual archaeology was after). The key, as historians always knew and Marshall Sahlins (2004) recently reminded anthropologists, is the interplay of individual Great Men or Women or Agents and those pesky Larger Forces.

Agency seems an unnecessarily roundabout way for archaeology to rediscover history. Beyond my difficulties with Agency as backdoor history, I have two more serious problems—one theoretical, the other operational. Theoretically, Agency seems to me far too *presentist*. It idealizes modern human behavior and cognition in eighteenth-, nineteenth-, and twentieth-century Europe and jams that font of all anomie into the past. Is it realistic to transpose modern Agency to other places and times? Or should that be a research question: Did these ancient people or that ancient society enjoy Agency as we understand it today? I'm not sure that Agency would make sense to a Pueblo elder today, much less a Pueblo elder of 1300. In pueblos, individuals are far subordinate to families, and families far subordinate to clans and villages. The notion of Great Men is abhorrent in pueblos (as it is, I'm sure, to Agency enthusiasts, who seem stridently populist). Are concepts mooted for Euro-American society valid or useful for thinking about Native American societies of a thousand years ago? At one point, decades ago, I was interested in cognitive archaeology, particularly the development of cognition over the past twenty-five thousand years (Lekson 1981); based on that schoolboy knowledge of the field, Agency strikes me as a question perhaps to be investigated, not a condition to be assumed.

That's my first problem with Agency: is it a universal condition? Enthusiasts have worked hard to get around the problem. But my second objection is operational, and it seems (to me) fatal. Agency focuses on individuals, but it is almost impossible at this point for archaeology to actually *see individual people*. "The individual in prehistory" was a short-lived fad of the 1980s. It faded fast because seeing individuals is astonishingly hard, like nanosecond sightings of subatomic particles that win the Nobel Prize. We couldn't track individuals from the kitchen to the privy, much less through lives and generations (although hope springs eternal: Hodder 2006). Indeed, we have problems with villages and migrations and "ethnic groups," especially when they shift position. Consider the bouncing ninth-century villages of chapter 4 or the vanishing Four Corners migrations of chapter 7. Where *did* they go? Or "cultural affiliation" under NAGPRA (chapter 8). We really can't answer those questions about big groups. What hope do we have for Agency of individuals?

Agent-based history becomes the sum of individual actions; recall Hodder: "The movement is built up from the micro-details of life" (Hodder 2006:144).For Agency enthusiasts, it seems wrong to speak of abstract categories like "the bull market" or "the Roman Empire." What to do with "the Spanish influenza"? Epidemics are, after all, only aggregates of individual infections. No historian or anthropologist would disallow climate change or Spanish influenza as Larger Forces to be reckoned with, but Agency insists that we frame the human (Great Man) side of the question *as individual action*s. That's very small scale—the smallest possible. Hohokam did nothing; Hohokam *individuals* did everything.

It's really hard to see the ragged proletariat as individuals, historically or archaeologically. It's easier to track public figures, such as leaders—the original Great Men. (Mayanists are good at this because Maya Great Men bragged, in stone.) Methodologically, we might be justified to focus on Great Men and Larger Forces simply because *we can see them*. But there is something unpleasant, undemocratic, unsouthwestern about privileging the privileged. In southwestern settings, we have been told since before archaeology became a profession that *there were no leaders*. Or no leaders we can see: "Southwestern societies present a particular challenge to agent-based [that is, Agency] approaches because the pivotal actors, the leaders and elites, are not readily visible"; "leaders are not distinguished by easily recognized indicators such as lavish wealth, coercion toward personal ends, elaborate and exclusive insignia, or individualized prominence in art and iconography" (Fish and Fish 2000c:155). Something more modest and unpretentious is likely, and therefore a bit harder to see archaeologically. Less conspicuous but hardly invisible.

I declined to pin my methodological hopes on theories that require us to *see individuals* and that discount (or euphemize) larger formations, like the French Revolution or the Teotihuacán hegemony. As Hodder notes above, we can see large-scale, cumulative results of individual actions (that is, we see archaeological things like Anasazi and Hohokam). So I will backslide occasionally into corporate Agency: "Anasazi did this," "Hohokam did that," and so forth. It's not fashionable, but it's useful: we lose a lot when we lose concepts like Renaissance or Great Depression or Mesoamerican Post-Classic. (For those who speak the tongue, yes, I am from time to time an undeconstructed reductionist—when it's useful to be so.)

30. For example, Okasha 2006.

31. For example, Cooley 2005.

32. Contrast, for example, Mississippian or Mayan archaeology. For many decades, Mississippianists focused on chiefs and chiefdoms, more or less to the exclusion of the rest of society, much as Mayan archaeology honed in on kings and elites to the exclusion of households. Since 1980, interests in archaeology have shifted to households, individuals, children. The decades since 1980 have become the era of the common man. Mississippian and Mayan archaeologies shifted with larger intellectual trends, redressing the imbalance. The overlooked little guy, the working stiff, and the underclass are now as prominent in Mississippian and Mayan archaeology as were chiefs a decade ago (e.g., Pauketat 2004, 2007; Robin 2003). This interest in the common man follows the movement in conventional history away from "kings and battles" and toward social history. That's fine. There was imbalance to be rebalanced in Mississippian and many other archaeologies and histories around the globe. But southwestern archaeology has the opposite problem—we've been working with the archaeology of common people for a century, more or less to the exclusion of kings and battles. We've been writing social not political history. Only lately did we admit *battles* (LeBlanc 1999). This book may be the first (and last?) to propose *kings*.

33. Clastres 1977. See also Miller, Rolands, and Tilley 1989; Patterson and Gailey 1987; Skalnik 1989.

34. Mills 2004.

35. In *The Rise of Bronze Age Society*, Kristiansen and Larsson highlight the movement and diffusion of institutions rather than artifacts: "Instead of traditional random studies of the spatial distribution of cultural traits, whose significance is then evaluated within a more general historical or evolutionary model, we propose to begin by studying the transmission and transformation of social institutions—economic, political, and religious—since all societies are organized around institutions.... By this the focus is shifted from tracing and discussing random similarities in material culture to studying the transmission and possible transformation of the structured material evidence of social institutions in time and space" (Kristiansen and Larsson 2005:11). Amen—although "random" seems harsh.

36. For example, Helms 1988.

37. Anderson 1999:fig. 15.5.

38. Anderson 1999:225–27.

39. Nelson 2000:318, 329. See also Nelson's contribution to McGuire et al. 1994.

40. Brotherston 1992:xi.

41. It's not that southwestern archaeology has ignored political formations. "Complexity" (that is, centralized hierarchy) was something of a southwestern obsession in the 1970s. See chapter 7's discussion of the Grasshopper–Chavez Pass debates and their effects (and for a quick summary of past and current approaches, see Feinman, Lightfoot, and Upham 2000; Lightfoot 1984; and Mills 2000). Southwestern studies of political developments, however, almost always focus on *particular times and places*. For example, what was the nature of Classic Hohokam leadership? What's missing is a narrative of political formations and developments as continuous, historical threads woven through the region's conventional culture history. That's what I'm trying to do in this book—combine others' arguments and conclusions (and my own, of course) about particular times and places into a continuous narrative.

42. Lekson 2006a. There also is a postmodern, post-structuralist reaction to parsimony. Parsimony smacks

too much of science, so complication! The post-structuralist take seems to be that everything is far more complicated than we can possibly imagine. Whatever your story, your narrative, *it's more complicated than that.* I overheard a post-structuralist colleague approve a graduate student's second or third thesis draft: "That complicates things! Good! Good!" Curiously, that postmodern reaction gets us to the same place: avoiding larger scales, bigger pictures, and sweeping generalizations. Metanarratives and Big History are anathema, perceived somehow as reactionary. Every story is necessarily local because human actions and motivations are terribly, terribly complicated and can be understood (if they can be understood at all) only locally, individually. History, in anthropology, thus becomes biography—a long-standing theme in historiography of course.

43. Marilyn Vos Savant, "Ask Marilyn," *Parade*, January 9, 2005, 16.

44. Spanish colonial policies, in contrast, were more interested in co-opting Natives into a new social order. Spanish colonization rolled over Native civilizations to be sure, but Spanish goals were different. Rather than eliminate Natives, use them as labor. Souls to save and hands to work. Anglo policies were importantly different. We couldn't make Indians work; they died of disease or withdrew into the wilderness. North of the Rio Grande, we ordered out. We replaced Natives with Africans in the East and with Chinese in the West. Natives themselves became superfluous to our requirements and had to go. We tried hard to make them vanish and then wept at their passing. If they were noble but conveniently vanishing savages in the present, it was ethically important that they were savages in the past too. It would be unpleasant to think that we had destroyed civilizations.

45. After presenting versions of this argument at meetings, I have been accosted by colleagues who think I am saying, "Disagree with Lekson and you're racist." That's absurd. Anthropologists and archaeologists of my acquaintance are anything *but* racist. Racists don't become anthropologists. But we should interrogate our assumptions—the things passed down from our teacher's teacher's teachers—early and often. Parsimony is one of those assumptions, or methodological dictums, that does not shine in the bright light of historical analysis. See chapter 8.

46. Byrkit 1992; Meinig 1971.

47. For example, Di Peso 1974.

48. For me, the most important southwestern environmental summary is Brown and Lowe's remarkable map (1980) and its accompanying book (Brown 1982). It lacks the time dimension of dendroclimatology and presents a snapshot in time—but what a snapshot! (I discuss the finer-grained dendroclimatological reconstructions that dominate much southwestern archaeology in chapter 6.) My tattered copy of Brown and Lowe—a detailed map, at 1:1,000,000, of "native" biotic communities—has moved from office wall to office wall for almost three decades. Over the longer term, the southwestern environment changed, but I do not dabble much here in the longer term (Paleo-Indian and Archaic periods). Thus Brown and Lowe remains my major resource for southwestern lands. The same treatment was expanded to all of North America, including Mexico (Brown, Reichenbacher, and Franson 1998), producing another amazing map, more useful for the continental scales I see emerging in American archaeology.

49. There are several possibilities for a north–south axis, none exact. The continental divide, if it had any decency, would run up the spine of the Chuska Mountains, but it does not. It meanders inconveniently to the east, leaving Chaco on the western slope. The New Mexico–Arizona state line is unacceptable to me because it imposes a modern political boundary on the Native past (even though it roughly corresponds to a line that did apparently mean something). I prefer US Highway 666—an order of magnitude more fabulous than Route 66—which meanders from Douglas, Arizona, to Blanding, Utah. "Triple 6" is remarkably close to the north–south axis I am trying to define (fig. 1.2). It tickles me to think that Triple 6 marks some ancient and mysterious Truth. Apparently, the numerical "mark of the devil" did not please the highway departments of Arizona, New Mexico, and Utah, which have spinelessly changed it to other, less apocalyptic designations, varying state by state.

Dates are equally difficult (see note 50, chapter 8). Scientists use BP (before present, where the present is 1950). Many others prefer BCE (before current era) and CE (current era). Here I present dates in terms of our conventional calendar, BC and AD. When a date is BC, I so specify. Since most of this book's action is firmly AD, to reduce clutter, I specify AD only when needed for clarity.

50. D. Brown 1982; Brown and Lowe 1980.

51. Brown, Reichenbacher, and Franson 1998:49.

52. Bison roamed the eastern border of the Southwest and were found in a few portions of the southern Southwest (perhaps the plains of San Agustin and the Casas Grandes Valley). Bison played a key role in the later chapters of southwestern history, and had the Old World not intervened, bison might have provided domestic animals missing from New World societies. I firmly believe that one attraction of the Rio Grande to migrating Anasazi was the lure of bison—the salmon of the Plains—to people reduced in their old homelands to rabbit and turkey.

53. LeBlanc 2002.

54. The Yuman languages of the lower Colorado are notably absent from this section and this book. The archaeology of that remarkably fertile region is so underdeveloped that it is impossible to integrate it with the richly textured archaeologies of Hohokam, Anasazi, and Mogollon. If the Southwest had a possible Nile, it should have been the lower Colorado River, but it didn't happen.

55. By "successful," I mean that the Apache maintained that way of life longer than almost any other southwestern people. Geronimo's wars, which ended in 1887, were in large part a struggle to live (and continue living) as hunter-gatherers. In the end, of course, Geronimo's Apaches and many others were prisoners of war, kept in concentration camps. Written passes from a camp at Ojo Caliente, New Mexico, survive in the National Archives. In formal military copperplate script, they allowed the bearer, an Apache, to gather herbs or to hunt game outside the reservation for a specified time—permits to hunt and gather.

56. Hendrickson and Minckley 1984.

57. Ferguson and Hart 1985:map 21.

58. The term *Anasazi* has been controversial in recent decades. The Pueblos (in particular the Hopi) are not happy with this Navajo-derived archaeological jargon. But *Anasazi* is archaeological jargon, *not* a Navajo word (Walters and Rogers 2001). This is an archaeological book. People who read it will be archaeologists or archaeology-savvy civilians. For those readers, *Anasazi* means something that *ancestral Pueblo* and *Hisatsinom* (the Hopi term) do not. Importantly, *Anasazi* avoids the specificity of those Pueblo-centric terms (Riggs 2007). *Ancestral Pueblo* assumes what is to be proved. It's not that I doubt that Hopi is closely related to Mesa Verde, but I'm not at all sure that everything and everyone at Mesa Verde were related to Hopi—or even represented in Hopi people's memories and histories. My constituents, if I have any, are the ancient people of Mesa Verde themselves, not the modern people of Hopi. The Hopi, happily, have no need of my services. The modern Pueblos are represented by their traditional and elected leaders, by their writers and poets and artists, and by their lawyers. The ancient Anasazi have archaeologists, for good or ill.

There's another consideration. About one-third of this book is an analytical history of southwestern archaeology—how it developed, what it did, how it operated. It's impossible to tell that story without using *Anasazi*, with its intended implication of separate but equal (or, originally, first among equals) with Hohokam and Mogollon. If you care to, imagine chapter 3 without *Anasazi*. Can't be done.

My use of *Anasazi* may get my book banned at Mesa Verde National Park. Following Hopi directives, the park store rid its shelves of books with *Anasazi* in the title. But as it turns out, Mesa Verde was fairly inconsequential in the history of the ancient Southwest.

59. Gregory and Wilcox 2007.

60. For example, Lewis and Wigen 1997; O'Gorman [1961]1972.

61. See, for example, Jerry Bentley's 1993 *Old World Encounters*, John Hobson's 2003 *The Eastern Origins of Western Civilization*, or Christopher Ehret's 2001 *An African Classical Age*.

62. The debate between Garcians and Acostans continued in the Mound Builder controversy, whose political and philosophical importance has been ably summarized by Roger Kennedy in *Hidden Cities* (1994). To demonstrate that the mounds were Native, the heirs of the Acostans had to eliminate the alternatives: Egyptians, Phoenicians, Lost Tribes, Lamanites, Atlanteans, and a whole rogue's gallery of exotic peoples (Wauchope 1962). The logic of the earliest American archaeology was far more negative than positive: the mounds were *not* Egyptian, *not* Phoenician, *not* this and *not* that. Archaeological attitudes toward distance— at least, transatlantic distance—became firmly negative in the process, an orthodoxy that continues into the present. Interaction over distance is, prima facie, suspect. The Acostans won.

63. *Native* attitudes toward distance can be inferred by the very rapidity with which the New World was settled, ten thousand years or more before Europeans arrived. By land and by sea, hunters with simple resources reached America and raced across its continents in a gigantic land rush. Their progeny settled and diversified. But amid the astonishing range of languages and societies, that initial experience of distance stuck: you *can* get there from here. Almost every Native group in North America has traditions of *starting somewhere else*, often a long way away. Their evident attitude toward distance was that distance was no barrier. That, I think, was a New World reality.

64. Flint and Flint 2005; Flint and Flint (eds.) 1997.

65. I would like to think that my interpretation of the Turk was my own, but I probably nicked it from Alice Kehoe. Readers interested in the Turk should consult Kehoe's "What the Turk Described" (2002:165–66). Indeed, Alice Kehoe has said or written most of the things I say in this book. I think most of my arguments are truly convergent. That is, we reached many of the same conclusions more or less independently. But I am honored and humbled to acknowledge that Alice was there long before me.

66. Sauer 1932:9.

67. Kehoe 2002:165.

68. Flint and Flint 2003.

69. Parmentier 1979.

70. Bandelier 1882.

71. Meltzer 1994.

72. MacNeish and Libby 2003.

73. Taylor et al. 2003:table 9.2.

74. Haynes and Agogino 1986; Hibben 1941; Stevens and Agogino 1975; but see MacNeish and Libby 2003:483.

75. Dillehay 1989, 2000.

76. Adovasio et al. 1998.

77. Wagner and McAvoy 2004.

78. Deloria 1995.

79. Dixon 1999, among many others.

80. Bradley and Stanford 2004.

81. Fitzhugh and Ward 2000.

82. Jones and Klar 2005.

83. Transpacific contacts, I'm told, are openly discussed in Andean archaeology. There was a time when they were taken with sufficient seriousness in Mesoamerica to merit chapters (pro and con) in the *Handbook of Middle American Indians* (Heine-Geldern 1966; Phillips 1966) and even books (e.g., Smith 1953). Good material (that is, intriguing scholarship) on transoceanic prehistory is buried under vast heaps of nonsense (eliciting a subgenre of debunking books, for example, Wauchope 1962, Williams 1991). The topic may be reemerging as quasi-legitimate but remains professionally quite dangerous (see Kehoe 1998, published, significantly, by Routledge; and Bradley and Stanford 2004).

Barry Cunliffe, author of the superb *Facing the Ocean* (2001), makes a good case that Pytheas the Greek visited Iceland about 320 BC (Cunliffe 2002). Pytheas wrote a book about his voyage that survived (in fragments and citations) for us to read. Pytheas, like the Spanish conquistadors and most European "explorers," had guides. He went to Iceland (if Cunliffe is correct) as supercargo of obliging barbarians. How many illiterate traders or fisherman preceded (and followed!) him to Iceland and beyond, leaving not a note, a mark for us to know? Surely a few—and maybe more.

And after the Vikings? Well, of course, Columbus was one of a large number of explorers who launched out of Portugal, Spain, and Venice (among other places) in the thirteenth, fourteenth, and fifteenth centuries. For example, the brothers Vivaldi, "who from Genoa in 1291 departed 'for the regions of India by way of the ocean,' thus apparently anticipating the task Columbus was to set himself on almost exactly 200 years later.... The Vivaldi were never heard of again, but it is likely that there were other journeys in the same direction" (Fernández-Armesto 1987:152).

And almost a century before Columbus, from 1405 to 1433, China sent huge fleets of huge ships exploring in every direction: India, the Philippines, Africa (Levathes 1994). These remarkable explorations are tarnished by recent enthusiasts who have suggested that in 1421 the Chinese not only discovered America but also visited ports around the world (Menzies 2003).

The problem here is that the question of transoceanic contacts—which seems to me legitimate—has been so marginalized by the profession that we see only marginal scholarship. We have pushed it to and perhaps beyond the fringe. How many undocumented, unofficial, unremembered expeditions paralleled or preceded the official, government-sponsored voyages? Columbus returned. Unlike the unfortunate Vivaldis, he was indeed heard from again. And the world changed. But anthropologically, statistically, or rationally, it seems likely that others preceded him with less success. We know of many failures after Columbus; many did not follow his route. People were trying to discover new things, not Columbus's "Indies" (e.g., Fernández-Armesto 1987, 2006). Columbus may have been a Great Man, but the Age of Exploration was one of those pesky historical Larger Forces.

84. In his dotage, Harold Gladwin suggested that Alexander's lost fleet rowed up the Gila, upsetting things (Gladwin 1979). *The Zuni Enigma* (Davis 2000) links the New Mexico Pueblo to Japan; I know several Zunis who are intrigued by the enigma—but no archaeologists. James Q. Jacobs (2007), who apparently discovered the "Chaco Meridian" before me, extends it north to Mount Wilson, the Big Horn Medicine Circle, and beyond. He notes that "the arc distance from Pueblo Bonito to Mount Wilson precisely equals 1/200th of the circumference of the earth" (2007). I have limits: no Macendnoi in Phoenix, no Nippon in Halona:wa, and no Santa on my meridian.

85. Summarized by Huckell 1996, 2005.

86. Cynthia Irwin-Williams's research on the Oshara tradition defined "the Archaic continuum that underlay the evolution of Pueblo sedentary society" (Irwin-Williams 1979:35; see also Irwin-Willliams 1973). Irwin-Willliams and others researching the Archaic assumed that cultural evolution occurred on relatively small scales —the region at most or the Arroyo Cuervo *en petit*; the introduction of maize was a monumental non-event.

87. Vierra 2005.

88. Huckel 2005:150.

Chapter 2

1. For example, Braniff 1993, 2002 and her chapters in Braniff 2001.

2. Through the pioneering scientific explorations of Bandelier, Hewett, Cummings, and others (discussed in text) and through the journalism of Lummis, Baxter, and other writers, the Southwest became *our* Southwest—"America's Orient" (in the words of Louise Lamphere, I believe). Britain had India; we had New Mexico. The tone was set for the next century's research: the Southwest was a region of North America, not Mesoamerica. It may have had distant connections to the south, but those connections were tenuous, singularly secondary to the Southwest's particular genius loci. The trappings of territorial and early statehood southwestern culture nodded to Spain and to Old Mexico, but the distillation was pure, local moonshine: the Santa Fe mystique. Much of "old" Santa Fe dates to the 1930s and the very conscious, considered efforts of its white upper classes. Fake, but it works. We want to believe in Santa Fe, "The City Different." And we want to believe in an ancient unchanging Southwest, peaceful and egalitarian. The Southwest was colonized first in fact, then in fictions.

3. Gallatin 1848.

4. Gallatin 1848:liv.

5. Gallatin 1848:lxxxiii.

6. Gallatin 1848:lxxxiv.

7. Gallatin 1848:xcvi–xcvii.

8. Smith 1988:13.

9. Fowler 2000:180–83.

10. Lange and Riley 1996.

11. Bandelier 1890–92; Lange and Riley (eds.) 1966, 1970; Lange, Riley, and Lange 1975, 1984.

12. Gustaf Nordenskiold, who conducted the first systematic archaeology at Mesa Verde, linked these ruins unequivocally to the modern Pueblos (Nordenskiold [1893]1979). But he published in Swedish (an English translation of his report appeared a few years later), and he was reviled by southwestern partisans as a European pirate, working in collusion with Wetherill's clan of pot hunters. The sheriffs arrested him (briefly); injunctions were sought. Nordenskiold had to wait many decades for recognition of his excellent archaeology (among other accounts, see Arrhenius 1984; Fowler 2000; Smith 1988).

13. Resek 1960.

14. Parmentier 1979.

15. Fiske and Lummis 1975; Houlihan and Houlihan 1986; Sarber 1977; Thompson 2001.

16. Lummis 1925:294–95.

17. Chauvenet 1983; Elliot 1987.

18. Bostwick 2006.

19. Reid and Whittlesey 2005b:46.

20. Judd 1950:11.

21. Fowler 2000.

22. Fowler 2000; Wilcox and Fowler 2002.

23. Green 1990; Hinsley and Wilcox 1996.

24. Quoted by Hinsley 1996a:3.

25. Snead 2005:35.

26. Neither Cummings nor Hewett produced satisfactory reports on their big projects. Of all early pioneer Southwesternists, Bandelier had the best record. His monumental *Final Report* (Bandelier 1890–92) stands even today as a primary reference. Alas, he never visited the Four Corners, but alone of the first pioneer archaeologists, Bandelier ventured into the Mogollon Mountains. In the early 1880s, those hills were alive, notoriously, with Apaches, who did not suffer fools or welcome strangers. The early battles between Apaches and outsiders, in the 1860s and 1870s, were local affairs, reported only in brief army accounts. Journalists brought the final Geronimo campaigns to the American public in unprecedented detail. Newspapers of the Gilded Age showed readers in Boston, Philadelphia, Washington, and Charleston a Southwest that was still

savage, riven by brutal conflicts. Thus the tracks of the early expeditions formed an intricate swirl of enormous loops around, but not through, the Mogollon uplands. After Bandelier, Walter Hough took the Museum– Gates Expedition into the Mogollon uplands in 1905—but by that time Geronimo was signing autographs at county fairs. Not surprisingly, Mogollon archaeology lagged behind that of the Plateau (Anasazi) and even to some extent Hohokam.

27. Fowler 2005:20.

28. For example, Lummis 1925.

29. For example, Dilworth 1996; Hinsley 1996b; McFeely 2001. Boston-bred Sylvester Baxter (1850–1927) wrote for *Harper's* and the *Boston Herald*; he was the quintessential easterner out west. He attached himself to the colorful Cushing at Fort Wingate in 1881, becoming the unofficial scribe of the Hemenway Expedition (Hinsley and Wilcox 1996). Baxter typified what James Byrkit (1992:355) calls "Mugwump Southwest dreamspinners": New England intellectuals who created or rather idealized a particular Southwest in the late nineteenth century. He began (in 1881) convinced that southwestern ruins were Aztec (for example, "Mysteries of Ancient Aztecs Unveiled by an Explorer from the Smithsonian Institution," Sylvester Baxter's 1881 newspaper account, reprinted in Hinsley and Wilcox 1996:45–54). He was soon captivated by Zuni and extolled the "primitive" virtues of the Pueblos. Baxter's Southwest was exotic and highly romantic (Hinsley 1996a).

30. Lummis 1925:5.

31. Lummis 1925:201.

32. Byrkit 1992:361.

33. Di Peso 1974; Kelley and Kelley 1974. See Riley 2005 for a *sostenuto* treatment.

34. I use *maize* most often and *corn* where it scans better. Key recent references include *Corn and Culture in the Prehistoric New World*, edited by Sissel Johannessen and Christine A. Hastorf (1994), and *Histories of Maize*, edited by John E. Staller, Robert H. Tykot, and Bruce F. Benz (2006).

35. Ford 1994, quoting Pueblo farmers.

36. For example, Boher 1994.

37. Mann 2005:194.

38. Adams 1994; Blake 2006; Doolittle and Mabry 2006; Hard et al. 2006; Huckell 2006; Matson and Dohm 1994; Roney and Hard 2002a, 2002b; Smiley 2002.

39. Cited in Roney and Hard 2002a:131.

40. Vierra and Ford 2006.

41. Matson 2005:286.

42. Haury 1962.

43. Altschul 1995.

44. Whittlesey and Ciolek-Torrello 1996:50; see also Doolittle and Mabry 2006.

45. Kohler 1993:273–74; Matson 2002, 2005.

46. Matson 2005:279, 281.

47. Matson 2005; B. Smith 2005; see also LeBlanc 2002. R. G. Matson was perhaps the first and certainly the strongest proponent of the model of the migration of maize onto the plateaus, which he finds "more than plausible, even compelling" (Matson 2005:281). Me too.

48. Hill 2001, 2002, 2006; see also Shaul and Hill 1998; contra Fowler 1983, among others.

49. Hill 2001:925; see also Carpenter, Sanchez, and Villalpando 2002; Matson 2002; Vierra 2005; Wilcox 1986b.

50. Washburn 1995:fig. 16. In Dorothy Washburn's *Living in Balance* (1995), a map of Hopi migrations "compiled by Eric Polingyouma, Bluebird Clan, Shungopavi" shows "*Yayniini*—the Beginning" slightly south of Mexico City. Polingyouma leads an ongoing project researching the geography of Hopi origins. In a recent (2006) public presentation, he and his group suggested that *Yayniini* might actually be farther south, perhaps in the Maya region. Other Hopi elders firmly believe that the migrations began at Teotihuacán. I have been told privately (but not confidentially) that Hopi histories and traditions specifically recall that the people who became Hopi began as "peasants" or lower-class workers in the great Mesoamerican cities, "building pyramids but not getting to use them." Note that many Hopis hold to the more familiar origin story in which the place of emergence was much closer, near the confluence of the Little Colorado and Colorado rivers at the upper end of the Grand Canyon (Voth 1905).

51. Hill 2001; Matson 2002, 2005.

52. David Wilcox's "Tepiman Corridor" (1986b). The underlying *linguistic* connections of Hohokam and southern Uto-Aztecan groups may help explain Hohokam's close *historic* connections to West Mexico, compared with Chaco (for example). Hohokam had broadband international connections, while Chaco had dial-up or, more likely, surface mail.

53. Mabry 2002:178.

54. Gregory 2001; B. Huckell 1996; L. Huckell 2006; Mabry (ed.) 1998; Wallace forthcoming.

55. Gregory 2001; Mabry (ed.) 1998.

56. Damp 2002.

57. For example, Huckell 2005; Roney and Hard 2002b.

58. For example, Gregory and Diehl 2002; Mabry 2005b; Roth 1996b; Whittlesey and Ciolek-Torrello 1996.

59. Wallace and Lindeman 2003:374–75.

60. Hard and Roney 2004, 2005; Hard et al. 2006; Roney and Hard 2002b.

61. Matson 1991.

62. Gregory and Diehl 2002.

63. For example, Chapman, Gossett, and Gossett 1985; Huckell 1995.

64. See Mabry 2005a:fig. 3.1.

65. Gibson 2001; Gibson and Carr 2004.

66. Of course, not every Mesoamericanist would call San Lorenzo a city or Olmec a state, but many do (reviewed in Pool 2007). The archaeology can support arguments for an Olmec "mother culture" and (of course) for annoyed ripostes from investigators invested in other areas who prefer their research areas and the Olmec heartland to be separate but equal "sisters." Although Poverty Point gets no mention in a recent textbook on Olmec (Pool 2007), I suspect that Gulf Coast archaeology will, in coming decades, encompass both (e.g., White 2005).

67. Cheetham 2006.

68. Gumerman and Dean 1989; Matson 1991, 2002, 2005.

69. The beginning dates for Basketmaker II are a matter of lively debate and hot dispute. R. G. Matson dates the earliest Basketmaker II to 400 BC, with the period starting even later over much of the Plateau (for example, 300 BC on the Rainbow Plateau; Geib and Spurr 2002). The counterargument: Kim Smiley (1994, 2002) dates maize and Basketmaker II in southeastern Utah to 2200 BC! The upper end of Basketmaker II, less controversially, hovers between AD 400 and 500 (e.g., Janetski 1993:227; Lipe 1999; Matson 2002, 2005; Reed 2000:6; Smiley 2002:51). I accept R. G. Matson's dates and round them off for Basketmaker II at 500 BC to AD 500.

70. Matson 1991, 2002, 2005.

71. Smiley 2002.

72. Matson 2002, 2005.

73. Coltrain, Janetski, and Carlyle 2006; Hard et al. 2006; Smiley 2002. It is quite possible that in the first enthusiastic rush into southern Arizona, Early Agricultural Period desert farmers spilled up onto the Plateau. Indeed, Kim Smiley may be right: the first farmers may have arrived at 2000 BC. There were small pit house villages in Chinle Wash that early (Gilpin 1994), and where there's one such site, there are probably more. As noted above, there were hints and fragments of Early Agricultural technologies at 1000 BC or even earlier in the east—canals at Zuni (Damp 2002)—but nothing came of them. A false start? Those early incursions apparently didn't succeed; there are no (known) Los Pozos–sized Early Agricultural sites on the Plateau. Over most of the area, maize or no maize, early Basketmaker II people remained low in density and highly, highly mobile (Lipe 1999). Indeed, caves or alcoves were the principal short-term residences (Smiley 2002). It was only in the latter part of Basketmaker II—after (in many places long after) 50 or 150 BC—that pit house settlements appeared and maize shifted from a dietary supplement to the economic focus (e.g., Gieb and Spurr 2002; Lipe and Pitblado 1999; Smiley 2002). That came first in the west. In the east (at Chaco, for example), the transition occurred later still, perhaps as late as AD 400 (Wills and Windes 1989).

Is this version of history a function of sampling? Are Zuni canals and Chinle pit houses the tip of the iceberg (as I argued for the Early Agricultural Period in the Tucson Basin and the Land Between)? I think not. Compared with the Land Between, the Four Corners and much of the Colorado Plateau are exceptionally well known archaeologically. The rarity of early canals and pit house villages on the Plateau is a good indication of what happened in history: the intense developments of the deserts failed to flourish when transposed upward in altitude and latitude.

74. Matson (1991) argues that on much of the Plateau, maize would be all or nothing; there was nothing else to eat. I partly disagree. I think maize could have been a hedge fund for small populations, although once populations gained size and embraced sedentism, maize was the only way to support them.

75. Smiley 2002:62.

76. Coltrain, Janetski, and Carlyle 2006; Lipe and Pitblado 1999.

77. Reed 2000:6.

78. For example, Smiley (2002) for southeastern Utah at 1000 BC; Geib and Spurr (2002) for the Rainbow Plateau at 300 BC.

79. LeBlanc 2002; LeBlanc et al. 2007; Matson 1991, 2002, 2005.

80. Coltrain, Janetski, and Carlyle 2006.

81. LeBlanc 2002.

82. R. G. Matson: "The evidence…supports three propositions: an east/west ethnic division among the BM II; the similarity of Eastern BM II with earlier Colorado Plateau Archaic; and of the Western BM II with the San Pedro Cochise," the Archaic of the southern deserts (Matson 2002:347; see also LeBlanc 2002). Western Basketmaker agricultural villages were Uto-Aztecan-speaking immigrants, while the eastern Basketmaker societies were locals adjusting to the intrusion.

Languages are important here: if we bring corn into the southern deserts with Uto-Aztecan-speaking peoples, it seems likely that peoples speaking related languages also colonized the western Plateau, and Hopi is a Uto-Aztecan language. The differences between eastern and western Basketmaker II may very well reflect differences, even to the level of language, with Uto-Aztecan/Hopi on the west and (perhaps) the other Pueblo languages (Keres? Zuni? even Tanoan?) being pushed to the eastern Plateau. Yet the material culture of eastern and western Basketmaker II— while distinct—is sufficiently similar that the whole package can be called Basketmaker II. Several scenarios come to mind. Southeastern farming groups, pushed onto the Great Plains, soon looked much like other Plains groups materially but maintained their languages. Houses and tools adapted to the Plains would have replaced (or displaced) material culture suited to the Southeast. Alternatively, if Uto-Aztecan speakers brought corn to the western Plateau, they might have required local groups wishing to join in the farming to change languages (that happened historically at Hopi). The local groups would have brought local tools and architecture time-tested and suited to the Plateau, which the Uto-Aztecan "founders" might well have adopted. However it transpired, I think Uto-Aztecan-speaking people (eventually becoming Hopi) brought farming to the western Plateau and then adopted or adapted much of the "indigenous" material culture. A division formed between a western Uto-Aztecan Plateau, with strong ties to the southern deserts (and Hohokam), and "Native" eastern Plateau Basketmaker II groups (who got corn from the Uto-Aztecan west). That split—history, language, perhaps even traditions of agricultural priority— may have structured subsequent history, perhaps for the next eight or ten centuries. (We will revisit this fundamental historical division in chapter 8.)

83. For example, Wallace 2003:fig. 1.11.

84. Blinman and Wilson 1993; Reed, Wilson, and Hays-Gilpin 2000.

85. Reed, Wilson, and Hays-Gilpin 2000; Wilson et al. 1996; see Whittlesey (1998) for a good recent review.

86. Ciolek-Torrello 1998.

87. Anderson and Mainfort 2002; Brose and Greber 1979; Carr and Case 2005; Charles and Buikstra 2006; DeBoer 2006; Mainfort and Sullivan 1998; Pacheco 1996.

88. Yerkes 2006. Hopewell offers a familiar example of an ancient American society that might be best understood through cosmology, ideology, and ritual (Byers 2004; Carr and Case 2005; Charles and Buikstra 2006; DeBoer 1997, 2006; Romain 2000). However, I question our current enthusiasm for ritual and ceremony in southwestern archaeology insofar as that emphasis deflects us from the equally important subjects of political and economic power (cf. Pacheco and Dancy 2006—Hopewell polities!). Compared with Hopewell, southwestern architecture is grindingly pragmatic and grimly materialist. Compared with Newark or Chillicothe, "ceremonial" objects and architecture of the early Southwest are singularly unimpressive. In the Pueblo area, archaeological evidence for ritual blooms late, after AD 1250–1300 (chapter 7). The British approaches to landscape and monuments (Bradley, Tilley, Thomas, and others) seem far more useful for the Ohio Valley than for the Phoenix Basin or Chaco Canyon (cf. Chapman 2006). This is not to say that ritual, ceremony, and ideologically charged landscapes are irrelevant. Of course they are relevant (Stein and Lekson 1992). I argue only that these approaches may not build the best foundation for understanding southwestern prehistory (Lekson 1996a). For all our fascination with ritual in the ancient Southwest, the archaeological evidence is slim compared with Hopewell earthworks or Neolithic henges.

Chapter 3

1. Bruce Trigger captured the spirit of those times in *A History of Archaeological Thought*: "In accordance with the belief that change had been minimal in prehistoric times, the systematic study of cultural variation in the archaeological record was oriented towards defining geographical rather than chronological patterns" (Trigger 2006:180). In 1914 William Holmes published a map that divided ancient North America into a dozen archaeological areas. Other anthropologists (Otis Mason, Clark Wissler) sliced and diced the Native

continent into more and finer subdivisions. Alfred Kroeber's *Cultural and Natural Areas of Native North America* (1939) almost tripled Holmes's total, a mapping more or less codified in Gordon Willey's classic 1966 text *An Introduction to American Archaeology*. Willey divided North and Middle America into about fifty archaeological areas. On average, that amounted to just shy of 500,000 square kilometers per "culture area"—about three-quarters the size of Texas, half of British Columbia, or twice Chihuahua. Those areas, of course, each contained up to twenty districts, which are usually treated as distinct subareas, independent in method and perhaps in fact. As far as I can tell, we've tweaked but not challenged Willey's maps.

2. *We know where almost all the big sites are.* A Clintonesque parse: *We* means southwestern archaeologists and institutions, including the personal knowledge of all my colleagues, plus the archives and databases of museums and agencies. *Know* includes casual or informal knowledge. Many archaeologists know big sites that have never been fully mapped, recorded, and filed with institutions that gather such data. Personal knowledge isn't optimal, but it can be extraordinarily useful (e.g., Adams and Duff [eds.] 2004; Adler 1996; Lekson [ed.] 2006). *Big* equals fifty or more rooms or pit houses, but of course some periods and places never had sites that large. *Sites* means towns and villages, which (as noted) excludes the vast majority of archaeological sites. And *almost all?* Eighty percent—an informed guess. I base that figure on my association with several big-site-gathering projects—Pueblo I, Pueblo II (Great Houses), Pueblo III, and Pueblo IV; conversations with other big site aficionados; and personal experience. Some of my work was in well-known places (for example, Chaco Canyon), but most, by choice, has been in poorly known or "unknown" regions (for example, the Rio Grande Valley in southern New Mexico, the upper Gila River). Even in those "unknown" areas, there were only a few "big sites" that were entirely new to science. The records might be spotty or even conversational, but someone, somewhere, sometime had visited and noted most of the big ruins. Thinking back on those experiences, I say 80 percent. The wild card is the Early Agricultural Period. I think there could be many Early Agricultural "big sites" out there, buried under meters of alluvium. So we know the locations of more than three-quarters of the post-500 villages in the Southwest.

3. Melinda Elliott (1995) provides a good introduction to this group.

4. Nordenskiold [1893]1979:170.

5. "Tom Outland's Story" in *The Professor's House* by Willa Cather, 1925.

6. Ann Phillips (1993:103–04) offers this account of "Ancient Aztec Relics" (see also McNitt 1966:35). Popular sentiment had not assimilated the new scientific facts. Through the end of the nineteenth century, it was widely accepted that cliff dwellings and the other ruins of the Four Corners were indeed Aztec—"the region of the dead cities of the ancient Aztecs" (Smith 1988:14, quoting a journalist's account of 1876). Wetherill's biographer excused "Ancient Aztec Relics" as a marketing ploy, "the word *Aztec* being a conscious misnomer, a concession to a wide-spread popular belief that the Cliff Dwellers had been Aztec, which Richard knew they were not" (McNitt 1966:35). But I suspect that Wetherill, at least early in his archaeological career, shared that widespread popular belief. See chapter 2.

7. See Atkins 1993.

8. Kidder and Guernsey 1919.

9. For example, Holmes 1886; Kroeber 1916; Spier 1917.

10. For example, Fewkes 1904, cited in Blinman 2000:42–43. Walking today around protected sites—where gophers bring up sherds the size of dinner plates and cattle and collectors are fenced out—we get a hint of what the Southwest must have been like a century ago: big sherds everywhere. Look for sherds today in the Mimbres Valley or at Chaco Canyon. They are gone, the largest taken as souvenirs and the remainder crushed by cattle. At most sites near a beaten track, you are lucky today to see sherds larger than your thumbnail. I compared the sherd collections taken in the 1920s from sites in southern New Mexico with those visible on the surface of those same sites today. The size and diversity of pottery in older collections dramatically exceeds those of today.

11. Hewett [1908]1993.

12. Givens 1992; Woodbury 1973.

13. Kidder, like Bandelier, Hewett, and Cummings, had firsthand experience across the Southwest and (unlike those other pioneers) that necessary East Coast cachet. Kidder was not a local boy; he was a wise man from the East. His *Introduction to the Study of Southwest Archaeology* (1924) was and is a classic, still in print (reprinted most recently in 2000). Similar attempts by Hewett (his handbooks of archaeological history, 1936, for example) and Cummings (1953) are largely forgotten, not-quite-rare books. Bandelier's *Final Report* (1890–92) is honored as a trove of original data—but not reprinted for the market.

14. Kidder [1924]1962:165.

15. Haury 1988.

16. Haury 1945.

17. Sayles 1935.

18. Sayles 1936.

19. Haury 1936, 1986.

20. Reid and Whittlesey 2005b:53–58, 2009; Wheat 1955.

21. In the early decades of the twentieth century, rivalries between Arizona and New Mexico museums and universities split the Anasazi into western (in Arizona) and eastern (in New Mexico). The same state line, farther south, conveniently divided Hohokam and Mogollon. New Mexico archaeologists would do the necessary work in the eastern Anasazi and Mimbres Mogollon areas; Arizona archaeologists claimed rights to western Anasazi and Hohokam. As noted with chagrin in chapter 1, there actually were historically meaningful divisions roughly along the state line or old Highway 666. But those divisions were time specific, effective in the sixth century but not in the eleventh (for example). East and west on the Plateau at least had real history. But the state-line distinction between Hohokam and Mimbres seems less useful and more a reflection of modern than ancient politics (chapters 4 and 5).

The tripartite division of Anasazi, Hohokam, and Mogollon corresponds roughly to the territories of modern Native peoples (chapter 1). Anasazi encompasses both Pueblo and Navajo. Hohokam, as defined by Gladwin and his cohorts, corresponds well to Pima and Papago (as they were called then; today O'odham). And the Mogollon uplands were the historic homes of Western, Chiricahua, and Mescalero Apache groups.

Archaeologists use these modern peoples as models for ancient history—but not as a one-to-one geographic fit. Pueblo lifestyles and cosmologies flesh out the dry bones of Anasazi archaeology. Most of the Anasazi region is today the homeland of Navajo (or Dine). Indeed, *Anasazi* is archaeological jargon borrowed from the Navajo, but the historical relationship of the modern Navajos to the ancient Anasazi is a matter of very contentious debate (chapter 7). There are intriguing parallels between traditional Navajo settlement and the Anasazi of the Chaco era (chapter 5). Take away sheep, and traditional Navajo farming may offer a reasonable model for Anasazi. Almost every Navajo farming community shares some part of its landscape with Anasazi ruins. Controversy also clouds links between Pima and Hohokam. In that case too, both used the same desert in something of the same way, with ditch irrigation but on vastly different scales. No one, including the Apache, claims lineal affinity between Apache and Mogollon, but Apaches (who grew limited amounts of corn when colonial troops did not burn their fields) have been repeatedly used both as models for early Mogollon (who grew a little corn) and as foils against which to contrast later Mogollon (who grew a great deal of corn). Navajos, Pueblos, Pimas, and Apaches show us how real people used real landscapes, and that's important (chapter 1).

22. Glyn Daniel, in *A Hundred and Fifty Years of Archaeology*, explained the great strides made in North American archaeology in the nineteenth century:

> This great story of the development of north American archaeology differs in many ways from the problems of Old World archaeology. In the first place, many of these prehistoric American cultures are interpreted far more completely than are European prehistoric cultures, because so many of the present-day Indians are living more or less as did their prehistoric ancestors, substantially unaltered by Spanish and American culture; in North America, to use Lummis's phrase, we can "catch our archaeology alive." Then, because of this, it is impossible to study North American archaeology except in the closest association with North American ethnology. (Daniel 1976:274)

23. Judd 1954.

24. Fowler 2005:22.

25. Benedict [1934]1989, emphasis added.

26. McFeely 2001. *Patterns of Culture*, originally published in 1934, is still in print, having gone through scores of editions and at least fourteen translations (as of 1960!). In American intellectual life (beyond our discipline), Benedict's *Patterns of Culture* was probably the most influential anthropology book written by an American until Carlos Castaneda met Don Juan and Jared Diamond won the Pulitzer. Of these three celebrated authors, capital-A Anthropology claims only Benedict, and she's been dead sixty years. What does this tell us?

27. Her descriptions also brought joy to Marxists; chapter 7 and Lekson 2006a.

28. Benedict [1934]1989:99.

29. Whittlesey 1998:228.

30. Reed, Wilson, and Hays-Gilpin 2000:209–11.

31. The first Anasazi black-on-white pottery may even have been contemporary with the red-on-brown. Some archaeologists date Anasazi black-on-white as early as 550 (Reed, Wilson, and Hays-Gilpin 2000; Toll and McKenna 1997).

Washburn (2006) offers the intriguing insight that Abajo red-on-black pottery, characteristic of the following Pueblo I Period in southeastern Utah (chapter 4), was "not the product of the local Anasazi, but may have come into the area with one of *the many northward movements of people that occurred through the occupation of the American Southwest*" (Washburn 2006:193, emphasis added).

32. For example, Diehl and LeBlanc 2001; Wallace 2003.

33. Wallace and Lindeman 2003:380.

34. For example, Ciolek-Torrello 1998.

35. For example, Doyel 1991a:238 ("dwellings of leaders").

36. Wallace and Lindeman 2003:380.

37. Wallace and Lindeman 2003:384.

38. Wallace and Lindeman 2003:398.

39. If you want conventional explanations, population pressure and new, more productive strains of maize might be a place to start. Compared with the Early Agricultural horizon, there are many more sites and presumably many more people. It's possible that sites of this period are just better preserved than the earlier villages, because some people (at least) moved away from the floodplain onto higher terraces that, unlike many hard-to-find, large Early Agricultural villages, were not subject to flooding and burial under floodplain sediments. But new site locations were probably prompted by too many people in the valleys to begin with. So it seems likely that people moved out—to escape Big House hierarchies?

McGuire (1992, 2001) influentially argued from burial data that Hohokam of this (and later) periods were egalitarian, but architecture contradicts that interpretation. McGuire notes, "There certainly must be a large number of other, alternative, interpretations that would fit these data" (2001:86). My alternative interpretation, following Wallace: the beginnings of hierarchy.

40. Doyel and Fish 2000:9; Mabry 2000a.

41. Adams 1994:table 16.9; Wallace and Lindeman 2003:380.

42. Ciolek-Torrello 1995:566; Wallace and Lindeman 2003:385–86.

43. Large Phoenix Basin canals absolutely required centralized decision making. But were "political leaders" really necessary? There are other ways to manage canals, other ways to run a railroad. Archaeologists delight to suggest (and to invent) alternative leadership strategies for southwestern societies—anything to avoid un-Puebloan, un-Benedictine hierarchies. Hohokam should be exempt from Benedictine strictures and orthodoxies; Hohokam was not Pueblo. But even here we seek simple alternatives: *Plausible Ethnographic Analogies for the Social Organization of Hohokam Canal Irrigation* (Hunt et al. 2005). As we shall see (chapters 4 and 5), Hohokam later developed ways to do their political business without kings, but clearly somebody (or some body or several bodies) was calling the shots. Political hierarchies emerged in the early Hohokam because hierarchies, I think, were the obvious model—the "default option" for North American farming societies. The emergence of leadership in early Hohokam reflects the larger world in which Hohokam came to be—Teotihuacán's world.

44. Doyel 1991a:244, acknowledging David Wilcox.

45. Gladwin et al. 1938; Haury 1976.

46. Love 2001:175.

47. For example, Haury 1976; Neitzel 1991; Wilcox 1987, 1991b.

48. Fish and Fish 1991:168.

49. Ferdon 1967; Haury 1976.

50. For example, Florescano 2006; compare previously accepted 700–750 end dates.

51. Kubler 1962:39.

52. Carrasco, Jones, and Sessions 2000; Florescano 2006.

53. Millon 1993:24.

54. Millon 1993:27; see also Cowgill 1997.

55. Fash and Fash 2000; Gugliotta 2007; Stuart 2000.

56. Aveni, Hartung, and Kelley 1982.

57. Spencer and Redmond 2004.

58. Clark 1997, 2004.

59. Foster 1999; Weigand 1999, 2000; Weigand and Beekman 1998; Williams 2003.

60. Nelson 1995, 1997.

61. I am a fairly firm believer in emergent order, leaders arising sui generis from the internal dynamics of settlements that reach or exceed a certain permanent size: about twenty-five hundred people (Lekson 1990a; Kosse 1990). But *sui generis* is *ceteris paribus*. Emergent order suggests (but does not demand) the natural laboratory or the computer model or—and this is important—archaic or original states (see chapter 8). The prin-

ciple applies *in isolation*. Emergent properties are inherent in the individuals or the aggregate of interest—the culture in the petri dish or agents in a computer model. But nothing in the Southwest was isolated from anything.

Hierarchical leadership appears in many towns and villages *smaller* than twenty-five hundred people. Almost all of those cases were secondary; leadership roles and institutions were in a sense learned behaviors. The historical events we read as "leadership" or "hierarchy" (or any other form of governance) seldom come from nowhere (that is, emerge parthenogenetically). Leadership, or its forms, was imported or exported and modified for local circumstances and local customs. There was only a handful of *primary* states in the whole world's long history; almost everything thereafter was *secondary*—borrowed, modified, or raised in reaction to other, older polities (a major theme of chapter 8). What is sauce for the state is sauce for less elaborate political formations. Shabik'eschee looking to Phoenix, for example.

62. Thinking about the effects of Mesopotamian urbanism on the uttermost fringes of Neolithic Europe, Andrew Sherratt (2004:79) laments, "For historical reasons—both the institutional separation of research activity and recent distrust of long-distance connections that smack of 'diffusionism'—the two areas are not often discussed in conjunction." Yet the rise of urban societies, he argues, had much to do with the end of Neolithic monumentalism, "as if the system had been wrenched from one path to another, ending a period of relative isolation and incorporating it in a wider world with different objectives and ideals" (Sherratt 2004:88). The continental scale of Sherratt's argument works well with Mesoamerica, the Southwest, and the Mississippi Valley.

Did ripples from Classic Period Mesoamerica contribute to the end of Hopewell monumentalism? Or to the rise of village leaders and hierarchies in the Tucson Basin? I submit yes and yes, at several removes, through chains of events and interactions perhaps too complex for archaeology ever to know in detail. But the fact that we can't reconstruct the details is no reason to ignore Teotihuacán, Teuchitlán, and Classic Mesoamerica. We should look harder or look differently, finding new ways to understand the data we have in hand.

63. Pit houses, most places they are used, were primarily winter residences (even if the summer residence was a sunshade next to the pit house) (Gilman 1987). A deeper pit provided more insulation than a shallow pit, both from the deeper living earth walls and from the additional excavated fill to layer over the roof and "plaster" the walls of the freestanding superstructure. Deep Mogollon pit houses had thick layers of earth on their roofs and minimal freestanding walls. The fill from a shallow Hohokam pit house would barely cover the roof, much less plaster the tall freestanding walls of the house. Were the walls of Hohokam pit houses plastered, or were they left (at least in part) as open thatch or pole screens, tight enough to keep out critters but letting in the evening breeze? (Of course, barrow pits at Hohokam sites might provide additional fill soil for construction, but barrow pits become common after the period discussed in this chapter.)

64. Similarities linking early Hohokam and early Mogollon are given more weight by archaeologists working in Arizona than by those working in the Mimbres area of southwestern New Mexico (e.g., Ciolek-Torrello 1998; Haury 1936, 1986; Whittlesey 1998 versus Diehl and LeBlanc 2001). That's changing (e.g., Creel and Anyon 2003), but few Mogollon archaeologists would accept my interpretations (e.g., Hegmon and Nelson 2006), and with good reason. For example, there are no clay figurines or trash mounds in early Mogollon, and, as noted, early Mogollon sites were on buttes and hilltops—unlike Hohokam sites. I am not suggesting that Mogollon *was* Hohokam, in the sense of presenting identical lists of interesting artifacts, but I think that southwestern New Mexico and the Phoenix Basin represent two ends of a desert axis of which the Phoenix Basin was clearly the senior partner. The "type sites" we think of when comparing Hohokam and Mogollon are hundreds of kilometers apart, in the Phoenix or Tucson basin on one hand and in the upper San Francisco or Mimbres valley on the other. The Land Between is poorly known, and archaeologists have argued over the San Simon area, Dragoon, and even the Tucson Basin. Hohokam or Mogollon? (For a good review, see Whittlesey, Ciolek-Torrello, and Sterner 1994.) That very ambiguity tells us something important: there was a material continuum between early Mogollon and early Hohokam.

65. Wheat 1955, emphasis added.

66. Unlike Anasazi and Hohokam, there is no Native or Native-derived name for Mogollon (a colonial Spanish governor) or Mimbres. The Natives of the Mimbres area, when Adolph Bandelier came through in the late nineteenth century, were Apaches, many of whom were busy defending their homelands with measured violence. There are no recorded discussions between early explorers and Native Apaches on their area's prehistory. Unlike the Navajo-inspired *Anasazi*, if the Apaches have a word for the ancient people (and they do), archaeologists don't use it.

Here, I call this period Early Pithouse, but technically the addition of redwares at about 550 moved the dial to the first phase of the Late Pithouse Period—that and a shift in settlement patterns. More on this below.

67. The Mimbres Valley and the other Mimbres Mogollon areas have not experienced the explosion of cultural resource management (CRM) work that led to the discovery of the remarkable Early Agricultural Period and Pioneer Period sites of the Tucson Basin. For example, it is generally believed that the advent of pottery signals a marked shift from the preceding Archaic, with a much greater reliance on maize (e.g., Diehl and LeBlanc 2001; Swanson and Diehl 2003). But there are only a few excavated Archaic structures in the Mimbres region, much less village sites (an absence of data acknowledged by Swanson, Diehl, and LeBlanc). We have essentially no idea what Late Archaic sites and subsistence were like in the Mimbres Mogollon area. There are tantalizing clues that it might be like Tucson's Early Agricultural Period; large sites with scores of visible pit house depressions, no ceramics, and Late Archaic projectile points are known (but not excavated) on tributaries of the upper Gila (Chapman, Gossett, and Gossett 1985) and a very few excavated Late Archaic pit structures with internal storage pits and postholes quite like those of the Tucson Basin (for example—I think!—NAN Ranch Room 71, dated ceramically to the Three Circle Phase; Shafer 2003:35–36). I strongly suspect that the Late Archaic of the Mimbres region more closely resembled the Early Agricultural of the Tucson Basin than the Oshara Tradition or other hunter-gatherer Anasazi Archaic models most often invoked for Mogollon.

68. Diehl and LeBlanc 2001.

69. The early Late Pithouse period was otherwise indistinguishable from the Early Pithouse Period, save for the addition of redware pottery. Thus site location on high points and the absence of redwares are the two defining criteria for the Early Pithouse Period. I wonder about this: unquestionably, many Early Pithouse sites are on high places, but some are not. The SU site, one of the most famous Early Pithouse Period sites, is on a low ridge, hardly a defensive setting. Many other Early Pithouse Period sites of my acquaintance are on river terraces, low knobs, and landforms too low and too gentle to be "high points." I suspect that Early Pithouse settlements lie buried under later Mimbres towns on lower terraces, nearer the creeks and streams—and more like contemporary Hohokam.

Early archaeology in the Mimbres Mogollon area focused almost entirely on pueblos. Like robbing banks because that's where the money is, we dug pueblos because that's where the pots were. Pit houses, discovered under the masonry room blocks, were a surprise. Big Mimbres sites represent centuries of use, from Late Archaic through Late Pithouse through Mimbres and post-Mimbres villages (Anyon and LeBlanc 1984; Creel 2006a; LeBlanc 1983; Lekson 2006c; Shafer 2003). These sites are stratigraphically dense and complex but not necessarily deep. Pueblos sit atop filled pit houses, pit houses cut into other pit houses, pits and features from later occupations intrude into earlier structures, and the whole has been churned by a century of the most intensive looting anywhere in the Southwest. What are the chances of seeing or isolating Early Pithouse structures—defined, if not on high points, by only the absence of redwares—at a long-lived, complexly stratified, badly looted Mimbres site? Slim at best.

70. Reviewed by Diehl and LeBlanc 2001.

71. LeBlanc's interpretation in Diehl and LeBlanc 2001.

72. Diehl's interpretation in Diehl and LeBlanc 2001.

73. Swanson and Diehl 2003:3. See also Gilman 1987; Lekson 2006b; Shafer 2003:218.

74. Diehl and LeBlanc 2001:103.

75. Reed 2000:7–8; Wilshusen 1999a.

76. Powell 2002:79.

77. Nichols 2002:70–71.

78. Chenault and Motsinger 2000; Wilshusen 1999a:177.

79. Altschul and Huber 2000:table 7.1; Gilpin and Benallie 2000:table 8.1; Reed and Wilcox 2000:85.

80. Gilpin and Benallie 2000:167.

81. Roberts 1929; Wills and Windes 1989. I estimate eighty to ninety pit houses.

82. Windes forthcoming.

83. My assessment of Shabik'eschee and 423—that those are two exceptional sites—is generally accepted by Basketmaker archaeologists. However, I was surprised and delighted to learn of an eleventh-hour rival, Cottonwood Seep, just south of Navajo, Arizona. Dennis Gilpin (personal communication, March 13, 2008) believes that Cottonwood has "as many as two-hundred to three-hundred structures[!]." My thanks to Dennis Gilpin for this information.

Cottonwood Seep is a district or complex of sites (but so are Shabik'eschee and 423). It has a much longer history of occupation compared with the Chaco sites (but we have only the shakiest understanding of the spans of Shabik'eschee and 423). Cottonwood Seep dates from 485 to 900. The Chaco sites started about the same time as Cottonwood Seep, but they almost certainly ended after only a century or so. The Cottonwood Seep site complex came to light through CRM—the Coronado Project (e.g., Marek, Greenwald, and Ahlstrom 1993). It may revise our views of Basketmaker III just as dramatically as the CRM Dolores Project changed our ideas about Pueblo I. I note with more than passing interest that Cottonwood Seep sits more or less on a line between Chaco and Phoenix, about halfway between the two centers.

84. Wills and Windes 1989.

85. Kantner 2004:66.

86. Roberts (1929) found *Glycimeris* shell armlets at Shabik'eschee, and my admittedly hopeful reading of the report places these among "the inordinate quantity of rare artifacts." *Glycimeris* armlets reappear on the Plateau centuries later, among the high-status burials of Pueblo Bonito; see chapter 5, note 131.

87. Pit House F was a Big House. More than twenty years ago, Lightfoot and Feinman (1982) drew the same conclusion (although not the Hohokam connection; that's mine). They said that large houses such as Pit House F at Shabik'eschee indicated leaders. Their suggestion met with methodological quibbles (Schiffer 1983) and southwestern archaeology's innate skepticism toward political leadership, but their argument was neither illogical nor at odds with the evidence. Five years ago, however, they recanted (Feinman, Lightfoot, and Upham 2000), accepting instead the conclusions of Windes and Wills (1989) that Shabik'eschee was seasonally occupied over many decades, with implications for a small-scale, cheerfully egalitarian social structure.

But recent work at other Basketmaker III sites suggests that many were more or less sedentary, and many other researchers now question Wills and Windes's seasonal Shabik'eschee (Reed 2000:9; Reed [ed.] 2000). I think Lightfoot and Feinman (1982) got it right the first time: large houses at Shabik'eschee mean leaders (e.g., Kantner 2004; from a different perspective, Kohler 1993).

88. Teague 1998.

89. Jernigan 1978.

Chapter 4

1. Dean 1991; Gladwin 1948.

2. The Southwest is extremely, almost embarrassingly well dated. There are now approximately forty thousand tree-ring dates—many to the very year. Of course, almost all those dates come from the Plateau, the Mogollon uplands, or the Rio Grande. A summary of Hohokam dates (as of 1988) listed 219 14C and 403 archaeomagnetic dates (Dean 1991:72). Ten years later, driven by CRM, those numbers quadrupled to almost 891 14C dates and 1,508 archaeomagnetic dates (Deaver 1997:565–66). The numbers continue to climb, with increasing proportions of CRM budgets marked for chronology. Obviously, the deserts lag behind the mountains and plateau in chronological precision, but twenty-four hundred independent dates would be a considerable achievement and an enviable resource in any other archaeological region of the world. (And there are now perhaps two thousand archaeomagnetic dates from all regions of the Southwest, extrapolating from Eighmy 2000:fig. 6.3.)

Tree-ring dating is a wonderful thing, but it sometimes sets unrealistic standards. Let me explain. Jeff Dean's classic dendrochronological study of two large, perfectly preserved cliff dwellings, Betatakin and Kiet Siel (chapter 6), with highly detailed construction and social histories, raised a very high bar (Dean 1969). Archaeologists *want to do that* and attempt to achieve similar precision at a Hohokam village flattened in a cotton field; an Anasazi pit house rescued from a roadway, with a score of burned beams in the fill; or a big Mogollon pueblo, all but destroyed by pot hunters and probed with a few tiny test pits. Or entire regions, fitting ceramic assemblages from surveyed sites to statistical curves, tacked down at various points by absolute dates. That sort of regression offers the (absurd) possibility of dating ceramic assemblages not just to a century or a decade but potentially to the day, month, and year. It's all a matter of decimal places in the coefficients. Carry the calculation out to four decimal points and you can name the hour of the day.

We do this because we have come to *expect precision*. That's the downside of tree rings. I worry that we are trying to make atomic chronometers out of sundials or bank calendars—that we are forcing coarse-grained, sherds-and-flakes data into five-year time blocks to fit the finer resolution of dendroclimatology. Overemphasis on chronological precision affects practice. We want dates; an excavation without dates is a failure. Thus burned structures get far more attention than unburned structures because burned structures can be dated (charred beams, 14C, archaeomagnetism on baked walls or features)—a silent bias in both Anasazi and (especially) Hohokam archaeology that may someday return to bite us.

3. Hinsley 1996b:196.

4. Hinsley 1996b:196.

5. Archaeology's appreciation of Native accounts waxes and wanes (chapter 7). The earliest pioneers paid attention; the first "new archaeology" rejected Native tales as unreliable myths. Land claims cases of the 1950s and 1960s (Indians sued the government for lost lands) briefly reengaged archaeology with Native traditions

and oral histories but subjected informants' testimony to the pitiless analysis of the courtroom. That association ended when New Archaeology (in the late 1960s) remanded traditional history back to "myth"—an aspect of "ideational" behavior impossible to research—and once again proclaimed Native accounts scientifically useless (chapter 5). Today archaeologists once again listen eagerly, even reverently, to Indians and their traditions. The pendulum has swung, perhaps too far back. But that story belongs in chapters 7 and 8.

6. Morris 1939:11.

7. Nash 2000:61.

8. Eighmy 2000:111.

9. Jeff Eighmy (2000), a master at archaeomagnetic dating, feels the future of the technique is bleak because of the closure of several laboratories and the retirement of key practitioners. That would truly be a shame.

10. T. T. Waterman was credited by some (specifically Kidder; see Woodbury 1993:92–94) as the catalyst of the Pecos Classification. T. T. had immediate misgivings. In an amusing article, Waterman (1929) critiqued his own creation and suggested in its place a cumbersome scheme of eleven "horizons" that were not necessarily chronological. His scheme is so baroque and cumbersome that I wonder whether it was a Sokal-style joke. Of course, no one used Waterman's second try, but I bet it got a good laugh. His was one of many attacks on the Pecos Classification, but the old standard stands. We still use it, and we still argue about it. Here's a thumbnail sketch, based on Linda Cordell's (1997:164–165) summary:

> *Basketmaker I*: Postulated pre-agricultural stage, no longer used. Now considered archaic.

> *Basketmaker II*: Agriculture and atlatl made, but pottery not present.

> *Basketmaker III*: Pit houses or slab houses make, pottery make, bow and arrow make, no cranial deformation (flattening of childrens' heads due to binding on cradle boards).

> *Pueblo I*: Cranial deformation; villages of above-ground, contiguous rectangluar rooms; true masonry.

> *Pueblo II*: Small masonry villages occur over a large geographic area.

> *Pueblo III*: Very large communities make, artistic elaboration, and specialization in crafts.

> *Pueblo IV*: Much of Pueblo area abandoned, particulatly the San Juan region; artistic elaboration declines.

> *Pueblo V*: from AD 1600 to present.

11. Gladwin and Gladwin 1934.

12. Fowler 2000; Hinsley 1986; Snead 2001. Rivalries were such that the Laboratory of Anthropology, Gila Pueblo, and the Museum of Northern Arizona each created its own laboratory for dendrochronology. Gladwin did not trust Douglas's techniques and developed his own. By 1950 these independent labs were gone, consolidated at the original Laboratory of Tree-ring Research at the University of Arizona.

13. Chauvenet 1983; Elliot 1987; Hinsley 1986.

14. Fowler 2000; Toulouse 1981.

15. Hewett almost never used the Pecos Classification, which did not fit the northern Rio Grande, his particular fiefdom. Nor did it fit Chaco, another of Hewett's neighborhoods: Chaco's Pueblo II Great Houses should have been Pueblo III. That misfit—Great Houses in Pueblo II—marks a central fact in Plateau prehistory, as we shall see in chapter 5. In place of the Pecos Classification, Hewett's students and collaborators at Chaco devised and refined a complicated phase system, which reached its culmination in the 1960s with three contemporary phases: Bonito, McElmo, and Hosta Butte (Vivian and Mathews 1965). The Chaco phase sequence has collapsed back to a series of sequential phases, once again (more or less) linked to Pecos stages (e.g., Lekson [ed.] 2006; Mathien 2005).

16. Haury 1988.

17. Haury 2004; Wilcox 2005c.

18. Fowler 2000:371–72.

19. Curiously, no single institution claimed the Four Corners. Perhaps the institution builders felt the Four Corners region was already sufficiently well known, a sucked orange. Bill Lipe (citing Walter Taylor 1954) refers to the area's archaeology from the 1930s through the 1960s as "gap filling." And the Four Corners' quartered political division must have discouraged ownership. Or—and I think this most likely—perhaps the region was too far away from each state's political and cultural capitals. In the early automotive era, nobody wanted to be that far away from Denver, Santa Fe, Tucson, or Salt Lake City. In any event, no research institute or museum rose in the Four Corners to rival the Museum of Northern Arizona, the Museum of New Mexico,

the Laboratory of Anthropology, the Arizona State Museum, Gila Pueblo, or the Amerind Foundation.

Southwestern Colorado, southeastern Utah, and northwestern New Mexico are always threatening, not entirely in jest, to secede from states that do not attend to them sufficiently. Northeastern Arizona is a whole different country—the Navajo Nation—with its own time zones. The University of Colorado might have been the obvious candidate to establish a research institution in Durango or Cortez, and indeed the university had a permanent field station at Mesa Verde for many years. Alas, nothing in life is truly permanent, and that center reverted to its landlords, the National Park Service. Into that vacuum, Crow Canyon Archaeological Center emerged in the 1980s as the leading Four Corners research institution. Originally (and loosely) affiliated with a distant university, Crow Canyon is now a stand-alone nonprofit in Cortez, Colorado. It does outstanding research.

20. Roberts 1935. The Pecos Classification equivalents are approximate, as we'd see them today and not precisely Roberts's reading.

21. It comes and goes: Ford, Schroeder, and Peckham 1972; Habicht-Mauche 1993; Wendorf 1954; Wendorf and Reed 1955. Currently, the San Juan is very much in the Rio Grande doghouse.

22. Wendorf 1954; Wendorf and Reed 1955.

23. Fowler 2000:371–72.

24. Colton 1946.

25. Colton 1946:table 1.

26. Colton 1960. In fact, Colton said "about 1065."

27. Colton 1960:7–8.

28. Territorial particularism in the 1940s and 1950s mirrors the last gasp of Boasian anthropology. Franz Boas, the dominant anthropologist of the first three or four decades of the twentieth century, was famed for collecting data and avoiding generalizations—no Big Pictures. This is not fair to Boas, who was historically minded and in fact a Big Picture guy. But he trained and inspired a generation or two of anthropologists to gather details and postpone (indefinitely) conclusions. Particularism was long gone in the ethnology of that time, but it held on, in one form or another, in southwestern archaeology.

29. Gladwin 1948; Gladwin et al. 1938.

30. Haury 1976.

31. Gladwin et al. 1938.

32. Gladwin 1948.

33. See also Di Peso 1956, 1979.

34. Gladwin 1948.

35. Wheat 1955:fig. 12.

36. Kidder (quoted in Nash 2000:63).

37. Haury 1976:343–348, 351–53.

38. Dean 1991.

39. Somehow, the identification of each Hohokam phase by a single, characteristic pottery type survived all the chronological debates and revisions. To me, one type/one phase seems problematic, particularly for the earliest phases of the old Hohokam sequence: Sweetwater, Estrella, and Snaketown. Those early phases are, of course, less well known than later Colonial and Sedentary periods. The three are now thought to span only about a century, and many chronologies compress them or run them in parallel but keep them as named phases (Sweetwater/Estrella, for example, is not uncommon). I suspect that Early Hohokam had a variety of pottery styles, house forms, and so on, which then sorted themselves out into the regularity of the Colonial and Sedentary periods. That would fit well with the version of Hohokam presented in this chapter.

I wonder too about a similar situation at the beginning of the Mogollon Late Pithouse Period: a rapid sequence of short-lived phases, each denoted by a particular pottery type (Anyon, Gilman, and LeBlanc 1981; Shafer 2003). Emil Haury defined the Early Mogollon sequence, and he made the same assumptions for Mogollon that he and Gladwin made for Hohokam: one type equals one phase. Modern Mimbres Mogollon work continues to use Haury's original phase names and definitions, but it may well be time to rethink both early Hohokam and early Mogollon systematics.

Pueblo I, the Anasazi archaeology of this era, has been described as a failed temporal (and spatial) systematic, with too many local phase sequences and too many phases: "This emphasis on local areas led to a remarkable proliferation of phases for Pueblo I manifestations. Kidder originally divided the entire San Juan Drainage into three subcultures—Chaco, Mesa Verde and Kayenta—but since his day at least 10 Pueblo I phases have been defined for his Mesa Verde subculture area alone" (Wilshusen and Ortman 1999:371–72). In all three areas, we have many trees but not many views of the forest.

40. Carrasco, Jones, and Sessions 2000; Florescano 2006.

41. Nelson 2000; see also Nelson 2006 and McGuire et al. 1994:244–52. Other reconstructions of the era differ in outline but agree in the specificity of historical detail (Di Peso 1974; Kelley and Kelley 1974). Mesoamerican archaeology does not shy away from historical narratives.

42. Nelson 2000:321.

43. Marcus 1989.

44. For example, *Mesoamerica after the Decline of Teotihuacán, AD 700–900* (Diehl and Berlo 1989).

45. Braniff 2001:239.

46. See also Di Peso 1974; Kelley 1986; Riley 2005.

47. Williams 2003.

48. Hohokam has long been connected (in the archaeological imagination) to the west coast of Mexico (e.g., Haury 1976; McGuire and Villalpando 2007b; Meighan 1999). A tantalizing case in point: Loma Alta and Hohokam. Dating between 100 and 350, the Loma Alta site sits about 30 kilometers northwest of the later Tarascan capital of Tzintzuntzan and about 1,800 kilometers from Phoenix. Patricia Carot noted that ceramics and cremations at Loma Alta were very like those of the Hohokam, where Loma Alta motifs may appear first in the very late Pioneer Period "et proliferent pendant les periodes Coloniale et Sedentaire" (Carot 2000:119). The cremated remains were fragmented, ground, and then buried in urns, "a funerary custom found at Loma Alta that has never been seen in other areas of the Occidente, and perhaps nowhere else in Mesoamerica" (Williams 2003). The time discrepancy is major but perhaps not a deal breaker. Carot suggests that shared iconography constitutes a "route" from Proto-Classic times to the Southwest, much like "la fameuse route de la turquoise" in the Classic and Post-Classic (Carot 2001:132).

Ceramics matter, but for individual or group identity, other media and modalities—house forms, for example, or personal adornment and clothing—might be even more significant. Patricia Anawalt (1992) notes the potential significance of clothing, and Lynne Teague links the turban headgear of Hohokam with the later Aztatlan centers of Chametla and Amapa (Teague 1998:fig. 8.2, ch. 5):

> The source of early Mesoamerican influence on the people of the Southwest has long been debated by archaeologists.... Textiles may help to resolve this issue.... The west coast of Mexico is unique in providing the full assemblage of nonlocal textile materials, technology, and structures found among the Hohokam and Mogollon of the desert Southwest. (Teague 1998:177)

Teague dates the arrival of this textile industry from the west coast of Mexico at about 700. Many archaeologists agree that about 750–800, peoples of the southern deserts *became* Hohokam.

49. *Hohokam Canon* is a regrettable neologism. Other archaeologists have offered names for this remarkable package of ritual/economics/governance—for example, *the Hohokam Cult* or *Rainbow Way* (Doyel 1994) or *the Hohokam Revitalization Movement* (Wallace and Lindeman forthcoming). I once suggested *Hohokam Ceremonial Complex (HCC)*, a counterpart for the Southeast Ceremonial Complex (SCC). *HCC* has the merit of ambiguity but somehow suggests hazardous waste. More importantly, in chapter 7 I suggest that the appropriate Southwest comparison to the Southeast's SCC is not HCC, but Pueblo IV (PIV). So SCCSE = HCCSW; SCCSE = PIVSW.

Please don't ask me about the content of Hohokam religion. It's remarkably difficult to get a handle on the core doctrines of major modern religions, even with popes and ayatollahs laying down the law. Attempting to determine the principles of an ancient religion—gone for almost a thousand years—is probably a waste of time. We might ferret out hints and details, but think how easy it would be to misunderstand major modern religions from only hints and details. But see Wilcox 1987, 1991b—a braver man than I—and Doyel and Wallace, above.

50. Abbott 2000:27.

51. Millon 1993; see also Cowgill 1997.

52. Abbott 2000; Cable 1991; Craig [ed.] 2001; Fish and Fish 1991, 2000c; Howard 1993.

53. Doolittle 1990:79.

54. Graybill et al. 2006.

55. Graybill et al. 2006:112.

56. Bayman 2001; Haury 1976; Wallace 1995; Wallace, Heidke, and Doelle 1995; Wallace and Lindeman forthcoming.

57. Haury 1976.

58. For example, Doyel 1991a, 1994:14, 2000c; McGuire and Villalpando 2007b; Wallace and Lindeman 2003; Whittlesey 1997, 2007:26–28; Wilcox 1987, 1991d. See also note 48.

59. Haury 1976:355, reaffirmed in Haury 1986. See Wallace, Heidke, and Doelle 1995.

60. Haury 1976:356–57.

61. Doyel 2000b:224; Doyel and Crary 1995.

62. Gladwin et al. [1938]1975; Haury 1976; Wilcox, McGuire, and Sternberg 1981.

63. Haury 1976:356.

64. Reviewed in Craig 2000b:139.

65. It has become a favorite pastime among Hohokam archaeologists to deflate that number and to show that Snaketown was, contra Haury, smaller or much smaller (e.g., Wilcox, McGuire, and Sternberg 1981; cf. Craig 2000a). Similar downsizings turned Los Pozos into a farmstead (chapter 2), made Shabik'eschee a piñon-gathering camp (chapter 3), and may someday make Cahokia vanish entirely (chapter 5).

66. Craig 2001a.

67. Craig 2001a:46.

68. Doyel 1987; Doyel, Fish, and Fish 2000.

69. Abbott 2000:37–40 (Abbott is not happy with hierarchical modularities); Howard 1985; Wilcox, McGuire, and Sternberg 1981.

70. Doelle, Huntington, and Wallace 1987; Howard 1985.

71. Abbott, Ingram, and Kobler 2006; Doyel 1974:fig. 4.10; contra S. Fish 1996.

72. Bayman 2002:77. Craig cites a scalar threshold at twelve hundred (from Feinman and Neitzel 1984:67–68), half my twenty-five hundred (Lekson 1990c), as "the approximate threshold for the presence of highly differentiated leaders with marked social differences. Thus the apparent increase in the number of status markers at Grewe during the Colonial period may be a reflection, in part, of demographic factors" (Craig 2000b:160).

73. See Craig (ed.) 2000.

74. Hackbarth 2000:7.

75. Bayman 2002:84–85.

76. Doyel 1991a:fig. 6; Haury 1986. At least in terms of floor areas and features, all that archaeologists can see. We see only the floors, not the actual Big House, which may have been distinguished by greater height, different materials, flashy finishes, or even flags and banners (Lekson 1990d). There is no archaeological evidence for any such architectural embellishments—but we'd never know, would we? Presumably, the importance of Big House leaders waned with the diminishing size of their trophy houses proportionately to the rising importance of Hohokam Canon leadership.

77. Lekson 2006c.

78. Suzanne and Paul Fish, in a recent review, summarize the situation: "Although there is unequivocal evidence for strong centralization and massive coordinated effort in some spheres, leaders are not distinguished by easily recognized indicators such as lavish wealth, coercion towards personal ends, elaborate and exclusive insignia, or individualized prominence in art and iconography" (Fish and Fish 2000c:155).

79. P. Fish and S. Fish 1991:168; S. Fish and P. Fish 2000b:378–81.

80. There are site hierarchies within canal communities: "Some sites are distinguished by ballcourts early in the Colonial period, and during this same interval, larger sites along the Salt and Gila canal networks show the beginnings of primacy" (Fish and Fish 1991:168). In the later Sedentary and Classic periods, several towns were notably larger than others sharing the same canal. These larger towns are often at the upper or lower ends of the canal. That is, these presumed seats of authority were nearest the diversion dams and intakes or at the end of the ditch. It is not clear, however, that this pattern was firmly established during the Colonial Period.

81. Marshall 2001; Wilcox 1991d; Wilcox and Sternberg 1983.

82. Scarborough and Wilcox 1991.

83. Hill and Clark 2001.

84. Hill and Clark 2001.

85. Santley, Berman, and Alexander 1991.

86. Gillespie 1991:344.

87. Wilcox 1991d:124.

88. Abbott 2000.

89. Bayman 2002:77.

90. Haury 1976; Marshall 2001.

91. Wilcox 1991d; Marshall 2001.

92. Wilcox presents three tables of dated ball courts: Colonial/Early Sedentary 37, Late Sedentary 57, and Early Classic 21 (Wilcox 1991d:tables 6.1, 6.2, 6.3). In each table, he notes the dating, court by court, and that information indicates the difficulties of dating this kind of architecture without excavation. Many temporal assignments are necessarily multiple—for example, Colonial/Late Sedentary. I recast these data using the earliest of each of Wilcox's court-by-court datings (for example, Colonial/Early Sedentary becomes Colonial,

and the chronological distribution of ball courts becomes Colonial 67, Sedentary 15, Early Classic 10). This is the worst kind of angels-on-the-head-of-a-pin scholasticism—reanalyzing a colleague's thrice-refined data, originally presented as approximate. But I call 'em as I see 'em. And a few knowledgeable Hohokam archaeologists agree that most ball courts were Colonial—off the record.

93. Abbott 2000:193.

94. Haury 1976; Wilcox 1987, 1991b.

95. White 2004.

96. In 1988, at the Arizona State Museum, I sought out a class of artifacts with which to test the Hohokam regional system defined by David Wilcox. Wilcox defined the system on the basis of ball courts. I thought it would be useful to look at an independent data set. I wanted an artifact class distributed over all or most of the "system," numbering in several thousands, with sufficient decorative content that I could play with designs, elements, motifs, and so on—and *not* pottery. I settled on pallets and visited museums throughout the country recording these very interesting artifacts, including careful 1:1 drawings of each. I spent a lot of quality time with pallets. After preliminary analysis and a conference paper, I got way too busy to do anything more with pallets. But I loved them dearly and passed the data on to a series of graduate students, finally hitting the jackpot with Devin White (2004).

97. Haury 1976:286.

98. Haury 1976:286.

99. Haury 1976:286.

100. White 2004.

101. White 2004:36.

102. Bayman 2002; Bradley 2000; Gladwin et al. 1938; Haury 1976.

103. For example, Bayman 2002; Marmaduke and Marynec 1993; Whittlesey 1997:619.

104. Bayman 2002:79–80, fig. 3.

105. Bayman 2002:80. And the rest of the outfit? Based on the very fragmentary evidence of textiles, Hohokam and Mogollon clothing was remarkably similar during this period and differed in materials, techniques, and forms from contemporary Anasazi clothing (Kent 1983; Teague 1998:176, fig. 8.1). Hohokam grew lots of cotton and before 1000 or so exported quite a bit to the western Anasazi—the region of Hohokam's initial and continued "influence" (Laurie Webster, personal communication, 2006). Western Anasazi may have traded cotton or cotton clothes east, into the Chaco region, but that is another story.

106. Elson and Clark 2007.

107. Rice, Simon, and Loendorf 1998:109.

108. By using the word *peripheries*, I lose half of the Hohokam archaeologists (if any) among my readers (if any). No one wants to work in a periphery (but for another view, see Sullivan and Bayman eds. 2007). *Peripheries* is tainted for some by its association with world systems theory, which many people discredit (for southwestern applications) on theoretical grounds (e.g., McGuire 1991:364; Whittlesey 1997).

But in the dictionary sense, there were indeed a core and peripheries for the Hohokam Canon. The core, of course, was Phoenix. Sites that look like colonies (in the sense of organized migrations) pop up in the peripheries: the Tonto Basin (most famously Haury 1932; see also Clark and Huckell 2004:8; Elson and Clark 2007, forthcoming; Elson, Gregory, and Stark 1995:446–49; Rice 1998:231), Gila Bend (Doyel 2000c [my interpretation, not his]; Wasley and Johnson 1965), the Verde (Ciolek-Torrello 1997; but see Fish, Pilles, and Fish 1980; McGuire 1991; Whittlesey 1997), the San Pedro (Clark et al. forthcoming); the Papagueria (Bayman 2007; McGuire 1991), and the Tucson Basin (Doelle and Wallace 1991; Kelley 1978). Were these colonies, or local people "changing clothes," or a bit of both? To my aging eyes, these sites look like Colonial Period colonies. Many younger, sharper archaeologists agree, at least to a degree (e.g., Wallace and Lindeman forthcoming).

109. For example, Elson and Clark 2007; McGuire 1991; Wallace and Lindeman 2008; Whittlesey 1997.

110. For example, Reid and Whittlesey 1997:89; Wallace, Heidke, and Doelle 1995.

111. Haury 1976:343–48, 351–53.

112. But see Carot 2000, 2001; Carot and Hers 2006.

113. Haury 1976:343–48.

114. McGuire and Villalpando 2007b; Wallace and Lindeman forthcoming; Whittlesey 2007:26–28; Wilcox 1986b, 1987, 1991b.

115. Craig 2001b; cf. Nelson 1986:167.

116. Lansing 2006.

117. Abbott 2000.

118. Hunt et al. 2005.

119. For example, Hunt et al. 2005; cf. Howard 1993:316; Yoffee, Fish, and Milner 1999; but wait for chapter 8!

120. Clastres 1977.

121. Craig 2000b:160.

122. Diehl and LeBlanc 2001.

123. Chapman, Gossett, and Gossett 1985; Lekson 2006b.

124. Lekson 2006b.

125. Creel and Anyon 2003:85–86; Hegmon 2002; Lekson 1993a, 1999b; Shafer 2003:8, 112, 202; but see Hegmon and Nelson (2007), who conclude that Mimbres and Hohokam were "in sync, but barely in touch."

126. Heckman and Whittlesey 2000:117–25.

127. Heckman and Whittlesey 2000:126. The key archaeological distinction between the Early and Late Pithouse periods is the addition of redware pottery to the ceramic inventory and, consequently, our ability to see Late Pithouse ceramic assemblages (dating after 550) at complex, multicomponent sites; see chapter 3. Early Hohokam red-on-buff was much like Mogollon red-on-brown (and Three Circle red-on-white for that matter). They were clearly made in different areas, by different people using different clays, but those different people shared a vision of what a pot should look like. The glory days of Mimbres black-on-white pottery, with its famous naturalistic art, lay in the future (chapter 5), but the origins of its naturalistic design almost certainly lay with Hohokam's Colonial Period depictions of animals and plants (Brody 2004; Jerry Brody, personal communication, 1998). Mimbres artists developed their own remarkable artistic tradition in their own idiom, but it did not come from nowhere. Michelle Hegmon and Margaret Nelson note that at the Mimbres Valley Galaz site, more than half the bowls from this time period had "Hohokam-like motifs and conventions" (Hegmon and Nelson 2007:fig. 5.9). Yet curiously, they minimize the importance of Hohokam–Mimbres dynamics in the Late Pithouse Period.

128. Wasley and Johnson 1965.

129. Cosgrove and Cosgrove 1932.

130. Creel 1989; Shafer 2003.

131. Garcia de Quevedo 2004; White 2004; see also Shafer 2003:202.

132. Lekson 1982, 2006b.

133. For example, Shafer 2003:39, 91.

134. "Red" Ellison, an old and honored avocational archaeologist (long since deceased) worked in the Mimbres area long before current and even emeritus archaeologists. Red once told me that there were two ball courts in the Mimbres Valley (both now destroyed) and a third at the huge Woodrow Ruin in the Gila Valley (Richard Ellison, personal communication, 1974). Red's "ball court" at Woodrow is still there. I have seen it, but I am not sure what to think about it. It's not Snaketown. Hohokam ball courts vary from towering berms to very subtle swales. Red could be right.

I worked in the Mimbres region for years before I saw my first Hohokam ball court. Any number of oddly shaped depressions on Mimbres sites that I long ago mapped as Mogollon pit houses might just as readily be interpreted as the shallower, less formal, less well-preserved Hohokam courts. We see what we expect to see (at least I do), and I *did not expect to see ball courts* in the Mimbres area. Perhaps they are not there. But after seeing Hohokam courts, I could not confidently say so or say, "no."

135. Haury 1989:108; Johnson 1961.

136. Anyon and LeBlanc 1980; Creel and Anyon 2003.

137. Creel and Anyon 2003.

138. Lekson 1982.

139. Creel and Anyon 2003; Lekson 1999a.

140. At one point (before recent Tucson Basin discoveries, discussed in chapter 3), I thought that Early Hohokam Big Houses might represent comparable structures, a carryover from the pan-southwestern brownware horizon (also chapter 3), but clearly that is not the case. Hohokam sites had multiple contemporary Big Houses, and they were domestic structures. Great Kivas in both Anasazi and Mogollon regions more closely parallel Hohokam ball courts. Like ball courts, Great Kivas served as foci and symbols of the community. Both could accommodate big crowds. But the activities carried out in ball courts and Great Kivas were rather different. Ball courts were open and public; Great Kivas were enclosed and private.

141. Lekson 1986; Minnis 1985.

142. Herrington 1982; Shafer 2003.

143. Lekson 2006b.

144. Creel and Anyon 2003; Diehl and LeBlanc 2001; Shafer 2003.

145. Creel and Anyon 2003; Lekson 2006b; Shafer 2003.

146. This period, between 900 and 1000–1025, has been the subject of much controversy, symptomatic of its transitional nature (e.g., LeBlanc 1986b; Lekson 1988, 1999a; Shafer 2003:40–54). We argue about the "Mangas Phase," the pit house to pueblo transition, and other awkward systematics, about the timing of the transition in one valley or another, about change or continuity in ceramics and architecture. Those arguments reflect the dynamic realities of the tenth century: all positions (and none) may be correct for particular places and specific times.

147. Gilman 1990; LeBlanc 1983; Shafer 2003.

148. See Hegmon 2002:336–37.

149. Creel and Anyon 2003:80; cf. Feinman, Lightfoot, and Upham 2000.

150. Breternitz, Robinson, and Gross 1986.

151. Potter and Chuipka 2007.

152. For example, Hayes 1964; Hayes and Lancaster 1975; Rohn 1977.

153. J. O. Brew 1946.

154. Morris 1939.

155. Wilshusen and Ortman 1999:374.

156. And Wilshusen's later studies, for example, Wilshusen and Ortman 1999.

157. Toll and Wilson 2000:33–34.

158. Kuckelman 2003; Wilshusen 2003.

159. Varien 1999.

160. The intricacies of these movements foreshadow or mirror those described in traditional Pueblo histories—for example, Zuni (Ferguson and Hart 1985:map 8; Washburn 1995:fig. 16). I was once dubious about intricate, complicated maps of Pueblo migrations, but after the convolutions of Pueblo I, anything seems possible.

161. This note originally read: "How should we understand that absence of evidence? Are big Pueblo I sites at Zuni or around Hopi present but unreported? I would be greatly surprised if the Zuni region did not have big Pueblo I sites—it has gobs of everything else archaeological. Someday a book like this one may be written with the Zuni area as the central focus, the lynchpin of the Anasazi world." In June 2008 I received messages from Keith Kintigh and Andrew Duff telling me of a very large Pueblo I site about 50 kilometers south of Zuni. This site is only sketchily known, but I believe them: it's big. And I suspect it is not alone.

162. For example, Powell 2002.

163. With thirty pit structures, Bad Dog Ridge, on a high bluff at Ganado, Arizona, is a possible exception (Gilpin and Benallie 2000). The dating is problematic (it may be Basketmaker III), but it's probably Pueblo I.

164. Reviewed in Powell 2002.

165. Chuipka and Potter 2007; Wilshusen and Ortman 1999.

166. Duke 1985; Potter and Chuipka 2007.

167. The recent Animas–La Plata project in the Ridges Basin tilted the balance of power from Blue Mesa to Sacred Ridge (Chuipka and Potter 2007:8). Wilshusen and Ortman (1999) estimated about two hundred pit structures at Blue Mesa; Chuipka and Potter reduce that to seventy-four, about the same number as at Ridges Basin (Potter and Chuipka 2007). I continue to use the names *Blue Mesa* and *Blue Mesa–Ridges Basin* in preference to *Ridges Basin*, because I suspect Blue Mesa was in fact larger in terms of numbers of pit houses (about one-fourth of Blue Mesa was bulldozed into an airport before archaeologists mapped the site). But Ridges Basin has much more interesting architecture, specifically *Sacred Ridge*, described in the text. Indeed, the whole complex might rightly be called Sacred Ridge, but I have an aversion to sacrality—too much of that already in southwestern archaeology! Whatever we call it, the Durango Pueblo I complex was originally thought to date toward the end of the Pueblo I Period, to the first half of the ninth century (Wilshusen and Ortman 1999). Dates from the ALP project indicate that it began somewhat earlier, about 750 to 810 (Chuipka and Potter 2007; Potter and Chuipka 2007). Blue Mesa itself produced dates from one structure at 831, so the Pueblo I sites lasted that long if not longer (in some form, perhaps diminished). Again, these datings (and other Pueblo I datings) will no doubt change with additional work (only a tiny fraction of Blue Mesa has been intensively investigated).

168. Jason Chuipka, personal communication, 2006.

169. Potter and Chuipka 2007. It's tempting to see the tower as a precursor to Chaco's "tower kivas" and the igloolike structure as an early version of the domed, upside-down basket ceilings of Chaco "kivas."

170. Potter and Chuipka 2007.

171. Potter and Chuipka 2007.

172. Why there, at Durango? Why not in the more densely settled districts near Mesa Verde? Symbolic landscapes and cosmologies we are only beginning to understand may have played roles in the rise of Blue Mesa–Ridges Basin. A north–south meridian structured a regional symbolic landscape (Lekson 1999b), or so

it seems. Blue Mesa–Ridges Basin was due north of Chaco Canyon, with its Basketmaker III megasites Shabik'eschee and 29 SJ 423 (chapter 3). The Blue Mesa–Ridges Basin complex stretches about 10 kilometers east to west. At Chaco Canyon, 10 kilometers is approximately the east-to-west distance from Shabik'eschee to Pueblo Bonito. Blue Mesa–Ridges Basin, the largest known Pueblo I site, was almost directly north of Chaco Canyon. Sacred Ridge, specifically, was due north of Hungo Pavi.

This is the first in a series of four notes about the Chaco Meridian. The others are in chapter 5, note 136; in chapter 6, note 54; and in chapter 7, note 207. I've relegated the argument to notes because the meridian is not central to the argument I am making and the political history I tell in chapter 8. But *it's there.*

173. Wilshusen and Van Dyke 2006:216.

174. This version of Pueblo I is my spin on personal communications with and research by Richard Wilshusen and Jason Chuipka.

175. Wilshusen 1999b; Wilshusen and Ortman 1999; Wilshusen and Van Dyke 2006.

176. Smith 1990.

177. Kidder 1927:491.

178. For example, Wilshusen 1989.

179. Gregson Schachner, commenting on McPhee Village and Dolores, observed, "In some sense, oversized pitstructures are regular domestic pitstructures writ large, having the same shape and structural layout…as smaller pitstructures, but including very formalized features…rarely or less frequently found in other types of pitstructures" (Schachner 2001:180–81). Indeed. In my view, oversized pit structures at McPhee (and elsewhere) represent attempts by individuals or families to co-opt communal rituals previously (and subsequently) housed in Great Kivas.

180. "When is a kiva?" was simply an exercise in pattern recognition. To get to the processual heart of the problem, the question became the pit house to pueblo transition: *How* did kivas arise in Pueblo I? We accepted that Pueblo I Indians had their kivas—those pit structures out in front of the pueblo. With the kiva removed from domestic architecture, the issue became why they left pit houses and moved upstairs into pueblos. So when is a *pueblo*? Archaeologists wrote books and articles about the pit house to pueblo transition; graduate students were quizzed about it on exams. That transition (we thought) happened at the time the first kivas appeared, so it was somehow wrapped up in the kiva business, in Pueblo I (hence the "I"—the first pueblos). In Basketmaker III, Anasazi lived in pit houses. By Pueblo II, they lived in pueblos. Of course, there were plenty of *pit structures* at Pueblo II (and III) sites, but we all knew those were kivas—right?

I disagreed. I thought Anasazi gave up on pit houses only at the beginning of Pueblo IV, around 1300. Without getting into all the details (Lekson 1988, 1989; cf. Adler 1993; Lipe and Hegmon 1989; Ware 2002a), let's cut to the chase: there was no pit-house-to-pueblo transition in Pueblo I because all those Pueblo I, II, and III pit structures were not kivas—*they were pit houses.* People were still living in them. They were also living in pueblos (the aboveground rooms), because kiva and pueblo were—together—elements of one house, differentiated spaces like our kitchens, bedrooms, and parlors. Anasazi homes (and especially the traditional pit house) hosted household ritual and ceremony, variably expressed in architecture. That's true of folk architecture everywhere. Consider the Navajo hogan, the traditional house, frequently the focus of very elaborate ritual—but still a family home. Pueblo I pit houses had sipapus, but that did not make them kivas, if by *kiva* we mean the ritual structures sitting in the plazas of Rio Grande pueblos today. In the Rio Grande, each village has one or two kivas; in Pueblo I, II, and III, each *family* had one. Pueblo I kivas and modern kivas simply cannot be the same thing.

If I had to pick a single architectural form that typified Anasazi, it wouldn't be Pueblo Bonito. It would be a pit house. Anasazi lived in pit houses for five centuries before Pueblo I and continued to live in newer, better, and improved pit houses right through Pueblo III, even after they added a few storerooms to the rear (Pueblo I) and after those storage rooms became larger and more formal (Pueblo II and III). Just as the pueblo part of the package from 500 to 1300 became better built and increasingly formal, so too did the attached pit house! Many archaeologists accept the received version of a pit house to kiva transition in Pueblo I yet still use the number of kivas at Pueblo II and Pueblo III ruins as an index of population, with each kiva equaling one household (e.g., Rohn 1983)!

In any event, the pit house to pueblo transition was framed as an independent local process in at least two-score studies, each focusing on a particular part of the Southwest, from the desert Mogollon to Mesa Verde. I myself once thought the change (in the Mimbres region) meant a phase shift in mobility, from high (Apache-like) to low (Hispanic farming village–like) (Lekson 2006b)—and I still like parts of that argument. But to treat the "transition" as a local ecological succession to a sort of climax architecture, repeated independently again and again in different valleys, unjustly downplays history and interconnection.

If *kiva* were simply archaeology jargon for a Pueblo I, II, or III pit house, this whole argument would not matter. But *kiva* is a powerful term, automatically invoking ceremony and ritual. A few examples: Ben Nelson (1995), in an otherwise admirable comparison of Chaco and La Quemada, follows convention and assumes that Pueblo I and II "kivas" at Chaco were kivas. Chaco outscored the northern Mesoamerican city in the most measurable indices of "complexity," yet Chaco *could not have been* hierarchical: "The symbolism associated with Chacoan kivas, as known ethnographically, is linked to collaboration and consultation, whereas that of the La Quemada temple/ballcourt/pyramid complex is related to hierarchical structure and repression" (Nelson 1995:615). Feinman, Lightfoot, and Upham (2000:465) make the same error, suggesting that Pueblo I and II "kivas" indicate "increasingly more corporate-oriented organizations after A.D. 700." Fish and Fish (2000c), who accept the old view of Pueblo I kivas, cite my initial anti-kiva article to support the statement "Archaeologists cannot agree on criteria that define kivas, yet they share remarkable consensus on what to call a kiva." Consensus? More like a bad habit I think.

The notion that Pueblo I pit structures were kivas (in a modern ethnographic sense) projects a rather unusual feature of the present back into the distant past. Time does not work that way, from present to past. If we recognize that time flows from past to present, how might we think about features such as "roofed sipa-pus," oversized pit structures in the Dolores Valley? We might ask, how was a household ritual feature (for roofed sipapus were common in regular houses at Dolores sites such as Grass Mesa) appropriated by one powerful family at McPhee Village (where roofed sipapus were limited to the oversized pit structure)? And through eight tumultuous centuries (chapters 5, 6, and 7), how was that feature reinterpreted and reconstituted in modern kivas that serve neither families nor elites but communities, clans, and sodalities?

Between Pueblo I and Pueblo III, there were epochal social and political reorganizations. After 1300, population crashed regionwide. After 1600, Pueblos were colonized, oppressed, reduced, and threatened with elimination. To imagine ritual continuities over that span may afford some of us comfort, in the twenty-first century, but it does little service to history. For those who wish to find the first kiva, I will suggest this: do not look at small round rooms in Pueblo I, Pueblo II, or Pueblo III sites, but rather at the large communal structures (Great Kivas), which appear at least as early as Shabik'eschee and may last, greatly changed, in the kivas of the modern Pueblos.

Indeed, Pueblo people never completely gave up pit houses. These continued to be built as emergency or pioneer architecture—for example, as temporary housing at a new village site, like the "soddies" of the Great Plains. Temporary pit houses continued in that role right through the early twentieth century.

181. Wilshusen and Ortman 1999.

182. LeBlanc 1999:119–152; Lekson 2002b.

183. Wilshusen and Ortman 1999.

184. Lipe, Morris, and Kohler 1988. The distinctive "street" or "row house" layout continued at several very large Pueblo II towns (Skunk Springs; chapter 5) and Pueblo II–III towns (Yellow Jacket; chapter 6). Streets also characterized several nineteenth-century pueblos, both east and west, and they are probably not a Spanish introduction.

185. This describes Grass Mesa in the Periman Subphase. The Great Kiva was junked partway through the village's life, an "oversized pit structure" appeared in the later Grass Mesa Subphase, and the site's final days were strange indeed: about one hundred "pocket pit houses" appeared rather suddenly in between existing features, followed by a final, flaming conflagration (Lipe, Morris, and Kohler 1988; Wilshusen and Ortman 1999). There's a story there if someone wants to tell it.

186. Lipe, Morris, and Kohler 1988.

187. Wilshusen and Van Dyke 2006; Windes 2007; Windes and Ford 1996.

188. Potluck in the proto-kiva? Feasting, to be sure, but who's serving whom? Evidence for feasting in the McPhee Big House could be interpreted as community potluck (Blinman 1989), as the Big House helping itself to other people's cooking, or both.

189. Wilshusen and Ortman 1999:391.

190. Kane 1989; Kohler 1993; Wilshusen and Van Dyke 2006.

Chapter 5

1. Marshall et al. 1979.

2. Powers, Gillespie, and Lekson 1983.

3. Wilcox and Sternberg 1983.

4. Crossley 2008:1–10.

5. Gladwin et al. 1938.

6. Haury 1936.

7. Kelley 1978.

8. Decades ago, Snaketown was designated an NPS unit, but local politics keep it closed. The recent declaration of the Agua Fria National Monument was driven in part by its ruins and petroglyphs, but even more by its scenery. Other Hohokam sites are preserved in state and local parks, such as Pueblo Grande and Mesa Grande in Phoenix and Fort Lowell Park in Tucson.

9. Geib 1996.

10. Smith 1985.

11. Mathien 2005.

12. Haury 1989.

13. Reid and Whittlesey 2005a.

14. Mills, Herr, and Van Keuren 1999.

15. Haury 1976:3.

16. Haury 1976:fig. 3.2.

17. For example, Abbott forthcoming; Crown 1991a; Wilcox 1991c, 1999a.

18. Haury 1976:355.

19. How are we to deal with Emil Haury's aesthetic judgments? Anthropological archaeology can't handle that kind of thing. Haury was almost apologetic, offering his opinions on Hohokam art as if expecting ridicule. But we lose a lot if we ignore Dr. Haury. He was a very smart man, and he was on to something. Aesthetic judgments color our thinking: why are we so impressed with Chaco masonry? It's nothing on Mitla. Why our passionate interest in Mimbres black-on-white? It was no better made than and was less widely traded than Red Mesa black-on-white. No matter how scientific we hope to be, aesthetics matter. So we might as well get them out in the open. Perhaps if we partied more with Classical archaeologists and the people over in art history, we would be more comfortable with those kinds of insights, which are quite valuable.

20. Wasley and Johnson 1965.

21. Taylor didn't like the way American prehistorians did history. He was particularly critical of Kidder, who no longer worked in the Southwest but hovered as an éminence grise over the region. (Kidder published his last major Pecos report in 1958. Yale University Press republished his *Introduction to the Study of Southwestern Archaeology* in 1962.) Taylor took Kidder to task for (what Taylor saw as) empty time-space systematics (culture history), without historical meat or anthropological content: "The influence of A. V. Kidder upon archaeological research in the Americas has been, and is now, of the greatest proportions," Taylor acknowledged (1948:46), setting up his target. But "when Kidder writes theory he often talks historiography and anthropology [but] when he directs fieldwork and publishes reports, he talks comparative chronicle" (Taylor 1948:67). Taylor wanted archaeology to be anthropology, with a strong historical component, and southwestern archaeology, in his opinion, was not getting that job done. Chaco and Mimbres came under Taylor's microscope as case studies, but Hohokam did not register in his *Study of Archaeology*.

22. Binford 1983.

23. In the 1970s, Glyn Daniel, in *A Hundred and Fifty Years of Archaeology*, summarized the Old World's bemused view of New Archaeology (my thanks to Jeffrey Boyer at the Museum of New Mexico for directing my attention to this charming quote):

> This new movement of the 1960s needs to be absorbed into standard thought and work: at the present moment [1976] it is, especially for non-American workers, bedeviled by jargon and by people who, apparently unable to speak and write in clear English, use such phrases as "the logico-deductive-evolutionary systems paradigm." We must never forget that these "new" American methods and concepts are developed in the study of the most unrewarding material: no steps were taken to the establishment of a higher culture or civilization in North America and there were no incentives to persuade students of North American Archaeology that they were dealing with events in the main stream of history. (Daniel 1976:372)

As I read this passage, our British cousins thought we were bored to tears by savage Indians and had turned to the consolations of theory. The strongest theory at that time was science, so we donned lab coats, grabbed clipboards, and spoke in logico-deductive tongues. Daniel's complaint was a bit rude, but I fear there was some truth in it.

24. The treatment of the last age's great men and women was one of several reasons I was never fond of New Archaeology. For me, a key document discrediting New Archaeology was Paul Martin's public renunciation of his career, published in *American Antiquity* and titled "The Revolution in Archaeology" (1971). Martin's was a

long, distinguished, and remarkably useful career. His first job, while he was still in graduate school, was state archaeologist of Colorado. After attending the first Pecos conference, he began a field program excavating Pueblo I sites and Chaco outliers in southwestern Colorado. He moved to the Mogollon uplands in 1939. His work, along with Haury's, was fundamental for Mogollon archaeology. He began his fieldwork in southwestern New Mexico. In 1956 he moved west to the Vernon area of upland Arizona, where he continued field research until his death early in 1974. At Vernon, he trained students who would become famous New Archaeologists.

In "The Revolution in Archaeology," he turned his back on "a 35-year professional investment," dismissing previous American archaeology and his own remarkable contributions to the Southwest as "at best, a stunted history…and, at worst, a kind of stamp-collecting" (Martin 1971:2). He rejected his past and embraced New Archaeology with the passion of a religious convert.

Perhaps New Archaeology saved Paul Martin's soul, but at the time, I thought the article sad and depressing. The man had done seminal work in the Anasazi and Mogollon regions; the first site reports I ever read were his, on the work around Reserve, New Mexico. Those reports provided the best information on Mogollon then available. I was not then, nor am I now, a paragon of respect for my elders, but I knew a bad thing when I saw it. When I read "The Revolution in Archaeology," I decided that New Archaeology was not a bandwagon on which I would jump.

New Archaeology offered revolutionary ideas, but a cynic might say that it was driven at least in part by boomer demography as much as philosophy of science. By the early 1960s, the first wave of boomers was coming of age, and too many perhaps got PhDs. They wanted professorships. Youth will be served: young scholars levered out deadwood culture historians by declaring the old ideas invalid, decayed, irrelevant. Amid all the careerism, the intellectual issues were of course real. The merits of New Archaeology were important, to be sure, but perhaps not worth the costs—for example, Paul Martin's public humiliation.

25. Di Peso 1974.

26. Di Peso, Rinaldo, and Fenner (eds.) 1974.

27. Binford 1962.

28. Plog 1974:8.

29. Binford, in "A Consideration of Archaeological Research Design" (1964), insisted that archaeologists should study regions, not just sites, because sites were adaptations to local ecologies. Okay—but how big was a region exactly? For that particular article, Binford's region was a bit larger than the Carlyle Reservoir in southern Illinois—a creek's watershed—the CRM project on which he was then engaged. The accepted scale for New Archaeology soon became the "drainage" or small watershed, about as much of a valley as a small dam might flood. Not too big, not too small, but just right for a dissertation (and, conveniently, about the size of many early CRM projects).

30. See Anthony 1990.

31. Euler and Gumerman 1978; Gumerman 1971; Judge 1981.

32. SARG (Southwest Anthropological Research Group) was an admirable attempt to escape the confines of single-scholar research. But SARG was not building large-scale, regional knowledge cumulatively—that is, by adding together information from many different research areas. It was testing theory with multiple, separate cases. Each SARG research area was a natural laboratory, and, as we shall see (chapter 6), the SARG surveys were multiple evaluations of the same hypotheses. Each area was considered sufficient for asking and answering questions independently.

My thesis project, a survey of a 10-mile segment of the Gila River, was SARG-like in scale. It was framed on New Archaeology scales (that is, convenient scales for a thesis) and completed in the mid-1970s, yet I doubt it would qualify as New Archaeology. I originally included a chapter highly critical of the new program's ahistoricity. I valued history highly, and I hated to see it go. My adviser (with my best interests in mind, I'm sure) threw out my New Archaeology critique. Probably just as well.

33. For example, Rohn's (1977) treatment of Farview at Mesa Verde.

34. Smith and Berdan 2003b:table 1.1. Nothing in North America would ever re-create or surpass Teotihuacán, although some cities would try (Carrasco, Jones, and Sessions 2000). Later Native histories revered Tollan and the Toltecs, a legendary city and people, great in trade, politics, and the arts; "re-creating the former glory of Tollan" was an Aztec obsession (Davies 1987:289). Jiménez Moreno, in the 1940s, placed Tollan and the Toltecs at Tula, and that was the accepted orthodoxy. But surely mythical Tollan at least in part also reflected the earlier and much greater Teotihuacán (Carrasco, Jones, and Sessions 2000).

35. For example, Pollard 2003a, 2003b; Townsend 1998.

36. Smith and Berdan 2003b:6–8.

37. Hassig 1992. *The Postclassic Mesoamerican World* (2003b), edited by Michael Smith and Francis Berdan, was my main source on the Post-Classic. The book is congenial to my views, in part because many of the con-

tributors are intrigued by world systems theory. I am not wedded to that particular approach, but I applaud its large scales and its openness to action at distance. Brockmann (2004) posits specific trade routes for the Early Post-Classic (that is, at and after 1000) in his reconstruction of Mesoamerican "trade under the sign of the feathered serpent."

38. Gerhard 1972.

39. M. Smith 2005.

40. Davies 1977 for the old Tula; Diehl 1983 and Guadalupe Mastache, Cobean, and Healan 2002 for the new. Was Tula the mythical Tollan? Generations of scholars before Jiménez Moreno identified Teotihuacán as fabulous Tollan, and a few modern scholars are cautiously reviving that idea, recognizing the conflation of time and space in myth and history (e.g., Boone 2000; Florescano 2006). (Twixt Teo and Tula / Tula was tiny / Teo tremendous—as the poet said.) And Tula keeps getting smaller and smaller. Tula, archaeologists now tell us, was the capital of a state but not the center of an empire (Smith and Berdan 2003a:25; Spence 2000). Tula's sphere of control is shrinking fast and may soon be reduced to an area smaller than the Southwest, perhaps smaller than Chaco's!

41. Jones 1995.

42. Chichén Itzá and Tula look alike. Both have big, important, monumental buildings that are almost identical. That simple fact, long recognized, forms a major theme in Post-Classic archaeology. Maya histories suggested that Chichén Itzá was founded by foreigners (the Itzá), who, logically enough, were identified by an earlier generation of archaeologists as the conquering Toltecs (e.g., Davies 1977; Diehl 1983:150–51; cf. Jones 1995). That dramatic reading has fallen from favor (Guadalupe Mastache, Cobean, and Healan 2002). But the remarkable architectural similarities remain, as Smith and Berdan cautiously remind us: "These two cities were clearly in contact with one another, but the nature of their interaction remains unclear" (2003b:4). Here's my point: Tula and Chichén Itzá were 1,125 kilometers apart.

43. Smith and Berdan 2003a:fig. 3.3.

44. McCafferty 2000:359.

45. Smith and Berdan 2003b.

46. Turner and Turner 1999.

47. Di Peso 1974; Kelley and Kelley 1974.

48. For example, Diehl 1983:152–53; Di Peso 1974.

49. Nelson 1997.

50. Hayes 1981; Turner and Turner 1999.

51. For an excellent review, see Nelson 2006.

52. The distances are daunting: 2,000 kilometers separate Chaco and Tula. There were states and cities between (and long stretches of simpler societies), of course, but 2,000 kilometers is still a long way to go, even with way stations and caravanserais. Recall that Tula and Chichén Itzá interacted in architecturally dramatic ways at distances of 1,125 kilometers. Swinging that radius of 1,125 kilometers north from Tula, it very nearly reaches modern Ciudad Chihuahua, at the southernmost edge of the greater Southwest. Several centuries later, northern Chihuahua would become the Southwest's center of gravity, closely connected to later Post-Classic polities (chapter 7).

53. Smith and Berdan 2003b:4.

54. Williams 2003.

55. Pollard 2003a.

56. Spence 2000:259. My main sources are Foster (1999); Kelley (2000); Mountjoy (1998, 2000, 2001); Sauer and Brand (1932); and Williams (2003). The Aztatlan horizon (not to be confused with the Aztecs' Aztlan, chapter 8; Wisconsin's Aztalan; or Phoenix's Azatlan, this chapter) seems to have had close ties to Cholula in central Mexico, whose influence "may have been in part religious, in part military, and in part mercantile" (Williams 2003:"Epiclassic"). Mountjoy provides this summary:

> The Aztatlan tradition was a widespread and relatively uniform cultural expansion over a considerable part of the west Mexican coast...[and] the highest development of Mesoamerican culture ever achieved in some areas of west Mexico. It is likely that at least one ceremonial/civic center of the Aztatlan tradition was established near the center of every large coastal river valley between Tomatlan, Jalisco, and the northern border of Sinaloa, as well as in strategic locations along routes of communication and commerce in many highland areas. (Mountjoy 2000:95)

57. Foster 1999; Garnot and Peschard F. 1995; Kelley 1986, 2000; Mountjoy 2000.

58. For example, Anawalt 1998; Edwards 1965, 1978.

59. Hosler 1988, 1994, 2003; see also Evans and Meggars 1966. This suggestion is supported by the isolated occurrence in West Mexico of the painted jay (*Cyanocorax dickeyi*), whose closest relation is the white-tailed jay,

an Ecuadorian species—presumably carried as supercargo on coastal vessels (Anawalt 1998:244; but I have recently learned that this interpretation may not survive genetic analysis).

60. West coastal maritime trade paralleled the much better known eastern coastal trade along the Gulf of Mexico and around the Yucatán (of which, more below). The archaeological world seems more comfortable with foot traffic than with marine trade, even if direct evidence on the ground is almost as evanescent as flotsam on the water. By land or by sea, little hard evidence remains. New World long-distance trade is *assumed* to be land based, even in the absence of roads, way stations, or caravanserais—no hard evidence of long-distance land travel beyond the inescapable facts of "exotic" objects out of place. By sea, we of course would not find a thousand-year-old wake or trail of jetsam marking an ancient boat's passage. Why accept one and not the other? A logical conundrum that reflects, I think, our flawed assumptions about the social developments of the ancient people we study (chapter 8): boats were somehow beyond them. They had them, even if we can't dig them up. Without documents, would archaeology ever know of Coronado's fleet, which reached the mouth of the Colorado? Several generations of archaeologists have speculated on the land routes (e.g., Flint and Flint 2003, 2005), but the sea remains beyond our ken.

Coastal trade was almost certainly a major factor in the story. The Post-Classic capital of Tututepec, in coastal Oaxaca, was a port of entry for southwestern turquoise, which was then crafted by lapidaries in the Mixteca Alta and traded to the Mesa Central and the Maya region (Michael Smith 2003:125).

Farther up the coast, this period saw the sudden rise of social complexity among the Chumash of southern California, contemporaries of Chaco, Cahokia, and the post-Aztatlan polities. Coincidence? California prehistory is generally understood as an isolated phenomenon (e.g., Arnold 2004; Arnold, Walsh, and Hollimon 2004; Erlandson and Jones 2003), despite possible pepperings of errant Polynesians (Jones and Klar 2005). I suspect that California archaeology—like southwestern archaeology—could benefit from a repositioning within the larger context of ancient North America.

I cannot refrain from mentioning the coastal, hopscotch distribution of earliest maize (Blake 2006:fig. 4-1). Maize appears first in the Rio Balsas region of Guerrero, then in the Southwest. Then maize appears more or less at the same time in isolated areas of northeastern Mexico, the middle Mississippi Valley, Ecuador, northern Chile, and southern Chile. That distribution may well be the result of uneven archaeological attention or the vagaries of preservation, but it's certainly provocative. I suspect that Pacific and Gulf coastal communications went deep into antiquity.

61. Notably more Mesoamerican objects, architecture, and ideas reached Colonial Period Hohokam (chapter 4) than reached the Plateau of that time (Doyel 1991b; Nelson 1986; Vargas 1995).

Routes from Anasazi and Mogollon to Aztatlan may have been direct, without (or around) Hohokam. Trade routes over the mountains and into the Pueblo Southwest have been suggested via the "Topia Gate" in Durango (Kelley 2000) and on a more northerly route due north from the area of Culiacán (Lekson 1999b). Culiacán was largely Late Post-Classic (chapter 7) and in fact was the principal city of the north coast when the Spanish arrived. It was the northernmost Mesoamerican city during Pueblo IV and V and the launching point for conquistadors into New Mexico.

We will revisit those linkages in chapter 7; they become clearer after 1200 (Riley 2005; Smith and Berdan (eds.) 2003). Smith and Berdan, considering "Mesoamerica and the American Southwest," note that eleventh-century, Early Post-Classic "patterns of interaction set the stage for continued exchange between Mesoamerican peoples and their distant neighbors during the Middle and Late Postclassic periods" (2003a:23).

62. To us, the obvious route from West Mexico to the Southwest ran northwest, through the string of Aztatlan cities on the Pacific and then over the flat coastal plain to the Tucson Basin and points north. Many scholars favor such a route, following Carl Sauer's seminal *Road to Cibola*. Sauer was a great historical geographer, unjustly overlooked by archaeologists. But, in my opinion, *Road to Cibola* began with a flawed premise: he assumed that Native routes were preserved in later Spanish roads because "the requirements of a man were the same as those of a horse" (Sauer 1932:1). In fact, Spanish conquistador armies—with cavalry, wagons, and herds of animals—faced very different transportation problems than did Native tumpline economies. Native routes might follow rivers or valleys, but many went straight up grades that precluded European horses and carts. Hand- and toeholds went straight up cliffs; steep (sometimes nearly vertical) Chacoan stairways cut the faces of mesas. The only way a horse goes up those Native routes is in pieces. When Carl Lumholtz explored the Sierra Madre, his guides proposed to follow "el camino de los antiguos" straight up and down alarmingly steep slopes. He (and his horse) rebelled against "the Mexican method of going uphill as straight as possible," and he made his guides cut new "zigzag" trails more suitable for (European) man and horse (Lumholtz 1902:33).

63. Bradley 1993, 2000; Teague 1998; Vargas 1995.

64. Estimates vary. Fowler (1997:185) thinks big at thirty thousand. Milner (1998:123) works very hard to

keep it small, "in the low thousands." Pauketat (2004:106) offers a reasonable estimate of ten to fifteen thousand, which I accept. The archaeologically savvy reader will not be surprised to learn that Timothy Pauketat (1994, 2004, 2007) is my main resource on Cahokia. His worldview and mine are for the most part in focus, with only slight parallax. Other important sources and inspirations include Emerson and Lewis 1991; Hall 2006; Kehoe 1998; Pauketat and Emerson 1997; Peregrine 1992; and, honored in the breach, Milner 1998.

New varieties of corn, or new appreciations of corn, made it possible: "During the Lohman [Phase], the crop was an important part of the diet, but was not a preferred foodstuff and appeared to be without ritual meaning. By the Stirling [Phase], the crop was fully absorbed into the culture, ritually as well as dietarily, as shown by the apparent importance of maize surplus as an elite gift and as a subject of iconographic representation" (Reber 2006:245).

65. Fowler et al. 1999.

66. Pauketat 2004.

67. Pauketat 2004:47–66; Smith 1990.

68. Trevelyan 2004.

69. Kozuch 2002.

70. For example, White 2005.

71. Reviewed in Goldstein 1991; Goldstein and Richards 1991.

72. See Brown 1996; Emerson et al. 2003.

73. Spiro is altogether fascinating (e.g., Brown 1996). This westernmost Mississippian center rivaled Paquimé (its southwestern contemporary) for sheer masses of interesting stuff. Both sites are justly famous for astonishing quantities of remarkable artifacts, many of distant origin. In addition to remarkable artifacts from Cahokia (Emerson et al. 2003), Spiro produced tens of thousands of shell beads from California (obtained via the Southwest?) (Kozuch 2002) and a blade of "Pachuca" obsidian from central Mexico (Barker et al. 2002). Its engraved shell motifs (Phillips and Brown 1978) have been compared with Huastecan designs with a predictable range of conclusions, pro and con. Parallels between Spiro and Paquimé are worth pursuing: both were large and late, both were at the edges of their respective regions, and both were filled with exotic, fabulous artifacts. Ports of trade?

Other Pachuca obsidian is known from the Southwest and the southern Plains, but it is routinely dismissed as probably historic (that is, brought by Native Mexican allies of Spanish conquistadors). There may be something in that, but that's also an easy out. The Spiro find shows that at least some of the other Mexican blades may be prehistoric. We have at the University of Colorado Museum a photograph taken many years ago of an obsidian prismatic blade, clearly a Mesoamerican piece, reportedly found by a pot hunter below the floor of a Mimbres Phase site in southwestern New Mexico. We have only the photograph; the object itself has vanished from a private collection in Silver City, New Mexico.

74. Of course, Macon Plateau's provenance is debated (Hally 1994, especially Williams; Hally and Rudolph 1986).

75. Southeastern and Mississippian archaeologies are far less open to suggestions of Mesoamerican "contacts" than is southwestern archaeology (Lekson and Peregrine 2004; and with a few short-lived exceptions, Griffin 1966; Wicke 1965). George Milner, in the best recent archaeological review of the eastern United States, dismisses such contacts as "ill-informed and strangely persistent speculation" (Milner 2004:162–63). Milner's is the prevailing view. Yet, looking from the Southwest, Cahokia looks far more like a Mesoamerican city than does any site in the Southwest. If one were to point at a Mesoamerican knockoff in North America, it would not be Chaco or Pueblo Bonito; it would be Cahokia.

I note with admiration the few brave Southeasternists looking toward Mesoamerica (e.g., Hall 2006; Kehoe 1998, 1999, 2005; White 2005; see also Bagatzky 1980) and the Mexican archaeologists looking right back (Davila Cabrera 2005; Zaragoza Ocaña 2005). The Huasteca, the extreme northeast of Mesoamerica, had a long and very interesting prehistory, beginning far back in the Pre-Classic, but the region came into its own during the Post-Classic. El Tajin is famous, but of more relevance here is a less well-known site, Tantoc, just west of Tampico. Tantoc was "la ciudad mas importante del noreste de Mexico" (Davila and Zaragoza 2002:66). Its great earthen (not masonry) pyramids recall the Mississippi Valley, and Davila and Zaragoza suggest a link between the two:

> Después de un prologado estancamiento durante el Clásico, floreció en el Epiclasico y el Posclasico Temprano, cuando se construyeron los basamentos colosales, distintivos de Tantoc de hoy en día...sin embargo, estos rasgos son comunes a las culturas llamadas Mound Builders del Sureste de Estados Unidos, principalmente de la región del Mississippi. En aquella época, esta estaba relacionada con la zona arquelógica llamada Cahokia, en Illinois, y con otras del Sureste de Norteamerica. (Davila and Zaragoza 2002:69)

The distances are indeed impressive. It is almost 1,500 kilometers, measured along the "Gilford Corridor" along the Texas coast, from Tampico to the Mississippi River and another 1,000 kilometers inland to Cahokia. A long way to walk. But the first 1,500 kilometers might have been by sea, and the rest by river. Evidence for circum-Caribbean and circum-Gulf maritime trade is much stronger than that of the Pacific coast. The Maya were great coastal navigators. Columbus was the first European to meet a Maya commercial "canoe" (Blom 1932); the ancient coastal commerce he observed around the Yucatán Peninsula may well have extended up the Gulf to Tampico and beyond. And Mississippian boat transport on rivers is widely attested.

Did people from Tantoc march up to Cahokia and show the locals how to stack dirt? Probably not—people around Cahokia already knew how to pile dirt in powerful ways. Tantoc and Cahokia and Lilbourn and Lake George and Emerald should all be considered together to truly understand the ancient history of North America. See Lekson and Peregrine 2004; Peregrine and Lekson 2006; and White 2005, among others.

A final observation: A major migratory bird flyway runs directly from the Yucatán to the Mississippi River valley and back again. For thousands of years, Native people observed annual migrations of millions of birds, north to south and south to north. That surely would have made an impression—there was land to the south, land to the north. It would not be astonishing if some bright young people (or crabby old people) at either end of the flyway had followed the birds. Indeed, we should expect it. Flyways are not "evidence," but they are as much a part of the effective environment as droughts or currents.

76. The Sedentary Period is nominally two centuries in length—900/950 to 1150—but it may have run a shorter span. Wallace (1995) argues that the stylistic shift that marks its beginning occurred as late as 1020. Doyel argues that the major disruptions and dislocations—depopulations at Snaketown and Grewe, for example—began about 1075, and those signaled the end of the Sedentary Period. If we use Wallace's dates as a starting point and Doyel's as an endpoint, the Sedentary Period was indeed short: 1020 to 1075.

77. Doyel 1981, 1991a.

78. Doyel 2000b:224.

79. Abbott, Smith, and Gallaga 2007.

80. Gasser and Miksicek 1985.

81. Abbott, Smith, and Gallaga 2007; Doyel 1991b.

82. Abbott 2000; for a good short summary of lower Gila settlements, Ravesloot 2007. From 900 to 1150, the Salt River "entered a nearly five-century period of low variation and few high annual discharges that defined optimal conditions for irrigation agriculture." The Gila, however, was highly variable and almost unmanageable, with floods in the 1070s and 1080s—about the time Hohokam fell apart (Graybill et al. 2006:112).

The sky played other roles too, perhaps determinative. Citing Bruce Masse—a celestial prophet in these matters—David Doyel notes "that a series of portentous naked-eye celestial events, such as comets and solar eclipses followed by floods, occurred in the [Hohokam] region. Between A.D. 1062 and 1156, five solar eclipses occurred, with the A.D. 1076 being the first total solar eclipse in 279 years. Multiple supernova events between A.D. 1054 and 1074, the eruption of Sunset Crater in A.D. 1064, and the appearance of Halley's Comet in A.D. 1066 were other celestial spectacles that occurred in rapid succession. Add to this the probability of high stream flows in A.D. 1052, 1079 and 1087 and a pattern emerges of naked-eye celestial events followed by floods" (Doyel 2000b:233–34). (Doyel uses a widely accepted date for the eruption of Sunset Crater. We are today less certain, but it seems likely that the volcano erupted in the last quarter of the eleventh century or possibly in the very early twelfth century; see chapter 6.) Bruce Masse is definitely on to something; see also Masse and Soklaw (2005) and Masse and Espenak (2006). Comets and eclipses must have been terribly important. In the eleventh century and the early twelfth, the second assistant undersecretary for portents and omens was undoubtedly busy.

83. Abbott 2003:208.

84. Three of the largest sites in Canal System 2—Pueblo Grande, La Ciudad, and Las Colinas—were extensively excavated by CRM projects (Abbott 2003; Rice 1987; and Gregory 1988; Gregory et al. 1988, respectively), and many other, smaller sites have been investigated to varying degrees. Even though Canal System 2 sits today under the city of Phoenix, the history of its settlement has been reconstructed in some detail by Jerry Howard and others (Howard and Huckleberry 1991) and ably summarized by David Abbott (Abbott 2000:25–34). I rely on Abbott's account here. During the full-bore Colonial Period (chapter 4), the major canal systems were engineered, surveyed, excavated, and built. Population boomed, and canals were expanded (causes and effects I leave to others). By the Early Sedentary, Salt River canals irrigated a manmade breadbasket unparalleled in Native North America.

85. Masse 1981, 1991.

86. Ravesloot 2007.

87. Graybill 1989; Graybill et al. 2006.

88. Abbott 2000:31.

89. Marshall 2001; Wilcox and Sternberg 1983.

90. "That an inland people, several hundred kilometers from the source of supply, should have been so heavily committed to using imported marine materials, is paradoxical" (Haury 1976:319). The Hohokam shell industry developed during the Colonial Period (Doyel 1991b:table 1; McGuire 1993; McGuire and Howard 1987; Nelson 1991). The timing and trajectory of the Hohokam shell industry are of course matters of debate. Nelson concluded that "during the later Colonial and even more in the Sedentary Period, Hohokam shell procurement, production, and exchange seem to have exhibited intense expansion" (Nelson 1991:89), and they continued through the Classic. McGuire and Howard (1987) argue that major shell manufacture in the Phoenix Basin dates to the Middle to Late Sedentary and continued through the Classic, when it became centralized and controlled.

Bradley's 1993 analysis suggests a western shell network from Hohokam to Sinagua and over to Chaco and Aztec, and an eastern sphere from Casas Grandes through Mimbres to Pecos. Her analysis, while pioneering, is on some counts problematic: her cluster analysis groups Bonito, Arroyo, and Aztec closely but puts Chetro Ketl in a different world. Perhaps that's true, and if so, it's truly interesting. But I suspect the parsing may reflect clustering of broad formal typologies rather than specific characteristics and attributes, and the conflation of several centuries of changing depositional contexts.

91. Mitchell and Foster 2000.

92. More than three-quarters of all Hohokam copper bells came from three caches at Gatlin (thirty-five), Snaketown (twenty-eight), and Romo Ruin in the Tucson Basin (twenty-five) (Vargas 1995). These spanned the Hohokam world: Gatlin west, Snaketown north-central, and Romo Ruin south. Only a half-dozen bells were found at all other Sedentary Period sites. Were those three big caches necklaces? Regalia? Costumes? Stockpiles? Offerings? Whatever their purpose, those three contexts are remarkably different from those in which copper bells were found in the Chaco Anasazi and Mimbres Mogollon areas—a bell here, a bell there.

93. Craig 2000b, 2001a.

94. For example, Howard and Huckleberry 1991.

95. Nelson 1986; cf. Crown 1991b.

96. Abbott 2000.

97. Many archaeologists believe that Sedentary societies were only weakly hierarchical, at most (Doyel 1981, 1991a; Fish 1999; Hunt et al. 2005; Wilcox 1991c; but see Abbott 2003; Howard 1993). Given the complexities of Hohokam material culture and the scale of its irrigation systems, there should have been kings—or puffed-up rulers by some other name more acceptable to modern ears. The scale of Hohokam irrigation of course required centralized decision making, presumably bureaucratized into institutions and priesthoods (e.g., Howard 1993). We can also assume that there were local leaders and elite lineages, carried over from their Pioneer Period beginnings through the Colonial and into the Sedentary. But they were local or, more accurately, *localized* by the Colonial explosion and the larger institutions of the Hohokam Canon.

Many archaeologists interpret *Strombus* shell trumpets as possible symbols of leadership among the Hohokam (e.g., Bayman 2002). Much like copper bells, these were conspicuously concentrated at only a few sites in the Hohokam world, most notably Grewe and Casa Grande (actually one big site), at Chaco (Pueblo Bonito) in the Anasazi area, and at Paquimé in the Chihuahuan region. Individual trumpets have been found at scores of other, smaller sites; Paquimé leads in the heavyweight division with more than 180!

Regarding the absence of Hohokam high-status burials, I was fortunate recently to view collections from a truly remarkable Hohokam cremation burial from the Silverbell-Coachline site just north of Tucson, Arizona. The site itself was not a major Hohokam settlement, but the burial was astonishing, with an assemblage of associated objects that might turn a Chaco lord green with envy. Perhaps this is an elusive Hohokam prince. Analyses are ongoing at the Center for Desert Archaeology in Tucson. I am confident that, whatever the conclusions, the Silverbell burial will be seen by some not as a Hohokam prince but as a very holy man—perhaps a very, very, very holy man.

98. For example, Wilcox 1991c.

99. For example, Doyel 1991a.

100. Craig (ed.) 2001b.

101. Doyel forthcoming.

102. Craig 2001:47.

103. Abbott, Smith, and Gallaga 2007:471.

104. Elson and Clark 2007, forthcoming.

105. Doelle and Wallace 1991.

106. Doyel and Elson 1985.

107. Whittlesey 1997.

108. Doyel 2000c.

109. White 2004.

110. Haury 1976:286.

111. White 2004.

112. It would take another book (almost as long as this one) to present and evaluate competing interpretations of Chaco Canyon. I've done selective evaluations elsewhere (Lekson 1999b, Lekson [ed.] 2006a), but in those papers I did not pretend to summarize every idea that's out there, nor do I here. Books and essays that have had the most impact on my thinking—positive and negative—include Cameron and Toll 2001; Cordell, Judge, and Piper 2001; Crown and Judge 1991; Crown and Wills 2003; Doyel [1992] 2001; Fagan 2005; Kantner 2003, 2004; Mathien 2005; Neitzel 2003; Nelson 1995; Sebastian 1992; Sofaer 1999; Vivian 1989, 1990, 1996, 2005; Wilcox 1999a, 2004, 2005b; and Wills 2000. A good one that came after the final draft of this book was finished: Van Dyke 2007b.

Since the end of Chaco Project fieldwork in 1978, there has been little new data from Chaco itself: new tree-ring dates from beams exposed in the ruins (Windes and Ford 1996); some startling hydrology, with a dam and lake at the canyon's end (Force et al. 2002); and much rethinking of old data (Lekson [ed.] 2006; Neitzel 2003). As a member of the Chaco Project, I thought we'd seen the last excavations at the canyon for at least my lifetime, and probably well after I shuffle off the scene. I am surprised and delighted that a major new project, the Chaco Stratigraphy Project, directed by Chip Wills and Patricia Crown of the University of New Mexico, is obtaining a whole heap of hot new data from Pueblo Bonito(!) by reopening trenches dug in the 1920s by Neil Judd. This is a major project, and it will undoubtedly change much (or all?) of what we think about Chaco. Everything you read in this chapter (and elsewhere) about Chaco will probably require revision, but that's an *excellent* thing! It means that we've learned something. See http://www.unm.edu/~chaco/index.html.

113. Windes 2007; Wilshusen and Van Dyke 2006.

114. Lekson 2006a; Smith 2005.

115. For example, Agnew, Mercer, and Sopher 1984; Doxiadis 1968; Fletcher 1995; Rapoport 1977; Smith (ed.) 2003.

116. Trigger 2003a:120; see also Cowgill 2004:526–27; Monica Smith 2003.

117. Lekson 1984:272.

118. Benson et al. 2006:301.

119. Expanded interpretations of Chaco's cityscape and how it worked can be found in Fritz 1978; Lekson (ed.) 2006; Sofaer 1999; and Van Dyke 2007b. See also papers in Lekson 2007, especially by Stein and others.

120. Van Dyke 2007a.

121. We have known this since the 1970s: Fritz 1978; see also Sofaer 1999 and Stein et al. 2007. For an excellent recent treatment, see Van Dyke 2007b.

122. Waterworks and gardens at Chaco represented a large, complex system of gathering and storing rainwater (Vivian 1990; Vivian et al. 2006). Chaco is a famously poor place to farm, and Chacoans knew it. Perhaps Chaco was not using its precious water to raise crops better farmed elsewhere. "One of the common features [of New World palaces]…was the importance of amenities such as gardens and waterworks. Although clearly elements of pleasure and delight, such additions surely played a profound symbolic role as representative of the ruler's control over the physical environment and presumably his intimate link with divine powers" (Pillsbury and Evans 2004:2). As at Post-Classic elite architecture elsewhere, Chaco water was architectural. Together with Great Houses and monuments, the control of water at the center of the San Juan Basin could have inspired something like awe.

123. Fletcher 1995:117.

124. Bernardini 1999; Lekson 1984; Neitzel 2003; Stein and Lekson 1992; Windes 1984, 1987; cf. Vivian 1990, the most important dissenter in this matter.

125. Kantner 1996; Neitzel 2003; Sebastian 1992.

126. Lekson 2006c; see also Wilcox 2004. David Wilcox suggested that Chaco Great Houses were palaces long before I did, first in a Forest Service report (Wilcox 1993a) and again in a published version of that first paper (Wilcox 2004). In my Chaco palace paper (Lekson 2006), I neglected to cite Dave's ideas and contributions—despite the fact that I was at the conference and wrote an introduction to the 2004 book! Just getting old I guess, but that's no excuse. I sincerely regret my error. As in so many things, Dr. Wilcox was there long before I was.

127. And *palace* shifts our frame of reference out of the useless catchall *intermediate societies* (archaeology's

dustbin for ancient North Americans) and into more useful comparisons and milieus: the Mesoamerican Post-Classic and Mississippian. See chapter 8, note 29.

128. Nelson 2004.

129. For example, Christie and Sarro 2006; Evans and Pillsbury 2004.

130. Webster and Inomata 2004:149.

131. Akins 2003. Very important people lived in Great Houses. Pueblo Bonito produced many high-status burials, particularly very rich crypt burials of two middle-aged men (Akins 2001, 2003; Akins and Schelberg 1984). I interpret the mass of human remains piled over the crypts as "retainers," but of course other inter-pretations are possible. These two men were buried in the mid-eleventh century, deep in much earlier rooms of the original, early-tenth-century "Old Bonito." Watch them closely: they sometimes vanish in Chacoan debates, dismissed (for example) as "a few unusual burials" (Mills 2002:66) or "two anomalous burials" (Van Dyke 2003:183). Heitman and Plog (2005:90) rightly decry "the extent to which these mortuary complexes are oversimplified and ignored." There are as many high-status burials from Chaco as from Cahokia, and unlike that great city on the Mississippi, Chaco has unambiguous, monumental elite residences: Great Houses!

Glycimeris shell bracelets/armlets, identified as "badges" of Hohokam identity and possibly as status markers of Basketmaker would-be elites (chapter 3, note 86), reappear on the Colorado Plateau in the anomalous burials of Pueblo Bonito. Twenty-six perfect bracelets and fifteen fragments were found near the right knee of Burial 14, associated with a *Strombus* shell trumpet (which many interpret as a marker of leadership in the Hohokam region). I thank Zonna Barnes for this information.

132. Lekson 1984, 2006c.

133. The Southwest was probably linked more closely to West Mexico than to central Mesoamerica. Ben Nelson reviews "Elite Residences in West Mexico":

> Some observable regularities include the following: (a) palaces may exist in the absence of urban development; (b) palaces were uncommon in West Mexico and probably were an exclusively [Late] Postclassic phenomenon; (c) at least as early as the Early Classic…the Elite built "proto-palaces"…(d) although operating within distinct local traditions, the architects of elite residences made use of common canons to connote power; (e) the architecture of social power often encompassed not only built space but the entire landscape [and he adds on page 75, "No West Mexican elite residence can be fully understood without following out its causeway connections, panoptical vistas, and astronomical alignments"]; (f) palaces per se tended to occur in areas of West Mexico that had contact with the Basin of Mexico and had developed economic, as well as ideational, bases of social power. (Nelson 2004:59)

Pueblo Bonito, Chetro Ketl, and their fellows fulfill those West Mexican palatial requirements. (I'm pretty sure that Chaco was a city, but for those who may not agree, perhaps Pueblo Bonito and Chetro Ketl "existed in the absence of urban development.") Chetro Ketl's colonnade (fig. 5.1) attempted to use formal "canons to connote power," and Great Houses surely existed as part of a much larger "landscape" of power, Chaco's cityscape.

Nelson himself goes on to apply curiously prescriptive presuppositions on what a palace should be and what it should do. Likely candidates are dismissed because their societies were not "the kind of setting in which palatial architecture was appropriate" (Nelson 2004:72). These words were written about West Mexico, but they summarize the same Procrustean logic used against elite residences and palaces in the Southwest (as in Nelson 1995).

Great House palaces are the strongest evidence for Chacoan lords and rulers. Their testimony seems over-whelming (to me; Lekson 2006c), yet there is stiff resistance (Vivian 1990; Mills 2002), as there was to earlier, calmer claims for Chacoan "chiefs," when that term was in vogue (e.g., Schelberg 1984). Recall Johnson's (1989) pronouncement, "Chaco data can support a basically egalitarian interpretation" (chapter 5). Essays reaching similar conclusions include those by respected arbiters such as Norman Yoffee (2001; Yoffee, Fish, and Milner 1999) and Colin Renfrew (2001). Linda Cordell and George Milner, in *Great Towns and Regional Polities* (1999:112), say: "There is little evidence that the large scale structures built in the Late Precolumbian Southwest were used as elite residences. The Great Houses of Chaco Canyon and Chacoan outliers were not palaces. They are most often considered examples of public architecture used for purposes other than, and in addition to, ordinary domestic tasks and were not restricted to a few high-status people and their immediate households." I disagree.

134. Corresponding to Anna Sofaer's 1999 lunar and solar: see note 136.

135. Judd 1964; Lekson 1984.

136. Orientation to the heavens and intervisibilities were basic to Great House architecture—recall West

Mexican "causeway connections, panoptical vistas, and astronomical alignments" (see n. 133). Intervisibilities mapped the city's communication and signaling (Fletcher 1995:117), but we can't be sure what messages were being sent or received.

I think that celestial orientations directly mirror ancient cosmology. We may never know the content of those cosmologies, but we can know them by their diverging alignments. I set great store by orientations of Great Houses, because they were not random. They were carefully patterned. The major Great Houses show two contrasting orientations, two cosmologies: a traditional southeast-facing orientation, aligned with the solstices, and a new north–south/east–west layout, aligned with the cardinal. (I rely heavily on Sofaer [1997]2007, 1999, tempered by questions raised by Malville 2007.)

What to call these alignments? Anna Sofaer and her colleagues first defined them at Chaco. My solstitial is her "lunar" (for lunar standstills), and my cardinal her "solar." I originally used her terms; solar and lunar make good theater and a great story. But I worry a bit about the lunar: solstice is about 60.4 degrees azimuth. Lunar majors were about 54.3; minors 67.1. Are proposed lunar alignments simply errors around intended solstice alignments? That is, might ancient errors measuring the solstice—a few degrees off either way—look to us like precise lunar major and minor standstills? These guys were working with naked eyes, not theodolites.

Precision (with any technology) comes from repeated measurements. Cardinals could be determined daily (even twice daily), measuring from the sun with a gnomon or by the stars. Solstices, of course, are on a yearly cycle. Lunar standstills happen over a much longer time, 18.6 years. We might expect decreasing precision in that order. I accept that my solstitial could in fact have been Sofaer's "lunar" or even a combination of solstice and lunar. For once, I will play it safe and use cardinal and solstitial. But my usage does nothing to diminish the important contributions of Sofaer and her colleagues (Sofaer [1997]2007, 1999).

The Anasazi world had a long-established north–south meridian axis, as old as Pueblo I and perhaps earlier (chapter 4, note 172). The cityscape of Chaco reflected that axis (Fritz 1978; Lekson 1999b), but Pueblo Alto appropriated a cosmological landscape alignment and incorporated it into palatial architecture, a personal or familial statement. Pueblo Alto itself was cardinal. It was sited directly on the north–south city axis (directly over an older monument; Windes 1987) and in some sense occupied and "controlled" that axis. The builders of Pueblo Alto claimed that previously abstract principle and aligned it to their purposes. I think this was a signal event in Chaco's history and the history of the ancient Southwest.

Chetro Ketl's and Pueblo Alto's notably differing orientations were both established about 1020 and marked two rival ideologies and perhaps purposes. I think Chaco was the scene of a cosmological tug-of-war, won by Pueblo Alto when its cardinality, and all it symbolized, was imposed over Pueblo Bonito's antique lines; the final construction at Pueblo Bonito was markedly cardinal. The remarkable north–south wall that bisects Bonito was built sometime after 1100. The orientation of that wall was so important that it ran over kiva roofs, requiring some terrifying engineering. A realignment of just a few degrees would have avoided that structural problem.

The orientations we see today from the cliffs are "as-builts": Pueblo Bonito, the oldest and most important building in the central canyon, began solstitial and ended cardinal. In Bonito's several rebuildings, unused foundations, and realignments, we can see cosmological arguments played out in bricks and mortar (Lekson 1984). Pueblo Bonito preserved its original alignment through the late eleventh century, but the last major construction was spectacularly cardinal: a precise north–south wall cuts across the plaza (suggesting moieties to some, but a political statement to me). The north–south wall at Pueblo Bonito has been described by one skeptical archaeoastronomer (who remains anonymous here) as "the only real ancient astronomy in Chaco Canyon."

Around 1100 Pueblo Alto and Pueblo Bonito aligned in architecture and, I think, politics. Chetro Ketl lost the struggle to control Chaco's cosmovision and continued to build, monumentally, in its traditional solstitial orientation. Cosmological and political struggles tore Chaco apart or at the very least contributed to its fall. When the time came to build a second capital (chapter 6), it was located due north at Aztec Ruins, honoring the meridian axis. But when the new city was actually built, it was laid out on solstitial principles (Fowler and Stein 2001). Was this Chetro Ketl's resurgence, a return to traditional cosmologies? Just as various additions to Pueblo Bonito were planned, initiated, overruled, and overbuilt (Lekson 1984; Stein, Ford, and Friedman 2003), interruptions and alternations from cardinal to solstitial may represent political arguments inscribed on symbolic landscapes.

137. Judge 1979.

138. Di Peso 1974.

139. Judge 1990.

140. I may be the last surviving believer in a redistributive food network in the San Juan Basin. Judge's original model was "tested" with pottery and lithics. Pots and rocks arrived in Chaco but apparently did not move

back out. Of course, redistribution was about *corn*, not about ceramics and lithics—a fact that was overlooked by most critics of the model. As it turns out, corn did move around the San Juan Basin—but again, apparently into Chaco and not back out (Benson et al. 2003). All these analyses focus on later Chaco. What's needed, of course, to test Judge's model, is an analysis of tenth- and early-eleventh-century corn, both at Chaco *and in the outliers*. I'm not holding my breath, nor should you. Right now I do not see any information developed since 1990 to confirm or deny early redistribution of corn at and through Chaco Canyon.

Intriguingly, Linda Manzanilla (1997) emphasizes that the importance of redistribution was not in "chief-doms" but in the early stages of urban societies—that is, the role of cities in emerging Mesoamerican polities. Were there Chaco parallels on very modest southwestern scales?

141. LeBlanc 1999; Lekson 2002b; but see Cole 2007.

142. Lewis Henry Morgan ([1881]1965) recognized Aztec Ruins—80 kilometers north of Chaco Canyon—as Chacoan. That is, Aztec Ruins was built in the style and on the scale of the huge Chaco Canyon Great Houses, a diagnosis confirmed by Earl Morris (1919–1928) (chapter 6). Aztec Ruins was pretty obvious. By the 1930s a number of much smaller Great House–like sites (only twenty or so rooms) had been found across the Plateau—on La Plata River (Morris 1939), at Lowry in southwestern Colorado (Martin 1936), at Chimney Rock near Pagosa Springs (J. J. Jeancon's excavations, summarized in Malville 2004), and—far to the south—at Village of the Great Kivas near Zuni (Roberts 1932). These sites were built, at least in part, in the style but not on the scale of the canyon. Early archaeologists typically explained smaller Great House–like sites as show-ing greater or lesser degrees of "Chacoan influence." But as the years passed, more and more small Great Houses popped up, clearly different from the local unit pueblos. Unit pueblo architecture varied from district to district, but the small Great Houses consistently showed the characteristic details of Pueblo Bonito and Chetro Ketl. Since mid-century, the total number of such sites has reached about two hundred over an area of up to 150,000 square kilometers (fig. 5.2) (Fowler and Stein 1992; Kantner and Kintigh 2006; Marshall et al. 1979; Powers, Gillespie, and Lekson 1983). Terminology suggested something more than vague influences: the small Great Houses were tagged outliers, with clear implications for their dependent relation to Chaco.

The term *outliers* was possibly unfortunate, perhaps prescient. As in most issues of archaeological interest, opinions vary on the closeness of the connection or even the disconnection of these sites to Chaco Canyon (e.g., Kantner and Kintigh 2006 versus Lekson 2006a). I think *outlier* is the right and proper term. I suggested the less-charged phrase *Chaco World* for the most recent evaluation of the matter (Kantner and Kintigh 2006), but in this book I extend Chaco's world to Tula and Cahokia, so that won't work. The terms *Chaco regional sys-tem* and *outliers* are cranky and old-fashioned, but so am I.

With the singular exceptions of Salmon and Aztec Ruins (chapter 6), none rivaled the huge Great Houses in and around Chaco Canyon; if you stacked up one hundred of the smallest outliers, they might make one Pueblo Bonito, with a bit left over.

Almost all outliers have a Great Kiva nearby, but that Great Kiva may or may not have been part of the Great House. It may have "belonged" to the community to which the Great House was central, continuing a long-standing Anasazi tradition. Many, probably most, outliers were associated with "roads" that some argue (Lekson 1999b, 2006a) were connected, symbolically or actually, to Chaco. Others argue otherwise (Kantner 2003; Roney 1992).

143. Sebastian 1992:152. Was the "regional system" economic, political, ritual, all of the above, none of the above? How did the "regional system" work exactly? I freely admit, I don't know. Scholars skeptical of Chaco regional aspirations (and they are legion) ask those questions pointedly (Kantner 2003; Neitzel 2000). When detailed answers are not forthcoming, absence of insight is taken as evidence of absence, and critics dismiss the empirical pattern itself. To me, this seems akin to demanding, upon initial discovery of a site, all the details of what happened there, and when details are not forthcoming, denying the site exists. We do have trial reconstructions of how the Chaco regional system might have worked (Lekson 1999b; Neitzel 2000; Wilcox 2004). I am not interested in exploring those models here. Rather, I am concerned with spatial scales and how they work for or against the perception of empirical patterns.

144. To explore questions of distance, I play with empirical data—what we actually see, on the ground—against archaeological perceptions—what we *think* about empirical data (fig. 5.12). What's out there, and what do archaeologists say about it?

Let's begin with Chimney Rock, a well-known outlier Great House with one of the most spectacular set-tings of any southwestern site (Eddy 1977; Malville 2004) (fig. 5.11). Chimney Rock, described in the title of a recent book as the "ultimate outlier" (Malville 2004), is the clearest, least ambiguous Chacoan Great House in the catalog: its Great House architecture contrasts remarkably with the local unit pueblo traditions of the Piedra Valley; it was spared the subsequent thirteenth-century reoccupations that obscured many Chacoan Great Houses in the northern San Juan; and it was clearly tied to Chaco through a visual communication system (smoke and mirrors) discovered by (then) high school student Katie Freeman (Freeman, Bliss, and Thompson 1996)—part of a much larger visual communication network originally recognized by Alden Hayes and Tom Windes (1975) and currently being researched by Ruth Van Dyke.

Chimney Rock was linked to Chaco via a single repeater station at Huerfano Peak, which is also visible from Farview House. Huerfano and Pueblo Alto are easily intervisible. The (probable) use of repeater stations makes this network a *system*—that is, a complicated arrangement that required cooperative or directed administration. I believe, but cannot currently demonstrate, that the visual communication system extended over the entire Chacoan region and very likely out to the 240-kilometer limits of the Chacoan world.

Nobody argues about Chimney Rock. It's an outlier, a *Chacoan* outlier, and the northeasternmost of the crew. At 140 kilometers from Chaco Canyon, Chimney Rock establishes a trial "radius" for Chaco's eleventh-century reach (fig. 5.12). (Please note: I am *not* claiming that Chaco's region was a perfect circle!) I projected Chimney Rock's radius to the west, and it neatly encompassed two other well-known Great Houses that I believe to be Chacoan: Farview House at Mesa Verde and White House at Canyon de Chelly (fig. 5.12). Compared with Chimney Rock, Farview and White House invite archaeological demurrals, but the vast majority of Chaco scholars agree (and we hold these truths to be self-evident) Farview House and White House are slam-dunk, lead-pipe-cinch outliers. These three sites—all about 140 to 150 kilometers from Chaco—offer a useful, empirically based scale for Chacoan regional dynamics. Extended south, 140–150 kilometers reaches Village of the Great Kivas at Zuni.

Of course, there were candidate Great Houses far beyond that radius. How far? Let's start in the better-known north and then work south. In the northern San Juan region, the Great House most distant from Chaco was Owen's Great House, near the head of Grand Gulch in Utah and approximately 240 kilometers from Chaco Canyon (fig. 5.12). The site also known as 42 SA 24584, discovered by Owen Severance and later recorded by Winston Hurst, is near the head of Grand Gulch in southeastern Utah. It includes a full suite of Great House features, including Great Kivas and roads, and dates from the Late Pueblo II to Early Pueblo III periods. That's as far out as anyone has ever claimed a Chacoan outlier. Striking a 240- to 250-kilometer arc catches all the would-be Great Houses and—intriguingly—cuts through a ruin near Reserve, New Mexico, approximately 245 kilometers from Chaco, that I and others believe to have been the southernmost candidate Great House: Aragon, now destroyed by a pot hunter's bulldozer. Aragon was first described by Walter Hough (1907:74):

> This ruin stands on the top of the ridge, upon a pyramidal base, which bears the traces of shaping, the sides of the ridge also having been graded.… The ruin from its elevated position may be seen from a long distance; when viewed from the southwest, it resembles a Mexican teocalli [pyramid].

From Hough's description and plates, Aragon was identified as a candidate outlier independently by Lekson (1999b) and LeBlanc (1989b). Another brief description in Schroeder and Wendorf (1954) notes a C-shaped pueblo of three stories, with eleventh- and twelfth-century ceramics, with a deep, round, masonry-walled Great Kiva. Photos in Hough show massive (perhaps core-and-veneer), carefully coursed walls at the pueblo and the Great Kiva. (The site was bulldozed in the 1970s.)

Those two concentric circles, or rather partial radii, are based more or less on data. I've come to think of 140–150 kilometers as the *inner circle* and 240–250 kilometers as the *outer limits* of Chaco's region (fig. 5.12). What do those terms mean, if anything? The inner-circle radius of 140–150 kilometers was arbitrary but archaeologically warranted: Chimney Rock is our surety that Chaco got at least that far. The outer limits at 240–250 kilometers could be excused as the twisted projections of a fevered imagination, yet Owen's Site is in almost every respect identical to outliers well within the 140-kilometer inner circle: Owen's is a cookie-cutter outlier, much like a hundred others. I think the 140- to 150-kilometer and 240- to 250-kilometer territorial limits are real.

Whatever it was, beyond that 240-kilometer radius (and perhaps within it) lie sites with which to define the gossamer, indefinite quality of "emulation." Much of the recent chatter about outliers revolves around "export" versus "emulation": were distant Great Houses Chaco colonies ("export"), or were they local yokels buying in ("emulation")? How to tell? If we seek really obvious potential emulators, I'd look for exceptional Chaco-era sites well beyond the limits of the most expansive interpretation of the Chacoan world (that is, more than 240 kilometers from Chaco)—sites that have large, massive, formal buildings, central to a community of relatively smaller, less formal, domestic structures (the "big bump" pattern of a Great House surrounded by a community of unit pueblos; Lekson 1991). That is, emulations might be seen in sites that are clearly beyond Chaco's political or economic reach but resemble it in functional patterns if not architectural details. In such places, local leaders took on the appearance, but not the obligations and entanglements, of Chacoan society.

Beyond the 240-kilometer radius, I think such sites occur in the Mimbres region (discussed in the text) and in the Fremont region, with sites such as Nawthis Village in east-central Utah, an unusually large, formal structure built of massive puddle adobe (Madsen 1989) that is remarkable in its Fremont context. A "big bump"? Another candidate, to the south, is Tla Kii (Haury 1985; contra Herr 2001 and Mills 2002)—not enormous but *something different* from contemporary settlements in its area. Unlike Woodrow Ruin (built of river cobbles) and Nawthis Village (adobe), Tla Kii has a few Chacoan details in wall construction, but all three represent "big bumps" among unit-pueblo-sized structures and, I suggest, all three are good places to begin to think about emulation.

If we learn how to use them, Woodrow Ruin and Nawthis (and perhaps Rio Grande sites such as the Bronze Trail Group; Wiseman and Darling 1986) can help us think about outliers, emulations, and interactions between Chaco Canyon and the middle San Juan. It's important to consider (absent bulk economies) the extent to which space does *not* structure society but society structures space. Of course, space and society are recursive and interacting, but we might first comprehend the nature (or at least the extent) of the Chacoan world and *then* attempt to understand its distances.

145. Malville 2004.

146. Dobyns 2002.

147. David Wilcox (e.g., 1999a, 2004), an early student of the question, offered estimates of distances and travel times for social interaction in southwestern regional systems. He initially proposed two measures: 11 miles (17.7 kilometers) for "daily intercourse between communities," which represents a round-trip of 22 miles (the distance a person can walk with a pack in a day), and 22 miles (35.4 kilometers) for a one-way day trip. At that pace, 140 kilometers represents a four-day walk, and 240 kilometers represents a seven-day walk. Wilcox interpreted these 11- and 22-mile distances in terms of social interaction, up to and including threats of force, and not long-distance economic interactions.

My analysis owes many debts to Wilcox's "macro-economies" (Wilcox 1991a, 1999a). Dr. Wilcox has been worrying about these matters longer than I. Our maps look superficially alike—there are only a few ways to draw circles—but we reach very different conclusions.

148. Lightfoot 1979.

149. For example, Sebastian 1992:88.

150. Drennan 1984:110.

151. Malville 2001:230. See also Santley and Alexander, who independently estimate an outer limit of 150 kilometers for Post-Classic "trafficking in bulky goods" (1992:44).

152. Recent chemical-sourcing research suggests that foodstuffs did indeed move about within Chaco's 150-kilometer inner circle (Benson et al. 2003, 2006), as did very large quantities of ceramics (Toll 2006) and construction timbers (Betancourt, Dean, and Hull 1986).

153. Chaco turquoise has a well-developed literature of its own (for a starting point, see Mathien 1997, 2005). Chaco's "control" of the mines is hypothetical but supported by a Chaco-esque "mining camp" near the mines (Wiseman and Darling 1986).

154. My views on Mimbres are my own and are not widely shared (Lekson 1989, 1990c, 1996b, 1999b, 2006b). For mainstream views, see Michelle Hegmon's (2002) excellent review "Recent Issues in the Archaeology of the Mimbres Region."

155. Anyon and LeBlanc 1984; Bradfield 1929; Cosgrove and Cosgrove 1932.

156. Because of its artistic, extremely valuable pottery, Mimbres attracted early archaeological attention (reviewed in Hegmon 2002; Lekson 2006b) and industrial-scale looting. Mimbres archaeology was essentially moribund after 1930, given up as a bad job, lost to looters. Interest revived with New Archaeology, which did not love art. Two major projects—the Mimbres Foundation (LeBlanc 1983) and the Upper Gila Project (Lekson 1990c)—salvaged scientific data from ravaged Mimbres sites. The successes of the Mimbres Foundation (e.g., Anyon and LeBlanc 1984, among many other publications) showed that Mimbres sites still had much to offer archaeology. Field research continued thereafter—steady, but at lower levels than Anasazi or Hohokam (or even upland Mogollon, for that matter). Three major research programs deserve particular mention. These are Harry Shafer's extensive excavations at the NAN Ranch Ruin (Shafer 2003), Darrell Creel's excavations at the very important Mimbres Valley site of Old Town (Creel 2006a), and the field program of Michelle Hegmon and Margaret Nelson in the eastern Mimbres area (e.g., Hegmon 2000; Nelson 1999; Nelson and Hegmon 2001).

157. The exception was Arthur Jelinek's University of Michigan Mimbres Area Survey, in the mid-1960s, the first of the new wave but with roots in the old school. The Mimbres Area Survey was by far the largest project (in geographic scale) in the Mimbres renaissance. A wide-ranging survey with limited test excavations, the Mimbres Area Survey recorded more than five hundred sites from the Rio Grande to the Arizona line and as

far south as the Mexican border. James Fitting's Upper Gila Project was a direct descendant of Jelinek's survey.

158. Watson, LeBlanc and Redman 1971.

159. For example, Nelson and Anyon 1996. But see note 171.

160. Lekson 2006b.

161. Lekson 1993a.

162. With that mention of black-on-white and corrugated, we open the can of worms that is Mimbres ceramic art. It is not possible to talk about Mimbres without slavering over pottery. The famous Mimbres black-on-white pottery is well represented in art museums and private collections around the world. (NAGPRA has not yet caught up with Mimbres; when it does, we can expect a fine brouhaha.) An exceptional Mimbres bowl will fetch tens or even hundreds of thousands of dollars at an art auction. The pottery itself was not technically remarkable (hand-formed, indifferently finished earthenware), but the designs—painted in black pigment on the white-slipped interior of bowls—appeal strongly to modern aesthetic sensibilities. Mimbres constitutes the most appealing, intriguing, and recognizable Native artistic tradition of North America.

Mimbres black-on-white pottery was "the pottery that should have been made at Chaco Canyon," according to Kidder (quoted in Cosgrove and Cosgrove 1932). I'm not sure what the people of Pueblo Bonito would have replied; they could have had Mimbres in the cupboard if they wanted, but they didn't. Only a few sherds of Mimbres black-on-white were found at Chaco Canyon.

Mimbres owed much to Late Pithouse Period types and styles—which owed much to Hohokam (chapter 4). But around 1000, Mimbres black-on-white pottery took a sharp turn toward Anasazi. Or perhaps that's the wrong way to put it: Mimbres took a turn that Anasazi followed. Mimbres was a Pueblo II type with many Pueblo III features. Mimbres band designs and framing lines presaged later Mesa Verde. Mimbres geometrics could have inspired Sosi and the other "busy" northeastern Arizona styles. Exterior "cartouche" designs on Pueblo II Mimbres pots anticipated classic Mesa Verde (late Pueblo III) and Pueblo IV types with that distinctive treatment. As with kachina images, many Pueblo III and IV "Anasazi" motifs appeared first on Mimbres. Much that was Mimbres stayed in Mimbres—too bizarre to travel perhaps. The kaleidoscopic complexity of Mimbres layouts defied analysis by even our brightest ceramicist, Anna Shepard (1948). No Anasazi designer would have attempted that many overlapping symmetries. Comparing Mimbres with contemporary and later Plateau types would be an eye-opener, I'm sure. Some Mimbres designs would have stumped M. C. Escher. After a long, careful, and intricate analysis of Mimbres's bizarre symmetries, Shepard concluded: "It is not practicable to attempt a quantitative summary of the relation of symmetry to structure because of the number of instances in which the order of drawing parts of the design is problematic. Complexity and variety combine to make structural analysis difficult" (Shepard 1948:290).

Was Mimbres black-on-white more like Anasazi or more like Mogollon? Anasazi and Mimbres geometric designs are clearly part of the same tradition, and even technical details like "slip slop" (a thin band of slip just below the rim on bowl exteriors) were similar. There were of course differences of style and technology, but the divergences between Mimbres and Gallup black-on-white (the most common type at Chaco) aren't that much greater than the differences between Gallup and many other Anasazi types—Kwahee or Black Mesa black-on-whites, for example. Consider Mimbres pottery from the perspective of Hohokam archaeology. Viewed through buff-colored glasses, Mimbres and Cibola look alike—compared with contemporary Hohokam buffwares. And Mimbres was "more like" Reserve or Gallup black-on-whites than it was "like" Mogollon red-on-brown and Three Circle red-on-white, its putative ancestors. That's a bald assertion, but I'm confident it would stand up to close analysis. Mimbres was Anasazi—and vice versa.

What to do about corrugated pottery? Corrugation is a hallmark of Anasazi. And in the Hohokam region, corrugated and, especially, indented corrugated sherds in Hohokam sites are understood as clear symptoms of Anasazi—that is, corrugated pottery comes from the north. But Mimbres was corrugating pottery perhaps earlier, and it was certainly closer to Hohokam. Take that same "Anasazi" corrugated sherd from a Tucson site east across the border into New Mexico and it becomes the final type in a long series of Mimbres utility wares.

Corrugated in the Hohokam area means Anasazi. The Mimbres utility ware tradition, which leads to corrugation in several interesting varieties, might "mean" Anasazi too. Or vice versa. The Mimbres sequence of textured types parallels, even presages, Anasazi types. Neck banded, shoulder corrugated, corrugated, indented corrugated (in a local Mimbres form) marched in lockstep—or in a three-legged race—across both sides of the Chaco–Mimbres line, but the Mimbres leg leads. The dating is less certain than we wish, but it appears that many ceramic developments happened first in Mimbres and later in Anasazi. Who's zooming whom?—to paraphrase a gifted chanteuse of the past.

The Mimbres ceramic tradition is ripe for reanalysis, recast as a key constituent of *southwestern* (inclusive of Anasazi) pottery. Tear down that wall! Look at Mimbres and Anasazi together. I am sure that startling new insights will come—and not all to the advantage of Anasazi.

163. For example, Haury 1986; Wheat 1955.

164. For example, LeBlanc 1986b.

165. Darrell Creel is cautiously open to this possibility (and even to—shudder!—some role for Chaco) and has said so in public (Creel 2006b). He met stiff resistance (Darrell Creel, personal communication, October 18, 2006). A recent review of Mimbres–Hohokam connections by Michelle Hegmon and Margaret Nelson (2007) reaffirms the accepted version: there were ceramic parallels between Mimbres and Hohokam in the Late Pithouse Period, but no traffic with Anasazi (and specifically Chaco) in the following Mimbres Phase (Hegmon and Nelson 2007:71–75). Hegmon and Nelson report an intriguing analysis of ceramic motifs (emphasizing pictorial images but not exclusively) at the large Mimbres Valley Galaz site, where external "motifs and conventions" shifted from Hohokam in the Late Pithouse Period to *Mesoamerica* in the Mimbres Phase. Mesoamerican motifs were translated into Mimbres idioms. They probably reflect the beginnings of eastern "end-run" routes of interaction around the old Hohokam-controlled corridors to West Mexico—and the growing importance of direct connections to Mesoamerica for both Mimbres *and* Chaco. Chaco (in my view) impacted Mimbres, while Mimbres played an important, decidedly nonperipheral role in the history of Chaco (and even more important roles in the reformation of later, post-Chacoan Plateau populations).

166. Lekson 1999a.

167. Late Pithouse Period domestic architecture in the Mimbres region (chapter 4) did not foreshadow the unit pueblo as Basketmaker III storage cysts prefigured "pueblo" structures on the Plateau. If anything, Mimbres pit houses resembled Hohokam courtyard groups. So I think Mimbres unit pueblos—the architectural form, not actual sites—came from the north. The question is in part entangled in the pit house to pueblo transition (chapter 4)—an event or process operating in near parallel in both Anasazi and Mimbres regions. The pit house to pueblo transition is a classic research question in both areas, but for some reason it is convenient to think that the Anasazi transition has nothing to say to the Mimbres, and vice versa. Surely, the same thing happening at the same time in two adjacent areas is, at the very least, curious.

Many small sites in the upper Gila show a clear pattern of the unit pueblo: five or six aboveground masonry rooms in direct association with a small, square, subterranean kiva (Lekson 1999a). I think the pattern is also evident, but obscured, in Harry Shafer's (1995, 2003) intermediate rooms at NAN and at comparable small nuclei ("core rooms") identified by LeBlanc at Swarts Ruin. The small, independent room blocks were there at least. Kivas were too, but their association with room blocks is less clear than in the upper Gila. Scores of small, square kivas are known from excavations in, under, and around big Mimbres pueblos, but the connection of a particular kiva with a particular six-room unit is not easily demonstrated.

That's not surprising. It's hard to pry the early levels out from under the considerable mass of a later, classic Mimbres pueblo: 150 rooms built, rebuilt, modified, remodeled over many decades, riddled with burial pits, and (much later) pothunted almost out of existence. That process wears hard on earlier structures—unit pueblos razed and buried beneath NAN Ranch, Swarts Ruin, Mattocks, and Old Town.

168. Lekson 1993b; Shafer 1999b:97; Swanson 2003; but see Diehl and LeBlanc 2001; Shafer 2003:133–34.

169. Herr 2001.

170. Oakes 1999.

171. We just can't get big Mimbres pueblos out of the local, Late Pithouse Period population (Lekson 1993b, 2006b). People had to come from somewhere else. Shafer (2003) draws those populations from nearby sources, upland Mimbres who left their mountain homes and rolled down to the river. It is my impression, from other surveys, that upland populations were largely late movements *out of the valley*. See also Margaret Nelson's post-Mimbres highlanders (Nelson 1999).

Another likely source might be valley-to-valley migrations—for example, from the Gila (heavily occupied in Late Pithouse times) to the Mimbres (heavily occupied in the later Mimbres Phase) (Nelson and Anyon 1996). But survey data do not seem to support that idea for Mimbres's latter days, however intriguing it might be (alas, see Lekson 2006b). I think the new people came from the north, from well beyond the northern limits of the Mimbres region—that is, from the Cibola Anasazi region. People spilled out from or escaped ahead of Chaco's enlarging domain. We know Anasazi (or at least northern Pueblo) peoples washed into southeastern Arizona and southwestern New Mexico in the late thirteenth century (chapters 6 and 7). Is it unthinkable that it also happened a few centuries earlier, during the Mimbres Phase?

172. The Pueblo II Expansion was a staple of southwestern culture histories written before the 1960s. John C. McGregor's 1941 map of Pueblo II showed an arrow from Pueblo II right into the Mimbres Valley. A later edition (McGregor 1965) politely deletes arrows into Mimbres Mogollon. McGregor got it right the first time. Fremont moved it north (Janetski 2002; Madsen 1989; Wormington 1955; but see Adovasio, Andrews, and Fowler 1982), Virgin Anasazi moved it west (Lyneis 1996; Shutler 1984), and Mimbres (Lekson various) moved it south.

Note, please, that the Pueblo II Expansion need not mean an actual movement of Anasazi peoples into previously Anasazi-free zones. Emulation, a- or en-culturation, cherry-picking—pay your money and take your choice—local people might well have adopted and adapted Anasazi-inspired products and practices. The empirical fact remains that right around 1000, many people in many areas around (but well beyond) the Anasazi started looking more Anasazi-like.

The Pueblo II Expansion suggests populations fleeing from Chaco—voting with their feet (a phrase, precisely apropos, I use repeatedly in this book). Large numbers of people went to the edges of the Plateau (and beyond). Demographically, the Pueblo II Expansion suggests a doughnut, with Chaco in the hole. Who was left to build palaces?

The Pueblo II Expansion to the west, north, and south is fairly well established. In some areas (Virgin Anasazi, Fremont, Mimbres), population shrank in the following Pueblo III. In others (Mogollon highlands, northern San Juan), it continued to increase. Pueblo II expansion to the east, into the Rio Grande, is a thornier and (frankly) stranger problem, precisely because subsequent developments (Pueblo III and IV) were so spectacular (chapter 7) and because Pueblo II ("Developmental," in Rio Grande terms) lasted longer there. A century of intense archaeological work in the northern Rio Grande has not discovered substantial occupations before 900 or 950—"substantial" compared with the Four Corners. A scattering of Pueblo II/Developmental unit pueblos and several medium-sized communities (such as Arroyo Negro in Santa Fe, one of the largest [Nusbaum 1935; Smiley, Stubbs, and Bannister 1953], and the Pojoaque Grant site north of Santa Fe [Wiseman 1995; Wiseman and Olinger 1991]) appeared between 950 and 1000. A few had Great Kivas (Peckham 1979; Stubbs 1954). These sites were variations on the unit pueblo communities characteristic of Anasazi at that time and had pottery recognized (in more rational times) as local variants of Pueblo II Anasazi Red Mesa styles and types.

Recent summaries by Steven Lakatos (2007) and Cherie Scheick (2008) (see also Adler 1993; Peckham 1979) demonstrate that the Pueblo II Developmental Period has been underestimated. But when I read those summaries and consider Pueblo II in the Four Corners, I'm left thinking that *comparatively* much less was going on in the Rio Grande. Lakatos and Schiek are correct: there was more Pueblo II/Developmental than we previously knew, but that's still not a heck of a lot compared with the San Juan Basin or the northern San Juan, with sites like Skunk Springs and Yellow Jacket. Or compared with the emerging Pueblo II powerhouses, Mimbres, Cibola, and Socorro (the south should enter this equation somehow). David Wilcox's atlas (Hill et al. 2004; Wilcox et al. 2006) shows it correctly: there were plenty of people in the Rio Grande at 1200, but a heck of a lot more to the west—and even more so at 1100. Compare the lists in Lakatos and Scheik with the lists of known Chacoan communities, which are only part of Pueblo II.

Some observations on the extended Rio Grande Developmental: like Kayenta at the western edge of the Anasazi world, the northern Rio Grande continued (apparently) the pattern of unit pueblos and pit structures well beyond the time of aggregated "pueblo" villages in the San Juan and Zuni–Acoma areas (chapter 6). After 1300, things get interesting (chapter 7): population rose dramatically, just as population fell dramatically in the Four Corners. Yet in conversations with practicing Santa Fe archaeologists, one hears that Tewa and Galisteo Basin demographics owed little or nothing to the Four Corners. If they are correct, we should all pity (and honor) PIV Rio Grande women of child-bearing age; their lives must have been nasty, brutal, abnormally fecund, and consequently short.

The Rio Grande was not the creation of migrating Mesa Verdeans. *Of course* there were local histories. *There are always local histories.* Taos, for example, may owe as much to the upper Republican as to the upper San Juan (e.g., Fowles 2004:23). But in Taos too there was a substantial influx of "Anasazi" during the Pueblo II Expansion—substantial migrations in from the Piedra area perhaps (Severin Fowles, personal communication, October 31, 2007).

173. Jett and Moyle 1986; cf. Bettison et al. 1999.

174. Lekson 1999b:fig. 2.19. Armadillos did not expand into the Southwest until very recent times (after 1850), and they are still rare indeed in New Mexico. An armadillo on a Mimbres pot could be explained in two ways. Someone from the Mimbres region traveled far enough south into Mexico to see an armadillo (it is not clear how far that would be at 1050), or someone from the Mimbres Valley stopped at a gas station in Texas. I favor the former. The Mimbres monkey is less certain. On one pot, a cavorting humanlike figure with a long curling tail holds two macaws (Lekson 1999b:fig. 2.19). The monkey manqué is of particular interest. Macaws—also depicted on pots and found in Mimbres sites—originated far to the south in southern Mexico; there too were the monkeys. Did people from the Mimbres region visit the jungles of western coastal Mexico? Probably.

175. Creel and McKusick 1994.

176. Hegmon and Nelson 2007.

177. Lekson 2006b.

178. I suggested that emulation Great Houses (that is, local copies) exist on the Gila and Mimbres (Duff and Lekson 2006; Lekson 1999b). My short list includes Woodrow Ruin, TJ Ruin, and the south room block at NAN. Woodrow Ruin, just below the Gila's dramatic exit from the Mogollon Mountains, was one of the two very largest Mimbres towns (the largest was at Redrock, 40 kilometers farther downstream on the Gila). At Woodrow, a prominent central room block, immediately adjacent to two huge Great Kivas, is remarkable for its very large rooms and (for Mimbres) rigid right-angle geometry. Mimbres architecture tends to collapse into low mounds, often very low mounds. The central room block at Woodrow *sticks up*, rather dramatically. It was probably not multistoried, however. The unexcavated central room block at TJ Ruin (another large Mimbres town at the head of the Gila) is, by consensus, the most likely multistoried Mimbres structure (e.g., McKenna and Bradford 1989; Shafer 2003; Darrell Creel, personal communication, 2004). TJ seems comparable to Woodrow— a massive (but not necessarily large) room block that *sticks up* amid more typical Mimbres ankle-high squalor. My third example, at NAN Ranch, is probably the most offensive, and I apologize in advance to Harry Shafer.

Shafer conducted more than a decade of research at the large NAN Ranch Ruin in the Mimbres Valley. His excellent report (Shafer 2003) mentions Chaco just three times: first, to deny any significant interaction between Chaco and Mimbres (page 5); second, to contrast Chaco's local sandstones and Mimbres's lack of any tabular stone suitable for building (page 56); and third, to contrast the south room block's east–west orientation with the north–south orientation of many Chaco buildings (page 95). But from the first time I saw the south room block during Shafer's excavations, I was struck by the massiveness of its walls (the north walls were three and four courses wide), the size of its rooms, and the geometric formality of its layout (contrasted with normal hodgepodge Mimbres buildings). It didn't stick up (the area had been leveled), but it stood out. Shafer would agree that the south room block was unusual (Shafer 2003:95), but I am sure he would not agree that it was a Mimbres emulation of a Chacoan Great House translated into Mimbres architectural technologies and idioms. But that's what it was—in my opinion.

The idea of emulation Great Houses is not particularly appealing to Mimbres archaeologists. I have, in a shoebox somewhere, a photo of a half-dozen Mimbres specialists standing on my "Great House" at Woodrow Ruin. They hold their right arms straight out, every thumb pointing down.

179. Several recent essays suggest that Mimbres may not have been all that egalitarian after all (Creel and Anyon 2003:80–83; Hegmon 2002:336–37). Creel and Anyon note, "At some point during the Classic Mimbres period, communal pit structures [Great Kivas] were apparently no longer needed as foci of community integration" with a shift to corporate household groups. Going corporate "does not mean there was a lack of leadership positions or individuals to fill them." They offer for our approval a remarkable burial at Old Town "as a clear indication that leaders could emerge and function within the established corporate structure" (which they then explain with analogies from Zuni and other pueblos) (Creel and Anyon 2003:86–87). I approve: there were Mimbres leaders, but I'm not sure Zuni is the right place to look for models of how those leaders led. Chaco would be more appropriate historically. Based on significant differentiation in burials, Hegmon places potential leaders in particular room blocks, "specifically, the 400 room block [its provenience designation, not its size] at Mattocks and the South Roomblock at NAN" (Hegmon 2002:336)—the latter, one of my candidates for an emulation Great House (see note 178).

180. Carlson 1982a; Schaafsma 1994. Of course, Mimbres kachinas might not mean the same things or act the same way as modern kachinas. And there was more to Mimbres than proto-kachinas, just as there is far more to Pueblo "religion" than kachina dances (e.g., Parsons [1939]1996). Harry Shafer (1995) has made an intriguing foray into Mimbres ideology, linking house form and cosmology (see also Shafer 2003). Many non-kachina ceremonial events are depicted on Mimbres pottery, and some of these appear familiar to Pueblo observers (e.g., Kabotie [1949]1982; see also Carr 1979; Moulard 1984; among others). Many (most?) interpretations of Mimbres ritual appeal to Pueblo practices, but there was also a very strong component of Mesoamerican imagery and reference (Schaafsma 1994; Thompson 1994).

181. For example, Di Peso 1974; Kelley and Kelley 1974; Schroeder 1965, 1966.

182. Nelson 1986; Vargas 1995:table 5.1.

183. Hargrave 1970; Haury 1976; Lange 1992; Nelson 1986.

184. Haury 1976:231.

185. Doyel 2000c:102.

186. What to do with Patayan, the problematic archaeology of the lower Colorado River (McGuire and Schiffer 1982; Stone 1991)? The lower Colorado should have been the Southwest's Nile Delta or (more appropriately) the Southwest's Mississippi Delta—a cradle of great and wonderful things. But its archaeology is so enigmatic and ill defined—basically, a distinctively non-Hohokam pottery and a broad-brush chronology—that I cannot reasonably integrate Patayan into my narrative. There are limits beyond which I cannot honorably

go—the difference, perhaps, between a respectable historical novel and a flat-out fantasy. I welcome the day when Patayan—with so much potential and so much warfare (later)—can play its proper role in the history of the ancient Southwest. My apologies to those ancient people—they may have done great things, but we don't yet know the details.

187. Darling and Lewis 2007; White 2007.

188. Doyel 2000c:125.

189. Schaafsma 1994:79; see also Ellis and Hammack 1968; Young 1994.

190. Kelley 2000; Lekson 1999b.

191. Bradley 1993, 2000; Creel and McKusick 1994; McGuire 1993; Vargas 1995.

192. By any route, macaws were a shipping nightmare. Bells and mirrors may have passed from hill tribe to hill tribe, "down the line" (as this form of exchange has been called). But that wouldn't work with macaws. Like corn (and metallurgy), the product is worthless without the knowledge to keep it going. Macaws are picky eaters, and they don't like most of what the desert Southwest has to offer. Yet macaws made it to Mimbres and the greater Southwest and survived to provide red and blue feathers for ritual and political insignia. Much later, at Paquimé (chapter 7), macaws were successfully bred, on impressive scales. I would not be surprised if Mimbres tried to breed macaws too.

193. Weigand and Harbottle 1993.

194. For example, Cosgrove and Cosgrove 1932 and my interpretation of McCluney 1968.

195. For example, Di Peso 1974; Hayes 1981; Kelley 1986.

196. Weigand and Harbottle 1993.

197. Helms 1988:264.

198. "Exotic goods and everyday chiefs," as Paul Goldstein (2000) suggested for a comparable New World situation. Ben Nelson, in a very similar interpretation, argues that "Mesoamerican styles and practices spread northward along a time series of newly aggregated social groups whose formation demanded the introduction of symbols and practices associated with hegemonic order" (Nelson 2000:318). Following Helms, he suggests that Chacoan leaders obtained selected Mesoamerican objects and symbols to buttress their power (Nelson 2006). I argued elsewhere (following Helms) that Mesoamerican objects and symbols were employed to legitimate and consolidate power—as badges of office, symbols of alliance, or rewards for service in a political prestige economy controlled by Chaco (Lekson 1999b:158).

The importance of these items in the Southwest is often downplayed by appeal to their rarity: "There aren't many"; "You could fit all the Mesoamerican artifacts into a bushel basket"; "There's only a handful." I do not understand that logic—rarity is a necessary attribute of rare things.

"Prestige goods economies" have taken a theoretical beating, but I still believe that baubles and bangles provide an extraordinary entrée into ancient political arrangements. I'm not thinking of prestige goods as *economic*. Rather, they were symbols of power. Defining Mesoamerica, Blanton and his colleagues described a geographic region united mainly by "elite-level communication," marked at least in part by the distribution of prestige goods (not an interconnected economy):

> That this kind of system relied primarily on elite-rank contacts meant that it rather easily spread over space. The only requirement was that the participating societies have at least a chiefdom level of sociocultural integration. In this way the boundaries of "Mesoamerica" could change markedly, at times extending down into Central America or, especially in Toltec times, into the southwestern part of the United States. (Blanton et al. 1993:220)

The lords of Chaco took on more and more trappings of the south. Toward the end of Chaco, in the early 1100s, they added a colonnade as the last, plaza-facing wall of Chetro Ketl. Colonnades were features of the Post-Classic and specifically were an architectural indication of important monumental buildings and palaces. At Chaco, they did not quite get it right. As with Mimbres monkeys, travelers perhaps described the feature to the stay-at-home architect. The result was a colonnade—sort of. The columns of Post-Classic colonnades, like those of Greek temples, rose from floor to ceiling. Chetro Ketl's short stubby columns sat atop a low footing wall, creating a facade more like a row of closely spaced windows than a forest of pillars.

199. When I write *king*, please do not think Louis XIV. Southwestern kings would have been more like Iron Age Irish kings—just barely kings. Kingship had been known in North America since Olmec (Diehl 2005; Fields and Reents-Budet 2005; and, although he eschews *king*, Pool 2007; for a sample of the inevitable counterarguments: Flannery and Marcus 2000). If there were kings in the Southwest, they were a very watered-down version of Mesoamerican kings—who themselves ranged from great and powerful emperors to jumped-up hill chiefs. Southwestern kings were nothing a seventeenth-century European monarch would recognize as a peer or cousin. But it is important to think of kingship from the point of view of the king and his

or her family. Kings come from lineages, families, or groups for which ruling is a duty and an obligation. After a few generations, that kind of thinking comes naturally. Some families were farmers, some were potters, some were priests, and some were kings.

In chapter 7 we will meet the Great Gambler, who ruled Chaco. A well-educated, cosmopolitan, yet traditional man from a Navajo clan near Chaco commented, "That person you people call 'the Great Gambler'— he was our king."

I replied, "There's no Navajo word for king."

"Yes, but if we had a word like that for him, that would be it: *king.*"

That is one of three reasons I use the term *king.* The second is to erase the political boundary between the United States (where only "chiefs" may apply; chapter 8) and Mexico (where kingship was two thousand years old before Chaco was a twinkle in the Gambler's eye). The third is to dredge southwestern polities out from the murky goop of intermediate societies.

Should I use another word, perhaps a Native or near-Native word? *Cacique? Almehenob? Cazonci? Gobernantes* (not exactly Native)? I think not—those words would imply a cut-and-paste transfer of office, and I'd rather let southwestern kings define themselves. They were neither Carib headman nor Tarascan emperors. But we have to call them *something.* Let's call them kings. Kingship, in various guises, was nearly universal in human experience (Oakley 2006) and nearly ubiquitous in North American polities.

200. Haury 1976 (affirmed by McGuire and Villalpando C. 2007b).

201. Lekson 1989.

202. Nelson 2006.

203. Lekson and Peregrine 2004.

Chapter 6

1. Johnson 2004; O'Brien, Lyman, and Schiffer 2005.

2. Cross-cultural archaeology was identified with the University of Michigan in general and with Dr. Binford in particular; for example, Binford 2001.

3. Sahlins and Service 1960; Service 1962.

4. For example, Service 1975. Archaeology discovered HRAF just as ethnology was becoming disenchanted with cross-cultural studies and "social science." In the late 1970s and early 1980s, ethnology and cultural anthropology drifted off toward humanism, away from science. HRAF had no part in that: "To humanistic anthropologists, the comparative project in general and HRAF in particular represent the apotheosis of positivistic behavioral science. The HRAF is clunky, hardware-heavy, artless, bureaucratic—in a word, uncool" (Tobin 1990:475). But processual archaeologists loved it.

5. A very popular book of the time was *Man's Rise to Civilization*, by Peter Farb (1968). It sold well (a minor best seller), went to a second edition in 1978, and was the *1491* of its day, introducing America to its Natives. And it was the public face of neo-evolution. Farb, a respected science writer and fellow of AAAS, used Service's band-tribe-chiefdom-state theory to showcase Native America. The Southwest was represented by Zuni; Farb placed them safely in the tribal zone. (Indeed, he used Zuni to introduce the category "tribe.") He had almost nothing good to say about Ruth Benedict and scorched her portrayal of Zuni as the "peaceful pueblo": "Benedict's view of Zuni is totally misleading; in fact, she never did sufficient field work there to justify her conclusions" (Farb 1968:81). He did, however, agree that Zuni, like all North American tribes, lacked "any strong political organization or permanent authority that might give stability.... The tribal 'chief' belongs to no political hierarchy or dominant group; he is merely a sort of consultant, an advisor who may or may not be listened to" (Farb 1968:71). For real chiefdoms, Farb looked to the Northwest Coast and the Mississippi Valley Natchez and for states, of course, to the "total power" of the Aztecs. Farb did not displace Benedict (she's still in print; he's not), but he did introduce the American reading public to neo-evolution and to the fact that for Native states, one must look to Mexico.

6. Doelle and Phillips 2005; Roberts, Ahlstrom, and Roth 2004.

7. As noted in chapter 5, CRM was unequally applied. In the Mogollon area, there were no big projects on the scale of Dolores, Black Mesa, the Central Arizona Project, or Tucson and Phoenix freeways. (Nor has Mogollon benefited from big Park Service projects such as Wetherill Mesa and Chaco. There is only one Mogollon archaeological park, Gila Cliff Dwellings—in fact, a Tularosa Phase site.) Most Mimbres projects were field schools, Earthwatch sessions or other low-budget projects—all good work, but on scales dwarfed by big CRM projects elsewhere in the Southwest. In southern New Mexico, the largest CRM projects were in the Jornada Mogollon (ahead of the army's tanks or the air force's missiles). I think this disparity in CRM

research is one reason Mimbres Mogollon remains undervalued in southwestern prehistory.

8. Gumerman 1991.

9. Dean 2000.

10. Historic preservation (and fiscal realities) protected the biggest and most complex sites, in national parks or in conservation easements and set-asides. When possible, construction avoided the largest sites. It was both a nice thing to do and good for the bottom line: digging a big site is very, very expensive. (The major exceptions to this situation were in the Phoenix and Tucson areas, where modern cities were established directly over ancient ruins, making avoidance impossible.) After the 1970s, sites in national parks were increasingly protected *from archaeologists*. For example, the University of Colorado's long research program at Mesa Verde ended in 1977. Today Mesa Verde actively discourages archaeological research. Apparently, they think we know all we need to know. They're wrong, and citizens are shortchanged. The NPS once mounted large research programs, typically in collaboration with universities, but that era came to a close with the end of Chaco Project in the late 1970s.

11. Watson, LeBlanc, and Redman 1971.

12. I once wrote (gratefully supported by your tax dollars) an archaeological overview of the BLM East Socorro Resource District—an entirely arbitrary block of land encompassing the east end of the Plains of St. Augustine, a few ridges running out from surrounding mountain ranges, and a short length of the Rio Grande Valley. No site in the East Socorro Resource District could possibly be understood without reference to the larger contexts from which it had been untimely ripped, but we were asked to develop a predictive model of site locations within that small area based on soils, drainages, and vegetation of the East Socorro "region." It was a strange job, but it paid the bills.

The old site files at central institutions, such as the Laboratory of Anthropology or the Arizona State Museum, were intended to be databases of ancient geography. With the rise of CRM, we realized the management potential of these files—before you built a dam, you could see whether there were any big ruins in the reservoir—and federal and state agencies began to support, financially, the operation of the site files. Paying the piper, they called the tune: the site files became tools for CRM—which was fine, but "pure research" projects now tend to bypass the site files and often create brand-new databases (e.g., Hill et al. 2004).

13. Stuart and Gauthier 1981 (reissued in a revised edition in 1984 by a university press).

14. For example, for the Anasazi area of southwestern Colorado: Eddy, Kane, and Nickens 1984; Lipe, Varien, and Wishusen 1999. I had some personal involvement with this process, writing an overview of southwestern New Mexico in 1992 (published, finally, as Lekson 2006b), and I served on an editorial committee supervising production of new overviews for Colorado (e.g., Lipe, Varien, and Wilshusen 1999). Almost every southwestern archaeologist of a certain age wrote a "regional overview" of a resource district, a special-use area, or a national forest at some point in the 1970s and 1980s. And where are these now?

15. Marshall et al. 1979; Powers, Gillespie, and Lekson 1983.

16. Wilcox and Sternberg 1983.

17. Cordell and Plog 1979:405.

18. Cordell and Plog 1979:408–09, 424.

19. SARG's question—Why were sites located where they were?—was meant to be a major anthropological research issue. In retrospect, the question seems a bit obvious; after much analysis, it was determined that proximity to water and arable land were pretty important (Euler and Gumerman 1978). To be fair, this truism was not presented as an earthshaking breakthrough. And the prediction of site locations—Why were sites located where they were?—had important implications for CRM. If agency archaeologists could predict where sites would be located, they could reroute roads or pipelines, avoid sites, and save everybody a lot of trouble. "Predictive modeling" became a hot topic in the 1980s and engaged some of the SARG leadership.

20. Dean 1988.

21. Plog et al. 1988.

22. For example, Graybill et al. 2006.

23. Gumerman et al. 2003.

24. Johnson, Kohler, and Cowan 2005; Kohler et al. 2007.

25. Kohler, Gumerman, and Reynolds 2005.

26. Kohler, Gumerman, and Reynolds 2005:80, 81.

27. Graybill et al. 2006:112.

28. I have reservations about agent-based modeling. Agent-based modeling has been around for several decades, without (so far) revolutionizing social sciences (e.g., Diermeier 2007). I have doubts about capital-A Agency too, from social theory (chapter 1). Agent-based modeling and Agency are two very different things, but they share a firm belief in the Common Man. My principal objection to agent-based models is literally

elitist: bottom-up models ignore top-down dynamics. It's foolish to ignore top-down dynamics. I'm more or less a populist, and I'm not in any sense an elite, but I don't discount the power of powerful people. A dumb president can really screw up things. So can a smart tyrant.

29. Wilcox and Masse (1981) tackled Pueblo IV about the same time.

30. Adler 1996.The conference, I blush to admit, was my idea.

31. Adams and Duff 2004. An atlas of the Southwest from 750 to 900—Pueblo I in the north, Late Pithouse in the south—is currently under way (Lisa Young, personal communication, 2008).

32. Gumerman 1991.

33. For example, Mathien and McGuire 1986. Southwest–Mexico is a long-established if minor theme in southwestern archaeology, with its own prehistoriography: Phillips 1989; Wilcox 1986a).

34. Hill et al. 2004; Wilcox 2005a; Wilcox et al. 2006.

35. Its compilation was largely the work of one researcher, the indefatigable David Wilcox (Museum of Northern Arizona). The vision and commitment came from the Center for Desert Archaeology, a nonprofit research organization sponsored by a respected CRM firm, Desert Archaeology, Inc. Dr. Wilcox has mapped, visited, and otherwise considered most of the big sites in the Southwest, and those he has not seen personally he has "visited" via documents. And he has always worked on admirably large scales. His encyclopedic knowledge has been tapped by the Coalescent Communities project, also admirably large in scale.

The project's name may be unfortunate: it assumes a dynamic ("coalescence") yet to be demonstrated. And I have misgivings about the preliminary conclusions of Hill and his colleagues (2004). They suggest that the prime mover of demographic change in the thirteenth century was demography itself: diminished health and negative population growth eliminated populations once thought to have migrated out of regions or to have transformed themselves into new social formations. I think they may confuse cause and effect. But I applaud the scale and the commitment to long-term research beyond the capacities of the single academic scholar.

The Desert Archaeology arrangement—a for-profit CRM firm (Desert Archaeology, Inc.) sponsoring a parallel nonprofit research and public education foundation (Center for Desert Archaeology)—has been followed by several other Arizona CRM organizations, with great success. New Mexico CRM organizations are following suit (the state museum's CRM organization, the Office of Archaeological Studies, recently won a national award for its public outreach). CRM long ago eclipsed the academy in fieldwork; now CRM-sponsored institutions are taking the lead in research. CRM replaces the old museum or Gila Pueblo model, with staffs working together on a region or theme. CRM firms can take on the long view, the wide scale, the collaborative strategies, and the public engagement that are not particularly rewarded in the academy.

36. Diehl (1983) and Hassig (1992) saw Tula's fall as the end of an empire. Smith and Berdan (2003a:25) relegate Tula's misfortune to a local matter.

37. Smith and Berdan 2003a:25–26.

38. McCafferty 2000.

39. Foster 1999; Kelley 1986, 2000; Smith and Berdan 2003a.

40. Riley 2005.

41. For example, Gerhard 1972.

42. Smith and Berdan 2003b:6–8. Smith, Berdan, and many of the authors in their volume are partial to world systems theory and assume that long-distance contacts were not just real, but really important. While I'm not entirely on board with world systems, I enjoy its supporters' attitudes about long-distance dynamics: early, often, and consequential. And they do not fear to generalize.

43. For example, Hassig 1992.

44. Pauketat 2004.

45. Hall 2006:217.

46. Knight and Steponaitis 1998.

47. For example, Reilly and Garber 2007.

48. For example, Townsend and Sharp 2004.

49. I've been fascinated by Chaco–Cahokia parallels for almost three decades (Lekson 1983; Lekson and Peregrine 2004). If the two were on different continents, their similar trajectories would delight a processual archaeologist, but there's the undeniable historical fact of Mesoamerica, a third element in the equation. Did Chaco and Cahokia go through the same processes, coincidentally at the same time? Or was Mesoamerica pulling the strings, with Chaco and Cahokia dancing to a Mexican tune? Or some combination of process and history?

50. Milner 1999.

51. The link between Chaco and Aztec Ruins was demonstrated monumentally on the landscape by the Great North Road, which runs due north out of Chaco to end…where? I thought (and think) that the North

Road ended at Aztec Ruins, and I found that fact curious; it connected two noncontemporary sites (Chaco, 850–1125, and Aztec, 1110–1280). The North Road, like most Chacoan roads, was not (primarily) a transportation corridor but rather a manifest connection between Chaco and Aztec, history written on the landscape. There are some strange notions about the North Road floating around; only some of them are mine. I think some of these strange notions require correction. So here's how I see it.

Emerging from the tangle of roads and walls outside Pueblo Alto, the North Road runs straight north across the largely flat San Juan Basin. Every 15 to 20 kilometers, there was a Chacoan structure alongside the road. The largest was Pierre's Site—a small Great House directly beside the road and another, larger structure (with attendant "shrines" or masonry arcs) atop a steep-sided mesa, 50 meters above and a few meters offset from the road itself. About 50 kilometers north of Chaco, the road reaches Kutz Canyon, at the southern edge of one of New Mexico's most spectacular badlands—deeply eroded canyons cut through banded cliffs of shale, clay, and sandstone (the Twin Angels Recreation Area, named for two spires on a badlands peak). At the canyon's edge, the North Road descended to the sandy canyon bottom, ran north another few kilometers, and then turned slightly to the west down Kutz Canyon to Salmon Ruins, a huge Chaco Great House on the San Juan River. Those were the conclusions of the San Juan Valley Archaeological Project (SJVAP), which first surveyed the North Road and excavated Salmon Ruins. In the interest of full disclosure, I worked for the SJVAP (but not on the North Road), and when I worked for the NPS, I helped survey Pierre's Site (named for the SJVAP archaeologist who studied the North Road, Pierre Morenon). So my notions on the North Road were formed by SJVAP: the thing ran from Chaco to Salmon Ruins.

That tidy interpretation was challenged by the Solstice Project, a research effort led by Anna Sofaer (1999) with the able assistance of Michael Marshall (1997). Their alternative interpretation was this: the North Road went to Kutz Canyon and stopped. It did not go to Salmon Ruins. Curiously, Marshall and Sofaer were the first to discover an elaborate wooden stairway that took the road down into Kutz Canyon. Still, they argued that the road was entirely symbolic, with north being the direction of death and Kutz Canyon representing the underworld or previous world from which Pueblo people had emerged (Marshall 1997).

I agree that the road was largely symbolic—but not entirely. Stairs and way stations show that people moved along it. I disagree very strongly that the road ended at the edge of Kutz Canyon. A few kilometers north of the stairway in the canyon (and only a few meters off the original north alignment) sits Twin Angels Pueblo, a Chaco Great House atop a tall mesa jutting out over Kutz Canyon and above the North Road's presumed route. The similarities to Pierre's Site are clear, including massive masonry arcs or shrines. It seems obvious, to me at least, that the road continued to and presumably beyond Twin Angels. The site is not a new discovery: Twin Angels Pueblo was excavated by Earl Morris in 1915 and reported a half century later in an article in *American Antiquity* (Carlson 1966). Unlike most Great Houses, Twin Angels has no surrounding community of small houses. Its sits in splendid isolation, with no reason for its existence except the North Road, which (I and others think) passed below. The road made a slight turn to the west at Twin Angels and ran straight down Kutz Canyon to Salmon Ruins on the San Juan River, directly opposite Kutz Canyon's mouth. In fact, that's what Twin Angels Pueblo was about: like many "road-related" Great Houses, it marked a turning point on the Great North Road, slightly off north and down Kutz Canyon to Salmon Ruins. When a Chaco road turned, it was almost always at a Great House (for example, Kin Ya'a). The Kutz canard: for some reason, people want to believe that the North Road ends at Kutz Canyon. It doesn't. It almost certainly goes on to Salmon Ruins— and probably, after a course correction back to due north, on to Aztec.

Ruth Van Dyke (2007b), in an interpretation as relentlessly cosmological as mine is political, briefly mentions Twin Angels Pueblo, misplaces it "northwest" of the putative Kutz Canyon terminus, and then ignores it. She goes on to interpret the North Road as if it did indeed end at Kutz Canyon. "The North Road might be better interpreted not as a physical path linking settlements, but rather as a symbolic statement of the importance of the direction north for Chacoans" (Van Dyke 2007b:149). On that we can agree, at least in part: the North Road was a monument symbolizing the historical connection of Aztec and Chaco, invoking a key cosmological direction, north (Lekson 1999b). People probably also walked on it from time to time.

Twin Angels Pueblo demonstrates that the road continued into and through Kutz Canyon. Salmon Ruins (one of the largest Great Houses ever built), at the mouth of the canyon, gives us a strong hint of where the road was headed. Somehow, Salmon and Aztec get lost in the rush to ritualize the North Road. Is it somehow simply coincidence that both Salmon and Aztec(!) were built on these lines? Did their locations result from some obscure, unrelated process(es) that just happened to put them *both* at places that certainly appear to reference north–south alignments and specifically the North Road?

Aztec Ruins was due north of Salmon Ruins, and because of the short "dog leg" down Kutz Canyon, Aztec was offset slightly west from the original North Road alignment. There are hints of north–south roads on the mesas between Salmon Ruins and Aztec (John R. Stein, personal communication, 2003). Sadly, the area today is crisscrossed by a web of newly bladed dirt roads and pipelines servicing hundreds of gas wells. It will be hard indeed to ferret out the prehistoric road—if any—from gas and oil developments. (CRM, working well pad by well pad, is challenged by large yet ephemeral features like roads.)

I am confident that the Great North Road went from Chaco to Salmon Ruins and then to Aztec. Which came first, the road or the ruins? We currently can't say. But the Great North Road and its end points formed a coherent cultural and political landscape—old and new capitals and a monument linking them in history and power.

52. Baker 2008. The importance of four-room units at Salmon, Aztec, and Wupatki probably continued an architectural pattern noted by Tom Windes at Pueblo Alto: the association of freestanding, paired-room units with road alignments and terminations (Windes 1987:vol. 1, 109–12).

53. Reed ed. 2006, Reed ed. 2008.

54. This is the "Chaco Meridian" (Lekson 1999b): the north–south alignment of Chaco, Aztec, and Paquimé, and the suggestion that their alignment had historical importance. That idea met an uneven reception. For the staunchly scientific, *meridian* suggested archaeoastronomy and New Agery. This kind of alignment suggests ley lines, and ley lines are trouble. I'm wary of archaeoastronomy, and I'm certainly not a New Ager. (If I ever get to the point where I need hocus-pocus and mumbo jumbo, I will join some old-time religion with a track record and eighteenth-century music. I suspect I can take care of that type of difficulty, however, with some good scotch.) For others, the whole thing is simply a huge coincidence: a beautiful fact killed by an ugly theory (a phrase I failed to credit to my friend Paul Minnis in 1999). Surely, southwestern history did not play out on such large scales? A principal argument of this book is, yes, southwestern history was indeed Big History. But large scales do not necessarily entail stuff like meridian alignments. Surely we can play geopolitical games without ley lines. *We* can, of course, but apparently *they* found them useful. The meridian, unfortunately, seems to be real.

The meridian surfaces in chapter 4, note 172, and chapter 5, note 136, but it first came to my attention (Lekson 1999b) in the events described in chapters 6 and 7, so I summarize it here. I defend it against several notable criticisms in chapter 7, note 207.

The story in 1999 was this: Chaco, Aztec, and Paquimé were three sequential capitals of shifting territories—not unlike early Chinese capitals but on a much smaller scale—and their positions were intentionally aligned on approximately the same meridian. Consider the evidence: three sites on a line. But not just any three sites—Chaco, Aztec, and Paquimé were sequentially the largest, most complicated, most cosmopolitan centers of their respective times and places. Nor just any direction—north was the only permanent, immutable direction available. The alignment was in fact a four-point problem, and each of the four points was, in its own way, unique. Coincidence? A statistical fluke? I described the probabilities elsewhere (Lekson 1999b:132–34), and the chances of a purely random alignment are very slim. The *fact* of the Great North Road linking Chaco and Aztec suggests, to me at least, that the alignment was not a statistical fluke. To accept the four-point alignment as intentional requires a slight stretch of the imagination, but to dismiss the alignment as a fluke requires heroic special pleading.

That was the 1999 version. As we've seen in chapters 3 and 4, things have become more interesting, with the addition of Basketmaker III centers (Shabik'eschee and 29 SJ 423) and Pueblo I centers (Blue Mesa–Ridges Basin) on approximately the same meridian. It's now a six-point problem (five sites and north), with each of the sites being unique in its time period (biggest, strangest, and so forth).

I originally suggested that the intent of the alignment was *positional legitimation*, much as Islam uses precise alignment toward Mecca (*qibla*) as a large-scale landscape mnemonic linking distant mosques to the holy city. This happened in the New World: long-distance alignments shaped the political and ritual landscapes of both Aztec and Inca (think of *ceques*). The Great North Road strongly suggests this kind of linkage between Chaco Canyon and Aztec Ruins. Intentional long-distance alignment upsets some of my colleagues, who feel that southwestern peoples were incapable of those sorts of things. I disagree very strongly with the limits placed a priori on ancient southwestern peoples (chapter 8), but I accept that my colleagues were properly skeptical of the meridian.

I'm thinking now that the alignment resulted from another social mechanism, less outré than a southwestern *qibla*. The alignments we see on the map could have resulted from the (comparatively) simple act of *moving in a direction*, carefully. We know that Chacoan designers could determine and use the cardinal with accuracy comparable to that of other naked-eye astronomers. If their intent (for whatever reason) was to go north or south with precision, the result would have been three (or five) sites aligned on a map. In some versions of the White House story (chapter 7), the people are indeed instructed to go straight south, with precision. Alfonso Ortiz offered this comment on Pueblo concerns for direction: "All peoples try to bring their definitions of group space somehow into line with their cosmologies, but the Pueblos are unusually precise about it" (Ortiz 1972:142).

So perhaps they were told to go north or south, and they did so with the unusual precision and care seen throughout Chacon built environments. In this scenario, the direction *back to* the starting point is less important than the direction *away from* the starting point—and the results are exactly the same. Occam's Razor is one of the most abused nostrums in the social sciences (chapter 1). But if simplicity makes complex histories easier to swallow, then dress the meridian in directional accuracy—and hold the *qibla*.

55. Brown, Windes, and McKenna 2008.

56. Based on early-twelfth-century pottery found in one of its rooms, Aztec North, built of adobe and facing south, may have been one of the first Great Houses built at Aztec Ruins (McKenna 1990). There are no tree-ring dates.

Aztec North interests me strangely. It's adobe (like Paquimé; chapter 7), and it faces south. While the city below lies snug in the valley bottom, Aztec North sits above on a high terrace, much like Pueblo Alto at Chaco Canyon. And like Pueblo Alto, Aztec North is cardinal—not precisely, but notably more cardinal than the Aztec cityscape with its solstitial master plan. To me, Aztec North seems a good candidate for Chaco's cardinal faction, first built and first abandoned at the new capital. Perhaps the first stirrings of Casas Grandes began as early as the late twelfth century at Aztec North.

57. Fowler and Stein 2001; McKenna and Toll 2001.

58. Quoted in Keen 1971:254.

59. Greiser and Moore 1995; Howe 1947.

60. Mark Elson, personal communication, 2007.

61. Sunset Crater may well have played a role in the removal of the Anasazi capital from Chaco to Aztec—north and away from the troubling omen. Projecting back from Aztec to omen, I'd bet the blasted thing blew its top around 1075–1080. Research on the timing is ongoing. As they say, time will tell.

62. Doyel 2000c.

63. Downum, Brennan, and Holmlund 1999:53.

64. Downum, Brennan, and Holmlund 1999.

65. Population spiked around Wupatki during the twelfth century, when population was apparently low to the north. Maybe a migration? (This suggestion came, casually, from Christian Downum, personal communication, 2000.) The middle/late twelfth century has been seen as a period of population decrease in the northern and middle San Juan (Lipe, Varien, and Wilshusen 1999, whose views I follow here), but it is the current opinion of researchers associated with Crow Canyon Archaeological Center that twelfth-century population remained more or less level at many multicomponent communities spanning "Chaco" Pueblo II and "Mesa Verde" Pueblo III periods (Scott Ortman and Mark Varien, personal communication, 2004). Either scenario has interesting implications for regional demographics, and for the histories of Salmon and Aztec ruins.

66. Macaws: Hargrave 1970; Haury 1976; Nelson 1986. Copper bells: Vargas 1995. Remarkable regalia: Wilcox 1999a. Wilcox notes that "emblems of ritual and political office, which probably derived from Chacoan models, were adopted in the Flagstaff-Verde Valley-Prescott area in the A.D. 1150–1250 period. They consisted of the turquoise-encrusted raptorial bird symbol…and the turquoise encrusted toad" (Wilcox 1999a:137–38). He argues that Chacoan ideology was modified and expanded by Wupatki—for example, with the addition of elaborate nose plugs (a West Mexican form).

67. Lekson 1999b; Lipe and Varien 1999b.

68. Laurie Reed, personal communication, 2007.

69. Aztec's region suffers from much the same skepticism that met Chaco's region three decades ago. Then, many archaeologists in Colorado and Utah denied adamantly that Chaco ever poached into Mesa Verde or the Great Sage Plain. After much hard work, that changed. We wore 'em down. Chaco in the northern San Juan is no longer a question of yes or no, but of how and when.

It's déjà vu all over again with Aztec. Not in my backyard! There's no Aztec at Mesa Verde (e.g., Lipe 2006). For some archaeologists (but certainly not for Lipe), it's almost as if there's *no Aztec*. In their discussion of Mesa Verde sacred landscapes, my colleagues Winston Hurst and Jonathan Till say, "Although no great-house site has been identified as a paramount ritual center for the entire Mesa Verde region, it is possible that certain major sites exerted ritual influence over a relatively large area." They go on to name "Yellow Jacket Pueblo, for example," and *never mention Aztec Ruins* (Hurst and Till 2006:77–78). Aztec is the obvious paramount ritual (and political and economic) center for the Mesa Verde region. It's just *off* center geographically (as was Chaco). Yellow Jacket (a huge site and dear to my heart) was just a big town—and not the "Four Corners Anasazi Ceremonial Center" it once aspired to be (Lange et al. 1986).

70. Lekson 1999b versus Lipe 2006.

71. Glowacki 2006; Kearney 2000; Kuckelman 2003; Lekson 1999b.

72. Circular and D-shaped bi- and tri-walled structures were found from Aztec to the Montezuma Valley in

southeastern Utah and south almost to Gallup, New Mexico. Tri-walls were the defining elements of Aztec's cityscape—John Stein's idea (Stein and McKenna 1988), which I appropriated (Lekson 1999b:fig. 3.6). The earliest tri-wall I know is attached to Pueblo del Arroyo at Chaco. It may date to the early 1100s. Significantly, the Pueblo del Arroyo tri-wall was one of the last things built at Chaco, and it was razed! They built it and then tore it down. All the other circular bi- and tri-walls date well after 1100—most, I think, in the thirteenth century.

Bi- and tri-walled structures probably mark the region of which Aztec Ruins was the center, the capital. Yellow Jacket's monumental bi-walled "Great Tower" (Kuckelman 2003) represents Aztec Ruins' presence at the largest Mesa Verde town—at least in my version of prehistory. Of course, there are arguments to the contrary (e.g., Glowacki 2006).

Our knowledge of bi- and tri-walled structures is less complete than our knowledge of Great Houses; one survey lists only sixteen, including three at Aztec (Glowacki 2006:table 3.5; see also Kearney 2000). To that number, I add bi-walls at Red Willow, near Gallup, New Mexico, and at Kin Li Chii, near Ganado, Arizona, for a total of eighteen. Almost all are within a 140-kilometer radius of Aztec Ruins. The single exception, Kin Li Chii, is 180 kilometers from the new Chaco.

Some archaeologists consider multi-walled D-shaped structures as variations on the tri-wall theme. Intriguingly, there are eighteen D-shaped structures, about the same number as circular bi- and tri-walls, and they have exclusive geographic distributions (Glowacki 2006:table 3.5). Most of the circular bi- and tri-walled structures were east of Cortez, Colorado, and most D-shaped structures were west of Cortez (Glowacki 2006:fig. 3.10). That's the kind of strong pattern that means something...but what?

There are no D-shaped structures at Aztec Ruins, *except of course Aztec West itself*. It's been suggested that the D-shaped structures—mimicking the form of classic Chaco sites such as Pueblo Bonito and Chetro Ketl—represented a mid-thirteenth-century revival of Chacoan ideologies (Bradley 1996), an idea with merit. Could circular versus D shapes signal yet another religious schism within Aztec's fragmenting world? Stay tuned.

73. Reyman's (1985) suggestion that tri-walls were circular stepped pyramids, like those of (much earlier) Teuchitlán in western Mexico, is worth considering. In his reconstruction, the central cylinder was three stories tall, the inner ring of concentric rooms was two, and the outer ring one. These were filled, much like platform mounds.

Based on the excavation of precisely one tri-wall, Reyman's solid-fill reconstruction seems to be incorrect. But what if he is right about stepped stories (an inner tower of three, a middle ring of two, and an outer ring of one story)? Bi-walls and tri-walls would then become towers and—if shorn of their surrounding concentric rooms—not unlike the ubiquitous towers of Pueblo III in the northern San Juan. That is, Mesa Verde towers might have been tri-walled structures without the outer rings of rooms.

74. Glowacki 2006:63.

75. Cameron 2008; Lipe 2006.

76. Lipe and Varien 1999b:303.

77. I use the word *unspeakable* literally and ironically. These were acts of appalling violence, differing from twentieth-century cruelties only in scale. One cannot imagine the horror of extended families cut to ribbons and their bodies, in pieces, tossed into kivas (Turner and Turner 1999; White 1992). I believe that these executions were public and meant to intimidate villagers from the surrounding countryside. Archaeology adds another meaning to *unspeakable* by censoring our knowledge of these events. One reason Dr. Turner was so obstreperous in his use of the media was that his views were literally forbidden at regional meetings: he was denied the podium. I don't approve of his sensationalism, but I can understand his frustrations with the field.

78. Billman, Lambert, and Leonard 2000; Turner and Turner 1999; White 1992.

79. Turner and Turner 1999.

80. Lipe 2006.

81. Lekson 2002b.

82. Kuckelman 2002; LeBlanc 1999.

83. Kuckelman 2003.

84. Ortman and Bradley 2002.

85. Adler 1996.

86. Haas and Creamer 1993; LeBlanc 1999.

87. Lekson and Cameron 1995.

88. Irwin-Williams 2006.

89. Earl Morris (1919–1928) described discrete, distinct "Chaco" and "Mesa Verde" occupations at Aztec Ruins. It seemed clear enough: the Chaco building went up in the early 1100s, the Great House was abandoned in the late 1100s or early 1200s, and Mesa Verde people (en route to the Rio Grande) took over the still serviceable buildings in the mid-1200s (Lekson and Cameron 1995). Cynthia Irwin-Williams, who excavated

Salmon Ruins, initially saw the same thing there: "The reoccupation of the town by non-Chacoan groups after nearly a century of abandonment and decay" (Irwin-Williams 1972:14). During the course of excavations at Salmon Ruins, scattered deposits, usually high in room fill, suggested a shadowy "intermediate" occupation. This has now become the Early San Juan Period, dated 1125 to about 1180, with a full-bore later occupation, now termed the Late San Juan Period, dated about 1180 to 1280 (Reed 2006:fig. 12.1).

I don't doubt the reality of the Early San Juan Period, but I wonder how extensive it was at Salmon Ruins. The "intermediate" was so ephemeral that its existence was a matter of heated debate when Irwin-Williams excavated the site. The architectural differences and discontinuities between Chacoan and Late San Juan (that is, Mesa Verde) occupations were striking and suggested a real break between the two.

I think Morris and Irwin-Williams were more right than wrong: there was a significant discontinuity between the initial post-Chaco period and the later Mesa Verde uses of Salmon and Aztec. The final Mesa Verde period was very much a "reoccupation," peasants taking over the palace.

90. The word *abandonment* is problematic. Pueblo people hold that the Four Corners is not now abandoned and has never been. They are, of course, correct—from their perspective. Even though Pueblo people no longer live there, the ancestral towns of the Four Corners are spiritually linked to modern Pueblos. The term is not so entangled in other parts of the world, where archaeology routinely studies abandonments. It's a common field of study. There's no better word in the thesaurus to describe the total depopulation of a region. As an archaeologist, I'd hate to see the southwestern situation disappear into euphemisms. Since this is an archaeology book, I use the word; but I apologize to Pueblo readers, and I hope this note informs readers who might not be aware of the problem.

Southwestern archaeology has been curiously ambivalent about collapse and abandonment. The events of this chapter (and the previous chapter) provide a study in two areas where I have research interests, Chaco and Mimbres. The awkward anomaly of Chaco (political power in the ancient Pueblo world) is minimized by abandonment and collapse. Chaco may have been unpleasantly odd, but at least *it did not last long*—a brief aberration, a short-course syndrome. (I disagree: Chaco moved north and re-created itself at Aztec.) In the south, where evidence of Mimbres collapse and abandonment seems far stronger than for Chaco, archaeologists work hard to keep post-Mimbres alive: no collapse, no abandonment (e.g., Hegmon and Nelson 2006; Nelson 1999; Nelson and Hegmon 2001). That interpretation of Mimbres could of course be entirely correct, but I'm struck by the extreme measures taken for Mimbres life support, curiously at odds with our unseemly haste to pull Chaco's plug. See also note 176, below.

91. Lipe 2006; Lipe and Varien 1999b; Roney 1995, 1996.

92. Out-migrations began long before 1275 and probably well before 1250. In the mid- to late twelfth century, population rose around the western, southern, and eastern margins of the old Chaco world—at Wupatki on the west (as noted above), around Zuni to the south, and—most contentiously—in the Rio Grande on the east. Rio Grande archaeologists seem uneasy with migrants from the Four Corners (see note 106), but demography probably demands in-migration: a notable climb in the Late Developmental Period with a dramatic spike around 1300 (Adler 1996; Adams and Duff 2004). And to the south? A recent study at Zuni suggests major in-migration between 1125 and 1225 but carefully notes "that the archaeological record provides no reason to believe that population movement into the survey area came from outside the broader Zuni area (that is, the area in which the Zuni ceramic types are dominant); that is, sites of this period had a lot of 'local' Zuni pottery types, particularly Tularosa black-and-white and Wingate black-and-red" (Kintigh, Glowacki, and Huntley 2004:443, 444, fig. 4). People were sloshing around in the Tularosa horizon (see note 98), and I expect they did the same in an as-yet-undefined Mesa Verde–Santa Fe carbon-painted horizon to the north, much as Sarah Schlanger suggests (page164, above).

93. Salzer 2000.

94. Dean 1996.

95. Lekson 2002b.

96. Hill et al. 2004. And perhaps there was no going back: the coincidence of several major climatic shifts around 1290 "changed the world," very much for the worse, in the Four Corners (Gregory and Nials 2007:71–74).

97. Greiser and More 1995.

98. Lekson 1996b. Tularosa black-on-white and associated types paralleled the contemporary Mesa Verde style far to the north. The northern edge of Tularosa was approximately Acoma, Zuni, and Wide Ruins in Arizona; the southern boundary may have followed a line from Truth or Consequences through Gila Cliff Dwellings to Safford, reaching the upper reaches of the Gila River and the Salt River.

We are told that Tularosa black-on-white evolved from local types across this large area, but, given so many parents, the end product was remarkably homogeneous. There are similarities, in fact, to contemporary Mesa

Verde styles (Franklin 1980), in both design and finish, and of course notable differences, all of which need not detain us here. A key difference was this: Mesa Verde black-on-white was most commonly in bowl forms (and of course jars too, but in normal southwestern proportions). Tularosa black-on-white was very predominately jar forms; bowls were rare. (Mesa Verde decorated both.) People of the Tularosa horizon carried their water in brightly decorated jars; they ate their meals from unpainted, smudged interior bowls. Tularosa black-on-white designs on jars were meant to be seen, to identify the user in some recognizable way. I will not speculate here what that ceramic horizon might have meant, but from the marked differences of display, I am pretty confident Tularosa meant *something*.

Many Tularosa horizon sites were extraordinarily large; a few around Zuni had as many as fourteen hundred rooms (Kintigh 1996). The big Zuni sites and several other "Tularosa" sites, such as Kin Tiel, were remarkable for their geometric formality—giant squares, circles, or ovals, almost Chacoan in their precision (Bernardini 2004; Kintigh 1985) (fig. 6.10). Most Tularosa sites were smaller and less formal of course, but largeness was characteristic—for example, on the east end, the Victorio site of five hundred rooms (Laumbach and Wakeman 1999); to the west, Turkey Creek (at Point of Pines) with three hundred rooms.

99. Cameron and Duff 2008; Kintigh, Glowacki, and Huntley 2004:445.

100. Turner and Turner 1999:fig. 3.1—only a few in the south, compared to the northern San Juan.

101. LeBlanc 1999:240–243.

102. Adams and Duff 2004; Adler 1996.

103. Hill et al. 2004.

104. Schlanger 2007:183.

105. Modern migrations are the subject of an enormous theoretical literature, mostly from economics and sociology (e.g., Brettell and Hollifield 2000; Castles and Miller 2003; for anthropology, Brettell 2000). Contemporary migration theory understandably focuses on the present. For example, *The Cambridge Survey of World Migration* (Cohen 1995) covers only the past three centuries. Contemporary and even historical migrations do not provide full—perhaps not even adequate—range for comprehensive theory. (Historical approaches are notoriously atheoretical—for example, Diner 2000.) Prehistory certainly offers situations not represented in modern migration—for example, the peopling of the New World and the Pacific. We will see nothing like that again until someone colonizes a planet.

Some recent migration theory is moving toward inclusion of prehistoric migrations (e.g., Demuth 2000; Marsella and Ring 2003, who cite Jared Diamond's *Guns, Germs and Steel* as a major source). It seems likely that the Southwest—with its rich demographic, environmental, and economic data—can contribute to migration theory by expanding the range of inquiry to premodern migrations and by clarifying methodology for their study.

The Southwest provided an early, classic study of archaeological migrations, Emil Haury's "Evidence at Point of Pines for a Prehistoric Migration from Northern Arizona" (1958). Haury described a remarkably clear Tusayan-Kayenta "site unit intrusion" from northeastern Arizona into a large Mogollon pueblo in the Mogollon highlands of southern Arizona (see also Dean 1996b:39–40; Lindsay 1987; Stone 2001, 2003, 2005). Haury marshaled a range of archaeological evidence; out-of-place ceramics, details of domestic architecture, "kivas," crop varieties, and Tusayan-Kayenta ritual objects made a strong case. Much of this evidence was remarkably well preserved by fire, which had destroyed the migrant barrio. The unfortunate aspect of Haury's otherwise admirable article was that it set the bar very high. Claims for migration were judged against Point of Pines's checklist and of course were most often found wanting. Several other Tusayan-Kayenta–like sites were located in southeastern Arizona (e.g., Di Peso 1958), but migrant sites with Point of Pines's extraordinary resolution were understandably quite rare elsewhere in the Southwest.

Pueblo traditional histories and "migration stories" suggest that migrations were the rule, not the exception. Yet we found remarkably few migration sites—sites *we* recognized as migrations. Was something wrong with our methods or assumptions (e.g., Lathrap 1956; Thompson 1958)?

In the late 1960s, New Archaeology marked a deliberate "retreat from migration" (Adams, VanGerven, and Levy 1978; Anthony 1990). For several decades, migration—if discussed at all—was dismissed as a "nonexplanation." For a couple decades, we really didn't think much about migrations. In the mid-1990s a flurry of studies and dissertations refocused on southwestern migration (e.g., Adler, VanPool, and Leonard 1996; Cameron 1995; Clark 2001; Lekson 1995; Lyons 2003; Mills 1998; Preucel 2005; Reid 1997; G. Rice 1998; Spielmann 1998; Stark, Clark, and Elson 1995; Wilshusen and Ortman 1999; Woodson 1999) and migration's logical counterpart, abandonment (e.g., Cameron and Tomka 1993; Glowacki 2006; Hill et al. 2004; Nelson and Hegmon 2001; Nelson and Schachner 2002). Migration has again become a major focus for southwestern archaeology.

There were at least three reasons for renewed interest. First, NAGPRA required archaeology to determine "cultural affiliations" of sites and remains, and that invariably involves migrations—a very real-world, practical application (e.g., Duke 1999; Perry 2003; Wozniak 1996). Second, collaborations with southwestern tribes (beyond NAGPRA) led to a new appreciation of oral histories and traditions, which often deal with migrations (e.g., Ferguson and Colwell-Chanthaphonh 2006; Ferguson and Hart 1985; Gregory and Wilcox 2007; Ortman 2007; Washburn 1995; see also Deloria 1995; Echo-Hawk 2000). And third, the 1990s saw an encompassing turn toward historicity in the social sciences (McDonald 1996); in southwestern archaeology, migrations are among the more obvious "events" (sensu Sewell 2005) with which to frame history.

Because of the "retreat from migration" from the 1960s to the 1990s, however, the methodology of migration lagged in the Southwest (reviews in Clark 2001 and Lyons 2003). NAGPRA "cultural affiliation" studies forced archaeologists to reengage with migration, working with the tools of the 1950s. Did pottery equal people? Or details of domestic architecture? If the Point of Pines model set the bar too high, where—realistically—should it be set? Questions like these guide NAGPRA cultural affiliation determinations made by field, museum, and agency archaeologists, with profound consequences for collections and cultural heritage.

106. For the Rio Grande, Adler 1996; Crown, Orcutt, and Kohler 1996. One reviewer of this book complained that the Rio Grande does not show up until chapters 6 and 7. Well, yes. You can say the same for Casas Grandes. They both got interesting after 1200. The Rio Grande went through a long and comparatively uneventful Developmental Period (650 to 1200), followed by a more intriguing Coalition Period (1200 to 1350) and then the very remarkable Classic Period (1350 to 1600). That's the standard view, and I accept it (see chapter 5, note 172). This is not to say that nothing happened in the Rio Grande before 1200, but what happened was (it seems) primarily of local interest. For example, big Developmental Period sites (such as Arroyo Negro near Santa Fe) would fit comfortably among many scores of other, bigger contemporary sites in the Four Corners. If we are looking for historical highpoints, Arroyo Negro does not challenge Chaco.

Before 1200 the action—*many* more sites and *many* more people—was clearly to the west and northwest. *Of course* there were people in the Rio Grande before 1200, but compared with the rest of the Southwest, the Rio Grande was not exceptional and is therefore effectively absent from chapters 1 through 5. During the Coalition Period (after 1200), things heated up: Coalition Period sites weighed in at fifty to sixty rooms (Adler 1996:appendix), but there were not many sites of that size. Most of the Coalition Period northern Rio Grande shows vegetal-painted pottery associations with a larger ceramic horizon that stretches back to the Four Corners (Roney 1995, 1996)—types called "frozen McElmo" by ceramic guru C. Dean Wilson (personal communication, 2007).

The Mesa Verde region began to see major out-migration prior to 1250. That's when the Rio Grande got large. Connecting the dots, we arrive at the long-accepted interpretation:

> Aggregation [into sites of fifty rooms or more] occurred in all areas [of the northern Rio Grande]…in the AD 1250 to 1300 period. In some areas, aggregation appears to have grown out of already existing patterns among the indigenous population, but in other areas, initial occupation occurs in aggregated forms, suggesting movement of aggregated communities from elsewhere. (Crown, Orcutt, and Kohler 1996:201)

That's interesting *but not exceptional*: it was happening all over the Southwest. It is during the Classic Period, with all those new people living in remarkably large villages, that the northern Rio Grande demands (and rewards) our attention; see chapter 7.

Some Santa Fe–based archaeologists reject this reading. They apparently think that Developmental sites are seriously underrepresented and that the startling population spike at 1250–1350 was mostly locals having babies (see chapter 5, note 172). I find this isolationism truly baffling—and a bit discouraging.

107. Lekson et al. 2002.

108. Clark 2001; Lyons 2003.

109. The University of Colorado's Pinnacle Ruin Project investigated migration at a Magdalena Phase (1300 to 1450), two-hundred-room pueblo located 50 kilometers northwest of Truth or Consequences, New Mexico, and 400 kilometers south of Mesa Verde National Park. Pottery from Pinnacle Ruin and other Magdalena Phase sites appears to be a late form of Mesa Verde black-on-white, and Magdalena Phase masonry more closely resembles that of the Mesa Verde region than any local traditions of southern New Mexico. Tens of thousands of people left the Mesa Verde region between 1250 and 1300; it is possible that a thousand Mesa Verde migrants founded the Magdalena Phase sites.

The Magdalena Phase comprises three large pueblos and a handful of smaller sites in southern New Mexico: the Gallinas Spring site (near Magdalena), investigated by unpublished field schools; the Roadmap site (near Truth or Consequences), currently investigated by Arizona State University; and Pinnacle Ruin. The University of Colorado conducted excavations at Pinnacle Ruin in 2000–2004. Our preliminary interpretations, based on the first two years' work at Pinnacle Ruin and review of notes and collections from the Gallinas

Spring site, was that the Magdalena Phase represented a possible Mesa Verde migration (Lekson et al. 2002).

Pinnacle Ruin is far beyond the conventional "Anasazi" region. Because of increased contrast with extant or indigenous groups, there is increased clarity in migration at or beyond the edges. Pinnacle Ruin was part of a broad arc of such situations in the thirteenth- and fourteenth-century southern Southwest, from southeastern Arizona through the Magdalena Phase area of southern New Mexico to the northern Rio Grande—migrations with which Pinnacle Ruin and the Magdalena Phase can be compared and contrasted.

Clear migrant sites in southeastern Arizona include Point of Pines, Reeve Ruin (Di Peso 1958) and other sites along the San Pedro River (Clark 2006), and sites such as Goat Hill along the Gila River (Woodson 1999). These sites very closely resemble Tusayan-Kayenta sites transposed several hundred kilometers to the south, and they meet most Point of Pines criteria (see note 105, above). As Stone (2003) has demonstrated, migrations deeper into southeastern Arizona were not all so clearly marked, archaeologically. The total size of the Tusayan-Kayenta immigration into southern Arizona was comparatively small, perhaps five hundred rooms in a score of sites (an estimate currently being refined by the Center for Desert Archaeology; Hill et al. 2004). The size of individual migrating groups was apparently small, with the largest migrant components totaling seventy rooms. The context into which they migrated varied: some groups moved into sparsely occupied valleys; other groups intruded into very large existing towns. Migrations on scales similar to Point of Pines, but with quite variable archaeological consequences, took place at the Grasshopper site (Reid and Whittlesey 2005a) and in the Silver Creek area (Mills 1998, 1999). Artifactual or architectural markers of ethnicity, such as those seen at Point of Pines, were "emphasized in some places, de-emphasized in others, and ignored altogether in still others" (Stone 2003:31). Cultural coherence and survival of prior cultural forms varied.

In contrast, northern Rio Grande migrations are far less obvious in terms of material culture. It has long been assumed that substantial numbers of Mesa Verde migrants joined existing pueblos on the Rio Grande (Cameron 1995; Duff and Wilshusen 2000), and numbers of potential migrants in the Mesa Verde area have been estimated in the tens of thousands (e.g., Kohler et al. 2007; Lipe and Varien 1999b). The Rio Grande was certainly occupied in the thirteenth and fourteenth centuries, in larger numbers than we had previously believed. But population reconstructions show a notable spike in the early fourteenth century that seems to require in-migration (Crown, Orcutt, and Kohler 1996; Hill et al. 2004). It seems likely that the Rio Grande in-migration was very large, but it is very difficult (compared with Point of Pines or Pinnacle Ruin) to "see" Four Corners migrant groups in the northern Rio Grande, which leads to the reasonable assumption that migration was undertaken by small *group-size* social units (families) joining existing villages, rather than larger migrant groups (clans, villages) establishing new towns (e.g., Cordell 1995). A key Rio Grande pottery type, Galisteo black-on-white, resembles Mesa Verde types (Breternitz, Rohn, and Morris 1974), and it was common in fourteenth-century components at some Rio Grande sites (e.g., Snead 2004). Its significance is a matter of debate (e.g., Habicht-Mauche 1993). Only a few "keyhole-shaped kivas" and two or three mugs are known from the northern Rio Grande—from an archaeological sample many times larger than the Magdalena Phase. Apparently, these migrant small groups integrated into existing large Rio Grande towns, losing their original "ethnic" identities—that is, low cultural coherence.

Pinnacle Ruin and the other Magdalena Phase sites fall somewhere between Point of Pines's clarity and the Rio Grande's murky situation. Magdalena Phase sites were probably new towns established in an empty frontier—pending clarification of the dating of Pinnacle Ruin and the nearby Tularosa Phase Victorio site (the focus of ongoing research). The total Magdalena Phase migration may have been eight hundred rooms, with three sites showing variable group sizes and the largest site, Gallinas Spring, perhaps reaching five hundred rooms. Pinnacle Ruin, with two hundred rooms, lacks the range of architectural and artifactual evidence of Point of Pines. The decorated ceramic evidence for migration is compelling (Laumbach 2006; Lincoln 2007), utility ceramics less so (Schleher and Ruth 2005; cf. Hegmon, Nelson, and Ennes 2000). Well-coursed walls at Pinnacle Ruin and Gallinas Spring had no precedents in southern New Mexico, but several cruder cobble walls at Pinnacle and Roadmap are not unlike those observed at the earlier Victorio site (Laumbach and Wakeman 1999). Where many Arizona sites replicate in remarkable detail the sites of the Tusayan-Kayenta "homeland," key elements of the Mesa Verde tradition—distinctive "keyhole-shaped kivas," mug and "kiva jar" ceramic forms, and ceremonial "tchamahia" celts—are absent at Magdalena sites—traditions left behind, perhaps, in the disruptions of Pueblo III in the Four Corners. (The Gallinas Spring site, however, reportedly had five kivas [Davis 1964]). Thus Magdalena Phase cultural coherence was much lower than at Point of Pines but arguably higher than at Rio Grande sites. While ceramic and architectural evidence, on balance, certainly suggest a migration, it is the *context* of Pinnacle Ruin and the Magdalena Phase sites—in empty frontier valleys—that most clearly indicates in-migration.

110. LeBlanc 1999:197–276.
111. Duff and Lekson 2006; Kintigh 1985, 1996; Kintigh, Glowacki, and Huntley 2004.

112. Lekson 1996b.

113. Brown 1973; Lekson 1996b, 2002a; Neuzil 2005.

114. Elson and Clark forthcoming; Elson, Stark, and Gregory 2000; G. Rice 1998.

115. Gladwin [1938]1975:266.

116. Doyel 1981.

117. Abbott 2000:195.

118. Rice 2001:304; see also LeBlanc 1999; Wallace and Doelle 2001; Wilcox 1989.

119. Downum 1993; Fish, Fish, and Villalpando 2007.

120. Abbott 2003; Graybill et al. 2006; Nials et al. 1989.

121. Abbott 2003:63, table 3.6.

122. Gladwin [1938]1975; Haury 1945.

123. "Little is known about Santan phase [Late Sedentary/Early Classic] platforms as the evidence remains concealed inside the massive mounds of later phases" (Doyel 2000a:305).

124. Fish and Fish 2000a; Fish, Fish, and Madsen 1992.

125. For example, Snaketown: Haury 1976; Grewe: Craig (ed.) 2000; Azatlan: Doyel and Crary 1996.

126. Craig 2000b, 2001a.

127. Fish and Fish 2000a:247.

128. Fish and Fish 2000a:252.

129. For example, Pueblo Grande; Abbott (ed.) 2003.

130. For example, Doyel 1991a:253.

131. Fish and Fish 2000a:261.

132. Fish and Fish 2000a:267–71.

133. Doyel 1974.

134. Doelle, Gregory, and Wallace 1995; Rice and Redman 2000.

135. Gregory 1987:fig. 7.

136. In chapter 4, I argued that ball courts were markers of the Colonial expansion, bending David Wilcox's (1991d) data to my evil purposes to make that case. Wilcox dates several ball courts at Classic sites to the Early Classic. I suspect that many ball courts were *used* in the Early Classic, as the Hohokam Canon waned before platform mound ideologies, but that most of those courts were carryovers from the Sedentary Period, mostly at exceptional Classic Period towns built atop Sedentary sites.

137. For example, Bostwick 1992; Doelle, Gregory, and Wallace 1995; Downum and Bostwick 2003; Elson and Abbott 2000; Gregory 1987; Lindauer 1992.

138. The openness of mounds changed in the Late Sedentary. Mound 16, for example, was surrounded by a circle of posts or poles. Was this a fence to keep things in or a palisade to keep riffraff out? Or an architectural embellishment (like "wainscoting" in Chaco kivas), the symbolism of which we have yet to understand? The posts around Mound 16 may have been the beginnings of the enclosing walls of later platform mounds, or Cahokia's Woodhenge or something like it.

139. Gregory 1987; Doyel 1991a, 2000a.

140. Gregory 1987:188.

141. Gregory 1987:188–89.

142. Downum and Bostwick 2003:169–70.

143. Doyel 2000a:305–08, fig. 13.5.

144. For example, Doelle, Gregory, and Wallace 1995:386.

145. Another angle on the question: unlike Mound 8 and Pueblo Grande, most excavated platforms in the Phoenix Basin and elsewhere (Tonto, Tucson, eastern Papagueria; Doelle, Gregory, and Wallace 1995:table 13.1) were *not* built directly over earlier low round mounds. Quo vadis continuity?

146. "(1) Classic period [platform mounds]…was an invention that occurred and radiated from one place [the Phoenix Basin]…(2) social differentiation thought to be represented by this form of mound had already developed in Phoenix Basin irrigation communities prior to the invention and spread of the Classic period form; and (3) these factors contributed to (and perhaps even encouraged) the rapid spread of the form across the Phoenix Basin" (Doelle, Gregory, and Wallace 1995:438).

147. For example, Downum and Bostwick 2003.

148. Fish and Fish 2000a, 2000c.

149. Compare Doelle, Gregory, and Wallace 1995:table 13.1.

150. Doelle, Gregory, and Wallace 1995:438.

151. Three platforms on (and beyond) the edges of the Hohokam world—Gatlin, Pueblo Viejo, and

Pueblo Bonito—are worth considering in this regard. The Gatlin mound (Wasley 1960) is a key exhibit in the argument for pre-Classic to Classic continuity (Gregory 1987) because it (1) was built in the pre-Classic Sedentary Period and (2) seems to combine the sloping facing of low mounds with the height and massiveness of the taller, later platforms. It is an intermediate form, the missing link, if we are hoping to find one, but it sits off to the west in splendid isolation from Phoenix.

Far to the east sits Pueblo Viejo, almost at the New Mexico line near Safford, Arizona. Pueblo Viejo had the easternmost Hohokam ball court and one of the largest. It also may have had an early platform mound. This structure, which has been variously identified as a Great House and a platform mound, has been dated to the twelfth century. Jesse Walter Fewkes described it as the "central mound": a massive, flat-topped rectangular structure looming over the surrounding site. Today Pueblo Viejo has been so badly damaged that this structure is impossible to identify; it is a sad fact that many of the most important sites in the southern Southwest are no longer intact. Joel Tyberg, in a study of collections from the site, noted that "archeomagnetic and ceramic evidence place the principal occupation of this structure to sometime in the twelfth century... [ceramic evidence consisted of] the prevalence of Hohokam style ceramics coupled with an almost complete lack of Salado polychromes" (Tyberg 2000:217, 218). Tyberg suggested that this structure might be a Hohokam Great House. William Doelle (personal communication, 2005) counters that it might be a platform mound. I think there is merit in *both* suggestions. Many later platforms, especially in the peripheries, consist of pueblolike structures with ground-floor rooms filled in and structures built atop (Doelle, Gregory, and Wallace 1995; Lindauer 1992). The central mound at Pueblo Viejo was probably something like that.

I offer my third extra-Phoenix example with real trepidation. It is two rectangular platforms at Chaco Canyon that assumed their final forms in the early twelfth century; their initial construction must have been even earlier. These are the contentious "trash mounds" of Pueblo Bonito: large, tall, masonry-enclosed rectangular platforms with carefully finished flat upper surfaces. They are comparable in form and size to large (but not the largest) Phoenix Basin platforms.

Two of these three distant platforms—Pueblo Bonito and Gatlin—predate 1150. The third, Pueblo Viejo, if it was indeed a platform, dates to sometime in the twelfth century. In the Phoenix Basin Classic, platforms "probably appear sometime between A.D. 1200 and 1250" (Doelle, Gregory, and Wallace 1995:437). I can't help but think that Hohokam, after 1150, wasn't selling—it was buying. Maybe platforms originated outside the Phoenix Basin and subsequently replaced the Hohokam Canon in its core area. Just a thought.

And, for horrified Hohokam readers, it could be worse: platforms out on the northern periphery perhaps *started out* as Chacoesque Great Houses. I refer to recent excavations in the Tonto Basin, which revealed some interesting progenitors for Tonto Basin platforms (Doelle, Gregory, and Wallace 1995; G. Rice 1998). Glen Rice summarizes the situation in the Tonto Basin around 1250:

> Platform mounds were shared ceremonial precincts serving the needs of residentially dispersed communities, and developed from earlier precincts that consisted of sets of big rooms.... At sites in the Phoenix Basin, the big rooms were arranged in pairs around low, flat topped mounds, but initially no rooms were built on the mound. Sometime after A.D. 1250, the Hohokam began placing the big rooms on top of the platforms, and by then they had developed the technique of constructing flat-topped mounds with vertical faced sides. (G. Rice 1998:235)

"Big-room" structures had rooms with floor areas in excess of 30 square meters (G. Rice 1998:64). Most had two to four of these huge rooms. "By the late 13th century, most had been transformed into platform mound centers" (G. Rice 1998:64). The current interpretation says these were not residences and probably served as "council chambers" (G. Rice 1998:64). To me they look like Great Houses—a century on down the line and transposed 300 kilometers, but not unlike the core rooms of Salmon Ruins or Aztec West. According to Glen Rice (1998:64), big-room structures were not residences because in one excavated example, the ceramics were all bowls (feasting) and the nearest residential compound was 500 meters distant. People weren't cooking there but eating.

Sounds like a (small) palace to me. Several big-room structures were physically subsumed into platform mounds. For example, V:5:76/700 the Pillar site was a big-room structure later "encased" in a platform (G. Rice 1998:fig 4.10). I find this case remarkably interesting: could this platform have started out as a Plateau Great House? Classic platform mounds were usually constructed by erecting an empty enclosure with stout adobe (or sometimes stone masonry) retaining walls and infilling the empty space within. The physics of the thing is interesting: it was asking much of a simple puddled-adobe retaining wall—a rectangle the size of a tennis court and head high—to hold back the many tons of earth piled within to create the mound. Before filling, the empty mound-in-becoming was subdivided with interior "cells" (which, to the untrained eye, look rather like rooms in a pueblo), presumably to even the strain. However they did it, they managed, and a large

Classic platform mound is indeed an impressive structure (see the discussion of Pueblo Grande, chapter 7).

152. Wallace 1995.

153. Fish, Fish, and Villalpando 2007; O'Donovan 2004.

154. Downum, Fish, and Fish 1994.

155. For example, Wallace and Doelle 2001; Wilcox 1979.

156. For example, Downum 1993; Downum, Fish, and Fish 1994.

157. Nelson 2007; O'Donovan 2004; Zavala 2006.

158. Nelson 2007.

159. Fish, Fish, and Villalpando 2007; Newell and Gallaga 2004.

160. McGuire and Villalpando 1993; but see O'Donovan 2004.

161. Whalen and Minnis (2003) summarized my 1999 argument accurately and fairly (hallmarks of their work). I may not do so well by them—if not, I apologize. But with all respect, I doubt their dating.

A review of Chihuahua chronology from my perspective: Di Peso developed a continuous (but not gradual!) history through three periods: Viejo (pre-Paquimé Pithouse horizons), Medio (Paquimé), and Tardio (post-Paquimé and Colonial). I suggested that the Viejo Period, which preceded Paquimé, ended about 1150 while Paquimé itself dated to the late 1200s or even after 1300 (Lekson 1999b). I thought that gap was interesting and meaningful, but Chihuahua researchers took it as a challenge and attacked it on two fronts: the central Casas Grandes area, the scene of Whalen and Minnis's work, and the southern margins, an area researched by Jane Kelley, Joe Stewart, and their colleagues. Whalen and Minnis (2003) are pushing back Medio; Stewart and colleagues (2004, 2005) are pushing forward Viejo. With two such talented teams pushing from either end, it seems inevitable that they will meet in the middle. Chronological continuity is *necessary* if one views Paquimé as a process. But it's not so inevitable if one sees Paquimé as a historical event.

When did the Medio Period begin? Di Peso (1974) wanted the Medio to start in the early or middle twelfth century, contemporary with Chaco. Whalen and Minnis (2003) prefer to start the Medio Period in the early or middle thirteenth century. I argued that most or all of Paquimé itself was early fourteenth century (Lekson 1999b), but for the Medio Period elsewhere, I am open to ideas. Kelley and Stewart's work on the southern margins supports a late-1200s dating (Stewart et al. 2004, 2005). The Medio Period and Paquimé need not march together: the city might rise later than the ceramics (and so forth) that define the period.

Dating in the Casas Grandes region relies on 14C. Paquimé itself produced only a handful of tree-ring dates (chapter 7), and other sites so far have none. Carbon 14 dating is far better than no dates, but it can be wonderfully elastic. Those seeking continuity can use the safer, longer spread of two-sigma readings; those looking for events might prefer the riskier, shorter spread of one-sigma readings or even intercepts. Both Whalen and Minnis (2003) and Stewart and others (2004, 2005) use two-sigma calibrated spans or ranges. That's sensible, conservative, blue chip. But we should bear in mind that a two-sigma span is not a date; it's simply the range within which the calendar date has a 67 percent chance of falling. Typically, two-sigma spans for the recent Chihuahua dates are 150 to 250 years, and of course many are considerably longer. We go, almost imperceptibly, from the target of a single, specific year to a span of two or three centuries—it's the nature of 14C. But in both vague impressions and closely reasoned arguments, it is important to remind ourselves that two-sigma spans are *not* chronological ranges—say, from 1278 to 1413—but a statistical smear. Somewhere in that smear is a real date, a single year, in which the corncob burned.

Whalen and Minnis (2003) date the Medio Period to the mid-thirteenth century, based on 14C dates from a nearby ruin, most of which have upper two-sigma limits between 1280 and 1300 (Whalen and Minnis 2003:table 1). That is, most dates are probably earlier than 1300—two chances out of three. It is important to note that almost all these dates were on wood fragments, not annuals. This point is really important: wood almost certainly biases dates *earlier* than the event to be dated, often several decades earlier. There is no rule of thumb, but fifty years off (that is, too early) is quite possible.

A critical bit of data in all of this is Gila Polychrome. I made the argument that Paquimé was post-1300 because every provenience with more than a few sherds included Gila Polychrome, which is firmly dated to 1300 and after. Was Gila Polychrome present at Whalen and Minnis's pre-1300 Medio site? Their presentation (Whalen and Minnis 2003) is silent on this critical question. I doubt that means Gila Polychrome was absent, since they note that much of the site was undeniably occupied in the fourteenth century, but was Gila Polychrome present in the rooms producing the putative pre-1300 14C dates? This is a straightforward question that I am confident they will answer in future publications.

Kelley and Stewart and Company work on the southern margins of the Casas Grandes region (Stewart et al. 2005). Of twenty-eight Medio Period dates they've reported (at the time of this writing), twenty-one have *lower* limits of two-sigma spans later than 1250 (Stewart et al. 2004, 2005:fig. 11.5). Looking at contexts and not individual dates, fourteen contexts have two-sigma spans that postdate 1250; two postdate 1200, three span a period from 1000 to 1400, and four *predate* 1200. I see these dates as strong evidence that the Medio Period began 1250 or later. Stewart and his colleagues seem to accept this view: "Most researchers believe that the Viejo Period ends with the beginning of the Medio Period at ca. A.D. 1200/1250" (Stewart et al. 2005:176). But in their conclusions, they offer the interesting statement, "The Medio Period…at Paquimé is currently thought to begin ca. 1130/1150 to 1250" (Stewart et al. 2005:188). "1130/1150" of course is the standing end date for Viejo, and if we seek continuity, then that's when Medio must begin.

What of the Viejo Period? When *did* it end? The Viejo Period is the province of Stewart and Kelley and friends; they have spent far more time in Viejo contexts, out on the southern edge of the Casas Grandes region, than have Whalen and Minnis in the heartland. (I think that disparity reflects, in part, a real paucity of Viejo Period sites in the Casas Grandes heartland.) In southern Chihuahua, Stewart, Kelley, and colleagues seem to be pushing the Viejo Period up to the early or mid-thirteenth century (Kelley et al. 1999, 2004). The gap is closed—continuity.

Is it? The latest intrusive ceramic type found at Viejo Period sites is Mimbres black-on-white, which, according to Harry Shafer, "came to an end shortly before 1140 in the Mimbres Valley and probably elsewhere outside the valley" (Shafer 2003:185; contra Nelson 1999). Mimbres black-on-white plays the same role in dating Viejo's end that Gila Polychrome plays in dating Medio's beginnings. Mimbres black-on-white is present in almost all Late Viejo assemblages throughout the Casas Grandes area, even to the far south, hundreds of kilometers from the Mimbres Valley (Burd Larkin 2006; Di Peso 1974; Stewart et al. 2005). Stewart and others accept claims for Mimbres through the 1200s and cite Oppelt (2002) for an end date of Mimbres black-on-white of 1250 (which comes, I assume, from Breternitz 1966—seriously out of date). They note somewhat circularly that "these temporal inferences are consistent with the radiocarbon data" (Stewart et al. 2005:187). They seem to accept that Mimbres black-on-white dates more than a century later in southern Chihuahua than in the Mimbres region. But with two-sigma spans, we can move the end of Viejo up to 1250—if that's what we want to do.

Chihuahua researchers may well push the Medio back beyond 1250 or move Viejo up to 1250. But remember the Hohokam chronology (chapter 4). If we learned nothing else from the Hohokam chronology wars, we learned that consummately careful scholars can make data do whatever the hell they want—especially 14C dates and ceramic seriations. (I myself do it occasionally; see chapters 2 through 7.)

I cannot conclude this note without another example, less consequential, but important to me. I suggested that there were no contexts or structures at Paquimé that, based on absolute dates or ceramics, could be confidently dated before about 1300 (and thus there was a gap between the earlier Viejo Period and the rise of that magnificent Medio Period city). Whalen and Minnis concede that "in a strict sense this statement is true" (2003:324) but counter that Di Peso excavated only one-quarter of the site and that pre-1300 contexts no doubt lie beneath unexcavated areas. I can respond that 25 percent is a pretty good sample and that sample included many structures that the excavator himself identified as Early (pre-1300) Medio Period. They weren't. I mention this quibble here mainly because it makes me proud—one of the few times in my career I have been chastened for cleaving too closely to data. I love it: "In a strict sense, this statement is true."

162. Whalen and Minnis 2003.

163. Di Peso 1974.

164. Lekson 1999b.

165. Whalen and Minnis 2003:328.

166. What do we mean by "local" and "distant"? Whalen and Minnis define local as *within the region* and cite "the broadest definition" (2003:314) of region as Andrew Duff's intentional circularity: "Regions are essentially the scale at which archaeologists believe social interactions were concentrated" (Duff 2000:71). Duff diplomatically leaves the definition open to the archaeologist. Dr. Jones, it's time to ask yourself *what you believe*: natural laboratory or Big History?

Whalen and Minnis work within the tradition of natural laboratories, although they do not use that term. They equate regions with "major topographic subdivisions, the Tucson Basin for instance" (Whalen and Minnis 2003:314). Sounds a lot like Binford's "research design," although the Tucson Basin is big for an old school natural lab. Natural laboratories don't work for the questions we now ask; topographic subdivisions probably won't do either. We can't understand the Tucson Basin, for example, without reference to Phoenix, at least during the Colonial Period (chapter 4)—not to mention the provenance of Tucson's Early Agricultural Period (chapter 2)! Chaco and Hohokam were both bigger than a drainage basin or a topographic subdivision, and I strongly suspect that Casas Grandes was bigger than Chaco or Hohokam. Large-scale dynamics—like migrations and "fallow valleys"—don't seem to scare anyone in Arizona or New Mexico, but they've yet to register in Chihuahua archaeology.

167. Lieberman 2003:460.

168. Whalen and Minnis 2001, forthcoming. Whalen and Minnis frame the problem in fascinating terms, antithetical to Lieberman (and me):

> When archaeological knowledge of an area is sparse, developmental models tend to focus on distant or external pressures for change. There is, in other words, an understandable tendency to argue from better-known cases, projecting their attributes into more obscure situations. This observation explains why explanations of change relying on external factors were so common in the early days of archaeology. As knowledge grows, local continuities often become more apparent, obviating the need for outside agents of change. (Whalen and Minnis 2003:315)

In very intriguing ways, Casas Grandes archaeology parallels the longer history of southwestern archaeology. The interpretative progression from Di Peso to Lekson to Whalen and Minnis and on to the post-processual Van Pools (chapter 7) links "archaeologies" and "histories." Southwestern archaeology moved from pioneer reconnaissance (chapter 2) to defining regions and boundaries (chapter 3) to establishing chronologies (chapter 4) and then to applying methods of the moment: New Archaeology (chapter 5), "Americanist" (chapter 6), or postmodern (chapter 7). That history mirrors stages of research: explore, map, date, and finally interpret to taste (culture history, adaptive processes, post-processual ritual or history).

I am reminded, in this sequence, of the "Real Mesoamerican Archaeologist" of Kent Flannery's *The Early Mesoamerican Village*. The RMA set forth his research agenda, comfortably familiar:

> I want to pick a valley which is a real hydrographic unit: you know, define it by the boundary of the watershed. Then I want to do a real settlement pattern survey. Then pick some really good sites, get the whole sequence. I want to know the ecological adaptation of the early villages to the area, and get some data on social and political organization. Make some real solid population estimates. Then I want…to pin down the trade wares and outside influences. (Flannery 1976:3; I omitted references specific to the Mesoamerican Formative.)

Flannery approved of the RMA's goals but objected to his methods. I object to his sequence. I'm not sure that outside influences should be last on our list of things to do.

Ontogeny recapitulates phylogeny. In my jaded view, Casas Grandes archaeology is marching through the same historical steps as southwestern archaeology, with positive results—and negative. On the positive side, we know a lot more now about Paquimé and the Casas Grandes region. On the negative, nothing that we've learned (as far as I can see) justifies making Paquimé provincial and local. I think Whalen and Minnis lean far too much toward "local" in their otherwise laudable efforts to bring Casas Grandes archaeology into the twenty-first century. Casas Grandes' ontogeny has reached the 1970s—enormous progress but still a few decades shy of today's archaeology.

That should not surprise us. Archaeology in Chihuahua had a late start, slower off the mark than Anasazi, Hohokam, and Mogollon. Understandably, "pioneering" continued into the 1930s (Brand 1935; Sauer 1935; Sayles 1936), through the 1940s (Lister 1946), and well into the 1960s. Indeed, it is still going on over much of Chihuahua. The original pioneer archaeologists were not to blame. Bandelier and Hewett spent time in Chihuahua, and Casas Grandes appeared on early regional maps, equal in cartographic emphasis to the San Juan Anasazi and Hohokam. But when southwestern archeology institutionalized with the Laboratory of Anthropology, the Museum of Northern Arizona, and the Arizona State Museum, no comparable institution developed in Las Cruces, El Paso, or Ciudad Chihuahua for the archaeology of Casas Grandes. In the end, it was the Amerind Foundation, which had previously confined itself to minor projects in southeasternmost Arizona, that took the plunge and investigated Paquimé, under the guidance of Charles Di Peso. In the late 1960s, DiPeso excavated Casas Grandes. He published both a regional map and a detailed chronology in 1974. Di Peso jumped the gun, leaping right over New Archaeology and processual archaeology and into something rather like post-processual historicity. He was postmodern before modern was post, decades ahead of his time. And thereafter, a hiatus.

In the 1980s, Chihuahua archaeology finally came of age, with a series of projects and programs from several Mexican, US, and Canadian institutions. Current researchers seem firm in the faith that more data will resolve issues *on the local level*. We may have to live through a period of righteous sequence building in Chihuahua, reliving the slow phylogeny of southwestern archaeology, before we can once again come to grips with real history, à la Di Peso. But perhaps we needn't wait that long. We know enough about Paquimé and *more than enough* about the larger picture to integrate Casas Grandes into the larger Southwest and North America.

169. Lekson 1999b:87–94.

170. LeBlanc 1986a.

171. Shafer 2003:5.

172. Hegmon et al. 1999; Nelson 1999.

173. Nelson 1999.

174. Creel 1999.

175. Shafer 2003:217.

176. Shafer 2003:217.

177. Mimbres really *did* end. The fragmentation of the old Mimbres world is reflected by the taxonomic confusion of archaeological practitioners working in various parts of the old Mimbres region (Terminal Mimbres, Post-Classic Mimbres, Black Mountain, Animas, El Paso, Tularosa, Cliff, and so on), and "it is probably no accident that the greatest terminological difficulties are associated with the period of change around A.D. 1150" (Hegmon et al. 1999:162). The period immediately post-Mimbres is fraught with archaeological difficulties. For varying views of post-Mimbres, see Creel 1999; Hegmon et al. 1999; and Shafer 1999a. For the version used here, see Lekson 2006b.

The pottery is particularly perplexing. Mimbres potters had for at least a century created some of the most vibrant ceramic art in the ancient Southwest. Around 1130 it's as if someone issued an edict and *painting stopped*. No more graven images! The art style might have survived in other media, particularly in remarkable pockets of Mimbres and post-Mimbres rock art scattered around southern New Mexico. Die-hard religious refugees hiding in the hills, like Christians in catacombs?

178. Nelson and LeBlanc 1986.

179. Nelson and Anyon 1996.

180. Creel 1999; Lekson 1999b.

181. Creel 1999.

182. LeBlanc 1980; Shafer 1999a.

183. Riley 2005:74–78; Schaafsma and Riley 1999:fig. 1; Shafer 1999a. The Early El Paso Phase was not a backwater, nor was it (entirely) an evolutionary step from the earlier, pit house Mesilla Phase. It is my impression that Jornada population jumps in the late-eleventh/early-twelfth century, much like the northern Rio Grande, and for exactly the same reasons: migrations of small groups out from Mimbres and into the desert. Black Mountain was more like Magdalena: intact communities in distinct villages, turning away from the past and changing the way they lived. The parallels are (nearly) precise.

184. Lekson 2002a:76.

185. For example, Hegmon et al. 1999 and, most notably, Blake, LeBlanc, and Minnis 1986, the baseline of Mimbres demography.

186. Minnis and LeBlanc 1979.

187. Lekson 2006b.

188. Art historians have linked the two pottery types, separated by a century (e.g., Brody 2004; Moulard 2005). I will argue in chapter 7 that Paquimé's rulers were both cosmopolitan and sophisticated, making use of symbol systems of distant societies in Mesoamerica (to their south) and historically linked societies in the Southwest (to their north). Barbara Moulard's "archaisms and emulations" are mirrored in the T-doors of Paquimé and its dependencies: a Chaco form revived and reinterpreted but referencing one of Paquimé's antique role models.

189. Lekson, Bletzer, and MacWilliams 2004.

190. Di Peso (1974:vol. 1) traveled over much of Chihuahua and did not see many Late Viejo Period sites (that is, sites that immediately predated Paquimé). Whalen and Minnis (2001, 2004) spent a couple decades looking *very hard* for Late Viejo/Early Medio sites and did not find many either.

There were, of course, Viejo Period sites (Di Peso 1974:vol. 1)—but not many, and they were small. Whalen and Minnis's survey "recorded only 15 sites with pure Viejo ceramic assemblages. These sites are small, with a mean area of only 0.7 ha" (Whalen and Minnis 2003:319). They suggest, hopefully, that there will be more Viejo hidden under later, larger Medio sites, and that makes sense—that's where Mimbres Late Pithouse Period components are found, underneath later Mimbres pueblos. At the southern end of Casas Grandes, only one of a dozen investigated Medio Period sites had Viejo Period underpinnings, and those were slim (Stewart et al. 2004). Viejo Period sites are indeed found in other parts of the Casas Grandes region, but they too are small and thin on the ground (Stewart et al. 2005:171).

Minnis and Whalen tacitly acknowledge the problem of insufficient Viejo populations in their "alternative scenario" for the rise of Paquimé, which "does not require so many local people" to populate the city (Whalen and Minnis 2003:328)—local people who probably weren't there. That alternative has Paquimé arising from the aggregation of many slightly earlier but smaller sites—Medio Period pueblos such as Tinaja. Possible—but we still need people to create the slightly earlier but smaller sites. Where does the buck stop?

191. Di Peso 1974.

192. Even before Di Peso, there were broad surveys of Chihuahua (e.g., Brand 1935; Sayles 1936). Di Peso compiled those surveys, added his own extensive observations, and produced a "big site" map of Medio Period settlement in the Casas Grandes region (Di Peso, Rinaldo, and Fenner 1974a:fig. 284–5). Like almost all of Di Peso's research on Casas Grandes, this map has been roundly criticized and questioned, largely, it seems, because Di Peso did it (I refrain from citing these criticisms; most are "personal communications"). Imprecise data are still data; we do not need UTMs measured to the meter to understand the fourteenth and fifteenth centuries. And give the devil his due: Di Peso knew a site when he saw one, and he was looking mainly at the biggest and most obvious ruins. In areas more recently resurveyed, archaeologists are finding *more* Medio Period sites than Di Peso, not fewer (Whalen and Minnis 2003). That result is only to be expected when comparing 1960s "windshield" surveys with full-coverage surveys of the 1980s and 1990s.

Di Peso's map is the best we have for the entirety of northwestern Chihuahua. Based on that map, it appears that numbers and sizes of sites (and presumably population) exploded in the thirteenth and fourteenth centuries. Chihuahua may well have been the most densely populated district in the greater Southwest of its era (contra Hill et al. 2004). Given the apparent paucity of Viejo Period archaeology, the astonishing numbers of post-1250 sites (shown on Di Peso's map) certainly suggest major in-migrations (Lekson, Bletzer, and MacWilliams 2004:61; this argument is Lekson's; Bletzer and MacWilliams are innocent). There was a lot of that going on in the thirteenth and fourteenth centuries north of the border. Why not south as well? The most likely candidates, in my view, are post-Mimbres peoples, followed (or perhaps pushed) by the cascade of thirteenth-century migrants from the Mogollon uplands and the Plateau.

193. Jane Kelley from the University of Calgary leads a major research effort in southern Chihuahua, defining the southern limits of the Casas Grandes region (and much more) (e.g., Kelley and MacWilliams 2005; Kelley et al. 2004; Kelley et al. 1999).

194. Pauketat 2004.

195. Whalen and Minnis 2001:318, citing Sebastian 1992.

196. Whalen and Minnis 2003:327.

Chapter 7

1. Native scholars point out that their histories began long before Coronado, and they are of course correct. But historians, however enlightened, still value what's written in documents over what's inferred from anthropology (e.g., Fernández-Armesto 2006:239–42).

2. And here's what I saw: Just as our cousins across the Atlantic seem to have read only the most strident of New Archaeology—and even today bristle at the mention of Watson, LeBlanc, and Redman's *Explanation in Archeology: An Explicitly Scientific Approach*—much of what we saw of the British post-processual was the hottest, most radical stuff: Routledge, Berg, the Theoretical Archaeology Group, edgy Web journals. It was almost masochistic: we read what hurt most. Both early processual and early post-processual manifestos were written to provoke.

We were perplexed at Ian Hodder and company's changing agendas. The Brits hit us rapid-fire with a new impossible philosopher, or a new impenetrable basic text, or a new unspeakable lexicon. "Theory of the month club" was one distinguished academic's acid observation as British archaeologists slipped deeper and deeper into the sloughs of continental philosophies. We wondered at the time what our counterparts—average British working archaeologists—thought of this stuff? Were they as bemused and bewildered as we were?

The first rush of post-processualism staked out strange territories, from which it later withdrew, sometimes gracefully, sometimes in fighting retreat. For example, hyper-relativism—there is no truth, there are no facts, no certainties. This was sure to annoy straightforward Americanists, and it did. After their moment in the spotlight, hyper-relativists grudgingly admitted there was a reality out there after all—a reality that we might perhaps hope to know. Many in the post-processual vanguard staked bold or outrageous claims and—after they'd made reputations and secured jobs—modified them. Whatever the intentions of the original proponents, post-processualism had a familiar, careerist subtext as Young Turks advanced over the shell-shocked bodies of stunned processualists. We'd done this one before, when New Archaeology blasted cultural history. Now, aging New-turned-processual archaeologists got a taste. It was lively while it lasted. And it reintroduced *history* into southwestern archaeology—which was a good thing I think.

3. Post-processual archaeology affected southwestern work—especially in the academy—beyond the renewed sense of history and historicity. Post-processual favorites sprouting up in the Southwest include symbols and meaning, agency and practice, gender, materiality, ritual, and postcolonial sensibilities (see Hegmon's 2003 inventory). I find (most of) these areas interesting. I once (long ago) dabbled in ritual landscapes, memory, and cognition. But for this book, I'm happy with history; that's enough for now.

I was puzzled, at the time, by the sources and foundational texts of American post-processual approaches. For example, why go to murky French social critics and agenda-driven British sociologists when historians (of every stripe and nationality) have been grappling with issues of "agency" (but calling it something else) for a very long time (chapter 1)? The scavenger hunt for philosophical inspiration took a nasty turn when British archaeologists hooked up with Heidegger. If one must shop for ideas, there are libraries filled with books by thinkers with less embarrassing baggage.

I'd rather shop at home. Freedom Fries and all that. I once thought I was an American realist, until I read more realism and had a long talk with Jane Kelley. American pragmatism has a few champions (Preucel 2006), but not all the pragmatists (better men than Heidegger!) survive close scrutiny ad hominem (Menand 2001; Novick 1998:150–54). For example, I'm not sure I really want to be Piercian. (Even in the world of ideas, one is known by the company one keeps.) I am not, however, an intellectual isolationist. I read as much British social theory as I can and as much French as I can stand (chapter 1), but I fail to be inspired, professionally, by analytical philosophy—that is, philosophy written by philosophers for philosophers. There are other, more cheerful inspirations, much closer to archaeology in disciplinary space: history and historiography, for example.

I despair when I see young scholars citing Henri Lefebvre (a dead French Marxist philosopher who pondered how people conceptualize space) but ignoring Amos Rapoport (a distinguished American anthropologist/architectural theorist, happily still with us, who studied how people cross-culturally *actually use space*). In the 1960s and 1970s, New Archaeology was (rightly) accused of "physics envy." Today it's "philosophy envy."

4. Hegmon 2003.

5. New Archaeology's explicitly scientific approach (that is, a largely ahistorical approach) carried over into processual archaeology and, to a large degree, into southwestern CRM archaeology. A key difference was that CRM laws and regulations were framed by historians or historically minded architects and preservationists (chapter 6). For example, of four National Register criteria applied to determine whether a threatened site should live or die, three were explicitly historical: "A. That are associated with events that have made a significant contribution to the broad patterns of our history; or B. That are associated with the lives of persons significant in our past; or C. That embody the distinctive characteristics of a type, period, or method of construction, or that represent the work of a master, or that possess high artistic values, or that represent a significant and distinguishable entity whose components may lack individual distinction." Almost all southwestern archaeology was done under much-beloved, catch-all criterion D: "That have yielded, or may be likely to yield, information important in prehistory or history." For National Register purposes, Indians were not involved unless some *real history*, involving named people, had happened: Geronimo slept here, Custer died here, and so forth.

NAGPRA sought to redress a long list of sins, both of omission and commission. I won't review what the law meant to Indians; I don't know. I have some ideas, but I'm not Indian. Most importantly for archaeology, "cultural affiliation studies" required by NAGPRA made us investigate migration archaeologically, informed by Native traditions and migration stories. Migrations had little credence in New and processual archaeology. A session on Mesa Verde to Rio Grande migration at the Southwest Symposium of 1992 was perhaps the first major airing of the renewed interest. Contra the point I'm trying to make here, the Southwest Symposium session represented "pure research," unrelated to NAGPRA (Cameron 1995). Work in the Tonto Basin, long suspected as a melting pot of ethnic mixing, brought migrations back into CRM (e.g., Elson, Stark, and Gregory 1995; Rice 1998). Interest in migrations never entirely ceased, even at the height of New Archaeology, especially at the University of Arizona (see Adams 1991; Haury 1958; Lindsay 1987; Reid and Whittlesey 1997). Thus the University of Arizona was well positioned for the era of NAGPRA and attendant interest in migrations, which have now become a major theme in dissertations and conference papers (e.g., Clark 2001; Lyons 2003).

6. My experiences with NAGPRA come from a museum perspective and differ considerably from experiences one would have in CRM or other fieldwork. My recent fieldwork has been on private lands where the law does not apply. Still, we consulted with many pueblos and other tribes and brought in key tribes for site visits. But NAGPRA as a law has not impacted my field research.

I spend a lot of my professional life (my day job, in the museum) apologizing to Indians for things other archaeologists did long ago. That's depressing. I needed to write this book as therapeutic archaeology, if only to avoid throwing myself in front of a train. I wanted to write about the Southwest as if I were writing about the British Neolithic, free from the guilt and angst of today's southwestern archaeology. I'll probably get gigged for it too.

The University of Colorado Museum of Natural History was slightly behind the NAGPRA curve when I was hired as curator of anthropology. Through the herculean efforts of Richard Wilshusen, Debbie Confer, and Jan Bernstein, we have now inventoried and published our collections and have consulted with more than fifty tribes from the Southwest, the Plains, and the Great Basin (bringing representatives to Boulder for lengthy meetings and collection tours). As a result, we've completed repatriations of several major collections and assisted with their reburial. Those experiences have changed my feelings about southwestern archaeology. What I've seen and heard has made me much harder on my field, more critical. Unless we are doing things that are actually interesting to larger audiences, we should probably hang up our trowels. Archaeologists talking and writing only for other archaeologists is not sufficient justification for the pain we've caused Indians. Archaeology will never, in my lifetime or yours, win favor among Indians (e.g., Deloria 1995). We must shop our wares elsewhere. I think archaeology has a place in American intellectual life: art, history, philosophy—and probably a place in science. We won't get there by turning inward and obsessing over theory.

7. Does pottery, after all these years, really equal people? In 1975 that was a ridiculed cliché; by 1995 it was a darn good question. Methodological recidivism: NAGPRA was a return to old, out-of-fashion ways, tracing culture history through traits and assemblages. That kind of culture history went out with flappers in raccoon coats—as did many of the original culture historians (*merci*, Pogo). We scramble for historical methods and use anything that works, reviving long-dormant ways of thinking and trying to devise scientific ways to follow people around the Southwest through material culture (NAGPRA discouraged osteological and genetic research). Pottery once again became people—or something like that.

I must note that, through the era of processual archaeology, University of Arizona research at Grasshopper Pueblo kept the porch light on for migration. Jeff Reid, Stephanie Whittlesey, and their colleagues thought about migration and ethnicity when most of us didn't. In part, that work reflected the history of the University of Arizona field schools in the Mogollon uplands of Arizona. It was hard to ignore migration at Point of Pines (Haury 1958).

8. We no longer even compare! A younger scholar, rejecting my advice to contrast two superficially different cases, asked, "Why would I want to compare apples and oranges?" I was nonplussed, stunned. I compare apples and oranges as a matter of course—it's almost second nature. Hours later, I thought of a snappy retort: "So we can tell which are the apples and which are the oranges!" I'm all for history, but the rejection of comparisons denies us archaeology's most robust tool. We might not be able to answer direct questions about the past, but we can always say one case is bigger, smaller, simpler, more complicated than another.

9. For example, Reid and Whittlesey 2005a:197; Upham 1982, 1986.

10. Reviewed by Cordell (1984:346–51, 1986, 1997:421–23), Hegmon (2005:214–16), McGuire and Saitta (1996), Spielmann (2005:199–201), and others. It was summarized from the Grasshopper perspective by Reid and Whittlesey (2005a:196–211) and from the Chavez Pass perspective by Upham and Plog (1986) and Feinman, Lightfoot, and Upham (2000). Articles arguing for political "complexity" (e.g., Cordell and Plog 1979; Upham 1982) began to appear about 1980. But these did not directly engage Grasshopper and Chavez Pass.

11. I see no reason not to include both Grasshopper and Chavez Pass in the larger Anasazi rubric of Pueblo IV—an assessment not shared by the principal scholars involved with those sites. Of course, by Pueblo IV, "Anasazi" was splintering into a number of increasingly distinct entities, presaging the Pueblos of today.

12. Reid and Whittlesey 2005a.

13. For example, Graves and Reid 1984; Meyer, Dawson, and Hanna 1996; Upham, Lightfoot, and Jewett 1989; Upham and Plog 1986; Whittlesey 1984.

14. The social and professional consequences of the acrimonious debate—professor against professor, grad students against grad students—colored subsequent considerations of political complexity in the Southwest. Students from that era are today's senior scholars; they almost uniformly eschew "complexity" in Grasshopper–Chavez Pass terms. Barbara Mills (2000:5) summarized the debates of the 1980s as "unproductive," but they produced at least one thing—a cohort of professionals who, quite understandably, chose to study things other than political complexity in the Southwest (Lekson 2005).

15. Brandt 1994; Ware 2001, 2002b; Whiteley 1998, 2004, but perhaps not a great deal more hierarchical; see McGuire and Saitta 1996.

16. Indeed, this view of the Pueblo Southwest goes back to Edgar Hewett and Harold Gladwin and their times (chapter 3). In that older view, the onward-and-upward progress of the Pueblos was truncated by invasions of warlike Athabaskans—not unlike events in the Europe of Hewett's time. That made a good story and lively history (Gladwin 1957), but the Athabaskans—Navajo and Apache—almost certainly entered the Southwest after the fall of Chaco and probably after the end of Aztec Ruins (Towner 1996).

There was nothing in the processual paradigm that precludes collapse. For example, Joseph Tainter's *The Collapse of Complex Societies* (1988) included Chaco as a case study. An excellent and too often overlooked work, *The Collapse of Complex Societies* is conspicuous by its absence in Chaco studies (including mine, mea culpa). It did not, apparently, merit mention in a recent comprehensive bibliography of Chaco studies (Mathien 2005) or in the spate of recent "trade" books on Chaco. For my part, the absence of Tainter from my writing reflects historical uncertainties: did Chaco really collapse, or did it move north? (I favor the latter.) *Something* collapsed in the thirteenth century, however, and fell hard. And something else collapsed in the Hohokam area in the fifteenth century and fell harder. The ancient Southwest is a fertile field for collapse studies (if I may be allowed a twisted metaphor), and I sense a return to Tainter's questions in works such as Hill et al. 2004 and Tim Kohler and others (2007) "Village Project" (chapter 6).

17. I find it extremely difficult—impossible, actually—to contradict Pueblo people on matters of their past. How can I suggest to an elder, firm in his faith, that my jumped-up version of Pueblo history is more accurate than his? I've been a party to many fruitful collaborations—writing books, planning exhibits, serving on public panels, and (of course) taking part in NAGPRA consultations. Other, harder-nosed archaeologists might hold their own in those situations, but not me. An example: in the mid-1980s I questioned aloud (and in print; Lekson 1988) the nature of ancient "kivas," suggesting that they were in fact pit houses (an argument reviewed in chapter 4). That didn't go over well with Pueblo colleagues. So from 1990 to 1998, I refrained— self-censored—from writing or lecturing on that theme. I'm back to it now, but only after demonstrating (I hope) to at least some Native scholars that my revisionist notions are not intended to undermine or belittle their history but instead to unfetter it from colonial restraints inherent in archaeology.

18. For example, Ezell 1963; Haury 1976.

19. For example, Di Peso 1956; Doelle 1981; Masse 1981.

20. See Whittlesey et al. 1994:194 and Doyel 1991a:266–67 for reviews of the issue. Archaeologists, beginning with Emil Haury, have worked hard to relate their work to Piman peoples and to engage, collaborate with, and advocate for Arizona tribes. But in 1976 Haury could declare that Hohokam was not Piman but Mesoamerican. It is rather difficult to imagine an Anasazi archaeologist, in the 1970s, declaring that Mesa Verde or Chaco was *not* Puebloan. That would have been literally unthinkable because the very basis of pioneer archaeology had been to show that Anasazi was indeed Puebloan and local (chapter 2).

Another factor in archaeology's free hand with Hohokam was social: Piman cultures were not reverentially idealized as were Pueblos. Leah Dilworth mordantly describes America's view of the Southwest, formed in the late nineteenth/early twentieth centuries

> At the bottom were the Apaches, a conquered people who remained unregenerate savages; then came groups like the Mojave and Pima Indians, who were primitive but harmless and doomed to disappear; then the Navajos, whose nomadic ways made them somewhat suspect but whose industriousness redeemed them; and finally the Pueblo Indians, peaceful and settled agriculturalists who lived in houses. (Dilworth 1996:95)

Zuni, Hopi, and the other Pueblos were elevated, without their leave or approval, as American icons (e.g., Dilworth 1996; Hinsley and Wilcox 1996; McFeely 2001). Pima people were not. Unfair, I know, but there it is. It was possible, through the 1980s, to write about a Hohokam decline without social consequences. It might have been blunt, but it wasn't rude.

21. ASU's Tonto Basin work began under the "elite" paradigm (Redman, Rice, and Pedrick 1992; Rice 1990), but during the long span of field and lab work and writing up the project (1989–1998), interests in the larger archaeological world shifted away from managerial elites to ritual. ASU's principal, Glen Rice, eventually concluded for the Tonto Basin: "Some of the mounds were essentially empty ceremonial centers, places where people visited but did not live, while other mounds were a combination of public rooms and private residences.... Although only a few people lived at the platform mound, it was 'owned' by all members of the settlement complex" (Rice 1998:236). Managers were transformed into "specialists responsible for conducting and preparing ceremonial activities" who did not have "heightened economic privileges" (Rice 1998:237; see also Downum and Bostwick 2003; Fish and Fish 2000c).

Alternative leadership toppled platform mound elites. Jerry Howard (1992:76) notes, the "suggestion that the primary role of platform mounds is ceremonial and not residential presents a radical new view that affects sociopolitical interpretation" of the Classic Period. And David Abbott, writing very carefully: "The platform mound probably glorified descent groups as a whole rather than individuals or elite families within the group. The mounds were public works that created spaces for communal ritual and were not oriented toward important living individuals by providing segregated and elevated locations for their residences" (Abbott 2003:213). The wind blows ritual:

> A corporate strategy was most likely the dominant mode of leadership at prehistoric Southwestern platform mound communities. This is true for both Early and Late Classic periods and is based on the association of ritual [exotic] goods and features with some mounds and the generally accepted function of the mounds as group-oriented integrative locales for the collection and dis-

pensing of ritual knowledge and power. However, it is also possible that groups with larger and more diverse mounds, such as those in the Phoenix Basin during the Late Classic Civano phase, had leaders who used a more mixed network/corporate strategy. (Elson and Abbott 2000:133–34)

On a slightly different tack, Fish and Fish argue that "Hohokam political ideology...engendered little tolerance or support for the personal aggrandizement of leaders as evidenced by extravagant dwellings.... It was compatible with highly centralized societal functions such as communal construction of public architecture, communal ritual and ceremony, concentrated storage in many mound precincts, and probably some degree of coordination of external affairs" (Fish and Fish 2006c:166)

22. Clark and Huckell 2004:9.

23. It wasn't all NAGPRA, of course. Reid and Whittlesey (1997)—staunch advocates of migration during the dark days of natural laboratories—suggest that Haury's theory was "the simplest and perhaps most satisfying...opposed by newer but not necessarily more accurate views" that "view the Classic period changes as a local phenomenon" (Reid and Whittlesey 1997:106). They cite evidence from physical anthropology that supports a "migration theory." Theirs was a brave stand: positing historical dynamics between the Plateau and the deserts was dangerous business. Michael Berry, in the early 1980s, dared to suggest that cyclic population peaks in Hohokam corresponded to population declines in Anasazi (Berry 1982). He was pilloried. In retrospect, I think Berry might have had some details wrong (as we all do, in everything we write) but he was on to something.

24. Doyel 1994.

25. For example, Dean and Ravesloot 1993.

26. But see Riley 2005 for a beleaguered defender of a Di Peso–esque Paquimé. Processual archaeology rules in Casas Grandes, but there are intriguing sorties by post-processual proponents. The region's archaeology is still so under-researched that post-processual approaches tend to wobble right off into art history, working with museum collections and iconography (e.g., Moulard 2005; Townsend 2005; VanPool 2003)—which is not necessarily a bad thing.

27. Neo-evolutionary thinking did not just fade away. Afficionados of the chiefdom produced closer and closer analyses of that institution, showing it to be a remarkably variable category (Earle 1997), and undeconstructed neo-evolutionaries developed an open-ended corporate-network, egalitarian-hierarchical matrix in which chiefdoms occupied a particular spot (Blanton et al. 1996). These efforts, in the long run, may prove more useful than many of the post-processual conceits.

28. For example, Miller and Tilley 1984.

29. Bender 1998.

30. Renfrew 2001. Lord Renfrew would probably not appreciate being labeled post-processual (see Renfrew 2007). I owe him an apology and an appreciation. I was instrumental in his invitation to consider Chaco, in my attempt to bring British and European insights to that perennial southwestern problem (Lekson 2006a). Colin Renfew was kind enough to fit Chaco into his busy, astonishingly productive life (Renfrew 2001), and my response here and elsewhere has been churlishly negative. I argue with his ideas, but I honor the man.

31. For example, Fish and Fish (2000c:154): "The Hohokam and other relatively complex prehistoric societies of the Southwest conform poorly to the dominant band-tribe-chiefdom-state classificatory scheme of the last several decades"; "they do not fit the variably defined criteria for chiefdom so well as do, for example, their North American contemporaries, the Mississippians." In some ways, that's not too surprising: eastern North America was a breeding ground for chiefdoms, anthropologically defined, just as the Southwest was a "type site" for Morgan's communalism. Bands-tribes-chiefdoms-states were denounced by a wide range of luminaries (e.g., Hegmon 2005; Yoffee 2005). The neo-evolutionary litany has become a shibboleth, marking those who use it as antiques or dangerous reactionaries. But we still think that way. As discussed in chapter 8, note 29, vaguely defined "intermediate societies" have taken the place of old tribes and chiefdoms.

32. Mills ed. 2000.

33. For example, Mills ed. 2000; Nelson 1995; VanPool, VanPool, and Phillips 2006; Yoffee 2001; Yoffee, Fish, and Milner 1999. For a good review, see Mills 2000b and Hegmon 2003, 2005.

34. Archaeologists scramble to find, or invent, alternative leadership strategies that can get Chaco built without vulgar political power. For example, Norman Yoffee (a keen observer of the Southwest scene) rejects neo-evolutionary nomenclature and proposes something new:

The term "rituality" is useful particularly because it is a neologism [which Yoffee credits to Robert Drennan] and owes nothing to neo-evolutionist theory. The term also must be unpacked, and the unique cluster of Chaco Canyon great houses and other structures must be explained in their own historical context, and not necessarily as a type of city or town in the nomenclature of Western urban geography. (Yoffee 2005:170)

Yoffee suggests that Chaco was unique (or at least something extraordinarily unusual; see also Nelson 1995; Van Dyke 2004; Wills 2000). Whatever Chaco was, apparently it cannot have been political: "It was the overarching ceremonial system that held diversity together in a ritual system, and this system is what made Chaco unique. However, bequeathed a legacy of neo-evolutionism, archaeologists aren't used to finding uniqueness, and it makes them uncomfortable" (Yoffee 2005:172–73).

Chaco and other southwestern entities are sometimes considered to have been hierocracies—a term I encountered a few years ago while looking up *hierarchy* in a really big dictionary but that Severin Fowles (2004) uses to better advantage. A hierocracy is a government of ecclesiastics (also the original meaning of hierarchy, to my surprise). Ritualities (I assume) were hierocracies. Yoffee sees ritual elites running Chaco. I do not doubt that Chaco's rulers mixed the ritual and the political—so did most Post-Classic rulers in Mesoamerica and most kings everywhere else. Most, perhaps all, governments were (somewhat) sacred before the Enlightenment. The separation of church and state is a modern experiment (and one that shows signs of failing). If we must choose one or the other, ritual or political, surely it is only a matter of emphasis. Is a government *more* sacred or *more* profane? Are you paying tithes or taxes?

In the end, does it matter? The household budget had been lightened by the same amount, gone to gods or to greedy heads or to greedy gods. Why are gods so often short of cash? (A question first posed by Paul Hewson.)

As noted in chapter 1, I use *politics* and *political* as indicative of more secular systems, but I assume that any ancient southwestern government was an indivisible mix of politics and "religious" ritual. At issue here is the nature of power. I contend that Chaco, on the face of the evidence, was consciously moving toward the Post-Classic virtues of population growth, long-distance exchange, militarism, and general small-polity-ness, with kings and elites (chapter 6). The rulers of Chaco were enjoying their roles, or at least giving that appearance; Trigger (2003a) sees as a near universal the rulers of early states conspicuously consuming and flaunting wealth. Chaco bosses were behaving like kings, or behaving *as they thought kings should behave* (chapter 8). And that's how Indians remember it too. At Chaco, people acted like lords.

35. Whalen and Minnis 2000, 2001. In the latter, Paquimé was considered a processual parallel to Chaco, which—following Sebastian 1992—the authors saw as very modestly political, somewhere in the "intermediate" range.

36. VanPool 2003. VanPool concludes that the lords of Paquimé were shaman priests. But her definition of shaman does not suggest a simple society: "Paquimé's social organization was more similar to the Mesoamerican system of shamanic leaders than the communal male religious practitioners in the American Southwest" (VanPool 2003:713). VanPool's "shamans," I suppose, could describe the guys running Palenqué—not feather-waving tribal practitioners but great lords whose duties included intercession and divination (Freidel, Schele, and Parker 1993). I think Chaco's leaders were like that too—not shamans (an unfortunate word) but more like Mesoamerican leaders than anything seen in the ethnographic Southwest.

37. Phillips and Sebastian 2004:242–43. Michelle Hegmon, in an excellent review of "Inequality in Southwest Villages," offers a similar caution: "I do not dispute the broad applicability of the alternative models of leadership to the Southwest. At the same time, I emphasize that 'alternative' strategies should not be assumed to be egalitarian. An archetype of corporate leadership is classic Teotihuacan, and even if the leaders of that great city were 'faceless,' no one is suggesting that they were not powerful or that inequality was minimal. The Southwest was not Teotihuacan, but we also should not forget Teotihuacan" (Hegmon 2005:228).

I reviewed the rise of alternative leadership models elsewhere (Lekson 2005), perhaps overharshly. If so, my apologies to Barbara Mills, the editor of the key volume on this topic (Mills ed. 2000), and to her contributors. It's a good book and a step forward! My acerbity stemmed from a fear of progress lost—one (big) step forward but two steps back. It had taken several decades of thankless prodding to nudge the field into a general, if reluctant, acceptance of complex political systems at Chaco, Hohokam, and Paquimé—pushing past, or aside, the red herrings of the Chavez Pass–Grasshopper debate. Reactions to and memories of Chavez Pass–Grasshopper made it hard to suggest political complexity *anywhere* in the Southwest—even places where it seemed nearly certain (such as Chaco and Paquimé). Yet that's how it was. The grudging recognition of non-Puebloan political arrangements at Chaco and Paquimé was also a big step forward. Just as those hard-won arguments were about to take the *next* step (chapter 8), all that work was threatened by a post-processual tide of ritual, ceremony, and communalism. Archaeology is quite capable of turning bloodthirsty tyrants into philosopher-poet-kings (and back again) on waves of methodological fashions—consider the Maya. I fear similar vacillations in the Southwest, driven not by data but by theoretical enthusiasms. Theories come and go, but (as I said elsewhere) the baby we just threw out with the neo-evolutionary bathwater might be the Lost Dauphin.

38. Today it is impossible to attend a conference, read a journal, listen to a campfire talk, or converse with

a graduate student without getting a huge dose of ritual. "Ritual was always central in the Southwest"—that's a quote from a student paper presented at an annual meeting of the Society for American Archaeology, but it's also the working assumption of many archaeologists, junior and senior. Ritual indeed plays a central role in modern (and ethnological) Pueblo life, or so I'm told. Pueblo spirituality appeals to many of us—we are reaching advanced ages when those sorts of things are of increasing interest.

But consider a less pleasant aspect: ritual may be so prominent in modern Pueblo life because *ritual was all they had left* after centuries of colonization and oppression. Pueblos survived the colonial experience in better shape than many tribes (they are still here, and they kept some of their lands), but Spain, Mexico, and the United States all replaced the economies, converted the religions, confiscated the lands, assimilated the peoples, and terminated the tribes. Deprived of political and economic power, they worked with what was left: ritual and religion. I am not suggesting that ritual was not important in precolonial times, merely that the emphasis was probably magnified by colonization. "Ritual was *always* central in the Southwest?" Ritual was always *present* in the Southwest, but other vectors of power were important too. Popé, who organized the stunningly successful Pueblo Revolt of 1680, is considered an anomaly: a leader who united the Pueblos in a common cause. I suspect that Popé was the last in a long line of leaders who mobilized Pueblo peoples toward political goals. In deeper history, those leaders were not occasional or situational but were permanent and institutional.

39. As mentioned in chapter 3, some archaeologists were hired by or for tribes to make the tribes' case. Other archaeologists worked for the federal government, disputing tribal claims. Those who worked for the tribes—for example, Florence Ellis and Ed Dittert—carried over the Pueblos' confidence and confidences into their academic lives.

40. Ethnology provided models for residence patterns, kinship systems, and so forth (e.g., Hill 1970; Longacre 1970), including the proper parameters that archaeologists might apply to ancient governance. The ethnologies themselves were not of historical interest; they merely set the upper limit, the evolutionary end point.

41. Josephy, Nagel, and Johnson 1999.

42. Biolsi and Zimmerman 1997.

43. Deloria 1995:17–18, 15.

44. A growing number of federal and state laws, as well as agency policies, encourage or require consultations between archaeologists and Indians (King 2004), but the passage of NAGPRA really got archaeology's attention because it impacted museum collections. "That belongs in a museum" is only one of many useful dicta from Dr. Jones. Archaeologists are trained from their earliest days that collections are sacrosanct, preserved in perpetuity. NAGPRA gave collections back to Indians.

Of course, archaeologists and museums had productive collaborations with Native Americans long before NAGPRA. Those collaborations were often individual to individual, collegial. A major change, in my opinion, was that after NAGPRA, consultations became regulated and routinized, "government to government." It's almost bureaucratized: people talk about the "consultation community" like a profession—and indeed it's heading that way. A different dynamic, but still very productive.

45. Not everyone, of course, treaded softly or wisely. Cannibalism and Kennewick Man, in a social vacuum, might be legitimate research topics. But the way they were researched and broadcast offended and provoked Native communities. We must carefully rethink and redefine what constitutes "legitimate" research!

46. Archaeologists don't want to hear it from other archaeologists either. Recall that Frank Roberts once referred to Pueblo IV as Regressive Pueblo (chapter 4), suggesting a degree of slippage from Pueblo II and Pueblo III (Roberts 1935). The label "regressive" was summarily, even angrily, rejected. I recall classroom lectures, decades after Roberts's faux pas, denouncing his term as ethnocentric, paternalistic, and fundamentally evil. All the poor guy did was suggest that Pueblo prehistory had ups and downs. His idea, however, was beyond the bounds of polite usage. Archaeology, then and now, preferred to see the ancient Southwest as a steady progress from deepest antiquity to the modern Pueblos.

47. My thinking on these matters owes much to Vine Deloria (1995), Keith Basso (1996), Roger Anyon and others (1997), Roger Echo-Hawk (1997, 2000), and Joe Watkins (2001), as well as general treatments of oral history by Vansina (1985) and Barber and Barber (2004). But far more important were conversations with many Pueblo, Navajo, and Pima people—and a long series of conversations with Vine Deloria.

Archaeologically specific southwestern histories have been produced by recent scholars such as Ekkehart Malotki (1993) and Wesley Bernardini (2005), and of course there are libraries of classic ethnologies from the first half of the twentieth century. Gordon Brotherston's works (1979, 1992) have also been inspirations—if sometimes cryptic, as many inspirations are.

48. Many details in origin stories are quite specific. I believe that the specificity of oral traditions decreases dramatically with distance in both time and place.

Time first: the more time since the event, the less the historical specificity of the account (Barber and Barber 2004; Mason 2006; Vansina 1985). Details decay as a matter of course and then shift in the service of larger purposes: truths, teachings, eschatology, cosmology, philosophy. The decades around 1300 were a watershed for Pueblo peoples. The fall of Pueblo II and Pueblo III political systems and the subsequent population movements of the late thirteenth century changed everything (chapter 6). If we could attach calendar dates to origin stories, events after 1300 would very likely be specific and "true." Before 1300, in my opinion, traditional stories offer broader outlines of history set in idealized landscapes. They are no less "true" but are seemingly less specific. Most Pueblo migration accounts are very precise for places occupied after 1250/1300 and schematic for places and events before 1300. Was White House Mesa Verde or Chaco? Or was it the general Four Corners region? I've heard all three interpretations.

Space next: places preserve history. People who stay at or near the scene of events may well remember details forgotten by those who do not. Keith Basso's influential book *Wisdom Sits in Places* (1996) reminds us that in nonliterate societies, the landscape itself was a text. Histories could be "written" on the land—think of Chaco roads—or invested in natural features. Places collected history, and under the right circumstances, those histories survived replacement of populations—they jumped ethnicities. It is my experience that Native groups value the accounts and traditions of other groups, be they related clans or different tribes, and remember what the people before them knew about a particular butte, river, or canyon—Chaco Canyon, for instance.

Incidents are often linked to mountains, springs, trees. When people leave those places behind, the specificity of historical detail necessarily decreases with time. People who once knew, intimately, a particular tree or mesa describe that place to younger generations. But younger generations do not see or experience that place. Over time, the key principles and lessons are passed on intact, but the details understandably fade. Thus Pueblo peoples speak of a general "White House" that encompasses Chaco, Aztec, and even Mesa Verde; modern-day Navajo people living around Chaco tell astonishingly specific stories of happenings at each and every Great House. Immigrants themselves, they learned Great House stories from Pueblo people at a time when those stories were still fresh in Pueblo lore. Navajos kept them fresh by living on the lands where it all happened. For Pueblos, away from the scene of events, the details may well have faded over centuries.

49. Hill et al. 2004:fig. 2. The Coalescent Communities reconstruction agrees with several others (see Wilcox et al. 2006): remarkable decline, regionally, starting several decades after 1300. As we shall see in the discussion of Paquimé's region, these reconstructions would look very different if we accepted Di Peso's (1974) survey data (Lekson, Bletzer, and MacWilliams 2004). In any event, after 1450, population in the north dropped catastrophically until the arrival of Europeans. Then things got worse.

50. For example, Naranjo 1995, 2006.

51. Reyman 1995.

52. See Washburn 1995:fig. 16.

53. For flawed but accessible accounts, see Waters (1977:67–71) and Courlander (1971:56–71). My version relies on discussions with a half-dozen Hopi elders, artists, and scholars, but there are scores of different versions of Hopi's Red City. Di Peso suggested that Paquimé might be Palatkwapi (Di Peso 1974:290; see also Waters 1977:68–69). Other archaeologists have suggested other locations: Casa Grande, Coronado's Chichitecale, or the archaeological site of Kwilleylekia. Kwilleylekia (Lekson 2002a), like the Red City, ended with a disastrous flood (cf. Courlander 1971:64), but floods, we know, are a common motif in myth and legend. Some Hopi scholars place the Red City in central or southern Mexico. They may well be right. (Hopi accounts of migrations out of Mexico are discussed in chapter 1.) Early accounts of Paquimé as a painted or mosaicked city (Obregon 1928) emphasized color, but was it red? Even today, Paquimé's tall earth walls turn pink with the rising and setting sun, but so do the Sandia Mountains.

54. The Aztecs were politically aggressive, militaristic, commercial—all the things that a successful Post-Classic polity should be (chapter 6). They thought big: their farthest province was 1,000 kilometers from Tenochtitlán (Smith and Berdan 2003a). Their empire was not a solid unit across those vast distances; like Europe in the nineteenth century, Mesoamerican empires were patchwork, discontinuous affairs. Late Post-Classic political entities encompassed distances comparable to Formative and Classic period horizons. Distances could be dealt with.

55. Gorenstein and Pollard 1983; Pollard 2003a.

56. Di Peso (1974) relied on Sahagun accounts of Aztecs for ethnohistoric color commentary. He might have done better illuminating Paquimé with *Relacion de Michoacan*.

57. Pollard 2003b.

58. Stone 2004.

59. Gorenstein and Pollard 1983:1.

60. Gorenstein and Pollard 1983:63.

61. Carpenter 2002; Kelly 1938; Lekson 1999b:appendix B; Riley 2005.

62. J. Charles Kelley, personal communication, 1979.

63. Anderson 1994, after Wright 1984.

64. An overview: Galloway and Jackson 2004.

65. Neitzel 1965.

66. The year 1300 is a date of convenience, a midpoint for events that spread over several decades (1275–1335). A recent, excellent summary of the Pueblo IV Period divides it into three subperiods: 1275–1325, 1325–1400, and 1400–1600 (Adams and Duff 2004). These periods reflect events in the Pueblo part of Arizona perhaps more closely than those in New Mexico, Chihuahua, and Hohokam Arizona. I have organized my thoughts into two subperiods, 1275–1450 and 1450–1600, and I use 1300 as a nominal date for a process or sequence of events that took several decades to play out.

67. Cordell 2006:266.

68. Should we call it art? Certainly, to modern eyes, the visual symbolic expressions of Anasazi and Pueblo IV are artistic—often stunningly so (Brody 1991). But many Indians and a few anthropologists object to the term *art*, with its European baggage. Ancient visual symbol systems were both more and less than individual creative expressions; they were more than something pretty to hang on the wall. In societies without writing, visual symbols were the medium of choice for targeted communication, for getting a message across. Those communications could be about identity, ethnicity, ritual and ceremony, use rights, status, history, or myriad other themes. I use *art* as a shorthand for more cumbersome terms (such as *visual symbol systems*), but with the knowledge that Pueblo IV "art" was central to and permeated all social relations—not, as it is for most of us today, as a category of objects.

69. There was plenty of color in early sandals, baskets, and other "perishable" artifacts (Cole 1994; Hays-Gilpin et al. 1998; Washburn and Webster 2006; Webster and Hays-Gilpin 1994) and in rock paintings (Brody 1991; Schaafsma 1980). For the most part, the rigid geometry of those polychromatic designs paralleled that of black-on-white pottery—or vice versa. They stand in contrast to the dynamic Pueblo IV styles.

70. Brody 1991; Carlson 1982b; Wright 2005.

71. For overviews of Pueblo IV polychrome and glaze-painted pottery, see Carlson (1982b) and Habicht-Mauche, Eckert, and Huntley (2006). Here's what happened between 1275 and 1325: around Zuni and the middle and upper Rio Grande, glaze-painted pottery (Eckert 2006; Habicht-Mauche, Eckert, and Huntley 2006); in east-central Arizona, the polychrome Fourmile style in White Mountain redwares (Carlson 1982b; Van Keuren 2000, 2006; Wright 2005—although "full of errors," as one careful reader noted) and the beginnings of Salado polychromes (Crown 1994); at Hopi (slightly later) and at Zuni, polychrome buffwares of the Sityaki style (Schachner 2006; Wilcox 2007); and at Casas Grandes, the florescence of the Chihuahua polychromes and their signature type, Ramos Polychrome (e.g., Powell 2006; Townsend 2005). Polychromes did not replace black-on-white everywhere of course. The simple geometric designs of Santa Fe black-on-white and other black-on-white types continued in pockets of the northern Rio Grande right through Pueblo IV. But in general:

> At about AD 1300, Pueblo peoples abandoned the seven-hundred-year-old Anasazi tradition of decorating white ceramics with black designs and began producing yellow, red and orange wares.... Dynamic asymmetric forms emphasizing birds—especially parrots and raptors—and snakes replaced the tight geometry and symmetry of earlier Pueblo ceramic traditions. (McGuire et al. 1994:252, citing Carlson 1970, 1982b)

72. Brody 1991; Carlson 1970; Hays-Gilpin and LeBlanc 2007; Schaafsma 1980, 1994, 2007; Teague 1998; Townsend 2005; Webster 2007a.

73. M. E. Smith 2003:125; Teague 1998; Townsend 2005.

74. Nicholson and Quiñones Keber 1994.

75. Boone and Smith 2003; Pohl 2003.

76. Reilly and Garber 2007:1.

77. Galloway 1989; Knight, Brown, and Lankford 2001; Reilly and Garber 2007.

78. Pauketat 2004.

79. Reilly and Garber 2007; Townsend and Sharp 2004.

80. Reilly and Garber 2007:6.

81. For example, Upham 1982.

82. Crown 1994.

83. Adams 1991.

84. Adams 1991; Schaafsma 1994.

85. For example, Crown 1994; Hays-Gilpin and Hill 2000; Hays-Gilpin and LeBlanc 2007; Riley 2005:92–97; Schaafsma 2007; VanPool, VanPool, and Phillips 2006.

86. For example, Webster 2007a; Young 1994.

87. If the new readings of SCC are correct, might that too represent a deliberate step back down the organizational ladder from the lords of Cahokia, just as Pueblo IV art reflected reorganization after Chaco—again perhaps paralleling Pueblo IV?

88. Charles Adams and Andrew Duff (2004) summarize settlement across the Pueblo IV world (see also Spielmann 1998; Wilcox and Masse 1981). According to Adams and Duff, after initial experiments with huge towns (several with 800 to more than 1,400 rooms), between 1250 and 1325 the villages dropped to a more manageable size, averaging about 200 rooms and increasing slightly to 325 rooms in 1325–1400. After 1400 town size rose "explosively" to 500 or more rooms. At least thirty Late Pueblo IV towns had more than 1,000 rooms, and several were twice that big (Adams and Duff 2004:appendix).

89. Huntley and Kintigh 2004; Kintigh, Glowacki, and Huntley 2004; Schachner 2006. "The brief jump to enormous size of some villages at Zuni in the late 1200s probably failed because the associated social organizational changes were not yet in place, resulting in fission" (Adams and Duff 2004:12). I think there was a scalar process at work. Adams and Duff (2004:11, 14) rightly emphasize that Pueblo villages become unstable at a population of about five hundred and reach a "hard" threshold at twenty-five hundred (citing Kosse 1990, 1996, among others). Egalitarian villages generally do not, and possibly cannot, exceed twenty-five hundred people. Even a five-hundred-person town is inherently unstable without governmental structures to hold things together: a king, a mayor, a police force, or some other centralized political structure, either in the town or elsewhere in the settlement system. Indeed, hierarchy may be an emergent property of settlement size (Kosse 1990; Lekson 1990c). And Pueblo villages after 1300 did not want hierarchy.

Art Rohn (1983) and others have noted that, historically, Pueblos approaching two thousand people almost invariably split into "daughter communities"; the same process was almost certainly at work among the prehistoric large towns of the fourteenth-century Rio Grande. The very largest, Sapawe and Kuapa, certainly exceeded the twenty-five-hundred-person limit—for a while. But they did not maintain large sizes for centuries, as did Chaco and Aztec, as well as Paquimé.

90. House form should be a primary interest of archaeology, but it is curiously understudied. That is strange because there is a well-developed literature in anthropology (Rapoport 1969, 1982) and in the hybrid field of vernacular architecture (e.g., Oliver 1997). Historically, we've placed far more value on pottery than house form—with the exception of so-called kivas. Square kivas were Kayenta; keyhole kivas were Mesa Verde; and so forth. That's house form sliding under the ritual radar.

91. Adams and Duff 2004:13.

92. For example, kachina ceremonialism; Schaafsma 1994.

93. Schachner 2006. Kintigh (2000) discusses the implications of ethnic heterogeneity for Zuni leadership strategies. Perhaps it was less of a problem than we might think: "Virtually everywhere we can identify immigration in the late 1200s and early 1300s evidences a sparse indigenous population or no apparent residential population prior to Pueblo IV aggregation" (Spielmann 2004:142).

94. Adams 2002; Rushforth and Upham 1992.

95. Adams and Duff 2004, especially Duff; Spielmann 1998.

96. Mills 1998; Wilcox et al. 2006.

97. Crown, Orcutt, and Kohler 1996; Kohler 2004; Riley 1995.

98. Graves and Spielmann 2000; Kohler, Van Pelt, and Yap 2000; Ware 2001, 2002b. Pueblo IV in the Rio Grande was more politically and economically structured than were the western Pueblos (Dozier 1970; Ware 2001, 2002b). Kohler, Van Pelt, and Yap argue, persuasively, for the emergence of market economies on the Rio Grande during Pueblo IV, in marked contrast to Zuni and Hopi: "Why should market economies develop in the northern Rio Grande at this time but not earlier or not elsewhere in the Southwest?" (Kohler, Van Pelt, and Yap 2000:203). There *were* markets earlier and elsewhere—in the Hohokam Sedentary Period (if not before) and very likely later in the Casas Grandes region, which (in my opinion) was more closely linked to the Rio Grande than to western Pueblos. I argued in chapter 5 that Chaco had a bulk-goods economy (as well as a political prestige economy), but whether the bulk goods were market or managed, I do not care to guess. In any event, the Rio Grande Pueblos probably did not have to invent markets.

99. Yes, Pueblo Bonito would fit in Poshu'ouinge's plaza. But put things into perspective: Pueblo Bonito was only one element of the Chaco cityscape, which covered more than 1,000 hectares to Poshu'ouinge's 4.

The Rio Grande pueblos were big towns, but they were big *towns*, not cities—and that's a critical difference. Chaco was a city (chapter 5). The Southwest had cities, and those cities had rulers and governments rather larger in scale than northern Rio Grande pueblo arrangements.

100. Adams and Duff 2004.

101. Adams and Duff 2004; Wilcox et al. 2006:fig. 6.

102. Dean, Doelle, and Orcutt 1994; Doelle 1995a, 2000; Riley 2005:106; Wilcox et al. 2006:fig. 7. Wilcox and others (2006:215) suggest that the drop in population after 1350–1400 was "nowhere as precipitous as Dean and Doelle have supposed." But as I read their chart (Wilcox et al. 2006:fig. 7), the Southwest north of modern Mexico was indeed a demographic train wreck. Only the inclusion of very generous estimates of late "statelets" in Sonora saves the day (Wilcox et al. 2006), raising the downslope from double black diamonds to the kiddie hill—still a plunge, but less adrenalized. The center of demographic gravity shifted southwest.

In chapter 6, I made a parallel argument for Chihuahua from 1250 to 1450 (that is, *before* the post-1400 drop), noting that Di Peso found a great many more Medio Period towns in the Casas Grandes region than the Viejo Period population could possible account for (Lekson, Bletzer, and MacWilliams 2004). I suspect that we both are right: southwestern populations shifted into Chihuahua during the fourteenth and fifteenth centuries and then crossed over the mountains into Sonora during the sixteenth and seventeenth centuries. Of course, they had to change pottery styles, architecture, and who knows what else, but they'd done that before, several times.

103. Schroeder 1979.

104. Wilcox et al. 2006:210.

105. Upham 1982.

106. Spielmann 2004.

107. Adams and Duff 2004.

108. LeBlanc 1999; Lekson 2002b; Spielmann 2004:142; Wilcox et al. 2006.

109. LeBlanc 1999.

110. "Devolution" (as it were) from politically complex to simpler societies has been mooted for other periods of southwestern prehistory. I trace that trajectory from Pioneer to Colonial and Sedentary Hohokam (chapter 4), after which things ramped up again, sharply. Steadman Upham long ago introduced the idea of "adaptive diversity"—sedentary southwestern peoples shifting to less sedentary lifestyles and back again (Upham 1984, 1994). Feinman, Lightfoot, and Upham argued that "the pithouse-to-pueblo transition marked a significant organizational shift to more corporate forms of political action that also characterize historic and modern Pueblos" (2000:449; see also Feinman 2000). They got the trajectory right but set the story several centuries too early. Jill Neitzel (2003) makes a similar argument that Chaco, and specifically Pueblo Bonito, moved from a hierarchical to a diffuse (corporate) structure of government. This is a brilliant suggestion, allowing Chaco to be both—hierarchy early, hierocracy late. But I think Neitzel's reconstruction is based on an incorrect temporal assignment of the elite burials at Pueblo Bonito (chapter 5) to early in Chaco's history. From the associated pottery, they were more likely later in the Chaco sequence. What happened in Pueblo IV had happened, repeatedly, throughout the history of the ancient Southwest: hierarchy breaking down into heterarchy.

111. The profusion of new ideas and "cults" in Pueblo IV tells us something about the homogeneity and stability of Chacoan ways, even in their attenuated (and eventually failed) continuation through Pueblo III times at Aztec Ruins. I'm not sure that we know very much about Chacoan "religion" (but see Kantner 2006; Mills 2002, 2004). Whatever Chaco religion was, it certainly wasn't Pueblo IV: the uniformity and redundancy of Chaco's visual symbol systems stand in astonishing contrast to the dynamic and varied ritual art of Pueblo IV.

Modern Pueblo ritual largely postdates Chaco and probably postdates the 1300 migrations—insofar as archaeology can see its material manifestations (e.g., Adams 1991; Plog and Solomento 1997; Schaafsma 1994; VanPool, VanPool, and Phillips 2006; but see Mills 2004). I agree with John Ware and Eric Blinman,

> that Pueblo social-ceremonial organization is fundamentally syncretic, that most Pueblo ceremonial organizations that survived into the historic period attained their ethnographic form during the late prehistoric period following the depopulation of the Colorado Plateau, and that the dynamics of structural collapse and migration were instrumental in creating the variety of ceremonial institutions that appeared during the fourteenth and fifteenth centuries. (Ware and Blinman 2000:382)

Peter Whitely, one of the most interesting and productive of ethnologists currently working with the Pueblos, presents a very reasonable view:

> We might usefully hypothesize some persistent, longue-durée Puebloan social thought from

inferred Chacoan sociopolitical structures. Devolution of power structures after the collapse of Chaco resulted in a variety of socio-structural replacements. It is reasonable to assume, however, that some basic elements in modes of production and social reproduction—both directly from Chaco and from coeval non-Chacoan Pueblo forms—persisted. (Whitely 2004:152)

Things may well have got going at Chaco—I'm betting, during the post-Chaco period at Chaco Canyon itself (if that phrase makes sense). Barbara Mills (2004), in an important essay on "the establishment and defeat of hierarchy" in the Pueblo Southwest, looked at three classes of Pueblo ritual artifacts—altars, ceremonial clothing, and staffs—and concluded that almost all date to the late thirteenth or fourteenth century, *except at Chaco*, where they might have been earlier (Mills 2004:244, 245). Artifacts closely resembling modern Pueblo altars and ceremonial staffs were found at Chetro Ketl and Pueblo Bonito, respectively (Vivian, Dodgen, and Hartman 1978). Painted wood very similar to the Chetro Ketl assemblage was also found at Aztec Ruins (Webster 2007b). Did post-Chaco ceremonial systems begin at Chaco itself? I have heard Hopi accounts that at least some aspects of ritual life did indeed originate at Chaco, and several versions of the White House story indicate that Pueblo people learned the proper ways to dance for kachinas as they were leaving that great city—that is, at the time White House fell.

The artifacts from Chetro Ketl are painted slats of wood that, when reassembled, certainly resemble altars (Vivian, Dodgen, and Hartman 1978). They also may include mobile-on-a-pole artifacts shown on Mimbres pots and found in Mogollon caves (Cosgrove 1947; Wasley 1962). The same can be said of staffs: they appear prominently in Mimbres ceramic art (and in rock art there and elsewhere). Some think that the earliest depictions of recognizable kachinas appear on the same Mimbres pottery (Carlson 1982a; cf. Brody 2004). Polly Schaafsma argues strongly for the "origins" of kachina ceremonialism in Mimbres area rock art (slightly later than Mimbres itself), inspired by masked ceremonies in Mexico. A possible scenario: kachina ceremonialism began in eleventh-century Mimbres, established a foothold in Chaco's final days, went through the refiner's fire of twelfth- and thirteenth-century Wupatki, and emerged, fully formed, along the Little Colorado River in the fourteenth century, spreading east from Hopi to the Rio Grande thereafter. That scenario could make everyone happy, but it probably won't.

112. For example, Parsons [1939]1996.

113. Whiteley 1998.

114. Pueblo people are not inclined to discuss the origins of their spiritual and religious beliefs with outsiders—having been burned by ethnologists who wrongfully published stories told in confidence. In light of past anthropological misbehavior, recent post-processual fascinations with Pueblo ritual make for unsettling reading. Are we doing it again? Perhaps we should not try to "understand" the details of Pueblo spiritual life. I suspect that many Pueblo colleagues and friends would agree: anthropological understanding is neither possible nor necessary. That's one big reason I wrote this book about politics and not ritual, even though ritual is today's hot topic. Pueblo colleagues thought that politics (at least the way I've handled it in past publications) would be less problematic than another study of kachina cults or medicine societies.

115. For example, Kuwanwisiwma 2004.

116. Noble 2004; Sofaer 1999; Warriner 2000.

117. Sofaer 1999.

118. Sofaer 1999.

119. Sofaer 1999.

120. Warriner 2000.

121. Noble 2004.

122. According to historians and anthropologists, Navajo people arrived in the Southwest many decades after Chaco ended. Navajos disagree. We also say that Navajos gained knowledge of Chaco's history from Pueblo people revisiting their old city, marrying into Navajo clans, or relocating to Navajo country when life in the Rio Grande or Acoma or Zuni got too lively. I know several Navajo people who would agree to that in part but not in full.

One thing we can agree upon, I think: because Navajos inhabited the old Chaco country, they were constantly aware of its ruins and landscapes and their histories (see note 48, above). Stories are invested in and reinforced by landscape features, including ruins. I think that Navajo clans remembered Chaco's details, which Pueblos far distant from Chaco forgot or glossed, because Navajos actually *lived on that land* (Kelley and Francis 1994, 2003; Warburton and Begay 2005). They saw these ruins daily, and they passed on their histories in that vivid, mnemonic setting. Living in, on, and around history keeps history alive and the details fresh in a different way than does telling and retelling at physical and temporal distance.

123. He has a name: Noqoilpi or Nááhwílbįįhí ("he who wins you by gambling" or "winner of people"). My

principal sources include Begay 2004, Goddard 1933, Mathews 1889, 1897, O'Bryan 1956, and conversations with Navajo people who live around Chaco Canyon. For an accessible summary, see Gabriel 1996:ch. 4 and appendix II. See also chapter 5, note 199.

124. My principal sources are Stirling 1942 and White 1932, supplemented by conversations with individuals from the pueblos of Acoma, Zia, and Zuni. "White House" is often identified specifically as Chaco and sometimes as Mesa Verde, but it may also refer to the larger region called here the eastern Anasazi or eastern Plateau—more of a concept or an idea than a place.

125. The city of Phoenix, independently of the highway CRM project, sponsored an important archival study of the platform mound (summarized in Downum and Bostwick 2003).

126. Soil Systems Publication in Archaeology 20, published in 1994, summarized in Abbott (ed.) 2003.

127. LeBlanc 1999; Rice 2001.

128. "The modal age at death was birth…newborns and young infants represented almost 20 percent" of the burials recovered by the CRM project (Sheridan 2003:85). The osteological data set the grim, bleak tone of *Centuries of Decline*'s Pueblo Grande (Abbott [ed.] 2003). Sheridan, Van Gerven, and their colleagues at the University of Colorado conducted detailed analyses of bone chemistry, pathologies, and of course demography of the site's remarkable burial population—more than eight hundred individuals (Sheridan 2001, 2003). Those studies, more dramatically than any other data (and often in contrast to other data), revealed the difficult, even desperate conditions of Pueblo Grande's "golden age" Classic Period. I'm not sure we would have *Centuries of Decline*—and this startling new view of the Classic Period—without osteology.

Reanalysis of the Pueblo Grande numbers (the human remains are no longer available for study) may lead to revision. Paul Fish (personal communication, October 22, 2007) informed me, "While your evaluation certainly represents the dominant position among Hohokam archaeologists, I believe a different one will emerge in the not so distant future. In part, this is influenced by a reanalysis of Classic period human remains (including Pueblo Grande) from published sources…[which suggest] a considerably brighter picture of health among Pueblo Grande populations." Conference papers by Rebecca Hill and Lorrie Lincoln-Babb (2008) suggest a healthier Late Classic, at Pueblo Grande and elsewhere. In many ways, that would make Hohokam's end even more interesting. Stay tuned.

129. Pueblo Grande and other large Hohokam Classic Period sites display the characteristics of "coalescent communities": population aggregation, multiethnic/multilingual composition, concern for defense, economic intensification, and increased long-distance interaction (Hill et al. 2004:698–99). Hill and colleagues contribute two additional cross-cultural aspects of coalescent communities that seem to me less likely for the Late Classic: egalitarian ideologies and collective leadership institutions. Platform mounds suggest—to me and to others—hierarchical political structures. As with everything interesting in archaeology, there are other views. The picture painted of coalescent communities is not too far off Rice's characterization of large Gila Phase sites in the Tonto Basin: big "syncretic villages" with both platform mounds and pueblos (Rice 1998:234–35).

130. James 2003; Kwiatowski 2003.

131. Abbott 2003:214; Howard 1993.

132. Elson and Abbott 2000:120–21.

133. (Doyel 2000a:fig. 13.5; Doyel and Fish 2000:10; see also Elson and Abbott 2000). The literature on platform mounds is large and diverse; summaries and shorter essays I found particularly useful include Doelle, Gregory, and Wallace 1995; Downum and Bostwick 2003; Doyel 2000a:303–09; forthcoming; Elson 2000; Gregory 1987; Lindauer 1992; Wilcox 1991c. David Doyel (2000a:fig. 13.5) offered a schematic evolutionary development for Hohokam mounds: pre-Classic dance platforms, Early Classic "temples," and finally Late Classic elite houses. I'm not sure I agree with the continuity of pre-Classic capped mounds and later Classic platforms, but the compromise seems reasonable to me.

134. See note 21, above.

135. Elevation for signaling? Mounds were regularly spaced along canal systems (Gregory and Nials 1985). "Mounds were ideally positioned for communication and decision making purposes related to hydraulic management" (Abbott 2000:201). Could they have a line-of-sight function, hence all those flashing pyrite mirrors?

136. Evidence for elite residence in the Late Classic, if not before, seems strong. Doelle, Gregory, and Wallace argue for elite residence during the Late Classic in the Phoenix Basin (that is, after 1200/1250): "The idea [of platform elite residence] may have derived from a single individual or group of individuals (at Pueblo Grande or Mesa Grande, for example), although the rapid spread of the innovation is most significant…. Rapid emulation of such a move by other 'elite' households could be expected due to the fact that the number of households involved was very small—probably only a few households in each of the 14 or 15 irrigation communities" (Doelle, Gregory, and Wallace 1995:438). But not in the provinces: "This is not to say that social differentiation was entirely lacking outside the Phoenix Basin…. [Outside the Phoenix Basin] it seems most

likely that construction and use of the mounds may have been the responsibility of ritual specialists at the household level, or one or more groups or lineages related to functions such as curing, dance or warfare. The access of such groups to restricted esoteric knowledge would have served to underwrite their authority" (Doelle, Gregory, and Wallace 1995:439). For intriguing reviews of (possibly) elite Classic Period burials, see Mitchell and Brunson-Hadley 2001 and Loendorf 2001.

137. Wilcox and Shenk 1977. Casa Grande was probably the Classic Period component of the enormous pre-Classic Grewe (discussed in chapters 4 and 5), moved slightly to the west along the major canal. You could argue that Grewe and Casa Grande represent two periods in one of the biggest, most important of all the Hohokam towns (Craig 2000b, 2001a), like the amalgamated Blue Mesa–Ridges Basin site(s) of chapter 4. People partial to Pueblo Grande or Los Muertos or Snaketown or Azatlan will promote the objects of their affection, of course, and indeed there were many very large Hohokam towns in the Classic Period.

138. I am aware that puddled adobe has a deeper history in Hohokam and the southern deserts, before Casa Grande (e.g., Cameron 1998). But think of Chaco. There was an earlier history of stone masonry on the Plateau, but nothing in the stonework of Pueblo I explained the masonry invented to build Bonito. I don't doubt that one led to the other, but the nature of the masonry changed, both in appearance and in physics. The issue is not stone qua stone, but the development of new masonry that could match the grand new Chacoan design (Lekson 1984). Likewise, the issue at Casa Grande is not so much the use of mud as mud, but the use of massive adobe walls to reach four stories. There were no precedents for *that* in the Hohokam desert. There might have been precedents to the southeast, in Chihuahua (more on this below).

139. Elson 1998:6; Wilcox and Shenk 1977:23, 38. We "normalized" Casa Grande by making it a platform mound, using this logic: when excavated, the first floor of Casa Grande was found to have been filled in, apparently intentionally. Casa Grande's filled first floor equates roughly to the filled cells of a platform mound: ergo, platform mound (Wilcox and Shenk 1977). All those extra stories were needed as an astronomical observatory, with cleverly placed windows letting in sunlight, moonlight, and starlight at appropriate times (this is *not* in Wilcox and Shenk 1977 but is one widely accepted reading of the building). Since the astronomers could have built equally useful observatories at ground level, out of poles and twine, the observatory hypothesis seems like special pleading—and perhaps a reaction against anything hinting at "Pueblo" in the Hohokam heartland.

Old accounts, which we have no reason to doubt, suggest that there were several similar multistoried structures in the Phoenix area. Very likely, there was another "casa grande"—with massive walls and a compact footprint—at Los Muertos on the Salt River, a good candidate for the largest of all Classic Period sites (Haury 1945), and there was probably another at Pueblo Grande (Wilcox 1993b). Whatever the final count, Casa Grande was certainly the largest of a few Hohokam Great Houses, all in the Phoenix Basin. Contrast the rarity of Hohokam "Great Houses" to the ubiquity of platform mounds, of which there were between 120 and 125 (Doelle 1995b; Doelle, Gregory, and Wallace 1995), or the earlier ball courts, which totaled twice that, almost 240 (Marshall 2001; Wilcox 1991d).

I've always been struck by similarities between Casa Grande and Casas Grandes (Paquimé), so much so that I once suggested that Casa Grande was an outpost of Paquimé (Lekson 2000). Casa Grande and smaller Hohokam "Great Houses" may have been something like Chaco outliers: big buildings, remarkable in form and construction, built in the style of a distant capital. I still think that may be the case, but the orthodox reading of Casa Grande—as a platform mound/Great House—makes a better story. As explained in chapter 1, story line is key to my selection from competing interpretations, including my own.

140. Evans and Hillman 1981.

141. Abbott 2003.

142. Gillespie 1989.

143. What are the physical traces of Plateau elites, or ideas of elites, in the Hohokam heartland? Don't look for pottery—the people who ruled Chaco and Aztec didn't make their own. They had people to do that. The signs are at once more subtle and more obvious: architecture and insignia.

The best and strongest evidence of Plateau elites *on the Plateau* is architectural: Great Houses. And for Classic Period elites, of course, the massive palacelike structures built on top of Late Classic Period platform mounds and purpose-built monuments such as Casa Grande. I think all were elite residences—palaces, not temples. Move Casa Grande north and build it of sandstone, and it would fit in at Aztec Ruins. It would be weird, like a tri-wall, but it would fit in. Yet, somehow, architecture standing alone (inescapably monumental) fails to convince archaeologists who want their data to come in bags—artifacts.

Insignia are artifacts, and emblems of office. David Wilcox (1999a:137–138) traced the origins of twelfth- and early-thirteenth-century "emblems of ritual and political office" in the Flagstaff–Verde Valley–Prescott area to Chaco. "A little later, the raptorial bird and toad emblems, and the nose plugs [a Flagstaff addition], were adopted by the Hohokam in the Phoenix Basin, and the people of the Tonto Basin, and many other peoples involved in the fourteenth century Salado macroregional system," which overlapped significantly with platform mounds. That is, a Chacoan ideology, modified at Wupatki, "was taken up by the Phoenix Basin Hohokam to help restructure their society. The time these emblems were adopted coincides with the moment when large structures began to be built on top of the Hohokam platform mounds" (Wilcox 1999a:137–38).

What about birds? Rich Lange (1992:fig. 36.3) demonstrates nearly exclusive geographic distributions of platform mounds and macaws. Platform mounds were Hohokam; macaws were Anasazi, Pueblo, and Casas Grandes. Like Pueblo III Aztec, perhaps the Classic Period Hohokam were cut off from distant West Mexican societies by Pueblo IV Paquimé.

144. Abbott 2003:225.

145. Abbott 2003:225.

146. Graybill et al. 2006:115.

147. Graybill et al. 2006.

148. Graybill et al. 2006. Graybill and colleagues believe that the 1382 floods "produced severe damage and substantial lateral erosion which immediately rendered the Civano phase systems inoperable and…effectively prevented any recovery" (2006:118; see also Nials, Gregory, and Graybill 1989).

149. Abbott 2003:225.

150. After the fall, the Phoenix Basin was not entirely empty. Small, scattered Polvoron Phase hamlets continued long after the mobs stormed the mounds (e.g., Chenault 2000), and perhaps a few of the old cities had stubborn remnants (Los Muertos?). But there is little chronometric or ceramic data to suggest that big Classic Hohokam sites survived past 1400 or, at latest, 1450.

151. Graybill et al. 2006:117.

152. For example, Bahr et al. 1994.

153. Bahr et al. 1994.

154. Bahr et al. 1994.

155. Teague 1993:fig. 1.

156. Teague 1993:443.

157. Fish, Fish, and Villalpando 2007; O'Donovan 2004:fig. 2.2.

158. S. Fish and P. Fish 2004; McGuire and Villalpando C. 2007a; McGuire et al. 1999; O'Donovan 2004.

159. McGuire et al. 1999; O'Donovan 2002.

160. Fish and Fish 2007.

161. Fish, Fish, and Villalpando 2007; McGuire and Villalpando C. 1993; Newell and Gallaga 2004.

162. O'Donovan 2004:40.

163. Hard and Roney 2007.

164. McGuire et al. 1999:142–43.

165. McGuire et al. 1999:146; but see Nelson 2007 for a review of Mesoamerican precedents for hilltop terracing.

166. Bandelier 1890–92:575.

167. Di Peso 1974; Di Peso, Rinaldo, and Fenner eds. 1974.

168. Whalen and Minnis 2000, 2001, 2003, 2004.

169. From the University of New Mexico, the Museum of New Mexico, and the University of Calgary, among others; Kelley et al. 2004; Whalen and Minnis 2004; Newell and Gallaga 2004; Reyman 1995; Schaafsma and Riley 1999; Woosley and Ravesloot 1993.

170. For example, Lekson 1983; Mathien and McGuire 1986; McGuire 1980.

171. Lekson 1999b.

172. According to Di Peso (1974:vols. 2, 5), Paquimé began as a dozen or more independent, widely spaced, single-story adobe compounds, which he erroneously dated to 1060 to 1205. These were followed in the early thirteenth century by an explosive "urban renewal" (Di Peso's term), creating the dense cityscape and monuments. A period of decline, ending in the mid-fourteenth century, was marked by strife and finally abandonment. Today most archaeologists agree that the Medio Period (and Paquimé) began later and lasted longer. The span 1200 to 1450 is generally accepted for the Medio Period (Dean and Ravesloot 1993; Whalen and Minnis 2001), but I think that may stretch things too far back in time; Paquimé itself began well after 1250, probably after 1300 (Lekson 1999b; see also chapter 6, note 161).

173. Paquimé's relationship to Late Classic Period Hohokam has been less often explored (Lekson 2000; McGuire 1993; VanPool, VanPool, and Phillips 2006; Wilcox 1991a, 1999a). In chapter 6, I wondered whether the dearth of southern exotics in Aztec's region was a matter of policy or an accident of history. I am inclined toward policy, at least in part, because a similar situation arose in the Hohokam area in the Classic Period.

The numbers and qualities of Mesoamerican objects and goods in southern Arizona plummeted (Doyel 2000b:235–36; McGuire 1993:109). Both Aztec and Phoenix showed remarkable declines in physical evidence for Mesoamerican interactions at a time when Paquimé—the Southwest's most Mesoamerican city—was gearing up and gaining traction.

Hohokam of the Classic Period was a formidable thing. Decline is something we see after the fact; between 1100 and 1200/1250, nothing in the greater Southwest came close to the mass and power of Phoenix—even Phoenix in trouble. Chaco and Hohokam were contemporary polities but probably not "*peer* polities." Phoenix and Chaco were *parallel* polities; Phoenix and Paquimé were peers.

The Rio Casas Grandes had never been part of the Hohokam sphere, and it could be argued that the Chihuahuan Desert differs sufficiently from the Sonoran that Paquimé was in an area of no economic interest to Hohokam (I doubt it: a canal's a canal, for a' that—as the poet might have said). But I think the lords of Casas Grandes had to consider Classic Period Hohokam rather more carefully than had the rulers of Chaco. Indeed, creating a rival desert polity at Paquimé was a bold act. Wars were being fought, farther south, over that sort of provocation (and we can assume that southwestern leaders were well aware of Post-Classic militarism).

We don't find much Chaco pottery in Phoenix or buffware at Bonito. But there were contact and commerce between Paquimé and the Hohokam world. Gila Polychrome—the red, white, and black badge of Salado—appears at Paquimé in quantity, and local "imitations" were produced (Escondida Polychrome). I hinted above (note 139) that the Hohokam Great Houses ("Casa Grande") may have been architecturally inspired by Paquimé ("Casas Grandes"). The historical decline of Phoenix and the rise of Paquimé were probably linked, in ways we do not yet understand—an open research question of paramount importance.

174. There is disagreement over the city plan of Paquimé. The excavated portions of the site run approximately north–south along the edge of a low terrace above the Rio Casas Grandes valley. Ruins of undetermined size extend down into the valley bottom, particularly along an alluvial ridge that parallels the terrace edge. Di Peso (1974) suggested that the dense "high-rise" formed a huge, inverted-U-shaped building (open to the south), including both terrace edge and alluvial ridge areas; the U surrounded a large central plaza. Other archaeologists question the existence of the lower, valley-bottom arm of the U, suggesting instead that Paquimé was essentially an L- or I-shaped architectural mass (cf. Di Peso 1974 and Lekson 1999c versus Phillips and Bagwell 2001 and Wilcox 1999b:98).

There is also disagreement about the construction techniques employed. Di Peso thought that Paquimé's walls were poured into forms, while many archaeologists believe that the walls were puddled by hand in low courses, a much simpler technique (reviewed in Schaafsma and Riley 1999). Adobe walls were not unknown in the southern Southwest before Paquimé (see note 138, above), but the use of massive walls (however constructed) to achieve multiple stories appears to be a Medio Phase innovation—much like Classic Period Hohokam at Casa Grande. Paquimé's rooms were large, tall, and typically rectangular, with heavily timbered upper-story floors and roofs. Many rooms were more complex, with odd L shapes and even more complicated forms (one room resembles an abstract butterfly). These shapes created small nooks and reentrants that accommodated shelflike "sleeping platforms." They also strengthened and internally buttressed multistoried walls by "folding" long walls into something like a piece of corrugated tin roof set on edge. Interlock enough of these many-angled walls and you have a building that can reach four stories or more. These unusual forms (and the massive width of walls) may have been necessary because puddled or poured adobe is far from ideal technology for multistoried building. Necessity for verticality was the mother of invention. But why that need? I suspect it was precisely the same ideological drive that raised Chacoan Great Houses to great heights.

175. See Pietzel 2007—but *not* Pietzel's interpretation.

176. Lekson 1983, 1999b, 1999c.

177. Lekson 1999b:fig. 3.3, 1999c.

178. Di Peso, Rinaldo, and Fenner 1974a:208–11; Lekson 1999b:appendix A.

179. I am particularly drawn to an unusual Casas Grandes pottery form, "hand drums"—open-ended, narrow-waisted tubes (Fenner 1974) that Gloria Fenner and Di Peso interpreted as percussion instruments. This form is not known from other regions of the Southwest, although there are contextual parallels to Chaco's cylinder vases (Lekson 1999b:96–98).

180. Moulard 2005.

181. Minnis 1988; VanPool and Leonard 2002; cf. Whalen and Minnis 2001:182–90.

182. Wilcox 2007:237.

183. Weigand and Harbottle 1993.

184. Whalen and Minnis 2000, 2001.

185. Architecturally, there is not a lot of differentiation within the "high-rise"—no obvious stratified

housing *within the city*. The "high-rise" was complex and dense, but uniform in its details: all the walls are immense, all the rooms are large and peculiarly configured, and key room features (fire pits, platforms, T doors) are homogeneously distributed. I think Paquimé was a city of palaces. The "high-rise" deconstructs into a dozen Great House–sized palaces, built shoulder to shoulder. Princely families, as in Chaco.

But where and how did the other half live? Perhaps the surrounding compounds (originally thought by Di Peso to be earlier than the "high-rise") were actually servants' quarters. Intriguingly, the only candidate kiva—room 38, unit 11 (a Mogollon-looking, Great Kiva–like, rectangular pit structure with a ramp entry)—was in a detached compound. Was that the social center for the working classes?

Burials at Paquimé have been interpreted as indicating several tiers of social or political ranking (Di Peso, Rinaldo, and Fenner 1974b:vol. 8, chs. 19–23; Ravesloot 1988). At the apex (in these earlier analyses) were secondary burials of defleshed bones in huge jars, deposited in a cryptlike space in a major platform mound or pyramid. The second tier (again, in these earlier analyses) had two adult males placed in wooden crypts in an otherwise unremarkable area of Paquimé, accompanied by remarkable quantities of grave goods. In the crypts and in the chambers above them were scores of disarticulated individuals. I interpret them as "retainers" (officials and kinsmen sacrificed when the king was buried), but less hierarchical interpretations have of course been offered (Ravesloot 1988; Whalen and Minnis 2001). Notably, in the rooms above the burial crypts were almost all the known ceramic hand drums, paralleling the cylinder jars of Pueblo Bonito. I suggest that the two males in the crypt were in fact the highest-ranking individuals, the lords of Paquimé. I have no idea whose bones were in the jars, but given that "trophy" long bones and skulls commonly hung from the rafters of Paquimé rooms (Di Peso 1974:562), they could have belonged to just about anybody. They might have been important people, but perhaps not so important to Paquimé in life as in death. Lower-status burials were scattered throughout the site, in the "high-rise" and compounds.

186. Whalen and Minnis 2001:189.

187. Johnson 1989:386.

188. Di Peso 1974; Lekson 1999b; Whalen and Minnis 2001.

189. Schaafsma and Riley 1999:fig. 1.

190. Di Peso 1974:328.

191. Whalen and Minnis 2001:194.

192. See also chapter 6, note 166. And see Whalen and Minnis (2001:194) for subdivisions of the three concentric zones. Insofar as is known, I-shaped ball courts were concentrated in the core, were largely absent from the middle zone, and reappear in the outer periphery (at sites such as Joyce Well). Other features and artifacts conspicuous at Paquimé follow similar distributions, with a "near-complete absence [in the middle zone] of almost all of the core features and facilities, from ball courts to birdcages to agricultural terrace systems" (Whalen and Minnis 2001:191). Some features, such as ball courts and platform hearths, appear in the outer periphery; others, such as bird pens, are absent there. Chacoan Great Kivas followed a similar distribution (Van Dyke 2007a): a heavy concentration at Chaco Canyon; an inner zone around Chaco, where these otherwise ubiquitous features are absent; and an outer zone where settlements routinely have these features.

Although Whalen and Minnis (and others) have done remarkable work, the evidence is far more fragmentary than it is for the far better-known Chaco and Hohokam regions. It will be decades before Chihuahuan archaeology enjoys the regional coverage taken for granted north of the border. For example, Di Peso describes "roads" from Paquimé throughout the Casas Grandes area, but these are all but unstudied. Roads visible in aerial images appear to be broad and formally constructed but not straight like Chaco's. Only slightly better known is the network of fire signaling stations—much like Chaco's line-of-sight communication network, with a central hub on Cerro de Moctezuma near Paquimé (Pietzel 2007; Swanson 2003). Apparently, a signaling system of stations on high points interconnected much of Paquimé's area—much like Chaco. Following out roads and communication systems is an obvious strategy, but even for over-researched Chaco, our knowledge of both remains incomplete. Paquimé's systems may require innovations in technique and, particularly, remote sensing options.

193. Kidder, Cosgrove, and Cosgrove 1949; McCluney 1962; Naylor 1995; Skibo, McCluney, and Walker 2002.

194. But see Douglas 2007.

195. Skibo, McCluney, and Walker 2002.

196. Whalen and Minnis put Joyce Well at the very outermost margins of their "intermediate peripheries… less closely tied into the core's political economy" (2001:194).

197. Kelley et al. 1999; MacWilliams and Kelley 2004.

198. Di Peso 1974:630; Lekson 2002a.

199. Lekson 2002a.

200. As noted in the text, Whalen and Minnis limit Paquimé's political control to its central core and limit its political economy to 150 kilometers. In southern New Mexico (which is far better known than other segments of the Casas Grandes region), arguments for meaningful connections to Casas Grandes have ranged as far abroad as Bloom Mound near Roswell (Kelley 1984:appendix 6; *not* her interpretation). Schaafsma and Riley (1999:fig. 1) extend the "Casas Grandes interaction sphere" as far as 330 kilometers north (to the vicinity of Truth or Consequences) and as far northeast as Bloom Mound (about 460 kilometers). To the south, Carlos Lazcano Sahagun, in his survey of Sierra Madre cliff dwellings, extends the "límite approximado del territorio Paquimé" almost as far south as Creel—more than 500 kilometers south of Paquimé (Lazcano Sahagun 1998).

201. Whalen and Minnis 2001.

202. There is a curious disparity in the ways archaeologists treat these two features at Paquimé. I-shaped ball courts were clearly Mesoamerican; there's nothing like them in the greater Southwest. We accept them as significant evidence of connections in part *because* the distances involved are great. T-shaped doorways are apparently less convincing; we question them as evidence of historical connection because they occur elsewhere in the greater Southwest. T doors were a general southwestern thing, right? Well, no, they were not. They shifted with the political winds, from Chaco to Aztec to Paquimé (Lekson 1999b:appendix A).

I am bemused by how we allow Paquimé to connect to societies far to the south but preclude historical connections to societies nearer (but still distant) within the Southwest. To write histories of Casas Grandes, Di Peso (1974) focused on Mesoamerica, while I (Lekson 1999b) highlighted Anasazi. Both were present, and both were important. We can't write Paquimé's history without crossing all our *t*'s and dotting all our *i*'s.

203. Lekson 1999b.

204. Di Peso (1974:409) called Paquimé a cardinal city. Its zigzagging walls run on the cardinals, as if it were laid out on giant graph paper or with the old children's toy Etch A Sketch. The Mound of the Cross, at the north end of the city, was a monument to cardinality, as was the remarkable serpent effigy mound, running north–south.

205. Lekson 1999b.

206. Helms 1988; see also chapter 5.

207. We can, if we dare, look beyond Paquimé to the largest (very) Late Post-Classic city in northwestern Mesoamerica: Culiacán (see note 61). When conquistadors set off for Cibola, they launched from Culiacán, the last and best civilized Mesoamerican city. For those keeping score, Culiacán, the northernmost sixteenth- and seventeenth-century Mesoamerican city, was pretty much due south of Paquimé (fourteenth and fifteenth centuries), and Aztec (twelfth and thirteenth centuries), and Chaco (tenth and eleventh centuries), and Blue Mesa (eighth and ninth centuries), and Shabik'eschee (sixth and seventh centuries). That's right, folks. They all line up on a north–south line: the Chaco Meridian. (See chapter 4, note 172; chapter 5, note 136; and chapter 6, note 54.)

Chaco Meridian (Lekson 1999b) got good reviews. I have a folder of clippings at the office; I haul it out and read them from time to time to cheer myself up. Archaeologists outside the Southwest seem to like the argument (e.g., Sahlqvist 2001), but many of my southwestern colleagues have rejected the idea—a few without reading the book! I am aware of four published criticisms of the *Chaco Meridian* from those who slogged through the whole thing (thank you!): Michael Whalen and Paul Minnis 2003, David Phillips forthcoming (and online), Gwinn Vivian 2001, and Brian Fagan 2005. I have not previously responded to these critiques. Here we go.

Whalen and Minnis

In "The Local and the Distant in the Origin of Casas Grandes," Whalen and Minnis (2003) fought on two fronts: against Di Peso's pochteca from the south and against my Chaco elites from the north (see also chapter 6, note 166). Pressed in a two-ocean war, they wisely ignored arguments about Chaco and Aztec—someone else's problem—but dug in for a hedgehog defense of Paquimé. By demonstrating that Casas Grandes was local, they could repel intruders, north and south, by rendering them superfluous and unnecessary. Whalen and Minnis certainly acknowledge distant contacts but hold firm that the primary sources of change were local.

My reading of Whalen and Minnis yields two basic points of contention with *Chaco Meridian*. First, I argued that the Rio Casas Grandes Valley was, just before Paquimé's Medio Period, an essentially empty niche. Second, I argued for major cultural disjunctures between the preceding Viejo Period and Paquimé's Medio Period. (Di Peso made the same arguments on slightly different grounds.) Whalen and Minnis disagree on both points. Their counterargument, as I understand it, is that a sufficient Viejo Period population, with satisfactory similarities to the Medio Phase and Paquimé, eliminates any need for distant deus ex machina, Chaco or pochteca. Let's consider material culture first, then demography.

The Viejo Period was fairly long: 700 to 1205 or 1250, depending on whom you believe (see chapter 6, note 161). Dean and Ravesloot (1993) say 1205. I say 1250. The Medio Period was 1205/1250 to 1450. If we accept my dating, Viejo was more than five centuries long; Medio about two centuries.

Material Continuities

The material differences between the Viejo Period at 1100 and the Medio Period at 1300 were remarkably well defined—as great as the differences between Pueblo I and Pueblo IV assemblages. The question, it seems, revolves around the boundary conditions at 1250. Sharp or fuzzy? I have no problem with a fuzzy boundary because I cannot image that Paquimé happened overnight. That was Di Peso's position, not mine. His history was more dramatic than mine and in many ways simpler. That's not a criticism. I am certain that Dr. Di Peso knew that actual events were lurching, twisted, and complicated, but a narrative necessarily evens out bumps and cuts corners. I think there was a run-up to Paquimé—but the run-up was short and the city itself was built quickly. In any event, Whalen and Minnis (2003; see also Kelley et al. 1999) argue for a fuzzy transition between the Viejo and Medio periods, with continuities in lithics, ceramics, and adobe architecture.

Let's not worry overmuch about lithics, because later southwestern lithics were overwhelmingly expedient. Usable materials were relatively abundant, so little effort went into 95 percent of tools—expedient flakes, and so forth. It probably does not help us evaluate the argument, that debitage and flake tools of the Viejo Period do indeed resemble debitage and flake tools of the Medio Period. The other 5 percent—points, knives, and drills—are potentially much more interesting and informative, but detailed studies of those more formal tools are only now beginning.

Did the Casas Grandes ceramic tradition emerge fully formed at 1300? Of course not! I see the Casas Grandes ceramic tradition originating as an earlier, broader polychrome horizon that stretched across the southern deserts (but apparently not Phoenix) (Doyel 1988). Continuities between Ramos Polychrome and the much earlier Mimbres traditions (see also Brody 2004; Moulard 2005) suggest to me a sudden jolt of Mimbres aesthetics into an otherwise unremarkable tricolor ceramic industry: Ramos Polychrome. As I argue here and in the text (chapter 6), that was because post-Mimbres people moved into the Casas Grandes region.

Whalen and Minnis (2003) argue that many of Paquimé's architectural details had appeared by 1250 (that is, pre-Paquimé, which I date to 1300). As noted elsewhere (chapter 6, note 161), their dating is based on 14C on wood and therefore is almost certainly early, perhaps decades early.

Another continuity might be adobe. Puddled adobe walls appeared in the desert before Paquimé. But I'm not sure they are the *same* walls as Paquimé's (see note 138, above). What made Paquimé famous (and made a loser out of me?) were architectural chops addressing an unhealthy fixation on the vertical. Unhealthy, because puddled or poured adobe is not a good medium for tall walls. Paquimé was remarkably tall—four or even five stories tall. As noted above, its multi-angled rooms reflect (at least in part) structural considerations: many corners made for stronger, more stable, multistoried walls. You don't see those shenanigans in Chacoan Great Houses because (after 1020) they had figured out multistoried sandstone masonry. Paquimé's massive walls and multi-angled rooms quickly became part of a new canon and showed up later in smaller, single-story sites, but not much before.

Demography

Chihuahua still lacks the detailed demographic data that drives cyber-Anasazi models. But it's clear that at the peak of the Medio Period, there must have been tens of thousands of people living in the central Casas Grandes area. The basic demographic question is, Were there enough Viejo Period people to create the densely settled Casas Grandes Valley in the Medio Phase? I addressed this question in chapter 6 and concluded no, probably not. But it cannot be stated too strongly (since many people seem to miss this point) that *Chaco Meridian* never suggested wholesale migration of tens of thousands of people from the Anasazi area into Chihuahua. No, I suggested that several hundred elites made the journey to the Rio Casas Grandes Valley, joining thousands of *other* in-migrants from nearer areas (specifically the Mimbres and post-Mimbres; chapter 6).

It was not an entirely "empty niche"—that's just an expression. There clearly were Viejo Period settlements just before the Medio Period—but not many, as noted in chapter 6, notes 190 and 192. My point is that the simple *presence* of Viejo sites does not prove (or disprove) a demographic trajectory leading to Paquimé. No one argued that there was *no* Viejo Period. Di Peso defined its phases at sites in the Casas Grandes Valley; I certainly did not dispute it. Both Di Peso and I, however, thought the Viejo Period sites were too thin on the ground, and there is little in the recent intensive surveys around Paquimé to contradict that conclusion possible that denser Viejo populations in southern Chihuahua (Kelley et al. 1999, Kelley et al. 2004) ad something to the mix.

Chihuahua is many decades away from the demographic detail that archaeologists now take for granted in the Four Corners states, so arguments for continuity or discontinuity remain just that—arguments. With the far greater investment in research in the Four Corners states, we have come to realize that movements, migrations, periodic abandonments, "fallow valleys," and reoccupations were *typical* and not extraordinary. Why would Chihuahua be different? Perhaps because of canal irrigation, à la Hohokam and Mimbres. If there were more Viejo sites, I'd be more inclined to consider local demographic growth—but that still would have no bearing on the influx of a few hundred elites from the north. The Medio Phase, as we know it today, was supported bottom-up by local people (Viejo and/or post-Mimbres), but it was *created by* elites, top-down. Shaman-priests or would-be kings, the upper classes most likely considered themselves different and distant, engaging ideologies from and exchanges with and probably even travels from and to far distant regions: Chaco and Mesoamerica. Rather than set out to prove Casas Grandes was a remarkable special case in the Southwest—*a truly local development*—would it not be wiser to inform its fledgling archaeology with insights (if not elites) from the north, particularly given the flamboyantly extroverted nature of Paquimé itself? However Casas Grandes began, it certainly did not live locally once it was going strong.

Phillips

The second critique of *Chaco Meridian* was by David A. Phillips Jr. (forthcoming and online). Phillips had four main objections: (1) the meridian was not straight (sites were not all exactly on the same longitude); (2) the chronologies were not precise (there's overlap between sequent centers); (3) insufficient attention was paid to Salmon Ruin, which was chronologically and geographically intermediate between Chaco and Aztec; and (4) people resident in the Rio Casas Grandes might not have welcomed a Chacoan intrusion. Phillips—a gentleman and scholar—graciously allowed me to respond on his Web page (see Phillips forthcoming), which I did, in a memo:

> To: David A. Phillips, Jr.
> From: Stephen H. Lekson
> Subject: Doctrinal errors, manifest heresies, and cardinal sins
>
> Date: April 6, 2000
> I read, in humility and abnegation, your dictum on my several theses, nailed first to the poster boards of the Society and propounded later in *Chaco Meridian*. Forgive me, David, for I have sinned. It has been many years since I've confessed to anything worse than simple indolence. I now freely and fully admit to errors clerical, numerical, cartographical. Mea, as they say, culpa. My soul is at risk, my reputation is in the tank. But, as I leave the Court of Higher Opinion, I mutter: "They still align." And the argument still works. At risk of full inquisition and final censorship, I respond to several (but not all) queries and charges, to wit:
>
> **Their errors negate my argument**
> The Meridian wobbles! I make no claims that ancient engineers were preternaturally precise. The meridian argument, in fact, is based on the realization that errors were unavoidable, theoretically predictable, and, indeed, observable in the careening route to the North Road. But the ancient importance of meridian alignment is independently affirmed by: (1) the final north–south wall in the plaza of Pueblo Bonito (built over a Great Kiva, when a two-degree deviation would have avoided that dangerous construction); (2) the "Cardinal City" of Paquimé—Di Peso's words; and (3) the Great North Road—as close to a large-scale meridian monument as any ancient ever built. Hammering these people for their errors is, I think, demanding false precision. They did the best they could, lacking chronometers and GPS, and their errors are key to my argument.
>
> **Chronological overlaps: The trains arrive before they leave the station**
> Just between you and me, I think the actual chronology went something like this: Chaco was really rolling from 1000 to 1110; Aztec boomed from 1110 to 1275; Paquimé began about 1275–1300 and ended either at 1450 with the rise of Culiacán, or maybe a century later with the arrival of European microbes. I used the "as is" tree-ring dates to avoid endless chronological digressions and exegeses. But the "as is" dates overlap, a little. Fine: if I were the High Panjandrum, I'd surely send a gang ahead to build a comfortable palace before I dragged my Royal Self over hill and dale to the new Pleasure Dome in Xanadu. (See "Salmon Ruins," below.)

In the dendrochronologically beglamoured Southwest, we have come to expect temporal precision. We find these little overlaps alarming. In most parts of the archaeological world, the temporal sequence of Chaco, Aztec, and Paquimé would be hailed as astonishingly tight. (I say this because I've presented the chronology to non-southwestern archaeologists; they hailed it as astonishingly tight.)

What about Salmon Ruins?
Salmon Ruins began at 1088, at Chaco's height—that is, they started their move out of Chaco while times were good, undercutting the standard climatic arguments. As a child of the '70s, I was raised to believe that ancient activities mirrored climatic shifts. But as a practitioner in the '00s, I must let ancient people act politically, making decisions free of the Natural Laboratory. The move from Chaco to Aztec and the move from Aztec to Paquimé were, I think, fundamentally political—hence the book's subtitle. They moved north out of Chaco long before the droughts of the 1130s. Perhaps the High Panjandrum wanted to leave that dry nasty canyon, and move to one of the lovely little creeks up north. That's Salmon Ruins—but the San Juan wasn't so lovely, after all; so they went to Aztec.

What about all those Casas Grandes people, before the new Lords arrived?
Well, what about 'em? Where are they? Mike Whalen and Paul Minnis have been looking for a decade, and they still can't find substantial remains of post-Mimbres, pre-Paquimé archaeology in the Rio Casas Grandes Valley and its surroundings—or such is my impression. I believe that the base population which built and supported Paquimé was living elsewhere during the 12th and 13th centuries—exactly as suggested by Ben Nelson and Roger Anyon for the valleys of the Chihuahua Desert north of the Border. If "fallow valleys" worked north of the line, why not south of the line, too? The missing links might be the early El Paso Phase or Jane Kelley's sites farther south. But—if you insist on looking at actual evidence—the evidence suggests that nobody was home in the Rio Casas Grandes in the 12th and 13th centuries. Indeed: where WERE the Casas Grandes people before the new Lords arrived?

Vivian

The third critical essay was Gwinn Vivian's (2001) review of *Chaco Meridian*—the book's only published negative review, as far as I know. Rather than engage the central argument (which he very ably summarized), Vivian went after the details—"at the risk of being labeled 'fine tuning.'" Fair enough: the details he disputes are important.

First, Vivian objects to Paquimé's "removal from the Mogollon tradition and its assignment to the Ancestral Pueblo world." If Paquimé was not part of Pueblo history, then apparently it's excused from any further entanglements with Anasazi—a problem of conventional scales I sought to identify (if not resolve) in *Chaco Meridian*. I argued that history played out without reference to conventional archaeological regions. The reality (and utility) of "Mogollon" is wearing thin. Whalen and Minnis (2003) seem convinced that Casas Grandes was indeed part of the Pueblo world. I agree with them (see also Kantner 2004).

Second, Vivian objects to my characterization of Chaco Great Houses as elite residences. He staunchly believes that Great Houses were "pueblos" (my term, not his). I honor his constancy: Vivian is among the last major scholars to support that time-honored view of Chaco. Current thinking, however, runs strongly against him. Chaco Great Houses were not pueblos—that is, not simple agricultural villages (Kantner 2004; Lekson 2007; Neitzel 2003; Van Dyke 2004).

Third, Vivian argues that "data to confirm a second Chacoan capital at Aztec are extremely tenuous." I'd answer that the great mass of architecture at the Aztec Ruins complex is its own best evidence, neither subtle nor obscure—and certainly not tenuous. Architecturally, the place was Chaco North. That interpretation (or variations on it) was suggested before *Chaco Meridian* and is now widely accepted (Brown, Windes, and McKenna 2008; Judge 1989; Lipe 2006; Wilcox 2004; cf. Reed 2004:59–60). Not everyone agrees that Aztec and Chaco were *capitals*, but that was the whole point of *Chaco Meridian*: to suggest political histories that we could not see because of inherited, unexamined systematics.

Fourth and finally, Vivian does not like the way I presented the argument: "circumstantial, anecdotal, [and] juristic." Mea culpa. I use whatever works. As Vivian notes, we do not yet have "a comparative archaeology of polities and their residual landscapes," but how are we to build methods for such an enterprise without first recognizing what those polities looked like? *Chaco Meridian* was an attempt to define polities and political histories in the Southwest that transcended conventional notions like "Anasazi" and "Mogollon," to expand beyond the old natural laboratories, and to push past Benedictine stereotypes of timeless Pueblo egalitarianism.

Fagan

In contrast to print and Web reviews, almost all of which were favorable, I've *heard* some scathingly negative comments about the book in conference exchanges. The most animated came from colleagues who later admitted that they'd never read the book. That happened at least three times I can recall, but I will not name names.

Brian Fagan—a friend and colleague—*did* read the book. He recommended its publication. We all make mistakes apparently. Six years later, Fagan dismissed *Chaco Meridian* as "an archaeological myth, which has no solid grounding in historical reality" (2005:212). Ouch! "No solid grounding"? Many trees died to make the paper to print the book to present the evidence to support the argument of *Chaco Meridian*. The book is about two hundred pages long, and I estimate that about half those pages are evidence and half argument. One hundred pages of evidence seems to me at least a start at "solid grounding." Fagan summarizes the argument but strangely never engages the evidence. Instead, he notes that "few archaeologists involved with any of the three sites accept Lekson's alignment as historical reality" (2005:212). Thus, the meridian becomes "archaeological myth." I wish Fagan had asked me to suggest some other referees. Archaeologists deeply involved with each of the three sites are of course the archaeologists least likely to welcome my suggestions. No surprise that *Chaco Meridian* was voted off the island. Fagan's *Chaco Canyon* is a popular book (and a good one too) and certainly not the place for intricate arguments about T-shaped doors, tree-ring dates, and other archaeological minutia. But it should be obvious that my book and its argument don't stand a chance in a popularity contest. *Chaco Meridian* basically tells southwestern archaeology that it's getting it wrong. Who's going to vote for *that*? If I wrote safe, popular stuff, everybody might believe my account of Chaco as a happy, peaceful, egalitarian place where people pretty much minded their own business, thinking hard about how to become Pueblo. But I don't. And they didn't. Fagan's Chaco is solidly old school, safe, and familiar:

> What was historical reality? It was an ancient one, a way of life finely tuned to an environment of unpredictable rainfall and marginal conditions for any form of agriculture. It was a way of life where people survived by being flexible, by blending agriculture and religion into a seamless, intensely symbolic existence, living, as they did, in the midst of a vast cultural landscape.… Chaco, Aztec, and other great houses were profoundly local phenomena, whatever elaboration they acquired through ritual acumen or food surpluses.… Behind all the panoply of carefully engineered rituals, lavish ceremonies, great houses and public display lay an eternal verity of the Ancestral Pueblo world—the endless rhythm of the seasons, of rain and drought, held together by agriculture and religion. (Fagan 2005:212–13)

Keep 'em simple: ancestral Pueblo as Zen farmers—a spiritualized stereotype of modern Pueblos. That view goes down well in Santa Fe and Sedona, and perhaps that's necessary in a popular volume. But it's not what happened at Chaco. Chaco was *different*. And *big*. And profoundly *not local*.

Et Alia

Finally, an addendum to this addendum: James Q. Jacobs of Central Arizona College informs me that he (not I) discovered and named the Chaco Meridian in 1990. I try to be fair, so let it be known that in 1990 Jacobs noticed that the Big Horn Medicine Wheel, Chaco, Aztec, and the Mimbres Valley were on longitude 108°. In 1991 he noticed that Casas Grandes and Mount Wilson were also on this longitude. He further notes that the distance from Mount Wilson to Pueblo Bonito was one two-hundredth of the circumference of the earth. Jacobs and I are talking about (some of) the same alignments, but I hope the reader notes that our interpretations differ markedly. I am not allying my arguments with Jacobs's or using his arguments to bolster mine. Our arguments have only the thinnest of commonalities—a line. Indeed, there is little glory, but much grief, in the Chaco Meridian. For my part, Jacobs is welcome to both. His website: http://jqjacobs.net/southwest/chaco_meridian.html.

208. Courlander 1971:56–71.

209. Waters 1977:67–71.

210. The city may have fallen to warfare, even massacre (Di Peso 1974; LeBlanc 1999:252–54; Ravesloot 1988), but the identity of its assailants is not clear. Internal strife? Foreign invasion? The projectile points found in its latest contexts look very much like Toyah points of western Texas (Lekson 1997). Intriguingly, Di Peso hints that an earthquake might have been involved (Di Peso 1974:fig. 16-2).

211. Di Peso 1974:319–325; LeBlanc 1999; Ravesloot 1988; cf. Rakita 2006:223–24.

212. Di Peso 1974:388–91; cf. Rakita 2007:229–31.

213. Lazcano Sahagun 1998. There were not, it seems, the terrible executions that marked Aztec's decline

in the Four Corners (chapter 6). Most Medio Period sites are not located in defensive settings (Whalen and Minnis 2001). Late Medio Period cliff dwellings, however, are well known from the Sierra Madre, west of Paquimé (Bagwell 2004; Lazcano Sahagun 1998), which suggests that at least some people were concerned with security.

214. Villagra [1610]1933:43–50.

215. Masse and Espenak 2006; Monnig 1939; Ninenger 1938. Bruce Masse suggests that the iron stone of the witch and the Casas Grandes meteorite might "conceivably derive from a single witnessed impact event" (Masse and Espenak 2006:237).

216. Braniff and Felger 1976; Doolittle 1988; Douglas 1995; Pailes 1978; Riley 1999.

217. Riley 1987, 2005:149–70.

218. Riley 1999:197.

219. I was not alone in discounting the Rio Sonora "statelets" (e.g., McGuire and Villalpando 1989).

220. Lekson, Bletzer, and MacWilliams 2004; Wilcox et al. 2006:fig. 6.

221. The Spanish king gave Pueblos land grants, typically 4 leagues square around the pueblo at that moment. Those grants pinned down Pueblos like butterflies on a board. Families and clans could move (and did, when threatened), but the pueblo—now defined as a town, not as a people—was fixed in place, legally defined and described. With the Treaty of Guadalupe Hidalgo, the United States promised to honor the land grants. We didn't, of course, but the principle was affirmed: Pueblo lands were set in cadastral concrete.

Meaning no disrespect, I truly wonder how Pueblo philosophies and worldviews adjusted to that startling new condition. After millennia of migration and "agricultural nomadism," they were no longer *allowed to move*. Surely, that change had an effect on beliefs and institutions? You may not get the middle place you want, so you work with the middle place you have.

Chapter 8

1. For example, Cooper Alarcón 1997; Keen 1971; Kubler 1991.

2. Canizares-Esguerra 2001:204.

3. O'Gorman [1961]1972:346.

4. Fowler 1987:234.

5. In 2005, when my text had reached an advanced (overripe?) stage, Carroll Riley published a book titled *Becoming Aztlan: Mesoamerican Influences in the Greater Southwest, AD 1200–1500*. While I owe a great deal to Riley's insights over the years (as evidenced by my citations), my interests in Aztlan grew independently of his and take a rather different tack. For Riley, Aztlan is an interesting historical myth; for me, Aztlan is a serious political issue.

6. Mexico's past attracted Anglo-American literary interest long before the United States won its independence (Wertheimer 1999). Colonial intellectual life was diverted by revolutions and political theorizing, but in postcolonial times, when the fireworks died down and solidity set in, American thinkers thought again about Aztecs.

7. Prescott [1843]1922:6.

8. Quoted in Keen 1971:391.

9. Harris 1968:137–140.

10. Paul Zolbrod, in an essay on "New World Ancientness," made the case that Henry James, in his 1879 biography of Nathaniel Hawthorne, denied statehood in the New World, "in sharp contrast to the old European and ancient Mediterranean ones":

> More than a century ago, Henry James set a benchmark for making that contrast. In his biography of Nathaniel Hawthorne, he asserted the bareness of America's native legacy. For him it included no such thing as a state "in the European sense of the word, and indeed barely a specific national name." (Zolbrod 2004:593)

A great quote, but alas, I won't use it in the text. In that biography, James (1879) quotes the preface to *Marble Faun*, in which Hawthorne bemoans "the difficulty of writing a romance about a country where there is no shadow, no antiquity, no mystery." It seems clear both from James's biography and from *Marble Fawn* that Hawthorne was referring to the young American nation of his day, not the Native past. But Zolbrod's projection is fair to the times, if not precisely fair to the texts.

11. Bernal 1980:143–44; Miller 2006:370.

12. Keen 1971:488–93.

13. Miller 2006:369–72.

14. Keen 1971:409.

15. Bandelier 1890–1892.

16. Chauvenet 1983:21. T. T. Waterman (he of the Pecos Classification) evaluated "Bandelier's contribution to the study of ancient Mexican social organization" and noted:

> There are two widely different schools of doctrine concerning the political and social institutions which the Spaniards encountered among the highly civilized natives of the Mexican plateau. One school consists of two investigators, Lewis H. Morgan and A. F. Bandelier. These two writers consider the famous Aztec "empire" was not an empire at all, but a loose confederation of democratic Indian tribes. They have been supported…*by the sentiments, if not in the published writings, of most American ethnologists.* The opposing school consists, broadly speaking, of the other scholars who have written on the subject. (Waterman 1917:249–50; emphasis added)

Waterman was critical of Bandelier's methods but concluded that "Bandelier's work…is a good beginning, and offers the proper foundation for a final study of Mexican society" and that Bandelier "may be regarded as finally confirming the most important of Morgan's conclusions" (Waterman 1917:276).

17. Hewett ran George Pepper (American Museum of Natural History) out of the canyon, legally, in 1902. Pepper's 1920 "report," published under duress, consisted of a selection of his field notes and little more. Neil Judd (Smithsonian Institution) would not publish reports on his 1920s work at Pueblo Bonito until 1954 (Judd 1954)—eight years after Hewett died! Both Pepper's and Judd's reports were in obscure museum technical series (although Judd's work was reported at the time in *National Geographic*). Hewett shared his views on Chaco with the reading public, publishing many articles in magazines and several books, the most important being *The Chaco Canyon and Its Monuments* (Hewett 1936b), which incorporated several earlier articles from *Art and Archaeology* magazine. He was a seemingly inexhaustible public speaker, and many of his speeches were republished in books and magazines. Hewett's Chaco saturated the market.

18. Bandelier and Hewett 1937; Hewett 1930, 1936a; and Hewett 1936b on Aztecs.

19. Benedict [1934]1989:ch. 3. Ruth Benedict had little to say about Aztec government (and less about the patriarch Morgan), but her Pueblos were definitely not states, *nor had they ever been.*

20. Aristotle said that the state was an association of men for the sake of the best moral life. At the other end of both alphabet and spectrum, Weber thought that the state was the monopoly of force. (Athens, even in decline, was a happier place than Weimar Germany.)

Ancient states that interest us most are those with family resemblances to modern nation-states—a "backstory for current politics" (A. T. Smith 2003:97). For Gordon Childe, to qualify as an ancient state (or civilization), the society of interest had to do things that Britain did better and later: read, write, innovate, conquer, administer, extract, coerce, and so forth. Many ancient states did these things *differently* of course (so Britain could do them *better*, later), but they *did them*. We most cherish those ancient states that best compare to (or most amusingly contrast with) imperial Britain, Gilded Age America, or the People's Republic of China—the states we are in. The process is not so much deliberately teleological as strangely selective, like studying evolution only through the hominid line. Thousands of statelike ancient governments failed to become the *kinds of states* we find most interesting, most worthy of study. These brilliant mistakes and fascinating failures are banished to "intermediate societies"—neither hunter-gatherer band nor state—a vast residual that holds the largest part of humanity's political history.

Two recent studies offer distinct views of ancient statehood. These are Feinman and Marcus's edited volume *Archaic States* (1998) and Norman Yoffee's *Myths of the Archaic State* (2005). They typify the two too-simple poles of contemporary archaeological thought that I caricatured in chapter 1: generalizing (*Archaic States*) and particularizing (*Myths of*). Bruce Trigger (2003a) bridges that divide, which he terms "rationalism" (generalizing) and "relativism" (particularizing): "There is far more cross-cultural uniformity than extreme relativism would allow but less than a purely rationalist explanation would indicate" (Trigger 2003a:11). Amen. Feinman and Marcus's (1998) *Archaic States* develops the familiar processual, evolutionary view. Although the contributors are varied in theory and practice, it is fair to characterize the aggregate as mainstream Americanist archaeology—a generalization, not a criticism. For Marcus and Feinman,

> Archaic states were societies with (minimally) two class-endogamous strata (a professional ruling class and a commoner class) and a government that was both highly centralized and internally specialized. Ancient states were regarded as having more power than the rank societies that preceded them, particularly in the areas of waging war, exacting tribute, controlling information, drafting soldiers, and regulating manpower and labor…. For some well-known states where texts are available, one could add to this the stipulation that archaic states were ruled by kings rather than chiefs, had standardized temples implying a state religion, had full-time priests rather than

shaman or part-time priests, and could hold on to conquered territory in ways no rank society could. (Marcus and Feinman 1998:4–5)

This is Childe brought up to date—more knowledgeable, more sophisticated, but essentially a list of things our states, modern states, did or do. And it needs no apology of course. We *should be interested*, archaeologically, in where modern states come from. But what about ancient statelike entities that did not obligingly prefigure the present?

Norman Yoffee, in *Myths of the Archaic State*, offers a "Nietzschean approach of declining to define changing historical entities in absolute terms" (2005:15). His approach seems, at first blush, more elastic, more relative. For Yoffee, states are strategies of governance marked by

> the emergence of a political center [which] depended on its ability to express the legitimacy of interaction among the different elements [of society]. It did this by acting through a generalized structure of authority, making certain decisions in disputes between members of different groups, including kin groups, maintaining the central symbols of society, and undertaking defense and expansion of the society. *It is this governmental center that I denominate as the "state," as well as the territory politically controlled by the governmental center.* (Yoffee 2005:17)

That broad characterization might admit many ancient societies not customarily considered states. But Yoffee is a stern judge, with very high standards. In the end, his case studies (with two interesting nonstate exceptions) are the perennial favorites of Childe, Durant, and Time-Life Books. Yoffee defends his selection with an argument bordering on connoisseurship:

> Neo-evolutionists spent much time attempting to decide whether a complex society was a state or a chiefdom.... I have tried to show the futility of those arguments and the emptiness of their categories. However, for those who persist in the quixotic venture, I submit "Yoffee's Rule" about how to identify the ineffable presence (or absence) of the earliest [primary] states: "If you have to argue about whether a society is a state or isn't, then it isn't." (Yoffee 2005:41)

It's all a matter of taste. (Yoffee's tongue, superbly discerning, sits firmly in cheek.) His high standards, however, are real and are shared by almost all who study states. They know states and they know, at sight, nonstates, states manqué, wannabe states.

I am in Carneiro's (1981) camp: things got interesting, politically, long before high-end "states." When the few started making decisions for the many and the decisions (and those few who made them) stuck, an interesting threshold had been crossed. This would be at a level previously known as chiefdom and now somewhere in the undifferentiated mass of "intermediate societies." What came after (for example, the state) was largely a matter of degree and of history, not a qualitative change. Strangely, my position (founded on antique, cross-cultural, neo-evolutionary arguments) reaches conclusions compatible with contemporary deconstructions of the state. There is much in Adam Smith's *The Political Landscape* (2003) that I find laudable, both in his insistence on large scales and history and in his doubts about "states" as conventionally construed. Contra Yoffee (2005), I do not see the ancient state as a phase shift, or a revolution, or a leap, or a Great Divide (cf. A. T. Smith 2003:81). States were metastasized polities or "chiefdoms" on steroids, each with its own particular history and trajectory, sprung from the tendency toward centralized decision making as an emergent property of human societies. That "tendency" reflects, I think, some hard-wired cognitive limits and group sizes (Fletcher 1995; Kosse 1990, 1994, 1996; Lekson 1990a; van der Leeuw 1981) and thus qualifies as the much reviled "process," something Smith might not appreciate.

But most importantly, we are not talking about "archaic" or "primary" states in the Southwest. So all rules are off.

21. Yoffee, Fish, and Milner 1999:262, 264. Yoffee's Rule avoids squabbling, which is good, but I fear its unintended consequences: compressing a great deal of significant political variability into a vast, undifferentiated underclass of "intermediate" or "middle-range" societies. When Yoffee invokes his rule, he does so with wit and discretion. But at many seminars and conferences, I have seen others (less discerning) wield Yoffee's Rule like an inviolate law of physics, simply to keep Chaco in its place or Cahokia in its place (or me in my place?).

We should not treat secondary states like primary states. But it is tempting to argue the case on Yoffee's and Marcus and Feinman's terms, the dimensions and qualities of primary states—if only to get the Southwest out of the dustbin of intermediate societies and a place at the table with real states. Bits and pieces of Chaco match phrases and clauses of several definitions of "state." Revisit Yoffee's thoughts on the state: "a political center [and its territory]...acting through a generalized structure of authority, making certain decisions in disputes between members of different groups, including kin groups, maintaining the central symbols of society, and undertaking defense and expansion of the society" (Yoffee 2005:17). Chaco did those things. (It may not have been called on to defend itself, because it had no active rivals or peers, but it surely maintained peace.) And it did those things on Mesoamerican scales (Nelson 1995). Marcus and Feinman want "two…strata (a professional ruling class and a commoner class) and a government that was both highly centralized and internally specialized." Chaco's archaeology is one of the world's clearest examples of stratified housing, palaces versus commoner-class dwellings. (That's what Chaco, as an archaeological phenomenon, is all about.) Chaco, on very small scales (and not very successfully), tried "waging war, exacting tribute, controlling information…and regulating manpower and labor." Other criteria are stipulated for "states where texts are available"—details of governance we shall never know for Chaco or other ancient southwestern polities.

22. Yoffee, Fish, and Milner 1999:267.

23. For example, Clark 1997; Fields and Reents-Budet 2005.

24. Smith and Schreiber 2005, 2006.

25. Fernández-Armesto 2003:52. Neo-evolutionary scenarios were strongly, and strangely, local. "Archaic" or "primary" states were, by definition, sui generis and therefore well suited to natural (local) laboratories. Sometimes those laboratories were pretty large: Mesopotamia, Oaxaca, and so forth. Newer, particularistic, anti-neo-evolutionary approaches can be even more local: "Chaco (and by extension the Southwestern history of which Chaco is a part) must be understood within its own history and experiences" (Yoffee 2005:172). But I have argued throughout this book that Chaco and other ancient southwestern cities were not isolates, that they were part of a *continental* history. The "natural laboratory" reached from Panama to the northern limits of maize agriculture and beyond (chapter 1). Indeed, why stop at Panama? Southwestern copper work owes its origins, ultimately, to Ecuador (Hosler 1994), and the earliest statelike polities were not in Mesoamerican but along the Peruvian coast.

26. The contributors to *Archaic States* asked two very pertinent questions: "How do third- and fourth-generation states differ from first- and second-generation states?…and what to call the polities on the periphery of states when they acquire some of the trappings of that state but are never really incorporated into it?" (Marcus and Feinman 1998:6). I submit that the Southwest is a very good place to find answers. Adam Smith, in his deconstruction of states, laments that "the processes of secondary state formation [are]…woefully undertheorized" (Smith 2003:82–83). While I am uncertain that a deluge of unrestrained "theorizing" will get us very far, the study of actual cases—for example, Chaco, Hohokam, and Paquimé—might help.

Or—above all!—Cahokia. Timothy Pauketat extricates Cahokia from the typological muddle of band-tribe-chiefdom-state by leaping over that morass and placing Cahokia with other *civilizations*, where it surely belongs. That smart maneuver sidesteps (or leapfrogs) the dilemma of "chiefdoms and other archaeological delusions" (the title of Pauketat's 2007 book) but leaves Cahokia as something of a historical oddity: "Like other apparent precocious places, Poverty Point or Chaco Canyon, Cahokia doesn't seem to fit one's expectations of a typical anything" (Pauketat 2007:135). Pauketat notes that "Cahokia really was too extreme to be called a chiefdom" (2007:136), but he avoids the term *state*. Claims in the 1980s for a Cahokia "Ramey State" (e.g., O'Brien 1989) smacked hard into the remarkably solid ghost of Lewis Henry Morgan and met virulent rejection.

"State" is not a good place for a Mississippianist to be, so Pauketat makes a great leap forward to *civilization*. I agree and applaud! But I think *state* might usefully reenter the Cahokia and Chaco conversation (to benefit from a century of state studies and scholarship) if we reinvent the North American states—Chaco and Cahokia—as Post-Classic *secondary* states.

27. Bruce Trigger's definition of state is even less particular, less limiting: "A state is a politically organized society that is regarded by those who live in it as sovereign or politically independent and has leaders who control its social, political, legal, economic, and cultural activities" (Trigger 2003a:94). Trigger is less excited about delimiting stateness than are Feinman, Marcus, and Yoffee. Indeed, Trigger's brief is "early civilizations," not "archaic" or "earliest" states. (And his notions of "early" are commendably elastic; his case studies include nineteenth-century Yoruba and sixteenth-century Aztecs and Incas.) His definition of state is happily vague; many societies might make the cut.

28. Yoffee, in *Myths of the Archaic State*, offers two familiar cases of "complex" societies that (he says) did not become states: Chaco and Cahokia. I leave Cahokia's case to others—it is far stronger than Chaco's (see, particularly, Pauketat 2004, 2007). Yoffee sees Chaco as a "rituality" rather than a "complex" polity (and certainly never, ever a chiefdom) "because it is apparent that Chacoan 'complexity' cannot be reduced to one or another of the canonical neo-evolutionist stages, and also that political and economic explanations cannot account for major aspects of Chacoan society" (Yoffee 2005:168; see also Yoffee 2001; Yoffee, Fish, and Milner 1999). Well, yes, Chaco, in evolutionary stages, is "intermediate," but Yoffee is not fond of evolutionary stages anyway, so that seems like an odd criticism. "Political and economic explanations" require a brief discursion into territory far more familiar to me than the archaeology of states: defending my arguments.

Yoffee argues against "three factors which have led Lekson (and other archaeologists) to campaign for Chacoan 'complexity'" (Yoffee 2005:168). First, "Chaco is larger, contains more parts, and is structurally more heterogeneous than earlier societies in the area." Second, Lekson (I continue, for clarity, in the third person) and other southwestern archaeologists confuse the complexity of research with complexity of the entity under study. Third, southwestern archaeologists confuse the "complexity" of the Santa Fe Institute (SFI) and its allies with political complexity.

Factors 2 and 3—confusing various complexities—are simply nonstarters. No one argues that a complex research process (detailed excavations, "an array of scientific research technologies," and so on) has any relationship to ancient political conditions. Archaeologists apply some of the most complicated and technical research conducted anywhere in archaeology to the Paleolithic, but nobody is talking about Neanderthal states. For the second confusion—political complexity for scientific complexity—it is true that many archaeologists initially mistook, but no longer mistake, SFI complexity for the political condition of the same name. Not me—that confusion has never numbered among my sins, current or past. I learned SFI complexity at SFI. Even Homer nods: Yoffee errs.

That leaves Yoffee's factor 1: Chaco was much bigger and far more complicated than anything that had come before and (as we have seen, with only one or two possible exceptions) came after in Pueblo prehistory. On this, Yoffee and I agree, as we also agree on the monumental nature of Great Houses and the evident high status of those who lived in them (Yoffee 2005:163–69).

29. We currently finesse the issue with "intermediate societies"—a relic of our neo-evolutionary heritage. "Intermediate" denotes the vast mass of societies that were more than preagricultural bands and less than primary states. I say *denotes* and not *defines* because "intermediate" is not a definition; it's a residual: if it's not hunter-gatherer and it's not a state, then it's intermediate. In effect, "intermediate" is simply a repackaging of tribes and chiefdoms, without the specificity of those earlier, now discredited tags. Advocates would say that vagueness is a virtue; I think "intermediate" is just a way for American archaeology to do business as usual. And it's a most unhelpful category that(as far as I can see) serves only to prevent societies north of Mexico from being considered states—and thereby understood alongside their sisters and peers in and around Mesoamerica. Whalen and Minnis (2001:189), when looking for appropriate cases for Paquimé comparisons, limit the field to intermediate societies—and thereby preclude any analysis that might suggest that Casas Grandes was a state. A similar situation hobbles Mississippian studies. Mississippian societies, as we all know, were intermediate, so that's where we look for parallels and insights. That's lauded as a sensible practice, but the "intermediate" category predetermines what should be determined through thoughtful analysis.

30. This matters. Many of my colleagues, scarred and scared by the Grasshopper–Chavez Pass debates and disenchanted with band-tribe-chiefdom-state neo-evolutionary schemes, feign boredom with questions of complexity, dismissing arguments as "unproductive" or even "silly." Obviously, I disagree. I think we've bumped up against a very interesting problem with real implications for several sister disciplines and we should see it through. Its solution may be difficult, with false starts and many stops, but that does not render the issue unproductive or silly.

31. I am no friend to academic fads and fashions, but "postcolonial" interests (an enthusiasm of the late 1990s and early 2000s) seem appropriate and even necessary for my field, southwestern archaeology. We truly need to examine "received wisdom" for colonial prejudices, brought forward from Morgan and the racist nineteenth century.

32. Carrasco 1971.

33. Braniff 2001; Di Peso 1974:48–58.

34. León-Portilla 2001; Townsend 1992.

35. By their own accounts, the Aztecs began as savages from the north, the Mongols of Mesoamerica. They didn't know which fork to use or whom to use it on. (Aztec leaders once served a potential ally his own daughter for dinner—the finer points of diplomacy apparently not yet learned.) But in a few generations, they were masters of one of the world's great civilizations. The last of Mexico's great Native civilizations, Aztecs adopted and adapted urban and social traditions from a long series of Mesoamerican civilizations from Mexico's deeper history. And so did the Southwest.

36. Hall 2006:217. For example, Fields and Zamudio-Taylor 2001; Hodge 1998; Townsend 1992:55.

37. Matos Moctezuma 1988:37.

38. Townsend 1992:55.

39. Riley 2005:206, n. 3.

40. Humboldt 1812; Rodriguez and Gonzales 2005.

41. For example, Anaya and Lomeli 1991.

42. For example, Fields and Zamudio-Taylor 2001. Armando Navarro's recent (2005) textbook on Chicano

political history, for example, is titled *Mexicano Political Experience in Occupied Aztlan.* Navarro is commendably careful about the archaeology: "The Aztecas or Mexica were Chichimecas ('the dog people') that originate from the area called Aztlan. Scholars are in a perpetual debate as to its actual location. Some argue that it was somewhere in the present-day Southwest in the United States, but disagreements remain. Still others propose that it was somewhere in northern Mexico" (Navarro 2005:40). In a later passage, he clarifies contemporary usage: Aztlan "means all the lands lost by Mexico to the United States in 1848 as the result of US imperialism, which today is considered the Southwest" (2005:390, n. 57). Navarro of course is only one voice—that of a '60s activist, now a respected academic, who is not happy with conciliatory, assimilationist trends. He concludes his history with a call to action along four possible lines—three within the current national structure and the fourth involving "a separate Chicano/Mexicano nation, Aztlan, or opt[ing] for Aztlan to be re-annexed to the motherland Mexico" (Navarro 2005:705). This is a textbook. Remember, separatism is not mainstream, but neither is it fringe. See also Chavez 1984 for a thoughtful analysis of "the Chicano image of the Southwest" and Jack Forbes's *Aztecas del Norte: The Chicanos of Aztlan* (1973) for a partisan account by a fine Native American scholar

Aztlan is present in higher education and in the formation and training of younger Latino leaders. Many US universities have MEChA (Movimiento Estudiantil Chicano de Aztlan) student groups—none separatist and many devoted to indigenous rights throughout the Americas and the world. A logical progression, it seems, from the Aztlan of the 1960s and '70s, rooted in civil rights.

43. Southwestern archaeologists would do well to understand Aztlan's powerful cultural influence on Latino movers and shakers. Today's Mexican American senior leadership—lawyers, journalists, mayors, senators, artists, and poets—matured alongside the Chicano movement, certainly *with it* if not always *of it.* Aztlan was a central idea in their intellectual and political environments. Archaeologists of my generation are not all old hippies, but flower power was undeniably a factor in our formative years. Similarly, Aztlan was part of the maturation of today's Latino leaders. It remains a powerful concept (far more potent today than fables of Haight-Ashbury).

To some degree, however, Aztlan may have been trumped by the tide of events. The huge immigrant demonstrations of spring 2006 show how many Latin Americans have entered the United States and how little they reference Aztlan. What does Aztlan mean to a man from Honduras—or to a Mexican national, for that matter? Aztlan was a rallying cry for Chicano civil rights—that is, for political activism by Mexican Americans *in the United States.* In my "video at ten" TV observations of the immigration demonstrations, I saw only a few overt references to Aztlan, specifically T-shirts with an angry Aztec asking, "Who's the illegal alien, pilgrim?" That relic of the '70s may well have come from Dad's closet. Young Mexican Americans of my acquaintance seem to accept Aztlan as an important historical theme in the Chicano movement but perhaps as less relevant to their generation as to their parents'.

44. Edgar Hewett, in a poetic mood, suggested that Casas Grandes might be the "charming Vale of Aztlan" (Hewett 1923:50). Casas Grandes was identified in colonial times as the last home of the Aztecs, before they left the Southwest for central Mexico (Humboldt 1812; see also Rodriguez and Gonzalez 2005). The timing is off by a couple centuries. Mexica (if we believe the Aztecs' politically driven "histories," which few archaeologists do) arrived in central Mexico about the same time people were leaving Mesa Verde. But large-scale movements and migrations long predated the "abandonment of the Four Corners." The idea of large groups of southwestern peoples moving south, out of the region and out of southwestern archaeology's field of view, is more than intriguing; it may well be important.

45. Who, after all, were the Aztecs? That question is almost as complex as my questions earlier about the nature of states. A wandering band of adventurers, Aztecs did not repopulate Mesoamerica or even central Mexico. The Aztecs were a ruling elite, sitting uneasily over a vast, ethnically diverse empire (Carrasco 1971; Townsend 1992). The name *Aztec* now marks their era; Aztec has become a horizon.

46. I've reached the unhappy conclusion that American anthropology may not be the best or most useful way to think about the ancient Southwest. There's too much baggage, carried over from nineteenth-century anthropology's peculiar relationship with its subject matter. And the subject matter did not care for subjugation: it is no secret that many—most?—Indians are dubious or dismissive of anthropology (chapter 7).

Archaeology today seems free to follow its muse: continental philosophers, agent-based modeling, art history. We might consider snipping anthropology's apron strings—despite the fact that almost all of us were trained to be anthropologists. European archaeology's provenance was not anthropology; its history was *history* (chapter 1). Perhaps American archaeology should start anew and think historically. History is not a panacea. It too can be colonial and racist. That's the attraction of Big History. World history deliberately decenters Europe and the West and looks at the world as a whole—things anthropology tries but sometimes fails to do. Big History corrects the biases that cripple American anthropological archaeology. It borrows the best of anthropology and buries the worst. Big History owes nothing to Lewis Henry Morgan.

47. See chapter 1. To recapitulate a bit, *connecting the dots* runs the same teleological risk as ethnographically driven prehistory: we know what happened next. In writing this history, I tried hard to be surprised when moving forward from Pueblo I to Pueblo II. "Never forget that people in the past did not know what came next.... To share the past's ignorance of itself, one must share its ignorance of what came next" (Vincent 2006:37). This is impossible of course, but I worked hard, studied diligently, and read broadly in pursuit of ignorance. "Everybody knew everything"—except what was going to happen next. "No coincidences" is obviously incorrect. There *were* coincidences. But southwestern archaeology has, for as long as I've been involved with it, operated with the assumption that it's *all* coincidences. Let's make the opposite error and see where that leads us. "Distances can be dealt with"—in the words of Alice Kehoe—and I make no apologies for my third maxim. To that method and those rules, I now add a goal: an *eventful history* (Sewell 2005), a story of changes, departures, crises, turning points, rises and falls. We've filled libraries with business-as-usual, everyday-life, corn-beans-and-squash archaeology. Those steady-state stories reinforce nineteenth-century notions that nothing much ever happened in Native North America—nothing that might be mistaken for civilization or for civilized history. Time for a story line.

48. My narrative features architecture over pottery and politics over climate. Mere mortals and their fragile crockery are dwarfed by palaces and pyramids, paraphrasing George MacDonald Fraser's appraisal of Cecile B. DeMille. I was trained, in polite conversation and archaeological discourse, to talk about the weather and avoid politics and religion. My mother and my mentors will be distressed, but I'm talking about politics—in the present case, politics and religion were probably the same thing. And I'm avoiding weather.

In southwestern archaeology, ceramic evidence rules. It is fair to say that southwestern archaeology, for most of its century-plus run, has been about ceramics: culture areas, cross-dating, influences and exchange, ethnicities. But I have reservations about pottery. Among other problems, *it moves.* Anna Shepard (1948) showed us that our assumptions about pottery as a baseline, foundational artifact class were misplaced, literally: for much of later southwestern prehistory, pottery moved around in astonishing quantities over remarkable distances. Architecture's provenance, in contrast, is unambiguous. Buildings don't move. Besides, my central theme is hierarchical political systems, and architecture is a very useful yardstick for politics. The technical literature on pottery is hugely bigger than serious studies of southwestern architecture (e.g., Morgan 1994). Let's put buildings in the spotlight for a change.

I deliberately mute climate. Dendroclimatology has become the tail wagging the archaeological dog (chapter 6). I respect floods and droughts in this history, for those environmental events surely shaped history. But I am interested in political decisions—"agency," if you wish (chapter 1)—over environment because for too long we've done precisely the reverse. The truth, which is indeed out there, lies somewhere in between.

49. This is my version of the ancient Southwest, speculative but based on facts. I hope the broad outlines are correct; I'm sure the details will change. I did not get it right. It's difficult to envision any archaeological statement that can be declared "right," beyond centimeter measurements of postholes or gram weights of arrowheads. Everything else archaeologists say or write about the past is interpreted or extrapolated and therefore is almost certainly, to varying degrees, in error. Thus I ask the reader to avoid *falsum in uno, falsum in omnibus* rejection, because details will *always* be wrong. Jacques Barzun (2000:569) calls this "the most illogical of thought-clichés: 'If I find this error on a small point, how can I trust the author on big ones?'"

History of course is notoriously malleable. Two biographies of the same president describe two very different men. Two histories of the fall of Rome reach startlingly different conclusions. Both biographies and both histories can win awards and good reviews (I am thinking of real books on my shelf, which need not be cited here). That's the nature of history. Barzun again: "A reader of history must be a reader of histories—several on the same topic—and a judge at leisure on the points in conflict" (2000:569).

50. When was then? Prehistories are customarily framed in years "before/after Christ" or "before present." BC/AD has the advantage of familiarity (even in its nonsectarian reformation, "before/after current era," or BCE), but the reference point has no real relevance to the history of the ancient Southwest. It seems strange to pin southwestern history to events in Palestine. For years "before present," the neutral "present" in BP is 1950—a year for which I have a strong personal partiality. There are excellent reasons for me to use 1950 as a benchmark. But BP counts backward while history marches forward. In BP terms, construction at Pueblo Bonito *began* in 1100 and *ended* in 800, before present. My basic premise is that the (ethnological) present is not a guide or goal for the ancient past and that projecting back from the present into the past is problematic. The BP flow is just wrong, rhetorically, for my purposes. For the last half of chapter 8, I use conventional BC/AD dates.

There would be real value in a chronology specific to the Southwest. For one thing, it would remind us that the Southwest has a respectably long history. Start the clock at 1500 BC, when maize-based villages took root in the Southwest. Dates calculated from that zero might be designated SW. From SW zero (and not quibbling over half decades), today becomes SW 3505. Hohokam rose about SW 2200, Chaco about SW 2520, Paquimé at SW 2750. Tut died in SW 175; Confucius arrived on the scene in 950; Brutus stabbed Julius in 1455; Mohammad's hegira from Mecca took place in 2122; William conquered England in 2565; Columbus discovered America in 2990; and Carter broke into the boy king's tomb in 3422. We, today, are three and a half millennia removed from the first farming villages of the Southwest. The Zunis of Cushing (SW 3390 or AD 1890) were more than eight centuries removed from Chaco's end (SW 2650 or AD 1125)—as far in time from Chaco as we are today from the high Middle Ages.

Time, through chapters 2–7, moves in approximately two-century increments. The biggest exception to that periodization was the first, 1500 BC to AD 500, providing backstory and stage setting (chapter 2). The first chapter of the actual history, AD 400 to 750 (chapter 3), covered 350 years. That long span could easily divide into two spans: 400 to 500/600 and 500/600 to 750. Thereafter, the political history of the ancient Southwest unfolded at a two-century pace—a rate that would gladden Emil Haury, who presupposed just such a stately two-century rhythm for his Hohokam.

The rate of change accelerated over the Southwest's long history, as seems so often the case globally. Things start slowly, gain momentum, and then rev into high and higher gears. The first two millennia of the Southwest (to 500) seem tame compared with the next thousand years. The pace picked up about 500 and got positively busy by about 750/800. Thereafter, changes multiplied at some sort of geometric rate. By 1500 things were happening so fast that it becomes hard to track history through archaeology (the murky, nebulous "Protohistoric"). After 1500, the Old World worked over the New. Changes then came even faster, all to the detriment of the Natives, but that's not part of our story here.

It may be that the impression of accelerating change reflects only increasing archaeological precision: we know the younger stuff better (in more detail) than the older stuff. That's true. Twenty years ago, we had no idea of the early agricultural villages of 1000 BC—not a clue. It seems cruel to dismiss those villages and the next two thousand years as uneventful (as I did in the preceding paragraph). People being people, we may be sure of it: things happened. Villages grew and splintered, great deeds were done, (little) wars were fought, great art was made (and much was lost), new ideas rose and a few survived the harsh filter of time and usage. But if archaeology has been rooting for the right truffles, southwestern societies from 1500 BC to AD 400/500 did not take major steps toward hierarchical government. To mix metaphors, the spoor of hierarchy is often quite visible—easy truffles to root. Those early villages did not leave such spoor, or truffles, or evidence so obvious that even an archaeologist could see it. This should not alarm us. Hierarchical political arrangements are rare, over the long, long span of human social history.

The tenth and eleventh centuries in the Southwest were at a place on the curve where the rapidity of change came about as fast as archaeology can see—even with a high-resolution lens (which the Southwest surely enjoys). Even faster change in the Protohistoric (fifteenth and sixteenth centuries) was too fast to see. With people moving around like Brownian molecules, we see only a larger pattern or secondary signs, but not the details. Thus the period from AD 500 to 1450—the heart of this book—is ideal for history: plenty of change but not so fast that it becomes a blur.

51. Lekson 2006a.
52. Benedict [1934]1989:80.

References

Abbott, David R.

2000   Ceramics and Community Organization among the Hohokam. Tucson: University of Arizona Press.

2003   The Politics of Decline in Canal System 2. *In* Centuries of Decline during the Hohokam Classic Period at Pueblo Grande. David R. Abbott, ed. Pp. 201–27. Tucson: University of Arizona Press.

Forthcoming   Middle Sedentary Period Regional Organization and Interaction: A Perspective from the Lower Salt River Valley and Adjoining Northern Uplands. *In* Hohokam Trajectories in World Perspective. Suzanne K. Fish and Paul R. Fish, eds. Amerind Studies in Archaeology. Tucson: University of Arizona Press.

Abbott, David R., ed.

2003   Centuries of Decline during the Hohokam Classic Period at Pueblo Grande. Tucson: University of Arizona Press.

Abbott, David R., Scott E. Ingram, and Brent G. Kobler

2006   Hohokam Exchange and Early Classic Period Organization in Central Arizona: Focal Villages or Linear Communities. Journal of Field Archaeology 31(3):285–305.

Abbott, David R., Alexa M. Smith, and Emiliano Gallaga

2007   Ballcourts and Ceramics: The Case for Hohokam Marketplaces in the Arizona Desert. American Antiquity 72:461–84.

Abu-Lughod, Janet L.

1989   Before European Hegemony: The World System A.D. 1250–1350. New York: Oxford University Press.

Adams, E. Charles

1991   The Origin and Development of the Pueblo Katsina Cult. Tucson: University of Arizona Press.

2002   Homol'ovi: An Ancient Hopi Settlement Cluster. Tucson: University of Arizona Press.

Adams, E. Charles, and Andrew I. Duff

2004   Settlement Clusters and the Pueblo IV Period. *In* The Protohistoric Pueblo World, A.D. 1275–1600. E. Charles Adams and Andrew I. Duff, eds. Pp. 3–16. Tucson: University of Arizona Press.

Adams, E. Charles, and Andrew I. Duff, eds.

2004   The Protohistoric Pueblo World, A.D. 1275–1600. Tucson: University of Arizona Press.

Adams, Karen A.
1994   A Regional Synthesis of *Zea mays* in the Prehistoric American Southwest. *In* Corn and Culture in the Prehistoric New World. Sissel Johannessen and Christine A. Hastorf, eds. Pp. 273–302. Boulder, CO: Westview.

Adams, William Y., Dennis P. VanGerven, and Richard S. Levy
1978   The Retreat from Migrationism. Annual Review of Anthropology 7:483–532.

Adler, Michael A.
1993   Why Is a Kiva? New Interpretations of Prehistoric Social Integrative Architecture in the Northern Rio Grande Region of New Mexico. Journal of Anthropological Research 49:319–46.

Adler, Michael A., ed.
1996   The Prehistoric Pueblo World, A.D. 1150–1350. Tucson: University of Arizona Press.

Adler, Michael A., Todd VanPool, and Robert D. Leonard
1996   Ancestral Pueblo Aggregation and Abandonment in the North American Southwest. Journal of World Prehistory 10(3):375–438.

Adovasio, James M.
1980   Prehistoric Basketry of Western North America and Mexico. *In* Early Native Americans. David L. Bowman, ed. Pp. 341–62. New York: Mouton.

Adovasio, James M., R. L. Andrews, and C. S. Fowler
1982   Some Observations on the Putative Fremont "Presence" in Southern Idaho. Plains Anthropologist 27(95):19–27.

Adovasio, James M., J. Donahue, D. R. Pedler, and R. Stuckenrath
1998   Two Decades of Debate on Meadowcroft Rockshelter. North American Archaeologist 19(4):317–41.

Agnew, John A., John Mercer, and David E. Sopher, eds.
1984   City in Cultural Context. Boston: Allen and Unwin.

Akins, Nancy J.
2001   Chaco Canyon Mortuary Practices, Archaeological Correlates of Complexity. *In* Ancient Burial Practices in the American Southwest. Douglas R. Mitchell and Judy L. Brunson-Hadley, eds. Pp. 167–90. Albuquerque: University of New Mexico Press.
2003   The Burials of Pueblo Bonito. *In* Pueblo Bonito: Center of the Chacoan World. Jill E. Neitzel, ed. Pp. 94–106. Washington, DC: Smithsonian Books.

Akins, Nancy J., and John D. Schelberg
1984   Evidence of Organizational Complexity as Seen from the Mortuary Practices at Chaco Canyon. *In* Recent Research in Chaco Prehistory. W. James Judge and John D. Schelberg, eds. Pp. 89–102. Reports of the Chaco Center 8. Albuquerque, NM: National Park Service.

Altschul, Jeffrey H., ed.
1995   The Archaic–Formative Transition in the Tucson Basin. Kiva 60(4). Special issue.

Altschul, Jeffrey H., and Edgar K. Huber
2000   Economics, Site Structure and Social Organization during the Basketmaker III Period: A View from the Lukachukai Valley. *In* Foundations of Anasazi Culture: The Basketmaker–Pueblo Transition. Paul F. Reed, ed. Pp. 145–60. Salt Lake City: University of Utah Press.

Anawalt, Patricia
1992   Ancient Cultural Contacts between Ecuador, West Mexico, and the American Southwest: Clothing Similarities. Latin American Antiquity 3(2):114–29.
1998   They Came to Trade Precious Things: Ancient West Mexican–Ecuadorian Contacts. *In* Ancient West Mexico: Art and Archaeology of the Unknown Past. Richard Townsend, ed. Pp. 233–49. Chicago: Art Institute of Chicago.

Anaya, Rudolfo, and Francisco Lomeli, eds.
1991   Aztlan: Essays on the Chicano Homeland. Albuquerque: University of New Mexico Press.

Anderson, David G.
1994   The Savannah River Chiefdoms: Political Change in the Late Prehistoric Southeast. Tuscaloosa: University of Alabama Press.

1999   Examining Chiefdoms in the Southeast: An Application of Multiscalar Analysis. *In* Great Towns and Regional Polities in the Prehistoric American Southwest and Southeast. Jill E. Neitzel, ed. Pp. 215–41. Albuquerque: University of New Mexio Press.

Anderson, David G., and Robert C. Mainfort Jr., eds.
2002   The Woodland Southeast. Tuscaloosa: University of Alabama Press.

Anthony, David W.
1990   Migration in Archaeology: The Baby and the Bathwater. American Anthropologist 92(4):895–914.

Anyon, Roger, T. J. Ferguson, Loretta Jackson, Lillie Lane, and Philip Vicenti
1997   Native American Oral Tradition and Archaeology: Issues of Structure, Relevance, and Respect. *In* Native Americans and Archaeologists: Stepping Stone to Common Ground. Nina Swidler, Kurt E. Dongoske, Roger Anyon, and Alan S. Downer, eds. Pp. 77–87. Walnut Creek, CA: AltaMira.

Anyon, Roger, Patricia A. Gilman, and Steven A. LeBlanc
1981   A Reevaluation of the Mogollon-Mimbres Archaeological Sequence. Kiva 46:209–25.

Anyon, Roger, and Steven A. LeBlanc
1980   The Architectural Evolution of Mogollon-Mimbres Communal Structures. Kiva 45:253–77.
1984   The Galaz Ruin. Albuquerque: University of New Mexico Press.

Arnold, Jeanne E., ed.
2004   Foundations of Chumash Complexity. Los Angeles: Costen Institute of Archaeology.

Arnold, Jeanne E., Michael R. Walsh, and Sandra E. Hollimon
2004   The Archaeology of California. Journal of Archaeological Research 12(1):1–73.

Arrhenius, Olof W.
1984   Stones Speak and Waters Sing: The Life and Works of Gustaf Nordenskiold. Mesa Verde, CO: Mesa Verde Museum Association.

Atkins, Victoria M., ed.
1993   Anasazi Basketmaker: Papers from the 1990 Wetherill–Grand Gulch Symposium. Cultural Resource Series 24. Salt Lake City, UT: Bureau of Land Management.

Aveni, Anthony F., H. Hartung, and J. Charles Kelley
1982   Alta Vista (Chalchihuites): Astronomical Implications of a Mesoamerican Ceremonial Outpost at the Tropic of Cancer. American Antiquity 47:316–35.

Bagatzky, Thomas
1980   Aspects of Aboriginal Trade and Communications between Northeast Mexico and Southwest Texas in the 16th Century. Anthropos 75:447–64.

Bagwell, Elizabeth A.
2004   Architectural Patterns along the Rio Taraises, Northern Sierra Madre Occidental, Sonora. Kiva 70:7–30.

Bahr, Donald, Juan Smith, William Smith Allison, and Julian Hayden
1994   The Short, Swift Time of Gods on Earth: The Hohokam Chronicles. Berkeley: University of California Press.

Baker, Larry L.
2008   Salmon Ruins: Architecture and Development of a Chacoan Satellite on the San Juan River. *In* Chaco's Northern Prodigies. Paul F. Reed, ed. Pp. 29-41. Salt Lake City: University of Utah Press.

Bancroft, Hubert Howe
1975   The Native Races of the Pacific States of North America, vol. 2. San Francisco: A. L. Bancroft.

Bandelier, Adolph F.
1882   The "Montezuma" of the Pueblo Indians. American Anthropologist 5(4):319–26.
[1887]1988 Histoire de la Colonisation et des Missions de Sonora, Chihuahua, Nouveau Mexique et Arizona Jusqu'a l'Annee 1700. Sources and Studies for the History of the Americas, vol. 14. Rome: Jesuit Historical Institute.

1890–92   Final Report of Investigations among the Indians of the Southwestern United States, Carried On Mainly in the Years from 1880 to 1885. American Series, vols. 3–4. Cambridge: Archaeological Institute of America.

Bandelier, Adolph F., and Edgar L. Hewett
1937   Indians of the Rio Grande Valley. Albuquerque: University of New Mexico Press.

Barber, Elizabeth Wayland, and Paul T. Barber
2004   When They Severed Earth from Sky: How the Human Mind Shapes Myth. Princeton, NJ: Princeton University Press.

Barker, Alex W., Craig E. Skinner, M. Steven Shakley, Michael D. Glascock, and J. Daniel Rogers
2002   Mesoamerican Origin for an Obsidian Scraper from the Precolumbian Southeastern United States. American Antiquity 67(1):103–08.

Barzun, Jacques
2000   From Dawn to Decadence: 1500 to the Present. New York: Harper Collins.

Basso, Keith
1996   Wisdom Sits in Places: Landscape and Language among the Western Apache. Albuquerque: University of New Mexico Press.

Bayman, James M.
2001   The Hohokam of Southwest North America. Journal of World Prehistory 15(3):257–311.
2002   Hohokam Craft Economies and the Materialization of Power. Journal of Archaeological Method and Theory 9(1):69–95.
2007   Papaguerian Perspectives on Economy and Society in the Sonoran Desert. *In* Hinterlands and Regional Dynamics in the Ancient Southwest. Alan P. Sullivan III and James M. Bayman, eds. Pp. 109–24. Tucson: University of Arizona Press.

Begay, Richard M.
2004   Tsé Bíyah 'Anii'áhí: Chaco Canyon and Its Place in Navajo History. *In* In Search of Chaco: New Approaches to an Archaeological Enigma. David Grant Noble, ed. Pp. 52–60. Santa Fe, NM: School of American Research Press.

Bellwood, Peter, and Colin Renfrew, eds.
2002   Examining the Farming/Language Dispersal Hypothesis. Cambridge: McDonald Institute for Archaeological Research.

Benavides, Alonso de
1954   Benavides' Memorial of 1630. Peter P. Forrestal, trans. Washington, DC: Academy of American Franciscan History.

Bender, Barbara
1998   Stonehenge: Making Space. Oxford: Berg.

Bender, Barbara, Sue Hamilton, and Chris Tilley
2007   Stone Worlds: Narrative and Reflexivity in Landscape Archaeology. Walnut Creek, CA: AltaMira.

Benedict, Ruth
[1934]1989   Patterns of Culture. Boston: Houghton Mifflin.

Benson, Larry, Linda Cordell, Kirk Vincent, Howard Taylor, John Stein, G. Lang Farmer, and Kiyoto Futa
2003   Ancient Maize from Chacoan Great Houses: Where Was It Grown? Proceedings of the National Academy of Sciences 100(22):13111-13115.

Benson, Larry, John Stein, Howard Taylor, Richard Friedman, and Thomas C. Windes
2006   The Agricultural Productivity of Chaco Canyon and Source(s) of Prehispanic Maize Found in Pueblo Bonito. *In* Histories of Maize. John Staller, Robert H. Tycot, and Bruce F. Benz, eds. Pp. 289-314. Burlington, MA: Academic Press.

Bentley, Jerry H.
1993   Old World Encounters: Cross-cultural Contacts and Exchanges in Pre-Modern Times. Oxford: Oxford University Press.
2002   The New World History. *In* A Companion to Western Historical Thought. Lloyd Kramer and Sarah Maza, eds. Pp. 393–431. Oxford: Blackwell.

Bentley, R. Alexander
2006   Academic Copying, Archaeology, and the English Language. Antiquity 80(307):196–201.

Bernal, Ignacio
1980   A History of Mexican Archaeology. London: Thames and Hudson.

Bernardini, Wesley
1998   Conflict, Migration, and the Social Environment: Interpreting Architectural Change in Early and Late Pueblo IV Aggregations. *In* Migrations and Reorganization: The Pueblo IV Period in the American Southwest. Katherine A. Spielmann, ed. Pp. 91–114. Anthropological Research Papers 51. Tempe: Arizona State University.
1999   Reassessing the Scale of Social Action at Pueblo Bonito, Chaco Canyon, New Mexico. Kiva 64:447–70.
2004   Hopewell Geometric Earthworks: A Case Study in the Referential and Experiential Meaning of Monuments. Journal of Anthropological Archaeology 23(3):331–56.
2005   Hopi Oral Tradition and the Archaeology of Identity. Tucson: University of Arizona Press.

Berry, Michael S.
1982   Time, Space and Transition in Anasazi Prehistory. Salt Lake City: University of Utah Press.

Betancourt, Julio L., Jeffrey S. Dean, and Herbert M. Hull
1986   Prehistoric Long-Distance Transport of Construction Beams, Chaco Canyon, New Mexico. American Antiquity 51:370–75.

Bettinger, Robert L.
2002   Why Corn Never Came to California. Electronic document, www.santafe.edu/files/gems/coevolutionV/bettinger.pdf, accessed June 2008.

Bettison, Cynthia Ann, Roland Shook, Randy Jennings, and Dennis Miller
1999   New Identifications of Naturalistic Motifs on Mimbres Pottery. *In* Sixty Years of Mogollon Archaeology. Stephanie M. Whittlesey, ed. Pp. 119–25. Tucson, AZ: SRI Press.

Billman, Brian R., Patricia M. Lambert, and Banks L. Leonard
2000   Cannibalism, Drought and Warfare in the Mesa Verde Region during the Twelfth Century A.D. American Antiquity 65:145–78.

Binford, Lewis R.
1962   Archaeology as Anthropology. American Antiquity 28:217–25.
1964   A Consideration of Archaeological Research Design. American Antiquity 29(4):425–41.
1983   Working at Archaeology. New York: Academic Press.
2001   Constructing Frames of Reference: An Analytical Method for Archaeological Theory Building Using Hunter-Gatherer and Environmental Data Sets. Berkeley: University of California Press.

Binford, Lewis R., and George I. Quimby
1963   Indian Sites and Chipped Stone Materials in the Northern Lake Michigan Area. Fieldiana: Anthropology 36(12). Chicago: Field Museum of Natural History.

Bintliff, John, ed.
1991   The Annales School and Archaeology. New York: New York University Press.

Biolsi, Thomas, and Larry J. Zimmerman, eds.
1997   Indians and Anthropologists: Vine Deloria, Jr., and the Critique of Anthropology. Tucson: University of Arizona Press.

Blake, Michael
2006   Dating the Initial Spread of *Zea mays*. *In* Histories of Maize. John E. Staller, Robert H. Tykot, and Bruce F. Benz, eds. Pp. 55–72. Burlington, MA: Academic Press.

Blake, Michael, Steven A. LeBlanc, and Paul E. Minnis
1986   Changing Settlement and Population in the Mimbres Valley, SW New Mexico. Journal of Field Archaeology 13:439–64.

Blanton, Richard E., Gary M. Feinman, Stephen A. Kowalewski, and Peter N. Peregrine
1996   A Dual-Processual Theory for the Evolution of Mesoamerican Civilizations. Current Anthropology 37:1–14.

Blanton, Richard E., Stephen A. Kowalewski, Gary M. Feinman, and Laura M. Finsten
1993   Ancient Mesoamerica: A Comparison of Change in Three Regions. Cambridge: Cambridge University Press.

Blinman, Eric
1989   Potluck in the Protokiva: Ceramics and Ceremonialism in Pueblo I Villages. *In* The Architecture of Social Integration in Prehistoric Pueblos. William D. Lipe and Michelle Hegmon, eds. Pp. 113–24. Occasional Paper 1. Cortez, CO: Crow Canyon Archaeological Center.
2000   The Foundations, Practice, and Limitations of Ceramic Dating in the American Southwest. *In* It's About Time: A History of Archaeological Dating in North America. Stephen E. Nash, ed. Pp. 41–59. Salt Lake City: University of Utah Press.

Blinman, Eric, and C. Dean Wilson
1993   Ceramic Perspectives on Northern Anasazi Exchange. *In* The American Southwest and Mesoamerica: Systems of Prehistoric Exchange. Jonathan E. Ericson and Timothy G. Baugh, eds. Pp. 65–94. New York: Plenum.

Blom, Frans Ferdinand
1932   Commerce, Trade and Monetary Units of the Maya. Middle America Research Series, 4. New Orleans: Tulane University.

Boher, Vorsila L.
1994   Maize in Middle American and Southwestern United States Agricultural Traditions. *In* Corn and Culture in the Prehistoric New World. Sissel Johannessen and Christine A. Hastorf, eds. Pp. 469–512. Boulder, CO: Westview.

Boone, Elizabeth Hill
2000   Venerable Place of Beginning: The Aztec Understanding of Teotihuacan. *In* Mesoamerica's Classic Heritage: From Teotihuacan to the Aztecs. David Carrasco, Lindsay Jones, and Scott Sessions, eds. Pp. 371–95. Boulder: University Press of Colorado.

Boone, Elizabeth Hill, and Michael E. Smith
2003   Postclassic International Styles and Symbol Sets. *In* The Postclassic Mesoamerican World. Michael E. Smith and Frances F. Berdan, eds. Pp. 186–93. Salt Lake City: University of Utah Press.

Bostwick, Todd W.
1992   Platform Mound Ceremonialism in Southern Arizona: Possible Symbolic Meanings of Hohokam and Salado Platform Mounds. *In* Proceedings of the Second Salado Conference. Richard C. Lange and Stephen Germick, eds. Pp. 78–85. Phoenix: Arizona Archaeological Society.
2006   Byron Cummings: Dean of Southwest Archaeology. Tucson: University of Arizona Press.

Boyle, Katie, Colin Renfrew, and Marsha Levine, eds.
2002   Ancient Interactions: East and West in Eurasia. Cambridge: McDonald Institute for Archaeological Research.

Bradfield, Wesley
1929   Cameron Creek Village. Santa Fe, NM: School of American Research.

Bradley, Bruce A.
1996   Pitchers to Mugs: Chacoan Revival at Sand Canyon Pueblo. Kiva 61(3):241–56.

Bradley, Bruce, and Dennis Stanford
2004   The North Atlantic Ice-edge Corridor: A Possible Route to the New World. World Archaeology 36(4):459–78.

Bradley, Ronna J.
1993   Marine Shell Exchange in Northwest Mexico and the Southwest. *In* The American Southwest and Mesoamerica: Systems of Prehistoric Exchange. Jonathan E. Ericson and Timothy G. Baugh, eds. Pp. 121–51. New York: Plenum.
2000   Networks of Shell Ornament Exchange: A Critical Assessment of Prestige Economies in the North American Southwest. *In* The Archaeology of Regional Interaction: Religion, Warfare, and Exchange across the American Southwest and Beyond. Michelle Hegmon, ed. Pp. 167–87. Boulder: University Press of Colorado.

Brand, Donald D.
1935   The Distribution of Pottery Types in Northwest New Mexico. American Anthropologist 37(2):287–305.

Brandt, Elizabeth A.
1994   Egalitarianism, Hierarchy, and Centralization in the Pueblos. *In* The Ancient Southwestern Community. W. H. Wills and Robert D. Leonard, eds. Pp. 9–23. Albuquerque: University of New Mexico Press.

Braniff C., Beatriz
1993   The Mesoamerican Northern Frontier and the Gran Chichimeca. *In* Culture and Contact: Charles C. Di Peso's Gran Chichimeca. Anne I. Woosley and John C. Ravesloot, eds. Pp. 65–82. Amerind Foundation New World Studies Series 2. Albuquerque: University of New Mexico Press.
2002   Fronteras e Intercambio: Mesoamerica, el "Southwest" y La Gran Chichimeca. *In* Boundaries and Territories: Prehistory of the U.S. Southwest and Northern Mexico. M. Elisa Villalpando, ed. Pp. 107–15. Anthropological Research Papers 54. Tempe: Arizona State University.

Braniff C., Beatriz, ed.
2001   La Gran Chichimeca: El Lugar de las Rocas Secas. CONACULTA Milan: Jaca Books.

Braniff C., Beatriz, and Richard S. Felger, eds.
1976   Sonora: Antropologia del Desierto: Primera Reunión de Antropologia e Historia del Noroeste. Coleccion Cientifica Diversa 27. Mexico City: Instituto Nacional de Antropología e Historia, Centro Regional del Noroeste.

Breternitz, David A.
1966   An Appraisal of Tree-Ring Dated Pottery in the Southwest. Tucson: University of Arizona Press.

Breternitz, David A., Christine K. Robinson, and G. Timothy Gross, eds.
1986   Dolores Archaeological Program: Final Synthetic Report. Denver, CO: Bureau of Reclamation.

Breternitz, David A., Arthur H. Rohn, and Elizabeth A. Morris, eds.
1974   Prehistoric Ceramics of the Mesa Verde Region. Ceramic Series 5. Flagstaff: Museum of Northern Arizona.

Brettell, Caroline B.
2000   Theorizing Migration in Anthroplogy: The Social Construction of Networks, Identities, Communities and Globalscapes. *In* Migration Theory: Talking Across Disciplines. Caroline B. Brettell and James F. Hollifield, eds. Pp. 97–135. New York: Routledge.

Brettell, Caroline B. and James F. Hollifield, eds.
2000   Migration Theory: Talking Across Disciplines. New York: Routledge.

Brew, J. O.
1946   The Archaeology of Alkali Ridge, Southeastern Utah. Papers of the Peabody Museum of American Archaeology and Ethnology, vol. 21. Cambridge, MA: Harvard University.

Brockmann, Andreas
2004   Trade under the Sign of the Feathered Serpent: Mesoamerica's Route into the Second Millennium. *In* The World in the Year 1000. James Heitzman and Wolfgang Schenkluhn, eds. Pp. 154–79. Lanham, MD: University Press of America.

Brody, J. J.
1991   Anasazi and Pueblo Painting. Albuquerque: University of New Mexico Press.
2004   Mimbres Painted Pottery. Revised ed. Santa Fe, NM: School of American Research Press.

Brose, David S., and N'omi Greber
1979   Hopewell Archaeology: The Chillicothe Conference. MCJA Special Paper 3. Kent, OH: Kent State University Press.

Brotherston, Gordon
1992   Book of the Fourth World: Reading the Native Americans through Their Literature. Cambridge: Cambridge University Press.

Brotherston, Gordon, ed.
1979   Images of the New World: The American Continent Portrayed in Native Texts. London: Thames and Hudson.

Brown, Cynthia Stokes
2007   Big History: From the Big Bang to the Present. New York: New Press.

Brown, David E., ed.
1982   Biotic Communities of American Southwest—United States and Mexico. Special issue, Desert Plants 4(1–4).

Brown, David E., and Charles H. Lowe
1980   Biotic Communities of the Southwest. General Technical Report RM-78. Fort Collins, CO: Rocky Mountain Forest and Range Experiment Station, USDA Forest Service.

Brown, David E., Frank Reichenbacher, and Susan E. Franson
1998   A Classification of North American Biotic Communities. Salt Lake City: University of Utah Press.

Brown, Gary M., Thomas C. Windes, and Peter J. McKenna
2008   Animas Anamnesis: Aztec Ruins or Anasazi Capital? In Chaco's Northern Prodigies. Paul F. Reed, ed. Pp. 231-250. Salt Lake City: University of Utah Press.

Brown, James A.
1996   The Spiro Ceremonial Center: The Archaeology of Arkansas Valley Caddoan Culture in Eastern Oklahoma. Memoirs of the Museum of Anthropology 29. Ann Arbor: University of Michigan.

Brown, Jeffrey Lawrence
1973   The Origin and Nature of Salado: Evidence from the Safford Valley, Arizona. PhD dissertation, Department of Anthropology, University of Arizona, Tucson.

Burd Larkin, Karin
2006   Community Reorganization in the Southern Zone of the Casas Grandes Culture Area of Chihuahua, Mexico. PhD dissertation, Department of Anthropology, University of Colorado, Boulder.

Byers, A. Martin
2004   The Ohio Hopewell Episode: Paradigm Lost and Paradigm Gained. Akron, OH: University of Akron Press.

Byrkit, James W.
1992   Land, Sky, and People: The Southwest Defined. Journal of the Southwest 34(3):257–387.

Cable, John S.
1991   The Role of Irrigation Agriculture in the Formation and Sociopolitical Development of Early Hohokam Villages in the Lowlands of the Phoenix Basin, Arizona. In Prehistoric Irrigation in Arizona: Symposium 1988. Cory D. Breternitz, ed. Pp 107-137. Publications in Archaeology 17. Phoenix, AZ: Soil Systems Inc.

Cable, John S., and David E. Doyel
1987   Pioneer Period Village Structure and Settlement Pattern in the Phoenix Basin. In The Hohokam Village: Site Structure and Organization. David E. Doyel, ed. Pp. 21–70. AAAS Publication 87-15. Glenwood Springs, CO: Southwestern and Rocky Mountain Division of the American Association for the Advancement of Science.

Cameron, Catherine C.
1998   Coursed Adobe Architecture, Style, and Social Boundaries in the American Southwest. In The Archaeology of Social Boundaries. Miriam T. Stark, ed. Pp. 183–207. Washington, DC: Smithsonian Institution Press.
2008   Chaco and After in the Northern San Juan: Excavations at the Bluff Great House. Tucson: University of Arizona Press.

Cameron, Catherine C., ed.
1995   Migration and the Movement of Southwestern Peoples. Special issue, Journal of Anthropological Archaeology 14(2).

Cameron, Catherine C., and Andrew I. Duff
2008 History and Process in Village Formation: Context and Contrasts from the Northern Southwest. American Antiquity 73(1):29–57.

Cameron, Catherine M., and H. Wolcott Toll, eds.
2001 The Organization of Production in Chaco Canyon. Special issue, American Antiquity 66:5–140.

Cameron, Catherine M., and Steve A. Tomka, eds.
1993 Abandonment of Settlements and Regions: Ethnoarchaeological and Archaeological Approaches. Cambridge: Cambridge University Press.

Cañizares-Esguerra, Jorge
2001 How to Write the History of the New World: Histories, Epistemologies, and Identities in the Eighteenth-Century Atlantic World. Stanford, CA: Stanford University Press.

Carlson, Roy L.
1966 Twin Angels Pueblo. American Antiquity 31:676–82.
1970 White Mountain Redware: A Pottery Tradition of East-central Arizona and Western New Mexico. Anthropological Papers 19. Tucson: University of Arizona Press.
1982a The Mimbres Kachina Cult. *In* Mogollon Archaeology: Proceedings of the 1980 Mogollon Conference. P. H. Beckett, ed. Pp. 147–57. Ramona, CA: Acoma Books.
1982b The Polychrome Complexes. *In* Southwestern Ceramics: A Comparative Review. Albert H. Schroeder, ed. Pp. 201–34. Arizona Archaeologist 15. Phoenix: Arizona Archaeological Society.

Carneiro, Robert L.
1981 The Chiefdom: Precursor of the State. *In* The Transition to Statehood in the New World. Grant D. Jones and Robert R. Kautz, eds. Pp. 37–79. Cambridge: Cambridge University Press.

Carot, Patricia
2000 Las Rutas al Desierto: de Michoacan a Arizona. *In* Nomadas y Sedentarios en el Norte de Mexico: Homenaje a Beatriz Braniff. Marie-Areti Hers, Jose Luis Mirafuentes, Maria de los Dolores Soto, and Miguel Vallebueno, eds. Pp. 91–112. Mexico City: Universidad Nacional Antonoma de Mexico.
2001 Le Site de Loma Alta, Lac de Zacapu, Michoacan, Mexique. Monographs in American Archaeology 9. BAR International Series 920. Oxford: Archaeopress.

Carot, Patricia, and Marie-Areti Hers
2006 La Gesta de los Toltecas Chichimecas y de los Purépechas en las Tierra de los Antiguous Pueblo Ancestrals. *In* La Vías del Noroeste I: Una Macrorregión Indígena Americana. Carlo Bonfiglioli, Arturo Gutiérrez, and María Eugenia Olavarría, eds. Pp. 47–82. Mexico City: Universidad Nacional Autónoma de México.

Carpenter, John P.
2002 Of Red Rims and Red Wares: The Archaeology of Prehispanic Sinaloa. *In* Boundaries and Territories: Prehistory of the U.S. Southwest and Northern Mexico. M. Elisa Villalpando, ed. Pp. 143–53. Anthropological Research Papers 54. Tempe: Arizona State University.

Carpenter, John P., Guadalupe Sanchez, and Maria Elisa Villalpando
2002 Of Maize and Migration: Mode and Tempo in the Diffusion of *Zea mays* in Northwest Mexico and the American Southwest. *In* Traditions, Transitions, and Technologies: Themes in Southwestern Archaeology. Sarah H. Schlanger, ed. Pp. 245–56. Boulder: University Press of Colorado.
2005 The Late Archaic/Early Agricultural Period in Sonora, Mexico. *In* The Late Archaic across the Borderlands: From Foraging to Farming. Bradley J. Vierra, ed. Pp. 13–40. Austin: University of Texas Press.

Carr, Christopher, and D. Troy Case, eds.
2005 Gathering Hopewell: Society, Ritual, and Ritual Interaction. Interdisciplinary Contributions to Archaeology. New York: Kluwer Academic/Plenum.

Carr, Pat
1979 Mimbres Mythology. El Paso: Texas Western Press.

Carrasco, David, Lindsay Jones, and Scott Sessions, eds.
2000   Mesoamerica's Classic Heritage: From Teotihuacan to the Aztecs. Boulder: University Press of Colorado.

Carrasco, Pedro
1971   The Peoples of Central Mexico and Their Historical Traditions. *In* Handbook of Middle American Indians, vol. 11, pt. 2: Archaeology of Northern Mesoamerica. Robert Wauchope, ed. Pp. 459–73. Austin: University of Texas Press.

Castells, Manuel
1996   The Information Age: Economy, Society, and Culture, vol 1.: The Rise of Network Societies. Oxford: Blackwell.
1997   The Information Age: Economy, Society, and Culture, vol. 2.: The Power of Identity. Oxford: Blackwell.
1998   The Information Age: Economy, Society, and Culture, vol 3.: The End of the Millennium. Oxford: Blackwell.

Castles, Stephen, and Mark J. Miller
2003   The Age of Migration: International Population Movements in the Modern World. 3rd ed. New York: Guilford.

Cather, Willa
1925   The Professor's House. New York: Grosset and Dunlap.

Chapman, Richard C., Cye W. Gossett, and William J. Gossett
1985   Class II Cultural Resources Survey, Upper Gila Water Supply Study, Central Arizona Project. MS on file, Bureau of Reclamation, Phoenix, AZ.

Chapman, Robert
2006   Middle Woodland/Hopewell: A View from Beyond the Periphery. *In* Re-creating Hopewell. Douglas K. Charles and Jane E. Buikstra, eds. Pp. 510–28. Gainesville: University Press of Florida.

Charles, Douglas K., and Jane E. Buikstra, eds.
2006   Re-creating Hopewell. Gainesville: University Press of Florida.

Chase, Diane Z., and Arlen F. Chase
1992   Mesoamerican Elites: Assumptions, Definitions, and Models. *In* Mesoamerican Elites: An Archaeological Assessment. Diane Z. Chase and Arlen F. Chase, eds. Pp. 3–17. Norman: University of Oklahoma Press.

Chase, Diane Z., and Arlen F. Chase, eds.
1992   Mesoamerican Elites: An Archaeological Assessment. Norman: University of Oklahoma Press.

Chase-Dunn, Christopher
2004   Modeling Dynamical Nested Networks in the Prehistoric U.S. Southwest. Paper presented at the workshop Analyzing Complex Macrosystems as Dynamic Networks, Santa Fe Institute, Santa Fe, NM, April 29–30.

Chase-Dunn, Christopher, and E. N. Anderson
2005   The Historical Evolution of World-Systems. New York: Palgrave MacMillan.

Chase-Dunn, Christopher, and Thomas D. Hall
1995   Cross-World-Systems Comparisons. *In* Civilizations and World Systems: Studying World-Historical Change. Stephen K. Sanderson, ed. Pp. 109–35. Walnut Creek, CA: AltaMira.
1998   World-Systems in North America: Networks, Rise and Fall and Pulsations of Trade in Stateless Systems. American Indian Culture and Research Journal 22(1):23–72.

Chase-Dunn, Christopher, and Thomas D. Hall, eds.
1991   Core/Periphery Relations in Precapitalist Worlds. Boulder, CO: Westview.

Chauvenet, Beatrice
1983   Hewett and Friends: A Biography of Santa Fe's Vibrant Era. Santa Fe: Museum of New Mexico Press.

Chavez, John R.
1984   The Lost Land: The Chicano Image of the Southwest. Albuquerque: University of New Mexico Press.

Cheetham, David
2006   The Americas' First Colony? Archaeology 59(1):42–46.

Chenault, Mark L.
2000   In Defence of the Polvoron Phase. *In* The Hohokam Village Revisited. David E. Doyel, Suzanne K. Fish, and Paul R. Fish, eds. Pp. 277–86. Fort Collins, CO: Southwestern and Rocky Mountain Division of the American Association for the Advancement of Science.

Chenault, Mark L., and Thomas N. Motsinger
2000   Colonization, Warfare, and Regional Competition: Recent Research into the Basketmaker III Period in the Mesa Verde Region. *In* Foundations of Anasazi Culture: The Basketmaker–Pueblo Transition. Paul F. Reed, ed. Pp. 45–65. Salt Lake City: University of Utah Press.

Chrisomalis, Stephen
2007   The Perils of Pseudo-Orwellianism. Antiquity 81(311):204–07.

Christian, David
2004   Maps of Time: An Introduction to Big History. Berkeley: University of California Press.

Christie, Jessica Joyce, and Patricia Joan Sarro, eds.
2006   Palaces and Power in Ancient America. Austin: University of Texas Press.

Chuipka, Jason P., and James M. Potter
2007   Blue Mesa Excavations, Animas–La Plata Project, vol. 3. SWCA Anthropological Research Paper 10. Phoenix, AZ: SWCA.

Ciolek-Torrello, Richard
1995   The Houghton Road Site, the Agua Caliente Phase, and the Early Formative Period in the Tucson Basin. Kiva 60:531–74.
1997   Prehistoric Settlement and Demography in the Lower Verde Region. *In* Vanishing River: Landscapes and Lives of the Lower Verde Valley: The Lower Verde Archaeological Project. Stephanie M. Whittlesey, Richard Ciolek-Torrello, and Jeffrey H. Altschul, eds. Pp. 531–95. Tucson, AZ: SRI Press.
1998   Sites of the Early Formative Period. *In* Early Farmers of the Sonoran Desert: Archaeological Investigations at the Houghton Road Site, Tucson, Arizona. Richard Ciolek-Torrello, ed. Pp. 229–55. Technical Series 72. Tucson: Statistical Research Inc.

Ciolek-Torrello, Richard, ed.
1998   Early Farmers of the Sonoran Desert: Archaeological Investigations at the Houghton Road Site, Tucson, Arizona. Technical Series 72. Tucson: Statistical Research Inc.

Clark, Grahame
1989   Prehistory at Cambridge and Beyond. Cambridge: Cambridge University Press.

Clark, Jeffrey J.
2001   Tracking Prehistoric Migrations: Pueblo Settlers among the Tonto Basin Hohokam. Anthropological Papers 65. Tucson: University of Arizona Press.

Clark, Jeffrey J., ed.
2006   Migrants and Mounds: Classic Period Archaeology along the Lower San Pedro River. Anthropological Papers 45. Tucson, AZ: Center for Desert Archaeology.

Clark, Jeffrey J., and Lisa W. Huckell
2004   Introduction. *In* 2000 Years of Settlement in the Tonto Basin: Overview and Synthesis of the Tonto Creek Archaeological Project. Jeffrey J. Clark and James M. Vint, eds. Pp. 1–41. Anthropological Papers 25. Tucson, AZ: Center for Desert Archaeology.

Clark, Jeffrey J., Patrick D. Lyons, Henry D. Wallace, J. Brett Hill, Anna A. Neuzil, and William H. Doelle
Forthcoming Migration, Coalescence, and Demographic Decline in the Lower San Pedro Valley and Safford Basin. *In* Hohokam Trajectories in World Perspective. Suzanne K. Fish and Paul R. Fish, eds. Amerind Studies in Archaeology. Tucson: University of Arizona Press.

Clark, Jeffrey J., and James M. Vint, eds.
2004   2000 Years of Settlement in the Tonto Basin: Overview and Synthesis of the Tonto Creek Archaeological Project. Anthropological Papers 25. Tucson, AZ: Center for Desert Archaeology.

Clark, John E.
1997   The Arts of Government in Early Mesoamerica. Annual Review of Anthropology 26:211–34.
2004   Mesoamerica Goes Public: Early Ceremonial Centers, Leaders, and Communities. *In* Mesoamerican Archaeology: Theory and Practice. Julia A. Hendon and Rosemary A. Joyce, eds. Pp. 43–72. Oxford: Blackwell.

Clark, John E., and Michelle Knoll
2005   The American Formative Revisited. *In* Gulf Coast Archaeology. Nancy Marie White, ed. Pp. 281–303. Gainesville: University Press of Florida.

Clastres, Pierre
1977   Societies against the State: The Leader as Servant and the Humane Uses of Power among the Indians of the Americas. New York: Urizen Books.

Cobb, Charles R., Jeffrey Maymon, and Randall H. McGuire
1999   Feathered, Horned, and Antlered Serpents: Mesoamerican Connections with the Southwest and Southeast. *In* Great Towns and Regional Polities in the Prehistoric American Southwest and Southeast. Jill E. Neitzel, ed. Pp. 165–81. Albuquerque: University of New Mexico Press.

Cohen, Robin, ed.
1995   The Cambridge Survey of World Migration. Cambridge: Cambridge University Press.

Cole, Sally J.
1994   Roots of Anasazi and Pueblo Imagery in Basketmaker Rock Art and Material Culture. Kiva 60:289–311.

Cole, Sarah
2007   Population Dynamics and Sociopolitical Instability in the Central Mesa Verde Region, A.D. 600–1280. MA thesis, Department of Anthropology, Washington State University, Pullman.

Colton, Harold S.
1946   The Sinagua: A Summary of the Archaeology of the Region of Flagstaff, Arizona. Bulletin 22. Flagstaff: Museum of Northern Arizona.
1960   Black Sand: Prehistory in Northern Arizona. Albuquerque: University of New Mexico Press.

Coltrain, Joan Brenner, Joel C. Janetski, and Shawn W. Carlyle
2006   The Stable and Radio-isotope Chemistry of Eastern Basketmaker and Pueblo Groups in the Four Corners Region of the American Southwest. *In* Histories of Maize. John E. Staller, Robert H. Tykot, and Bruce F. Benz, eds. Pp. 275–87. Burlington, MA: Academic Press.

Cooley, Alexander
2005   Logics of Hierarchy: The Organization of Empires, States, and Military. Ithaca, NY: Cornell University Press.

Cooper Alarcón, Daniel
1997   The Aztec Palimpsest: Mexico in the Modern Imagination. Tucson: University of Arizona Press.

Cordell, Linda S.
1984   Prehistory of the Southwest. Orlando, FL: Academic Press.
1986   Status Differentiation and Social Complexity in the Prehistoric Southwest: A Discussion. *In* Status, Structure, and Stratification: Current Archaeological Reconstructions. Marc Thompson, Maria Teresa Garcia, and Francois J. Kense, eds. Pp. 191–95. Proceedings of the 16th Annual Conference. Alberta: Archaeological Association of the University of Calgary.
1995   Tracing Migration from the Receiving End. Journal of Anthropological Archaeology 14(2):203–11.
1997   Archaeology of the Southwest. 2nd ed. San Diego, CA: Academic Press.
2006   Rio Grande Glaze Paint Ware in Southwestern Archaeology. *In* The Social Life of Pots: Glaze Wares and Cultural Dynamics in the Southwest, AD 1250–1680. Judith A. Habicht-Mauche, Suzanne L. Eckert, and Deborah L. Huntley, eds. Pp. 253–71. Tucson: University of Arizona Press.

Cordell, Linda S., and Don D. Fowler, eds.
2005   Southwest Archaeology in the Twentieth Century. Salt Lake City: University of Utah Press.

Cordell, Linda S., and George J. Gumerman
1989   Cultural Interaction in the Prehistoric Southwest. *In* Dynamics of Southwest Prehistory. Linda

S. Cordell and George J. Gumerman, eds. Pp. 1–17. Washington, DC: Smithsonian Institution Press.

Cordell, Linda S., and George J. Gumerman, eds.
1989   Dynamics of Southwest Prehistory. Washington, DC: Smithsonian Institution Press.

Cordell, Linda S., W. James Judge, and June-el Piper, eds.
2001   Chaco Society and Polity: Papers from the 1999 Conference. Special Publication 4. Albuquerque: New Mexico Archaeological Council.

Cordell, Linda S., and George R. Milner
1999   The Organization of Late Precolumbian Societies in the Southwest and Southeast. *In* Great Towns and Regional Polities in the Prehistoric American Southwest and Southeast. Jill E. Neitzel, ed. Pp. 109–13. Albuquerque: University of New Mexico Press.

Cordell, Linda S., and Fred Plog
1979   Escaping the Confines of Normative Thought: A Reevaluation of Puebloan Prehistory. American Antiquity 44:405–29.

Cosgrove, C. B.
1947   Caves of the Upper Gila and Hueco Areas in New Mexico and Texas. Papers of the Peabody Museum of Archaeology and Ethnology, vol. 24, no. 2. Cambridge, MA: Harvard University.

Cosgrove, Harriet B., and C. B. Cosgrove
1932   The Swarts Ruin. Papers of the Peabody Museum of Archaeology and Ethnology, vol. 15, no. 1. Cambridge, MA: Harvard University.

Courlander, Harold
1971   The Fourth World of the Hopi. Albuquerque: University of New Mexico Press.

Cowgill, George L.
1997   State and Society at Teotihuacán, Mexico. Annual Review of Anthropology 26:129–61.
2004   Origins and Development of Urbanism: Archaeological Perspectives. Annual Review of Anthropology 33:525–49.

Craig, Douglas B.
2000a   Rewriting Prehistory in the Hohokam Heartland. Archaeology Southwest 14(3):1–4.
2000b   The Demographic Implications of Architectural Change at the Grewe Site. *In* The Hohokam Village Revisited. David E. Doyel, Suzanne K. Fish, and Paul R. Fish, eds. Pp. 139–66. Fort Collins, CO: Southwestern and Rocky Mountain Division of the American Association for the Advancement of Science.
2001a   The Demographic Implications of Architectural Change at Grewe. *In* The Grewe Archaeological Research Project, vol. 3: Synthesis. Douglas B. Craig, ed. Pp. 37–49. Anthropological Papers 99-1. Flagstaff, AZ: Northland Research.
2001b   Domestic Architecture and Household Wealth at Grewe. *In* The Grewe Archaeological Research Project, vol. 3: Synthesis. Douglas B. Craig, ed. Pp. 115–29. Anthropological Papers 99-1. Flagstaff, AZ: Northland Research.

Craig, Douglas B., ed.
2000   The Grewe Archaeological Research Project, vol. 1: Project Background and Feature Descriptions. Anthropological Papers 99-1. Flagstaff, AZ: Northland Research.
2001   The Grewe Archaeological Research Project, vol. 3: Synthesis. Anthropological Papers 99-1. Flagstaff, AZ: Northland Research.

Creel, Darrell
1989   A Primary Cremation at the NAN Ranch Ruin, with Comparative Data on Other Cremations in the Mimbres Area, New Mexico. Journal of Field Archaeology 16:309–29.
1999   The Black Mountain Phase in the Mimbres Area. *In* The Casas Grandes World. Curtis Schaafsma and Carroll Riley, eds. Pp. 107–20. Salt Lake City: University of Utah Press.
2006a   Excavations at the Old Town Ruin, Luna County, New Mexico, 1989–2003. Cultural Resources Series 16, vol. 1. Santa Fe, NM: Bureau of Land Management.
2006b   Architecture at the Baca and Pruitt Sites: Thoughts on the "Typical" Mimbres Village and the Dim View of Northern Influence. Paper presented at the 14th Mogollon Conference, Tucson, AZ, October 13, 2006.

Creel, Darrell, and Roger Anyon
2003   New Interpretations of Mimbres Public Architecture and Space: Implications for Cultural Change. American Antiquity 68:67–92.

Creel, Darrell, and Charmion McKusick
1994   Prehistoric Macaws and Parrots in the Mimbres Area, New Mexico. American Antiquity 59(3):510–24.

Croissant, Jennifer L.
2000   Narrating Archaeology. In It's About Time: A History of Archaeological Dating in North America. Stephen E. Nash, ed. Pp. 186–206. Salt Lake City: University of Utah Press.

Crossley, Pamela Kyle
2008   What Is Global History? Cambridge: Polity.

Crown, Patricia L.
1991a   The Hohokam: Current Views of Prehistory and the Regional System. In Chaco and Hohokam: Prehistoric Regional Systems in the American Southwest. Patricia L. Crown and W. James Judge, eds. Pp. 135–57. Santa Fe, NM: School of American Research Press.
1991b   The Role of Exchange and Interaction in Salt-Gila Basin Hohokam Prehistory. In Exploring the Hohokam: Prehistoric Desert Peoples of the Southwest. George J. Gumerman, ed. Pp. 383–416. Albuquerque: University of New Mexico Press.
1994   Ceramics and Ideology: Salado Polychrome Pottery. Albuquerque: University of New Mexico Press.

Crown, Patricia L., and W. James Judge
1991   Synthesis and Conclusions. In Chaco and Hohokam: Prehistoric Regional Systems in the American Southwest. Patricia L. Crown and W. James Judge, eds. Pp. 293–308. Santa Fe, NM: School of American Research Press.

Crown, Patricia L., and W. James Judge, eds.
1991   Chaco and Hohokam: Prehistoric Regional Systems in the American Southwest. Santa Fe, NM: School of American Research Press.

Crown, Patricia L., Janet D. Orcutt, and Timothy A. Kohler
1996   Pueblo Cultures in Transition: The Northern Rio Grande. In The Prehistoric Pueblo World, A.D. 1150–1350. Michael A. Adler, ed. Pp. 188–204. Tucson: University of Arizona Press.

Crown, Patricia L., and W. H. Wills
2003   Modifying Pottery and Kivas at Chaco: Pentimento, Restoration or Renewal? American Antiquity 68(3):511–32.

Cummings, Byron
1953   The First Inhabitants of Arizona and the Southwest. Tucson, AZ: Cummings Publication Council.

Cunliffe, Barry
2001   Facing the Ocean: The Atlantic and Its Peoples. Oxford: Oxford University Press.
2002   The Extraordinary Voyage of Pytheas the Greek. New York: Penguin Books.

Curtin, Philip D.
1984   Cross-cultural Trade in World History. Cambridge: Cambridge University Press.

Damp, Jonathan
2002   Early Irrigation on the Colorado Plateau near Zuni Pueblo, New Mexico. American Antiquity 67:665–76.
2007   Zuni Emergent Agriculture: Economic Strategies and the Origins of Zuni. In Zuni Origins: Toward a New Synthesis of Southwestern Archaeology. David A. Gregory and David R. Wilcox, eds. Pp. 118–32. Tucson: University of Arizona Press.

Daniel, Glyn
1962   The Idea of Prehistory. Cleveland, OH: World Publishing Company.
1976   A Hundred and Fifty Years of Archaeology. Cambridge, MA: Harvard University Press.
1981   A Short History of Archaeology. London: Thames and Hudson.

Dark, K. R.
1998   The Waves of Time: Long-term Change and International Relations. London: Continuum.

Darling, J. Andrew, and Barnaby V. Lewis
2007   Ancient Trails of the Arid Southwest. Archaeology Southwest 21(4):16-17.

Davies, Nigel
1977   The Toltecs until the Fall of Tula. Norman: University of Oklahoma Press.
1987   The Aztec Empire. Norman: University of Oklahoma Press.

Davila Cabrera, Patricio
2000   La Frontera Noreste de Mesoamerica: Un Puente Cultural Hacia el Mississippi. *In* Nomadas y
            Sedentarios en el Norte de Mexico: Homenaje a Beatriz Braniff. Marie-Areti Hers, Jose Luis
            Mirafuentes, Maria de los Dolores Soto, and Miguel Vallebueno, eds.
            Pp. 79–90. Mexico City: Universidad Nacional Antonoma de Mexico.
2005   Mound Builders along the Coast of Mexico and the Eastern United States. *In* Gulf Coast
            Archaeology. Nancy M. White, ed. Pp. 87–107. Gainesville: University Press of Florida.

Davila Cabrera, Patricio, and Diana Zaragoza Ocana
2002   Tantoc: Una Cuidad en la Huasteca. Arqueologia Mexicana 9(54):66–69.

Davis, Emma Lou
1964   Anasazi Mobility and Mesa Verde Migrations. PhD dissertation, Department of Anthropology,
            University of California, Los Angeles.

Davis, Nancy Yaw
2000   The Zuni Enigma. New York: W. W. Norton.

Dean, Jeffrey S.
1969   Chronological Analysis of Tsegi Phase Sites in Northeastern Arizona. Papers of the
            Laboratory of Tree-Ring Research 3. Tucson, AZ: Laboratory of Tree-Ring Research.
1988   A Model of Anasazi Behavioral Adaptation. *In* The Anasazi in a Changing Environment.
            George J. Gumerman, ed. Pp. 25–44. Cambridge: Cambridge University Press.
1991   Thoughts on Hohokam Chronology. *In* Exploring the Hohokam: Prehistoric Desert Peoples
            of the Southwest. George J. Gumerman, ed. Pp. 61–149. Albuquerque: University of New
            Mexico Press.
1996a   Demography, Environment and Subsistence Stress. *In* Evolving Complexity and
            Environmental Risk in the Ancient Southwest. J. A. Tainter and B. Bagley Tainter, eds.
            Pp. 25–56. Reading, MA: Addison-Wesley.
1996b   Kayenta Anasazi Settlement Transformation in Northeastern Arizona, A.D. 1150–1350. *In* The
            Prehistoric Pueblo World, A.D. 1150–1350. Michael A. Adler, ed. Pp. 29–47. Tucson: University
            of Arizona Press.
2002   Late Pueblo II–Pueblo III in Kayenta-Branch Prehistory. *In* Prehistoric Culture Change
            on the Colorado Plateau: Ten Thousand Years on Black Mesa. Shirley Powell and
            Francis E. Smiley, eds. Pp. 121–57. Tucson: University of Arizona Press.

Dean, Jeffrey S., ed.
2000   Salado. Albuquerque: University of New Mexico Press.

Dean, Jeffrey S., William H. Doelle, and Janet D. Orcutt
1994   Adaptive Stress: Environment and Demography. *In* Themes in Southwest Prehistory. George
            J. Gumerman, ed. Pp. 53–86. Santa Fe, NM: School of American Research Press.

Dean, Jeffrey S., and John C. Ravesloot
1993   The Chronology of Cultural Interaction in the Gran Chichimeca. *In* Culture and Contact.
            Anne I. Woosley and John C. Ravesloot, eds. Pp. 83–103. Albuquerque: University of New
            Mexico Press.

Deaver, William L.
1997   Chronological Issues of the LVAP. *In* Vanishing River: Landscapes and Lives of the
            Lower Verde Valley: the Lower Verde Archaeological Project. Stephanie M. Whittlesey,
            Richard Ciolek-Torrello, and Jeffrey H. Altschul, eds. Pp. 531–95. Tucson, AZ: SRI Press.

DeBoer, Warren R.
1997   Ceremonial Centers from the Cayapas (Esmeraldas, Ecuador) to Chillicothe (Ohio, USA).
            Cambridge Archaeological Journal 7(2):225–53.
2006   Salient Representations of the American Past. *In* A Pre-Columbian World. Jeffrey Quilter and
            Mary Miller, eds. Pp. 137–85. Washington, DC: Dumbarton Oaks.

Deloria, Vine, Jr.
1969   Custer Died for Your Sins: An Indian Manifesto. New York: MacMillan.
1995   Red Earth, White Lies: Native Americans and the Myth of Scientific Fact. New York: Scribner.

Demuth, Andreas
2000   Some Conceptual Thoughts on Migration Research. *In* Theoretical and Methodological
            Issues in Migration Research. Biko Agozino, ed. Pp. 21–58. Aldershot, UK: Ashgate.

Diamond, Jared
1997   Guns, Germs and Steel: The Fates of Human Societies. New York: W. W. Norton.
2005   Collapse: How Societies Choose to Fail or Succeed. New York: Penguin Group.

Diehl, Michael W.
2000   Some Thoughts on the Study of Hierarchies. *In* Hierarchies in Action: Cui Bono?
            Michael. W. Diehl, ed. Pp. 11–30. Occasional Paper 27. Carbondale, IL: Center for
            Archaeological Investigations.
2007   Mogollon Trajectories and Divergences. *In* Zuni Origins: Toward a New Synthesis of
            Southwestern Archaeology. David A. Gregory and David R. Wilcox, eds. Pp. 146–62. Tucson:
            University of Arizona Press.

Diehl, Michael W., and Steven A. LeBlanc
2001   Early Pithouse Villages of the Mimbres Valley and Beyond: The McAnally and Thompson
            Sites in Their Cultural and Ecological Contexts. Papers of the Peabody Museum of
            Archaeology and Ethnology, vol. 83. Cambridge, MA: Harvard University Press.

Diehl, Richard A.
1983   Tula: The Toltec Capital of Ancient Mexico. London: Thames and Hudson.
2005   The Olmecs: America's First Civilization. London: Thames and Hudson.

Diehl, Richard A., and Janet Catherine Berlo, eds.
1989   Mesoamerica after the Decline of Teotihuacán, A.D. 700–900. Washington, DC: Dumbarton
            Oaks Research Library and Collection.

Diermeier, Daniel
2007   Arguing for Computation Power. *Review of* Generative Social Science by Joshua M. Epstein.
            Science 318(5852):918–19.

Dillehay, Tom D.
1989   Monte Verde: A Late Pleistocene Settlement in Chile. Washington, DC: Smithsonian
            Institution Press.
2000   The Settlement of the Americas: A New Prehistory. New York: Basic Books.

Dilworth, Leah
1996   Imagining Indians in the Southwest: Persistent Visions of a Primitive Past. Washington, DC:
            Smithsonian Institution Press.

Diner, Hasia R.
2000   History and the Study of Immigration: Narratives of the Particular. *In* Migration Theory:
            Talking Across Disciplines. Caroline B. Brettell and James F. Hollifield, eds. Pp. 27–42. New
            York: Routledge.

Di Peso, Charles C.
1956   The Upper Pima of San Cayetano del Tumacacori: An Archaeological Reconstruction of the
            Ootam of Pimeria Alta. Publication 8. Dragoon, AZ: Amerind Foundation.
1958   The Reeve Ruin of Southeastern Arizona: A Study of Prehistoric Western Pueblo Migration
            into the Middle San Pedro Valley. Dragoon, AZ: Amerind Foundation.
1974   Casas Grandes: A Fallen Trading Center of the Gran Chichimeca, vols. 1–3. Dragoon, AZ:
            Amerind Foundation.
1979   Prehistory: The Southern Periphery. *In* Handbook of North American Indians, vol. 9:
            Southwest. Alfonso A. Ortiz, ed. Pp. 152–161. Washington, DC: Smithsonian Institution.

Di Peso, Charles C., John B. Rinaldo, and Gloria J. Fenner
1974a   Casas Grandes: A Fallen Trading Center of the Gran Chichimeca, vol. 5: Architecture.
            Dragoon, AZ: Amerind Foundation.
1974b   Casas Grandes: A Fallen Trading Center of the Gran Chichimeca, vol. 8: Bone-Economy-
            Burials. Dragoon, AZ: Amerind Foundation.

Di Peso, Charles C., John B. Rinaldo, and Gloria J. Fenner, eds.
1974   Casas Grandes: A Fallen Trading Center of the Gran Chichimeca, vols. 4–8. Dragoon, AZ: Amerind Foundation.

Dixon, E. James
1999   Bones, Boats and Bison: Archaeology and the First Colonization of Western North America. Albuquerque: University of New Mexico Press.

Dobres, Marcia-Anne, and John E. Robb
2000   Agency in Archaeology: Paradigm or Platitude? *In* Agency in Archaeology. Marcia-Anne Dobres and John E. Robb, eds. Pp. 3–17. London: Routledge.

Dobres, Marcia-Anne, and John E. Robb, eds.
2000   Agency in Archaeology. London: Routledge.

Dobyns, Henry F.
2002   Indoamerica and the Greater Southwest: Ropes, Bags, and Backpack Frames. *In* Culture and Environment in the American Southwest: Essays in Honor of Robert C. Euler. David A. Phillips Jr. and John A. Ware, eds. Pp. 169–76. SWCA Anthropological Research Paper 8. Phoenix, AZ: SWCA.

Doelle, William H.
1981   The Gila Pima in the Late Seventeenth Century. *In* The Protohistoric Period in the North American Southwest, A.D. 1450–1700. David R. Wilcox and W. Bruce Masse, eds. Pp. 57–70. Anthropological Research Papers 24. Tempe: Arizona State University.
1995a   Tonto Basin Demography in a Regional Perspective. *In* The Roosevelt Community Development Study: New Perspectives on Tonto Basin Prehistory. Mark D. Elson, Miriam T. Stark, and David A. Gregory, eds. Pp. 201–26. Anthropological Papers 15. Tucson, AZ: Center for Desert Archaeology.
1995b   Regional Platform Mound Systems: Background and Inventory (appendix F). *In* The Roosevelt Community Development Study: New Perspectives on Tonto Basin Prehistory. Mark D. Elson, Miriam T. Stark, and David A. Gregory, eds. Pp. 555–60. Anthropological Papers 15. Tucson, AZ: Center for Desert Archaeology.
2000   Tonto Basin Demography in a Regional Perspective. *In* Salado. Jeffrey S. Dean, ed. Pp. 81–105. Albuquerque: University of New Mexico Press.

Doelle, William H., David A. Gregory, and Henry D. Wallace
1995   Classic Period Platform Mound Systems in Southern Arizona. *In* The Roosevelt Community Development Study: New Perspectives on Tonto Basin Prehistory. Mark D. Elson, Miriam T. Stark, and David A. Gregory, eds. Pp. 385–440. Anthropological Papers 15. Tucson, AZ: Center for Desert Archaeology.

Doelle, William H., Frederick W. Huntingon, and Henry D. Wallace
1987   Rincon Phase Community Structure in the Tucson Basin. *In* The Hohokam Village: Site Structure and Organization. David E. Doyel, ed. Pp. 71–96. AAAS Publication 87-15. Glenwood Springs, CO: Southwestern and Rocky Mountain Division of the American Association for the Advancement of Science.

Doelle, William H., and David A. Phillips Jr.
2005   From the Academy to the Private Sector: CRM's Rapid Transformation within the Archaeological Profession. *In* Southwest Archaeology in the Twentieth Century. Linda S. Cordell and Don D. Fowler, eds. Pp. 97–108. Salt Lake City: University of Utah Press.

Doelle, William H., and Henry D. Wallace
1991   The Changing Role of the Tucson Basin in the Hohokam Regional System. *In* Exploring the Hohokam: Prehistoric Desert Peoples of the Southwest. George J. Gumerman, ed. Pp. 279–345. Albuquerque: University of New Mexico Press.

Doolittle, William E.
1988   Pre-Hispanic Occupance in the Valley of Sonora, Mexico: Archaeological Confirmation of Early Spanish Reports. Anthropological Papers 48. Tucson: University of Arizona Press.
1990   Canal Irrigation in Prehistoric Mexico: The Sequence of Technological Change. Austin: University of Texas Press.

Doolittle, William E., and Jonathan B. Mabry
2006   Environmental Mosaics, Agricultural Diversity, and the Evolutionary Adoption of Maize in the American Southwest. *In* Histories of Maize. John E. Staller, Robert H. Tykot, and Bruce F. Benz, eds. Pp. 109–21. Burlington, MA: Academic Press.

Douglas, John E.
1995   Autonomy and Regional Systems in the Late Prehistoric Southern Southwest. American Antiquity 60:240–57.
2007   Making and Breaking Boundaries in the Hinterlands: The Social and Settlement Dynamics of Far Southeastern Arizona and Southwestern New Mexico. *In* Hinterlands and Regional Dynamics in the Ancient Southwest. Alan P. Sullivan III and James M. Bayman, eds. Pp. 97–108. Tucson: University of Arizona Press.

Downum, Christian E.
1993   Between Desert and River: Hohokam Settlement and Land Use in the Los Robles Community. Anthropological Papers 57. Tucson: University of Arizona Press.
2007   Cerro de Trincheras in Southern Arizona: Review and Current Status of the Debate. *In* Trincheras Sites in Time, Space, and Society. Suzanne K. Fish, Paul R. Fish, and Elisa Villalpando, eds. Pp. 101–36. Amerind Foundation New World Series. Tucson: University of Arizona Press.

Downum, Christian E., and Todd W. Bostwick
2003   The Platform Mound. *In* Centuries of Decline during the Hohokam Classic Period at Pueblo Grande. David R. Abbott, ed. Pp. 166–200. Tucson: University of Arizona Press.

Downum, Christian E., Ellen Brennan, and James P. Holmlund
1999   An Architectural Study of Wupatki Pueblo (NA 405). Archaeological Report 1175. Flagstaff: Northern Arizona University.

Downum, Christian E., Paul R. Fish, and Suzanne K. Fish
1994   Refining the Role of Cerro de Trincheras in Southern Arizona Settlement. Kiva 59:271–96.

Doxiadis, Constantinos A.
1968   Ekistics: An Introduction to the Science of Human Settlements. New York: Oxford University Press.

Doyel, David E.
1981   Late Hohokam Prehistory in Southern Arizona. Scottsdale, AZ: Gila Press.
1988   Rio Rico Polychrome: Ceramic Interaction along the Southern Borderlands. *In* Research on Tucson Basin Prehistory: Proceedings of the Second Tucson Basin Conference. William H. Doelle and Paul R. Fish, eds. Pp. 349–72. Anthropological Papers 10. Tucson, AZ: Institute for American Research.
1991a   Hohokam Cultural Evolution in the Phoenix Basin. *In* Exploring the Hohokam: Prehistoric Desert Peoples of the Southwest. George J. Gumerman, ed. Pp. 231–78. Albuquerque: University of New Mexico Press.
1991b   Hohokam Exchange and Interaction. *In* Chaco and Hohokam: Prehistoric Regional Systems in the American Southwest. Patricia L. Crown and W. James Judge, eds. Pp. 225–52. Santa Fe, NM: School of American Research Press.
1994   Charles Corradino Di Peso. American Antiquity 59:9–20.
2000a   In Pursuit of Salado in the Sonoran Desert. *In* Salado. Jeffrey S. Dean, ed. Pp. 295–314. Albuquerque: University of New Mexico Press.
2000b   The Santan Phase in the Phoenix Basin. *In* The Hohokam Village Revisited. David E. Doyel, Suzanne K. Fish, and Paul R. Fish, eds. Pp. 221–44. Fort Collins, CO: Southwestern and Rocky Mountain Division of the American Association for the Advancement of Science.
2000c   Settlement Organization at Gila Bend. *In* The Hohokam Village Revisited. David E. Doyel, Suzanne K. Fish, and Paul R. Fish, eds. Pp. 101–38. Fort Collins, CO: Southwestern and Rocky Mountain Division of the American Association for the Advancement of Science.
Forthcoming Late Prehistoric Reorganization and Dissolution in the Salt River Valley, Arizona. *In* Hohokam Trajectories in World Perspective. Suzanne K. Fish and Paul R. Fish, eds. Amerind Studies in Archaeology. Tucson: University of Arizona Press.

Doyel, David E., ed.
1974   Excavations in the Escalante Ruin Group, Southern Arizona. Tucson: Arizona State Museum, University of Arizona.

1987   The Hohokam Village: Site Structure and Organization. AAAS Publication 87-15. Glenwood Springs, CO; Southwestern and Rocky Mountain Division of the American Association for the Advancement of Science.

[1992]2001   Anasazi Regional Organization and the Chaco System. Anthropological Papers 5. Albuquerque: Maxwell Museum of Anthropology, University of New Mexico.

Doyel, David E., and Joseph S. Crary

1996   Prehistoric Regional Dynamics in the Lower Verde Area. *In* The Bartlett Reservoir Cultural Resources Survey. Teresa L. Hoffman, ed. Pp. 85-109. Archaeological Consulting Services Cultural Resources Report No. 92. Tempe, AZ: Archaeological Consulting Services.

Doyel, David E., and Mark D. Elson, eds.

1985   Hohokam Settlement and Economic Systems in the Central New River Drainage, Arizona. Soil Systems Publications in Archaeology 4. Phoenix, AZ: Soil Systems, Inc.

Doyel, David E., and Suzanne K. Fish

2000   Prehistoric Villages and Communities in the Arizona Desert. *In* The Hohokam Village Revisited. David E. Doyel, Suzanne K. Fish, and Paul R. Fish, eds. Pp. 1–35. Fort Collins, CO: Southwestern and Rocky Mountain Division of the American Association for the Advancement of Science.

Doyel, David E., Suzanne K. Fish, and Paul R. Fish, eds.

2000   The Hohokam Village Revisited. Fort Collins, CO: Southwestern and Rocky Mountain Division of the American Association for the Advancement of Science.

Doyel, David E., and Stephen H. Lekson

1992   Regional Organization in the American Southwest. *In* Anasazi Regional Organization and the Chaco System. David E. Doyel, ed. Pp. 15–21. Anthropological Papers 5. Albuquerque: Maxwell Museum of Anthropology, University of New Mexico.

Doyel, David E., and Fred Plog, eds.

1980   Current Issues in Hohokam Prehistory: Proceedings of a Symposium. Anthropological Research Papers 23. Tempe: Arizona State University.

Dozier, Edward P.

1970   The Pueblo Indians of North America. New York: Holt, Reinhart, and Winston.

Drennan, Robert D.

1984   Long Distance Transport Costs in Pre-Hispanic Mesoamerica. American Anthropologist 86(1):105–12.

Duff, Andrew I.

1998   The Process of Migration in the Late Prehistoric Southwest. *In* Migrations and Reorganization: The Pueblo IV Period in the American Southwest. Katherine A. Spielmann, ed. Pp. 31–52. Anthropological Research Papers 51. Tempe: Arizona State University.

2000   Scale, Interaction and Regional Analysis in Late Pueblo Prehistory. *In* The Archaeology of Regional Interaction. Michelle Hegmon, ed. Pp. 71–98. Boulder: University Press of Colorado.

Duff, Andrew I., and Stephen H. Lekson

2006   Notes from the South. *In* The Archaeology of Chaco Canyon: An Eleventh-Century Pueblo Regional Center. Stephen H. Lekson, ed. Pp. 315–38. Santa Fe, NM: School of American Research Press.

Duff, Andrew I., and Richard H. Wilshusen

2000   Prehistoric Population Dynamics in the Northern San Juan Region, A.D. 950–1300. Kiva 66(1):167–90.

Duke, Philip G.

1985   Fort Lewis College Archaeological Investigations in Ridges Basin, Southwest Colorado: 1965–1982. Occasional Papers 4. Durango, CO: Center of Southwest Studies, Fort Lewis College.

Duke, Philip G., ed.

1999   Affiliation Conference on Ancestral Peoples of the Four Corners. Durango, CO: Center of Southwest Studies, Fort Lewis College.

Earle, Timothy K.
1997   How Chiefs Come to Power: The Political Economy in Prehistory. Stanford, CA: Stanford
            University Press.

Earle, Timothy K., ed.
1991   Chiefdoms: Power, Economy, Ideology. Cambridge: Cambridge University Press.

Echo-Hawk, Roger C.
1997   Forging a New Ancient History for Native America. *In* Native Americans and Archaeologists:
            Stepping Stone to Common Ground. Nina Swidler, Kurt E. Dongoske, Roger Anyon, and
            Alan S. Downer, eds. Pp. 88–102. Walnut Creek, CA: AltaMira.
2000   Ancient History in the New World: Integrating Oral Traditions and the Archaeological
            Record in Deep Time. American Antiquity 65:267–90.

Eckert, Suzanne L.
2006   The Production and Distribution of Glaze-Painted Pottery in the Pueblo Southwest. *In* The
            Social Life of Pots: Glaze Wares and Cultural Dynamics in the Southwest, AD 1250–1680.
            Judith A. Habicht-Mauche, Suzanne L. Eckert, and Deborah L. Huntley, eds. Pp. 34–59.
            Tucson: University of Arizona Press.

Eddy, Frank W.
1977   Archaeological Investigations at Chimney Rock Mesa: 1970–1972. Memoirs of the Colorado
            Archaeological Society 1. Boulder: Colorado Archaeological Society.

Eddy, Frank W., Allen E. Kane, and Paul R. Nickens
1984   Southwest Colorado Prehistoric Context. Denver: Colorado Historical Society.

Edwards, Clinton R.
1965   Aboriginal Sail in the New World. Southwestern Journal of Anthropology 21(4):351–58.
1978   Pre-Columbian Maritime Trade in Mesoamerica. *In* Mesoamerican Communication Routes
            and Cultural Contacts. Thomas A. Lee Jr. and Carlos Navarrete, eds. Pp. 199–209. New World
            Archaeological Foundation Papers 40. Provo, UT: Brigham Young University.

Ehret, Christopher
2001   An African Classical Age: Eastern and Southern Africa in World History, 1000 BC to AD 400.
            Charlottesville: University of Virginia Press.

Eighmy, Jeffrey L.
2000   Thirty Years of Archaeomagnetic Dating. *In* It's About Time: A History of Archaeological
            Dating in North America. Stephen E. Nash, ed. Pp. 105–23. Salt Lake City: University of Utah
            Press.

Elliot, Malinda
1987   The School of American Research: A History. Santa Fe, NM: School of American Research
            Press.
1995   Great Excavations. Santa Fe, NM: School of American Research Press.

Ellis, Florence Hawley, and Laurens Hammack
1968   The Inner Sanctum of Feather Cave, a Mogollon Sun and Earth Shrine Linking Mexico and
            the Southwest. American Antiquity 33:25–44.

Elson, Mark D.
1998   Expanding the View of Hohokam Platform Mounds: An Ethnographic Perspective.
            Anthropological Papers 63. Tucson: University of Arizona Press.
2000   Southwest Platform Mounds from an Ethnographic Perspective. *In* The Hohokam Village
            Revisited. David Doyel, Suzanne K. Fish, and Paul R. Fish, eds. Pp. 345–72. Fort Collins, CO:
            Southwestern and Rocky Mountain Division of the American Association for the
            Advancement of Science.

Elson, Mark D., and David R. Abbott
2000   Organizational Variability in Platform Mound-Building Groups in the American Southwest.
            In Alternative Leadership Strategies in the Prehispanic Southwest. Barbara J. Mills, ed.
            Pp. 117–35. Tucson: University of Arizona Press.

Elson, Mark D., and Jeffrey J. Clark
2007   Rethinking the Hohokam Periphery: The Preclassic Period in the Tonto Basin. *In*

Hinterlands and Regional Dynamics in the Ancient Southwest. Alan P. Sullivan III and James M. Bayman, eds. Pp. 31–49. Tucson: University of Arizona Press.

Forthcoming Tonto Basin Prehistoric Settlement. *In* Hohokam Trajectories in World Perspective. Suzanne K. Fish and Paul R. Fish, eds. Amerind Studies in Archaeology. Tucson: University of Arizona Press.

Elson, Mark D., and David A. Gregory
1995 Tonto Basin Chronology and Phase Sequence. *In* The Roosevelt Community Development Study: New Perspectives on Tonto Basin Prehistory. Mark D. Elson, Miriam T. Stark, and David A. Gregory, eds. Pp. 61–77. Anthropological Papers 15. Tucson, AZ: Center for Desert Archaeology.

Elson, Mark D., David A. Gregory, and Miriam T. Stark
1995 New Perspectives on Tonto Basin Prehistory. *In* The Roosevelt Community Development Study: New Perspectives on Tonto Basin Prehistory. Mark D. Elson, Miriam T. Stark, and David A. Gregory, eds. Pp. 441–79. Anthropological Papers 15. Tucson, AZ: Center for Desert Archaeology.

Elson, Mark D., Miriam T. Stark, and David A. Gregory
2000 Tonto Basin Local Systems: Implications for Cultural Affiliation and Migration. *In* Salado. Jeffrey S. Dean, ed. Pp. 167–91. Albuquerque: University of New Mexico Press.

Elson, Mark D., Miriam T. Stark, and David A. Gregory, eds.
1995 The Roosevelt Community Development Study: New Perspectives on Tonto Basin Prehistory. Anthropological Papers 15. Tucson, AZ: Center for Desert Archaeology.

Emerson, Thomas E., Randall E. Hughes, Mary R. Hynes, and Sarah U. Wisseman
2003 The Sourcing and Interpretation of Cahokia-Style Figurines in the Trans-Mississippi South and Southeast. American Antiquity 68(2):287–313.

Emerson, Thomas E., and R. Barry Lewis
1991 Cahokia and the Hinterlands. Urbana: University of Illinois Press.

Ericson, Jonathan E., and Timothy G. Baugh, eds.
1993 The American Southwest and Mesoamerica: Systems of Prehistoric Exchange. New York: Plenum.

Erlandson, Jon M., and Terry Jones, eds.
2003 Catalysts to Complexity: Late Holocene Societies of the California Coast. Los Angeles: Cotsen Institute of Archaeology.

Euler, Robert C., and George J. Gumerman, eds.
1978 Investigations of the Southwestern Anthropological Research Group: Proceedings of the 1976 Conference. Flagstaff: Museum of Northern Arizona.

Evans, Clifford, and Betty J. Meggars
1966 Mesoamerica and Ecuador. *In* Handbook of Middle American Indians, vol. 4: Archaeological Frontiers and Connections. Gordon F. Ekholm and Gordon R. Willey, eds. Pp. 243–64. Austin: University of Texas Press.

Evans, John H., and Harry Hillman
1981 Documentation of Some Lunar and Solar Events at Casa Grande, Arizona. Anthropological Papers 22. Pp. 133–35. Ramona, CA: Ballena.

Evans, Susan Toby, and Joanne Pillsbury, eds.
2004 Palaces of the Ancient New World. Washington, DC: Dumbarton Oaks.

Ezell, Paul H.
1963 Is There a Hohokam–Pima Culture Continuum? American Antiquity 29:61–66.

Fagan, Brian
2005 Chaco Canyon. Oxford: Oxford University Press.

Farb, Peter
1968 Man's Rise to Civilization as Shown by the Indians of North America from Primeval Times to the Coming of the Industrial State. New York: Dutton.

Farwell, Robin Y.
1981 Pit Houses: Prehistoric Energy Conservation? El Palacio 87(3):43–47.

Fash, William L., and Barbara W. Fash
2000   Teotihuacan and the Maya Mesoamerica's Classic Heritage: From Teotihuacan to the Aztecs. *In* Mesoamerica's Classic Heritage: From Teotihuacan to the Aztecs. David Carrasco, Lindsay Jones, and Scott Sessions, eds. Pp. 433–63. Boulder: University Press of Colorado.

Feinman, Gary M.
1991   Hohokam Archaeology in the Eighties: An Outside View. *In* Exploring the Hohokam: Prehistoric Desert Peoples of the Southwest. George J. Gumerman, ed. Pp. 461–83. Albuquerque: University of New Mexico Press.
2000   Corporate/Network: New Perspectives on Models of Political Action and the Puebloan Southwest. *In* Social Theory in Archaeology. Michael Brian Schiffer, ed. Pp. 31–51. Salt Lake City: University of Utah Press.
2005   The Institutionalization of Leadership and Inequality: Integrating Process and History. *In* A Catalyst for Ideas: Anthropological Archaeology and the Legacy of Douglas W. Schwartz. Vernon L. Scarborough, ed. Pp. 101–20. Advanced Seminar Series. Santa Fe, NM: School of American Research Press.

Feinman, Gary M., Kent G. Lightfoot, and Steadman Upham
2000   Political Hierarchies and Organizational Strategies in the Puebloan Southwest. American Antiquity 65:449–70.

Feinman, Gary M., and Joyce Marcus, eds.
1998   Archaic States. Santa Fe, NM: School of American Research Press.

Feinman, Gary M., and Jill Neitzel
1984   Too Many Types: An Overview of Sedentary Prestate Societies in the Americas. *In* Advances in Archaeological Theory and Method 7. Michael B. Schiffer, ed. Pp. 39–102. Orlando, FL: Academic Press.

Feinman, Gary M., Linda M. Nicholas, and Steadman Upham
1996   A Macroregional Comparison of the American Southwest and Highland Mesoamerica in Pre-Columbian Times: Preliminary Thoughts and Implications. *In* Pre-Columbian World Systems. Peter N. Peregrine and Gary M. Feinman, eds. Pp. 65–76. Madison, WI: Prehistory Press.

Fenner, Gloria J.
1974   Ceramic Hand Drums. *In* Casas Grandes: A Fallen Trading Center of the Gran Chichimeca, vol. 6: Ceramics and Shell, by Charles C. Di Peso, John B. Rinaldo, and Gloria J. Fenner. Pp. 356–65. Dragoon, AZ: Amerind Foundation.

Ferdon, Edwin N., Jr.
1967   The Hohokam "Ballcourt": An Alternative View of Its Function. Kiva 33:1–14.

Ferguson, T. J., and Chip Colwell-Chanthaphonh
2006   History Is in the Land: Multivocal Tribal Traditions in Arizona's San Pedro Valley. Tucson: University of Arizona Press.

Ferguson, T. J., and E. Richard Hart
1985   A Zuni Atlas. Norman: University of Oklahoma Press.

Fernández-Armesto, Felipe
1987   Before Columbus: Exploration and Colonization from the Mediterranean to the Atlantic, 1129–1492. Philadelphia: University of Pennsylvania Press.
2001   Civilizations: Culture, Ambition, and the Transformation of Nature. New York: Free Press.
2003   The Americas: A Hemispheric History. New York: Modern Library.
2006   Pathfinders: A Global History of Exploration. New York: W. W. Norton.

Fewkes, Jesse Walter
1904   Two Summers' Work in Pueblo Ruins. *In* Twenty-second Annual Report of the Bureau of American Ethnology, 1900-1901, part 1:3-126.
1913   Casa Grande, Arizona. *In* Twenty-eighth Annual Report of the Bureau of American Ethnology. Pp. 25–179. Washington, DC: Government Printing Office.

Fields, Virginia, and Victor Zamudio-Taylor, eds.
2001   The Road to Aztlan: Art from a Mythic Homeland. Los Angeles: Los Angeles County Museum of Art.

Fields, Virginia M., and Dorie Reents-Budet, eds.
2005   Lords of Creation: The Origins of Sacred Maya Kingship. London: Scala Publishers; Los
            Angeles: Los Angeles County Museum of Art.

Fish, Paul R., and Suzanne K. Fish
1991   Hohokam Political and Social Organization. *In* Exploring the Hohokam: Prehistoric Desert
            Peoples of the Southwest. George J. Gumerman, ed. Pp. 151–75. Albuquerque: University of
            New Mexico Press.
2004   Unsuspected Multitudes: Expanding the Scale of Hohokam Agriculture. *In* The Archaeology
            of Global Change: The Impact of Humans on Their Environments.
            Charles L. Redman, Steven R. James, Paul R. Fish, and J. Daniel Rogers, eds. Pp. 208–23.
            Washington, DC: Smithsonian Books.

Fish, Paul, Peter Pilles, and Suzanne Fish
1980   Colonies, Traders and Traits: The Hohokam in the North. *In* Current Issues in Hohokam
            Prehistory: Proceedings of a Symposium. David Doyel and Fred Plog, eds. Pp. 151–75.
            Anthropological Research Papers 23. Tempe: Arizona State University.

Fish, Paul R., and J. Jefferson Reid, eds.
1996   Interpreting Southwestern Diversity: Underlying Principles and Overarching Patterns.
            Anthropological Research Papers 48. Tempe: Arizona State University.

Fish, Suzanne K.
1996   Dynamics of Scale in Southern Deserts. *In* Interpreting Southwestern Diversity.
            Paul R. Fish and J. Jefferson Reid, eds. Pp. 107–14. Anthropological Research Papers 48.
            Tempe: Arizona State University.
1999   How Complex Were the Southwestern Great Towns' Polities? *In* Great Towns and Regional
            Polities in the Prehistoric American Southwest and Southeast. Jill E. Neitzel, ed. Pp. 45–58.
            Albuquerque: University of New Mexico Press.

Fish, Suzanne K., and Paul R. Fish
2000a   The Marana Mound Site: Patterns of Social Differentiation in the Early Classic Period. *In* The
            Hohokam Village Revisited. David E. Doyel, Suzanne K. Fish, and Paul R. Fish, eds. Pp.
            245–75. Fort Collins, CO: Southwestern and Rocky Mountain Division of the American
            Association for the Advancement of Science.
2000b   Civic-Territorial Organization and the Roots of Hohokam Complexity. *In* The Hohokam
            Village Revisited. David E. Doyel, Suzanne K. Fish, and Paul R. Fish, eds. Pp. 373–90. Fort
            Collins, CO: Southwestern and Rocky Mountain Division of the American Association for the
            Advancement of Science.
2000c   Institutional Contexts of Hohokam Complexity and Inequality. *In* Alternative Leadership
            Strategies in the Prehispanic Southwest. Barbara J. Mills, ed. Pp. 154–67. Tucson: University
            of Arizona Press.
2004   In the Trincheras Heartland: Initial Insights from Full-Coverage Survey. *In* Surveying the
            Archaeology of Northwest Mexico. Gillian E. Newell and Emiliano Gallaga, eds. Pp. 47–63.
            Salt Lake City: University of Utah Press.
2007   Regional Heartlands and Transregional Trends. *In* Trincheras Sites in Time, Space, and
            Society. Suzanne K. Fish, Paul R. Fish, and M. Elisa Villalpando, eds. Pp. 165–94. Amerind
            Foundation New World Series. Tucson: University of Arizona Press.

Fish, Suzanne K., and Paul R. Fish, eds.
2007   The Hohokam Millennium. Santa Fe, NM: School for Advanced Research Press.
Forthcoming Hohokam Trajectories in World Perspective. Amerind Studies in Archaeology. Tucson:
            University of Arizona Press.

Fish, Suzanne K., Paul R. Fish, and John H. Madsen, eds.
1992   The Marana Community in the Hohokam World. Anthropological Papers 56. Tucson:
            University of Arizona Press.

Fish, Suzanne K., Paul R. Fish, and M. Elisa Villalpando, eds.
2007   Trincheras Sites in Time, Space, and Society. Amerind Foundation New World Series. Tucson:
            University of Arizona Press.

Fiske, T. L., and K. Lummis
1975   Charles F. Lummis: The Man and His West. Norman: University of Oklahoma Press.

Fitzhugh, William W., and Elisabeth I. Ward
2000   Vikings: The North Atlantic Saga. Washington, DC: Smithsonian Institution Press.

Flannery, Kent V.
1976   Research Strategy and Formative Mesoamerica. *In* The Early Mesoamerican Village. Kent V. Flannery, ed. Pp. 1–11. New York: Academic Press.

Flannery, Kent V., and Joyce Marcus
2000   Formative Mexican Chiefdoms and the Myth of the "Mother Culture." Journal of Anthropological Archaeology 19(1):1–37.

Fletcher, Roland
1995   The Limits of Settlement Growth: A Theoretical Outline. New Studies in Archaeology. Cambridge: Cambridge University Press.

Flint, Richard, and Shirley Cushing Flint
2005   Documents of the Coronado Expedition, 1539–1542: "They were not familiar with His Majesty, nor did they wish to be his subjects." Dallas, TX: Southern Methodist University Press.

Flint, Richard, and Shirley Cushing Flint, eds.
1997   The Coronado Expedition to Tierra Nueva: The 1540–1542 Route across the Southwest. Niwot: University Press of Colorado.
2003   The Coronado Expedition: From the Distance of 460 Years. Albuquerque: University of New Mexico Press.

Florescano, Enrique
2006   Teotihuacan in Mesoamerican Political History. *In* A Pre-Columbian World. Jeffrey Quilter and Mary Miller, eds. Pp. 287–311. Washington, DC: Dumbarton Oaks.

Forbes, Jack D.
1973   Aztecas del Norte: The Chicanos of Aztlan. Greenwich, CT: Premier Books.

Force, Eric R., Gwinn Vivian, Thomas C. Windes, and Jeffrey S. Dean
2002   Relation of "Bonito" Paleo-Channels and Base-Level Variations to Anasazi Occupation, Chaco Canyon, New Mexico. Arizona State Museum Archaeological Series 94. Tucson: University of Arizona.

Ford, James A.
1969   A Comparison of Formative Cultures in the Americas; Diffusion or the Psychic Unity of Man. Smithsonian Contributions to Knowledge 11. Washington, DC: Smithsonian Institution Press.

Ford, Richard I.
1994   Corn Is Our Mother. *In* Corn and Culture in the Prehistoric New World. Sissel Johannessen and Christine A. Hastorf, eds. Pp. 513–26. Boulder, CO: Westview.

Ford, Richard I., Albert H. Schroeder, and Stewart L. Peckham
1972   Three Perspectives on Pueblo Prehistory. *In* New Perspectives on the Pueblos. Alfonso A. Ortiz, ed. Pp. 22–40. Albuquerque: University of New Mexico Press.

Foster, Michael S.
1999   The Aztatlán Tradition of West and Northwest Mexico and Casas Grandes. *In* The Casas Grandes World. Curtis F. Schaafsma and Carroll L. Riley, eds. Pp. 149–63. Salt Lake City: University of Utah Press.

Foster, Michael S., and Shirley Gorenstein, eds.
2000   Greater Mesoamerica: The Archaeology of West and Northwest Mexico. Salt Lake City: University of Utah Press.

Foster, Michael S., and Phil C. Weigand, eds.
1985   The Archaeology of West and Northwest Mesoamerica. Boulder, CO: Westview.

Fowler, Andrew P., and John R. Stein
1992   The Anasazi Great House in Space, Time and Paradigm. *In* Anasazi Regional Organization and the Chaco System. 2nd ed. David E. Doyel, ed. Pp. 101–31. Anthropological Papers 5. Albuquerque: Maxwell Museum of Anthropology, University of New Mexico.

Fowler, Catherine S.

1983   Some Lexical Clues to Uto-Aztecan Prehistory. International Journal of American Linguistics 49(3):224-257.

Fowler, Don D.

1987   Uses of the Past in the Service of the State. American Antiquity 52:229–48.

2000   A Laboratory for Anthropology: Science and Romanticism in the American Southwest, 1846–1930. Albuquerque: University of New Mexico Press.

2005   The Formative Years: Southwest Archaeology, 1890–1910. *In* Southwest Archaeology in the Twentieth Century. Linda S. Cordell and Don D. Fowler, eds. Pp. 16–26. Salt Lake City: University of Utah Press.

Fowler, Melvin L.

1997   The Cahokia Atlas: A Historical Atlas of Cahokia Archaeology. Revised ed. Urbana: Illinois Transportation Archaeological Research Program, University of Illinois.

Fowler, Melvin L., Jerome Rose, Barbara Vander Leest, and Steven A. Ahler

1999   The Mound 72 Area: Dedicated and Sacred Space in Early Cahokia. Reports of Investigations 54. Springfield: Illinois State Museum.

Fowles, Severin

2004   Tewa versus Tiwa: Northern Rio Grande Settlement Patterns and Social History, A.D. 1275–1540. *In* The Protohistoric Pueblo World, A.D. 1275–1600. E. Charles Adams and Andrew I. Duff, eds. Pp. 17–25. Tucson: University of Arizona Press.

Frank, Andre Gunder, and Barry K. Gills, eds.

1993   The World System: Five Hundred Years or Five Thousand? London: Routledge.

Franklin, Hayward H.

1980   Stylistic Similarities between Mesa Verde B/W and the White Mountain Redwares. Paper presented at the Annual Meeting of the Society for American Archaeology, Philadelphia, PA, April 24–27.

Freeman, Katherine, Robert Bliss, and Jennifer Thompson

1996   Visual Communication between Chimney Rock and Chaco Canyon. Paper presented at the Oxford V Conference on Archaeoastronomy, Santa Fe, NM, August 3–13.

Freidel, David, Linda Schele, and Joy Parker

1993   Maya Cosmos: Three Thousand Years on the Shaman's Path. New York: W. Morrow.

Friedman, Jonathan, and Christopher Chase-Dunn, eds.

2005   Hegemonic Declines, Past and Present. Boulder, CO: Paradigm.

Fritz, John

1978   Paleopsychology Today: Ideational Systems and Human Adaptation in Prehistory. *In* Social Archaeology: Beyond Subsistence and Dating. C. L. Redman, M. J. Berman, E. V. Curtin, W. T. Langhorne, N. M. Versaggi, and J. C. Wanser, eds. Pp. 37–59. New York: Academic Press.

Gabriel, Kathryn

1996   Gambler Way: Indian Gaming in Mythology, History and Archaeology in North America. Boulder, CO: Johnson Books.

Gaddis, John Lewis

2002   The Landscape of History: How Historians Map the Past. Oxford: Oxford University Press.

Gallatin, Albert H.

1848   Ancient Semi-Civilizations of New Mexico, Rio Gila, and Its Vicinity. Proceedings of the American Ethnological Society 2, pp. liii–xcvii.

Galloway, Patricia, ed.

1989   The Southeastern Ceremonial Complex: Artifacts and Analysis. Lincoln: University of Nebraska Press.

Galloway, Patricia, and Jason Baird Jackson

2004   Natchez and Neighboring Groups. *In* Handbook of North American Indians, vol. 14: Northeast. Raymond D. Fogelson, ed. Pp. 598–615. Washington, DC: Smithsonian Institution.

Garcia de Quevedo, Susan L.
2004   Trade, Migration, or Emulation: A Study of Stone Palettes from the Mimbres Region. MA thesis, Department of Anthropology, University of Oklahoma, Norman.

Gardiner, Juliet, ed.
1988   What Is History Today? Atlantic Highlands, NJ: Humanities Press International.

Gardner, Andrew, ed.
2004   Agency Uncovered: Archaeological Perspectives on Social Agency, Power, and Being Human. London: UCL Press.

Garnot R., Jaime, and Alejandro A. Peschard F.
1995   The Archaeological Site of El Cañon del Molino, Durango, Mexico. *In* The Gran Chichimeca: Essays on the Archaeology and Ethnohistory of Northern Mesoamerica. Jonathan E. Reyman, ed. Pp. 146–78. Worldwide Archaeology Series 12. Aldershot, UK: Avebury.

Gasser, Robert, and Charles Miksicek
1985   The Specialists: A Reappraisal of Hohokam Exchange and the Archaeobotanical Record. *In* Proceedings of the 1983 Hohokam Symposium, Part II. Alfred E. Dittert Jr. and Donald E. Dove, eds. Pp. 483–98. Occasional Paper 2. Phoenix: Arizona Archaeological Society.

Geib, Phil R.
1996   Glen Canyon Revisited. Salt Lake City: University of Utah Press.

Geib, Phil R., and Kimberly Spurr
2002   The Forager to Farmer Transition on the Rainbow Plateau. *In* Traditions, Transitions, and Technologies: Themes in Southwestern Archaeology. Sarah H. Schlanger, ed. Pp. 224–44. Boulder: University Press of Colorado.

Gerhard, Peter
1972   A Guide to the Historical Geography of New Spain. Cambridge: Cambridge University Press.

Gibson, Jon L.
2001   The Ancient Mounds of Poverty Point: Place of Rings. Gainesville: University Press of Florida.

Gibson, Jon L., and Philip J. Carr, eds.
2004   Signs of Power: The Rise of Cultural Complexity in the Southeast. Tuscaloosa: University of Alabama Press.

Giddens, Anthony
1979   Central Problems in Social Theory. Berkeley: University of California.
1987   Social Theory and Modern Sociology. Stanford, CA: Stanford University Press.

Gillespie, Susan D.
1989   The Aztec Kings: The Construction of Rulership in Mexican History. Tucson: University of Arizona Press.
1991   Ballgames and Boundaries. *In* The Mesoamerican Ballgame. Vernon L. Scarborough and David R. Wilcox, eds. Pp. 317–345. Tucson: University of Arizona Press.

Gilman, Patricia A.
1987   Architecture as Artifact: Pit Structures and Pueblos in the American Southwest. American Antiquity 52:538–64.
1990   Social Organization and Classic Mimbres Period Burials in the SW United States. Journal of Field Archaeology 17:457–69.

Gilpin, Dennis
1994   Lukachukai and Salina Springs: Late Archaic/Early Basketmaker Habitation Sites in the Chinle Valley, Northeastern Arizona. Kiva 60:203–18.

Gilpin, Dennis, and Larry Benallie Jr.
2000   Juniper Cove and Early Anasazi Community Structure West of the Chuska Mountains. *In* Foundations of Anasazi Culture: The Basketmaker–Pueblo Transition. Paul F. Reed, ed. Pp. 161–73. Salt Lake City: University of Utah Press.

Givens, Douglas R.
1992   Alfred Vincent Kidder and the Development of Americanist Archaeology. Albuquerque: University of New Mexico Press.

Gladwin, Harold S.

[1938]1975   Conclusions. *In* Excavations at Snaketown, Material Culture. Harold S. Gladwin, Emil W. Haury, E. B. Sayles, and Nora Gladwin, eds. Pp. 247–69. Tucson: University of Arizona Press.

1947   Men out of Asia. New York: Whittlesey House.

1948   Excavations at Snaketown IV, Reviews and Conclusions. Medallion Papers 38. Globe, AZ: Gila Pueblo.

1957   A History of the Ancient Southwest. Portland, ME: Bond Wheelwright.

1979   Mogollon and Hohokam A.D. 600–1100. Medallion Papers 40. Santa Barbara, CA: privately printed.

Gladwin, Harold S., Emil W. Haury, E. B. Sayles, and Nora Gladwin

[1938]1975   Excavations at Snaketown, Material Culture. Tucson: University of Arizona Press.

Gladwin, Winifred, and Harold S. Gladwin

1934   A Method for Designation of Cultures and Their Variations. Medallion Papers 15. Globe, AZ: Gila Pueblo.

Glowacki, Donna M.

2006   The Social Landscape of Depopulation: The Northern San Juan, A.D. 1150–1300. PhD dissertation, Department of Anthropology, Arizona State University, Tempe.

Goddard, Earle Pliny

1933   Navajo Texts. Anthropological Papers, vol. 34, no. 1. New York: American Museum of Natural History.

Goldstein, Lynne G.

1991   The Implications of Aztalan's Location. *In* New Perspectives on Cahokia. James B. Stoltman, ed. Pp. 209–27. Monographs in World Archaeology 2. Madison, WI: Prehistory Press.

Goldstein, Lynne G., and John D. Richards

1991   Ancient Aztalan: The Cultural and Ecological Context of a Late Prehistoric Site in the Midwest. *In* Cahokia and the Hinterlands. T. E. Emerson and R. B. Lewis, eds. Pp. 193–206. Urbana: University of Illinois Press.

Goldstein, Paul S.

2000   Exotic Goods and Everyday Chiefs. Latin American Antiquity 11(4):335–61.

Gorenstein, Shirley, and Helen Perlstein Pollard

1983   The Tarascan Civilization: A Late Prehispanic Cultural System. Publications in Anthropology 28. Nashville, TN: Vanderbilt University.

Graves, Michael W., and J. Jefferson Reid

1984   Social Complexity in the American Southwest: A View from East-central Arizona. *In* Recent Research in Mogollon Archaeology. S. Upham, F. Plog, D. Batcho, and B. Kauffman, eds. Pp. 266–75. New Mexico State University Museum Occasional Papers 10. Las Cruces: New Mexico State University.

Graves, Michael W., and Katherine A. Spielmann

2000   Leadership, Long-distance Exchange and Feasting in the Protohistoric Rio Grande. *In* Alternative Leadership Strategies in the Prehispanic Southwest. Barbara J. Mills, ed. Pp. 45–59. Tucson: University of Arizona Press.

Graybill, Donald A.

1989   The Reconstruction of Prehistoric Salt River Streamflow. *In* The 1982–1984 Excavations at Las Colinas: Environment and Subsistence. Donald A. Graybill, ed. Pp. 25–28. Archaeological Series 162, vol. 5. Tucson: Arizona State Museum.

Graybill, Donald A., David A. Gregory, Gary S. Funkhouser, and Fred L. Nials

2006   Long-term Streamflow Reconstructions, River Channel Morphology, and Aboriginal Irrigation Systems along the Salt and Gila Rivers. *In* Environmental Change and Human Adaptation in the Ancient American Southwest. David E. Doyel and Jeffrey S. Dean, eds. Pp. 69–123. Salt Lake City: University of Utah Press.

Green, Jesse, ed.

1990   Cushing at Zuni: The Correspondence and Journals of Frank Hamilton Cushing, 1879–1884. Albuquerque: University of New Mexico Press.

Gregg, Josiah
1844   Commerce of the prairies; or, The journal of a Santa Fé trader, during eight expeditions across the great western prairies, and a residence of nearly nine years in northern Mexico. New York: H. G. Langley.

Gregory, David A.
1987   The Morphology of Platform Mounds and the Structure of Classic Period Hohokam Sites. *In* The Hohokam Village: Site Structure and Organization. David E. Doyel, ed. Pp. 183–210. AAAS Publication 87-15. Glenwood Springs, CO: Southwestern and Rocky Mountain Division of the American Association for the Advancement of Science.
1991   Form and Variation in Hohokam Settlement Patterns. *In* Chaco and Hohokam: Prehistoric Regional Systems in the American Southwest. Patricia L. Crown and W. James Judge, eds. Pp. 159–93. Santa Fe, NM: School of American Research Press.

Gregory, David A., ed.
1988   The 1982–1985 Excavations at Las Colinas: The Mound 8 Precinct. Archaeological Series 162, vol. 3. Tucson: Arizona State Museum.
2001   Excavations in the Santa Cruz Floodplain: The Early Agricultural Period Component at Los Pozos. Technical Report 99-4. Tucson, AZ: Center for Desert Archaeology.

Gregory, David A., William L. Deaver, Suzanne K. Fish, Ronald Gardiner, Robert W. Layhe, Fred L. Nials, and Lynn S. Teague
1988   The 1982–1984 Excavations at Las Colinas: The Site and Its Features. Archaeology Series 162, vol. 2. Tucson: Arizona State Museum.

Gregory, David A., and Michael W. Diehl
2002   Duration, Continuity, and Intensity of Occupation at a Late Cienega Phase Settlement in the Santa Cruz River Floodplain. *In* Traditions, Transitions, and Technologies: Themes in Southwestern Archaeology. Sarah H. Schlanger, ed. Pp. 200–23. Boulder: University Press of Colorado.

Gregory, David A., and Fred Nials
1985   Observations Concerning the Distribution of Classic Period Hohokam Platform Mounds. *In* Proceedings of the 1983 Hohokam Symposium. A. E. Dittert Jr. and D. E. Dove, eds. Pp. 378–88. Occasional Papers 2. Phoenix: Arizona Archaeological Society.
2007   The Environmental Context of Linguistic Differentiation and Other Cultural Developments in the Prehistoric Southwest. *In* Zuni Origins: Toward a New Synthesis of Southwestern Archaeology. David A. Gregory and David R. Wilcox, eds. Pp. 49–76. Tucson: University of Arizona Press.

Gregory, David A., and David R. Wilcox, eds.
2007   Zuni Origins: Towards a New Synthesis of Southwestern Archaeology. Tucson: University of Arizona Press.

Greiser, Sally T., and James L. Moore
1995   The Case for Prehistoric Irrigation in the Northern Southwest. *In* Soil, Water, Biology, and Belief in Prehistoric and Traditional Southwestern Agriculture. H. Wolcott Toll, ed. Pp. 189–95. Special Publication 2. Albuquerque: New Mexico Archaeological Council.

Griffin, James B.
1966   Mesoamerica and the Eastern United States in Prehistoric Times. *In* Handbook of Middle American Indians, vol. 4: Archaeological Frontiers and Connections. Gordon F. Ekholm and Gordon R. Willey, eds. Pp. 111–31. Austin: University of Texas Press.

Guadalupe Mastache, Alba, Robert H. Cobean, and Dan M. Healan
2002   Ancient Tollan: Tula and the Toltec Heartland. Boulder: University Press of Colorado.

Gugliotta, Guy
2007   The Maya: Glory and Ruin. National Geographic 212(2):68–109.

Gumerman, George J., ed.
1971   The Distribution of Prehistoric Population Aggregates. Anthropological Reports 1. Prescott, AZ: Prescott College Press.
1972   Proceedings of the Second Annual Meeting of the Southwestern Anthropological Research Group. Anthropological Reports 3. Prescott, AZ: Prescott College Press.

1988 The Anasazi in a Changing Environment. Cambridge: Cambridge University Press.
1991 Exploring the Hohokam: Prehistoric Desert Peoples of the Southwest. Albuquerque: University of New Mexico Press.
1994 Themes in Southwest Prehistory. Santa Fe, NM: School of American Research Press.

Gumerman, George J., and Jeffrey S. Dean
1989 Prehistoric Cooperation and Competition in the Western Anasazi Area. *In* Dynamics of Southwest Prehistory. Linda S. Cordell and George J. Gumerman, eds. Pp. 99–148. Washington, DC: Smithsonian Institution Press.

Gumerman, George J., and Murray Gell-Mann, eds.
1994 Understanding Complexity in the Prehistoric Southwest. Reading, MA: Addison-Wesley.

Gumerman, George J., Alan C. Swedlund, Jeffrey S. Dean, and Joshua M. Epstein
2003 The Evolution of Social Behavior in the Prehistoric American Southwest. Artificial Life 9:435–44.

Gunn, Joel D.
2000 A.D. 536 and Its 300-Year Aftermath. *In* The Years without Summer: Tracing A.D. 536 and Its Aftermath. Joel D. Gunn, ed. Pp. 5–20. BAR International Series 872. Oxford: Archaeopress.

Haas, Jonathan, ed.
2001 From Leaders to Rulers. New York: Kluwer Academic/Plenum.

Haas, Jonathan, and Winifred Creamer
1993 Stress and Warfare among the Kayenta Anasazi of the Thirteenth Century A.D. Fieldiana Anthropology 21. Chicago: Field Museum of Natural History.
1997 Warfare among the Pueblos: Myth, History, and Ethnography. Ethnohistory 44:235–61.

Habicht-Mauche, Judith A.
1993 The Pottery from Arroyo Hondo Pueblo, New Mexico: Tribalization and Trade in the Northern Rio Grande. Santa Fe, NM: School of American Research Press.

Habicht-Mauche, Judith A., Suzanne L. Eckert, and Deborah L. Huntley, eds.
2006 The Social Life of Pots: Glaze Wares and Cultural Dynamics in the Southwest, AD 1250–1680. Tucson: University of Arizona Press.

Hackbarth, Mark
2000 Spectacular Finds in the 1930s. Archaeology Southwest 14(3):6–7.

Hall, Robert L.
2006 Exploring the Mississippian Big Bang at Cahokia. *In* A Pre-Columbian World. Jeffrey Quilter and Mary Miller, eds. Pp. 187–229. Washington, DC: Dumbarton Oaks.

Hally, David J., ed.
1994 Ocumlgee Archaeology 1936–1986. Athens: University of Georgia Press.

Hally, David J., and James L. Rudolph, eds.
1986 Mississippi Period Archaeology of the Georgia Piedmont. Laboratory of Archaeology Series, report 24. Athens: University of Georgia.

Hammond, George P., and Agapito Rey
1966 The Rediscovery of New Mexico 1580–1594. Albuquerque: University of New Mexico Press.

Hard, Robert J., and John R. Roney
2004 Late Archaic Period Hilltop Settlements in Northwestern Chihuahua, Mexico. *In* Identity, Feasting, and the Archaeology of the Greater Southwest. Barbara J. Mills, ed. Pp. 276–94. Boulder: University Press of Colorado.
2005 The Transition to Farming on the Rio Casas Grandes and in the Southern Jornada Mogollon Region. *In* The Late Archaic across the Borderlands: From Foraging to Farming. Bradley J. Vierra, ed. Pp. 141–86. Austin: University of Texas Press.
2007 Cerro de Trincheras in Northwestern Chihuahua: Arguments for Defense. *In* Trincheras Sites in Time, Space, and Society. Suzanne K. Fish, Paul R. Fish, and M. Elisa Villalpando, eds. Pp. 11–52. Amerind Foundation New World Series. Tucson: University of Arizona Press.

Hard, Robert J., A. C. MacWilliams, John R. Roney, Karen R. Adams, and William Merrill
2006 Early Agriculture in Chihuahua, Mexico. *In* Histories of Maize. John E. Staller, Robert H. Tykot, and Bruce F. Benz, eds. Pp. 471–85. Burlington, MA: Academic Press.

Hargrave, Lyndon L.
1970 Mexican Macaws: Comparative Osteology and Survey of Remains from the Southwest. Anthropological Papers 20. Tucson: University of Arizona Press.

Harmon, Marcel J.
2006 Religion and the Mesoamerican Ball Game in the Casas Grandes Region of Northern Mexico. *In* Religion in the Prehispanic Southwest. Christine S. VanPool, Todd L. VanPool, and David A. Phillips Jr., eds. Pp. 185–217. Lanham, MD: AltaMira.

Harris, Marvin
1968 The Rise of Anthropological Theory. New York: T. Y. Crowell.

Hassig, Ross
1992 War and Society in Ancient Mesoamerica. Berkeley: University of California Press.

Haury, Emil W.
1932 Roosevelt 9:6, a Hohokam Site of the Colonial Period. Medallion Papers 11. Globe, AZ: Gila Pueblo.
1936 The Mogollon Culture of Southwestern New Mexico. Medallion Papers 20. Globe, AZ: Gila Pueblo.
1945 The Excavation of Los Muertos and Neighboring Ruins in the Salt River Valley, Southern Arizona. Papers of the Peabody Museum of American Archaeology and Ethnology, vol. 24, no. 1. Cambridge, MA: Harvard University.
1958 Evidence at Point of Pines for a Prehistoric Migration from Northern Arizona. *In* Migrations in New World Culture History. Raymond H. Thompson, ed. Pp. 1–8. University of Arizona Bulletin 29(2), Social Science Bulletin 27. Tucson: University of Arizona.
1962 The Greater American Southwest. *In* Courses toward Urban Life. Robert J. Braidwood and Gordon R. Willey, eds. Pp. 106–31. Viking Fund Publications in Anthropology 32. New York: Wenner-Gren Foundation for Anthropological Research.
1976 The Hohokam: Desert Farmers and Craftsmen. Tucson: University of Arizona Press.
1985 Tla Kii Ruin. *In* Mogollon Culture in the Forestdale Valley, East-central Arizona. Emil W. Haury, ed. Pp. 1–133. Tucson: University of Arizona Press.
1986 Thoughts after Sixty Years as a Southwestern Archaeologist. *In* Emil W. Haury's Prehistory of the American Southwest. J. Jefferson Reid and David E. Doyel, eds. Pp. 435–64. Tucson: University of Arizona Press.
1988 Gila Pueblo Archaeological Foundation: A History and Some Personal Notes. Kiva 54(1):i–ix, 1–77.
1989 Point of Pines, Arizona: A History of the University of Arizona Archaeological Field School. Anthropological Papers 50. Tucson: University of Arizona.
2004 Reflections on the Arizona State Museum: 1925 and Ensuing Years. Journal of the Southwest 46(1):129–63.

Hayes, Alden C.
1964 The Archaeological Survey of Wetherill Mesa, Mesa Verde National Park, Colorado. Archaeological Research Series 7A. Washington, DC: National Park Service.
1981 A Survey of Chaco Canyon Archaeology. *In* Archaeological Surveys of Chaco Canyon, New Mexico. A. C. Hayes, D. M. Brugge, and W. J. Judge, eds. Pp. 1–68. Publications in Archaeology 18A. Washington, DC: National Park Service.

Hayes, Alden C., and James A. Lancaster
1975 Badger House Community, Mesa Verde National Park. Publications in Archaeology 7E. Washington, DC: National Park Service.

Hayes, Alden C., and Thomas C. Windes
1975 An Anasazi Shrine in Chaco Canyon. *In* Collected Papers in Honor of Florence Hawley Ellis. Theodore R. Frisbie, ed. Pp. 143–56. Papers of the Archaeological Society of New Mexico 2. Norman, OK: Hooper.

Haynes, C. Vance, Jr., and George A. Agogino
1986 Geochronology of Sandia Cave. Washington, DC: Smithsonian Institution Press.

Hays-Gilpin, Kelley, and Jane H. Hill
2000 The Flower World in Prehistoric Southwest Material Culture. *In* The Archaeology of Regional Interaction: Religion, Warfare, and Exchange across the American Southwest and Beyond.

Michelle Hegmon, ed. Pp. 411–28. Boulder: University Press of Colorado.

Hays-Gilpin, Kelley, and Steven A. LeBlanc
2007   Sikyatki Style in Regional Context. *In* New Perspectives on Pottery Mound Pueblo.
            Polly Schaafsma, ed. Pp. 109–36. Albuquerque: University of New Mexico Press.

Hays-Gilpin, Kelley Ann, Ann Cordy Deegan, and Elizabeth Ann Morris, eds.
1998   Prehistoric Sandals from Northeastern Arizona. Anthropological Papers 62. Tucson:
            University of Arizona Press.

Heckman, Robert A., Barbara K. Montgomery, and Stephanie M. Whittlesey, eds.
2000   Prehistoric Painted Pottery of Southeastern Arizona. Technical Series 77. Tucson: Statistical
            Research, Inc.

Heckman, Robert A., and Stephanie M. Whittlesey
2000   Concluding Thoughts. *In* Prehistoric Painted Pottery of Southeastern Arizona.
            Robert A. Heckman, Barbara K. Montgomery, and Stephanie M. Whittlesey, eds.
            Pp. 117–27. Technical Series 77. Tucson, AZ: Statistical Research, Inc.

Hedrick, Basil C., J. Charles Kelley, and Carroll L. Riley, eds.
1974   The Mesoamerican Southwest: Readings in Archaeology, Ethnohistory and Ethnology.
            Carbondale: Southern Illinois University Press.

Hegmon, Michelle
2000   Corrugated Pottery, Technological Style, and Population Movement in the Mimbres Region
            of the American Southwest. Journal of Anthropological Research 56(2):217–40.
2002   Recent Issues in the Archaeology of the Mimbres Region of the North American Southwest.
            Journal of Archaeological Research 10(4):307–57.
2003   Setting Theoretical Egos Aside: Issues and Theory in North American Archaeology. American
            Antiquity 68:213–43.
2005   Beyond the Mold: Questions of Inequality in Southwest Villages. *In* North American
            Archaeology. Timothy R. Pauketat and Diana DiPaolo Loren, eds. Pp. 212–34. Malden, MA:
            Blackwell.

Hegmon, Michelle, ed.
2000   The Archaeology of Regional Interaction: Religion, Warfare, and Exchange across the
            American Southwest and Beyond. Boulder: University Press of Colorado.

Hegmon, Michelle, and Stephanie Kulow
2005   Painting as Agency, Style as Structure: Innovations in Mimbres Pottery Designs from
            Southwest New Mexico. Journal of Archaeological Method and Theory 12(4):313–34.

Hegmon, Michelle, and Margaret C. Nelson
2007   In Sync, but Barely in Touch: Relations between the Mimbres Region and the Hohokam
            Regional System. *In* Hinterlands and Regional Dynamics in the Ancient Southwest.
            Alan P. Sullivan III and James M. Bayman, eds. Pp. 70–96. Tucson: University of Arizona
            Press.

**Hegmon, Michelle, Margaret C. Nelson, Roger Anyon, Darrell Creel, Steven A. LeBlanc, and
Harry J. Shafer**
1999   Scale and Time-Space Systematics in the Post–A.D. 1100 Mimbres Region of the North
            American Southwest. Kiva 65:143–66.

Hegmon, Michelle, Margaret C. Nelson, and Mark J. Ennes
2000   Corrugated Pottery, Technological Style, and Population Movement in the Mimbres Region
            of the American Southwest. Journal of Anthropological Research 56(2):217–40.

Heine-Geldern, Robert
1966   The Problem of Transpacific Influences in Mesoamerica. *In* Handbook of Middle American
            Indians, vol. 4: Archaeological Frontiers and Connections. Gordon F. Ekholm and Gordon R.
            Willey, eds. Pp. 277–95. Austin: University of Texas Press.

Heitman, Carolyn, and Stephen Plog
2005   Kinship and the Dynamics of the House: Rediscovering Dualism in the Pueblo Past. *In* A
            Catalyst for Ideas: Anthropological Archaeology and the Legacy of Douglas W. Schwartz.
            Vernon L. Scarborough, ed. Pp. 69–100. Advanced Seminar Series. Santa Fe, NM: School of
            American Research Press.

Helms, Mary W.

1979   Ancient Panama: Chiefs in Search of Power. Austin: University of Texas Press.

1988   Ulysses' Sail: An Ethnographic Odyssey of Power, Knowledge, and Geographical Distance. Princeton, NJ: Princeton University Press.

1993   Craft and the Kingly Ideal: Art, Trade, and Power. Austin: University of Texas Press.

2006   Glimpses of a Common Cosmos? A Brief Look South and North of Panama. *In* A Pre-Columbian World. Jeffrey Quilter and Mary Miller, eds. Pp. 107–35. Washington, DC: Dumbarton Oaks.

Hendon, Julia A., and Rosemary A. Joyce, eds.

2004   Mesoamerican Archaeology: Theory and Practice. Oxford: Blackwell.

Hendrickson, Dean A., and W. L. Minckley, eds.

1984   Ciénegas: Vanishing Climax Communities of the American Southwest. Special issue, Desert Plants 6(3).

Herr, Sarah A.

2001   Beyond Chaco: Great Kiva Communities on the Mogollon Rim Frontier. Anthropological Papers 66. Tucson: University of Arizona Press.

Herr, Sarah A., and Jeffrey J. Clark

2002   Mobility and the Organization of Prehispanic Southwest Communities. *In* The Archaeology of Tribal Societies. William A. Parkinson, ed. Pp. 123–54. Archaeological Series 15. Ann Arbor, MI: International Monographs in Prehistory.

Herrington, LaVerne

1982   Water-Control Systems of the Mimbres Classic Phase. *In* Mogollon Archaeology. Patrick H. Beckett, ed. Pp. 75–90. Ramona, CA: Acoma Books.

Hers, Marie-Areti, Jose Luis Mirafuentes, Maria de los Dolores Soto, and Miguel Vallebueno, eds.

2000   Nomadas y Sedentarios en el Norte de Mexico: Homenaje a Beatriz Braniff. Mexico City: Universidad Nacional Antónoma de México.

Hewett, Edgar L.

[1908]1993   Ancient Communities in the American Desert. Archaeological Society of New Mexico Monograph Series 1. Tucson: University of Arizona.

1923   Anahuac and Aztlan: Retracing the Legendary Footsteps of the Aztecs. Art and Archaeology 16(1–2):35–50.

1930   Ancient Life in the American Southwest. Indianapolis, IN: Bobbs-Merrill.

1936a   Ancient Life in Mexico and Central America. Indianapolis, IN: Bobbs-Merrill.

1936b   The Chaco Canyon and Its Monuments. Santa Fe, NM: School of American Research; Albuquerque: University of New Mexico.

Hibben, Frank C.

1941   Evidences of Early Occupation in Sandia Cave, New Mexico and Other Sites in the Sandia-Manzano Region. Smithsonian Miscellaneous Collections, vol. 99, no. 23. Washington, DC: The Smithsonian Institution.

Hill, J. Brett, Jeffery J. Clark, William H. Doelle, and Patrick D. Lyons

2004   Prehistoric Demography in the Southwest: Migration, Coalescence, and Hohokam Population Decline. American Antiquity 69:689–716.

Hill, James N.

1970   Broken K Pueblo: Prehistoric Social Organization in the American Southwest. Anthropological Papers 8. Tucson: University of Arizona Press.

Hill, Jane H.

2001   Proto-Uto-Aztecan: A Community of Cultivars in Central Mexico? American Anthropologist 103:913–34.

2002   Proto-Uto-Aztecan Cultivation and the Northern Devolution. *In* Examining the Farming/Language Dispersal Hypothesis. Peter Bellwood and Colin Renfrew, eds. Pp. 331–40. Cambridge: McDonald Institute for Archaeological Research.

2006   The Historical Linguistics of Maize Cultivation in Mesoamerica and North America. *In* Histories of Maize. John E. Staller, Robert H. Tykot, and Bruce F. Benz, eds. Pp. 631–45. Burlington, MA: Academic Press.

Hill, Rebecca J., and Lorrie Lincoln-Babb
2008 Hohokam Classic Period Health: Centuries of Decline? Paper presented at the Annual Meeting of the Society for American Archaeology, Vancouver, BC, March 27–30.

Hill, Warren D., and John E. Clark
2001 Sports, Gambling, and Government: America's First Social Compact? American Anthropologist 103(2):331–45.

Hinsley, Curtis M.
1986 Edgar Lee Hewett and the School of American Archaeology in Santa Fe, 1906–1912. *In* American Archaeology, Past and Future. David J. Meltzer, Don D. Fowler, and Jeremy A. Sabloff, eds. Pp. 217–36. Washington, DC: Smithsonian Institution Press.
1996a Boston Meets the Southwest. *In* The Southwest in the American Imagination: The Writings of Sylvester Baxter, 1881–1889. Curtis M. Hinsley and David R. Wilcox, eds. Pp. 3–33. Tucson: University of Arizona Press.
1996b The Promise of the Southwest: A Humanized Landscape. *In* The Southwest in the American Imagination: The Writings of Sylvester Baxter, 1881–1889. Curtis M. Hinsley and David R. Wilcox, eds. Pp. 181–206. Tucson: University of Arizona Press.

Hinsley, Curtis M., and David R. Wilcox, eds.
1996 The Southwest in the American Imagination: The Writings of Sylvester Baxter, 1881–1889. Tucson: University of Arizona Press.

Hirth, Kenneth
1992 Interregional Exchange as Elite Behavior: An Evolutionary Perspective. *In* Mesoamerican Elites: An Archaeological Assessment. Diane Z. Chase and Arlen F. Chase, eds. Pp. 18–29. Norman: University of Oklahoma Press.

Hobson, John M.
2003 The Eastern Origins of Western Civilization. Cambridge: Cambridge University Press.

Hodder, Ian
1987 The Contribution of the Long Term. *In* Archaeology as Long-term History. Ian Hodder, ed. Pp. 1–8. Cambridge: Cambridge University Press.
1990 The Domestication of Europe. Oxford: Blackwell.
1991 Reading the Past: Current Approaches to Interpretation in Archaeology. 2nd ed. Cambridge: Cambridge University Press.
1999 The Archaeological Process: An Introduction. Oxford: Blackwell.
2006 The Leopard's Tale: Revealing the Mysteries of Catalhoyuk. London: Thames and Hudson.

Hodder, Ian, ed.
1987 Archaeology as Long-term History. Cambridge: Cambridge University Press.

Hodder, Ian, and Scott Hutson
2003 Reading the Past. 3rd ed. Cambridge: Cambridge University Press.

Hodge, Mary G.
1998 Archaeological Views of Aztec Culture. Journal of Archaeological Research 6(3):197–238.

Holden, Constance, ed.
2005 Sensitivity or Censorship? Science 307:1197.

Holmes, William Henry
1878 Report of the Ancient Ruins in Southwestern Colorado, Examined During the Summers of 1875 and 1876. *In* Hayden Survey, 1874–1876: Mesa Verde and the Four Corners, by W. H. Jackson and W. H. Holmes. Pp. 383–408. Annual Report of the United States Geological and Geographical Survey of the Territories, 1878. Washington, DC: Government Publishing Office.
1886 Pottery of the Ancient Pueblos. Fourth Annual Report of the Bureau of Ethnology for 1882–83. Washington, DC: Bureau of Ethnology.
1914 Areas of American Culture Characterization Tentatively Outlined as an Aid in the Study of Antiquities. American Anthropologist, n.s. 16(3):413–46.

Hornborg, Alf, and Carole L. Crumley
2007 The World System and the Earth System: Global Socioenvironmental Change and Sustainability since the Neolithic. Walnut Creek, CA: Left Coast Press.

Hosler, Dorothy
1988   Ancient West Mexican Metallurgy: South and Central American Origins and West Mexican Transformations. American Anthropologist 90:832–55.
1994   The Sounds and Colors of Power: The Sacred Metallurgical Technology of Ancient West Mexico. Cambridge, MA: MIT Press.
2003   Metal Production. *In* The Postclassic Mesoamerican World. Michael E. Smith and Frances F. Berdan, eds. Pp. 159–71. Salt Lake City: University of Utah Press.

Hough, Walter
1907   Antiquities of the Upper Gila and Salt River Valleys in Arizona and New Mexico. Bulletin 35. Washington, DC: Bureau of American Ethnology.

Houlihan, Patrick T., and Betsy E. Houlihan
1986   Lummis in the Pueblos. Flagstaff, AZ: Northland.

Housley, R. A., and G. Coles, eds.
2004   Atlantic Connections and Adaptations: Economies, Environments and Subsistence in Lands Bordering the North Atlantic. Oxford: Oxbow.

Howard, Jerry B.
1985   Courtyard Groups and Domestic Cycling: A Hypothetical Model of Growth. *In* Proceedings of the 1983 Hohokam Symposium. Alfred E. Dittert Jr. and David E. Dove, eds. Pp. 311–26. Occasional Paper 2. Phoenix: Arizona Archaeological Society.
1992   Architecture and Ideology: An Approach to the Functional Analysis of Platform Mounds. *In* Proceedings of the Second Salado Conference. Richard C. Lange and Stephen Germick, eds. Pp. 69–77. Occasional Paper. Phoenix: Arizona Archaeological Society.
1993   A Paleohydraulic Approach to Examining Agricultural Intensification in Hohokam Irrigation Systems. *In* Research in Economic Anthropology, suppl. 7. Vernon L. Scarborough and Barry L. Isaac, eds. Pp. 263–324. Greenwich, CT: JAI Press.

Howard, Jerry B., and Gary A. Huckleberry, eds.
1991   The Operation and Evolution of an Irrigation System: The East Papago Canal Study. Publications in Archaeology 18. Phoenix, AZ: Soil Systems.

Howe, Sherman S.
1947   My Story of the Aztec Ruins. Farmington, NM: Times Hustler.

Huckell, Bruce B.
1995   Of Marshes and Maize: Preceramic Agricultural Settlements in the Cienega Valley, Southeastern Arizona. Tucson: University of Arizona Press.
1996   The Archaic Prehistory of the North American Southwest. Journal of World Prehistory 10(3):305–73.
2005   The First 10,000 Years in the Southwest. *In* Southwest Archaeology in the Twentieth Century. Linda S. Cordell and Don D. Fowler, eds. Pp. 142–56. Salt Lake City, UT: University of Utah Press.

Huckell, Lisa W.
2006   Ancient Maize in the American Southwest. *In* Histories of Maize. John E. Staller, Robert H. Tykot, and Bruce F. Benz, eds. Pp. 97–107. Burlington, MA: Academic Press.

Huddleston, Lee Eldridge
1967   Origins of the American Indians; European Concepts, 1492–1729. Austin: University of Texas Press.

Humboldt, Alexander von
1812   Atlas géographique et physique du royaume de la Nouvelle-Espagne. Paris: G. Dufour.

Humborg, Alf, and Carole Crumley, eds.
2007   The World System and the Earth System. Walnut Creek, CA: Left Coast.

Hunt, Robert C., David Guillet, David R. Abbott, James Bayman, Paul Fish, Suzanne Fish, Keith Kintigh, and James A. Neely
2005   Plausible Ethnographic Analogies for the Social Organization of Hohokam Canal Irrigation. American Antiquity 70:433–56.

Huntley, Deborah L., and Keith W. Kintigh
2004   Archaeological Patterning and Organizational Scale of Late Prehistoric Settlement Clusters in

the Zuni Region of New Mexico. *In* The Protohistoric Pueblo World, A.D. 1275–1600. E. Charles Adams and Andrew I. Duff, eds. Pp. 62–74. Tucson: University of Arizona Press.

Hurst, Winston, and Jonathan Till
2006 Mesa Verdean Sacred Landscapes. *In* The Mesa Verde World. David Grant Noble, ed. Pp. 75–84. Santa Fe, NM: School of American Research Press.

Hutchinson, Art, and Jack E. Smith, comp.
1991 Proceedings of the Anasazi Symposium 1991. Mesa Verde, CO: Mesa Verde Museum Association.

Irwin-Williams, Cynthia
1972 The San Juan Valley Archaeological Program. *In* The Structure of Chacoan Society in the Northern Southwest, Investigations at the Salmon Site—1972. Cynthia Irwin-Williams, ed. Pp. 1–14. Contributions in Anthropology 4(3). Portales: Eastern New Mexico University.
1973 The Oshara Tradition: Origins of Anasazi Culture. Contributions in Anthropology 5(1). Portales: Eastern New Mexico University.
1979 Post-Pleistocene Archaeology, 7000–2000 BC. *In* Handbook of North American Indians, vol. 9: Southwest. Alfonso Ortiz, ed. Pp. 31–42. Washington, DC: Smithsonian Institution.
2006 The Structure of Chacoan Society at Salmon Ruins. *In* Thirty-Five Years of Archaeological Research at Salmon Ruins, New Mexico. Paul F. Reed, ed. Pp. 349-366. Tucson, AZ: Center for Desert Archaeology; Bloomfield, NM: Salmon Ruins Museum.

Irwin-Williams, Cynthia, ed.
1972 The Structure of Chacoan Society in the Northern Southwest, Investigations at the Salmon Site—1972. Contributions in Anthropology 4(3). Portales: Eastern New Mexico University.

Jacobs, James Q.
2007 The Chaco Meridian. Electronic document, http://www.jqjacobs.net/southwest/chaco_meridian.html, accessed July 2007.

James, Henry, Jr.
1879 Hawthorne. London: Macmillan.

James, Steven R.
2003 Hunting and Fishing Patterns Leading to Resource Depletion. *In* Centuries of Decline during the Hohokam Classic Period at Pueblo Grande. David R. Abbott, ed. Pp. 70–81. Tucson: University of Arizona Press.

Janetski, Joel C.
1993 The Archaic to Formative Transition North of the Anasazi: A Basketmaker Perspective. *In* Anasazi Basketmaker: Papers from the 1990 Wetherill–Grand Gulch Symposium. Victoria M. Atkins, ed. Pp. 223–41. Cultural Resource Series 24. Salt Lake City, UT: Bureau of Land Management.
2002 Trade in Fremont Society: Contexts and Contrasts. Journal of Anthropological Archaeology 21:344–70.

Jennings, Jesse D., ed.
1956 The American Southwest: A Problem in Cultural Isolation. *In* Seminars in Archaeology: 1955. Robert Wauchope, ed. Pp. 59–127. Memoirs of the Society for American Archaeology 11. American Antiquity 22(2):pt. 2.

Jernigan, E. Wesley
1978 Jewelry of the Prehistoric Southwest. Albuquerque: University of New Mexico Press.

Jett, Stephen C., and Peter B. Moyle
1986 The Exotic Origins of Fishes Depicted on Prehistoric Mimbres Pottery. American Antiquity 51:688–720.

Johannessen, Sissel, and Christine A. Hastorf, eds.
1994 Corn and Culture in the Prehistoric New World. Boulder, CO: Westview.

Johnson Alfred E.
1961 A Ball Court at Point of Pines, Arizona. American Antiquity 26(4):563–567

Johnson, Amber L., ed.
2004 Processual Archaeology. Westport, CT: Praeger.

Johnson, David C., Timothy A. Kohler, and Jason Cowan
2005   Modeling Historical Ecology, Thinking About Contemporary Systems. American Anthropologist 107(1):96–107.

Johnson, Gregory A.
1989   Dynamics of Southwestern Prehistory: Far Outside Looking In. *In* Dynamics of Southwest Prehistory. Linda S. Cordell and George J. Gumerman, eds. Pp. 371–89. Washington, DC: Smithsonian Institution Press.

Jones, Lindsay
1995   Twin City Tales: A Hermeneutical Reassessment of Tula and Chichen Itza. Niwot: University Press of Colorado.

Jones, Terry, and Kathryn A. Klar
2005   Diffusionism Reconsidered: Linguistic and Archaeological Evidence for Prehistoric Polynesian Contact with Southern California. American Antiquity 70:457–84.

Josephy, Alvin M., Jr., Joane Nagel, and Troy Johnson, eds.
1999   Red Power: The American Indians' Fight for Freedom. 2nd ed. Lincoln: University of Nebraska Press.

Joyce, Rosemary A.
2002   The Languages of Archaeology: Dialogue, Narrative, and Writing. Malden, MA: Blackwell.
2004   Mesoamerica: A Working Model for Archaeology. *In* Mesoamerican Archaeology: Theory and Practice. Julia A. Hendon and Rosemary A. Joyce, eds. Pp. 1–42. Malden, MA: Blackwell.

Judd, Neil M.
1950   Pioneering in Southwestern Archaeology. *In* For the Dean: Essays in Anthropology in Honor of Byron Cummings on His Eighty-ninth Birthday, September 20, 1950. Erik K. Reed and Dale S. King, eds. Pp. 11–28. Tucson: Hohokam Museums Association; Santa Fe, NM: Southwestern Monuments Association.
1954   The Material Culture of Pueblo Bonito. Smithsonian Miscellaneous Collections, vol. 124. Washington, DC: Smithsonian Institution.
1964   The Architecture of Pueblo Bonito. Smithsonian Miscellaneous Collections, vol. 147, no. 1. Washington, DC: Smithsonian Institution.

Judge, W. James
1979   The Development of a Complex Cultural Ecosystem in the Chaco Basin, New Mexico. *In* Proceedings of the First Conference on Scientific Research in the National Parks, vol 2. R. M. Linn, ed. Pp. 901–06. Transaction and Proceedings Series 4. Washington, DC: National Park Service.
1981   Transect Sampling in Chaco Canyon. *In* Archaeological Surveys of Chaco Canyon, New Mexico. A. C. Hayes, D. M. Brugge, and W. J. Judge, eds. Pp. 107–37. Publications in Archaeology 18A. Washington, DC: National Park Service.
1989   Chaco Canyon–San Juan Basin. *In* Dynamics of Southwest Prehistory. Linda S. Cordell and George J. Gumerman, eds. Pp. 209–61. Washington, DC: Smithsonian Institution Press.
1990   Resource Distribution and the Chaco Phenomenon. *In* The Chimney Rock Archaeological Symposium. E. McKim Malville and Gary Matlock, eds. Pp. 35–36. General Technical Report RM-227. Fort Collins, CO: US Forest Service.

Kabotie, Fred
[1949]1982   Mimbres Designs: An Interpretation. Salisbury, CT: Lime Rock.

Kane, Allen E.
1989   Did the Sheep Look Up? Sociopolitical Complexity in Ninth-Century Dolores Society. *In* The Sociopolitical Structure of Prehistoric Southwestern Societies. Steadman Upham, Kent G. Lightfoot, and Roberta A. Jewett, eds. Pp. 307–62. Boulder, CO: Westview.

Kankainen, Kathy, ed.
1995   Treading in the Past: Sandals of the Anasazi. Salt Lake City: University of Utah Press.

Kantner, John W.
1996   Political Competition among the Chaco Anasazi of the American Southwest. Journal of Anthropological Archaeology 15(1):41–105.
2003   Rethinking Chaco as a System. Kiva 69:207–27.

2004   Ancient Puebloan Southwest. Cambridge: Cambridge University Press.

2006   Religious Behavior in the Post-Chaco Years. *In* Religion in the Prehispanic Southwest. Christine S. VanPool, Todd L. VanPool, and David A. Phillips Jr., eds. Pp. 31–51. Lanham, MD: AltaMira.

Kantner, John W., ed.

2003   The Chaco World. Special issue, Kiva 69(2).

Kantner, John W., and Keith W. Kintigh

2006   The Chaco World. *In* The Archaeology of Chaco Canyon: An Eleventh-Century Pueblo Regional Center. Stephen H. Lekson, ed. Pp. 153–88. Santa Fe, NM: School of American Research Press.

Kantner, John W., and Nancy M. Mahoney, eds.

2000   Great House Communities across the Chacoan Landscape. Anthropological Papers 64. Tucson: University of Arizona Press.

Kearney, Mary Ellen

2000   An Interpretive, Functional Assessment of Bi-wall and Tri-wall Structures, Northern San Juan Area of the Southwestern United States. MA thesis, Department of Anthropology, California State University, Fullerton.

Keen, Benjamin

1971   The Aztec Image in Western Thought. New Brunswick, NJ: Rutgers University Press.

Kehoe, Alice B.

1998   The Land of Prehistory: A Critical History of American Archaeology. New York: Routledge.

1999   The Postclassic along the Northern Frontiers of Mesoamerica. *In* The Casas Grandes World. Curtis F. Schaafsma and Carroll L. Riley, eds. Pp. 201–05. Salt Lake City: University of Utah Press.

2002   America before the European Invasions. London: Longman.

2005   Wind Jewels and Paddling Gods: The Mississippian Southeast in the Postclassic Mesoamerican World. *In* Gulf Coast Archaeology. Nancy M. White, ed. Pp. 260–80. Gainesville: University Press of Florida.

Kelley, J. Charles

1966   Mesoamerica and the Southwestern United States. *In* Handbook of Middle American Indians, vol. 4: Archaeological Frontiers and Connections. Gordon F. Ekholm and Gordon R. Willey, eds. Pp. 95–110. Austin: University of Texas Press.

1986   The Mobile Merchants of Molino. *In* Ripples in the Chichimec Sea. Frances Joan Mathien and Randall H. McGuire, eds. Pp. 81–104. Carbondale: Southern Illinois University Press.

2000   The Aztatlan Mercantile System: Mobile Traders and the Northwestward Expansion of Mesoamerican Civilization. *In* Greater Mesoamerica: The Archaeology of West and Northwest Mexico. Michael S. Foster and Shirley Gorenstein, eds. Pp. 137–54. Salt Lake City: University of Utah Press.

Kelley, J. Charles, and Ellen Abbott Kelley

1974   An Alternative Hypothesis for the Explanation of Anasazi Culture History. *In* Collected Papers in Honor of Florence Hawley Ellis. Theodore R. Frisbie, ed. Pp. 178–223. Papers of the Archaeological Society of New Mexico 2. Santa Fe: Archaeological Society of New Mexico.

Kelley, Jane H.

1984   The Archaeology of the Sierra Blanca Region of Southeastern New Mexico. Anthropological Papers 74. Ann Arbor: Museum of Anthropology, University of Michigan.

Kelley, Jane H., and A. C. MacWilliams

2005   The Development of Archaeology in Northwest Mexico. *In* Southwest Archaeology in the Twentieth Century. Linda S. Cordell and Don D. Fowler, eds. Pp. 81–96. Salt Lake City: University of Utah Press.

Kelley, Jane H., Joe D. Stewart, A. C. MacWilliams, and Karen R. Adams

2004   Recent Research in West-Central Chihuahua. *In* Identity, Feasting, and the Archaeology of the Greater Southwest. Barbara J. Mills, ed. Pp. 295–310. Boulder: University Press of Colorado.

Kelley, Jane H., Joe D. Stewart, A. C. MacWilliams, and Loy C. Neff
1999   A West Central Chihuahuan Perspective on Chihuahuan Culture. *In* The Casas Grandes World. Curtis F. Schaafsma and Carroll L. Riley, eds. Pp. 63–83. Salt Lake City: University of Utah Press.

Kelley, Klara, and Harris Francis
1994   Navajo Sacred Places. Bloomington: Indiana University Press.
2003   Abalone Shell Buffalo People: Navajo Narrated Routes and Pre-Columbian Archaeological Sites. New Mexico Historical Review 78(1):29–58.

Kelly, I.
1938   Excavations at Culiacán, Sinaloa. Ibero-Americana 25. Berkeley: University of California Press.

Kelly, Isabel T.
1978   The Hodges Ruin: A Hohokam Community in the Tucson Basin. Anthropological Papers 30. Tucson: University of Arizona Press.

Kelly, Roger E.
1963   The Socio-Religious Roles of Ball Courts and Great Kivas in the Prehistoric Southwest. MA thesis, Department of Anthropology, University of Arizona, Tucson.

Kennedy, Roger G.
1994   Hidden Cities: The Discovery and Loss of Ancient North American Civilization. New York: Free Press.

Kent, Kate Peck
1983   Prehistoric Textiles of the Southwest. Albuquerque: University of New Mexico Press.

Kidder, Alfred Vincent
[1924]1962   An Introduction to the Study of Southwestern Archaeology. New Haven, CT: Yale University Press.
1927   Southwestern Archaeological Conference. Science 68:489–91.

Kidder, Alfred Vincent, Harriet S. Cosgrove, and Cornelius B. Cosgrove
1949   The Pendleton Ruin, Hidalgo County, New Mexico. Contributions to American Anthropology and History 50. Publication 585. Washington, DC: Carnegie Institute.

Kidder, Alfred Vincent, and Samuel J. Guernsey
1919   Archaeological Explorations in Northeastern Arizona. Bureau of American Ethnology Bulletin 65. Washington, DC: Government Printing Office.

King, Adam, and Jennifer A. Freer
1995   The Mississippian Southeast: A World-Systems Perspective. *In* Native American Interactions: Multiscalar Analyses and Interpretations in the Eastern Woodlands. Michael S. Nassaney and Kenneth E. Sassaman, eds. Pp. 266–88. Knoxville: University of Tennessee Press.

King, Thomas F.
2004   Cultural Resource Laws and Practice. Walnut Creek, CA: AltaMira.

Kintigh, Keith W.
1985   Settlement, Subsistence and Society in Late Zuni Prehistory. Anthropological Papers 44. Tucson: University of Arizona Press.
1996   The Cibola Region in the Post-Chaco Era. *In* The Prehistoric Pueblo World, A.D. 1150–1350. Michael A. Adler, ed. Pp. 131–45. Tucson: University of Arizona Press.
2000   Leadership Strategies in Protohistoric Zuni Towns. *In* Alternative Leadership Strategies in the Prehispanic Southwest. Barbara J. Mills, ed. Pp. 95–116. Tucson: University of Arizona Press.

Kintigh, Keith W., Donna M. Glowacki, and Deborah L. Huntley
2004   Long-term Settlement History and the Emergence of Towns in the Zuni Area. American Antiquity 69:432–56.

Knapp, A. Bernard
1992   Archaeology and Annales: Time, Space, and Change. *In* Archaeology, Annales, and Ethnohistory. A. Bernard Knapp, ed. Pp. 1–22. Cambridge: Cambridge University Press.

Knapp, A. Bernard, ed.
1992   Archaeology, Annales, and Ethnohistory. Cambridge: Cambridge University Press.

Knight, Vernon James, Jr., James A. Brown, and G. E. Lankford
2001   On the Subject Matter of Southeastern Ceremonial Complex Art. Southeastern Archaeology 20:129–41.

Knight, Vernon James, Jr., and Vincas P. Steponaitis, eds.
1998   Archaeology of the Moundville Chiefdom. Washington, DC: Smithsonian Institution Press.

Kohl, Philip L.
2007   The Making of Bronze Age Eurasia. Cambridge: Cambridge University Press.

Kohler, Timothy A.
1993   News from the Northern American Southwest: Prehistory on the Edge of Chaos. Journal of Archaeological Research 1(4):267–321.

Kohler, Timothy A., ed.
2004   Archaeology of Bandelier National Monument: Village Formation on the Pajarito Plateau, New Mexico. Albuquerque: University of New Mexico Press.

Kohler, Timothy A., George J. Gumerman, and Robert G. Reynolds
2005   Simulating Ancient Societies: Computer Modeling Is Helping Unravel the Archaeological Mysteries of the American Southwest. Scientific American 293(1):77–84.

Kohler, Timothy A., C. David Johnson, Mark Varien, Scott Ortman, Robert Reynolds, Zian Kobti, Jason Cowan, Kenneth Kolm, Schaun Smith, and Lorene Yap
2007   Settlement Ecodynamics in the Prehispanic Central Mesa Verde Region. In Model-Based Archaeology of Socionatural Systems. Timothy A. Kohler and Sander E. van der Leeuw, eds. Pp. 61–104. Santa Fe, NM: School for Advanced Research Press.

Kohler, Timothy A., Matthew W. Van Pelt, and Lorene Y. L. Yap
2000   Reciprocity and Its Limits: Considerations for a Study of the Prehispanic Pueblo World. In Alternative Leadership Strategies in the Prehispanic Southwest. Barbara J. Mills, ed. Pp. 180–206. Tucson: University of Arizona Press.

Kosse, Krisztina
1990   Group Size and Social Complexity: Thresholds in the Long-term Memory. Journal of Anthropological Archaeology 9:275–303.
1994   The Evolution of Large, Complex Groups: A Hypothesis. Journal of Anthropological Archaeology 13:35–50.
1996   Middle-Range Societies from a Scalar Perspective. In Interpreting Southwestern Diversity. Paul R. Fish and J. Jefferson Reid, eds. Pp. 87–96. Anthropological Research Papers 48. Tempe: Arizona State University.

Kowalewski, Stephen A.
1996   Clout, Corn, Copper, Core-Periphery, Culture Area. In Pre-Columbian World Systems. Peter N. Peregrine and Gary M. Feinman, eds. Pp. 27–37. Madison, WI: Prehistory Press.
2004   The New Past: From Region to Macroregion. Social Evolution and History 3(1):81–105.

Kozuch, Laura
2002   Olivella Beads from Spiro and the Plains. American Antiquity 67:697–709.

Kristiansen, Kristian, and Thomas Larsson
2005   The Rise of Bronze Age Society: Travels, Transmissions and Transformations. Cambridge: Cambridge University Press.

Kristiansen, Kristian, and Michael Rowlands, eds.
1998   Social Transformations in Archaeology. London: Routledge.

Kroeber, Alfred L.
1916   Zuni Potsherds. Anthropological Papers, vol. 18, pt. 1. New York: American Museum of Natural History.
1939   Cultural and Natural Areas of Native North America. Berkeley: University of California Press.

Kubler, George
1962   The Shape of Time: Remarks on the History of Things. New Haven, CT: Yale University Press.
1975   History—or Anthropology—of Art? Critical Inquiry 1(4):757–67.
1991   Esthetic Recognition of Ancient Amerindian Art. New Haven, CT: Yale University Press.

Kuckelman, Kristin A.

2002   Thirteenth-Century Warfare in the Central Mesa Verde Region. *In* Seeking the Center Place: Archaeology and Ancient Communities in the Mesa Verde Region. Mark D. Varien and Richard H. Wilshusen, eds. Pp. 233–53. Salt Lake City: University of Utah Press.

2003   The Archaeology of Yellow Jacket Pueblo. Electronic document, http://www.crowcanyon. org/publications/yellow_jacket_pueblo.asp., accessed June 2007.

Kuper, Adam

2005   The Reinvention of Primitive Society. 2nd ed. London: Routledge.

Kuwanwisiwma, Leigh J.

2004   Yuplo:yvi: The Hopi Story of Chaco Canyon. *In* In Search of Chaco: New Approaches to an Archaeological Enigma. David Grant Noble, ed. Pp. 41–47. Santa Fe, NM: School of American Research Press.

Kwiatowski, Scott M.

2003   Evidence for Subsistence Problems. *In* Centuries of Decline during the Hohokam Classic Period at Pueblo Grande. David R. Abbott, ed. Pp. 48–69. Tucson: University of Arizona Press.

LaBianca, Øystein S., and Sandra Arnold Scham, eds.

2006   Connectivity in Antiquity: Globalization as a Long-term Historical Process. London: Equinox.

Lakatos, Steven A.

2007   Cultural Continuity and the Development of Integrative Architecture in the Northern Rio Grande Valley of New Mexico, A.D. 600–1200. Kiva 73(1):33–68.

Lange, Charles H., and Carroll L. Riley

1996   Bandelier: The Life and Adventures of Adolf Bandelier. Salt Lake City: University of Utah Press.

Lange, Charles H., and Carroll L. Riley, eds.

1966   The Southwestern Journals of Adolph F. Bandelier, 1880–1882. Albuquerque: University of New Mexico Press.

1970   The Southwestern Journals of Adolph F. Bandelier, 1883–1884. Albuquerque: University of New Mexico Press.

Lange, Charles H., Carroll L. Riley, and Elizabeth M. Lange, eds.

1975   The Southwestern Journals of Adolph F. Bandelier, 1885–1888. Albuquerque: University of New Mexico Press.

1984   The Southwestern Journals of Adolph F. Bandelier, 1889–1892. Albuquerque: University of New Mexico Press.

Lange, Fred, Nancy Mahaney, Joe Ben Wheat, and Mark L. Chenault

1986   Yellow Jacket: A Four Corners Anasazi Ceremonial Center. Boulder, CO: Johnson Books.

Lange, Richard C.

1992   Pots, People, Politics, and Precipitation: Just Who or What Are the Salado Anyway? *In* Proceedings of the Second Salado Conference. Richard C. Lange and Stephen Germick, eds. Pp. 325–33. Occasional Paper. Phoenix: Arizona Archaeological Society.

Lange, Richard C., and Stephen Germick, eds.

1992   Proceedings of the Second Salado Conference. Occasional Paper. Phoenix: Arizona Archaeological Society.

Lansing, J. Stephen

2006   Perfect Order: Recognizing Complexity in Bali. Princeton, NJ: Princeton University Press.

Lathrap, Donald W.

1956   An Archaeological Classification of Culture Contact Situations. *In* Seminars in Archaeology: 1955. Robert Wachope, ed. Pp. 1–30. Memoirs 11. Salt Lake City, UT: Society for American Archaeology.

Laumbach, Karl W., and James L. Wakeman

1999   Rebuilding an Ancient Pueblo: The Victorio Site in Regional Perspective. *In* Sixty Years of Mogollon Archaeology. Stephanie M. Whittlesey, ed. Pp. 183–89. Tucson, AZ: SRI Press.

Laumbach, Toni S.

2006   Glaze Wares and Regional Social Relationships on the Rio Alamosa. *In* The Social Life of Pots: Glaze Wares and Cultural Dynamics in the Southwest, AD 1250–1680. Judith A. Habicht-Mauche, Suzanne L. Eckert, and Deborah L. Huntley, eds. Pp. 142–62. Tucson: University of Arizona Press.

Lazcano Sahagun, Carlos

1998   Explorando un Mundo Olvidado: Sitios Perdidos de la Cultura Paquimé. Mexico City: Editorial México Desconocido.

LeBlanc, Steven A.

1980   The Post Mogollon Periods in Southwestern New Mexico: The Animas/Black Mountain Phase and the Salado Period. *In* An Archaeological Synthesis of South-central and Southwestern New Mexico. Steven A. LeBlanc and Michael E. Whalen, eds. Pp. 271–316. MS on file, New Mexico State Historic Preservation Division, Santa Fe.

1983   The Mimbres People. London: Thames and Hudson.

1986a   Aspects of Southwestern Prehistory: A.D. 900–1400. *In* Ripples in the Chichimec Sea. Frances Joan Mathien and Randall H. McGuire, eds. Pp. 81–104. Carbondale: Southern Illinois University Press.

1986b   Development of Archaeological Thought on the Mimbres Mogollon. *In* Emil W. Haury's Prehistory of the American Southwest. J. Jefferson Reid and David E. Doyel, eds. Pp. 297–304. Tucson: University of Arizona Press.

1989a   Cultural Dynamics in the Southern Mogollon Area. *In* Dynamics of Southwest Prehistory. Linda S. Cordell and George J. Gumerman, eds. Pp. 179–207. Washington, DC: Smithsonian Institution Press.

1989b   Cibola. *In* Dynamics of Southwest Prehistory. Linda S. Cordell and George J. Gumerman, eds. Pp. 337–69. Washington, DC: Smithsonian Institution Press.

1998   Settlement Consequences of Warfare during the Late Pueblo III and Pueblo IV Periods. *In* Migration and Reorganization. Katherine A. Spielmann, ed. Pp. 115–35. Anthropological Research Papers 51. Tempe: Arizona State University.

1999   Prehistoric Warfare in the American Southwest. Salt Lake City: University of Utah Press.

2000   Regional Interaction and Warfare in the Late Prehistoric Southwest. *In* The Archaeology of Regional Interaction. Michelle Hegmon, ed. Pp. 41–70. Boulder: University Press of Colorado.

2002   Conflict and Language Dispersal: Issues and a New World Example. *In* Examining the Farming/Language Dispersal Hypothesis. Peter Bellwood and Colin Renfrew, eds. Pp. 357–65. Cambridge: McDonald Institute for Archaeological Research.

LeBlanc, Steven A., Lori S. Cobb Kreisman, Brian M. Kemp, Francis E. Smiley, Shawn W. Carlyle, Anna N. Dhody, and Thomas Benjamin

2007   Quids and Aprons: Ancient DNA from Artifacts from the American Southwest. Journal of Field Archaeology 32:161–75.

Lekson, Stephen H.

1981   Cognitive Frameworks and Chacoan Architecture. New Mexico Journal of Science 21(1):27-36.

1982   Architecture and Settlement Plan in the Redrock Valley of the Gila River, Southwestern New Mexico. *In* Mogollon Archaeology. Patrick H. Beckett, ed. Pp. 61–73. Ramona, CA: Acoma Books.

1983   Chacoan Architecture in Continental Context. *In* Proceedings of the Anasazi Symposium 1981. Jack E. Smith, ed. Pp. 183–94. Mesa Verde, CO: Mesa Verde Museum Association.

1984   Great Pueblo Architecture of Chaco Canyon. Publications in Archaeology 18B. Albuquerque, NM: National Park Service.

1986   Mimbres Riverine Adaptations. *In* Mogollon Variability. C. Benson and S. Upham, eds. Pp. 181–90. Occasional Paper 15. Las Cruces: New Mexico State University Museum.

1988   The Idea of the Kiva in Anasazi Archaeology. Kiva 53:213–34.

1989   An Archaeological Reconnaissance of the Rio Grande Valley in Sierra County, New Mexico. Artifact 27(2). Special issue.

1990a   Mimbres Archaeology of the Upper Gila, New Mexico. Anthropological Papers 30. Tucson: University of Arizona Press.

1990b	Sedentism and Aggregation in Anasazi Archaeology. *In* Perspectives on Southwestern Prehistory. Paul Minnis and Charles Redman, eds. Pp. 333–40. Boulder, CO: Westview.
1990c	Cross-cultural Perspectives on the Community. *In* On Vernacular Architecture: Paradigms of Environmental Response. Mete Turan, ed. Pp. 122–145. Aldershot, UK: Avebury.
1991	Settlement Patterns and the Chaco Region. *In* Chaco and Hohokam. Patricia L. Crown and W. James Judge, eds. Pp. 31–55. Santa Fe, NM: School of American Research Press.
1993a	Chaco, Hohokam and Mimbres: The Southwest in the 11th and 12th Centuries. Expedition 35(1):44–52.
1993b	The Surface Archaeology of Southwestern New Mexico. Artifact 30(3). Special issue.
1995	Introduction. *In* Migration and the Movement of Southwestern Peoples. Catherine M. Cameron, ed. Special issue, Journal of Anthropological Archaeology 14(2):99–103.
1996a	Landscape with Ruins: Archaeological Approaches to Built and Unbuilt Environments. Current Anthropology 37(5):886–92.
1996b	Southwestern New Mexico and Southeastern Arizona, A.D. 900 to 1300. *In* The Prehistoric Pueblo World, A.D. 1150–1350. Michael A. Adler, ed. Pp. 170–76. Tucson: University of Arizona Press.
1997	Points, Knives, and Drills of Chaco Canyon. *In* Ceramics, Lithics, and Ornaments of Chaco Canyon: Analysis of Artifacts from the Chaco Project, 1971–1978, vol. 3: Lithics and Ornaments. F. J. Mathien, ed. Pp. 659–99. Reports of the Chaco Center 11. Santa Fe, NM: Division of Cultural Research, National Park Service.
1999a	Unit Pueblos and the Mimbres Problem. *In* La Frontera: Essays in Honor of Patrick H. Beckett. Meliha Duran and David Kirkpatrick, eds. Pp. 105–25. Archaeological Society of New Mexico 25. Albuquerque: Archaeological Society of New Mexico.
1999b	The Chaco Meridian: Centers of Political Power in the Ancient Southwest. Walnut Creek, CA: AltaMira.
1999c	Was Casas a Pueblo? *In* The Casas Grandes World. Curtis F. Schaafsma and Carroll L. Riley, eds. Pp. 84–92. Salt Lake City: University of Utah Press.
2000	Salado in Chihuahua. *In* Salado. Jeffrey S. Dean, ed. Pp. 275–94. Albuquerque: University of New Mexico Press.
2002a	Salado Archaeology of the Upper Gila, New Mexico. Anthropological Papers 67. Tucson: University of Arizona Press.
2002b	War in the Southwest, War in the World. American Antiquity 67:607–24.
2005	Complexity. *In* Southwest Archaeology in the Twentieth Century. Linda S. Cordell and Don D. Fowler, eds. Pp. 157–73. Salt Lake City: University of Utah Press.
2006a	Chaco Matters. *In* The Archaeology of Chaco Canyon: An Eleventh-Century Pueblo Regional Center. Stephen H. Lekson, ed. Pp. 3–44. Santa Fe, NM: School of American Research Press.
2006b	The Archaeology of the Mimbres Region, Southwestern New Mexico, USA British Archaeological Reports International Series 1466. Oxford: Archaeopress.
2006c	Lords of the Great House: Pueblo Bonito as a Palace. *In* Palaces and Power in the Americas, from Peru to the Northwest Coast. Jessica Joyce Christie and Patricia Joan Sarro, eds. Pp. 99–114. Austin: University of Texas Press.

Lekson, Stephen H., ed.

2006	The Archaeology of Chaco Canyon: An Eleventh-Century Pueblo Regional Center. Santa Fe, NM: School of American Research Press.
2007	The Architecture of Chaco Canyon, New Mexico. Salt Lake City: University of Utah Press.

Lekson, Stephen H., Michael Bletzer, and A. C. MacWilliams

2004	Pueblo IV in the Chihuahuan Desert. *In* The Protohistoric Pueblo World, A.D. 1275–1600. E. Charles Adams and Andrew I. Duff, eds. Pp. 53–61. Tucson: University of Arizona Press.

Lekson, Stephen H., and Catherine M. Cameron

1995	The Abandonment of Chaco Canyon, the Mesa Verde Migrations, and the Reorganization of the Pueblo World. Journal of Anthropological Archaeology 14(2):184–202.

Lekson, Stephen H., Curtis P. Nepstad-Thornberry, Brian E. Yunker, David P. Cain, Toni Sudar-Laumbach, and Karl W. Laumbach

2002	Migrations in the Southwest: Pinnacle Ruin, Southwestern New Mexico. Kiva 68:73–101.

Lekson, Stephen H., and Peter N. Peregrine

2004	A Continental Perspective for North American Archaeology. SAA Archaeological Record, vol. 4, no. 1:15–19.

León-Portilla, Miguel

2001   Aztlan: From Myth to Reality. *In* The Road to Aztlan: Art from a Mythic Homeland. Virginia Fields and Victor Zamudio-Taylor, eds. Pp. 20–33. Los Angeles: Los Angeles County Museum of Art.

Lepper, Bradley T.

2006   The Great Hopewell Road and the Role of the Pilgrimage in the Hopewell Interaction Sphere. *In* Re-creating Hopewell. Douglas K. Charles and Jane E. Buikstra, eds. Pp. 122–33. Gainesville: University Press of Florida.

Levathes, Louise

1994   When China Ruled the Seas: The Treasure Fleet of the Dragon Throne, 1405–1433. Oxford: Oxford University Press.

Lewis, Martin W., and Karen E. Wigen

1997   The Myth of Continents: A Critique of Metageography. Berkeley: University of California Press.

Lieberman, Victor

2003   Strange Parallels: Southeast Asia in Global Context, c. 800–1830, vol. 1: Integration on the Mainland. Cambridge: Cambridge University Press.

Lightfoot, Kent G.

1979   Food Redistribution among Prehistoric Pueblo Groups. Kiva 44:319–30.

1984   Prehistoric Political Dynamics: A Case Study from the American Southwest. De Kalb, IL: NIU Press.

Lightfoot, Kent G., and Gary M. Feinman

1982   Social Differentiation and Leadership Development in Early Pithouse Villages in the Mogollon Region of the American Southwest. American Antiquity 47:64–86.

Lincoln, Gail Bleakney

2007   Exploring Migration: Magdalena Black-on-white at Gallinas Spring Ruin and Pinnacle Ruin. MA thesis, Department of Anthropology, University of Colorado, Boulder.

Lindauer, Owen

1992   Architectural Engineering and Variation among Salado Platform Mounds. *In* Proceedings of the Second Salado Conference. Richard C. Lange and Stephen Germick, eds. Pp. 50–56. Occasional Paper. Phoenix: Arizona Archaeological Society.

Lindauer, Owen, and John H. Blitz

1997   Higher Ground: The Archaeology of North American Platform Mounds. Journal of Archaeological Research 5(2):169–207.

Lindsay, Alexander

1987   Anasazi Population Movements to Southeastern Arizona. American Archaeologist 6:190–98.

Lipe, William D.

1999   Basketmaker II (1000 B.C.–A.D. 500). *In* Colorado Prehistory: A Context for the Southern Colorado River Basin. William D. Lipe, Mark D. Varien, and Richard H. Wilshusen, eds. Pp. 132–65. Denver: Colorado Council of Professional Archaeologists.

2006   Notes from the North. *In* The Archaeology of Chaco Canyon: An Eleventh-Century Pueblo Regional Center. Stephen H. Lekson, ed. Pp. 261–313. Santa Fe, NM: School of American Research Press.

Lipe, William D., and Michelle Hegmon, eds.

1989   The Architecture of Social Integration in Prehistoric Pueblos. Occasional Paper 1. Cortez, CO: Crow Canyon Archaeological Center.

Lipe, William D., J. N. Morris, and Timothy A. Kohler

1988   Dolores Archaeological Projects: Anasazi Communities at Dolores: Grass Mesa Village. Denver: US Department of the Interior, Bureau of Reclamation.

Lipe, William D., and Bonnie L. Pitblado

1999   Paleoindian and Archaic Periods. *In* Colorado Prehistory: A Context for the Southern Colorado River Basin. William D. Lipe, Mark D. Varien, and Richard H. Wilshusen, eds. Pp. 95–131. Denver: Colorado Council of Professional Archaeologists.

Lipe, William D., and Mark D. Varien

1999a   Pueblo II (A.D. 900–1150). *In* Colorado Prehistory: A Context for the Southern Colorado River Basin. William D. Lipe, Mark D. Varien, and Richard H. Wilshusen, eds. Pp. 242–89. Denver: Colorado Council of Professional Archaeologists.

1999b   Pueblo III (A.D. 1150–1300). *In* Colorado Prehistory: A Context for the Southern Colorado River Basin. William D. Lipe, Mark D. Varien, and Richard H. Wilshusen, eds. Pp. 290–352. Denver: Colorado Council of Professional Archaeologists.

Lipe, William D., Mark D. Varien, and Richard H. Wilshusen, eds.

1999   Colorado Prehistory: A Context for the Southern Colorado River Basin. Denver: Colorado Council of Professional Archaeologists.

Lister, Robert H.

1946   Survey of the Archaeological Remains in Northwest Chihuahua. Southwesterrn Journal of Anthropology 2(4):433–53.

1964   Contributions to Mesa Verde Archaeology I: Site 499, Mesa Verde National Park. University of Colorado Studies, Series in Anthropology 9. Boulder: University of Colorado Press.

Lister, Florence C. and Robert H. Lister

1966   Chihuahua: Storehouse of Storms. Albuquerque, NM: University of New Mexico Press.

Loendorf, Chris

2001   Salado Burial Practices. *In* Ancient Burial Practices in the American Southwest: Archaeology, Physical Anthropology, and Native American Perspectives. Douglas R. Mitchell and Judy L. Brunson-Hadley, eds. Pp. 123–48. Albuquerque: University of New Mexico Press.

Longacre, William A.

1970   Archaeology as Anthropology: A Case Study. Anthropological Papers 17. Tucson: University of Arizona Press.

Longacre, William A., ed.

1970   Reconstructing Prehistoric Pueblo Societies. Albuquerque: University of New Mexico Press.

Love, Tina K.

2001   Hohokam Figurines from the Grewe Site. *In* The Grewe Archaeological Research Project, vol. 2: Material Culture, pt. 1: Ceramic Studies. David R. Abbott, ed. Pp. 161–76. Anthropological Papers 99-1. Flagstaff, AZ: Northland Research.

Lowenthal, David

1985   The Past Is a Foreign Country. Cambridge: Cambridge University Press.

Lumholtz, Carl

[1902]1973 Unknown Mexico; a record of five years' exploration among the tribes of the western Sierra Madre; in the tierra caliente of Tepic and Jalisco; and among the Tarascos of Michoacan. New York: C. Scribner's Sons.

Lummis, Charles F.

1925   Mesa, Cañon and Pueblo. New York: The Century Co.

Lyneis, Margaret M.

1996   Pueblo II–Pueblo III Change in Southwestern Utah, the Arizona Strip, and Southern Nevada. *In* The Prehistoric Pueblo World, A.D. 1150–1350. Michael A. Adler, ed. Pp. 11–28. Tucson: University of Arizona Press.

Lyons, Patrick D.

2003   Ancestral Hopi Migrations. Anthropological Papers 68. Tucson: University of Arizona Press.

Mabry, Jonathan B.

1998   Conclusions. *In* Archaeological Investigations of Early Village Sites in the Middle Santa Cruz Valley: Analysis and Synthesis, Part II. Jonathan B. Mabry, ed. Pp. 757–91. Anthropological Papers 19. Tucson, AZ: Center for Desert Archaeology.

2000a   The Red Mountain Phase and the Origins of Hohokam Villages. *In* The Hohokam Village Revisited. David E. Doyel, Suzanne K. Fish, and Paul R. Fish, eds. Pp. 37–63. Fort Collins, CO: Southwestern and Rocky Mountain Division of the American Association for the Advancement of Science.

2000b   Wittfogel Was Half Right: The Ethnology of Consensual Hierarchies in Irrigation Management. *In* Hierarchies in Action: Cui Bono? Michael W. Diehl, ed. Pp. 284–94.

Occasional Paper 27. Carbondale, IL: Center for Archaeological Investigations.

2002   The Role of Irrigation in the Transition to Agriculture and Sedentism in the Southwest. *In* Traditions, Transitions, and Technologies: Themes in Southwestern Archaeology. Sarah H. Schlanger, ed. Pp. 178–99. Boulder: University Press of Colorado.

2005a   Diversity in Early Southwestern Farming Systems and Optimization Models of Transitions to Agriculture. *In* Subsistence and Resource Use Strategies of Early Agricultural Communities in Southern Arizona. Michael W. Diehl, ed. Pp. 113–52. Anthropological Papers 34. Tucson, AZ: Center for Desert Archaeology.

2005b   Changing Knowledge and Ideas about the First Farmers in Southeastern Arizona. *In* The Late Archaic across the Borderlands: From Foraging to Farming. Bradley J. Vierra, ed. Pp. 41–83. Austin: University of Texas Press.

Mabry, Jonathan B., ed.
1998   Archaeological Investigations of Early Village Sites in the Middle Santa Cruz Valley: Analysis and Synthesis, Part II. Anthropological Papers 19. Tucson, AZ: Center for Desert Archaeology.

MacNeish, Richard S.
2003   Early Inhabitants of the Americas: Pendejo Cave and Beyond. *In* Pendejo Cave. Richard S. MacNeish and Jane G. Libby, eds. Pp. 173–89. Albuquerque: University of New Mexico Press.

MacNeish, Richard S., and Jane G. Libby
2003   Pendejo Cave. Albuquerque: University of New Mexico Press.

MacWilliams, A. C., and Jane H. Kelley
2004   A Ceramic Boundary in Central Chihuahua. *In* Surveying the Archaeology of Northwest Mexico. Gillian E. Newell and Emiliano Gallaga, eds. Pp. 247–64. Salt Lake City: University of Utah Press.

Madsen, David B.
1989   Exploring the Fremont. Salt Lake City: Utah Museum of Natural History.

Mainfort, Robert C., Jr., and Lynne P. Sullivan, eds.
1998   Ancient Earthen Enclosures of the Eastern Woodlands. Gainesville: University Press of Florida.

Malotki, Ekkehart, ed.
1993   Hopi Ruin Legends: Kiqötutuwutsi. Lincoln: University of Nebraska Press.

Malville, J. McKim
2007   Rethinking the Astronomy of the Sun Dagger. Paper presented at the 80th Pecos Conference, Pecos, NM, August 10–11.

Malville, J. McKim, ed.
2004   Chimney Rock: The Ultimate Outlier. Lanham, MD: Lexington Books.

Malville, Nancy J.
2001   Long-Distance Transport of Bulk Goods in the Pre-Hispanic American Southwest. Journal of Anthropological Archaeology 20:230–43.

Mann, Charles C.
2005   1491: New Revelations of the Americas before Columbus. New York: Alfred A. Knopf.

Manning, Patrick
2003   Navigating World History: Historians Create a Global Past. New York: Palgrave MacMillan.

Manzanilla, Linda
1997   Early Urban Societies. *In* Emergence and Change in Early Urban Societies. Linda Manzanilla, ed. Pp. 3–39. New York: Plenum.

Marcus, Joyce
1989   From Centralized Systems to City-States: Possible Models for the Epiclassic. *In* Mesoamerica after the Decline of Teotihuacan, A.D. 700–900. Richard A. Diehl and Janet Catherine Berlo, eds. Pp. 201–08. Washington, DC: Dumbarton Oaks Research Library and Collection.

Marcus, Joyce, and Gary M. Feinman
1998   Introduction. *In* Archaic States. Gary M. Feinman and Joyce Marcus, eds. Pp. 3–13. Santa Fe, NM: School of American Research Press.

Marek, Marianne, David H. Greenwald, and Richard V. N. Ahlstrom, eds.
1993   The Coronado Project: Anasazi Settlement Overlooking the Puerco Valley, Arizona, vol. 1.
            SWCA Anthropological Research Paper 3. Flagstaff, AZ: SWCA.

Marmaduke, William S., and Richard J. Marynec, eds.
1993   Shelltown and the Hind Site. Flagstaff, AZ: Northland Research.

Marsella, Anthony J., and Erin Ring
2003   Human Migration and Immigration: An Overview. *In* Migration. Lenore Loeb Adler and Uwe
            P. Gielen, eds. Pp. 3–22. Westport, CT: Praeger.

Marshall, John T.
2001   Ballcourt. *In* The Grewe Archaeological Research Project, vol. 1: Project Background and
            Feature Descriptions. Douglas B. Craig, ed. Pp. 109–24. Anthropological Papers 99-1.
            Flagstaff, AZ: Northland Research.

Marshall, Michael P.
1997   The Chacoan Roads: A Cosmological Interpretation. *In* Anasazi Architecture and American
            Design. Baker H. Morrow and V. B. Price, eds. Pp. 62–74. Albuquerque: University of New
            Mexico Press.

Marshall, Michael P., John R. Stein, Richard W. Loose, and Judith E. Novotny
1979   Anasazi Communities of the San Juan Basin. Santa Fe, NM: State Historic Preservation Bureau.

Martin, Debra L., and David W. Frayer
1997   Troubled Times: Violence and Warfare in the Past. War and Society, vol. 3. Amsterdam:
            Gordon and Breach.

Martin, Paul S.
1936   Lowry Ruin in Southwestern Colorado. Anthropological Series, vol. 23, no. 1. Chicago: Field
            Museum of Natural History.
1959   Digging into History. Popular Series, Anthropology 38. Chicago: Chicago Natural History
            Museum.
1971   The Revolution in Archaeology. American Antiquity 36:1–8.

Martin, Paul S., and Fred Plog
1973   The Archaeology of Arizona: A Study of the Southwest Region. Garden City, NJ:
            Doubleday/Natural History Press.

Martin, Simon
2006   On Pre-Columbian Narrative: Representations Across the Word-Image Divide. *In* A Pre-
            Columbian World. Jeffrey Quilter and Mary Miller, eds. Pp. 55–105. Washington, DC:
            Dumbarton Oaks.

Mason, Ronald J.
2006   Inconstant Companions: Archaeology and North American Oral Traditions. Tuscaloosa:
            University of Alabama Press.

Masse, W. Bruce
1981   Prehistoric Irrigation Systems in the Salt River Valley. Science 214:408–15.
1991   The Quest for Subsistence Sufficiency and Civilization in the Sonoran Desert. *In* Chaco and
            Hohokam: Prehistoric Regional Systems in the American Southwest. Patricia L. Crown and
            W. James Judge, eds. Pp. 195–223. Santa Fe, NM: School of American Research Press.

Masse, W. Bruce, and Fred Espenak
2006   Sky as Environment: Solar Eclipses and Hohokam Cultural Change. *In* Environmental
            Change and Human Adaptation in the American Southwest. David E. Doyel and Jeffrey S.
            Dean, eds. Pp. 228–80. Salt Lake City: University of Utah Press.

Masse, W. Bruce, and Robert Soklow
2005   Black Suns and Dark Times: Cultural Responses to Solar Eclipses in the Ancient Puebloan
            Southwest. *In* Current Studies in Archaeoastronomy. J. W. Fountain and R. M. Sinclair, eds.
            Pp. 47–67. Durham, NC: Carolina Academic Press.

Mathews, Washington
1889   Noqoilpi, the Gambler: A Navajo Myth. Journal of American Folklore 2(5):1–19.
1897   Navajo Legends. Boston: American Folklore Society.

Mathien, Frances Joan

1997   Ornaments of the Chaco Anasazi. *In* Ceramics, Lithics and Ornaments of Chaco Canyon, vol. 3: Lithics and Ornaments. Frances Joan Mathien, ed. Pp. 1119–1219. Publications in Archaeology 18G. Santa Fe, NM: National Park Service.

2005   Culture and Ecology of Chaco Canyon and the San Juan Basin. Studies in Archaeology 18H. Santa Fe, NM: National Park Service.

Mathien, Frances Joan, and Randall H. McGuire, eds.

1986   Ripples in the Chichimec Sea: New Considerations of Southwestern–Mesoamerican Interactions. Carbondale: Southern Illinois Press.

Matos Moctezuma, Eduardo

1988   The Great Temple of the Aztecs. London: Thames and Hudson.

Matson, R. G.

1991   The Origins of Southwestern Agriculture. Tucson: University of Arizona Press.

2002   The Spread of Maize Agriculture into the U.S. Southwest. *In* Examining the Farming/Language Dispersal Hypothesis. Peter Bellwood and Colin Renfrew, eds. Pp. 341–56. Oxford: McDonald Institute Monographs. McDonald Institute for Archaeological Research.

2005   Many Perspectives but a Constant Pattern. *In* The Late Archaic across the Borderlands. Bradley J. Vierra, ed. Pp. 279–99. Austin: University of Texas Press.

2007   The Archaic Origins of Zuni: Preliminary Explorations. *In* Zuni Origins: Toward a New Synthesis of Southwestern Archaeology. David A. Gregory and David R. Wilcox, eds. Pp. 97–117. Tucson: University of Arizona Press.

Matson, R. G., and Karen M. Dohm

1994   Introduction. Special issue. Kiva 60(2):159–63.

Matson, R. G., and Karen M. Dohm, eds.

1994   Anasazi Origins: Recent Research on the Basketmaker II. Kiva 60(2).

McCafferty, Geoffrey G.

2000   Tollan Cholollan and the Legacy of Legitimacy during the Classic–Postclassic Transition. *In* Mesoamerica's Classic Heritage: From Teotihuacan to the Aztecs. David Carrasco, Lindsay Jones, and Scott Sessions, eds. Pp. 341–67. Boulder: University Press of Colorado.

McCluney, Eugene B.

1962   Clanton Draw and Box Canyon. Research Monograph 26. Santa Fe, NM: School of American Research Press.

1968   A Mimbres Shrine at the West Baker Site. Archaeology 21(3):196–205.

McDonald, Terrence J., ed.

1996   The Historic Turn in the Human Sciences. Ann Arbor: University of Michigan Press.

McFeely, Eliza

2001   Zuni and the American Imagination. New York: Hill and Wang.

McGregor, John C.

1941   Southwestern Archaeology. New York: J. Wiley and Sons; London: Chapman and Hall.

1965   Southwestern Archaeology. 2nd ed. Urbana: University of Illinois Press.

McGuire, Randall H.

1980   The Mesoamerican Connection in the Southwest. Kiva 46:3–38.

1989   The Greater Southwest as a Periphery of Mesoamerica. *In* Centre and Periphery. T. C. Champion, ed. Pp. 40–61. London: Allen and Unwin.

1991   On the Outside Looking In: The Concept of Periphery in Hohokam Archaeology. *In* Exploring the Hohokam: Prehistoric Desert Peoples of the Southwest. George J. Gumerman, ed. Pp. 347–82. Albuquerque: University of New Mexico Press.

1992   Death, Society, and Ideology in a Hohokam Community. Boulder, CO: Westview.

1993   The Structure and Organization of Hohokam Exchange. *In* The American Southwest and Mesoamerica: Systems of Prehistoric Exchange. Jonathan E. Ericson and Timothy G. Baugh, eds. Pp. 95–119. New York: Plenum.

2001   Ideologies of Death and Power in the Hohokam Community of La Ciudad. *In* Ancient Burial Practices in the American Southwest: Archaeology, Physical Anthropology, and Native American Perspectives. Douglas R. Mitchell and Judy L. Brunson-Hadley, eds. Pp. 27–44. Albuquerque: University of New Mexico Press.

2002   The Meaning and Limits of the Southwest/Northwest: A Perspective from Northern Mexico. *In* Boundaries and Territories: Prehistory of the U.S. Southwest and Northern Mexico. M. Elisa Villalpando, ed. Pp. 173–83. Anthropological Research Papers 54. Tempe: Arizona State University.

McGuire, Randall H., E. Charles Adams, Ben A. Nelson, and Katherine Spielmann
1994   Drawing the Southwest to Scale: Perspectives on Macroregional Relations. *In* Themes in Southwest Prehistory. George J. Gumerman, ed. Pp. 239–65. Santa Fe, NM: School of American Research Press.

McGuire, Randall H., and Ann V. Howard
1987   The Structure and Organization of Hohokam Shell Exchange. Kiva 52:113–46.

McGuire, Randall H., and Dean I. Saitta
1996   Although They Have Petty Captains, They Obey Them Badly: The Dialectics of Prehispanic Western Pueblo Social Organization. American Antiquity 61:197–216.

McGuire, Randall H., and Michael B. Schiffer
1982   Hohokam and Patayan: Prehistory of Southwestern Arizona. New York: Academic Press.

McGuire, Randall H., and Maria Elisa Villalpando C.
1989   Prehistory and the Making of History in Sonora. *In* Columbian Consequences I: Archaeological and Historical Perspectives on the Spanish Borderlands West. David Hurst Thomas, ed. Pp. 159–77. Washington, DC: Smithsonian Institution Press.
1993   An Archaeological Survey of the Altar Valley, Sonora, Mexico. Archaeology Series 184. Tucson: Arizona State Museum.
2007a   Excavations at Cerro de Trincheras. *In* Trincheras Sites in Time, Space, and Society. Suzanne K. Fish, Paul R. Fish, and M. Elisa Villalpando, eds. Pp. 137–64. Amerind Foundation New World Series. Tucson: University of Arizona Press.
2007b   The Hohokam and Mesoamerica. *In* The Hohokam Millennium. Suzanne K. Fish and Paul R. Fish, eds. Pp. 57–63. Santa Fe, NM: School for Advanced Research Press.

McGuire, Randall H., Maria Elisa Villalpando C., Victoria D. Vargas, and Emiliano Gallaga M.
1999   Cerro de Trincheras and the Casas Grandes World. *In* The Casas Grandes World. Curtis F. Schaafsma and Carroll L. Riley, eds. Pp. 134–46. Salt Lake City: University of Utah Press.

McIntosh, Susan Keech, ed.
1999   Beyond Chiefdoms: Pathways to Complexity in Africa. Cambridge: Cambridge University Press.

McKenna, Peter J.
1990   An Artifact Collection from the Terrace Community, Aztec Ruins National Monument, New Mexico. Santa Fe, NM: Southwest Cultural Resources Center, National Park Service.

McKenna, Peter J., and James E. Bradford
1989   The TJ Ruin, Gila Cliff Dwellings National Monument. Professional Paper 21. Santa Fe, NM: Southwest Cultural Resources Center, National Park Service.

McKenna, Peter J., and H. Wolcott Toll
2001   Regional Patterns of Great House Development among the Totah Anasazi, New Mexico. *In* Anasazi Regional Organization and the Chaco System. 2nd ed. David E. Doyel, ed. Pp. 133–43. Anthropological Papers 5. Albuquerque: Maxwell Museum of Anthropology, University of New Mexico.

McNeill, J. R., and William H. McNeill
2003   The Human Web: A Bird's-Eye View of World History. New York: W. W. Norton.

McNitt, Frank
1966   Richard Wetherill: Anasazi. Revised ed. Albuquerque: University of New Mexico Press.

Meighan, Clement W.
1999   The Mexican West Coast and the Hohokam Region. *In* The Casas Grandes World. Curtis F. Schaafsma and Carroll L. Riley, eds. Pp. 206–12. Salt Lake City: University of Utah Press.

Meinig, D. W.
1971   Southwest: Three Peoples in Geographical Change, 1600–1970. Oxford: Oxford University Press.

Meltzer, David J.

1994   The Discovery of Deep Time: A History of Views on the Peopling of the Americas. *In* Method and Theory for Investigating the Peopling of the Americas. Robson Bonnichsen and D. Gentry Steele, eds. Pp. 7–26. Corvallis, OR: Center for the Study of the First Americans.

Menand, Louis

2001   The Metaphysical Club. New York: Farrar, Straus and Giroux.

Menzies, Gavin

2003   1421: The Year China Discovered America. New York: William Morrow.

Mera, H. P.

1940   Ceramic Clues to the Prehistory of North Central New Mexico. Archaeological Survey Bulletin 8. Santa Fe, NM: Laboratory of Anthropology,

Mewshaw, Michael

1997   The Existential Burger. New York Times, April 6:35.

Meyer, Daniel A., Peter C. Dawson, and Donald T. Hanna, eds.

1996   Debating Complexity. Proceedings of the Twenty-sixth Annual Chacmool Conference. Alberta: Archaeological Association of the University of Calgary.

Miller, Daniel, Michael Rowlands, and Christopher Tilley, eds.

1989   Domination and Resistance. One World Archaeology. London: Allen Unwin.

Miller, Daniel, and Christopher Tilley, eds.

1984   Ideology, Power, and Prehistory. Cambridge: Cambridge University Press.

Miller, Mary

2006   The Study of the Pre-Columbian World. *In* A Pre-Columbian World. Jeffrey Quilter and Mary Miller, eds. Pp. 363–76. Washington, DC: Dumbarton Oaks.

Millon, Rene

1993   The Place Where Time Began. *In* Teotihuacan. Kathleen Berrin and Esther Pasztory, eds. Pp. 17–43. New York: Thames and Hudson.

Mills, Barbara J.

1998   Migration and Pueblo IV Community Reorganization in the Silver Creek Area, East Central Arizona. *In* Migrations and Reorganization: The Pueblo IV Period in the American Southwest. Katherine A. Spielmann, ed. Pp. 65–80. Anthropological Research Papers 51. Tempe: Arizona State University.

1999   The Reorganization of Silver Creek Communities from the 11th to 14th Centuries. *In* Living on the Edge of the Rim. Barbara J. Mills, Sarah A. Herr, and Scott Van Keuren, eds. Pp. 505–11. Arizona State Museum Archaeology Series 192. Tucson: Arizona State Museum.

2000   Alternative Models, Alternative Strategies: Leadership in the Prehispanic Southwest. *In* Alternative Leadership Strategies in the Prehispanic Southwest. Barbara J. Mills, ed. Pp. 3–18. Tucson: University of Arizona Press.

2002   Recent Research on Chaco: Changing Views on Economy, Ritual and Society. Journal of Archaeological Research 10(1):65–117.

2004   The Establishment and Defeat of Hierarchy: Inalienable Possessions and the History of Collective Prestige Structures in the Pueblo Southwest. American Anthropologist 106(2):238–51.

Mills, Barbara J., ed.

2000   Alternative Leadership Strategies in the Prehispanic Southwest. Tucson: University of Arizona Press.

Mills, Barbara J., Sarah A. Herr, and Scott Van Keuren, eds.

1999   Living on the Edge of the Rim. Archaeology Series 192. Tucson: Arizona State Museum.

Milner, George R.

1998   The Cahokia Chiefdom: The Archaeology of a Mississippian Society. Washington, DC: Smithsonian Institution Press.

1999   Warfare in Prehistoric and Early Historic Eastern North America. Journal of Archaeological Research 7(2):105–51.

2004   The Moundbuilders: Ancient Peoples of Eastern North America. London: Thames and Hudson.

Minnis, Paul E.

1985   Social Adaptations to Food Stress, a Prehistoric Southwestern Example. Chicago: University of Chicago Press.

1988   Four Examples of Specialized Production at Casas Grandes, Northwestern Chihuahua. Kiva 53:181–93.

Minnis, Paul E., and Steven A. LeBlanc

1979   Destruction of Three Sites in Southwestern New Mexico. *In* Vandalism of Cultural Resources. Dee F. Green and Steven A. LeBlanc, eds. Pp. 69–78. Albuquerque, NM: USDA Forest Service, Southwestern Region.

Minnis, Paul E., and Charles L. Redman, eds.

1990   Perspectives on Southwestern Prehistory. Boulder, CO: Westview.

Mitchell, Douglas R., and Judy L. Brunson-Hadley

2001   An Evaluation of Classic Period Hohokam Burials and Society: Chiefs, Priests, or Acephalous Complexity? *In* Ancient Burial Practices in the American Southwest: Archaeology, Physical Anthropology, and Native American Perspectives. Douglas R. Mitchell and Judy L. Brunson-Hadley, eds. Pp. 45–67. Albuquerque: University of New Mexico Press.

Mitchell, Douglas R., and Judy L. Brunson-Hadley, eds.

2001   Ancient Burial Practices in the American Southwest: Archaeology, Physical Anthropology, and Native American Perspectives. Albuquerque: University of New Mexico Press.

Mitchell, Douglas R., and Michael S. Foster

2000   Hohokam Shell Middens along the Sea of Cortez, Puerto Peñasco, Sonora, Mexico. Journal of Field Archaeology 27:27–41.

Mitchell, Peter

2005   African Connections: Archaeological Perspectives on Africa and the Wider World. Walnut Creek, CA: AltaMira.

Mithen, Steven

2003   After the Ice: A Global Human History, 20,000–5000 BC. London: Weidenfeld and Nicolson.

Monnig, Oscar

1939   How the Casas Grandes, Chihuahua, Mexico, Meteorite Got to Washington, D.C. Popular Astronomy 47:152–54.

Morgan, Lewis Henry

[1881]1965   Houses and House-Life of the American Aborigines. Chicago: University of Chicago Press.

Morgan, William N.

1994   Ancient Architecture of the Southwest. Austin: University of Texas Press.

Morgenroth, Silke

2001   "X" Never, Ever Marks the Spot: Archaeology and Culture Studies. *In* A Companion to Cultural Studies. Toby Miller, ed. Pp. 154–68. Malden, MA: Blackwell.

Morris, Earl H.

1919–1928 The Aztec Ruin. Anthropological Papers, vol. 26, nos. 1–5. New York: American Museum of Natural History.

1939   Archaeological Studies in the La Plata District, Southwestern Colorado and Northwestern New Mexico. Publication 519. Washington, DC: Carnegie Institution of Washington.

Morris, Ian

2000   Archaeology as Cultural History. Oxford: Blackwell.

Morss, Noel

1954   Clay Figurines of the American Southwest. Papers of the Peabody Museum of American Archaeology and Ethnology, vol. 49, no. 1. Cambridge, MA: Harvard University.

Moulard, Barbara L.

1984   Within the Underworld Sky: Mimbres Ceramic Art in Context. Pasadena, CA: Twelvetrees.

2005   Archaism and Emulation in Casas Grandes Painted Pottery. *In* Casas Grandes and the Ceramic Art of the Ancient Southwest. Richard Townsend, ed. Pp. 66–97. Chicago: Art Institute of Chicago; New Haven, CT: Yale University Press.

Mountjoy, Joseph B.

1998 The Evolution of Complex Societies in West Mexico: An Evolutionary Perspective. *In* Ancient West Mexico: Art and Archaeology of the Unknown Past. Richard Townsend, ed. Pp. 251–65. Chicago: Art Institute of Chicago.

2000 Prehispanic Cultural Development along the Southern Coast of West Mexico. *In* Greater Mesoamerica: The Archaeology of West and Northwest Mexico. Michael S. Foster and Shirley Gorenstein, eds. Pp. 81–106. Salt Lake City: University of Utah Press.

2001 Aztatlan Complex. *In* Archaeology of Ancient Mexico and Central America, An Encyclopedia. Susan Toby Evans and David L. Webster, eds. Pp. 57–59. New York: Garland.

Naranjo, Tessie

1995 Thoughts on Migrations by Santa Clara Pueblo. Journal of Anthropological Archaeology 14(2):247–50.

2006 "We Came from the North, We Came from the South": Some Tewa Origin Stories. *In* The Mesa Verde World. David Grant Noble, ed. Pp. 49–57. Santa Fe, NM: School of American Research Press.

Nash, Stephen E.

2000 Seven Decades of Archaeological Tree-ring Dating. *In* It's About Time: A History of Archaeological Dating in North America. Stephen E. Nash, ed. Pp. 60–82. Salt Lake City: University of Utah Press.

Nassaney, Michael S., and Kenneth E. Sassaman

1995 Introduction: Understanding Native American Interactions. *In* Native American Interactions: Multiscalar Analyses and Interpretations in the Eastern Woodlands. Michael S. Nassaney and Kenneth E. Sassaman, eds. Pp. xix–xxxviii. Knoxville: University of Tennessee Press.

Nassaney, Michael S., and Kenneth E. Sassaman, eds.

1995 Native American Interactions: Multiscalar Analyses and Interpretations in the Eastern Woodlands. Knoxville: University of Tennessee Press.

Navarro, Armando

2005 Mexicano Political Experience in Occupied Aztlan. Walnut Creek, CA: AltaMira.

Naylor, Thomas H.

1995 Casas Grandes Outlier Ballcourts in Northwest Chihuahua. *In* The Gran Chichimeca: Essays on the Archaeology and Ethnohistory of Northern Mesoamerica. Jonathan E. Reyman, ed. Pp. 224–39. Worldwide Archaeology Series 12. Aldershot, UK: Avebury.

Neitzel, Jill E.

1991 Hohokam Material Culture and Behavior: The Dimensions of Organizational Change. *In* Exploring the Hohokam: Prehistoric Desert Peoples of the Southwest. George J. Gumerman, ed. Pp. 177–230. Albuquerque: University of New Mexico Press.

2000 What Is a Regional System? Issues of Scale and Interaction in the Prehistoric Southwest. *In* The Archaeology of Regional Interaction. Michelle Hegmon, ed. Pp. 25–40. Boulder: University Press of Colorado.

Neitzel, Jill E., ed.

1999 Great Towns and Regional Polities in the Prehistoric American Southwest and Southeast. Albuquerque: University of New Mexico Press.

2003 Pueblo Bonito: Center of the Chacoan World. Washington, DC: Smithsonian Books.

Neitzel, Robert S.

1965 Archaeology of the Fatherland Site: The Grand Village of the Natchez. Anthropological Papers, vol. 51, no.1. New York: American Museum of Natural History.

Nelson, Ben A.

1995 Complexity, Hierarchy, and Scale: A Controlled Comparison between Chaco Canyon, New Mexico, and La Quemada, Zacatecas. American Antiquity 60:597–618.

1997 Chronology and Stratigraphy at La Quemada, Zacatecas, Mexico. Journal of Field Archaeology 24(1):85–109.

2000 Aggregation, Warfare, and the Spread of the Mesoamerican Tradition. *In* The Archaeology of Regional Interaction: Religion, Warfare, and Exchange across the American Southwest and Beyond. Michelle Hegmon, ed. Pp. 317–37. Boulder: University Press of Colorado.

2004   Elite Residences in West Mexico. *In* Palaces of the Ancient New World. Susan Toby Evans and
            Joanne Pillsbury, eds. Pp. 59–81. Washington, DC: Dumbarton Oaks.
2006   Mesoamerican Objects and Symbols in Chaco Canyon Contexts. *In* The Archaeology of
            Chaco Canyon: An Eleventh-Century Pueblo Regional Center. Stephen H. Lekson, ed.
            Pp. 339–71. Santa Fe, NM: School of American Research Press.
2007   Crafting of Places: Mesoamerican Monumentality in Cerro de Trincheras and Other Hilltop
            Sites. *In* Trincheras Sites in Time, Space, and Society. Suzanne K. Fish, Paul R. Fish, and M.
            Elisa Villalpando, eds. Pp. 230–46. Amerind Foundation New World Series. Tucson:
            University of Arizona Press.

Nelson, Ben A., and Roger Anyon
1996   Fallow Valleys: Asynchronous Occupations in Southwestern New Mexico. Kiva 61:275–94.

Nelson, Ben A., and Steven LeBlanc
1986   Short-term Sedentism in the American Southwest. Albuquerque: University of New Mexico
            Press.

Nelson, Margaret C.
1999   Mimbres during the Twelfth Century. Tucson: University of Arizona Press.

Nelson, Margaret C., and Michelle Hegmon
2001   Abandonment Is Not as It Seems: An Approach to the Relationship between Site and
            Regional Abandonment. American Antiquity 66:213–35.

Nelson, Margaret C., and Gregson Schachner
2002   Understanding Abandonments in the North American Southwest. Journal of Archaeological
            Research 10(2):167–206.

Nelson, Richard S.
1986   Pochetcas and Prestige: Mesoamerican Artifacts in Hohokam Sites. *In* Ripples in the
            Chichimec Sea. Frances Joan Mathien and Randall H. McGuire, eds. Pp. 155–82. Carbondale:
            Southern Illinois University Press.
1991   Hohokam Marine Shell Exchange and Artifacts. Arizona State Museum Archaeological Series
            179. Tucson: University of Arizona.

Neuzil, Anna A.
2005   In the Aftermath of Migration: Assessing the Social Consequences of Late 13th and 14th
            Century Population Movements into Southeastern Arizona. PhD dissertation, Department of
            Anthropology, University of Arizona, Tucson.

Newell, Gillian E., and Emiliano Gallaga, eds.
2004   Surveying the Archaeology of Northwest Mexico. Salt Lake City: University of Utah Press.

Nials, Fred L., David A. Gregory, and Donald A. Graybill
1989   River Steamflow and Hohokam Irrigation Systems. *In* The 1982–1984 Excavations at Las
            Colinas: Environment and Subsistence. Donald A. Graybill, ed. Pp. 59–76. Archaeological
            Series 162, vol. 5. Tucson: Arizona State Museum.

Nichols, Deborah L.
2002   Basketmaker III: Early Ceramic Period Villages in the Kayenta Region. *In* Prehistoric Culture
            Change on the Colorado Plateau: Ten Thousand Years on Black Mesa. Shirley Powell and
            Francis E. Smiley, eds. Pp. 66–75. Tucson: University of Arizona Press.

Nicholson, H. B., and Eloise Quiñones Keber, eds.
1994   Mixteca-Puebla: Discoveries and Research in Mesoamerican Art and Archaeology. Culver City,
            CA: Labyrinthos.

Ninenger, H. H.
1938   Meteorite Collecting among Ancient Americans. American Antiquity 4:39–43.

Noble, David Grant, ed.
1991   The Hohokam: Ancient People of the Desert. Santa Fe, NM: School of American Research
            Press.
2004   In Search of Chaco: New Approaches to an Archaeological Enigma. Santa Fe, NM: School of
            American Research Press.
2006   The Mesa Verde World: Explorations in Ancestral Pueblo Archaeology. Santa Fe, NM: School
            of American Research Press.

Nordenskiold, Gustaf
[1893] 1979 The Cliff Dwellers of Mesa Verde. Glorieta, NM: Rio Grande.

Novick, Peter
1998   That Noble Dream: The "Objectivity Question" and the American Historical Profession. Cambridge: Cambridge University Press.

Nuñez Cabeza de Vaca, Alvaro
2003   The Narrative of Cabeza de Vaca. Rolena Adorno and Patrick Charles Pautz, eds. Lincoln: University of Nebraska Press.

Nusbaum, Jesse
1935   Archaeological Field Work in North America in 1934, pt. 2. American Antiquity 1(2):133–40.

Oakes, Yvonne R.
1999   Synthesis and Conclusions. Vol. 6 of Archaeology of the Mogollon Highlands. Yvonne R. Oakes and Dorothy A. Zamora, eds. Archaeology Notes 22. Santa Fe: Museum of New Mexico.

Oakley, Francis
2006   Kingship: The Politics of Enchantment. Oxford: Blackwell.

Obregon, Baltasar
1928   Obregon's history of 16th century explorations in western America, *entitled* Chronicle, commentary, or relation of the ancient and modern discoveries in New Spain and New Mexico, Mexico, 1584. George P. Hammond and Agapito Rey, eds. and trans. Los Angeles: Wetzel.

O'Brien, Michael J., R. Lee Lyman, and Michael Brian Schiffer
2005   Archaeology as a Process: Processualism and Its Progeny. Salt Lake City: University of Utah Press.

O'Brien, Patricia J.
1989   Cahokia: The Political Capital of the "Ramey" State? North American Archaeologist 10:275–92.

O'Bryan, Aileen
1956   The Story of Noqoilpi, the Great Gambler. *In* The Dine: Origin Myths of the Navaho Indians. Aileen O'Bryan, ed. Pp. 48–63. Bureau of American Ethnology Bulletin 163. Washington, DC: Government Printing Office.

O'Donovan, Maria
2002   New Perspectives on Site Function and Scale of Cerro de Trincheras, Sonora, Mexico. Archaeological Series 195. Tucson: Arizona State Museum.
2004   The Role of Cerro de Trincheras Site in the Northwest Mexican and the American Southwest Landscape. *In* Surveying the Archaeology of Northwest Mexico. Gillian E. Newell and Emiliano Gallaga, eds. Pp. 27–45. Salt Lake City: University of Utah Press.

O'Gorman, Edmundo
[1961]1972 The Invention of America: An Inquiry into the Historical Nature of the New World and the Meaning of Its History. Westport, CT: Greenwood.

Okasha, Samir
2006   Evolution and the Levels of Selection. Oxford: Clarendon.

Oliver, Paul, ed.
1997   Encyclopedia of the Vernacular Architecture of the World. New York: Cambridge University Press.

Oppelt, Norman T.
2002   List of Southwestern Pottery: Types and Wares. Greeley, CO: Oppelt Publications.

Ortiz, Alfonso
1972   Ritual Drama and the Pueblo World View. *In* New Perspectives on the Pueblo. Alfonso Ortiz, ed. Pp. 135–61. Albuquerque: University of New Mexico Press.

Ortman, Scott G.
2007   Population Biology in the Four Corners to Rio Grande Migration. Paper presented at the 72nd Annual Meeting, Society for American Archaeology, Austin, TX, April 26–28.

Ortman, Scott G., and Bruce A. Bradley
2002   Sand Canyon Pueblo. *In* Seeking the Center Place. Mark D. Varien and Richard H. Wilshusen, eds. Pp. 41–78. Salt Lake City: University of Utah Press.

Pacheco, Paul J., ed.
1996   A View from the Core: A Synthesis of Ohio Hopewell Archaeology. Columbus: Ohio Archaeological Council.

Pacheco, Paul J., and William S. Dancey
2006   Integrating Mortuary and Settlement Data on Ohio Hopewell Society. *In* Re-creating Hopewell. Douglas K. Charles and Jane E. Buikstra, eds. Pp. 3–25. Gainesville: University Press of Florida.

Pailes, Richard A.
1978   The Rio Sonora Culture in Prehistoric Trade Systems. *In* Across the Chichimec Sea. C. L. Riley and B. C. Hendrick, eds. Pp. 20–39. Carbondale: Southern Illinois University Press.

Pailes, Richard A., and Joseph W. Whitecotton
1995   The Frontiers of Mesoamerica: Northern and Southern. *In* The Gran Chichimeca: Essays on the Archaeology and Ethnohistory of Northern Mesoamerica. Jonathan E. Reyman, ed. Pp. 13–45. Worldwide Archaeology Series 12. Aldershot, UK: Avebury.

Parmentier, Richard J.
1979   The Pueblo Mythological Triangle: Poseyemu, Montezuma, and Jesus in the Pueblos. *In* Handbook of North American Indians, vol. 9: Southwest. Alfonso Ortiz, ed. Pp. 609–22. Washington, DC: Smithsonian Institution.

Parsons, Elsie Clews
[1939]1996 Pueblo Indian Religion, vols. 1 and 2. Lincoln: University of Nebraska Press.

Patterson, Thomas C., and Christine W. Gailey, eds.
1987   Power Relations and State Formation. Washington, DC: American Anthropological Association.

Pauketat, Timothy R.
1994   The Ascent of Chiefs: Cahokia and Middle Mississippian Politics in Native North America. Tuscaloosa: University of Alabama Press.
2001   Practice and History in Archaeology. Anthropological Theory 1(1):73–98.
2004   Ancient Cahokia and the Mississippians. Case Studies in Early Societies. Cambridge: Cambridge University Press.
2007   Chiefdoms and Other Archaeological Delusions. Lanham, MD: AltaMira.

Pauketat, Timothy R., and Thomas E. Emerson, eds.
1997   Cahokia: Domination and Ideology in the Mississippian World. Lincoln: University of Nebraska Press.

Pearson, Mike, and Michael Shanks
2001   Theatre/Archaeology. London: Routledge.

Peckham, Stewart
1979   When Is a Rio Grande Kiva? *In* Collected Papers in Honor of Bertha Pauline Dutton. Albert H. Schroeder, ed. Pp. 55–86. Papers of the Archaeological Society of New Mexico 4. Albuquerque, NM: Albuquerque Archaeological Society Press.

Pedersen, Susan
2002   What Is Political History Now? *In* What Is History Now? David Cannadine, ed. Pp. 36–56. Houndmills, UK: Palgrave Macmillan.

Pepper, George H.
1920   Pueblo Bonito. Anthropological Papers 27. New York: American Museum of Natural History.

Peregrine, Peter N.
1992   Mississippian Evolution: A World-Systems Perspective. Madison, WI: Prehistory Press.
1995   Networks of Power: The Mississippian World System. *In* Native American Interactions: Multiscalar Analyses and Interpretations in the Eastern Woodlands. Michael S. Nassaney and Kenneth E. Sassaman, eds. Pp. 247–65. Knoxville: University of Tennessee Press.

Peregrine, Peter N., and Gary M. Feinman, eds.
1996   Pre-Columbian World Systems. Madison, WI: Prehistory Press.

Peregrine, Peter N., and Stephen H. Lekson
2006   Southeast, Southwest, Mexico: Continental Perspectives on Mississippian Polities. *In*
            Leadership and Polity in Mississippian Societies. Brian Butler and Paul Welch, eds. Pp.
            351–364. Occasional Papers 33. Carbondale, IL: Center for Archaeological Investigations.

Perry, Elizabeth M.
2003   Animas–La Plata Cultural Resources Project: Cultural Affiliation Study. Cultural Resources
            Report 02-624. Durango, CO: SWCA Environmental Consultants.

Phillips, Ann
1993   Archaeological Expeditions into Southeastern Utah and Southwestern Colorado between
            1888–1898 and the Dispersal of the Collections. *In* Anasazi Basketmaker: Papers from the
            1990 Wetherill–Grand Gulch Symposium. Victoria M. Atkins, ed. Pp. 103–18. Cultural
            Resource Series 24. Salt Lake City, UT: Bureau of Land Management.

Phillips, David A., Jr.
1989   Prehistory of Chihuahua and Sonora, Mexico. Journal of World Prehistory 3(4):373–401.
2002   Mesoamerican–Southwestern Relationships: An Intellectual History. *In* Culture and
            Environment in the American Southwest: Essays in Honor of Robert C. Euler. David A.
            Phillips Jr. and John A. Ware, eds. Pp. 177–95. Anthropological Research Paper 8. Phoenix:
            SWCA Environmental Consultants.
Forthcoming *The Chaco Meridian*: A Skeptical Analysis. *In* Mogollon Archaeology: Collected Papers from
            the Eleventh Mogollon Conference, 20th Anniversary Volume. Patrick H. Beckett, ed. Pp.
            189–214. Las Cruces, NM: COAS Publishing and Research. (Available on http://www.unm.
            edu/~dap/meridian/meridian.html, accessed Oct. 14, 2008.)

Phillips, David A., Jr., and Elizabeth Arwen Bagwell
2001   How Big Was Paquimé? Poster presentation, 66th Annual Meeting, Society for American
            Archaeology, New Orleans, April 19–22.

Phillips, David A., Jr., and Lynne Sebastian
2004   Large-Scale Feasting and Politics: An Essay on Power in Precontact Southwestern Societies.
            In Identity, Feasting, and the Archaeology of the Greater Southwest. Barbara J. Mills, ed.
            Pp. 233–58. Boulder: University Press of Colorado.

Phillips, David A., Jr., and Lynne Sebastian, eds.
2001   Examining the Course of Southwest Archaeology: The Durango Conference, September
            1995. Special Publication 3. Albuquerque: New Mexico Archaeological Council.

Phillips, Philip
1966   The Role of Transpacific Contacts in the Development of New World Pre-Columbian
            Civilizations. *In* Handbook of Middle American Indians, vol. 4: Archaeological Frontiers and
            Connections. Gordon F. Ekholm and Gordon R. Willey, eds. Pp. 296–315. Austin: University
            of Texas Press.

Phillips, Philip, and James A. Brown
1978   Pre-Columbian Shell Engravings from the Craig Mound at Spiro, Oklahoma, pts. 1–2.
            Cambridge, MA: Peabody Museum Press.

Pietzel, Todd
2007   Surveying Cerro Moctezuma, Chihuahua, Mexico. Kiva 72(3):353–69.

Pillsbury, Joanne, and Susan Toby Evans
2004   Palaces of the Ancient New World: An Introduction. *In* Palaces of the Ancient New World.
            Susan Toby Evans and Joanne Pillsbury, eds. Pp. 1–6. Washington, DC: Dumbarton Oaks.

Plog, Fred T.
1974   The Study of Prehistoric Change. New York: Academic Press.
1983   Political and Economic Alliances on the Colorado Plateau, A.D. 400–1450. *In* Advances in
            World Archaeology, vol. 2. F. Wendorf and A. E. Close, eds. Pp. 289–330. New York: Academic
            Press.

Plog, Fred, George J. Gumerman, Robert C. Euler, Jeffrey S. Dean, Richard H. Hevly, and Thor N. V. Karlstrom
1988   Anasazi Adaptive Strategies: The Model, Predictions, and Results. *In* The Anasazi in a Changing Environment. George Gumerman, ed. Pp. 230–76. Cambridge: Cambridge University Press.

Plog, Stephen
1997   Ancient Peoples of the American Southwest. New York: Thames and Hudson.

Plog, Stephen, and Julie Solometo
1997   The Never-Changing and the Ever-Changing: The Evolution of Western Pueblo Ritual. Cambridge Archaeological Journal 7(2):161–82.

Pohl, John M. D.
2003   Ritual and Iconographic Variablity in Mixteca-Puebla Polychrome Pottery. *In* The Postclassic Mesoamerican World. Michael E. Smith and Frances F. Berdan, eds. Pp. 201–06. Salt Lake City: University of Utah Press.

Pollard, Helen Perlstein
2000   Tarascans and Their Ancestors: Prehistory of Michoacán. *In* Greater Mesoamerica: The Archaeology of West and Northwest Mexico. Michael S. Foster and Shirley Gorenstein, eds. Pp. 59–70. Salt Lake City: University of Utah Press.
2003a   The Tarascan Empire. *In* The Postclassic Mesoamerican World. Michael E. Smith and Frances F. Berdan, eds. Pp. 78–86. Salt Lake City: University of Utah Press.
2003b   West Mexico beyond the Tarascan Frontier. *In* The Postclassic Mesoamerican World. Michael E. Smith and Frances F. Berdan, eds. Pp. 55–57. Salt Lake City: University of Utah Press.

Pool, Christopher A.
2007   Olmec Archaeology and Early Mesoamerica. Cambridge: Cambridge University Press.

Potter, James M., and Jason Chuipka
2007   Early Pueblo Communities and Cultural Diversity in the Durango Area: Preliminary Results from the Animas–La Plata Project. Kiva 72:407–30.

Powell, Melissa S., ed.
2006   Secrets of Casas Grandes. Santa Fe: Museum of New Mexico Press.

Powell, Shirley
1983   Mobility and Adaptation: The Anasazi of Black Mesa, Arizona. Carbondale: Southern Illinois University Press.
2002   The Puebloan Florescence and Dispersion: Dinnebito and Beyond, A.D. 800–1150. *In* Prehistoric Culture Change on the Colorado Plateau: Ten Thousand Years on Black Mesa. Shirley Powell and Francis E. Smiley, eds. Pp. 79–117. Tucson: University of Arizona Press.

Powell, Shirley, and Francis E. Smiley, eds.
2002   Prehistoric Culture Change on the Colorado Plateau: Ten Thousand Years on Black Mesa. Tucson: University of Arizona Press.

Powers, Robert P., ed.
2005   The Peopling of Bandelier: New Insights from the Archaeology of the Pajarito Plateau. Santa Fe, NM: School of American Research Press.

Powers, Robert P., William B. Gillespie, and Stephen H. Lekson
1983   The Outlier Survey: A Regional View of Settlement in the San Juan Basin. Reports of the Chaco Center 3. Albuquerque, NM: National Park Service.

Prescott, William Hickling
[1843]1922 History of the Conquest of Mexico. London: Chatto and Windus.

Preucel, Robert W.
2005   Ethnicity and Southwestern Archaeology. *In* Southwest Archaeology in the Twentieth Century. Linda S. Cordell and Don D. Fowler, eds. Pp. 174–93. Salt Lake City: University of Utah Press.
2006   Archaeological Semiotics. Malden, MA: Blackwell.

Quilter, Jeffrey, and Mary Miller, eds.
2006   A Pre-Columbian World. Washington, DC: Dumbarton Oaks.

Rakita, Gordon F. M.

2006   Ancestors and Elites: Emergent Complexity, Ritual Practices, and Mortuary Behavior at Paquimé, Chihuahua, Mexico. *In* Religion in the Prehispanic Southwest. Christine S. VanPool, Todd L. VanPool, and David A. Phillips Jr., eds. Pp. 219–33. Lanham, MD: AltaMira.

Randsborg, Klavs

1991   The First Millennium A.D. in Europe and the Mediterranean: An Archaeological Essay. Cambridge: Cambridge University Press.

Rapoport, Amos

1969   House Form and Culture. Englewood Cliffs, NJ: Prentice-Hall.

1977   Human Aspects of Urban Form: Towards a Man-Environment Approach to Urban Form and Design. Oxford: Pergamon.

1982   The Meaning of the Built Environment: A Nonverbal Communication Approach. Beverly Hills, CA: Sage.

1990   History and Precedent in Environmental Design. New York: Plenum.

Ravesloot, John C.

1988   Mortuary Practices and Social Differentiation at Casas Grandes, Chihuahua, Mexico. Anthropological Papers 49. Tucson: University of Arizona Press.

2007   Changing Views of Snaketown in a Larger Landscape. *In* The Hohokam Millennium. Suzanne K. Fish and Paul R. Fish, eds. Pp. 91–97. Santa Fe: School for Advanced Research Press.

Rebere, Eleanora A.

2006   A Hard Row to Hoe: Changing Maize Use in the American Bottom and Surrounding Areas. *In* Histories of Maize. John E. Staller, Robert H. Tykot, and Bruce F. Benz, eds. Pp. 235–48. Burlington, MA: Academic Press.

Redman, Charles L., Steven R. James, Paul R. Fish, and J. Daniel Rogers, eds.

2004   The Archaeology of Global Change: The Impact of Humans on Their Environments. Washington, DC: Smithsonian Books.

Redman, Charles L., Glen E. Rice, and Kathryn E. Pedrick, eds.

1992   Developing Perspectives on Tonto Basin Prehistory. Anthropological Field Studies 26. Tempe: Arizona State University.

Redmond, Elsa M., ed.

1998   Chiefdoms and Chieftaincy in the Americas. Gainesville: University Press of Florida.

Reed, Lori Stephens, C. Dean Wilson, and Kelley A. Hays-Gilpin

2000   From Brown to Gray: The Origins of Ceramic Technology in the Northern Southwest. *In* Foundations of Anasazi Culture: The Basketmaker–Pueblo Transition. Paul F. Reed, ed. Pp. 203–20. Salt Lake City: University of Utah Press.

Reed, Paul F.

2000   Fundamental Issues in Basketmaker Archaeology. *In* Foundations of Anasazi Culture: The Basketmaker–Pueblo Transition. Paul F. Reed, ed. Pp. 3–16. Salt Lake City: University of Utah Press.

2004   The Puebloan Society of Chaco Canyon. Westport, CT: Greenwood.

2006   Chronology of Salmon Pueblo. *In* Thirty-Five Years of Archaeological Research at Salmon Ruins, New Mexico, vol. 1: Introduction, Architecture, Chronology and Conclusions. Paul F. Reed, ed. Pp. 287–96. Tucson, AZ: Center for Desert Archaeology; Bloomfield, NM: Salmon Ruins Museum.

Reed, Paul F., ed.

2000   Foundations of Anasazi Culture: The Basketmaker–Pueblo Transition. Salt Lake City: University of Utah Press.

2003   Anasazi Archaeology at the Millennium: Proceedings of the Sixth Occasional Anasazi Symposium. Tucson, AZ: Center for Desert Archaeology.

2006   Thirty-Five Years of Archaeological Research at Salmon Ruins, New Mexico, vol. 1: Introduction: Architecture, Chronology and Conclusions. Tucson, AZ: Center for Desert Archaeology; Bloomfield, NM: Salmon Ruins Museum.

2008   Chaco's Northern Prodigies: Salmon, Aztec, and the Ascendency of the Middle San Juan Region after AD 1100. Salt Lake City: University of Utah Press.

Reed, Paul F., and Scott Wilcox
2000   Distinctive and Intensive: The Basketmaker III to Early Pueblo I Occupation of Cove-Redrock
            Valley, Northeastern Arizona. *In* Foundations of Anasazi Culture: The Basketmaker–Pueblo
            Transition. Paul F. Reed, ed. Pp. 69–93. Salt Lake City: University of Utah Press.

Reid, J. Jefferson
1986   Measuring Social Complexity in the American Southwest. *In* Status, Structure, and
            Stratification: Current Archaeological Reconstructions. Marc Thompson, Maria Teresa
            Garcia, and Francois J. Kense, eds. Pp. 167–73. Proceedings of the 16th Annual Conference,
            Alberta: Archaeological Association of the University of Calgary.
1997   Return to Migration, Population Movement, and Ethnic Identity in the American Southwest.
            In Vanishing River. Stephanie M. Whittlesey, Richard Ciolek-Torrello, and Jeffrey H. Altschul,
            eds. Pp. 629–38. Tucson, AZ: SRI Press.

Reid, J. Jefferson, and David E. Doyel, eds.
1986   Emil W. Haury's Prehistory of the Southwest. Tucson: University of Arizona Press.

Reid, J. Jefferson, and Stephanie M. Whittlesey
1997   The Archaeology of Ancient Arizona. Tucson: University of Arizona Press.
2005a   Thirty Years into Yesterday: A History of Archaeology at Grasshopper Pueblo. Tucson:
            University of Arizona Press.
2005b   Seven Years That Reshaped Southwest Prehistory. *In* Southwest Archaeology in the Twentieth
            Century. Linda S. Cordell and Don D. Fowler, eds. Pp. 47–59. Salt Lake City: University of
            Utah Press.
2009   Prehistory, Personality, and Place: Emil W. Haury and the Mogollon Controversy. Tucson:
            University of Arizona Press.

Reilly, F. Kent, III, and James F. Garber, eds.
2007   Ancient Objects and Sacred Realms: Interpretations of Mississippian Iconography. Austin:
            University of Texas Press.

Renfrew, Colin
2001   Production and Consumption in a Sacred Economy: The Material Correlates of High
            Devotional Expression at Chaco Canyon. American Antiquity 66:14–25.
2003   Figuring It Out: What Are We? Where Do We Come From? The Parallel Visions of Artists
            and Archaeologists. London: Thames and Hudson.
2007   Brief Reply to Leo S. Klejn. Antiquity 80(310):985–86.

Resek, Carl
1960   Lewis Henry Morgan: American Scholar. Chicago: University of Chicago Press.

Reyman, Jonathan E.
1985   A Reevaluation of the Bi-wall and Tri-wall Structures in the Anasazi Area. *In* Contributions to
            the Archaeology and Ethnohistory of Greater Mesoamerica. W. J. Folan, ed. Pp. 293–334.
            Carbondale: Southern Illinois University Press.
1995   Pala'tkwabi: Red Land of the South. *In* The Gran Chichimeca: Essays on the Archaeology and
            Ethnohistory of Northern Mesoamerica. Jonathan E. Reyman, ed. Pp. 320–35. Worldwide
            Archaeology Series 12. Aldershot, UK: Avebury.

Reyman, Jonathan E., ed.
1995   The Gran Chichimeca: Essays on the Archaeology and Ethnohistory of Northern
            Mesoamerica. Worldwide Archaeology Series 12. Aldershot, UK: Avebury.

Rice, Glen E.
1987   La Ciudad: A Perspective on Hohokam Community Systems. *In* The Hohokam Village: Site
            Structure and Organization. David E. Doyel, ed. Pp. 127–58. AAAS Publication 87-15.
            Glenwood Springs, CO: Southwestern and Rocky Mountain Division of the American
            Association for the Advancement of Science.
1998   Migration, Emulation, and Tradition in Tonto Basin Prehistory. *In* A Synthesis of Tonto Basin
            Prehistory: The Roosevelt Archaeology Studies, 1989 to 1998. Glen E. Rice, ed.
            Pp. 231–41. Anthropological Field Studies 41. Office of Cultural Resource Management.
            Tempe: Arizona State University.
2001   Warfare and Massing in the Salt and Gila Basins of Central Arizona. *In* Deadly Landscapes:

Case Studies in Prehistoric Southwestern Warfare. Glen E. Rice and Steven A. LeBlanc, eds. Pp. 289–329. Salt Lake City: University of Utah Press.

Rice, Glen E., ed.
1990   A Design for Salado Research. Roosevelt Monograph Series 1, Anthropological Field Studies 22. Tempe: Office of Cultural Resource Management, Arizona State University.
1998   A Synthesis of Tonto Basin Prehistory: The Roosevelt Archaeology Studies, 1989 to 1998. Anthropological Field Studies 41. Tempe: Office of Cultural Resource Management, Arizona State University.

Rice, Glen E., and Steven A. LeBlanc, eds.
2001   Deadly Landscapes: Case Studies in Prehistoric Southwestern Warfare. Salt Lake City: University of Utah Press.

Rice, Glen E., and Charles L. Redman
2000   Compounds, Villages, and Mounds: The Salado Alternative. In The Hohokam Village Revisited. David E. Doyel, Suzanne K. Fish, and Paul R. Fish, eds. Pp. 317-344. Fort Collins: Southwestern and Rocky Mountain Division of the American Association for the Advancement of Science.

Rice, Glen E., Arleyn Simon, and Christopher Loendorf
1998   Production and Exchange of Economic Goods. In A Synthesis of Tonto Basin Prehistory: The Roosevelt Archaeology Studies, 1989 to 1998. Glen E. Rice, ed. Pp. 105–30. Anthropological Field Studies 41. Tempe: Office of Cultural Resource Management, Arizona State University.

Rice, Prudence M.
1998   Contexts of Contact and Cultural Change: Peripheries, Frontiers, and Boundaries. In Studies in Culture Contact. James G. Cusick, ed. Pp. 44–66. Occasional Paper 25. Carbondale, IL: Center for Archaeological Investigations.
2004   Maya Political Science: Time, Astronomy, and the Cosmos. Austin: University of Texas Press.

Riggs, Charles R.
2007   Cultural Sensitivity, Science and Ethical Imperatives: Contemporary Archaeology in the Southwestern United States. In Archaeology and Capitalism: From Ethics to Politics. Yannis Hamilakis and Philip Duke, eds. Pp. 83–97. Walnut Creek, CA: Left Coast.

Riley, Carroll L.
1987   The Frontier People: The Greater Southwest in the Protohistoric Period. Albuquerque: University of New Mexico Press.
1991   The Sonoran Connection: Road and Trail Networks in the Protohistoric Period. In Ancient Road Networks and Settlement Hierarchies in the New World. Charles D. Trombold, ed. Pp. 132–44. Cambridge: Cambridge University Press.
1995   Rio del Norte: People of the Upper Rio Grande from Earliest Times to the Pueblo Revolt. Salt Lake City: University of Utah Press.
1999   The Sonoran Statelets and Casas Grandes. In The Casas Grandes World. Curtis F. Schaafsma and Carroll L. Riley, eds. Pp. 193–200. Salt Lake City: University of Utah Press.
2005   Becoming Aztlan: Mesoamerican Influences in the Greater Southwest, AD 1200–1500. Salt Lake City: University of Utah Press.

Riley, Carroll L., and Basil C. Hedrick, eds.
1978   Across the Chichimec Sea: Papers in Honor of J. Charles Kelley. Carbondale: Southern Illinois University Press.

Roberts, Frank H. H., Jr.
1929   Shabik'eshchee Village: A Late Basketmaker Site in the Chaco Canyon. Bulletin 92. Washington, DC: Bureau of American Ethnology.
1932   Village of the Great Kivas on the Zuni Reservation, New Mexico. Bureau of American Ethnology Bulletin 111. Washington, DC: Smithsonian Institution.
1935   A Survey of Southwestern Archaeology. American Anthropologist 37:1–35.

Roberts, Heidi, Richard V. N. Ahlstrom, and Barbara Roth
2004   From Campus to Corporation: The Emergence of Contract Archaeology in the Southwestern United States. Washington, DC: Society of American Archaeology.

Robin, Cynthia
2003   New Directions in Classic Maya Household Archaeology. Journal of Archaeological Research
            11(4):307–56.

Rodriguez, Roberto, and Patrisia Gonzales
2005   Amoxtli San Ce Tojuan: We Are One—Nosotros Somos Uno. San Fernando, CA: Xicano
            Records and Film.

Roehner, Bertrand M., and Tony Syme
2002   Pattern and Repertoire in History. Cambridge, MA: Harvard University Press.

Rohn, Arthur H.
1977   Cultural Change and Continuity on Chapin Mesa. Lawrence: Regents Press of Kansas.
1983   Budding Urban Settlements in the Northern San Juan. *In* Proceedings of the Anasazi
            Symposium 1981. Jack E. Smith, ed. Pp. 175–80. Mesa Verde, CO: Mesa Verde Museum
            Association.

Romain, William F.
2000   Mysteries of Hopewell: Astronomers, Geometers, and Magicians of the Eastern Woodlands.
            Akron, OH: University of Akron Press.

Roney, John R.
1992   Prehistoric Roads and Regional Integration in the Chacoan Region. *In* Anasazi Regional
            Organization and the Chaco System. David E. Doyel, ed. Pp. 123–31. Anthropological Papers
            5. Albuquerque: Maxwell Museum of Anthropology, University of New Mexico.
1995   Mesa Verde Manifestations South of the San Juan River. Journal of Anthropological
            Archaeology 14(2):170–83.
1996   The Pueblo III Period in the Eastern San Juan Basin and Acoma-Laguna Areas. *In* The
            Prehistoric Pueblo World, A.D. 1150–1350. Michael A. Adler, ed. Pp. 145–69. Tucson:
            University of Arizona Press.

Roney, John R., and Robert J. Hard
2002a   Transitions to Agriculture: An Introduction. *In* Traditions, Transitions, and Technologies:
            Themes in Southwestern Archaeology. Sarah H. Schlanger, ed. Pp. 129–36. Boulder:
            University Press of Colorado.
2002b   Early Agriculture in Northwestern Chihuahua. *In* Traditions, Transitions, and Technologies:
            Themes in Southwestern Archaeology. Sarah H. Schlanger, ed. Pp. 160–77. Boulder:
            University Press of Colorado.

Roth, Barbara J.
1996a   Introduction: Early Hunters, Gatherers, and Farmers in the Southern Southwest. *In* Early
            Formative Adaptations in the Southern Southwest. Barbara J. Roth, ed. Pp. 1–4. Monographs
            in World Archaeology 25. Madison, WI: Prehistory Press.

Roth, Barbara J., ed.
1996b   Early Formative Adaptations in the Southern Southwest. Monographs in World Archaeology
            25. Madison, WI: Prehistory Press.

Rushforth, Scott, and Steadman Upham
1992   A Hopi Social History. Austin: University of Texas Press.

Sahlins, Marshall
2004   Apologies to Thucydides: Understanding History as Culture, and Vice Versa. Chicago:
            University of Chicago Press.

Sahlins, Marshall, and Elman R. Service, eds.
1960   Evolution and Culture. Ann Arbor: University of Michigan Press.

Sahlqvist, Leif
2001   Territorial Behaviour and Communication in a Ritual Landscape. Human Geography
            83(2):79–102.

Salzer, Matthew W.
2000   Temperature Variability and the Northern Anasazi: Possible Implications for Regional
            Abandonment. Kiva 65:295–318.

Sanderson, Stephen K., ed.
1995   Civilizations and World Systems: Studying World-Historical Change. Walnut Creek, CA: AltaMira.

Santley, Robert S., and Rani T. Alexander
1992   The Political Economy of Core-Periphery Systems. *In* Resources, Power and Interregional Interaction. Edward M. Schortman and Patricia A. Urban, eds. Pp. 23–49. New York: Plenum.

Santley, Robert S., Michael J. Berman, and Rani T. Alexander
1991   The Politicization of the Mesoamerican Ballgame and Its Implications for the Interpretation of the Distribution of Ballcourts in Central Mexico. *In* The Mesoamerican Ballgame. Vernon L. Scarborough and David R. Wilcox, eds. Pp. 3–24. Tucson: University of Arizona Press.

Sarber, Mary A.
1977   Charles F. Lummis: A Bibliography. Tucson: University Library, University of Arizona.

Sauer, Carl
1932   Road to Cibola. Ibero-Americana 3. Berkeley: University of California Press.
1935   Aboriginal Population of Northwestern Mexico. Ibero-Americana 5. Berkeley: University of California Press.

Sauer, Carl, and Donald Brand
1932   Aztatlán: Prehistoric Mexican Frontier on the Pacific Coast. Ibero-Americana 1. Berkeley: University of California Press.

Sayles, Edwin B.
1935   An Archaeological Survey of Texas. Medallion Papers 17. Globe, AZ: Gila Pueblo.
1936   An Archaeological Survey of Chihuahua. Medallion Papers 22. Globe, AZ: Gila Pueblo.

Scarborough, Vernon L., and David R. Wilcox, eds.
1991   The Mesoamerican Ballgame. Tucson: University of Arizona Press.

Schaafsma, Curtis F., and Carroll L. Riley, eds.
1999   The Casas Grandes World. Salt Lake City: University of Utah Press.

Schaafsma, Polly
1980   Indian Rock Art of the Southwest. Santa Fe, NM: School of American Research Press.
1994   The Prehistoric Kachina Cult and Its Origins as Suggested by Southwestern Rock Art. *In* Kachinas in the Pueblo World. Polly Schaafsma, ed. Pp. 63–79. Albuquerque: University of New Mexico Press.
2000   Warrior, Shield, and Star: Imagery and Ideology of Pueblo Warfare. Santa Fe, NM: Western Edge.
2007   The Pottery Mound Murals and Rock Art, Implications for Regional Interaction. *In* New Perspectives on Pottery Mound Pueblo. Polly Schaafsma, ed. Pp. 137–66. Albuquerque: University of New Mexico Press.

Schaafsma, Polly, ed.
1994   Kachinas in the Pueblo World. Albuquerque: University of New Mexico Press.
2007   New Perspectives on Pottery Mound Pueblo. Albuquerque: University of New Mexico Press.

Schaafsma, Polly, and Karl A. Taube
2006   Bringing the Rain: An Ideology of Rain Making in the Pueblo Southwest and Mesoamerica. *In* A Pre-Columbian World. Jeffrey Quilter and Mary Miller, eds. Pp. 231–85. Washington, DC: Dumbarton Oaks.

Schachner, Gregson
2001   Ritual Control and Transformation in Middle-Range Societies: An Example from the American Southwest. Journal of Anthropological Archaeology 20:168–94.
2006   The Decline of Zuni Glaze Ware Production in the Tumultuous Fifteenth Century. *In* The Social Life of Pots: Glaze Wares and Cultural Dynamics in the Southwest, AD 1250–1680. Judith A. Habicht-Mauche, Suzanne L. Eckert, and Deborah L. Huntley, eds. Pp. 124–41. Tucson: University of Arizona Press.

Scheick, Cherie L.
2008   The Late Developmental and Early Coalition of the Northern Middle Rio Grande. Kiva 73(2):131–54.

Schelberg, John D.

1984   Analogy, Complexity, and Regionally Based Perspectives. *In* Recent Research in Chaco Prehistory. W. James Judge and John D. Schelberg, eds. Pp. 5–21. Reports of the Chaco Center 8. Albuquerque, NM: National Park Service.

Schele, Linda, and David Freidel

1990   A Forest of Kings: The Untold Story of the Ancient Maya. New York: William Morrow.

Schiffer, Michael B.

1983   Toward the Identification of Formation Processes. American Antiquity 48:675–706.

Schlanger, Sarah H.

2007   Poor Mesa Verde: So Far from Heaven, So Close to Chaco. *In* Hinterlands and Regional Dynamics in the Ancient Southwest. Alan P. Sullivan III and James M. Bayman, eds. Pp. 163–84. Tucson: University of Arizona Press.

Schlanger, Sarah H., ed.

2002   Traditions, Transitions, and Technologies: Themes in Southwestern Archaeology. Boulder: University Press of Colorado.

Schleher, Kari L., and Susan M. Ruth

2005   Migration or Local Development? Technological Analysis of Corrugated Wares at the Pinnacle Ruin, Southwest New Mexico. Pottery Southwest 24(3–4):2–14.

Schoenwetter, James

2005   *Review of* America before the European Invasions, by Alice Kehoe. American Antiquity 70:790–91.

Schortman, Edward M., and Patricia A. Urban, eds.

1992   Resources, Power and Interregional Interaction. New York: Plenum.

Schroeder, Albert H.

1965   Unregulated Diffusion from Mexico into the Southwest Prior to AD 700. American Antiquity 30:297–309.

1966   Pattern Diffusion from Mexico into the Southwest after AD 600. American Antiquity 31:683–704.

1979   Pueblos Abandoned in Historic Times. *In* Handbook of North American Indians, vol. 9: Southwest. Alfonso Ortiz, ed. Pp. 236–54. Washington, DC: Smithsonian Institution.

Schroeder, Alfred H., and Fred Wendorf

1954   Excavations near Aragon, New Mexico. *In* Highway Salvage Archaeology. Fred Wendorf, ed. Pp. 53–65. Santa Fe: Museum of New Mexico.

Sebastian, Lynne

1992   The Chaco Anasazi: Sociopolitical Evolution in the Prehistoric Southwest. Cambridge: Cambridge University Press.

Service, Elman R.

1962   Primitive Social Organization. New York: Random House.

1975   Origins of the State and Civilization. New York: Norton.

Service, Robert

2007   Comrades! A History of World Communism. Cambridge, MA: Harvard University Press.

Sewell, William H., Jr.

2005   Logics of History: Social Theory and Social Transformation. Chicago: University of Chicago Press.

Shafer, Harry J.

1995   Architecture and Symbolism in Transitional Pueblo Development in the Mimbres Valley, SW New Mexico. Journal of Field Archaeology 22(1):23–47.

1999a   The Mimbres Classic and Postclassic: A Case for Discontinuity. *In* The Casas Grandes World. Curtis Schaafsma and Carroll Riley, eds. Pp. 121–33. Salt Lake City: University of Utah Press.

1999b   The Classic Mimbres Phenomenon and Some New Interpretations. *In* Sixty Years of Mogollon Archaeology: Papers from the Ninth Mogollon Conference, Siver City, New Mexico, 1996. Stephanie M. Whittlesey, ed. Pp. 95–105. Tucson, AZ: SRI Press.

2003   Mimbres Archaeology at the NAN Ranch Ruin. Albuquerque: University of New Mexico Press.

Shanks, Michael, and Christopher Tilley
1987   Reconstructing Archaeology. Cambridge: Cambridge University Press.

Shaul, David Leedom, and Jane H. Hill
1998   Tepimans, Yumans, and Other Hohokam. American Antiquity 63:375–96.

Shepard, Anna O.
1948   The Symmetry of Abstract Design with Special Reference to Ceramic Decoration. Contributions to American Anthropology and History 47. Publication 574. Washington, DC: Carnegie Institution.

Sheridan, Susan Guise
2001   Morbidity and Mortality in a Classic-Period Hohokam Community. *In* Ancient Burial Practices in the American Southwest: Archaeology, Physical Anthropology, and Native American Perspectives. Douglas R. Mitchell and Judy L. Brunson-Hadley, eds. Pp. 191–222. Albuquerque: University of New Mexico Press.
2003   Childhood Health as an Indicator of Biological Stress. *In* Centuries of Decline during the Hohokam Classic Period at Pueblo Grande. David R. Abbott, ed. Pp. 82–106. Tucson: University of Arizona Press.

Sherratt, Andrew
2004   Material Resources, Capital, and Power: The Coevolution of Society and Culture. *In* Archaeological Perspectives on Political Economies. Gary M. Feinman and Linda M. Nicholas, eds. Pp. 79–103. Salt Lake City: University of Utah Press.

Shott, Michael J.
2005   Two Cultures: Thought and Practice in British and North American Archaeology. World Archaeology 37(1):1–10.

Shutler, Richard, Jr.
1984   Lost City: Pueblo Grande de Nevada. Anthropological Papers 5. Carson City: Nevada State Museum.

Simmons, Alan H., Ann Lucy Wiener Stodder, Douglas D. Dykeman, and Patricia A. Hicks
1989   Human Adaptations and Cultural Change in the Greater Southwest. Arkansas Archaeological Survey Research Series 32. Fayetteville: Arkansas Archaeological Survey.

Simpson, James Hervey
1850   Journal of a Military Reconnaissance from Santa Fe, New Mexico, to the Navajo Country. *In* Report of the Secretary of War to the 31st Congress, 1st Session, Senate Executive Document 65. Union Office, Washington, DC.

Skalník, Peter, ed.
1989   Outwitting the State. New Brunswick, NJ: Transaction Publishers.

Skibo, James M., Eugene B. McCluney, and William H. Walker
2002   The Joyce Well Site: On the Frontier of the Casas Grandes World. Salt Lake City: University of Utah Press.

Smiley, Francis E.
1994   The Agricultural Transition in the Northern Southwest: Patterns in the Current Chronometric Data. Kiva 60:165-189.
2002   The First Black Mesa Farmers: The White Dog and Lolomai Phases. *In* Prehistoric Culture Change on the Colorado Plateau: Ten Thousand Years on Black Mesa. Shirley Powell and Francis E. Smiley, eds. Pp. 37–65. Tucson: University of Arizona Press.

Smiley, Terah A., Stanley A. Stubbs, and Bryant Bannister
1953   A Foundation for the Dating of Some Late Archaeological Sites in the Rio Grande Area, New Mexico. University of Arizona Bulletin 24(3), Laboratory of Tree-ring Research Bulletin 6. Tucson, AZ: Laboratory of Tree-Ring Research.

Smith, Adam T.
2003   The Political Landscape: Constellations of Authority in Early Complex Polities. Berkeley: University of California Press.

Smith, Bruce D.

1992   Mississippian Elites and Solar Alignments: A Reflection of Managerial Necessity, or Levers of Social Inequality? *In* Lords of the Southeast: Social Inequality and the Native Elites of Southeastern North America. A. W. Baker and Timothy R. Pauketat, eds. Pp. 11–30. Anthropological Papers of the American Anthropological Association, vol. 3, no. 1. Washington, DC: American Anthropological Association.

2005   Documenting the Transition to Food Production along the Borderlands. *In* The Late Archaic across the Borderlands: From Foraging to Farming. Bradley J. Vierra, ed. Pp. 300–16. Austin: University of Texas Press.

Smith, Bruce D., ed.

1990   The Mississippian Emergence. Washington, DC: Smithsonian Institution Press.

Smith, Duane A.

1988   Mesa Verde National Park: Shadows and Centuries. Lawrence: University Press of Kansas.

Smith, Jack E.

1985   Mesas, Cliffs and Canyons: The University of Colorado Survey of Mesa Verde National Park, 1971–1977. Mesa Verde, CO: Mesa Verde Museum Association.

Smith, Jack E., ed.

1983   Proceedings of the Anasazi Symposium 1981. Mesa Verde, CO: Mesa Verde Museum Association.

Smith, Marian, ed.

1953   Asia and North America: Transpacific Contacts. Memoirs 9. American Antiquity 18(3):pt. 2. Salt Lake City, UT: Society for American Archaeology.

Smith, Michael E.

2003   Key Commodities. *In* The Postclassic Mesoamerican World. Michael E. Smith and Frances F. Berdan, eds. Pp. 117–25. Salt Lake City: University of Utah Press.

2005   City Size in Late Postclassic Mesoamerica. Journal of Urban History 31:403–34.

2007   Form and Meaning in the Earliest Cities: A New Approach to Ancient Urban Planning. Journal of Planning History 6(1):3–47.

Smith, Michael E., and Frances F. Berdan

2003a   Spatial Structure of the Mesoamerican World System. *In* The Postclassic Mesoamerican World. Michael E. Smith and Frances F. Berdan, eds. Pp. 21–31. Salt Lake City: University of Utah Press.

2003b   Postclassic Mesoamerica. *In* The Postclassic Mesoamerican World. Michael E. Smith and Frances F. Berdan, eds. Pp. 3–13. Salt Lake City: University of Utah Press.

Smith, Michael E., and Frances F. Berdan, eds.

2003   The Postclassic Mesoamerican World. Salt Lake City: University of Utah Press.

Smith, Michael E., and Katharina J. Schreiber

2005   New World States and Empires: Economic and Social Organization. Journal of Archaeological Research 13:189–229.

2006   New World States and Empires: Politics, Religion, and Urbanism. Journal of Archaeological Research 14:1–52.

Smith, Monica

2003   Introduction: The Social Construction of Ancient Cities. *In* The Social Construction of Ancient Cities. Monica Smith, ed. Pp. 1–36. Washington, DC: Smithsonian Books.

Smith, Monica, ed.

2003   The Social Construction of Ancient Cities. Washington, DC: Smithsonian Books.

Smith, Watson

1990   When Is a Kiva? And Other Questions about Southwestern Archaeology. Raymond H. Thompson, ed. Tucson: University of Arizona Press.

Snead, James E.

2001   Ruins and Rivals: The Making of Southwest Archaeology. Tucson: University of Arizona Press.

2004   Ancestral Pueblo Settlement Dynamics: Landscape, Scale and Context in the Burnt Corn Community. Kiva 69:243–69.

2005   Paradigms, Professionals, and the Making of Southwest Archaeology. *In* Southwest

Archaeology in the Twentieth Century. Linda S. Cordell and Don D. Fowler, eds. Pp. 27–46. Salt Lake City: University of Utah Press.

Snow, Charles Percy
1959   The Two Cultures and the Scientific Revolution. Cambridge: Cambridge University Press.

Sofaer, Anna, producer
1999   The Mystery of Chaco Canyon. Video. Oley, PA: Bullfrog Films.

Sofaer, Anna
[1997]2007   The Primary Architecture of the Chacoan Culture: A Cosmological Expression. *In* The Architecture of Chaco Canyon, New Mexico. Stephen H. Lekson, ed. Pp. 225–54. Salt Lake City: University of Utah Press.

Spence, Michael W.
2000   From Tzintzuntzan to Paquimé: Peers or Peripheries in Greater Mesoamerica? *In* Greater Mesoamerica: The Archaeology of West and Northwest Mexico. Michael S. Foster and Shirley Gorenstein, eds. Pp. 255–61. Salt Lake City: University of Utah Press.

Spencer, Charles S., and Elsa M. Redmond
2004   Primary State Formation in Mesoamerica. Annual Review of Anthropology 33:173–99.

Spielmann, Katherine A.
2004   Clusters Revisited. *In* The Protohistoric Pueblo World, A.D. 1275–1600. E. Charles Adams and Andrew I. Duff, eds. Pp. 137–43. Tucson: University of Arizona Press.
2005   Ethnographic Analogy and Ancestral Pueblo Archaeology. *In* Southwest Archaeology in the Twentieth Century. Linda S. Cordell and Don D. Fowler, eds. Pp. 194–203. Salt Lake City: University of Utah Press.

Spielmann, Katherine A., ed.
1991   Farmers, Hunters, and Colonists: Interaction between the Southwest and the Southern Plains. Tucson: University of Arizona Press.
1998   Migration and Reorganization: The Pueblo IV Period in the American Southwest. Anthropological Research Papers 51. Tempe: Arizona State University.

Spier, Fred
1996   The Structure of Big History: From the Big Bang until Today. Amsterdam: Amsterdam University Press.

Spier, Leslie
1917   An Outline for the Chronology of Zuñi Ruins. Anthropological Papers, vol. 18, no. 3. New York: American Museum of Natural History.

Staller, John E., Robert H. Tykot, and Bruce F. Benz, eds.
2006   Histories of Maize: Multidisciplinary Approaches to the Prehistory, Linguistics, Biogeography, Domestication and Evolution of Maize. Burlington, MA: Academic Press.

Stark, Miriam T., Jeffrey J. Clark, and Mark D. Elson
1995   Social Boundaries and Cultural Identity in the Tonto Basin. *In* New Perspectives on Tonto Basin Prehistory. Mark D. Elson, Miriam T. Stark, and David A. Gregory, eds. Pp. 343–68. Anthropological Papers 15. Tucson, AZ: Center for Desert Archaeology.

Stearns, Peter N.
2001   Cultures in Motion: Mapping Key Contacts and Their Imprints in World History. New Haven, CT: Yale University Press.

Stein, John R., Dabney Ford, and Richard Friedman
2003   Reconstructing Pueblo Bonito. *In* Pueblo Bonito. Jill E. Neitzel, ed. Pp. 33–60. Washington, DC: Smithsonian Books.

Stein, John R., Richard Friedman, Taft Blackhorse, and Richard Loose
2007   Revisiting Downtown Chaco. *In* The Architecture of Chaco Canyon. Stephen H. Lekson, ed. Pp. 199–223. Salt Lake City: University of Utah Press.

Stein, John R., and Stephen H. Lekson
1992   Anasazi Ritual Landscapes. *In* Anasazi Regional Organization and the Chaco System. David E. Doyel, ed. Pp. 87–100. Anthropological Papers 5. Albuquerque: Maxwell Museum of Anthropology, University of New Mexico.

Stein, John R., and Peter J. McKenna
1988   An Archaeological Reconnaissance of a Late Bonito Phase Occupation near Aztec Ruins National Monument, New Mexico. Santa Fe, NM: Southwest Cultural Resources Center, National Park Service.

Stevens, Dominique E., and George A. Agogino
1975   Sandia Cave: A Study in Controversy. Contributions in Anthropology, vol. 7, no. 1. Portales: Eastern New Mexico University.

Stewart, Joe D., Arthur C. MacWilliams, and Jane H. Kelley
2004   Archaeological Chronology in West-Central Chihuahua. *In* Surveying the Archaeology of Northwest Mexico. Gillian E. Newell and Emiliano Gallaga, eds. Pp. 205–45. Salt Lake City: University of Utah Press.

Stewart, Joe D., Jane H. Kelley, Arthur C. MacWilliams, and Paula J. Reimer
2005   The Viejo Period of Chihuahua Culture in Northwestern Mexico. Latin American Antiquity 16(2):169–92.

Stirling, Matthew W.
1942   Origin Myth of Acoma, and Other Records. Bulletin 135. Washington, DC: Bureau of American Ethnology.

Stone, Connie L.
1991   The Linear Oasis: Managing Cultural Resources along the Lower Colorado River. Cultural Resource Series 6. Phoenix, AZ: Bureau of Land Management,

Stone, Cynthia L.
2004   In Place of Gods and Kings: Authorship and Identity in the Relacio'n de Michoaca'n. Norman: University of Oklahoma Press.

Stone, Tammy
2001   Prehistoric Community Integration in the Point of Pines Region of Arizona. Journal of Field Archaeology 27(2):197–208.
2003   Social Identity and Ethnic Interaction in the Western Pueblos of the American Southwest. Journal of Archaeological Method and Theory 10(1):31–67.
2005   Late Period Pithouses in the Point of Pines Region of Arizona. Kiva 70:273–92.

Stuart, David
2000   "The Arrival of Strangers": Teotihuacan and Tollan in Classic Maya History. *In* Mesoamerica's Classic Heritage: From Teotihuacan to the Aztecs. David Carrasco, Lindsay Jones, and Scott Sessions, eds. Pp. 465–513. Boulder: University Press of Colorado.

Stuart, David E, and Rory P. Gauthier
1981   Prehistoric New Mexico Background for Survey. Santa Fe: State of New Mexico Historic Preservation Bureau.

Stubbs, Stanley A.
1954   Summary Report on an Early Pueblo Site in the Tesuque Valley, New Mexico. El Palacio 61(2):43–45.

Stuhr, Joanne, ed.
2002   Talking Birds, Plumed Serpents and Painted Women: The Ceramics of Casas Grandes. Tucson: University of Arizona Press.

Sullivan, Alan P., III, and James M. Bayman
2007   Conceptualizing Regional Dynamics in the Ancient Southwest. *In* Hinterlands and Regional Dynamics in the Ancient Southwest. Alan P. Sullivan III and James M. Bayman, eds. Pp. 3–10. Tucson: University of Arizona Press.

Sullivan, Alan P., III, and James M. Bayman, eds.
2007   Hinterlands and Regional Dynamics in the Ancient Southwest. Tucson: University of Arizona Press.

Swanson, Steven J.
2003   Documenting Prehistoric Communication Networks: A Case Study in the Paquimé Polity. American Antiquity 68:753–67.

Swanson, Steven J., and Michael W. Diehl
2003   Mimbres Pithouse Dwellers. Archaeology Southwest 17(4):3.

Tainter, Joseph A.
1988   The Collapse of Complex Societies. Cambridge: Cambridge University Press.

Tainter, Joseph A., and Bonnie Bagley Tainter, eds.
1996   Evolving Complexity and Environmental Risk in the Prehistoric Southwest. Reading, MA: Addison-Wesley.

Tanner, Helen Hornbeck
2006   The Land and Water Communication Systems of the Southeastern Indians. *In* Powhatan's Mantle: Indians in the Colonial Southeast. 2nd ed. Gregory A. Waselkov, Peter H. Wood, and Tom Hatley, eds. Pp. 27–42. Lincoln: University of Nebraska Press.

Taylor, R. E., G. E. Cunnar, J. S. Schneider, C. A. Prior, D. Kirner, R. Burky, and B. A. Morrison
2003   Radiocarbon Chronology of Pendejo Cave. *In* Pendejo Cave. Richard S. MacNeish and Jane G. Libby, eds. Pp. 173–89. Albuquerque: University of New Mexico Press.

Taylor, Walter W.
1948   A Study of Archaeology. American Anthropological Association Memoir 69.
1954   Southwestern archaeology, its history and theory. American Anthropologist n.s. 56: 561–575.

Teague, Lynn S.
1993   Prehistory and the Traditions of the O'Odham and Hopi. Kiva 58:435–54.
1998   Textiles in Southwestern Prehistory. Tucson: University of Arizona Press.
2000   Outward and Visible Signs: Textiles in Ceremonial Contexts. *In* The Archaeology of Regional Interaction: Religion, Warfare, and Exchange across the American Southwest and Beyond. Michelle Hegmon, ed. Pp. 429–47. Boulder: University Press of Colorado.

Thayer, William M.
1890   Marvels of the New West: A Vivid Portrayal of the Stupendous Marvels in the Vast Wonderland West of the Missouri River. Norwich, CT: Henry Bill.

Thomas, Hugh
1992   The Real Discovery of America: Mexico, November 8, 1519. Mount Kisco, NY: Moyer Bell.

Thomas, Julian, ed.
2000   Interpretive Archaeology: A Reader. London: Leicester University Press.

Thompson, Marc
1994   The Evolution and Dissemination of Mimbres Iconography. *In* Kachinas in the Pueblo World. Polly Schaafsma, ed. Pp. 93–105. Albuquerque: University of New Mexico Press.

Thompson, Mark
2001   American Character: The Curious Life of Charles Fletcher Lummis and the Rediscovery of the Southwest. New York: Arcade.

Thompson, Raymond H., ed.
1958   Migrations in New World Culture History. University of Arizona Bulletin 29(2), Social Science Bulletin 27. Tucson: University of Arizona.

Tilley, Christoper, ed.
1993   Interpretative Archaeology. Providence, RI: Berg.

Tobin, Joseph
1990   The HRAF as Radical Text? Cultural Anthropology 5(4):473–87.

Toll, H. Wolcott
2006   Organization of Production. *In* The Archaeology of Chaco Canyon: An Eleventh-Century Pueblo Regional Center. Stephen H. Lekson, ed. Pp. 117–51. Santa Fe, NM: School of American Research Press.

Toll, H. Wolcott, and Peter J. McKenna
1997   Chaco Ceramics. *In* Ceramics, Lithics, and Ornaments of Chaco Canyon: Analyses of Artifacts from the Chaco Project, 1971–1978, vol. 1: Ceramics. Frances Joan Mathien, ed. Pp. 17–530. Publications in Archaeology 18G. Santa Fe, NM: National Park Service.

Toll, H. Wolcott, and C. Dean Wilson
2000   Locational, Architectural, and Ceramic Trends in the Basketmaker III Occupation of the La
            Plata Valley, New Mexico. *In* Foundations of Anasazi Culture: The Basketmaker–Pueblo
            Transition. Paul F. Reed, ed. Pp. 19–43. Salt Lake City: University of Utah Press.

Toulouse, Betty
1981   The Laboratory's Early Years: 1927–1947. El Palacio 87(3):7–13.

Towner, Ronald H.
1996   The Archaeology of Navajo Origins. Salt Lake City: University of Utah Press.

Townsend, Richard F.
1992   The Aztecs. London: Thames and Hudson.
2005   Casas Grandes in the Art of the Ancient Southwest. *In* Casas Grandes and the Ceramic Art of
            the Ancient Southwest. Richard F. Townsend, ed. Pp. 14–65. Chicago: Art Institute of
            Chicago; New Haven, CT: Yale University Press.

Townsend, Richard F., ed.
1998   Ancient West Mexico: Art and Archaeology of the Unknown Past. Chicago: Art Institute of
            Chicago.
2005   Casas Grandes and the Ceramic Art of the Ancient Southwest. Chicago: Art Institute of
            Chicago; New Haven, CT: Yale University Press.

Townsend, Richard, and Robert V. Sharp, eds.
2004   Hero, Hawk, and Open Hand: American Indian Art of the Ancient Midwest and Southeast.
            Chicago: Art Institute of Chicago; New Haven, CT: Yale University Press.

Toynbee, Arnold
1934–1961   A Study of History, vols. 1–10. Oxford: Oxford University Press.

Trevelyan, Amelia M.
2004   Miskwabik: Metal of Ritual: Metallurgy in Precontact Eastern North America. Lexington:
            University Press of Kentucky.

Trigger, Bruce G.
1989   A History of Archaeological Thought. Cambridge: Cambridge University Press.
2003a   Understanding Early Civilizations: A Comparative Study. Cambridge: Cambridge University
            Press.
2003b   Introduction: Understanding the Material Remains of the Past. *In* Artifacts and Ideas: Essays
            in Archaeology. Bruce G. Trigger, ed. Pp. 1–30. New Brunswick, NJ: Transaction.
2006   A History of Archaeological Thought. 2nd ed. Cambridge: Cambridge University Press.

Turner, Christy G., II, and Jacqueline A. Turner
1999   Man Corn: Cannibalism and Violence in the Prehistoric American Southwest. Salt Lake City:
            University of Utah Press.

Tyberg, Joel Jay
2000   Influences, Occupation, and Salado Development at the Solomonsville Site. MA thesis,
            Department of Anthropology, University of Colorado, Boulder.

Upham, Steadman
1982   Polities and Power: An Economic and Political History of the Western Pueblos. Studies in
            Archaeology. New York: Academic Press.
1984   Adaptive Diversity and Southwestern Abandonment. Journal of Anthropological Research
            40(2):235–56.
1986   Interpretations of Prehistoric Political Complexity in the Central and Northern Southwest.
            In Status, Structure, and Stratification: Current Archaeological Reconstructions. Marc
            Thompson, Maria Teresa Garcia, and Francois J. Kense, eds. Pp. 175–80. Proceedings of the
            16th Annual Conference. Alberta: Archaeological Association of the University of Calgary.
1994   Ten Years After: Adaptive Diversity and Southwestern Archaeology. Journal of
            Anthropological Research 50(2):155–57.

Upham, Steadman, ed.
1990   The Evolution of Political Systems: Sociopolitics in Small-Scale Sedentary Societies.
            Cambridge: Cambridge University Press.

Upham, Steadman, Kent G. Lightfoot, and Roberta A. Jewett
1989   The Sociopolitical Structure of Prehistoric Southwestern Societies. Boulder, CO: Westview.

Upham, Steadman, and Fred Plog
1986   Interpretation of Prehistoric Political Complexity in the Central and Northern Southwest: Toward a Mending of the Models. Journal of Field Archaeology 13(2):223–38.

van der Leeuw, Sander
1981   Information Flows, Flow Structures and the Explanation of Change in Human Institutions. *In* Archaeological Approaches to the Study of Complexity. Sander van der Leeuw, ed. Pp. 229–312. Amsterdam: University of Amsterdam.

Van Dyke, Ruth M.
2003   Memory and the Construction of Chacoan Society. *In* Archaeologies of Memory. Ruth M. Van Dyke and Susan E. Alcock, eds. Pp. 180–200. Oxford: Blackwell.
2004   Memory, Meaning and Landscape: The Late Bonito Chacoan Landscape. American Antiquity 69:413–31.
2007a   Great Kivas in Time, Space and Society. *In* The Architecture of Chaco Canyon, New Mexico. Stephen H. Lekson, ed. Pp. 93–126. Salt Lake City: University of Utah Press.
2007b   The Chaco Experience: Landscape and Ideology at the Center Place. Santa Fe, NM: School for Advanced Research Press.

Van Keuren, Scott
2000   Ceramic Decoration as Power: Late Prehistoric Design Change in East-central Arizona. *In* Alternative Leadership Strategies in the Prehispanic Southwest. B. J. Mills, ed. Pp. 79–94. Tucson: University of Arizona Press.
2006   Decorating Glaze-Painted Pottery in East-central Arizona. *In* The Social Life of Pots: Glaze Wares and Cultural Dynamics in the Southwest, AD 1250–1680. Judith A. Habicht-Mauche, Suzanne L. Eckert, and Deborah L. Huntley, eds. Pp. 86–104. Tucson: University of Arizona Press.

VanPool, Christine S.
2003   The Shaman-Priests of the Casas Grandes Region, Chihuahua, Mexico. American Antiquity 68:696–717.

VanPool, Christine S., and Todd L. VanPool
1999   The Scientific Nature of Postprocessualism. American Antiquity 64:33–53.

VanPool, Todd L., and Robert D. Leonard
2002   Specialized Ground Stone Production in the Casas Grandes Region of Northern Chihuahua. American Antiqity 67:710–30.

VanPool, Todd L., Christine S. VanPool, and David A. Phillips Jr.
2006   The Casas Grandes and Salado Phenomena: Evidence for a Religious Schism in the Greater Southwest. *In* Religion in the Prehispanic Southwest. Christine S. VanPool, Todd L. VanPool, and David A. Phillips Jr., eds. Pp. 235–51. Lanham, MD: AltaMira.

Vansina, Jan
1985   Oral Tradition as History. Madison: University of Wisconsin Press.
2004   How Societies Are Born: Governance in West Central Africa before 1600. Charlottesville: University of Virginia Press.

Van West, Carla R.
1994   Modeling Prehistoric Agricultural Productivity in Southwestern Colorado: A GIS Approach. Reports of Investigations 67. Pullman: Washington State University, Department of Anthropology.

Vargas, Victoria D.
1995   Copper Bell Trade Patterns in the Prehispanic U.S. Southwest and Northwest Mexico. Archaeological Series 187. Tucson: Arizona State Museum.

Varien, Mark D.
1999   Sedentism and Mobility in a Social Landscape: Mesa Verde and Beyond. Tucson: University of Arizona Press.

Varien, Mark D., and Richard H. Wilshusen, eds.
2002   Seeking the Center Place: Archaeology and Ancient Communities in the Mesa Verde Region. Salt Lake City: University of Utah Press.

Varien, Mark D., Scott G. Ortman, Timothy A. Kohler, Donna M. Glowacki, and C. D. Johnson
2007   Historical Ecology in the Mesa Verde Region: Results from the Village Ecodynamics Project. American Antiquity 72:273–99.

Vierra, Bradley J., ed.
2005   The Late Archaic across the Borderlands: From Foraging to Farming. Austin: University of Texas Press.
2007   The Northern Rio Grande. Special issue, Kiva 73(2).

Vierra, Bradley J., and Richard I. Ford
2006   Early Maize Agriculture in the Northern Rio Grande Valley, New Mexico. *In* Histories of Maize. John E. Staller, Robert H. Tykot, and Bruce F. Benz, eds. Pp. 497–510. Burlington, MA: Academic Press.

Villagra, Gaspar Pérez de
[1610] 1933 History of New Mexico, by Gaspar Pérez de Villagrá, Alcalá, 1610; translated by Gilberto Espinosa; introduction and notes by F. W. Hodge. Los Angeles, CA: The Quivira Society.

Villalpando, M. Elisa
2000   The Archaeological Traditions of Sonora. *In* Greater Mesoamerica: The Archaeology of West and Northwest Mexico. Michael S. Foster, and Shirley Gorenstein, eds. Pp. 241–53. Salt Lake City: University of Utah Press.

Villalpando, M. Elisa, ed.
2002   Boundaries and Territories: Prehistory of the U.S. Southwest and Northern Mexico. Anthropological Research Papers 54. Tempe: Arizona State University.

Vincent, John
2006   An Intelligent Person's Guide to History. 3rd ed. London: Duckworth Overlook.

Vivian, Gordon R., and Tom W. Mathews
1965   Kin Kletso: A Pueblo III Community in Chaco Canyon, New Mexico. Technical Series 6(1). Tucson, AZ: Southwest Parks and Monuments Association.

Vivian, R. Gwinn
1989   Kluckhohn Reappraised: The Chacoan System as an Egalitarian Enterprise. Journal of Anthropological Research 45(1):101–13.
1990   The Chacoan Prehistory of the San Juan Basin. San Diego: Academic Press.
1996   "Chaco" as a Regional System. *In* Interpreting Southwestern Diversity. Paul R. Fish and J. Jefferson Reid, eds. Pp. 45–53. Anthropological Research Papers 48. Tempe: Arizona State University.
2001   Chaco Reconstructed. Cambridge Archaeological Journal 11(1):142–44.
2005   Clyde Kluckhohn, Chaco, and the Puebloan World. *In* Inscriptions: Papers in Honor of Richard and Nathalie Woodbury. Regge N. Wiseman, Thomas C. O'Laughlin, and Cordelia T. Snow, eds. Pp. 199–207. Paper 31. Albuquerque: Archaeological Society of New Mexico.

Vivian, R. Gwinn, Carla R. Van West, Jeffrey S. Dean, Nancy J. Akins, Mollie S. Toll, and Thomas C. Windes
2006   Ecology and Economy. *In* The Archaeology of Chaco Canyon: An Eleventh-Century Pueblo Regional Center. Stephen H. Lekson, ed. Pp. 45–65. Santa Fe, NM: School of American Research Press.

Vivian, R. Gwinn, Dulce N. Dodgen, and Gayle H. Hartman
1978   Wooden Ritual Artifacts from Chaco Canyon, New Mexico. Anthropological Papers 32. Tucson: University of Arizona Press.

Vokes, Arthur W., and David A. Gregory
2007   Exchange Networks for Exotic Goods in the Southwest and Zuni's Place in Them. *In* Zuni Origins: Toward a New Synthesis of Southwestern Archaeology. David A. Gregory and David R. Wilcox, eds. Pp. 318–57. Tucson: University of Arizona Press.

Voth, Henry R.
1905   Traditions of the Hopi. Publication 96, Anthropological Series 8. Chicago: Field Museum of Natural History.

Wagner, Daniel P., and Joseph M. McAvoy
2004   Pedoarchaeology of Cactus Hill. Geoarchaeology 19(4):297–322.

Wallace, Henry D.
1995   Decorated Buffware and Brownware Ceramics. *In* Roosevelt Community Development Study: Ceramic Chronology, Technology and Economics. J. J. Heidke and M. T. Stark, eds. Pp. 19–84. Anthropological Papers 14. Tucson, AZ: Center for Desert Archaeology.

Wallace, Henry D., ed.
2003   Roots of Sedentism: Archaeological Excavations at the Valencia Vieja, a Founding Village in the Tucson Basin of Southern Arizona. Anthropological Papers 29. Tucson, AZ: Center for Desert Archaeology.

Wallace, Henry D., and William H. Doelle
2001   Classic Period Warfare in Southern Arizona. *In* Deadly Landscapes: Case Studies in Prehistoric Southwestern Warfare. Glen E. Rice and Steven A. LeBlanc, eds. Pp. 239–87. Salt Lake City: University of Utah Press.

Wallace, Henry D., James E. Heidke, and William H. Doelle
1995   Hohokam Origins. Kiva 60(4):575–618.

Wallace, Henry D., and Michael W. Lindeman
2003   Valencia Vieja and the Origins of Hohokam Culture. *In* Roots of Sedentism: Archaeological Excavations at the Valencia Vieja, a Founding Village in the Tucson Basin of Southern Arizona. Henry D. Wallace, ed. Pp. 371–405. Anthropological Papers 29. Tucson, AZ: Center for Desert Archaeology.
Forthcoming Cultural Florescence in a Regional Center: Hohokam Cultural Development in the Tucson Basin, A.D. 500 to 1150. *In* Hohokam Trajectories in World Perspective. Suzanne K. Fish and Paul R. Fish, eds. Amerind Studies in Archaeology. Tucson: University of Arizona Press.

Wallerstein, Immanuel
1974   The Modern World-System. New York: Academic Press.
1980   Mercantilism and the Consolidation of the European World-Economy, 1600–1750. New York: Academic Press.
1989   The Second Era of Great Expansion of the Capitalist World-Economy, 1730–1840s. San Diego: Academic Press.
1995   Hold the Tiller Firm: On Method and the Unit of Analysis. *In* Civilizations and World Systems: Studying World-Historical Change. Stephen K. Sanderson, ed. Pp. 239–247. Walnut Creek, CA: AltaMira Press.

Walters, H., and H. C. Rogers
2001   "Anasazi" and "Anaasázi": Two Words, Two Cultures. Kiva 66:317–26.

Warburton, Miranda, and Richard M. Begay
2005   An Exploration of Navajo–Anasazi Relationships. Ethnohistory 52(3):533–61.

Ware, John A.
2001   Chaco Social Organization: A Peripheral View. *In* Chaco Society and Polity: Papers from the 1999 Conference. Linda S. Cordell, W. James Judge, and June-el Piper, eds. Pp. 79–93. Special Publication 4. Albuquerque: New Mexico Archaeological Council.
2002a   What Is a Kiva? The Social Organization of Early Pueblo Communities. *In* Culture and Environment in the American Southwest: Essays in Honor of Robert C. Euler. David A. Phillips Jr. and John A. Ware, eds. Pp. 79–88. SWCA Anthropological Research Paper 8. Phoenix, AZ: SWCA.
2002b   Descent Group and Sodality: Alternative Pueblo Social Histories. *In* Traditions, Transitions, and Technologies: Themes in Southwestern Archaeology. Sarah H. Schlanger, ed. Pp. 94–112. Boulder: University Press of Colorado.

Ware, John A., and Eric Blinman
2000   Cultural Collapse and Reorganization: The Origin and Spread of Pueblo Ritual Sodalities. *In* The Archaeology of Regional Interaction: Religion, Warfare, and Exchange across the American Southwest and Beyond. Michelle Hegmon, ed. Pp. 381–409. Boulder: University Press of Colorado.

Warriner, Gary, prod., dir.
2000   Chaco. Video. Seattle, WA: Camera One.

Washburn, Dorothy K.
1995   Living in Balance: The Universe of the Hopi, Zuni, Navajo, and Apache. Philadelphia: University of Pennsylvania Museum.
2006   Abajo Ceramics: A Non-local Design System amidst the Anasazi. *In* Southwestern Interludes: Papers in Honor of Charlotte J. and Theodore R. Frisbie. Regge N. Wiseman, Thomas C. O'Laughlin, and Cordelia T. Snow, eds. Pp. 193–202. Papers of the Archaeological Society of New Mexico 32. Albuquerque: Archaeological Society of New Mexico.

Washburn, Dorothy K., and Laurie D. Webster
2006   Symmetry and Color Perspectives on Basketmaker Cultural Identities. Kiva 71:235–64.

Wasley, William W.
1960   A Hohokam Platform Mound at the Gatlin Site, Gila Bend, Arizona. American Antiquity 26:244–62.
1962   A Ceremonial Cave on Bonita Creek, Arizona. American Antiquity 27(3):380–94.

Wasley, William W., and Alfred E. Johnson
1965   Salvage Archaeology in Painted Rocks Reservoir, Western Arizona. Anthropological Papers 9. Tucson: University of Arizona Press.

Waterman, T. T.
1917   Bandelier's Contribution to the Study of Ancient Mexican Social Organization. University of California Publications in American Archaeology and Ethnology 12(7):249–82.
1929   Culture Horizons in the Southwest. American Anthropologist 31(3):367–400.

Waters, Frank
1977   Book of the Hopi. New York: Penguin Group.

Watkins, Joe
2001   Indigenous Archaeology: American Indian Values and Scientific Practice. Walnut Creek, CA: AltaMira.

Watson, Patty Jo, Steven A. LeBlanc, and Charles L. Redman
1971   Explanation in Archeology: An Explicitly Scientific Approach. New York: Columbia University Press.

Wauchope, Robert
1962   Lost Tribes and Sunken Continents: Myth and Method in the Study of American Indians. Chicago: University of Chicago Press.

Webster, David
2006   The Mystique of the Ancient Maya. *In* Archaeological Fantasies. Garrett G. Fagan, ed. Pp. 129–53. London: Routledge.

Webster, David, and Takeshi Inomata
2004   Identifying Subroyal Elite Palaces at Copan and Aguateca. *In* Palaces of the Ancient New World. Susan Toby Evans and Joanne Pillsbury, eds. Pp. 149–80. Washington, DC: Dumbarton Oaks.

Webster, Laurie
2007a   Ritual Costuming at Pottery Mound. *In* New Perspectives on Pottery Mound Pueblo. Polly Schaafsma, ed. Pp. 167–206. Albuquerque: University of New Mexico Press.
2007b   Painted Wood from Aztec Ruins. Paper presented at the 70th Annual Pecos Conference, Pecos, NM, August 10–11.
2007c   Mogollon and Zuni Perishable Traditions and the Question of Zuni Origins. *In* Zuni Origins: Toward a New Synthesis of Southwestern Archaeology. David A. Gregory and David R. Wilcox, eds. Pp. 270–317. Tucson: University of Arizona Press.

Webster, Laurie D., and Kelley Hays-Gilpin
1994   New Trails for Old Shoes: Sandals, Textiles, and Baskets in Basketmaker Culture. Kiva 60:313–27.

Weigand, Phillip C., and Garman Harbottle
1993   The Role of Turquoise in the Ancient Mesoamerican Trade Structure. *In* The American Southwest and Mesoamerica: Systems of Prehistoric Exchange. Jonathan E. Ericson and Timothy G. Baugh, eds. Pp. 159–77. New York: Plenum.

Weigand, Phillip C.
1999   The Architecture of the Teuchitlan Tradition of Mexico's Occidente. *In* Mesoamerican Architecture as a Cultural Symbol. Jeff Karl Kowalski, ed. Pp. 40–57. New York: Oxford University Press.
2000   The Evolution and Decline of a Core of Civilization: The Teuchitlan Tradition and the Archaeology of Jalisco. *In* Greater Mesoamerica: The Archaeology of West and Northwest Mexico. Michael S. Foster and Shirley Gorenstein, eds. Pp. 43–58. Salt Lake City: University of Utah Press.

Weigand, Phillip C., and Christopher S. Beekman
1998   The Teuchitlán Tradition: Rise of a Statelike Society. *In* Ancient West Mexico: Art and Archaeology of the Unknown Past. Richard Townsend, ed. Pp. 35–51. Chicago: Art Institute of Chicago.

Wendorf, Fred
1954   A Reconstruction of Northern Rio Grande Prehistory. American Anthropologist 56:200–27.

Wendorf, Fred, and Erik K. Reed
1955   An Alternate Reconstruction of Northern Rio Grand Prehistory. El Palacio 62(5–6):131–73.

Wertheimer, Eric
1999   Imagined Empires: Incas, Aztecs, and the New World of American Literature, 1771–1876. Cambridge: Cambridge University Press.

Wesche, Alice M.
1981   Runs Far, Son of the Chichimecs. Santa Fe: Museum of New Mexico Press.

Whalen, Michael E., and Paul E. Minnis
2000   Leadership at Casas Grandes. *In* Alternative Leadership Strategies in the Prehispanic Southwest. Barbara J. Mills, ed. Pp. 168–79. Tucson: University of Arizona Press.
2001   Casas Grandes and Its Hinterland: Prehistoric Regional Organization in Northwest Mexico. Tucson: University of Arizona Press.
2003   The Local and the Distant in the Origin of Casas Grandes, Chihuahua, Mexico. American Antiquity 68:314–32.
2004   After the Survey: Further Research around Paquimé, Chihuahua, Mexico. *In* Identity, Feasting, and the Archaeology of the Greater Southwest. Barbara J. Mills, ed. Pp. 311–25. Boulder: University Press of Colorado.
Forthcoming The Neighbors of Casas Grandes: Medio Period Communities of Northwest Chihuahua, Mexico. Tucson: University of Arizona Press.

Wheat, Joe Ben
1955   Mogollon Culture Prior to A.D. 1000. American Anthropological Association Memoir 82. Washington, DC: American Anthropological Association.

White, Devin Alan
2004   Hohokam Palettes. Arizona State Museum Archaeological Series 196. Tucson: University of Arizona.

White, Devin Allen
2007   Transportation, Integration, Facilitation: Prehistoric Trail Networks of the Western Papagueria. PhD dissertation, Department of Anthropology, University of Colorado, Boulder.

White, Hayden
1987   The Content of Form: Narrative Discourse and Historical Representation. Baltimore, MD: Johns Hopkins University Press.

White, Leslie A.

1932   The Acoma Indians. *In* 47th Annual Report of the Bureau of American Ethnology for the Years 1929–1930. Pp. 17–192. Washington, DC: Bureau of American Ethnology.

White, Nancy Marie, ed.

2005   Gulf Coast Archaeology: The Southeastern United States and Mexico. Gainesville: University Press of Florida.

White, Tim D.

1992   Prehistoric Cannibalism at Mancos 5MTUMR-2346. Princeton, NJ: Princeton University Press.

Whiteley, Peter M.

1998   Rethinking Hopi Ethnography. Washington, DC: Smithsonian Institution Press.

2004   Social Formations in the Pueblo IV Southwest: An Ethnological View. *In* The Protohistoric Pueblo World, A.D. 1275–1600. E. Charles Adams and Andrew I. Duff, eds. Pp. 144–55. Tucson: University of Arizona Press.

Whittlesey, Stephanie M.

1984   Uses and Abuses of Mogollon Mortuary Data. *In* Recent Research in Mogollon Archaeology. S. Upham, F. Plog, D. Batcho, and B. Kauffman, eds. Pp. 276–84. Occasional Paper 10. Las Cruces: New Mexico State University.

1997   Rethinking the Core-Periphery Model of the Pre-Classic Period Hohokam. *In* Vanishing River: Landscapes and Lives of the Lower Verde Valley: The Lower Verde Archaeological Project. Stephanie M. Whittlesey, Richard Ciolek-Torrello, and Jeffrey H. Altschul, eds. Pp. 597–628. Tucson, AZ: SRI Press.

1998   Early Formative Stage Ceramics and Cultural Affiliation. *In* Early Farmers of the Sonoran Desert: Archaeological Investigations at the Houghton Road Site, Tucson, Arizona. Richard Ciolek-Torrello, ed. Pp. 209–28. Technical Series 72. Tucson, AZ: Statistical Research Inc.

2000   *Review of* Chaco Meridian. Journal of Field Archaeology 27(2):359–64.

2007   Not the Northeast Periphery: The Lower Verde Valley in Regional Context. *In* Hinterlands and Regional Dynamics in the Ancient Southwest. Alan P. Sullivan III and James M. Bayman, eds. Pp. 11–30. Tucson: University of Arizona Press.

Whittlesey, Stephanie M., ed.

1999   Sixty Years of Mogollon Archaeology: Papers from the Ninth Mogollon Conference, Silver City, New Mexico, 1996. Tucson, AZ: SRI Press.

Whittlesey, Stephanie M., and Richard Ciolek-Torrello

1996   The Archaic–Formative Transition in the Tucson Basin. *In* Early Formative Adaptations in the Southern Southwest. Barbara J. Roth, ed. Pp. 49–72. Monographs in World Archaeology 25. Madison, WI: Prehistory Press.

Whittlesey, Stephanie M., Richard Ciolek-Torrello, and Jeffrey H. Altschul, eds.

1997   Vanishing River: Landscapes and Lives of the Lower Verde Valley: The Lower Verde Archaeological Project. Tucson, AZ: SRI Press.

Whittlesey, Stephanie M., Richard Ciolek-Torrello, and Matthew A. Sterner

1994   Southern Arizona the Last 12,000 Years: A Cultural-Historic Overview for the Western Army National Guard Aviation Training Site. Technical Series 48. Tucson, AZ: Statistical Research, Inc.

Wicke, Charles R.

1965   Pyramids and Temple Mounds: Mesoamerican Ceremonial Architecture in Eastern North America. American Antiquity 30(4):409–20.

Wilcox, David R.

1979   Implications of Dry-laid Masonry Walls on Tumamoc Hill. Kiva 45:15–38.

1986   A Historical Analysis of the Problem of Southwestern–Mesoamerican Connections. *In* Ripples in the Chichimec Sea. Frances Joan Mathien and Randall H. McGuire, eds. Pp. 9–44. Carbondale: Southern Illinois University Press.

1986   The Tepiman Connection: A Model of Mesoamerican–Southwestern Interaction. *In* Ripples in the Chichimec Sea. Frances Joan Mathien and Randall H. McGuire, eds. Pp. 135–54. Carbondale: Southern Illinois University Press.

1987   The Evolution of Hohokam Ceremonial Systems. *In* Astronomy and Ceremony in the

Prehistoric Southwest. John B. Carlson and W. James Judge, eds. Pp. 149–67. Papers of the
Maxwell Museum of Anthropology 2. Albuquerque, NM: Maxwell Museum of Anthropology.

1989 Hohokam Warfare. *In* Cultures in Conflict: Current Archaeological Perspectives.
D. C. Tkaczuk and B. C. Vivian, eds. Pp. 163–72. Proceedings of the Twentieth Annual
Chacmool Conference. Calgary: University of Calgary.

1991a Changing Contexts of Pueblo Adaptations, A.D. 1250–1600. *In* Farmers, Hunters, and
Colonists: Interaction between the Southwest and the Southern Plains. Katherine A.
Spielmann, ed. Pp. 128–54. Tucson: University of Arizona Press.

1991b Hohokam Religion: An Archaeologist's Perspective. *In* The Hohokam: Ancient People of the
Desert. David Grant Noble, ed. Pp. 47–59. Santa Fe, NM: School of American Research Press.

1991c Hohokam Social Complexity. *In* Chaco and Hohokam: Prehistoric Regional Systems in the
American Southwest. Patricia L. Crown and W. James Judge, eds. Pp. 135–57. Santa Fe, NM:
School of American Research Press.

1991d The Mesoamerican Ballgame in the American Southwest. *In* The Mesoamerican Ballgame.
Vernon L. Scarborough and David R. Wilcox, eds. Pp. 101–25. Tucson: University of Arizona
Press.

1993a The Evolution of the Chacoan Polity. *In* The Chimney Rock Archaeological Symposium.
J. McKim Malville and Gary Matlock, eds. Pp. 76–90. General Technical Report RM-2276.
Fort Collins, CO: USDA Forest Service Rocky Mountain Experiment Station.

1993b Pueblo Grande in the Nineteenth Century. *In* Archaeology of the Pueblo Grande Platform
Mound and Surrounding Features, vol. 1: Introduction to the Archival Project and History
of Archaeological Research. Christian E. Downum and Todd W. Bostwick, eds. Pp. 43–71.
Anthropological Papers 1. Phoenix, AZ: Pueblo Grande Museum.

1999a A Peregrine View of Macroregional Systems in the North American Southwest, A.D. 750–1250.
In Great Towns and Regional Polities in the Prehistoric American Southwest and Southeast.
Jill E. Neitzel, ed. Pp. 115–41. Albuquerque: University of New Mexico Press.

1999b A Preliminary Graph-Theoretic Analysis of Access Relationships at Casas Grandes. *In* The
Casas Grandes World. Curtis F. Schaafsma and Carroll L. Riley, eds. Pp. 93-104. Salt Lake City:
University of Utah Press.

2004 The Evolution of the Chacoan Polity. *In* Chimney Rock: The Ultimate Outlier. J. McKim
Malville, ed. Pp. 163–200. Lanham, MD: Lexington Books.

2005a Big Issues, New Syntheses. Plateau 2(1):8–21.

2005b Things Chaco: A Peregrine Perspective. Plateau 2(1):38–51.

2005c Creating a Firm Foundation: The Early Days of the Arizona State Museum. Journal of the
Southwest 47(3):375–410.

2007 Discussion of Pottery Mound Essays and Some Alternative Proposals. *In* New Perspectives on
Pottery Mound Pueblo. Polly Schaafsma, ed. Pp. 229–50. Albuquerque: University of New
Mexico Press.

Wilcox, David R., and Don D. Fowler

2002 The Beginnings of Anthropological Archaeology in the North American Southwest: From
Thomas Jefferson to the Pecos Conference. Journal of the Southwest 44(2):121–234.

Wilcox, David R., David A. Gregory, J. Brett Hill, and Gary Funkhouser

2006 The Changing Contexts of Warfare in the North American Southwest, A.D. 1200–1700. *In*
Southwestern Interludes: Papers in Honor of Charlotte J. and Theodore R. Frisbie. Regge N.
Wiseman, Thomas C. O'Laughlin, and Cordelia T. Snow, eds. Pp. 203–32. Paper 32.
Albuquerque: Archaeological Society of New Mexico.

Wilcox, David R., and W. Bruce Masse, eds.

1981 The Protohistoric Period in the North American Southwest, A.D. 1450–1700. Anthropological
Research Papers 24. Tempe: Arizona State University.

Wilcox, David R., Thomas R. McGuire, and Charles Sternberg

1981 Snaketown Revisited. Arizona State Museum Archaeological Series 155. Tucson: University of
Arizona.

Wilcox, David R., and Lynette O. Shenk

1977 The Architecture of Casa Grande and Its Interpretation. Arizona State Museum
Archaeological Series 115. Tucson: University of Arizona.

Wilcox, David R., and Charles Sternberg
1983   Hohokam Ball Courts and Their Interpretation. Arizona State Museum Archaeological Series 160. Tucson: University of Arizona.

Wilder, Joseph Carleton, ed.
1992   The Southwest Defined. Journal of the Southwest 34:257–387. Tucson: University of Arizona Press.

Willey, Gordon R.
1966   An Introduction to American Archaeology. Englewood Cliffs, NJ: Prentice-Hall.

Willey, Gordon R., and Phillip Phillips
1958   Method and Theory in American Archaeology. Chicago: University of Chicago Press.

Willey, Gordon R., and Jeremy A. Sabloff
1980   A History of American Archaeology. 2nd ed. San Francisco: W. H. Freeman.

Williams, Eduardo
2003   Prehispanic West México: A Mesoamerican Culture Area. Foundation for the Advancement of Mesoamerican Studies, Crystal River, FL. Electronic document, http://www.famsi.org/research/williams/index.html, accessed January 2006.

Williams, Mark
2004   The Origins of the Macon Plateau Site. In Ocumlgee Archaeology, 1936–1986. David J. Hally, ed. Pp. 130–37. Athens: University of Georgia Press.

Williams, Stephen
1991   Fantastic Archaeology: The Wild Side of North American Prehistory. Philadelphia: University of Pennsylvania Press.

Wills, W. H.
1988   Early Prehistoric Agriculture in the American Southwest. Santa Fe, NM: School of American Research Press.
2000   Political Leadership and the Construction of Chaco Great Houses. In Alternative Leadership Strategies in the Prehispanic Southwest. Barbara J. Mills, ed. Pp. 19–44. Tucson: University of Arizona Press.

Wills, W. H., and Robert D. Leonard, eds.
1994   The Ancient Southwestern Community: Models and Methods for the Study of Prehistoric Social Organization. Albuquerque: University of New Mexico Press.

Wills, W. H., and Thomas C. Windes
1989   Evidence for Population Aggregation and Dispersal during the Basketmaker III Period in Chaco Canyon, New Mexico. American Antiquity 54:347–69.

Wilshusen, Richard H.
1989   Unstuffing the Estufa: Ritual Floor Features in Anasazi Pit Structures and Pueblo Kivas. In The Architecture of Social Integration in Prehistoric Pueblos. William D. Lipe and Michelle Hegmon, eds. Pp. 89–111. Occasional Paper 1. Cortez, CO: Crow Canyon Archaeological Center.
1999a   Basketmaker III (A.D. 500–750). In Colorado Prehistory: A Context for the Southern Colorado River Basin. William D. Lipe, Mark D. Varien, and Richard H. Wilshusen, eds. Pp. 166–95. Denver, CO: Council of Professional Archaeologists.
1999b   Pueblo I (A.D. 750–900). In Colorado Prehistory: A Context for the Southern Colorado River Basin. William D. Lipe, Mark D. Varien, and Richard H. Wilshusen, eds. Pp. 196–241. Denver, CO: Council of Professional Archaeologists.

Wilshusen, Richard H., ed.
2003   The Yellow Jacket Project: Reports, Collections, History. Electronic document, http://yellowjacket.colorado.edu/, accessed June 2008.

Wilshusen, Richard H., and Scott G. Ortman
1999   Rethinking the Pueblo I Period in the San Juan Drainage: Aggregation, Migration, and Cultural Diversity. Kiva 64:369–99.

Wilshusen, Richard H., and Ruth M. Van Dyke
2006   Chaco's Beginnings. In The Archaeology of Chaco Canyon: An Eleventh-Century Pueblo

Regional Center. Stephen H. Lekson, ed. Pp. 211–60. Santa Fe, NM: School of American Research Press.

Wilson, C. Dean, Eric Blinman, James M. Skibo, and Michael Brian Schiffer
1996   Designing Southwestern Pottery: A Technological and Experimental Approach. *In* Interpreting Southwestern Diversity: Underlying Principles and Overarching Patterns. Paul R. Fish and J. Jefferson Reid, eds. Pp. 249–56. Anthropological Research Papers 48. Tempe: Arizona State University.

Windes, Thomas C.
1984   A New Look at Population in Chaco Canyon. *In* Recent Research on Chaco Prehistory. W. James Judge and John D. Schelberg, eds. Pp. 75–87. Reports of the Chaco Center 8. Albuquerque, NM: Division of Cultural Research, National Park Service.
2007   Gearing Up and Piling On: Early Great Houses in the Interior San Juan Basin. *In* The Architecture of Chaco Canyon, New Mexico. Stephen H. Lekson, ed. Pp. 45–92. Salt Lake City: University of Utah Press.

Windes, Thomas C., ed.
1987   Investigations at the Pueblo Alto Complex, Chaco Canyon, New Mexico, 1975–79, vols. 1 and 2. Publications in Archaeology 18F. Santa Fe, NM: National Park Service.
Forthcoming Early Puebloan Occupations in the Chaco Region. Excavation and Survey of Basketmaker III and Pueblo I Sites, Chaco Canyon, New Mexico. Reports of the Chaco Center, No. 13. Santa Fe: National Park Service.

Windes, Thomas C., and Dabney Ford
1996   The Chaco Wood Project: The Chronometric Reappraisal of Pueblo Bonito. American Antiquity 61:295–310.

Wiseman, Regge N.
1995   Reassessment of the Dating of the Pojoaque Grant Site (LA 835), a Key Site in the Rio Grande Developmental Period. *In* Pots and Rocks: Papers in Honor of Helene Warren. Meliha S. Duran and David T. Kirkpatrick, eds. Pp. 237–47. Papers of the Archaeological Society of New Mexico 21. Albuquerque: Archaeological Society of New Mexico.

Wiseman, Regge N., and J. Andrew Darling
1986   The Bronze Trail Group: More Evidence for a Cerrillos–Chaco Turquoise Connection. *In* By Hands Unknown: Papers on Rock Art and Archaeology. Anne Poore, ed. Pp. 115–43. Papers of the Archaeological Society of New Mexico 12. Santa Fe, NM: Ancient City.

Wiseman, Regge N., and Bart Olinger
1991   Initial Production of Painted Pottery in the Rio Grande: The Perspective from LA 835, the Pojoaque Grant Site. *In* Puebloan Past and Present: Papers in Honor of Stewart Peckham. Meliha S. Duran and David T. Kirkpatrick, eds. Pp. 209–17. Papers of the Archaeological Society of New Mexico 17. Albuquerque: Archaeological Society of New Mexico.

Wolf, Eric R.
1982   Europe and the People without History. Berkeley: University of California Press.

Woodbury, Richard B.
1973   Alfred V. Kidder. Leaders of Modern Anthropology. New York: Columbia University Press.
1993   Sixty Years of Southwestern Archaeology: A History of the Pecos Conference. Albuquerque: University of New Mexico Press.

Woodson, Mark Kyle
1999   Migrations in Late Anasazi Prehistory: The Evidence from the Goat Hill Site. Kiva 65:63–84.

Woosley, Anne I., and John C. Ravesloot, eds.
1993   Culture and Contact: Charles C. Di Peso's Gran Chichimeca. Amerind Foundation New World Studies Series 2. Albuquerque: University of New Mexico Press.

Wormington, H. M.
1955   A Reappraisal of the Fremont Culture with a Summary of the Archaeology of the Northern Periphery. Proceedings, no. 1. Denver, CO: Denver Museum of Natural History.

Wozniak, Frank E., ed.
1996   Cultural Affiliations: Prehistoric Cultural Affiliations of Southwestern Indian Tribes. Albuquerque, NM: USDA Forest Service.

Wright, Barton, ed.
1988   The Mythic World of the Zuni. Albuquerque: University of New Mexico Press.

Wright, Henry T.
1984   Prestate Political Formations. *In* On the Evolution of Complex Societies. Timothy K. Earle, ed. Pp. 43–77. Malibu, CA: Undena.

Wright, Richard B.
2005   Style, Meaning, and the Individual Artist in Western Pueblo Polychrome Ceramics after Chaco. Journal of the Southwest 47(2):259–325.

Yerkes, Richard W.
2006   Middle Woodland Settlements and Social Organization in the Central Ohio Valley: Were the Hopewell Really Farmers? *In* Re-creating Hopewell. Douglas K. Charles and Jane E. Buikstra, eds. Pp. 50–61. Gainesville: University Press of Florida.

Yoffee, Norman
2001   The Chaco "Rituality" Revisited. *In* Chaco Society and Polity: Papers from the 1999 Conference. Linda S. Cordell, W. James Judge, and June-el Piper, eds. Pp. 63–78. NMAC Special Publication 4. Albuquerque: New Mexico Archaeological Council.
2005   Myths of the Archaic State: Evolution of the Earliest Cities, States, and Civilizations. Cambridge: Cambridge University Press.

Yoffee, Norman, Suzanne K. Fish, and George R. Milner
1999   Communidades, Ritualities, Chiefdoms: Social Evolution in the American Southwest and Southeast. *In* Great Towns and Regional Polities in the Prehistoric American Southwest and Southeast. Jill E. Neitzel, ed. Pp. 261–71. Albuquerque: University of New Mexico Press.

Young, Biloine Whiting, and Melvin L. Fowler
2000   Cahokia: The Great Native American Metropolis. Chicago: University of Illinois Press.

Young, M. Jane
1994   The Interconnection between Western Puebloan and Mesoamerican Ideology/Cosmology. *In* Kachinas in the Pueblo World. Polly Schaafsma, ed. Pp. 108–20. Albuquerque: University of New Mexico Press.

Zaragoza Ocaña, Diana
2005   Characteristic Elements Shared by Northeastern Mexico and the Southeastern United States. *In* Gulf Coast Archaeology. Nancy M. White, ed. Pp. 245–59. Gainesville: University Press of Florida.

Zavala, Bridgte M.
2006   Elevated Spaces: Exploring the Symbolic at Cerro de Trincheras. *In* Religion in the Prehispanic Southwest. Christine S. VanPool, Todd L. VanPool, and David A. Phillips Jr., eds. Pp. 135–45. Lanham, MD: AltaMira.

Zolbrod, Paul
2004   Introduction: New World Ancientness. Journal of the Southwest 46(4):593–95.

Zubrow, Ezra B. W.
1974   Prehistoric Carrying Capacity, a Model. Menlo Park, CA: Cummings.

Index

255nn12 and 14–15; steady development school, 2–3

Archaeomagnetic dating, 73

Archaic, 27–29, 38–47, 266n86

Architecture. *See also* Architecture, Anasazi; Ball courts; Big Houses; Kivas; Platform mounds; Political hierarchies and architecture: defensive, 160, 167, 171–172, 226; D-shaped structures, 308n72; and governance, 228–229, 333n143; Hohokam, 23, 167–169, 231, 240–241; houses, 23, **118**, 135–136. (*See also* Unit pueblos); Mesoamerican influence, 140; Mimbres, 94, 282n146; Paquimé, 210–211, 244–245, 335n174, 338n207; towers, **97**

Architecture, Anasazi, 23, **123**, 228–229; Basketmaker III, 65–68, **66, 67, 68**; bi-wall structures, 158, 308n72, 309n73; Chaco, 125–126, 128, 293n136; Plateau, 233; Pueblo IV, 195; tri-wall structures, 154–155, 158, **159**, 308n72, 309n73; T-shaped doors, 211, 213, 337n202; unit pueblos, **95**, 100, 102, **123**, 123–124, **124**, 126, 135

Arizona State Museum (ASM), 75

Art, 30, 193–194, 328n68. *See also* Pottery

Artificial Anasazi Project, 149

Aztatlan, 114, 115–116, 224, 243, 287n56

Aztec Ruins. *See also* Chaco Meridian: Aztec West, **153**; canals, 163, 244; and Chaco, 153–155, 158, 295n142, 305n51, 308n61; construction, 154–155, 308n56, 309n72; cultural region, 158, 160, 308n69; failure, 160, 163, 172, 239; location, 306n51; and Morgan, 295n142; in Native histories, 246; orientations, 238, 308n56; reoccupation, 309n89; site plan, **155**; tri-wall structures, 154–155, 158, 308n72, 309n73

Aztecs, 191, 327n54. (*See also* Aztlan); heritage, 218–219; Mesa Verde as, 270n6; migrations, 33; and Morgan, 221, 343n16; origins, 223–224, 225, 346nn35 and42, 347nn44–45; Southwest as original home, 26, 31; Western histories of, 218, 219

Aztlan: Casas Grandes as, 347n44; and early archaeologists, 33, 34–36; location, 224; and Mexican Americans, 217, 224, 347nn42–43; Southwest as, 26, 31

Bad Dog Ridge, 65

Ball courts: dating, 279n92; and governance, 121; Hohokam, 85–86, **86**, 120–121, 133, 240–241; Mimbres, 90, 92, 281n134; at Paquimé, 213, 337n202; and platform mounds, 169, 170, 240, 314n136, 315n151; purpose, 231, 281n140; size, 232; and system distances, 133; at Wupatki, 157, 158, 238

Bancroft. Hubert Howe, 219

Bandelier, Adolph, 33–35; attitude toward Aztecs, 220, 343n16; Mogollon expeditions, 266n26; and Native Americans, 187; and Paquimé, 209; steady development view, 2

Basketmaker II (Plateau), 45–46, 268n69, 269n82

Basketmaker III, **57**, 65–68, **66, 67, 68**, 229, 274n83

Basketmaker III (Plateau), 274n83

Basketmaker Periods, 276n10

Benedict, Ruth, 55–56, 198, 250–251, 271n26, 303n5

Benedictine Fallacy, 56

Bentley, Jerry, 5

Berdan, Frances, 112–113, 151–152

Big History, 5, 6, 256n18, 256n20, 347n46

Big Houses: and governance, 228–229; and Great Houses, 102; Hohokam, 58, **60**, 84–85, 86, 279n76; oversized pit houses as, 99–100; at Shabik'eschee, 229

Binford, Lewis, 109, 286n29

Bison, 263n52

Black Mountain ruin, 175–176, 319n183

Blinman, Eric, 330n111

Blue Mesa-Ridges Basin, 96–98, **97**, 282n167

Boas, Franz, 177n28

Bostwick, Todd, 170

Braniff, Beatriz, 31, 80

Brew, J. O., 95

Brotherston, George, 12

Burials. *See* Death rituals

Cabeza de Vaca, 25

Cahokia, 114–115, 234; and Chaco, 140, 152–153, 305n49; collapse, 152–153; and maize, 289n64; and Mesoamerica, 115–116, 140, 222, 289n75; in Native histories, 26; and Southeast Ceremonial Complex, 194; spread of governance model, 11; and statehood issue, 221, 345n26

Canals: Anasazi, 156, 163, 244; communities, 84, 119, 236, 279n80; development of, 41, 226, 227; and governance, 16, 59, 228, 272n43; Hohokam, 80–82, **82**, 117–120, **120**, 135, 236; Las Capas, 41; and migrations, 230; Mimbres, 93–94, 135, 232; Piman, 19; and relocation, 167

Carbon 14 (14C) dating, 73

Cardinal orientation, 238. *See also* Chaco Meridian; Aztec North, 308n56; in Chaco, 294n136; Great Houses, 127, 293n136; Paquimé, **210**, 211, 213, 245, 337n204

Carot, Patricia, 278n48

Casa Grande, 202–203, **203, 204**, 246, 333nn137–139

Casas Grandes. *See* Paquimé

Casas Grandes (Di Peso), 109–110

Casas Grandes: A Fallen Trading Center of the Gran Chichimeca (Di Peso), 185

Centuries of Decline during the Hohokam Classic Period (Abbott), 166

Ceremony. *See* Ritual and ceremony

Cerro de Trincheras, **207**, 207–209

Cerro Juanaqueña, 42, **43**, 44–45, 171, 226

Chaco, 234–236. *See also* Chaco Meridian; Pueblo Bonito; and archaeologists, 122–123; and Aztec

Ruins, 153–155, 158, 295n142, 305n51, 308n61; and Cahokia, 140, 152–153, 305n49; Chetro Ketl, **104,** 126–127, 238, 294n136; as city, **125,** 125–126, 293n133; collapse, 172, 243, 322n16; D-shaped structures, 309n72; economy, 128–129, 132–133, 235, 294n140; governance, 186–187, 238, 324n34, 330n110; Great Houses, 123–124, 125–127, 128; Great North Road, 305n51, 307n54, 339n207; and Hohokam, 204–205, 333n143; Hungo Pavi, **122;** and McPhee Village, 102; and Mesoamerica, 126, 139, 140, 222, 292n127, 302n198; migrations from, 136; and Mimbres, 237; Native histories, 198, 199–200, 242, 246; orientation, 294n136; origins, 127–130; outliers, **130,** 130–132, **131,** 295nn142–144, 296n144; Pax Chaco, 129, 160; platform mounds, 315n151; political hierarchies, 129, 140, 204–205, 333n143; Pueblo Alto, 126–127, 238, 294n136; and Salmon Ruins, 154, 306n51; and statehood issue, 223, 344n21, 345n28; and Toltecs, 113; and Tularosa, 166; and West Mexico, 293n133

Chaco Meridian, 129–130, 154, 214, 282n172, 293n136, 305nn51 and 54, 337n207

Change, tradition of, 249

Chavez Pass, 183, 186

Chetro Ketl, **104,** 126–127, 238, 294n136

Chichén Itzá, 113, 234, 287n42

Chichimeca, 14, 223–224, 253n3, 346n42

Chiefdoms, 11, 192, 260n28, 302n199, 324n31

Chimney Rock, **130,** 131

Cholula, 113

Chronologies, **22;** classifications, 73–78, 276nn10 and 15; establishing, 49, 269n1; and increasing complexity concept, 183–184, 322n16; Paquimé, 316n161; and pottery, 51; and precision, 275n2; and southwestern archaeology, 318n168, 348n50; stratigraphy, 51

Chuipka, Jason, 282n167

Cibola, 24–25

Cienegas, 16

Cities, 227–228. See also Cahokia; Chaco; Paquimé

Classic Period (Hohokam), 166–171, **201,** 201–209; Casa Grande, 202–203, **203, 204,** 246, 333nn137–139; coalescent communities during, 332n129; governance, 279n80; platform mounds, 62, 184, 332n136; power during, 335n173

Classic Period (Mesoamerica). See Teotihuacán

Climate, 143–144, 148–149, 155–156, 206

Clothing, 114, 278n48, 280n105

Clovis, 27

Coalescent Communities project, 150, 189, 305n35, 327n49

Coalition Period (Rio Grande), 311n106

Colonialism: in archaeology and anthropology, 187, 250; attitudes, 217, 219–220; land grants, 35, 216, 342n221; results, 24, 251; Spanish, 247–248,

263n44

Colonial Period (Hohokam), 78, **79,** 80–89; Big Houses, 84–85, 86, 279n76; courtyard groups, 84, **84;** figurines, 60, **81;** and macaws, 138; mounds, 62; and rise of Chaco, 129; shell production, 291n90

Colonnades, 302n198

Colton, Harold, 75, 76–77

Communal societies. See Egalitarianism

Comparative civilizations genre, 256n20

Conquistadors, 24–27, 28–29, 218, 247, 265nn83–84, 288n62

Copper bells, 121, 291n92

Cordell, Linda, 147–148, 192–193, 276n10, 293n133

Corn. See Maize

Cotton, 59, 68, 280n105

Cottonwood Seep, 274n83

Courtyard groups, 84, **84,** 167–169, 231

Craig, Douglas, 83–84

Creel, Darrell, 301n179

Cremation. See Death rituals

Cross-cultural analysis, 144–145, 177, 255n18

Culiacán, 192, 337n207

Cults, 193, 194

Cultural affiliation studies, 321n5

Cultural resource management (CRM): Dolores Archaeological Program, 94, 95; and Hohokam, 108, 145; and Mimbres, 274n67; and New Archaeology, 146, 321n5; and scale, 105–106, 146, 305n35; and southwestern archaeology, 143, 145–147, 303n7, 304n10

Culture history, 2, 144

Cummings, Dean, 36, 54, 75

Daniel, Glyn, 255n12, 271n22, 285n23

Dating methods: accuracy, 49, 95, 96; archaeomagnetic, 73; carbon 14, 73; early, 38; and Paquimé, 316n161; stratigraphy, 51; tree-ring, 71–73, 76, 143–144, 148, 275n2, 316n161

Dean, Jeffrey, 78, 275n2

Death rituals: Anasazi, 23, 126, 293n131; Hohokam, 87, 121–122, 291n97; Mesoamerica, 278n48, 336n185; Mimbres, 90–91, 174–175, 232; Mogollon, 23

Deloria, Vine, Jr., 187

Dendrochronology. See Tree-ring dating

Dendroclimatology, 143–144, 148–149

Dendrohydrology, 148

Devolution, 330n110

Diehl, Michael, 43

Dilworth, Leah, 323n20

Di Peso, Charles: background of, 185; importance of, 318n168; and New Archaeology, 109–110; overview of work, 253n3; and Palatkwapi, 327n53; and Paquimé, 172, 176, 209–210, 212, 213, 214, 224n172, 316n161, 336n192

Distances. *See also* Chaco Meridian: in archaeological thinking, 249; and ball courts systems, 133; Chaco, 126, 132, 295n144; and conquistadors, 24; and Great Houses, 160; Mesoamerica, 62–64, 113, 273n62, 287n52, 290n75; Mississippian, 115, 290n75; Native attitudes, 264n63; and Pueblo people, 20–21; scale of, 9; time to traverse, 297n147; and trade, 132–133, 297n147; and world systems theory, 305n42

Doelle, William, 171

Dolores Archaeological Program, 94, 95, 99

Douglas, Andrew Ellicott, 72

Downum, Chris, 170

Doyel, David, 60, 170

Drennan, Robert, 132

D-shaped structures, 308n72

DuBois, Robert, 73

Duff, Andrew, 317n166

Early San Juan Period, 310n89

Ecology. *See* Environment

Economies. *See also* Trade: Chaco, 128–129, 132–133, 235, 294n140; and environment, 18–20, 128; Hohokam, 59, 81, 86, 117; Hopi, 245; market, 117, 329n98; Mesoamerican prestige goods, 302n198; Paquimé, 211–212, 213, 245

Effigy mounds, 211, 245

Egalitarianism: Benedict and Zuni, 55–56, 198, 303n5; challenged, 185–186; and Great Kivas, 233; Hohokam, 230, 231–232; Mimbres, 137, 301n179; and Morgan, 34; and post-processual archaeology, 186; and southwestern archaeology, 10, 262n32; in villages, 226, 329n89

Elites. *See* Political hierarchies

Ellison, "Red," 281n134

El Paso Phase, **175**, 319n183

El Toro. *See* Hewitt, Edgar Lee

Emergent order, 272n61

Environment: and Anasazi, 235, 243; and archaeology, 144, 145–146, 147–148; climate, 143–144, 148–149, 155–156, 206; and dendroclimatology, 143; and economies, 18–20, 128; floods, 148, 149, 205–206, 243, 334nn148 and 150; and Hohokam, 243; landscape as text, 327n48, 331n122; rainfall, 162–165, 233, 310n90; and societal changes, 148; vegetation, 15–17, 126, 292n122

"Escaping the Confines of Normative Thought" (Cordell and Plog), 147–148

Ethnography/ethnology, 49, 54–56, 249, 271nn22 and 26, 326n40

Explorers. *See* Conquistadors

Fagan, Brian, 341n207

Fallow valley model, 174

Farb, Peter, 303n5

Farming: canal communities, 84, 119, 236, 279n80;

first desert villages, 41–45, **42, 43, 44**; and migrations, 226, 267n47; Mogollon Pithouse Period, 65; Navajo, 271n21; patterns, 16–17; Plateau, 19–20, 40, 45–46, 68, 225, 227, 233, 268nn73–74; rainfall/dry, 229, 239; San Juan Basin, 128

Feinman, Gary M., 343n20, 345n21

Fernández-Armesto, Felipe, 222, 345n25

Fewkes, Jesse Walter, 187, 315n151

Firecracker Pueblo, **175**

Fish, Paul, 167, 284n180, 324n21

Fish, Suzanne, 167, 284n180, 324n21

Floods, 148, 149, 205–206, 243, 334nn148 and 150

Ford, James A., 257n22

423 site, 65, 66–67, 68

Fourmile Polychrome, **193**

Fungus models, 148

Galaz Ruins, 135, **135**, 136

Gallatin, Albert, 32–33, 34

Gallina Spring, 313n109

Galton's Problem, 177, 258n23

Garcia, Gregorio, 24

Gatlin platform mound, 314n151

Gila Polychrome, 167, 316n161, 335n175

Gila Pueblo, 52, 75

Gladwin, Harold S.: Hohokam chronology, 77–78; on Hohokam Classical Period, 166, 167; and increasing complexity concept, 322n16; overview of work, 52–54, 75, 253n3; and Salado, 167

Glycimeris shell bracelets/armlets: at Anasazi sites, 67, 68, 275n86, 293n131; appearance of, 59; as Hohokam marker, 87–88, **88**, 231; and Mimbres burials, 90–91

Governance. *See also* Egalitarianism; Political hierarchies; Ritual and governance: alternative models, 186–187, 324n34, 325nn35–38; Anasazi, 67, 68, 102, 103, 236, 238, 275n87, 330n110; and architecture, 228–229, 333n143; and canals, 16, 59, 228, 272n43; and cardinal directions, 238; chiefdoms, 11, 192, 260n28, 302n199, 324n31; devolution, 197, 330n110; and Great Kivas, 102; and Great Men concept, 261n29; importance of focus on, 260n28; Mesoamerica, 11–12, 62, 63, 191, 204–205, 222, 231–232, 236, 325n36; modern Pueblos, 183, 198; and platform mounds, 332n135; and post-processual archaeology, 180; and processual archaeology, 182–183; and southwestern archaeology, 10, 260n28; statehood issue, 221, 222–223, 343n20, 344n21, 345nn26–28, 346n29; and Uto-Aztecan migrations, 46

Grain (in archaeology), defined, 106

Grasshopper, 183, 186

Grass Mesa, 100, **101**, 102, 283n185

Great Drought and migrations, 162–165, 310n90

Great Gambler, 200, 331n123

Great Houses. *See also* Pueblo Bonito: Anasazi Pueblo I,

102–103; atop platform mounds, 243; Aztec Ruins, 154, 308n56; as ceremonial structures, 186; Chaco, **104**, 123–124, 125–127, 128, 234–235, 293n133; changes in function, 160, 162; development of, 123–124; and economy, 235; Mimbres, 237; Mimbres emulations, 301n178; orientation, 127, 293n136; outliers, **130**, 130–132, 236, 295nn142–144, 296n144, 306n51; pit structures in, 233; as platform mounds, 315n151; and political hierarchies, 126–127, 293n133; and unit pueblos, 160; Wupatki, 157, 238

Great Kivas: Basketmaker III, 67; Chaco, 236; Chaco outliers, 295n144; and governance, 102, 229, 233; Hohokam, 92, 281n140; Mimbres, 92, 232; Mogollon, 92, **93**; as precursors to modern kivas, 99; purpose, 92, 281n140; Wupatki, 238

Great Men concept, 261n29, 326n38

Great North Road, 305n51, 307n54, 339n207

Great Towns and Regional Polities (Cordell and Milner), 293n133

Gregory, David, 43, 170, 171

Grewe: ball court, 86, 121; Big Houses, 84–85, 229; figurines, 60; location, **57**; population, 83

Gumerman, George, 147, 148, 149

Guzmán, Nuño de, 25

Haury, Emil: aesthetic judgments, 285n19; on Anasazi migrations, 311n105; and Arizona State Museum, 75; and farming, 29, 40, 41, 266n86; and Hohokam, 77, 78, 82–83, 108, 277n39, 324n23; and Mogollon, 53; and Pima, 323n20; and Salado, 167, 184; and Snaketown, 108

Helms, Mary, 139

Hewitt, Edgar Lee, 74; and Aztecs, 220–221; and Casas Grandes, 347n44; and chronology, 276n15; control of Chaco archaeology, 221, 343n17; and eastern archaeological expeditions, 37; ethnological approach of, 54; importance to southwestern archaeology, 35, 36, 52; and increasing complexity concept, 322n16; and Native Americans, 187

Hierocracies, 325n34

Hill, Jane, 40, 41

Hinsley, Curtis, 72

Histories, 26, 31–32, 266n2. *See also* History, Western; Native histories

History, Western: and archaeology, 2, 180–181, 253n3, 254n10; of Aztecs, 218, 219; biases, 348n49; coincidences in, 9; and increasing complexity concept, 183–184, 322n16; and NAGPRA, 181–182, 321nn5–6, 322n7; nationalism in, 31–32, 266n2; and parsimony concept, 12–14, 262n42

History of Archaeological Thought, A (Trigger), 269n1

History of the Conquest of Mexico (Prescott), 34–35, 219

Hodder, Ian, 254n10, 255n11

Hohokam. *See also* Hohokam Canon; Hohokam governance; *specific sites*: and Anasazi, 68, 103, 129, 232, 235–236; ball courts, 85–86, **86**, 120–121, 133, 240–241; Big Houses, 58, **60**, 84–85, 86, 279n76; canals, 80–82, **82**, 117–120, **120**, 135, 236; chronology, **22**, 71–72, 77–78, 277n39; clothing, 280n105; death rituals, 291n97; decline and downfall, 205–206, 237, 243, 334nn148 and 150; defining, 21–22, 58; descendants, 271n21; economy, 59, 81, 86, 117; expansion, 232; figurines, 60, **61**, **81**; and Gladwin, 52–53; and Great Houses, 157–158; Great Kivas, 92, 281n140; houses, 23, 273n63; and Mesoamerica, 60, 138, 139–140, 191, 278n48, 335n175; migrations of, 23, 246; migrations to, 184, 239, 324n23; and Mimbres, 90–94, 134–135, 136, 232, 281n127, 298n162, 299nn165 and 167; and Mogollon, 64, 65, 273n64; as orphan of archaeology, 107; Phoenix, 57; platform mounds, 184–185, 240–241; population, 116; pottery, 20–21, 53, 56, **117**; region, **6**, **131**; ritual and ceremony, 22, 58, 121, 206; shell production, 87–88, **88**, 90–91, **91**, 231, 291n90; and statehood issue, 223; villages and towns, 23, 83–85, **84**, 91–92, 117, **119**, 167; and West Mexico, 63, 83, 89, 114, 278n48

Hohokam Canon: collapse, 122, 171, 172; death rituals, 87; defining, 80, 103; development and expansion, 82–83, 88, 280n108; as unifying ideology, 230–231, 240–241; variant names, 278n49

Hohokam governance: and Chaco elites, 204–205, 333n143; egalitarian strain in, 230, 231–232, 236; and Hohokam Canon, 80, 103; and platform mounds, 184, 323n21; political hierarchies, 58, 84–85, 121, 169, 206–207, 279n76, 291n97; and site hierarchies, 279n80

Hopewell, 47

Hopi: economy, 245; governance, 183; migrations to, 196; migration stories, 41, 191, 214, 246, 267n50, 327n53; and Red City, 214, 246; ritual and ceremony, 331n111

Howard, Jerry, 323n21

Huasteca, 289n75

Huddleston, Lee Eldridge, 24

Humanities and archaeology, 2, 4–5, 179–181, 254n9, 255n12, 255nn14–15, 320nn2–3

Human Relations Area File (HRAF), 144, 303n4

Hundred and Fifty Years of Archaeology, A (Daniel), 271n22, 285n23

Hungo Pavi, 122

Hunter-gatherers, 19, 226

Hurst, Winston, 308n69

Increasing complexity concept, 2–3, 183–184, 260n28, 262n41, 322n16

Indians. *See* Native American headings; *specific pueblos; specific tribes*

Inhumation. *See* Death rituals

Interconnections, 6, 8, 256n22

319n177; death rituals, 90–91, 174–175, 232; defining, 64; governance, 137, 301n179; Great Kivas, 92; and Hohokam, 90–94, 134–135, 136, 232, 281n127, 298n162, 299nn165 and 167; houses, 94, 135–136, 282n146; ideology change, 241; kachina societies, 137, 301n180; and Mesoamerica, 136, 138–139, 140, 237, 299n165, 300n174; migrations of, 174, 175–176, 241, 244, 319n183; migrations to, 136, 299n171; and modern Pueblos, 133, 237; and Mogollon, 21; name, 6; and Paquimé, 174, 176, 211; pit structures, 136, 299n167; region, 6, 57; ritual and ceremony, 331n111; trade, 237; unit pueblos, 94, 135–136, 299n167; villages, 90, 93, 137; and West Mexico, 138–139, 140

Minnis, Paul: Chaco Meridian, 337n207; defining regions, 317n166; Paquimé governance, 212, 335n185; Paquimé origins, 172–173, 176–177, 316n161, 318n168, 319n190; Paquimé region, 212, 213

Mississippian. See also Cahokia: archaeology of, 262n32; chiefdoms, 11, 324n31; distances in, 115; governance, 324n31; mounds, 115; Moundville, 152–153; Native stories of, 26; Poverty Point, 45; Vacant Quarter, 29

Mixteca-Puebla pottery, 194

Mogollon. See also specific sites: and archaeology, 53, 107–108, 266n26; and Aztatlan, 288n61; characteristics, 22; chronology, 77–78, 277n39; clothing, 280n105; descendants, 271n21; Great Kivas, 92, 93; migrations from, 24, 196; migrations to, 136, 239, 311n105; and Mimbres, 21; name, 6; pit houses, 48, 273n63; pottery, 22, 56, 57–58, 274n69; pueblos, 178; ritual and ceremony, 23; villages, 23, 89–90, 92

Mogollon Rim, 15, 53

Morgan, Lewis Henry: and anthropology, 34; and Aztec Ruins, 295n142; and Aztecs, 221, 343n16; colonial attitudes, 217, 219–220; communalism, 186, 324n31; and neo-evolutionism, 145

Morris, Earl, 72, 95, 309n89

Mounds, capped, 60, 62, 115, 169–170, 241. See also Platform mounds

Mounds, effigy, 211

Moundville, 152–153, 192

Mountjoy, Joseph B., 287n56

Museum of New Mexico, 74

Museum of Northern Arizona (MNA), 75, 76

NAGPRA. See Native American Graves Protection and Repatriation Act (1990, NAGPRA)

NAN Ranch Ruin, 301n178

Naranjo, Santiago, 54

Natchez Indians, 192

Nationalism, 31–32, 225, 266n2

Native American Graves Protection and Repatriation Act (1990, NAGPRA): and history, 181–182,

321nn5–6, 322n7; and migrations, 190; and New Archaeology, 311n105; and political divisions, 147; and southwestern archaeology, 187–188, 326nn44–45

Native Americans. See also Native histories: American attitudes toward, 217, 218, 219–220; and archaeologists, 180, 187–189, 326nn44–45; European attitudes, 24, 263n62; land claims, 35, 187, 216, 342n221

Native Americans, modern, 18, 322n6. See also specific pueblos; specific tribes

Native histories, 189; and archaeologists, 72, 275n5, 276n5; of Aztec (Ruins), 246; of Aztecs' origins, 223–224, 225, 346n35; of Cahokia, 26; of Casa Grande, 203; of Chaco, 198, 199–200, 242, 246; of Hohokam, 206; of Hopi migrations, 41, 191, 214, 246, 267n50, 327n53; of migrations, 190, 244, 311n105, 327n48; as myths, 54; of Paquimé, 214, 244, 245; and tradition of change, 249

Navajos, 17, 19–20, 247, 271n21, 331n122

Nawthis Village, 297n144

Nelson, Ben, 11–12, 14, 79–80, 284n180, 293n133, 302n198

Nelson, Margaret, 174

Neo-evolutionism, 145, 186–187, 303n5, 324nn27 and 31, 345n25

New Archaeology: and anthropology, 108–109; British view, 285n23; and Chaco, 128–129; and CRM, 146; and diffusion, 257n22; and ethnology, 326n40; legacies, 144; and migration, 311n105; and Mimbres, 134; and Native Americans, 180, 187, 276n5; overview of, 2, 105–106; and Fred Plog, 109, 110; and scale, 110–111, 186nn29 and 32; and science, 321n5

"New World History, The" (Bentley), 5

Nonhierarchical societies. See Egalitarianism

Nordenskiold, Gustav, 50, 266n12

Olmec, 45, 268n66

"On Pre-Columbian Narrative" (Martin), 3–4

O'odham, 184, 206, 271n21

Oral tradition. See Native histories

Orientations, 127, 293n136, 308n56. See also Chaco Meridian

Origins of the American Indians: European Concepts 1492-1729 (Huddleston), 24

Ortman, Scott, 282n167

Owen's Great House, 296n144

Pacific Coast, 114, 138

Palatkwapi, 191, 214, 246, 327n53

Paleo-Indians, 27

Pallets, 87, 87, 91, 120–121, 280n96

Papago. See O'odham

Paquimé, xii, 208. See also Chaco Meridian; and archaeology, 185, 209, 324n26; architecture, 210–211,

244–245, 335n174; as Aztlan, 347n44; cardinal orientation, **210**, 211, 213, 245, 337n204; and Casa Grande, 333n139; chronology, 316n161; collapse, 246; death rituals, 336n185; governance, 185, 212, 325n36, 335n185; and Hohokam, 335n175; and Mimbres, 241, 244; Mound of the Cross, **210**; Native histories, 214, 244, 245; origins, 172–177, 243, 244, 316n161, 318n168, 319n190, 320n192, 324n172; outliers, 246; as Palatkwapi, 191, 214, 246, 327n53; political hierarchies, 185; pottery, 211, 212, 335n179, 338n207; region, **131**; and Spiro Mounds, 289n73; and statehood issue, 223; trade, 211–212, 213, 245; and Tula, 113

Parsimony concept, 12–14, 220, 262n42

Patayan, 53, 301n186

Patterns of Culture (Benedict), 55–56, 271n26

Pax Chaco, 129, 160, 235, 236

Pecos Classification, 73–76, 99, 276nn10 and15

Pecos Pueblo, 34

Peñasco Blanco, 128, 129

Petroglyphs, **30**

Phillips, Ann, 270n6

Phillips, David A., Jr., 186–187, 339n207

Phoenix, 57. *See also* Hohokam

Pierre's Site, 306n51

Pima, 17–18; ancestors, 184, 271n21; economy, 19; and Haury, 323n20; histories, 243

Pinnacle Ruin Project, 311n109

Pioneer Period (Hohokam), 58–60, **60, 61,** 62, 80, 84

Pithouse Period (Mogollon), 64–65, 78, **79,** 89–94, 274n69

Pit structures, 273n63, 283n180; Anasazi, 65–67, **66,** 99, 268n73, 283n179; development, 41, 233; and Great Houses, 123; Mimbres, 64–65, 89–90, 94, 136, 237, 274n69, 282n146, 299n167; Mogollon, **48,** 64; as ritual loci, 23; Snaketown, **118**

Plateau. *See also* Anasazi: architecture, 233; defined, 14; environment, 16; farming, 19–20, 40, 45–46, 68, 225, 227, 233, 268nn73–74; Hohokam and eastern, 232; languages, 269n82; migrations to, 45–46; Shabik'eschee, **57,** 65–68, **68,** 229; villages, 47, 227, 229, 233, 268n73

Platform mounds, **142**. *See also* Casa Grande; and ball courts, 169, 170, 240, 314n136, 315n151; as ceremonial structures, 186; Chaco, 315n151; compared to capped mounds, 169–170, 241; development and spread, 62, 169–171, 314nn138 and 146, 315n151; and governance, 171, 231, 314n151, 332n135; Great Houses atop, 243; Hohokam outliers, 314n151; Marana site, **168,** 169; Paquimé, 245; Pueblo Grande, 201; purposes, 184–185, 202, 332nn129 and 136

Plog, Fred, 109, 110, 147–148, 183

Point of Pines, 313n109

Political hierarchies. *See also* Political hierarchies and architecture: after Aztec (Ruins), 239–240; Anasazi, 99, 102, 103, 183, 228–230, 233, 284n180; breakdown, 330nn110–111; Chaco, 129, 140, 234–235; development of, 273n61; emblems, 333n143; Hohokam, 58, 84–85, 121, 169, 279n76, 291n97; Hohokam with Chaco elites, 204–205, 333n143; Mesoamerica, 11–12; models ignoring, 148, 304n28; Natchez, 192; in Native histories, 199–200, 246; Paquimé, 185, 212, 245, 335n185; replaced by ritual authorities, 242; in Southwest, 10; symbols, 242; between towns, 232

Political hierarchies and architecture, 59; Big Houses, 58, 272n39; Great Houses, 126–127, 293n133; kivas, 284n180; platform mounds, 171, 184, 202, 314n151, 323n21, 332nn129 and 136; tri-wall structures, 158

Politics. *See* Political hierarchies

Politics and Power: An Economic and Political History of the Western Pueblos (Upham), 183

Popé, 326n38

Poshu'ouinge, 196, **196,** 329n99

Positional legitimation, 307n54

Post-Classic (Mesoamerica), 111–116, 126, 150–152, 191–192, 234, 327n54

Post-Middle (Mississippian), 153

Post-processual archaeology, 179–181, 185, 186, 320nn2–3, 324n26

Post-structural archaeology, 259n27

Potter, James M., 282n167

Pottery. *See also* Pottery, Anasazi; Pottery, Mimbres: Abajo red-on-black, 272n31; brownware, 46–47, 56, 57–58, 226; corrugated, 298n162; and cults, 194; and dating, 51, 73, 316n161; Fourmile Polychrome, **193;** Hohokam, 21–22, 53, 56, **117;** and migrations, 164, 313n109; Mixteca-Puebla, 194; Mogollon, 22, 56, 57–58, 274n69; Paquimé, 211, 212, 335n179, 338n207; redware, 56–57, 98, 274n69, 281n127; Salado, 167, 316n161, 335n175; in southwestern archaeology, 348n48

Pottery, Anasazi: black-on-white, 98, 163, 193, **193,** 310n98, 313n109, 328n71; corrugated, 298n162; development of, 57, 271n31; glaze paint, 98–99; Mesa Verde mugs, 164; signature, 21, 56

Pottery, Mimbres: absence of designs, 241, 319n177; black-on-white, 281n127, 298n162, 317n161; Mesoamerican motifs, 136, 138, 300n174; red-on-brown, 94

Poverty Point, 45

Practice in archaeology, 260n29

Predictive modeling, 148, 304n19

Prescott, William H., 34–35, 219

Prestige goods economies, 302n198

Primary states, 222, 345n26

Prime objects, 62

Processual archaeology, 143, 144, 149–150, 176–177, 180, 181, 185, 186, 321n5, 324n26

Pueblo Alto, 126–127, 238, 294n136

Stunned by the night skies in the Gila Wilderness, college sophomore Stephen Lekson determined to work outdoors in the Southwest. Archaeology seemed preferable to ditch digging or other forms of honest labor. He took an interest in his chosen profession, reading widely if not wisely, and it seemed to him that Chaco, Mimbres, and Salado were the three glamour kids of the ancient Southwest. Sometime during the Nixon administration, he took a solemn, if not entirely sober, vow to work in all three areas, producing monographs in each. (He later realized that Hohokam and Casas Grandes were far more interesting than his trio of usual suspects.) With moderate determination and a metric ton of luck, he maneuvered himself into research positions in each region and wrote his books. Near the end of the Carter administration, he married the distinguished Southwestern archaeologist Catherine Cameron (blameless for Lekson's eccentricities). He earned his doctorate from the University of New Mexico in the Reagan era by outlasting his professors. After a decade with the National Park Service and shorter stints with the Arizona State Museum, the Museum of New Mexico, and Crow Canyon Archaeological Center, he landed at the University of Colorado Museum of Natural History, where he has been curator of anthropology through one Clinton presidency and a double dose of Bush. Among his other books are *Archaeology of the Mimbres Region, Salado Archaeology of the Upper Gila*, and *Great Pueblo Architecture of Chaco Canyon* (the trifecta); *Nana's Raid* (Apache history); and *Chaco Meridian* (an outré claim that ancient political centers were linked by a meridian—which, much to his surprise, turns out to be [probably] correct). In his spare time, he undertook a study of Hohokam museum collections and wrote widely if not wisely about Casas Grandes.